Alan Rogers'
Good Camps Guide

BRITAIN and IRELAND
2001

Quality Camping and Caravanning Parks

THE ALAN ROGERS'
Good camps guide

Compiled by: Deneway Guides & Travel Ltd

Cover design: Design Section, Frome

Cover photography: 'Bluebells' by S&O Matthews

Maps created by Customised Mapping (01985 844092)
contain background data provided by GisDATA Ltd.
Maps are © Customised Mapping and GisDATA Ltd. 2000.

Clive Edwards, Lois Edwards & Sue Smart have asserted
their rights to be identified as the authors of this work.

First published in this format 2000

© **Haynes Publishing & Deneway Guides & Travel Ltd 2000**

Published by: Haynes Publishing, Sparkford, Nr Yeovil, Somerset BA22 7JJ
in association with
Deneway Guides & Travel Ltd, West Bexington, Dorchester, Dorset DT2 9DG

British Library Cataloguing-in-Publication Data:
A catalogue record for this book is available from the British Library.

ISBN: 0 901586 76 5

Printed in Great Britain by J H Haynes & Co Ltd

Contents

Introduction

The new Millennium started sadly for us when we heard that our founder, Alan Rogers, had died. Alan was 81 years of age when he died in January, and although he had no day-to-day involvement with the Guides for many years, we had remained friends, and he could always be relied upon to provide wise counsel when needed for advice as an 'eminence grise'.

Alan published the first of the Guides that still bear his name back in 1968, introducing it with the words "I would like to stress that the camps which are included in this book have been chosen entirely on merit, and no payment of any sort is made by them for their inclusion".

As campers and caravanners ourselves it was this objective approach that attracted us to become regular readers of his Guides, and which eventually lead to our taking over the editing and publishing of the Guides when Alan retired in 1986.

Whilst the content and scope of the Guides have expanded considerably in the fourteen years since we took over, mainly due to the huge growth in the number of campsites throughout the UK and Europe during those years, our selection of sites to be featured still employs exactly the same philosophy as Alan defined almost thirty years ago.

We would like to take this opportunity to pay tribute to Alan, and to thank him for providing us with the opportunity to enjoy what must be one of the most interesting jobs in Tourism.

The Alan Rogers' Approach to Selecting Sites

Firstly, and most importantly, our selection is based entirely on our own rigorous inspection. Parks cannot buy their way into our guides – indeed the extensive Site Report which is written by us, not by the site owner, is provided free of charge so we are free to say what we think and to provide an honest description. This is written in plain English and without the use of icons or symbols.

The criteria which we use when selecting sites are numerous, but the most important by far is the question of good quality and standards. Whatever the size of the site, whether it's part of a campsite chain, or even a local authority site, makes no difference in terms of it being required to meet our exacting standards in terms of its quality. In other words, irrespective of the size of the site, or the number of facilities offered, the essentials (the welcome, the pitches, the sanitary facilities the cleanliness and the general maintenance) must all be of a good standard.

Our selection of sites is designed to cater for a wide variety of preferences, from those seeking a small peaceful campsite in the heart of the countryside, to those looking for an 'all singing, all dancing' site in a popular seaside resort, and for those with more specific needs such as sports facilities, cultural or historical attractions, even sites for naturism.

We rely on our small, dedicated team of Site Assessors, all of whom are experienced campers, caravanners or motorcaravanners, to visit and recommend parks, following which our Sites Director makes the final decision on those to be included in the following year's guide. Once a park is included, it will be regularly inspected to ensure that standards are being maintained. We also appreciate the feedback we receive from many of our readers, and we always make a point of following up complaints, suggestions or recommendations for possible new sites. However, should you have a specific complaint about a park this should be addressed to the Park Operator at the time, preferably in person. Please bear in mind that although we are interested to hear about any complaints, we have no contractual relationship with the sites featured in our guides and are therefore not in a position to intervene in any dispute between a reader and a park.

How to use the Guide

A few words of explanation regarding the layout may be useful:

Regions and counties

For England we have used official Tourist Board Regions and the counties. For Wales and Scotland, where there are many official regions, we have adopted our own regional structure based on the needs of the average holidaymaker. For Ireland (North and South) we use the counties.

Index

Not one, but two – on pages 247-251 you will find each campsite indexed by its number, and on pages 244-246 you will find an index of the villages or towns nearest to where the sites are situated.

Maps

These appear on pages 253-256. The approximate position of each campsite is indicated on the map by the symbol: O and the name of the site. The colour of the symbol indicates whether the campsite is open all year or not. The maps are intended to help you find the approximate location of campsites, not to navigate by! Each Site Report includes succinct directions as to how to find the site, based on the assumption that you will be using a proper road map, such as those produced by the Ordnance Survey, the AA or RAC, etc. and for convenience we have also included an Ordnance Survey Grid Reference in our Site Report in respect of sites in mainland Britain.

The Site Reports

These are really self-explanatory, but please remember that all prices shown are per night, and all telephone numbers assume that you are 'phoning from within the country where the site is situated - thus if you want to telephone a site from abroad you will need to prefix the number with the appropriate International Dialling Code.

Example of an entry:

---

number park name, nearest village, town

These details should identify the park's location to within a mile or so on any medium scale map - finer details are given in the directions section at the foot of the main report.

summary line

main text	**Charges**
A description of the park in which we try to give an idea of the general features of the park - its size, its situation, its strengths and weaknesses, the quality and adequacy of the toilet block, special amenities and any special local attractions. Some things may be assumed unless the report states otherwise: that the toilet block has free hot showers, hot water in washbasins, mirrors, some razor points and chemical toilet disposal, and that dogs are accepted on leads. Throughout the reports the word `site' is used in the sense of park or campsite itself, not your individual place on the park, which we have called a 'pitch'. Practically all our parks now have electrical connections to some pitches and we include details of the amperage available. We try to tell you if the park does not take any particular type of normal touring unit - caravans, motorcaravans and tents - however, if you have an unusual unit (e.g. American motorhome or commercial vehicle) it is advisable to check with the park first to make sure that there are no special restrictions.	**Open** **Address** **Tel** **Fax** **E-mail** (if available)

Directions: **Reservations**
Given last, separated from the main text in order that they may be read   General adminis-
and assimilated more easily by a navigator en route. It is possible that a   trative detail is
few may have changed due to road improvement schemes, etc. since we   given in the right
visited the park. If this has happened we trust that any delay caused is or   hand column
was of only minor proportions. The 6-figure Ordnance Survey Grid   - see below.
Reference (O.S.GR:) point is provided by the park for those wishing to
locate a site by this means.

General information:

Grouped under the headings of charges, opening dates, address, telephone and reservations.

Charges are the latest provided by the parks. In those few cases where 2000 or 2001 prices are not given, we try to give a general guide. The pricing structures vary considerably and we try to be as uniform and succinct as possible in what is included since some parks have a simple tariff, while others have a vast complex of possibilities. The same is true of reservations and what is written cannot wholly replace the official park tariff and reservation form.

Please note that the opening dates are those advised to us during the early autumn of the previous year - park operators can, and sometimes do, alter these dates before the start of the following season - often for good reasons - so if you intend to visit a park shortly after its published opening date, or shortly before its closing date, it really is wise to check that it will actually be open at the time required. Similarly some parks operate a restricted service during the low season, only opening some of their facilities (e.g.

5

swimming pools) during the main season - where we know about this, and have the relevant dates, we indicate it, but if you are at all doubtful again it is wise to check.

We note an ever increasing number of 'special' pitches under a variety of fancy names (for example, Executive, Panorama, Super). These provide a range of extra facilities such as waste water disposal, TV and phone connections, patios, etc. and they are often booked up well in advance. We would suggest that readers interested is such pitches should contact the park concerned to check exactly what is provided and to pre-book if that is what they want. Disabled readers are also advised to telephone the park of their choice before turning up to ensure that facilities are appropriate to their particular needs.

Special thanks are due to Chris and Gerry Bullock for being out and about, continuing their work on facilities provided by parks for disabled visitors. See pages 242-243 for their comments and recommendations. The Disabled Discrimination Act (DDA) 2000 requires parks to make reasonable adjustments for wheelchair users and persons with disabilities.

Quick Reference Sections

Our Guide includes several Quick Reference Sections, (see pages 235-240) which should enable you to quickly identify those parks that are open all year, those which welcome dogs, and those which don't, parks where fishing facilities are available, those where there are facilities for launching small boats, those where there are bicycles for hire, those with riding stables or golf courses nearby, and those which are strictly 'adults only'.

Alan Rogers' Discounts

We have been able to negotiate special 'Alan Rogers' discounts with some of the parks featured in this Guide, and with a number of tourist attractions, whereby on presentation of a current edition of the Guide, readers will be able to enjoy a reduction compared with the normal public price. Details are shown in the relevant Site Report or, in the case of attractions, on the relevant advertisement page.

 Where a park offers a discount to our readers this is indicated in the Site Report by a small Alan Rogers' Logo, and a brief description of the discount available.

Our Site Assessors

Finally we'd like to say a special thank you to to our Site Assessors for all their efforts and hard work; and for the many miles they travel, their patience with our detailed site reports and their commitment to the philosophy of the guides.

We are, of course, also out and about ourselves, visiting Parks, talking to owners and readers, and generally checking on standards, new developments, etc. We wish all our readers thoroughly enjoyable Camping and Caravanning in 2001, and let's hope for some good weather!

Lois Edwards MA, FTS
Clive Edwards BEd, FTS
Sue Smart   Directors

David Bellamy Names His "Wildlife Wonderlands"

The annual David Bellamy Conservation Awards are granted to parks which can demonstrate the excellence of their conservation work. Gold, silver and bronze levels are available in what Professor Bellamy describes as the 'Green Olympics' for the parks industry. The scheme is run in conjunction with the British Holiday & Home Parks Association.

Conservationist David Bellamy believes that British holiday parks can provide a truly exciting way to experience the natural world. Professor Bellamy says he has been amazed at what many parks have done in the cause of conservation, including the creation of 'thrilling wildlife wonderlands' for holidaymakers to enjoy. Parks that received David Bellamy Conservation Awards for 2000 that are featured in this guide are identified with their Gold, Silver or Bronze award noted at the end of their editorial entry (e.g. Bellamy gold). Each winning park has had its environmental achievements assessed by both David Bellamy and an independent nature group, and many offer the opportunity to add a fascinating new dimension of wildlife discovery to your holiday stay.

NEW FOR 2001

The Alan Rogers Travel Service

for the Channel Islands and Ireland

Last year we launched a new Readers' Travel Service for pitch and ferry reservations at campsites in France.This has proved so sucessful both in terms of convenience and because, by packaging pitch reservations and ferry bookings together, we can offer the lowest possible prices. For 2001 we are delighted to be able to extend our Travel Service to many other countries as well as France, including selected campsites in Ireland and the Channel Islands.

Why not take a look at our web site at **www.alanrogers.com**

This is the ultimate 'one stop low cost holiday solution' for independent campers, caravanners and motorcaravanners, providing a pre-booked service that eliminates doubt and hassle for you, whereby we'll book a pitch and a low cost ferry, and if required provide travel and/or breakdown insurance too. We'll even provide a comprehensive Travel Pack including maps and directions, etc. as well.

At some campsites you can save even more money by combining the Alan Rogers Travel Service booking system with the highly sucessful Camping Cheques low season 'go-as-you-please' arrangements *(see below)*.

THE ALAN ROGERS'
travel service

Get the site you want
Get the dates you want
Get the ferry you want
Get the price you want

The all-season "leave it to us solution " We'll book your chosen Alan Rogers' approved campsite(s) - choose from nearly 200 across Europe. We'll organise your low cost ferry and insurance as well as providing a comprehensive Travel Pack with maps and directions too. We're with you all the way!

Call us now for your FREE colour Readers Travel Guide
01892 55 98 98   www.alanrogers.com

12 nights pitch fees + ferry for car and caravan and passengers from £315.00 Save Money, and Take It Easy!

No more trying to contact foreign sites direct
No more doubt as to whether your pitch really is booked
No more ringing round all the ferry companies for the best price
No more foreign currency booking fees

The low season 'go as you please' solution. With around 200 sites across Europe, all committed to fully open facilities in low season, there's no need to commit yourself to a fixed itinerary Move freely from site to site as you wish, and enjoy incredibly low ferry prices as well. This discount scheme offers fantastic savings

Enjoy the freedom   Enjoy the flexibility
Enjoy the ferry prices   Enjoy the savings

Call us now on 01892 559855 for your free Camping Cheque brochure
www.campingcheque.co.uk
10 Camping Cheques + ferry for car and passengers from £239

SUPER-LOW FERRY PRICES GUARANTEED

Camping Cheques now operate in Britain and Ireland. The ten parks involved are clearly identified in this guide with the words CAMPING CHEQUES at the foot of the right hand column of the editorial report.

England

South West Tourism

Isles of Scilly, Cornwall, Devon, Somerset, Bath, Bristol,
South Gloucestershire, Wiltshire and Dorset

Address: Woodwater Park, Exeter, Devon EX2 5WT
Tel: 0870 442 0830 Fax: 0870 442 0840
E-mail: post@swtourism.co.uk
Internet: http://www.westcountryholidays.com

The West Country - land of contrasts and home to some of Britain's most adventurous millennium projects. One of the premier holiday destinations in Britain, the West Country with it's mild climate and diverse scenery is unbeatable for the variety of places to visit and activities.

Cornwall

Stretching from the craggy cliffs of Land's End to the surf haven of Bude, Cornwall has over 300 miles of coastline on offer. The South West Coast Path enables even the laziest walker to choose from bracing cliff views at Tintagel Castle - home to King Arthur, traditional fishing villages of Polperro and Mevagissey or golden sandy beaches at Newquay or Falmouth. This is the land that has inspired artists whose work can be seen at The Tate Gallery in St Ives. Fans of the Lost Gardens of Heligan can now look forward to the Eden Project, an amazing new garden of tropical and native plants all under huge greenhouses that are bigger than football pitches.

Devon

Home to the English Riviera with the cosmopolitan atmosphere of Torquay, Paignton and Brixham on the palm fringed south coast. Nearby Salcombe and Dartmouth with the Royal Britannia Naval College, now open to the public, stands proud over the Dart Estuary are popular for watersports. Further west is the dramatic moorland of Dartmoor with wild ponies and granite tors. Clovely, Ilfracombe and Lynton on the North coast are a stark contrast to the green moorland with long golden beaches and pretty harbours. For shopping and heritage visit the cities of Plymouth for The Hoe, Barbican area and National Marine Aquarium or the cathedral city of Exeter with it's beautiful Tudor buildings.

Somerset

The west is covered by Exmoor where you can travel by steam train from Bishop's Lydeard to the coast at Minehead. Visit lush gardens at Hestercombe and historic Forde Abbey. Glastonbury Tor and Abbey have links to past dating thousands of years and while the caves and Gorge at Cheddar are spectacular. Weston Super Mare bustles with the noise of families as they enjoy the carnival atmosphere while the city of Taunton has a great range of shops, theatres and cafes.

Bath

Dating back to the 41h century AD, this historic city is poised once more to come alive as the Spa Resort of Britain when in 2001 visitors to the city will be able to enjoy water treatments and holistic therapy at The Bath Spa Project. Another reason to visit the city is the beautiful Georgian architecture of the Royal Crescent and The Circus.

Bristol

A modern vibrant city which has experienced a dramatic transformation in the past few years. '@Bristol', a brand new attraction for all ages takes you to a world where you can explore science and technology for yourself. The Harbourside now has a row of cafes, theatres and bars overlooking the city and the waterfront. Visit Harvey's Cellars to watch craftsmen fill the famous Bristol Blue bottles with delicious sherry or go aboard the SS Gt Britain at the Docks.

Wiltshire

Marked by canals and magnificent chalk horses cut into the hillsides that overlook the rolling Salisbury Plain. Stonehenge remains Wiltshire's most famous landmark with nearby Avebury completing the prehistoric picture. Located an hour from London, this county is also home to pretty villages with duck ponds such as Biddestone and Lacock which features in many television dramas. Steam -The Museum of the Great Western Railway and the Designer Outlet Village at Swindon offer a great day out of history and shopping.

Dorset

Land of Thomas Hardy and one of the best coastlines in the country for fossils which can be found along the three mile stretch of Chesil Beach or the cliffs of Lyme Regis. The seaside town of Weymouth is popular due to it's bustling nightlife and charming Georgian town houses.

002 Cardinney Camping Park, Crows an Wra, Penzance

Unpretentious small park near Lands End beauty spots.

A friendly Geordie welcome awaits from the owner, Kevin Lindley, when you visit Cardinney, which is perfectly situated for visiting the famous Lands End beauty spots and tourist attractions and also within easy driving distance of small Cornish beaches and coves. The level field is semi-divided into three areas and is neatly kept with some landscaping. Bushes and a central Cornish stone wall, allow for 105 marked pitches, 56 with 10A electricity and some with hardstanding. The facilities are simple compared to many of the more sophisticated sites in Cornwall, the toilet block originally built over 30 years ago but adapted over the years to provide three showers (free) and six washbasins for each sex. Razor points, hair dryers, a baby cubicle and chemical disposal, plus laundry facilities and one outside dishwashing sink with hot water. The combined café and bar acts as reception and a social point providing breakfast, takeaway at most times and good cheer in the evenings. Games room with TV, pool table and video games. Public phone and tourist information chalet. Fishing 3 miles, bicycle hire 5 miles. Coastal, cliff top walks, surfing beaches and the Minnack Open Air Theatre near.

Directions: Park is signed before Crows an Wra on main Penzance - Lands End A30 road, 5 miles west of Penzance. O.S.GR: SW426285.

Charges 2001:
-- Per unit incl. 2 adults £5.00 - £8.00; extra adult £2.00; child (2-15 yrs) £1.00; electricity £1.75.
-- Less for over 2 weeks.
-- Credit cards accepted.
Open:
1 February - 30 Nov.
Address:
Crows an Wra,
St Buryan, Cornwall
TR19 6HX.
Tel:
(01736) 810880.
FAX: (01736) 810998.
E-mail: cardinney@ btinternet.com.
Reservations:
Made with £10 per week deposit.

003 Ayr Holiday Park, St. Ives

Family park with holiday homes within walking distance of St. Ives, with superb views.

On first arrival Ayr Park seems to be all holiday homes, but behind them is a series of naturally sloping fields, with marvellous views over St. Ives Bay and Porthmeor beach, providing 40 touring pitches. Level, hard-core, terraced areas also provide places for motorhomes and vans, 35 with electricity (16A). The toilet block, with various parts, is modern and well maintained with free, hot, controllable showers (some accessed from the outside and some with toilet), hot water to washbasins, vanity style, hairdryer, three dishwashing sinks with hot water under cover and good laundry facilities. With the extra field for tents open in July/Aug, the facilities could be a little hard-pressed, but were coping well when we visited in August. Amenities include a games room with pool table, TV, hot drinks and snack machines, adventure play area and football field, and a public telephone. Motorcaravan service. Spa shop near. St. Ives centre and supermarkets are within easy walking distance, also the Tate Gallery. Direct access to the coastal footpath. One dog per pitch, up to medium size, is permitted but contact the park as dogs are not allowed on St. Ives beaches in high season. Bellamy silver.

Directions: 300 yds after leaving the A30 turn left on A3074 at mini-roundabout following signs for St. Ives for heavy vehicles and day visitors (not town centre). After 2 miles join B3311, then B3306 1 mile from St. Ives (octagonal building on left). Still heading for St. Ives turn left at a mini-roundabout through residential areas. Park entrance is 600 yds at Ayr Terrace. O.S.GR: SW515388.

Charges 2000:
-- Per adult £2.35 - £3.70; child (5 -16 yrs) £1.10 - £1.80; caravan or tent £4.40 - £7.00; car £1.20; motorcaravan £4.90 - £7.50; awning £2.00 - £3.85; m/cycle £1.20; dog £1.05; electricity £2.25.
-- VAT included.
-- Credit cards accepted.
Open:
Easter/1 April - 31 Oct.
Address:
Higher Ayr, St. Ives, Cornwall TR26 1EJ.
Tel:
(01736) 795855.
FAX: (01736) 798797.
E-mail: andy@ayrholiday park.demon.co.uk.
Reservations:
Made with £35 deposit.

004 Trevalgan Holiday Farm, St Ives

Friendly, smallish, 'no frills' site.

We already have two very different sites in the St Ives area and Trevalgan is different yet again. Based on a working farm on the cliffs 1½ miles west of St Ives, it provides 120 clearly marked pitches (43 with 16A electricity) in a level stone walled field, which vary in size as the park is very popular with walkers. A purpose built toilet block has curtained washbasins, controllable hot showers with seat and curtain, plus baby room, laundry and washing up, chemical disposal and even a hot drinks machine. Reception has a small shop (1/6-15/9) and a Farm House Kitchen with takeaway (July/Aug), popular for breakfast or evening meals. There is a games field, children's play area, pets corner and crazy golf. A games room in a barn has table tennis, pool, fruit machines and an upstairs TV room. Gas available. There is direct access to the coastal path and it is 25 minutes to St Ives. Fishing 3 miles, bicycle hire, riding, golf, all within 2 miles. In July/Aug. there is a bus service once a day from the park to St Ives (10 am. returning 5 pm). With tractor rides (high season), plus farm and hill trails it is quite an original type of park. A member of the Countryside Discovery group. Bellamy silver.

Directions: Approach site down a narrow Cornish lane from the B3306 St Ives - Lands End road, following sign. O.S.GR: SW490400.

Charges 2000:
-- Per adult £3.50 - £5.50; child 3-14 yrs £2.50 - £4.50, under 3 yrs £1.50; dog 50p; electricity £2.50.
-- Credit cards accepted.
Open:
Easter - 30 September.
Address:
Trevalgan Farm, St Ives, Cornwall TR26 3BJ.
Tel:
(01736) 796433.
FAX: as phone.
E-mail: trevalgan @aol.com.
Reservations:
Contact park.

9

Cornwall

005 Polmanter Tourist Park, Halestown, nr. St. Ives

Family owned farm park with pool, just outside St. Ives.

Polmanter is a good example of a sympathetic conversion of a farm from agricultural to leisure use and the Osborne family have developed the park well. The converted farm buildings provide a cosy bar lounge overlooking the heated swimming pool, toddler's pool and sunbathing area. Good value meals are served in the bar (Easter, then Whitsun - mid Sept) and there is a family area with high chairs, an upstairs games room with pool and table tennis and the new conservatory between the bar and the pool provides extra space for families (open all day, with a hot drinks machine). Occasional entertainment is organised in season. The 240 tourist pitches (no statics) are well spaced in several fields with growing shrubs and hedges and connecting tarmac roads. There are 16 hardstandings, 190 electric hook-ups (16A) and 80 deluxe pitches with electricity, water and waste water. The toilet blocks vary - as the park has grown, so extra blocks have been added. There are now four, the latest being modern and good, the others refurbished and tiled. All still incorporate the ideas of the first block, which include a wall cupboard for clothes in each shower to keep them dry. Heating is available, showers are free and there are two fully equipped en-suite family shower rooms, plus a baby changing room. There are hairdryers, chemical disposal, extra dishwashing sinks in the new block and good laundry provision including free irons. Activities include two full size tennis courts, two children's play areas with large wooden climbing frame on a sand base, a sports field and a games room with two pool tables, table tennis and games machines. Well stocked, self service shop (shop and pool Whitsun - mid Sept). It is a busy park with a happy atmosphere within 1½ miles of St Ives - a footpath leads from the park (20 minutes downhill) or there is a bus service from the park in high season hourly, 10 am. - midnight. Golf 1 mile, fishing, riding, bicycle hire and boat launching facilities within 2 miles. Dogs are accepted on leads (but not on the St. Ives beaches in high season) with a large exercise field provided and there are walks from the park. The park gates are closed midnight - 6.30 am. with outside parking. A member of the Best of British group.

Charges 2000:
-- Per unit incl. 2 persons, car and awning £9.00 - £14.00; extra adult £3.00 - £4.50; child (3-15 yrs) £2.00 - £3.50; electricity (16A) £2.00; multi-service pitch £3.00; dog £1.00; extra car or pup tent £1.00.
-- VAT included.
-- Credit cards accepted.
Open:
Easter - 31 October (full facilities to 10 Sept).
Address:
Halestown, St. Ives, Cornwall TR26 3LX.
Tel:
(01736) 795640.
FAX: as phone.
E-mail: phillip_osborne @hotmail.com.
Reservations:
Made with £30 deposit. For 15/7-26/8 only: multiples of 7 nights with arrival on Fri, Sat or Sunday for electric pitches, multiples of 7 nights but any day arrival for non-electric pitches.

`Camping Cheque'

Directions: Take B3074 to St. Ives from the A30 and then first left at a mini-roundabout taking 'Holiday Route' (B3311) to St. Ives (Halestown). At T-junction turn right for Halestown, right again at the Halestown Inn then first left. O.S.GR: SW509392.

001 Chacewater Park, Chacewater, Truro

Quiet, value-for-money park exclusively for adults over 30 only.

For those who want to be away from the hectic coastal resorts and to take advantage of the peace and quiet of an 'adults only' park, this will be an excellent value for money choice. Chacewater has a pleasant rural situation and the site is run with care and attention by Richard Peterken and his daughters Debbie and Mandy, providing 100 level touring pitches, 60 with hardstanding, in two large field areas (with a slight slope) edged with young trees or in smaller bays formed by hedging. There are 20 fully serviced pitches with electricity, water, drainage and sewage connections and one area for dog owners. The main toilet block provides free hot water throughout, vanity style washbasins, well equipped showers and two en-suite units, along with covered washing up sinks, a laundry room and chemical disposal facilities. This block has now been supplemented by a new one providing similar facilities near reception. Reception is not at the entrance but through the park to one side in a pleasant courtyard area and it also provides a small library. Dog field. Truro is only 5 miles and there is a good choice of beaches north or south within 5-10 miles.

Charges 2001:
-- Per unit incl. 2 adults from £9.00; extra person £4.00; electricity 95p; dog £1.00; extra car £1.00.
-- Weekly rates for pre-booked pitches.
-- Discounts for senior citizens excl. August.
-- VAT included.
-- Credit cards accepted.
Open:
1 May - 30 September.
Address:
Cox Hill, Chacewater, Truro TR4 8LY.
Tel:
(01209) 820762.
FAX: (01209) 820544.
E-mail: chacepark @aol.com.
Reservations:
Made with £20 deposit per week or part week, balance on arrival.

Directions: Chacewater can be approached either from the A390 road or from the A30. Park is ½ mile west of the village - follow signs. O.S.GR: SW742439.

006 River Valley Country Park, Relubbus, Penzance

Quiet touring park in natural environment for caravans and some tents, east of Penzance.

An attractive, spacious park in a pleasant river valley, run by Brian and Eileen Milson, River Valley provides 150 large, well spaced and level touring pitches. In nooks and bays around the perimeters of small meadows or in natural clearings, all are clearly defined by shrubs or hedges. Trees have been planted to supplement these or in the more open areas to edge the individual pitch spaces, making the park very attractive. Most pitches have electrical connections (15A), some have hardstanding and there are special sections for families, couples, tents, dogs, etc. Three good quality, well spaced, tiled toilet blocks are large enough, clean and well maintained. Hot water is free in the washbasins, showers and the 12 covered dishwashing sinks. Two male and two female family shower rooms have been added in the block at the far end, there are a few private cabins for ladies and a make-up room with hair dryers, which also provides tourist information, plus separate laundry facilities and baby bath. Water points around the park, chemical disposal and motorcaravan service point (fresh water top up and waste water emptying). There are 38 caravan holiday homes, some privately owned, in more or less separate areas, beside the river at the far end of the park or on the hillside at the back. Shop with reception and public phone. There is no children's playground, but lots of very tame ducks on the river. A fence separates the park from the river and there is a pleasant walk for 2½ miles alongside it, useful for dog walks (poop-scoops provided). St Michael's Mount is only 3 miles and can be reached by footpath. Much of the valley is a protected nature reserve and the park encourages wildlife by not using weedkillers and by leaving parts un-cut - badgers, foxes, herons, kingfishers and glow-worms are regular visitors. Bicycle hire 5 miles, riding or golf 3 miles. A member of the Best of British group. Bellamy silver.

Charges 2000:
-- Per unit incl. 2 adults £6.00 - £11.00; extra adult £1.00 - £3.25; child 50p - £1.25; awning/pup tent £1.00; dog £1.00; electricity £1.50.
-- Min. charge 2 adults per vehicle; large motorcaravans add £1.00.
-- VAT included.
-- Credit cards accepted.

Open:
All year except Jan. and Feb.

Address:
Relubbus, Penzance, Cornwall TR20 9ER.

Tel:
(01736) 763398
FAX: as phone.
E-mail: rivervalley@ surfbay.dircon.co.uk.

Reservations:
Any period with deposit (£20) and fee (£1).

see colour advert between pages 32/33

Directions: From A30 at St Michaels Mount roundabout, take A394 towards Helston. At next roundabout take B3280 to Relubbus. In approx. 3 miles in village turn left just over a small bridge. O.S.GR: SW566320.

011 Calloose Caravan Park, Leedstown, Hayle

Friendly, family rural touring park with swimming pool and a few holiday caravans.

This park is quietly situated in an inland valley and covering 8½ acres, about 4 miles from Hayle, with an extra ½ mile to the beaches beyond, 9 to St. Ives on the north coast and 6 to Helston and Praa Sands on the south. Attractively landscaped with almost a tropical feel, units are personally sited. The terrain is mainly flat but is dry, with two slightly raised areas on terraces. There are 120 tourist pitches (96 with 16A electricity, 8 with water and 28 gravel hardstandings) close together with individual markers, and 17 caravan holiday homes. In the main meadow areas, pitches are arranged round the perimeter with some free space in the middle. Both toilet blocks are well kept and provide washbasins in cubicles, free hot showers, family shower room, baby room, en-suite unit for disabled visitors, dishwashing sinks under cover and chemical disposal. A heated swimming pool (40 x 20 ft. open mid-May to mid-Sept) with separate paddling pool, is neatly landscaped with sunbathing terrace and access for disabled people. The shop and off-licence is well stocked (including gas) and a large, recreation block with themed bar and family room adjoins. Bar meals are served (daily in the main season, slightly restricted in early season), with takeaway (mid-May - late Sept), with entertainment most evenings in the main season including weekly barbecues in peak season. TV lounge, pool table, games room with skittle alley, all-weather tennis court, crazy golf (floodlit), table tennis and an adventure playground. Four acres of recreation fields include dog exercise fields, a full size football pitch and mountain bike scramble track. Laundry room, first aid room and public phones. Sun lounger and mountain bike hire and extensive local information are available in reception. All public areas have wheelchair access. The village with shops, pubs, etc. is within walking distance. Golf 4 miles, fishing 2 miles, riding 5 miles. A popular park, booking is essential. Bellamy silver.

Charges 2000:
-- Per unit incl. 2 persons £7.00 - £13.00; awning free; extra person (over 3 yrs) £1.00 - £3.00; pup tent (max. 1.8 x 1.2 m) £1.00 - £2.00; dog £1.00 - £2.50; electricity (10A) £2.00; 'super' pitch plus £2.00.
-- VAT included.
-- Credit cards accepted.

Open:
1 April - 30 September.

Address:
Leedstown, Hayle, Cornwall TR27 5ET.

Tel:
(01736) 850431.
FAX: as phone.

Reservations:
Made with £20 deposit per pitch, balance on arrival.

Directions: From B3280 and B3302 crossroads in Leedstown take B3302 towards Hayle. First right, then left on ½ mile access road to park. O.S.GR: SW599353.

11

Cornwall

008 Maen Valley Holiday Park, Falmouth

Long established park in sheltered valley with a relaxed atmosphere.

Maen Valley has two beaches within a mile, a range of activities nearby from sailing, windsurfing, fishing and diving to tennis coaching, access to the coastal path and many well known Cornish gardens near by. In a south facing, sheltered valley, a clear stream runs through the park and the mature woods provide walks. Its principal interest is in holiday cottages and caravan holiday homes (many privately owned, plus 70 to let) but there are also 18 places for touring caravans or motorhomes, on a separate level area with views at the top of the park near the second entrance, with electricity and a small, simple toilet block. A club (evenings and weekend lunches) provides social life and food. The club, bar and restaurant open Whitsun - 20 Sept. Other amenities include a shop (all season, 8.30-11am. and 4-7 pm), crazy golf and skittles. There is a pub in the village. Falmouth is 2 miles (5-10 minutes by car or there is an hourly bus service). Bellamy silver.

Charges 2000:
-- Per adult £4.00 - £6.00; child (3-16 yrs) £1.00 - £2.00; dog £1.00; electricity £2.00.
-- Credit cards accepted.
Open:
Easter - 31 October.
Address:
Falmouth, Cornwall TR11 5BJ.
Tel:
(01326) 312190.
FAX: (01326) 211120.
Reservations:
Made with £20 deposit.

Directions: From Truro, follow signs for Falmouth on A39. At first roundabout pass Asda then turn right at next roundabout signed Maenporth and industrial estates (on Bickland Water Road). Park is on right after 1½ miles. The first turning leads to the bottom of the valley and reception and is steep and narrow. The second entrance 100 yds further on is easier for caravans. O.S.GR: SW789311.

Maen Valley HOLIDAY PARK

Situated in a tranquil, sheltered, well wooded valley. Ideal touring centre and within walking distance to safe sandy beaches. Sailing, golf & other amenities.

Modern holiday caravans and chalets for hire
Touring van area with electrical hook-ups

• CARAVANS • CHALETS •

TELEPHONE 01326 312190 FOR FREE COLOUR BROCHURE

045 Pennance Mill Farm Chalet and Camping Park, Maenporth

Friendly, relaxed park for all units on working farm near Falmouth.

Pennance Mill Farm has been in the hands of the Jewell family for three generations and is listed as a typical Cornish farmstead – you can still watch the cows being milked and enjoy tractor rides. The touring site is situated in three sheltered south-facing, fairly level meadows with views over the fields and it provides for 70 pitches, 50 of which have 16A electricity. There are two toilet blocks, the first near the entrance is the original one but it is well kept and also provides a washing machine, dryer and laundry sinks. The new block in the top meadow is heated and well equipped with controllable showers, covered washing up sinks and chemical toilet disposal. Children have a small play meadow with a swing and climbing frame, and table tennis. An old mill wheel reminds one of the site's origins. You book in at the farmhouse and it is possible to get basic provisions and some locally produced specialities, in the little farm shop (open 09.00-10.30 and 17.30-18.30). Calor and camping gas are also available and a telephone. Continue on past the site for half a mile and you come to the sandy beach at Maenporth and, within walking distance, are tennis courts, golf course and pitch and putt. Also across the road and up a footpath you can reach Mean Valley Holiday Park (see entry above) where you can use their shop and club bar, enjoy good value food and where there is a nice atmosphere and some entertainment.

Charges 2000:
-- Per adult £2.50 - £3.00; child (over 3 yrs.) £1.00; pitch £2.50 - £3.00; awning £1.00; dog 50p; electricity £2.00.
Open:
Easter - November.
Address:
Maenporth, Falmouth, Cornwall TR11 5HY.
Tel:
(01326) 317431 or 312616.
FAX: (01326) 317431.
Reservations:
Contact park.

Directions: As for Maen Valley (no. 008, above) but continue past Mean Valley entrance down hill and site is on left as road bends right. O.S.GR: SW789307.

018 Carnon Downs Caravan and Camping Park, Truro

Quiet, quality, family park centrally situated for touring Cornwall.

This is a thoughtfully laid out, level park with attractive hedging and flowering shrubs providing some pleasant bays for caravans, run personally by Tony and Sarah Birch. Gravel roads connect 135 pitches, 120 with electricity (10/15A) and 15 with hardstanding. Of these 13 are fully serviced. The tent pitches, some with electricity, are well spaced around the outside of two level fields, the centre of one for goal posts and adventure-type play equipment, the other containing the reception and shop (for basics, gas and papers) where you receive a warm welcome, a neatly presented layout plan of the park, tourist and touring information pack. Two well cared for toilet blocks can be heated and provide good facilities including vanity style washbasins with mirrors - for ladies, three in one block are in cubicles. The showers are unisex, equipped with stool, shelf and curtain and, once you have got used to the idea, it works well. One block has been well refurbished to include three very good family bath/shower rooms, one suitable for use by disabled people or mothers and toddlers. There are two good laundries, one in each block, and a mother and toddler room (heated), including two baby sinks and a full sized bath, is to be found in the round-house next to the TV and information room. The round-house used to house the donkeys that turned the mill which once operated on the site! There is a recycling centre and a motor-caravan service point (ask at reception). Although one side of the park is next to the A39 road, it is well screened with a band of mature woodland so noise should be minimal. Excellent wooded dog walks around the site and two large fields. A 'Brewsters' pub is 100 yds across the road. Fishing 3 miles, riding or bicycle hire 2 miles, golf 1 mile. The park is well situated to explore the tip of Cornwall. Caravan storage. Bellamy gold.

Directions: From Truro take A39 Falmouth road. There is direct access from the Carnon Downs roundabout after 3 miles. O.S.GR: SW805406.

Charges 2000:
Per unit incl. 2 persons £7.25 - £12.75; extra adult £2.00; child (5-14 yrs) £1.70; electricity (10/15A) £2.00; all-service hardstanding £2.00; small 2 man tent plus car less £1.00, walker or cyclist (single) less £3.00, double less £2.00.
-- Credit cards accepted.
-- VAT included.

Open:
Easter/1 April - 31 Oct.

Address:
Carnon Downs, nr. Truro, Cornwall TR3 6JJ.

Tel:
(01872) 862283.
FAX: (01872) 862800.
E-mail: park@carnon-downs.co.uk.

Reservations:
Made with £20 deposit p/week; contact park.

010 Leverton Place Caravan Park, Truro

Neat, well kept park with swimming pool and other amenities, just west of Truro.

About 6 miles from the northern coast of Cornwall and not much more from the southern, Leverton Place has been well designed and laid out along continental lines and is now part of the Caravan Club 'managed under contract' scheme although non-members are very welcome. The pitches are attractively arranged in groups in a series of secluded bays with neat, well drained lawns divided up by access roads, hedges and shrubs. There is provision for 107 touring units of any type with 7 chalets and 13 caravans to let. Pitches are marked, 100 with electrical connections (10A), 39 with hardstanding and 14 fully serviced with their own water, waste drainage, full hardstanding and picnic bench. There are four toilet blocks serving the touring section, a central one providing 15 individual en-suite shower rooms, heated in winter, including one which is specifically designed for disabled people. It is a good, well maintained provision with two excellent dishwashing and laundry kitchens. The newest block near reception has a state-of-the-art chemical disposal and boot washing facility. Motorcaravan service point. An attractive walled patio area, complete with palm trees, provides a 18 m. long pool (heated mid May - mid Sept), a paddling pool, takeaway, lounge bar and bistro (mid May - mid Sept) with terraced sitting out area overlooking the pool. The bar opens each evening and perhaps at other times, but is sufficient distance from the pitch areas so as not to be intrusive. Shop with gas beside reception, open all day, all year. Two children's playgrounds and two games rooms, both with pool, one with table tennis. First aid room. Bicycles, roller skates and skate boards not allowed. Winter caravan storage. Two well stocked fishing lakes are 400 yds, riding or golf 2 miles. A quality site, well worth consideration.

Directions: Park is 3 miles west of Truro, signed from A390 road ½ mile from village of Threemilestone on road to Chacewater. O.S.GR: SW770451.

Charges 2000:
-- Per pitch 22 July - 31 Aug. £10.00, otherwise £1.00; adult £3.25 - £4.00; child (5-16 yrs) £1.10 - £1.20; dog free - £1.00; electricity £1.45 - £2.20; fully serviced pitch plus £2.00.
-- VAT included.
-- Credit cards accepted.

Open:
All year.

Address:
Truro, Cornwall TR4 8QW.

Tel:
(01872) 560462.
FAX: (01872) 560668.

Reservations:
Made with deposit of £20 per week or part for high season, £5 at other times.

Cornwall

039 Trelowarren Touring Caravan and Camping Park, Mawgan

Delightful park in grounds of Cornish Manor with Craft and Countryside Centre.

There is a sense of timelessness about Trelowarren - perhaps it is the mature parkland or the mellow manor house, home to the Vyvyan family since 1427. Whatever, it is a beautiful, tranquil park set on the eastern side of the Lizard Peninsula, close to the Helford river. Access from the main road is via a single track road for a mile but it is well worth it. Set in 20 acres, there are three distinctive areas for camping all with neatly cut grass, providing 125 places for caravans and motorcaravans and 75 for tents. First is the walled gardens with some pitches on a slight slope and with its own, if basic, small sanitary block with toilets, washbasins and chemical disposal. Second is the apple orchard edged by the woods with a secluded area known as the quarry at the lower end, with some level but mainly sloping pitches. The third area is more open, with views across the valley and running parallel to the orchard, separated by stone walls. It has some mature trees and the main toilet block. There are 25 level hardstandings here that fit even the large American motorhomes. Sanitary facilities in original stone buildings are modern and attractively equipped with free, comfortably sized showers with good heavy curtain dividers, some washbasins in cubicles for ladies, and a bath. Five washing up sinks are under cover, and a laundry room provides three sinks, a washing machine and dryer. En-suite facility for disabled visitors and a baby room with three sinks. Motorcaravan service point. Reception, a public telephone, takeaway (1/7-3/9) and a little 'Inn' complete the amenities on the site. However, through a small door, just past the walled garden, is the stable courtyard with a delightful bistro, licensed and open at lunch-times and some evenings (with jazz and folk music). A Countryside Centre charts the development of the Lizard from pre-history to the present day and is a must to try and understand this unique area, which is now home to the Goonhilly Earth Station. The Trelowarren Pottery and Weaving Centre and the various exhibitions organised by the Cornwall Craft Association, not to mention the house and gardens (being rebuilt to the original design but incorporating 20th century techniques, plants and architectural incident) and woodland walks (way-marked), make this a most attractive place to spend time - something for everyone in a most relaxing, yet interesting, setting.

Charges 2000:
--Per person £3.25 - £4.00; child (3-16 yrs) £1.50 - £1.95; dog, extra car or boat £1.00; electricity £1.80, -- Pitch and awning incl. -- No credit cards.

Open:
1 April/Easter - 30 Sept, (as are all other facilities on the park which are open to the public).

Address:
Mawgan,
Nr. Helston
Cornwall TR12 6AF.

Tel:
(01326) 221637.
FAX: (01326) 221440.

Reservations:
Made with £10 deposit; contact park.

Directions: From Helston take A3083 (Lizard). Just after Culdrose Air Station turn left on B3293, signed St. Keverne. Avoid turnings to Gweek and Mawgan and watch for Trelowarren signs on left before Goonhilly. O.S.GR: SW719239.

007 Silver Sands Holiday Park, Kennack Sands, nr. Helston

Small, 'away-from-it-all', peaceful park in a remote part of the Lizard.

On a corner of the Lizard peninsula, the most southerly part of mainland Britain, (an area of outstanding natural beauty), only reached after passing Culdrose Naval Base and Goonhilly Earth Station down a single track road, one finds Silver Sands - tucked away behind two other parks which provide holiday homes with very little else. A ½ mile footpath leads down through a small valley to the twin beaches of Kennack Sands (one is dog-free) divided by a small headland. This is generally an unspoilt walking area under the care of English Nature. The park itself has 16 caravan holiday homes for hire, along with 14 large touring pitches with 5A electricity, divided into bays by shrubs and bushes. An adjoining tent field has similar pitches (4 with electricity) where shrubs are growing and pitches in bays are slightly sloping. An additional, undeveloped three-acre field can be used for walking, kite flying, etc. The sanitary block is old and quite quaint, but is well maintained. It has showers, a laundry room, baby unit, chemical disposal, hair drying area, dishwashing sinks (H&C) and a microwave. Reception, in an elderly static van, has good tourist information. There is play equipment for under six's opposite reception, with swings and a sand pit in other areas. Public phone. A shop is 20 yards on the next site and a pub is within walking distance. Fishing 1 mile, bicycle hire 5 miles, boat launching 2 or 7 miles, riding 5 miles, golf 6 miles. A member of the Countryside Discovery group. Bellamy silver.

Charges 2001:
-- Per touring unit incl. 2 persons £6.00 - £7.50; extra adult £1.40 - £2.50; child (3-13 yrs) £1.30 - £1.90; awning or extra pup tent £1.00; dog £1.30 - £1.60; extra car or boat £1.20; electricity £1.60. -- Less £2 for cyclists or hikers with pup tent. -- No credit cards.

Open:
1 May - 15 September.

Address:
Kennack Sands, Ruan Minor, Helston, Cornwall TR12 7LZ.

Tel:
(01326) 290631.
FAX: as phone.
E-mail: silversnds @aol.com.

Reservations:
Made with 25% deposit, min. £30; balance on arrival.

Directions: From Helston take A3038 Lizard road. After Culdrose turn left on B3293 passing Goonhilly after 4 miles. At the next crossroads turn right (signed Kennack Sands, continue for 1½ miles then left to Gwendreath on single track road - site is 1 mile. O.S.GR: SW732170.

013 Liskey Touring Park, nr. Truro

Quiet, family park under new ownership, centrally situated for touring central Cornwall.

Liskey is pleasantly landscaped with rockery plants and well manicured grass and first impressions of loving care are carried all through the park. The first small building is a room for TV, excellent tourist information and a library. It can also be used by families for board games should the weather turn inclement. Next comes reception, a comfortable room with settee and chairs, where milk, bread, papers and gas are also sold (Truro supermarkets are 3 miles). The main, slightly sloping camping area is beautifully landscaped with trees, shrubs and heathers and level, well spaced pitches have good views across the countryside. A strictly touring site, 46 of the 60 pitches have 10A electricity and 12 are fully serviced with level hardstanding and a gravel area for awnings. There are all weather pea-gravel pitches for tents. There is a feeling of spaciousness, mainly because the owners do not try to fit in too many units. Breathable groundsheets are welcome on the grassy pitches. The central toilet block is clean, well maintained and can be heated. There is free hot water, some washbasins in cubicles, comfortable push-button showers, a bathroom (50p) and chemical disposal. Everywhere is tiled and there are free hairdryers, hand-dryers and soap. The laundry room is also well equipped and dishwashing sinks are under cover, also with free hot water. Motorcaravan service point. An adventure playground and playing field with volleyball and basketball nets should keep older children out of mischief and, should it be wet, there is a play barn with pea-gravel base with more adventure-type equipment and table tennis. For under 5s there is a fenced play area with a large selection of equipment. No bikes, skateboards or roller-blades are allowed. A boules pitch has been added. Dogs are accepted on short leads with a good dog walk provided. Winter caravan storage. A pub with good food and real ale is only 600 yds. and buses to Truro pass the gate. Coarse fishing ¼ mile, bicycle hire 3 mile, riding 2 miles, golf 1 mile. Within 5 miles are beaches and facilities for tennis and boat launching. Liskey is a good place for the family that can amuse itself without the need for discos and gaming machines.

Directions: From A30 take A390 to Truro. At next roundabout turn right (signed Threemilestone) and immediately at mini-roundabout, right again towards Chacewater. Park is 600 yds on right past Leverton Place. O.S.GR: SW772452.

Charges 2000:
-- Per unit incl. 2 persons £6.50 - £10.50; extra adult £2.50 - £3.50, teenager (13-17 yrs) £1.50 - £2.00, child (3-12 yrs) £1.20 - £1.50; first dog free - £1.00, extra dog £1.00; electricity (10A) £1.70; tent power unit incl. electricity £2.70; serviced pitch £2.20 - £3.20.
-- Low season discounts for over 50s, fully retired.
-- No single sex groups.
-- Credit cards accepted.
Open:
1 April - 22 September.
Address:
Greenbottom, Truro, Cornwall TR4 8QN.
Tel:
(01872) 560274.
FAX: no phone.
E-mail: enquiries @liskey.co.uk.
Reservations:
Made with £3 deposit per night booked or payment in full if less than 5 days.

Cornwall

014 Penrose Farm Touring Park, Goonhavern, nr. Truro

Well cared for, quality, family park in popular area.

Penrose Farm is a level, sheltered, touring only park on the edge of the village of Goonhavern. The 100 pitches are spread over five fields, with flower beds and bushes set amongst them. These flowers and all those at the entrance to the park are very colourful and give the park a neat, orderly and well cared for feel. The very enthusiastic owners, Colin and Joanne, take great delight in getting to know their customers, many of whom come every year, and pride in the facilities they provide. The refurbished toilet block is tiled throughout and kept spotless by Joanne. It provides vanity style washbasins, adjustable showers with stool and four excellent family rooms containing an adjustable shower, washbasin, WC and hairdryer. One of these rooms is accessible for wheelchairs. All these amenities are enhanced with beautiful pot plants and flowers like a 'mini' Kew Gardens. Children have an excellent adventure playground and an indoor animal centre with guinea pigs, rabbits and miniature goats to stroke and cuddle and fish, terrapins and birds to admire. The reception area has tourist information and a small shop sells gas and basic needs (Easter, then May - Sept). The laundry is well equipped and dishwashing sinks are provided, all with free hot water. Chemical disposal. Dogs are allowed on leads with a large exercise field provided. Colin is constantly re-appraising the pitches, always trying to ensure that each unit has plenty of space and doesn't feel overcrowded. There are 52 pitches with 16A electricity and 8 pitches with hardstanding (4 with electricity). It really is a very neat and tidy well run park. Caravan storage available. It is only a short walk to the village and its popular pub, and buses to Newquay stop in the village. The superb beach at Perranporth is only 2½ miles away. Bicycle hire can be arranged, fishing or riding ½ mile, golf 1 mile. To retain its quiet family image, there are no plans for bars or entertainment and only couples and families are admitted.

Charges 2001:
-- Per unit incl. 2 persons £8.00 - £12.00; extra person (5 yrs and over) £3.00; awning, extra car, dog free; electricity (16A) £2.00.
-- Families and couples only.
-- Less 50p for over 60s if booked.
-- VAT included.
-- Credit cards accepted.

Open:
1 April - 30 September.

Address:
Goonhavern, nr. Truro, Cornwall TR4 9QF.

Tel:
(01872) 573185.
E-mail: col@penrose99.freeserve.co.uk.

Reservations:
Made with £30 deposit.

Alan Rogers' Discount

 Less £1 p/night excl. 15/7-31/8

Directions: Take A30 from Exeter past Bodmin and Indian Queens. Just after wind farm take B3285 to Perranporth. Park is on the left as you enter Goonhavern village. O.S.GR: SW790535.

012 Silverbow Park, Goonhavern, nr Perranporth

Select, quiet and spacious, well kept park with pool, 2½ miles back from the sea.

J23

Silverbow has been developed by the Taylor family over many years and they are justifiably proud of their efforts. Particularly seeking to encourage couples and quiet families with young children (no teenagers over 12), they believe Silverbow is a way of life and staying is an experience - they have certainly created a relaxed and tranquil atmosphere. Hard work, planting and landscaping has provided a beautiful park set in 21 acres which has, in the past, taken part in the well known 'Gardens Scheme'. There are 90 good-sized tourist pitches, including 69 'super' pitches in a newly developed area, with electricity, water and drainaway, which are even larger. Many are on a slight slope with some attractive views. There is much free space not used for camping, including an excellent sports area with two all-weather and one grass tennis courts (free coaching in season), two outdoor badminton courts, short mat bowls, a children's adventure playground on sand and a general play field, as well as wild meadow and wooded areas ideal for walks. More recently, a natural area with ponds has been created to encourage wild-life (the first park in Cornwall to gain a Bellamy gold award for conservation). An attractive, kidney shaped, heated swimming pool and small paddling pool (mid-May - mid-Sept) sheltered by high garden walls is a real tropical sun trap. There is a games room with pool table, table tennis and tourist information. In a separate part are 15 park-owned, high quality leisure homes. The park is 2½ miles from the long sandy beach at Perranporth (30 minutes walk away from traffic) and 6 miles from Newquay. Three toilet blocks, all of excellent quality with private cabins for each sex, fully controllable free hot showers, four family shower/toilet rooms, two accessible for wheelchairs, and one bath on payment for each sex. Six enclosed dishwashing sinks. Laundry room. Recycling bins. Freezer service. Public phone. Shop (mid May - mid Sept). A pub is within walking distance. Concessionary green fees are available at Perranporth golf club. Gliding, riding and fishing are nearby. Mountain biking from the park (but no bikes on site). Bellamy gold.

Goonhavern. O.S.GR: SW781531.

Charges 2001:
-- Per unit incl. 2 adults £6.00 - £14.00; extra adult under 50 yrs £3.00 - £5.50; extra child 2-12 yrs or adult over 50 yrs £2.00 - £3.60; dog free - £1.50; fully serviced pitch incl. electricity £3.00.
-- Children over 12 yrs with or without parents not accepted.
-- Discounts available
-- VAT included.

Open:
2 May - 10 October.

Address:
Goonhavern, nr Truro, Cornwall TR4 9NX.

Tel:
(01872) 572347.

Reservations:
Made with £20 p/week deposit (Sat. - Sat. only 17/7-21/8).

Directions: Entrance is directly off the main A3075 road ½ mile south of

031 Trekenning Tourist Park, Newquay

Pretty, inland family park with an attractive garden pool.

Trekenning is owned by John Fynn, his daughter Tracey and son-in-law Dave and they have succeeded in developing a popular park with good facilities, a nice change from the 'all singing, all dancing' Newquay sites. Easy access just off the A39 roundabout at St Columb Major leads to a large sloping field with neatly cut grass and all the facilities in the opposite corner. In total there are 75 pitches, 68 with 10A electricity. Some have been levelled, others are tucked away at a lower level shaded by tall trees and a well hidden tent field with just a water point is edged by a wooded small stream. There are two sanitary blocks, one providing normal showers and vanity style washbasins, the other with two en-suite bathrooms and six large family showers, well refurbished. There is a laundry room, covered dishwashing sinks and chemical disposal. The star of the show is undoubtedly the kidney shaped pool and paddling pool which are in a garden-like setting with gazebos and sun loungers, with a terraced lawn and patio at the top. This leads to the games room and cosy upstairs bar. 'Eatery' and takeaway facilities (all July/Aug). Entertainment is provided every night in the main season (ie. singers, quiz nights, connect-4 nights, discos on Fridays). Barbecue areas and a sand based children's play area contained within a low stone wall in the main field complete the facilities. Public telephone. Fishing 1 mile, riding and golf 2 miles, bicycle hire 6 miles. The A39 runs parallel to one side of the site, so road noise is possible. Bellamy silver.

Directions: Take A3059 turning to Newquay from St Columb Major then turn immediately left; park is signed (this was the old road). O.S.GR: SW907625.

Charges 2000:
-- Per adult £3.75 - £5.40; child (3-15 yrs) £2.55 - £3.90; electricity £2.90; extra vehicle £1.10; dog £2.00.
-- No pitch charges.
-- VAT included.
-- Credit cards accepted.

Open:
Easter/1 April - 30 September

Address:
Newquay, Cornwall TR8 4JF.

Tel:
(01637) 880462.
FAX: (01637) 880500.
E-mail: trekenning @aol.com.

Reservations:
Made with £20 deposit.

Cornwall

017 Trevella Caravan and Camping Park, Crantock, Newquay

Orderly touring park close to sea, with pool and fishing lakes; some caravans for hire.

One of the best known and most respected of Cornish parks with its colourful flower-beds and driveway, a regular winner of a 'Newquay in Bloom' award, Trevella is also one of the first to fill up and has a longer season than most. Well organised, the pitches are in a number of adjoining meadows, most of which are on a slight slope. Of the 250 pitches for touring units (any type), some 200 can be reserved and these are marked, individual ones. Over 200 pitches have electricity (10A), with 33 'premium' serviced pitches (with hardstanding, electricity and TV hook-ups, water, waste water, sewage). Attractively and centrally situated, a free heated swimming pool with sunbathing area is open (weather permitting) like the shop, etc. from Easter - Oct. The nearest beach is ½ mile on foot, 1 mile by car and Newquay is 2 miles. There are pubs and restaurants at Crantock, 1 mile. Trevella is essentially a quiet family touring park with an accent on orderliness and cleanliness; on-site evening activities are limited. The sanitary facilities are kept very clean, the three blocks providing sufficient coverage with individual washbasins with shelf, in private cabins for ladies, free hot water to plentiful washing-up sinks and controllable showers, hair dressing room, baby room and launderette. There is a well stocked supermarket, a post box and telephone and a freezer pack service. Nicky's Kitchen offers hot dishes and snacks to take away or eat there, open late. A games room has pool tables and table tennis, there is a separate TV room, crazy golf, a large adventure playground, separate play and sports area and a pets corner. Access is free to three fishing lakes, two on site (permits from reception); some fishing instruction, and wildlife talks for youngsters in season. A pleasant walk is possible around the lakes, a protected nature reserve, and it is also possible to walk to Crantock beach but the tides must be checked first. Shuttle bus service to Newquay in high season. Riding 1 mile, golf 3 miles. A member of the Best of British group. Bellamy gold.

Charges 2000:
-- Per adult £3.00 - £5.50; child (3-16 yrs) £1.50 - £2.75; car 60p - 80p; dog 50p - £1.20; electricity £2.40; full services incl. electricity £5.50.
-- Families and couples only.
-- Credit cards accepted.
-- VAT included.

Open:
Easter - 31 October.

Address:
Crantock, Newquay, Cornwall TR8 5EW.

Tel:
(01637) 830308 (24 hr). FAX: (01872) 571254. E-mail: trevella@ compuserve.com.

Reservations:
Made with £20 deposit and £2 booking fee (16/7-27/8: Fri/Fri or Sat/Sat only).

Directions: To avoid Newquay leave A30 or A392 at Indian Queens, straight over crossroads with A39 and A3058, left at A3075 junction and first right at camp sign. O.S.GR: SW802598.

016 Newperran Tourist Park, Rejerrah, nr. Newquay

Large capacity, open touring-only park, with pool and close to popular beaches.

This is a level park in rural Cornish countryside and on high ground making it quite open but also giving excellent views of the coast and surrounding district. Although it has its own manager, it is under the same family ownership and direction as Trevella Park, with the same sort of standards. Newperran is a little further back from the sea, but only 2½ miles from Perranporth beach, and there is a free heated swimming pool on site. Those who prefer traditional camping to a holiday camp atmosphere should appreciate this park. This is not to say that it is without facilities; it certainly has its full share of amenities, but it is a quiet park used mainly by families and with few evening activities. It does now have an attractive 'village inn' with a garden, open every evening, more in high season. The park consists of a number of flat, well drained, hedged meadows divided into 250 individual pitches. Some fields have larger and reservable plots, with more free space in the middle. There are 113 electrical connections (10A) including 13 'all-service' pitches. Sanitary facilities comprise four clean, permanent blocks with free hot water in washbasins (most in cabins) and hot showers. There are two bathrooms, hair dressing room, a unit for disabled visitors, washing up sinks and a launderette. Good self-service licensed shop. Cafe with hot snacks to eat there or take away. TV room with some children's video shows. Activities for children include an adventure playground and a separate play area for under-fives, crazy golf, a children's room and an activity programme in season. Free fishing at Trevella. Riding or golf 2 miles. Goonhavern village is within walking distance with pubs and post office. A member of the Best of British group.

Charges 2000:
-- Per adult £3.00 - £5.50; child (3-16 yrs) £1.50 - £2.75; car 60p - 80p; dog 50p - £1.00; electricity (10A) £2.30; full services incl. electricity £5.50.
-- VAT included.
-- Credit cards accepted.

Open:
Mid-May - mid-Sept.

Address:
Rejerrah, Newquay, Cornwall TR8 5QJ.

Tel:
(01872) 572407. (1/10-1/5: (01637) 830308). FAX: (01872) 571254. E-mail: trevella@ compuserve.com.

Reservations:
Advised in high season; made with £20 p/w deposit and £2 fee.

Directions: Turn off A3075 to west at camping sign 7 miles south of Newquay and just north of Goonhavern village. O.S.GR: SW794546.

Trevella & Newperran

CARAVAN AND CAMPING PARK | TOURIST PARK

Both parks have spotless facilities including modern toilet and shower blocks with individual wash cubicles, razor points, babies room, hairdressing room, hairdriers, launderette, crazy golf, games room, TV room, cafe, shop and off licence, free heated swimming pools and adventure play areas.

GOLD

THE FAMILY RUN HOLIDAY PARKS

Our parks are renowned for their cleanliness and hygiene and we spare no effort to maintain this reputation.
- Concessionary green fees at Perranporth's excellent links golf course.
- Nature reserve and well stocked lake at Trevella offers Free Fishing (no closed season).

VOTED TWO OF THE TOP 10 TOURING PARKS IN CORNWALL

TREVELLA PARK
22 CRANTOCK, NEWQUAY, CORNWALL TR8 5EW.   TEL: 01637 830308
www.trevella.co.uk

Trevella just outside Newquay and its seven golden beaches. A breathtakingly beautiful secluded family park. As well as touring pitches there are holiday caravans for hire with toilet, shower and colour Satellite TV.

NEWPERRAN TOURIST PARK
22 REJERRAH, NEWQUAY, CORNWALL TR8 5QJ.   TEL: 01872 572407
www.newperran.co.uk

Newperran has been developed from a small Cornish farm in a picturesque, beautifully cared for setting. It is a level park with perimeter pitching ideal for caravans, tents, motor homes and the perfect family holiday.

TELEPHONE FOR COLOUR BROCHURES
01637 830308 (24 HOURS)
OR WRITE FOR BROCHURE TO THE SITE OF YOUR CHOICE.

Cornwall

020 Newquay Holiday Park, Newquay

Well run park with swimming pools and other amenities near town.

This park lies peacefully on a terraced hillside only just outside the town, 2 miles from the beaches and town centre. The main feature of the park is an attractively laid out group of three heated swimming pools with giant water slide (lifeguards in attendance) and surrounding 'green' sunbathing areas. Mainly a touring park, it has 356 marked pitches for any type of unit in a series of hedged fields, some sloping, with some fields just for caravans and others for tents, plus 138 caravan holiday homes (for hire). Most pitches are individual ones marked out by lines on ground but with nothing between them. Electricity points (16A) are provided for caravans and tents, plus 10 special 'star' pitches with hardstanding, water and drainage. The sanitary installations include two good-sized, modern blocks with washbasins set in flat surfaces with free hot water and fairly basic free hot showers with pre-mixed hot water which runs for four minutes and stops, with an extra block for the main season when they may be under pressure. There is a baby bath, covered external dishwashing sinks with hot water and chemical disposal points. Gas is available. Entertainment each night with live music, discos etc. is provided in the site's Fiesta Club which also has a bar, TV lounge and games room with pool and snooker tables (all open when the site is open). Amusement arcade. Well stocked self-service shop and takeaway food bar (both all season, and good value). Full launderette with free ironing. Activities include a pitch and putt course, crazy golf, a good children's playground, children's club and recreation field for football and volleyball. Fishing and bicycle hire 2 miles, golf 200 yds, riding 2½ miles. Bus service to Newquay from site. No dogs or pets are accepted. Bellamy gold.

Directions: Park is east of Newquay on A3059 road 1 mile east of junction with A3058. O.S.GR: SW853626.

Charges 2001:
-- Per adult £3.25 - £6.10; child (3-15 yrs) free - £4.10; vehicle 85p; electricity (16A) free - £2.50; star pitch supplement £3.50.
-- Min. charge per night in high season £13.05.
-- Families and mixed couples only.
-- VAT included.
-- Credit cards accepted.

Open:
Mid May - mid Sept.

Address:
Newquay, Cornwall TR8 4HS.

Tel:
(01637) 871111. FAX: (01637) 850818. E-mail: bookings@ newquay-holiday-parks.co.uk.

Reservations:
Advised for peak season; made with £18.50 deposit p/week plus £10 cancellation insurance (peak weeks Sat. - Sat. only).

022 Trevornick Holiday Park, Holywell Bay, Newquay

Large, busy, modern, family park for all touring units near sandy beach, with wide ranging amenities.

Trevornick, once a working farm, is now a modern, well-run touring park providing a wide range of facilities. The park has recently won the coveted 'Investors in People' award (one of the first parks to do so) and this is reflected in the standards and management of resources and in the welcoming attitude of the staff. The park has grown to provide caravanners and campers (no holiday caravans) with 450 grass pitches (386 with electricity) in five level fields and two terraced areas (few trees, but some good views), providing 'all singing, all dancing' facilities for family holidays. Five toilet blocks of a standard modern design provide washbasins in vanity style, toilets, coin-operated showers (20p) and include a family shower room, two bathrooms (50p), baby bath, dishwashing and laundry facilities, chemical disposal and facilities for disabled visitors. The farm buildings now provide the setting for the farm club (recently refurbished) with licensed facilities and food, children's rooms, games room, cafeteria 'De caff' with terrace and takeaway, plus much entertainment every night in season. The Trawlers' Bar serves meals and drinks for families (with TV), and there is a well stocked supermarket with fresh bread made on site (both from late May). Activities include a good sized, outdoor, heated and supervised pool (also late May) with slide, sauna, a super Fort Knox style adventure playground, crazy golf, Kiddies Club and indoor adventure play area (supervised for 2-8 year olds at a small charge). Dogs are accepted in one field only with a walk provided. The rest of the development has provided an 18 hole golf course, pitch and putt, a small, quiet club with bar meals and lovely views out to sea, Holywell Bay 'fun' park next door (site fun pass gives reduced rates) and recently much improved coarse fishing with three lakes. The sandy beach is 5 minutes by car or 20 minutes walk through the sand dunes past the Holywell. Bicycle hire on site. Boat launching 4 miles, riding within 1 mile. The park offers 60 'Eurotents' to hire (pre-erected, fully equipped tents sleeping 6; cot and TV hire available). A busy, happy park with lots to do.

Charges 2000:
-- Per adult £3.00 - £5.75; child (4-14 yrs) free - £3.75; car 80p; electricity £2.75 - £3.00; dog £1.75.
-- Families and couples only.
-- VAT included.
-- Credit cards accepted.

Open:
Easter -mid September.

Address:
Holywell Bay, Newquay, Cornwall TR8 5PW.

Tel:
(01637) 830531.
FAX: (01637) 831000.
E-mail: info@ trevornick.co.uk.

Reservations:
Made with £20 deposit per week (Sat. to Sat. only July/Aug).

Directions: From A3075 approach to Newquay - Perranporth road, turn towards Cubert and Holywell Bay. Continue through Cubert to park on the right. O.S.GR: SW776586.

...we've got the holiday for you! **Relax**
*Whether you are campers or tourers we have everything you need for a **brilliant** holiday. **Superb** location overlooking Holywell Bay. First-class facilities and a wonderful friendly atmosphere.*

'You deserve the best...!' 5 STAR GRADED PARK ★ ★ ★ ★ ★

...for a great fun holiday! **Smile**
*Glorious safe swimming and surfing beach. Amazing full entertainment programme, **marvellous** children's club, heated pool, coarse fishing and a **brilliant** 18-hole golf course. You'll have a fantastic time!*

Phone NOW for a copy of our brochure to find out more
☎ **01637 830531**
www.trevornick.co.uk · email: info@trevornick.co.uk

HOLYWELL BAY · NEWQUAY · CORNWALL TR8 5PW

Cornwall

021 Hendra Holiday Park, Newquay

Holiday park with comprehensive entertainment programme and new water park.

Hendra is a long-established holiday park for the family that likes to be entertained, as the entertainment programme here is very comprehensive. There are comedians, show bands, cabaret, dancing, bingo, discos, plus entertainment and clubs for children. The 600 pitches are on various well mown, slightly sloping grass fields with country views and mature trees, some more sheltered than others. There are tarmac roads and lighting and 200 pitches have electrical connections (16A). Some landscaped hardstanding 'super' pitches have individual water, electricity, light, sewer drainage and satellite TV connections (dogs are not accepted on these pitches). Many pitches also have water, drainage and hardstanding. There are caravan holiday homes for hire but they are separate from the tourers. The entrance and reception are very attractive with a mass of well tended flower beds which, along with the other facilities, form an attractive, village-like centre to the park. The 'star of the show' at Hendra is now the new Oasis complex consisting of a 30 m. indoor, heated fun pool with three flumes, river rapids, water falls and beach. Timed 1¼ hour sessions cost £2 per family group (max. 4 persons). The new outdoor heated pool with grass sunbathing area is free to campers. The complex is open to the public - really a mini water-park. Hendra's well stocked shop, various bars and restaurants open all season (limited hours in early season), even for breakfast, including a fish and chip bar and Mario's pizzeria, which is only open in the main season. The three toilet blocks have been refurbished to provide vanity style washbasins, free showers and some facilities for babies and disabled visitors. Large launderette, chemical disposal and motorcaravan services, plus gas supplies. Activities are well catered for with large playing fields, tennis court, minigolf, adventure play area, table tennis, pool tables and also a very large array of slot machines. A children's club and entertainment for everyone are organised in the club complex. Fishing or riding 1 mile, bicycle hire or golf 2 miles. Dogs are accepted in some areas of the park (small dog walk provided). The park is only 1½ miles from Newquay and its fabulous surfing beaches and a bus to the town passes the gate.

Charges 2000:
-- Per adult £3.30 - £5.15; child (3-14 yrs) free - £3.50; vehicle £1.00; awning free; 'super' pitch (electricity, water, chemical disposal, TV point, hardstanding, no dogs) £7.50; hardstanding pitch (electricity, water and drainage) £3.85; electricity only £2.80; dog £1.50.
-- Families and mixed couples only.
-- Various special offers.
-- VAT included.
-- Credit cards accepted.
Open:
February - end October.
Address:
Newquay,
Cornwall TR8 4NY.
Tel:
(01637) 875778.
FAX: (01637) 879017.
E-mail: hendra.cornwall @dial.pipex.com.
Reservations:
Made with deposit (£20) and fee (£3).

Directions: Park is on left side of A392 Indian Queens - Newquay road at Newquay side of Quintrell Downs. O.S.GR: SW833601.

024N Southleigh Manor Naturist Holiday Club, St. Columb Major

Welcoming family naturist site in the mature grounds of a large house with heated pool.

For those who have ventured to try the naturist sites in our French guide and who also may appreciate that special ambience at home, we are happy to include Southleigh Manor, now under the new ownership of Aideen and Roy Dougan and son Lawrence. The respect that the naturist has for the environment and for fellow beings provides a very special, caring atmosphere and this can be truly experienced on this site. The 50 pitches have been developed in the south facing, sheltered, lawned garden and orchard with mature trees. There are 2 hardstandings and 48 electrical connections (5/10A), plus 10 touring vans to let. The purpose built toilet block has identical, well equipped, unisex units at each end, well maintained, with a laundry room in the middle. Chemical disposal. Small shop - bread, milk, papers and tourist information (late May - 31 Aug). A sun room and leisure suite including sauna, spa bath and exercise equipment, are in the house. The small open air swimming pool is heated and can therefore be used all season. Other facilities include boules, croquet (in the walled garden), volleyball, minigolf and a children's play area with tree house and gaily painted train. Dogs are permitted on leads. Fishing 4 miles, bicycle hire 7 miles, riding 2 miles, golf 5 miles. You will be encouraged to get involved, with barbecues and social evenings and the opportunity to enjoy Cornwall's naturist beaches and many tourist attractions, which combine to provide a relaxed holiday atmosphere.

Charges guide:
-- Per unit incl. 2 adults £11.50 - £12.50; extra adult £2.30 - £2.40; child (13 yrs and under) £1.10 - £1.35; extra pup tent £1.10; electricity £1.95; dog 95p.
-- Club membership £2.50 per couple/family for stay.
-- No credit cards.
-- VAT included.
Open:
April - 20 September.
Address:
St. Columb Major,
Cornwall TR9 6HY.
Tel:
(01637) 880938.
FAX: as phone.
Reservations:
Made with £40 deposit.

Directions: From north on A30 Bodmin - Truro road, after village of Victoria pass crossroad (Roche Cross) and go under iron railway bridge and then first right on A3059 towards St Mawgan and St Columb. Site is on left in 3 miles. From A39, take A3059 at Newquay/St Columb roundabout and site is on right, almost immediately. O.S.GR: SW904622.

015 Sea View International, Gorran, nr. Mevagissey

First class, quality park with landscaped pool area and near safe beaches.

Sea View is one of the best examples of a well cared for, quality park and this is reflected in the number of awards it has won in the last 20 years. Now in the hands of the third generation of the Michell family, the park is constantly being improved with the aim of providing quality camping for the discerning camper. Although somewhat exposed, the park is a mass of colour with flower beds full of colourful bedding plants and flowering shrubs and has well manicured grass of exceptional quality. The area around the swimming pool is particularly attractive, with sunbathing areas with free sun-beds on tiled terraces surrounded by flowers creating private little areas, all with magnificent views of the sea and the distant headland (the pool is open all season, heated end May-mid Sept). The toilet blocks are excellent - centrally positioned, well maintained, with good quality fittings and central heating. The large showers are free and there are vanity style wash-basins, baby baths, facilities for disabled visitors (two showers and WCs), a hairdressing area with free hairdryers, plus bathrooms (on payment). The toilet and washbasin block has been extended to provide an enlarged dishwashing area with two small campers' kitchens (one with a microwave, one with a mini-grill and hob), a well equipped laundry and excellent chemical disposal facilities, all fully tiled. A covered, flowered walkway connects these excellent facilities which are topped by a handsome clock tower. A motorcaravan service point with car washing facilities is nearby. A shop (July-end Sept) and takeaway (Whit-mid Sept) are near the park entrance and reception provides plenty of tourist information, plus gas. There are no bars, restaurant or evening entertainment which seems to be the main reason many return year after year - booking for July/Aug. is advisable. Many of the 165 large, level pitches have views, all have 16A electricity and 47 are fully serviced, including hardstandings suitable for large motorhomes. There are 38 caravan holiday homes for hire. The excellent large playing field has plenty of room for leisure activities including tennis, volleyball, badminton, football, putting, table tennis, crazy golf and an adventure playground (all free). Bicycle hire on site. A barbecue area with tables and seats and a nice touch is a very descriptive weather map which is updated daily. Fishing lakes are planned for 2001. A large exercise field is provided for dogs (not certain breeds). Public phones. Anyone not restricted by school holidays will find May and June a particularly good time to visit, the gardens of Heligan and Trelissick and Lanhydrock House being at their best at that time. The area is full of places to visit from theme parks to the seal sanctuary, not forgetting the safe beaches, one of which is only a ½ mile walk from the park. Fishing ½ mile, boat launching 2 miles, riding 1 mile, golf 9 miles. A member of the Best of British group. Bellamy gold.

Charges 2000:
-- Per unit incl. 2 persons and awning £6.90 - £16.50; extra adult £1.00 - £4.00; child (5-14 yrs) £1.00 - £3.00; pup tent (outside 18/7-27/8) free - £2.00; electricity £1.90; dog (limited breeds and numbers) free - £2.00; extra car free - £1.00; special facility pitch £2.00 - £2.90.
-- VAT included.
-- Credit cards accepted.

Open:
1 April - 3 October.

Address:
Boswinger,
Gorran, St Austell,
Cornwall PL26 6LL.

Tel:
(01726) 843425.
FAX: (01726) 843358.
E-mail: enquiries@
SeaViewInternational.
com.

Reservations:
Min 7 nights, w/e - w/e,
28/7-1/9. other times, any length, with £30 deposit and £2 fee.

Alan Rogers' Discount

 Free hot welcome drink

see colour advert between pages 32/33

Directions: From St Austell take B3273 towards Mevagissey; one mile before Mevagissey village turn right at Gorran and camp sign and continue towards Gorran for 5 miles. Fork right at camp sign and follow signs to park. O.S.GR: SW991412.

Cornwall

025 Pentewan Sands Holiday Park, Mevagissey

Family park with private beach and swimming pool; some hire caravans and chalets.

Pentewan Sands is a popular park with an ideal position right beside a wide sandy beach, managed by the park, which offers safe bathing and direct flat access with no roads to cross. There is carefully monitored public access to the beach through the park. A busy, 32 acre park with lots going on, there are 480 individual touring pitches, 380 with electricity, and 112 caravan holiday homes for hire. The pitches are of reasonable size on level grass with nothing between them, and are marked by frontage stones, mostly in rows adjoining access roads. The three main toilet blocks serve their purpose well, receiving heavy use in peak season. There is free hot water in nearly all washbasins, many in vanity style, a few for ladies in semi-private cabins, free hot showers, two bathrooms and a baby room, plus facilities for disabled people, well equipped laundry room, washing up sinks and chemical disposal. A good sized free heated swimming pool (about 72 x 26 ft) with small children's pool (supervised and open Whitsun - mid Sept) is adjacent to the Clubhouse and bowling centre. The Clubhouse contains two licensed bar lounges upstairs and a further one downstairs opening on to the pool area, open all day and serving good value food (Whitsun - mid-Sept). A full entertainment programme, beach activities, water sports and a children's club are organised, and there is a small water sports centre on the beach. Other activities include an adventure playground, tennis courts (one full size, one compact) and bicycle hire. Riding or golf 2 miles. The sailing club adjoining offers membership to campers, scuba diving, windsurfing courses, etc. Slipway and boat launching service (Whitsun - mid Sept). No jet-skis are permitted and no 4WD vehicles allowed on the beach. The site has a large, self-service shop (from Easter but hours may be limited), a bistro, bar meals and fast food (Whit-mid-Sept). Freezer service for ice packs, battery charging service, gas, public phones and motorcaravan service point. Caravan and boat storage available. There is access to the Pentewan Valley Trail, a six mile route for cycling or walking following the old carriageway to Mevagissey with its throngs of tourists (only two miles by the main road). The park has been owned by the Tremayne family for 60 years, along with the beach, and there are links with the award winning Lost Gardens of Heligan nearby. Dogs are not accepted.

Directions: From St. Austell ring road take B3273 for Mevagissey. Park is 3½ miles, where the road meets the sea. O.S.GR: SX018468.

Charges 2000:
-- Per unit incl. 2 adults £6.25 - £15.95; extra adult £1.55 - £3.40; child (3-15 yrs) £1.00 - £2.55; awning free; extra small tent, boat or car £1.50 - £1.75; electricity (10A) £2.70.
-- Sea front pitch plus 10-20%.
-- VAT included.
-- Credit cards accepted.

Open:
Easter/1 April - 31 Oct.

Address:
Pentewan, nr. St. Austell, Cornwall PL26 6BT.

Tel:
(01726) 843485.
FAX: (01726) 844142.
E-mail: info@ pentewan.co.uk.

Reservations:
Made Sat - Sat or Wed - Wed with deposit (£35-£75, acc. to season), £4 booking fee and compulsory cancellation insurance (£3-£6).

'Camping Cheque'

see colour advert between pages 32/33

Alan Rogers' Discount

Discount for low season booked stays - 7 nights for price of 5.
(Both parks)

041 Pengrugla Park, Mevagissey

Peaceful park in mature garden setting.

Pengrugla is now owned by Pentewan Sands and the Tremayne family, and we are happy to feature the park to complement the Pentewan Site with its busy beach life and many activities. Part of Pengrugla's boundary actually edges The Lost Gardens of Heligan although nothing can be seen. At some time the land used to develop Pengrugla must have been part of the Gardens and one can enjoy the mature trees and flowering shrubs which have been further landscaped to provide an attractive situation for a number of privately owned holiday homes. These face out over a part of the 'Lost Valley' of Heligan fame and are interspersed with touring pitches, with some below on sloping grass and others in a more level situation amongst trees and shrubs. There are 100 good sized touring pitches, 80 with 16A electricity. A modern, heated and tiled toilet block is central and it provides vanity style washbasins and comfortably sized pre-set showers with divider and seat. A heated unisex bathroom is provided, plus three dishwashing sinks under cover, a laundry room with two washing machines, two dryers, iron and board, but no hand washing sinks, and chemical disposal. Reception at the entrance also has a small shop for basics with some tourist gifts and coffee also available (Whitsun - 14 Sept). A good adventure playground completes the on-site amenities but the many facilities of Pentewan Sands are open to Pengrugla visitors - see above. Dogs are welcome. There is access to the Pentewan Trail to ride or cycle into Mevagissey or Pentewan. Riding 4 miles, golf 5 miles.

Directions: From St Austell ring road take B3273 for Mevagissey. After 3½ miles, pass Pentewan Sands, continue up hill and turn right following site signs. Park is on left just before reaching Heligan Gardens. O.S.GR: SW999464.

Charges 2000:
-- Per pitch incl. 2 adults, caravan/tent and car £6.10 - £14.40; extra adult £2.00 - £3.00; extra child £1.00 - £2.00; extra tent, car or boat £1.25; dog £1.00; electricity £2.10.
-- Credit cards accepted.

Open:
1 April - 31 October.

Address:
St. Ewe, St Austell, Cornwall PL26 6ER.

Tel:
(01726) 842714.
FAX: (01726) 844414.
E-mail: info@ pentewan.co.uk.

Reservations:
Made with deposit (£35-£75, acc. to season); write to Pentewan Sands (see above).

see colour advert between pages 32/33

026 Penhaven Touring Park, Pentewan, Mevagissey

Family owned touring park with swimming pool, one mile from sandy beach.

Penhaven is a grassy, level 13 acre park, with the road on one side (this can be a little noisy on busy Saturdays) and a river on the other. There is a bridge from the site giving access to the Pentewan Valley Trail, a two mile walk or cycle ride to Pentewan village and beach along this quiet, traffic free track, with links to Mevagissey via Heligan. Owned and developed by the Hackwell family for over 10 years, the park comprises three fields with 105 good sized pitches which are numbered, 80 with 10A electricity, 5 with hardstanding and 4 fully serviced. The North field is used for rallies and has a refurbished 'portacabin' style unit near with washbasins, toilets and a shower. The South field is used as a ball game area, for caravan storage and as a tent area for 35 tents on a 28 day licence (no tarmac road and no lighting). The Middle field has all the main facilities which include a heated swimming pool (mid May - early Sept), unsupervised and with a paved sunbathing surround and loungers. There is a small fenced play area for children on sand and grass. Reception also incorporates the shop which has a wide variety of goods for sale. The tiled toilet block can be heated and provides washbasins, toilets and showers (a little cramped). There are also three family shower rooms (key on request with deposit) and one unit for use by disabled visitors. All hot water is free, there are dishwashing sinks under cover and a well equipped laundry with washing lines provided. Chemical disposal and motorcaravan services. Telephone. Dogs are welcome on a lead and exercised off site (there is a wood over the river). During high season a van on site sells takeaway snacks and there is a restaurant in the nearby village of London Apprentice. Buses pass the gate for St Austell and Mevagissey. Fishing near, boat launching 1 mile, golf 3 miles, riding 8 miles. Bicycle hire on site. The park adjoins the cycle trail to Mevagissy. Heligan Gardens are nearby, the new Eden Project is 4 miles. A busy park, but away from the hectic coastal sites, Penhaven will probably appeal to people who don't want a bar and evening entertainment.

Charges 2000:
-- Per unit incl. 2 persons £8.80 - £18.00; extra adult £3.35 - £4.45; child (5-15 yrs) £1.60; extra car, boat or trailer £1.50; electricity (10A) £2.10; dog 80p.
-- VAT included.
-- Credit cards accepted.

Open:
1 April - 31 Oct.

Address:
Pentewan, St Austell, Cornwall PL26 6DL.

Tel:
(01726) 843687. FAX: (01726) 843870. E-mail: penhaven. cornwall@virgin.net.

Reservations:
Made for min. 3 days with £20 deposit per week.

Directions: From St Austell on A390, take B3273 to Mevagissey and park is on left, 1 mile from London Apprentice before Pentewan. O.S.GR: SX008481.

019 Polruan Holidays Camping & Caravanning, Polruan, nr. Fowey

Quiet rural site in elevated situation not far from Fowey.

With 11 holiday homes for hire and 32 touring pitches, this is a very pleasant little site in an elevated situation with sea views. The holiday homes are arranged in a neat circle, with a central area for some tourers, including 7 pitches with gravel hardstanding and electricity. The remaining touring pitches are in an adjacent field with 4 electricity hook-ups, which is part level for motorcaravans and part on a gentle slope for tents. There are marvellous sea views, but it could be a little exposed when the wind blows off the sea. A raised picnic area, with a table provided, gives more views across the estuary to Fowey. The small sanitary block is centrally situated and has been refurbished, providing three controllable hot shower for each sex, washbasins with H&C, plenty of hooks and mirrors, a washing-up and a laundry sink (H&C), plus a washing machine - in the ladies. There are chemical disposal and motorcaravan service facilities, two fresh water taps and waste water points. Reception (with a small terrace) doubles as a small shop for basics and gas, and provides a freezer for ice packs, plenty of local tourist information and bus timetables (for Looe, etc). There are recycling bins, a public telephone and a large, sloping field for children's play with swings and seat. Riding or bicycle hire 3 miles, fishing ½ mile, golf 10 miles. This is a nice little park in a popular tourist area, within walking distance (down-hill all the way, and vice-versa!) of the village, where there are various hostelries and a passenger ferry to Fowey. A member of the Countryside Discovery group. Bellamy silver.

Charges 2000:
-- Per unit £6.50 - £10.00; tent £4.50 - 10.00; electricity £2.00.
-- No credit cards.

Open:
Easter - October.

Address:
Polruan-by-Fowey, Cornwall PL23 1QH.

Tel:
(01726) 870263. FAX: as phone. E-mail: polholiday @aol.com.

Reservations:
Advised for July/Aug. - contact park.

Directions: From main A390 at East Taphouse take B3359 towards Looe. After 5 miles fork right signed Bodinnick and ferry. Watch for signs for Polruan and site to left. Follow these carefully along narrow Cornish lanes to site on right just before village. O.S.GR: SX133509.

Cornwall

009 Trethem Mill Touring Park, St Just-in-Roseland, nr. St Mawes

Well kept, peaceful, rural family park on the Roseland Peninsula.

St Mawes is a very popular, pretty village on the Roseland peninsula, which is itself an `area of outstanding natural beauty'. Being only three miles away, Trethem Mill is well placed for either sailing, walking the coastal path around the peninsula, visiting the gardens of Trelissick or Heligan, or simply lazing on the nearby beaches. The Akeroyd family continue to work hard to turn Trethem Mill into a park of which to be proud. The centrally located toilet block has been refurbished to a very high standard and it is kept spotlessly clean. Centrally heated in cooler weather, there is an ample supply of hot water, vanity style washbasins, push-button, free showers, soap and hand-dryers and a baby room. The laundry is well equipped and dishwashing sinks are provided, plus chemical disposal. Also in the central area is reception and shop, which is only small but very well stocked and licensed. Trethem is a strictly touring park with 84 pitches, of which 50 have 16A electricity and with several now classified as 'all-weather'. The pitches are large, most on slightly sloping ground, and are clearly divided by hedging giving your own area. Generally there is a good spacious feel to the site, with tarmac circular access roads. At the busiest times an extra field, also with tarmac access, is brought into use. Children have a games room, TV room and a well equipped, fenced playground (closed at 9 pm). Hire and sale of wet suits. Freezer for ice packs (free). Public telephone. The park has been carefully landscaped and is a mass of colour, the area around reception being particularly pretty where a small watermill has been built amongst the flowers - the sound of gently flowing water is very relaxing - and there are pet animals (do not feed). A large field alongside the park is used as a recreation and ball game area, with a separate dog walk. Fishing 1½ miles, boat launching 2 miles, bicycle hire 4 miles, riding 8 miles, golf 6 miles. Trethem Mill aims to attract couples and families who seek peace and tranquillity, and can manage without a bar and on site entertainment.

Charges 2000:
-- Per unit incl. 2 adults £6.50 - £10.00; per person, hiker or cyclist £3.50 - £5.00; extra adult £2.00 - £2.50; child (4-16 yrs) £1.50 - £2.00; electricity £2.00; dog £1.00; extra car or pup tent £1.00.
-- Credit cards accepted.
Open:
1 April - 18 October.
Address:
St Just-in-Roseland, nr. St Mawes, Truro, Cornwall TR2 5JF.
Tel:
(01872) 580504. FAX: (01872) 580968. E-mail: reception@ trethem-mill.co.uk.
Reservations:
Made with £30 deposit.

Directions: From Tregony follow A3078 to St Mawes. Approx. 2 miles after passing through Trewithian, watch for caravan and camping sign. O.S.GR: SW862364.

028 Powderham Castle Tourist Park, Lanlivery, nr. Lostwithiel

Tranquil, sheltered family touring park well situated for exploring Cornwall.

This is a most pleasant, peaceful park with plenty of green space and a natural, uncommercialised atmosphere which has been enhanced by careful planting of trees and shrubs to form a series of linked paddocks with a small unfenced stream running through. The nearest beach at Par is some 4 miles. The park has 38 private caravan holiday homes in a separate field and 75 numbered touring pitches, all with electricity connections (5/10A) and 7 with hardstanding, spread round the perimeter of the paddocks, each with 10-15 pitches (awning groundsheets to be lifted alternate days). Dustbin and water points around the park are well hidden by trees and bushes. The single central toilet block is a good one with free hot water in the washbasins (with shelf and mirror), heated shower areas with hot showers on payment, curtained cubicles in the ladies', hairdryers and a family washroom with shower, basin, WC, etc. Separate dishwashing area with five sinks (free hot water), fully equipped laundry room and chemical disposal. It is quite a walk from some pitches and a torch would be useful. Activities include a badminton court, games room with table tennis and pool, TV room and a putting green. A large, well equipped children's activity play area with a super range of adventure type equipment on grass is in one of the hedged paddocks with a fenced paddling pool. Motorcaravan service point. Seasonal pitches and caravan storage available. Telephone. The village pub is within walking distance. Fresh water fishing 1½ miles or sea fishing 3 miles, bicycle hire 4 miles, riding 2 miles, golf 1½ miles. Indoor tennis courts (Bodmin) and a swimming pool are near. There are several good local restaurants and the new Eden Project is very close.

Charges 2001:
-- Per unit £3.50 - £5.00; adult £1.70 - £2.60; child (3-16 yrs) 60p - £1.30; electricity £1.75; awnings (without groundsheet), extra small tent, car free.
-- No single sex groups (excl. bona fide organisations).
-- No credit cards.
-- VAT included.
Open:
Easter/1 April - 31 Oct.
Address:
Lanlivery, nr. Lostwithiel, Cornwall PL30 5BU.
Tel:
(01208) 872277
Reservations:
Made with £20 deposit.

Alan Rogers' Discount

 Less 10%

Directions: Park approach road leads off A390 road 1½ miles southwest of Lostwithiel. Follow white or brown camping signs. No other approach roads are advised. O.S.GR: SX083592.

029 Carlyon Bay Caravan & Camping Park, Bethesda, Carlyon Bay

Spacious, tranquil, family owned park, 5 minutes walk from busy sandy beach.

Open meadows edged by mature woodland, well cared for by the Taylor family, provide a beautiful holiday setting with a blue flag beach 5 minutes walk from the top gate at this park. The original farm buildings have been converted and added to, providing an attractive centre to the park, also home for the owners, with a certain individuality of design which is very pleasing, particularly in the three modern, impressively tiled toilet blocks. These are now a feature of the park, being of excellent quality and design and providing a mix of facilities from vanity style washbasins to en-suite toilets and basins, comfortable, roomy, pre-set showers with divider, shelf, etc, facilities for hair-care and make-up and thoughtful provision for babies - almost 'home from home'! Dishwashing sinks with hot water are under cover at all the blocks. Fully equipped laundry room (hot water metered) with free irons and a well hidden chemical disposal point. The 180 pitches in five areas are spacious and allow for a family meadow, a dog free meadow, and an area for couples, etc. All are on flat, terraced or gently sloping grass with flowers and shrubs in some areas. The 104 pitches with electricity (5/10A) are marked. There is even a 'discreet' area, well screened and hidden, for naturists. The only official naturist beach in Cornwall, Polgaver Bay, at the far end of Carlyon Bay can be reached by walking over the cliff tops. The attractive kidney shaped, heated pool (Easter-Sept) with children's paddling pool, is walled and paved for sunbathing and is part of the central area, along with a canopied entertainment area, TV lounge, crazy golf, table tennis, pool table and barbecue area. Two children's play areas, one adventure type. Modern reception with a good little shop and takeaway (May-mid Sept). Socially the park provides entertainment in high season for families and children but those who wish for more can choose between the Cornish Leisure World complex on the beach, with its pool, bars and discos, or the social club near the entrance to the park which welcomes campers. For the more active, there is also a golf course opposite the entrance and the coastal footpath passes near. All Cornwall's attractions are within touring distance. Buses to St. Austell and Fowey run from the park entrance.

Charges guide:
-- Per unit incl. 2 persons and car £7.00 - £16.00; extra adult £3.00 - £3.50; child (3-17 yrs incl.) £1.50 - £2.50; awning or small pup tent free - £1.00; extra car £1.00; dog £1.00 - £1.50; electricity £2.00.
-- Motorcaravan less £1.00, hiker/tent less £2.00 per night.
-- VAT included.
-- Credit cards accepted.

Open:
April - October.

Address:
Bethesda, Carlyon Bay, St. Austell, Cornwall PL25 3RE.

Tel:
(01726) 812735. FAX: (01726) 815496. E-mail: jeff@ globalnet.co.uk.

Reservations:
Made with £30 deposit and £2 fee (min. 6 nights 19/7-17/8).

Directions: From Plymouth direction on A390, pass Lostwithiel and 1 mile after village of St Blazey, turn left at roundabout beside Britannia Inn. After 400 yds turn right on a concrete road and right again at site sign. O.S.GR: SX053526.

046 Croft Farm Touring Park, Luxulyan, Bodmin

Secluded park for all units one mile from the new Eden Project.

Croft Farm was once part of a larger site and you pass some of the residential homes on the way in. Mature trees and shrubs edge most of the site, except for an open top field. A number of mobile homes are on site, some privately owned and some for hire, along with three holiday cottages. For 2001 there will be 35 pitches in the top field with good views and 22 in the original mature areas, with 10A electricity for the majority of these and 5 will have hardstanding. The heated toilet block is of older design but has been neatly updated to provide vanity style basins, showers with a plastic door and plenty of room to change with a good seat, a baby room and one en-suite basin and toilet for ladies. Dishwashing sinks under cover, and one laundry sink with spin dryer. The park has won a Bellamy Gold award and it is the first time we have seen recycling complete with compost unit. The woodland trail is also part of the conservation effort and takes you through the rest of the park's natural areas which are indeed left very natural! A grass area here has adventure type play equipment. Games room with pool and amusement machines and a useful room of tourist information. Reception has a newspaper ordering service and keeps basic necessities such as milk. The village pub is ¾ mile.

Charges 2000:
-- Per unit incl. 2 adults £7.70 - £10.50; extra adult £2.00; child (5-15 yrs) £1.20; electricity £2.00; awning £1.00; dog 50p; small tent per person £2.80 - £3.25; extra car 50p.
Open:
21 March - 31 October
Address:
Luxulyan, Bodmin, Cornwall, PL30 5EQ.
Tel:
(01726) 850228.
FAX: (01726) 850492
E-mail: lynpick@globalnet.co.uk.
Reservations:
Made with £20 deposit p/week or £3 p/night for shorter visits.

Directions: From A391 Bodmin - St Austell road follow directions for the Eden project. At entrance to the project continue straight on for approx. 1 mile, and site is on the left side of this road in the direction of Luxulyan. O.S.GR: SX045588.

033 Killigarth Manor Caravan Park, Polperro, nr. Looe

Busy park for all units with much on site entertainment and holiday caravans to hire.

A substantial part of Killigarth Estate is occupied by caravan holiday homes but a separate part is allocated to touring units. Approached by a tree lined drive, this provides 202 marked, level or gently sloping grass pitches, of which 75 are taken by seasonal units. There are 73 electric hook-ups (16A) for tourers, plus well placed bins and water points. One large, spacious toilet block has pre-set showers (no divider, bench outside), vanity style washbasins, dryers, soap, hairdryers, washing up facilities under cover and a chemical disposal point. In peak season the block is supplemented by 'portacabin' style toilet facilities. Facilities for disabled visitors are in the main block and a very well equipped laundry with free hot water for sinks. The heart of the site is the Talland Suite providing a large bar and entertainment hall with family room, amusements and games areas, restaurant, takeaway and bar snacks, heated indoor pool (adult £2, child £1), fitness centre with gym, sauna and sun bed, and a sun terrace with beautiful views. Early evening `young entertainment' is followed later by live shows, discos or groups and a programme of competitions, quizzes or family films in a big screen cinema. A children's playground is beside the pool area (plus an additional one in the camping area). Well stocked mini-market (all season) and an information room. Tennis court (£3 p/hour), bicycle hire, a skittle alley, croquet, draughts, badminton and crazy golf. Fishing and boat launching approx. 1 mile. Bus service in high season. Dogs are accepted but not in the leisure areas. This park is popular with families with children of all ages and there is much to do in the area.

Charges guide:
-- Per pitch £2.80 - £6.00; adult £3.00 - £3.60; child (3-16 yrs) £1.50 - £1.80; electricity £1.90.
-- Pup tents not permitted to share a pitch with another unit.
-- Special offers available.
-- VAT included.
-- Credit cards accepted.
Open:
4 April - 25 October.
Address:
Polperro, Looe, Cornwall PL13 2JQ.
Tel:
(01503) 272216.
FAX: (01503) 272065.
Reservations:
Made (Sat. - Sat. in main season) with £30 deposit.

Directions: From Looe take A387 towards Polperro. After 3½ miles, fork left past bus shelter and phone box at Killigarth sign. Site is ¼ mile. O.S.GR: SX213519.

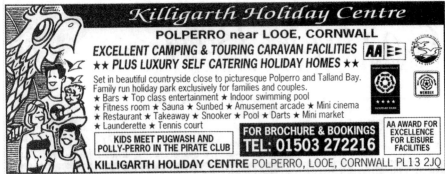

042 Looe Valley Holiday Park, nr. Looe

Large touring park near sea, with live entertainment and heated outdoor pool.

This park is situated between the two picturesque fishing villages of Looe and Polperro. Covering 63 acres, there is space for 573 units, with 30 pitches used for caravan holiday homes for letting and 40 for seasonal lets, plus some for 'Eurotents' to hire. The touring pitches are all numbered and marked in three spacious, gently sloping fields, well mown and with 280 electric hook-ups (10A). The pitches are of good size in alternating rows on marker lines - it could be crowded in peak season, although the pitch size is conducive to some privacy. Off peak there would be plenty of room. Four toilet blocks serve the whole area and are more than sufficient for peak periods. One modernised block can be heated when required and they provide all expected facilities. Hot water is free everywhere, dishwashing facilities are adequate and there is a launderette. The park has a wide range of facilities - in fact it is a self-contained holiday park with an extensive entertainment centre and live entertainment during the season. The clubhouse has a ballroom, large bar, disco room, three TV rooms, games and amusement rooms and a full restaurant with breakfast available as well (Whitsun - mid Sept) and takeaway facilities. A large self-service, licensed shop is open from late May. There is an outdoor heated swimming pool, 18 hole crazy golf course, two children's play areas and a children's club in season. Public phone and dog exercise area. Caravan storage. The nearest beach, of sand and rocks, is 1½ miles away at Talland.

Charges guide:
-- Per pitch incl. all persons, awning £7.00 - £10.90; boat, trailer or extra car £1.50; dog £1.50; electricity £2.00.
-- Various special offers.
-- VAT included.
Open:
Easter - end September.
Address:
Polperro Road,
Looe,
Cornwall PL13 2JS.
Tel:
(01503) 262425.
FAX: as phone.
Reservations:
Contact park.

see colour advert between pages 32/33

Directions: Park entrance is off the north side of the A387, 2 miles west of Looe. O.S.GR: SX228536.

040 Trelay Farmpark, Pelynt, by Looe

Small, quietly situated park with lovely views and some caravan holiday homes.

Situated a little back from the coast, just over three miles from Looe and Polperro in a rural situation, this is a neat, tidy and quiet park (there is no farm adjacent). On your right as you drive in, and quite attractively arranged amongst herbaceous shrubs, are caravan holiday homes (13 privately owned, 6 to let by the park). The touring area is behind and slightly above, on level to gently sloping, neatly cut grass. An oval hard-core road connects the good sized, numbered pitches which border the site and back onto hedges, the majority with rural views. There are 23 pitches with electricity hook-ups, with a further 30 pitches for tents, etc. Outside the main season the central area is kept for ball games, together with a water and refuse point. An excellent chalet-type, purpose built toilet block is to one side. Light, airy, spacious and centrally heated in cool weather, it is a good facility. Well equipped and maintained, it provides semi-private washbasins (H&C) and large comfortable, pre-set showers. In this building, but in separate smaller rooms, are two dishwashing sinks and a laundry sink (all H&C), washing machine and a dryer. Separate chemical disposal. For disabled visitors, an en-suite unit (with ramp) is accessed by key from reception. There is also a baby bath here. A public phone, tourist information including map sales and loan, gas supplies and free use of a fridge/freezer complete the provision. You will receive a good welcome from the enthusiastic owners, Heather and Graham Veale, who live in the chalet bungalow near the entrance where the small reception is located. The village with pub and shops is within ½ mile. Fishing or riding 3 miles.

Charges 2001:
-- Per unit incl. 2 persons £7.00 - £8.50; extra person under 5 yrs £1.00, over 5 yrs £2.00; dog 50p.
-- No credit cards.
Open:
1 April - end October.
Address:
Pelynt, by Looe,
Cornwall PL13 2JX.
Tel:
(01503) 220900.
FAX: as phone.
Reservations:
Advised for July/Aug;
contact park.

Directions: From A390 Lostwithiel road take B3359 south at Middle or East Taphouse towards Looe and Polperro. Site is signed ½ mile past Pelynt on the left. From Looe take A387 towards Polperro and after 2 miles turn right onto B3359 towards Pelynt. Site is signed 1 mile on right. O.S.GR: SX210545.

Cornwall

032 Polborder House Caravan and Camping Park, Looe

Small, neat touring park just back from sea with good views, personally run by owners.

Polborder House may appeal to those who prefer a quiet, well kept little family site to the larger ones with many activities. With good country views, up to 31 units can be taken on well tended grass. Pitches are marked with some hedging, 28 with electricity (10A). A number of hardstandings and 4 serviced pitches have been added. The sanitary block with coded entry is well kept, of ample size and provides free hot water in vanity style washbasins with curtained hot showers on payment. There is a baby room, a laundry room (H&C) with washing machine, spin and tumble dryers and iron, and three covered sinks outside for dishwashing (free hot water). A unit for disabled visitors has a ramped approach. Rubbish is recycled and there are chemical disposal and motorcaravan service facilities. Licenced shop for gas and basics, with tourist information, public phone and toddler's play area. A restaurant is 500 m. The owners live on the park. Five caravan holiday homes for hire, plus two holiday bungalows (Jan - Nov). Fishing, golf and boat launching within 2 miles, riding 8 miles. Seaton is 2 miles, Looe 2½ and the nearest beach 20-25 minutes walk from a gate in the corner of the park.

Directions: Park is ¾ mile south of B3253; turn off 2 miles east of Looe following signs to park and Monkey Sanctuary; care is needed with narrow road. O.S.GR: SX283555.

Charges 2000:
-- Per unit incl. 2 persons £6.00 - £9.50; extra person £1.50 - £2.00; child (4-15 yrs) 75p - £1.00; awning or child's tent £1.00; dog 75p; electricity £1.80.
-- Credit cards accepted.
-- VAT included.
Open:
1 April - 31 October.
Address:
Bucklawren Road, St Martin's-by-Looe, Cornwall PL13 1QR.
Tel:
(01503) 240265.
FAX: (01503) 240700.
E-mail: rlf.polborder @virgin.net.
Reservations:
Any period, £15 deposit.

Alan Rogers' Discount

Less 50p per night per pitch

036 Lakefield Caravan Park and Equestrian Centre, Camelford

Small touring park with BHS and RDA approved equestrian centre.

Lakefield was previously a working farm and, with only 40 pitches, well spaced and in sight of the small lake (fenced) and its feathered inhabitants, it is no wonder that the owners, Maureen and Dennis Perring, know all the campers. The pitches are all on level grass with 24 electric hook-ups (16A). The toilet block is clean and bright, providing the shelves, hooks, stools etc. which make life easier, a washing machine and dryer in the ladies', a dishwashing and a laundry sink outside, but under cover and chemical disposal. Hot water is free (no facilities for visitors with disabilities). The white-washed shop/reception, converted from one of the old barns and including a fascinating picture gallery, is open all day and all season which impressed us for such a small site. A tea room offers cream teas, cakes and sandwiches. A dozen picnic tables are dotted about the site, and some children's play equipment on grass, a separate dog walking field and bridleway access, gas supplies and a pay phone complete the facilities. In a barn is an animal corner with calves, lambs, chickens, etc. and 'Wabbit World' is fascinating. A BHS approved riding school on site offers lessons and hacks with qualified supervision and instruction and 25 horses, from miniature Shetlands to thoroughbreds. All abilities are catered for (sand menage, show jumping paddock, beginners cross country course and pony rides) and it is the Riding for the Disabled (RDA) Centre for north Cornwall. Pony days and activity days are organised. Mountain bike hire. Fishing (sea 4 miles, coarse 5 miles), golf 2 miles. Tintagel, Boscastle, Bodmin Moor and the many beaches and coves of the north Cornwall coast wait to be explored. Cornwall's first wind farm watches over the site. Torches may be useful.

Charges 2000:
-- Per unit incl. 2 adults £6.00 - £10.00; extra adult or child (5 yrs or over) 50p; dog, awning or extra car 50p; electricity £2.00.
-- No credit cards.
Open:
1 April - 31 October.
Address:
Lower Pendavey Farm, Camelford, Cornwall PL32 9TX.
Tel:
(01840) 213279.
FAX: as phone.
E-mail: lakefield@ pendavey.fsnet.co.uk.
Reservations:
Made with £20 deposit per week.

Directions: Follow B3266 north from Camelford. Park access is directly from this road on left, just before turn for Tintagel, clearly signed. O.S.GR: SX097852.

023 Glenmorris Park, St Mabyn

Family run, quiet park in north Cornwall.

The beaches of north Cornwall and the wilds of Bodmin Moor are all an easy drive away from Glenmorris Park and the Camel Trail for either cycling or walking all the way to Bodmin, Wadebridge or Padstow is only 2 miles. The amenities at the park include a heated, outdoor swimming pool and paddling pool (late May - early Sept), surrounded by sheltered, paved and grass sunbathing areas. Alongside is an excellent adventure playground which is fenced, with a bark safety base and, in the same building as reception, there is a games room for teenagers. Bodmin and Wadebridge are only 5 or 6 miles for supermarkets, etc. There is no bar but the local village inn has a good reputation for food. A quiet, family run park, Glenmorris has fairly modern sanitary facilities which are clean and well maintained. Washbasins are in vanity style units with hair-dryers, all hot water is free and showers are pre-set. There are dishwashing sinks, a laundry with washing machine, dryer and iron and chemical disposal. Of the 75 pitches, 52 have 16A electricity and all are reasonably level and well drained on well mown grass. Dogs are accepted on a lead and a good dog walk is provided (a large, well mown field). Fishing, riding or golf 3 miles, bicycle hire 5 miles. Some caravan holiday homes for rent. Caravan storage. All in all, this is a pleasant park in which to relax or to use as a base to explore the towns and beaches of Cornwall. A member of the Countryside Discovery group.

Directions: From Bodmin or Wadebridge on A389, take B3266 north signed Camelford. At village of Longstone turn left signed St Mabyn and brown camping sign. Site is 400 yds on right. Ignore all other signs to St Mabyn. O.S.GR: SX053735.

Charges 2000:
-- Per unit incl. 2 adults and awning £5.00 - £7.50; extra adult £1.00 - £2.25; child (3-16 yrs) 75p - £1.50; extra vehicle or pup tent free - £1.00; electricity (16A) £2.00; hiker or cyclist's tent (2 adults, no car) £5.00 - £6.50.
-- Weekly rate available.
-- Credit cards accepted.
Open:
Easter - 31 October.
Address:
Longstone Road,
St Mabyn,
Cornwall PL30 3BY.
Tel:
(01208) 841677.
FAX: as phone.
E-mail: glenmorris.
cornwall@virgin.net.
Reservations:
Made with £15 deposit - contact park for details.

043 Trerethern Touring Park, Padstow

Spacious park with marvellous views within walking distance of Padstow.

Trerethern is a traditional park of wide open fields, although there have been attempts to divide it up with hedging which is developing nicely in places despite the rabbits and the elements. There is room for 300 units but only 100 are taken so there is plenty of open space and the views across Bodmin Moor and the estuary are marvellous. The grass is neatly cut and the pitches mostly level, although there is a gentle slope in parts. Electricity (10A) is available on 65 pitches, there are 10 water points and 7 hardstanding places for motorcaravans, 5 of these with electricity plus an emptying point. A unique feature of the site is the four individual en-suite washrooms for use with the 'Kernow' pitches (which also have water and facilities for waste water and TV reception). These come with their own key and are for private use while on site, plus a pass key for the shower room (see below for cost). There are also two sanitary blocks with controllable free hot showers, two washbasins in cabins in the smaller block, otherwise in open rows; they are simple but clean and tidy. A toilet with washbasin with ramped access is provided at the back of the main toilet block at the far side of the park. There is also a dishwashing and laundry facility with two washing machines and a dryer. The small block which also houses the private units is locked at night so if you need the loo in the night it could be a little walk! A children's play area and the reception cum shop for gas and basic needs near the entrance complete the facilities. The owners live on site and ensure a well run and orderly park. Padstow itself is a mile away either by public footpath from the site through the fields (20-30 minutes) downhill or for bicycles by the road. A bus service passes (the site is a request stop) and reception holds timetables. The nearest beach is at Padstow, others are within 5 miles. Riding or fishing 2 miles, golf 5 miles. Note: Rick Steine has now opened a bistro alongside his restaurant so you may just get a reservation!

Directions: Park is signed from the A389, SSW of Padstow. O.S.GR: SW912739.

Charges 2000:
-- Per unit £3.00 - £4.00; adult £2.00 - £3.00; child (under 15 yrs) £1.00 - £1.50: awning or extra tent £1.00; dog 40p; extra vehicle £2.00 - £3.00; electricity £2.00; 'Kernow' pitch incl. electricity £4.00 - £5.00.
-- No credit cards.
Open:
Easter/1 April - 2 Oct.
Address:
Padstow,
Cornwall PL28 8LE.
Tel:
(01841) 532061.
FAX: as phone.
E-mail:
camping.trerethern
@btinternet.com.
Reservations:
Made with deposit (£15 p/week).

Cornwall

038 Wooda Farm Park, Bude

Spacious, quality, family run farm park with views of sea and countryside.

This well organised and cared for park with some nice touches is part of a working farm, 1¾ miles from the sandy, surfing beaches of Bude, in peaceful farmland with plenty of open spaces (some up and down walking) and marvellous views. The 200 pitches, spread over four meadows, are on level or gently sloping grass, 160 with electricity (10A), 21 with hardstanding and 21 grass, hedged 'premium' pitches (electricity, water, waste water) linked by tarmac roads. There are 55 holiday units beside the shop and reception at the entrance. Three well maintained toilet blocks, one heated, have free hot water. They provide fully tiled showers with seat and hooks, washbasins in vanity style with shelf and hand dryer, a unit suitable for disabled people, a baby room with small bath and two new private family washrooms including shower and bath - a very nice addition. Six washing up sinks (H&C) are under cover. Two laundry rooms with washing machines, tumble dryers, sinks with hot water and iron and board. A comprehensive range of facilities is provided from Spr. B.H - Sept. These include a self-service shop with off-licence (8.30 - 8.30 in main season), attractive courtyard bar with bar meals and a pleasant restaurant, Linney's Larder, with home cooking (closed Mon. and Sat. outside main season). A children's play area is in a separate field on grass, with plenty of room for ball games, a 9 hole 'fun' golf course (clubs provided), plus a woodland walk (where the pixies can be found) and an orchard walk. There is a small farm museum and friendly farm animals - children (and adults) are welcome to assist at feeding time! Tractor and trailer rides, pony riding and trekking, archery and clay pigeon shooting with tuition are provided according to season and demand, likewise barn dances. Games room with TV, table tennis and pool. Coarse fishing is available in a 1½ acre lake (permits from reception, £1.50 per half day, £2.50 per day). Dogs are accepted (not certain breeds) with a large exercise field. Public telephone. Caravan storage. The local village inn is five minutes walk. There is much to do in the area - the Leisure Centre and Splash Pool in Bude itself, sandy beaches with coastal walks, and Tintagel with King Arthur's Castle and Clovelly nearby. A member of the Best of British group.

Directions: Park is north of Bude at Poughill; turn off A39 on north side of Stratton on minor road for Coombe Valley, following signs at junctions. O.S.GR: SS225080.

Charges 2000:
-- Per unit incl. 2 persons £7.50 - £11.00; extra adult £1.50 - £2.50; child (3-15 yrs) £1.00 - £1.50; awning/pup tent £1.00 - £1.50; dog £1.00 - £1.50; electricity (10A) £2.00; fully serviced pitch (incl. electricity) plus £3.50 - £4.50, with TV point £4.50 - £6.00.
-- VAT included.
-- Credit cards accepted.

Open:
Easter/1 April - October.

Address:
Poughill,
Bude,
Cornwall EX23 9HJ

Tel:
(01288) 352069.
FAX: (01288) 355258.
E-mail: enquiries@
wooda.co.uk

Reservations:
Made with £20 p/week deposit.

037 Budemeadows Touring Holiday Park, Poundstock, nr. Bude

Attractive, family run touring park with pool, south of Bude, 1 mile from beach.

Budemeadows is maturing well with growing hedging and trees and though close to the A39 through road, offers a good, quiet option being only about a mile from the sandy surfing beaches at Widemouth Bay and 3 miles from Bude with all its amenities. It has been thoughtfully planned and provides large, separated (low hedging or fencing) pitches, some slightly sloping but with panoramic rural views, others more sheltered and nearer the facilities. Some 146 units of any type are taken and there is plenty of room for these numbers with 80 electrical connections (10A) and 26 hardstandings. An attractive feature is the centrally situated, fenced pool area with a comfortably heated pool and toddlers pool (also heated), patio and grass sunbathing area, and gazebos. The pine clad toilet block can be heated and is of good quality with free hot water in all washbasins, good controllable showers and six washing up sinks under cover; six private cabins for ladies with basin and WC, one for men. There are three family shower units, a bathroom, a baby bath and changing room, laundry room with tourist information, chemical disposal and motorcaravan service facilities. This has now been supplemented by a new block of similar design, with toilets and washbasins en-suite and full facilities for visitors with disabilities. Shop (Spr. B.H. - mid Sept). Gas is available. A large adventure playground, picnic tables and brick built barbecues are provided. Mobile 'Catch a Snack' van calls evenings in high season. Public phone. TV and games room with pool table and board games. Large scale chess set, outdoor table tennis and skittles. Boat launching in Bude, lake fishing 5 miles, riding 3 miles, golf 4 miles. Caravan storage. Holiday chalet for rent. The owners live on site.

Directions: Park entrance is from a lay-by to the east off the A39 just north of a turning to Widemouth Bay. O.S.GR: SS216017.

Charges 2000:
-- Per adult £4.45 - £5.99; child (3-14 yrs) £2.75 - £3.50; dog £1.00 - £1.50; electricity £2.99 - £1.99.
-- Pitch and awning included.
-- VAT included.
-- Credit cards accepted.

Open:
All year.

Address:
Poundstock,
Bude,
Cornwall EX23 0NA.

Tel:
(01288) 361646.
FAX: as phone.
E-mail: wendyjo@
globalnet.co.uk.

Reservations:
Made with deposit (£5 p/night or £35 p/week); contact park.

For everything about caravanning,
motor caravanning and camping, go to
www.oakwood-village.co.uk

RIVER DART COUNTRY PARK
at Ashburton, South Devon

Set in 90 acres of native & exotic parkland, adjoining National Trust woodland

All the facilities you would expect, plus:

- Shop & Bar
- Tennis courts
- Swimming pool
- Children's adventure play zones
- Canoeing & Fishing

**Holne Park, Ashburton
Newton Abbot Devon TQ13 7NP**

01364 652511

Perfect holidays begin with perfect locations

The best of both worlds

Pentewan Sands, the site by the sea

Discover the magic of Pentewan Sands, nestled in the arms of a quiet bay on the Cornish Riviera, with almost half a mile of private, sandy beach. A family park ideal for swimming, sailing, windsurfing and fishing. Great facilities including: large heated swimming pool, launching slipway, Beach Club with 2 bars and entertainment, restaurant and take away, large shop and launderette.

The perfect base to explore Cornwall in the quieter times of the year and ideally located to visit the nearby Eden Project. Over 450 large level pitches for tents, tourers and motor homes; most have electric hook-ups and some are right next to the beach! A large selection of luxury 2 and 3 bedroom modern caravans also available.

Pentewan Sands
Holiday Park

Pengrugla, the quiet site in the countryside

Enjoy the peace and tranquillity of Pengrugla, our second site. Set in the heart of the Cornish countryside and right next door to the world famous Lost Gardens of Heligan. Small and quiet, our beautifully landscaped park has views over open countryside towards St Austell Bay.

Set amongst mature trees our touring pitches have easy access, clean shower blocks, launderette, a children's play area and ample electric hook-ups. Self-catering caravans are also available. With lots of local walks dogs are welcome.

Guests at Pengrugla may also enjoy all the facilities of Pentewan Sands just 1.5 miles away. Pengrugla is ideally located to visit the amazing Eden Project and only 1 mile from the historic fishing village of Mevagissey.

PENGRUGLA

Call now for your FREE brochure | **01726 843485** | **www.pentewan.co.uk**
Write to: Dept AR, Pentewan Sands Ltd, St Austell, Cornwall PL26 6BT or Email: info@pentewan.co.uk

Countryside Discovery

Our peace and quiet is worth shouting about

Experience the Peace & Tranquility of Britain's most beautiful countryside

COUNTRYSIDE DISCOVERY

For a **FREE** brochure with full details of all our parks and types of accommodation, please telephone our brochure line on –
01986 788646

Britain's best rural holiday parks

030 Colliford Tavern Campsite, Colliford Lake, nr. St. Neot

Quality 'tavern' site on Bodmin Moor.

Colliford Tavern must be unique, quietly situated high on the moor near Colliford Lake but hidden and protected by tall pines. The project has been developed over the last 9 years by the Edwards family with much care and attention and offers a family run free house with excellent, home cooked food and ale in an old world atmosphere complete with 90 year old well and accommodation. There is a dining room, family room with terrace, garden, water wheel and a good fenced play area. For family get-togethers it is an ideal venue 'away from it all' with some original suggestions for food which can be quite special or very simple - ask for the mix and match bar menu or the 'thatched trout'! The camping area, however, is quiet and simple and has been kept very natural with short grass (helped by the rabbits) and sheltered from the moor by tall pines. The main field provides 40 fairly level pitches with 19 electric hook-ups (16A) and 6 hardstandings backing on to the pine trees. The smaller, lower area is nearer to all the facilities. The modern, pine fitted toilet block is well equipped and carefully maintained with free hot water, baby room, unit for disabled people (no shower), laundry sink and spin dryer, two washing up sinks and a good chemical disposal facility. Service wash and tumble dry available Monday to Friday. No barbecues are allowed. A dog exercise area is at far end of the site. Reception is in the 'Tavern' building and emergency bread and milk is available, but grocery orders can be supplied by the local village store at Mount. The gate is closed at night but there is a 24 hour bell. Ideally situated for Colliford Lake and the Moor with its rich history, flora and fauna, be it for walking, fly fishing or birdwatching, the park is also suitable for excursions to the north or south coast. Occasionally some family entertainment is provided.

Charges guide:
-- Per unit incl. 1 adult £6.00 - £6.75, 2 adults £8.00 - £10.00; extra person (over 4 yrs) £2.00 - £2.75; electricity £1.95; dog 50p.
-- VAT included.
-- Credit cards accepted.
Open:
Easter - end September.
Address:
Colliford Lake, nr. St. Neot, Liskeard, Cornwall PL14 6PZ.
Tel:
(01208) 821335.
FAX: as phone.
Reservations:
Advised for high season and made with £10 deposit, plus £5 for electric hook-up.

Directions: Approaching on the A30 travelling south, pass the Jamaica Inn on the right and site is signed a further 1-1½ miles on the left. Follow for ½ mile and site is signed beside Colliford Lake Park. O.S.GR: SX168730.

035 Whitsand Bay Holiday Park, Millbrook, nr. Torpoint

Self-contained, family holiday park with magnificent views, for all units.

Whitsand Bay must be one of the most unusual places to stay and is, in fact, a designated ancient monument in an 'area of outstanding natural beauty'. The site has been converted from a Coastal Gun Battery built in 1890 to protect Plymouth and the views are magnificent across to Plymouth and the Tamar Estuary with Dartmoor in the background, over the sea towards the Rame peninsula, Whitsand Bay and west to the Lizard and Bodmin Moor. Covering 27 acres, some wild and natural you can explore the original gun emplacements and enjoy the views or venture into the dark, damp underground tunnels and earthworks. It is obvious that the Clubhouse, laundry and chapel are part of the original fortifications, solidly constructed. In fact the laundry room was part of the Quartermaster's store and the Battery Club has been developed to provide a cosy bar with family area alongside a larger bar and dance hall/disco area with entertainment in high season. Approaching the site along the clifftop road is deceptive as the earth-works completely hide what is, in essence a self contained village including holiday caravans and chalets of older design to let. The 120 marked grass touring pitches, connected by tarmac roads, vary in size, are terraced and enjoy mainly landward views. Sixty have electricity (16A) and quite a few are taken by seasonal lets. The two toilet blocks are acceptable with metered showers - we understand they are shortly to be upgraded. Each block has a washing up sink and chemical disposal. Children are catered for with an indoor, heated pool and paddling pool, adventure play area, multi-sport court, amusement arcade and table tennis, not to mention the 'Kids Club'. There is a small sun terrace beside the pool, a sauna, sun-bed, a café open all day in season, with takeaway, well stocked shop and barbecue area, beside the bars and entertainment. A steep 200 ft. cliff path provides access to Whitsand Bay (unsuitable for small children or the infirm - other beaches near). Fishing ½ mile, boat slipway 2 miles, golf 2 miles. Torch useful.

Charges 2000:
--Per pitch incl. adults, children (max. 6), awning and space for car £8.00 - £16.00; electricity (16A) £2.00; dog £1.00; two-man tent with car £5.00 - £10.00; woodland mini-pitches for cyclists or walkers less 50%.
-- Club membership free.
-- VAT included .
-- Credit cards accepted.
Open:
March to December.
Address:
Millbrook, Torpoint, Cornwall PL10 1JZ.
Tel:
(01752) 822597
FAX: (01752) 823444
E-mail: rob@whitsand-bayholidays.co.uk.
Reservations:
Made with £10 deposit p/week.

Directions: Using Torpoint ferry, disembark on A374 Liskeard road for 3 miles. At village of Antony fork left for Millbrook (B3274) and continue for 2 miles to T-junction. Turn left for Whitsand Bay, then almost immediately right following narrow road overlooking the bay for a further 2 miles. Park is hidden on the left - watch for sign. O.S.GR: SX417506.

Cornwall / Devon

044 Dolbeare Caravan and Camping Park, Landrake, nr. Saltash

Neat and tidy site close to Plymouth, open all year.

Bob and Ruth Mahy will make you very welcome at their small, but well kept park. In a rural setting, but very easily accessible from the main A38, the park consists of a large rectangular field of neatly cut grass edged with trees and sloping slightly at the top, connected by a gravel roadway. Caravans and motor-caravans go around the edge, with some terraced pitches with hardstanding, and tents tend to go in the central area where there is also play equipment and water and refuse points. All 60 pitches are numbered and of comfortable size, 51 with electricity (16A). An extra field doubles as a rally and games field and part is set aside for a dog exercise area. The well kept heated sanitary block to one side of the field provides vanity style washbasins with hot and cold water, pre-set showers with curtain and seat, plus two outside, but covered washing up sinks. A chemical disposal point is carefully sited behind a door with bolt. The laundry is next to reception at the entrance and provides a sink (H&C), washing machine, dryer, iron and board. Reception doubles as a small shop for basics including gas (limited hours out of main season). The Mahys have thoughtfully provided leaflets on 'Where to Eat', 'Where to Walk', and 'Suggestions for what to do' with a good supply of tourist information with maps in a caravan near the caravan storage area. A boules pitch is opposite reception (a set of boules can be hired). The site barrier is closed 11 pm. to 7.30 am. Dog kennels nearby can provide day care from £3.50, but the drawback is that there could be some noise depending on season and wind direction. A very usefully situated park said to be 20 minutes from everywhere - Plymouth, beaches, National Trust properties, Dartmoor and Bodmin Moor, etc. Fishing 3 miles, golf 8 miles.

Charges 2001:
-- Per unit incl. 2 adults and car £7.50 - £8.50; extra adult £2.00; child (5-16 yrs) £1.00; electricity £1.50 - £1.80; awning £1.00; small tent per person £2.50 - £3.00.
Open:
All year.
Address:
St. Ive Road, Landrake, Saltash, Cornwall PL12 5AF.
Tel:
(01752) 851332.
E-mail: dolbeare@ compuserve.com.
Reservations:
Contact park.

Directions: After crossing the Tamar Bridge into Cornwall, continue on A38 for a further 4 miles. In village of Landrake turn right following signs and site is ¾ mile on right. O.S.GR: SX366616.

081 Riverside Caravan Park, Plymouth

Good sized touring park with heated outdoor pool, close to main holiday routes.

Riverside is well placed for those visiting Plymouth, the maritime capital of the southwest, using the car ferries or en-route to Cornwall. It is also ideally situated for touring Dartmoor and south Devon. Although under 4 miles from the city centre, its location on the banks of the River Plym in a wooded valley is a quiet one. Attractive shrubs and trees, flower beds, well kept grass and tarmac roads give a neat, park-like appearance. Over 220 units of any type are taken on flat, numbered pitches, including 170 with 10A electrical connections and 60 winterised, ie. with hardstanding. There is a separate area for tents and a large, hard area is retained for late arrivals and large American motorhomes. In the centre of the park arranged around a patio are a lounge bar (fully open from July with nightly entertainment), coffee bar and restaurant with takeaway meals (6-10 pm), games and TV rooms and a play area. A sheltered and heated swimming pool (60 x 30 ft) with children's paddling pool, is open from Spr. B.H. to mid-Sept. The two sanitary blocks, one subdivided into two, are of different construction and have been modernised and decorated somewhat haphazardly. They have free hot water in the washbasins (some in private cabins with toilets for ladies in one block), showers (some with two taps and pre-set, but giving adequate flow) and indoor dishwashing sinks. Hair dryers, shaver points and hand dryers. Laundry facilities and irons available on loan. A shop at the entrance is open to all (Spr. B.H. - mid-Sept). Public phones and post box. Fishing on site, riverside walks up to Dartmoor. Bicycle hire 3 miles, boat slipway 2 miles, tennis and dry ski slope 1 mile. An added advantage is that the site is security patrolled at night.

Charges 2000:
-- Per adult £2.50 - £3.00; child (3-10 yrs) £1.10 - £1.25; pitch £2.50 - £4.00; electricity £2.00 - £2.50; awning free - £1.00; dog, extra car or boat £1.00.
-- Special breaks for the over-50s.
-- No single sex groups.
-- Credit cards accepted.
Open:
All year.
Address:
Longbridge Road, Marshmills, Plymouth, Devon PL6 8LD.
Tel:
(01752) 344122.
E-mail: info@riverside-caravanpark.com.
Reservations:
Made with £15 deposit per week or part week.

Directions: From A38 dual-carriageway from Exeter, take Marsh Mill exit (the first signed to Plymouth city centre). Follow good camp site signs to third exit, turning left after a few yards. O.S.GR: SX518576.

34

079 Harford Bridge Park, Peter Tavy, nr. Tavistock

Attractive, mature park on west Dartmoor bordering the delightful River Tavy.

Harford Bridge has an interesting history - originally the Wheal Union tin mine until 1850, then used as a farm campsite from 1930 and taken over by the Royal Engineers in 1939, it is now a quiet, rural park inside the Dartmoor National Park. It is bounded by the River Tavy on one side and the lane from the main road to Peter Tavy village on the other, with Harford Bridge, a classic granite moorland bridge, at the corner. With 16½ acres, the park provides 120 touring pitches well spaced on a level grassy meadow with some shade from mature trees and others recently planted; 40 pitches have electricity and 8 have 'multi services'. Out of season or by booking in advance you may get one of the delightful spots bordering the river (these without hook-up facilities). Holiday caravans (13) and chalets (7, some centrally heated and double glazed for all year use) are available for hire, neatly landscaped in their own area. The single toilet block is older in style but has been recently refurbished. Kept perfectly clean, well decorated and properly maintained, hot water is free throughout. The facilities include hand and hair dryers (free), baby bathroom, washing up sinks, a good launderette and drying room, freezer pack facility and chemical disposal. At the entrance to the park a central grassy area is left free for games, which is also used by the town band, village fete, etc. It is overlooked by the shop, stocked with camping accessories, postcards, stamps, etc. but not groceries (Easter-end Sept). While the river (unfenced) will inevitably mesmerise youngsters and ducks and chickens attract their interest, a super central adventure play area on a hilly tree knoll will claim them. Two Wickstead stainless steel slides, a 45 year old carnival carousel round-about and tunnels are just part of a well presented, safe and marvellous provision. Games room with additional campers' information, table tennis and separate TV room. Tennis court (free). Fly fishing (by licence, £3 p/day, £10 p/week). Bicycle hire, riding and golf, all within 2½ miles. Two barbecue areas. Well behaved dogs are accepted and a 4 acre exercise field is provided. With its own and the local history, plus its situation, this is a super place to stay. Bellamy gold.

Charges 2001:
-- Per unit, incl. 2 persons £6.00 - £10.50; extra adult £2.00 - £2.50; child £1.00 - £1.50; dog 90p; electricity £2.00; awning £1.00; extra car 50p.
-- Less 10% for stays over 7 days (not electricity or fishing).
-- Credit cards accepted.
-- VAT included.
Open:
Late March - early Nov.
Address:
Peter Tavy,
Tavistock,
Devon PL19 9LS.
Tel:
(01822) 810349.
FAX: (01822) 810028.
E-mail: enquiry@harford-bridge.co.uk.
Reservations:
Made for any length with first night's fees.

Directions: Two miles north of Tavistock, off A386 Tavistock - Okehampton road, take the road to Peter Tavy. O.S.GR: SX504768.

080 Higher Longford Caravan & Camping Park, nr. Tavistock

Quiet, small, family run park, ideal for staying on lower slopes of Dartmoor.

Situated within the National Park boundaries, this small park has views up to the higher slopes of the moor. The site has a sheltered touring field where 40 level pitches are arranged on each side of a circular access road, two smaller touring areas for 12 units and a seasonal camping field for a further 80. Facilities include 49 electrical hook-ups and an area of hardstanding for poor weather. Residential caravans and chalets for hire are in a separate area adjacent and some attractive converted cottages also for hire form a courtyard area with the farmhouse, reception and bar. The main toilet block is alongside the touring field providing roomy, free showers, smallish washbasins and one en-suite cabin for ladies, hand and hair dryers and dishwashing, all with plentiful, free hot water. This is supple-mented by extra heated facilities in the courtyard, which include showers with a communal dressing area. Extra smart chemical disposal (like a wishing well), full laundry facilities and a washing line, motorcaravan service point. Within the 14th century farmhouse is a small licensed shop, open on demand, with gas and some fresh farm produce. It adjoins a pleasant, cosy bar and restaurant with open fire and TV, where takeaway or full meals are offered (all April-Oct), and a spacious conservatory, useful in poor weather. Tourist information and public phone. Caravan storage. Dogs are welcome with an exercise field provided. Higher Longford is an ideal centre for touring Dartmoor, either by car, on foot, or astride a local pony (riding stables nearby). Game or coarse fishing 3 miles, Tavistock golf course 1 miles, bicycle hire or riding 3 miles. Plymouth and the cross channel ferries are 30 minutes' drive, Tavistock is 3 miles, with a good market and Goose Fair in October. Bellamy gold.

Charges 2000:
-- Per unit incl. 1 person £6.50 - £7.50, 2 persons £7.50 - £8.50, family (2 adults, 2 children) £9.00 - £10.00; extra adult £2.00; extra child (over 3 yrs) £1.00; electricity £1.75.
-- Less 50p per night for booked stays over 7 nights.
-- No credit cards.
-- VAT included.
Open:
All year.
Address:
Moorshop,
Tavistock,
Devon PL19 9LQ.
Tel:
(01822) 613360.
FAX: (01822) 618722.
Reservations:
Made with £5 deposit.

Directions: Park is clearly signed from B3357, 2 miles from Tavistock. O.S.GR: SX520747.

Devon

104 Old Cotmore Farm, Stokenham, nr. Kingsbridge

Charming, small and secluded park two miles from Start Point, for all units.

Sue and John Bradney own Old Cotmore Farm - that is the farmhouse, two cottages and a small touring site. The only livestock to be seen now are a few chickens and ducks, including a curious black Indian Runner duck who patrols the site, and maybe some horses. They have worked hard to improve the facilities and now provide 30 pitches, all with electric hook-up, on neatly cut grass. Partly in a garden type situation to one side of the drive with some pitches sloping, and partly on a level, smallish field with children's play equipment in the centre. Pitches here tend to be used for families with children, with those on the other side of the drive kept for adults only. A small stream runs along one side with a pretty, fenced pond area and bridge near the entrance. Reception is past the pitches towards the farmhouse and adjoining the toilet block which has been converted from original buildings. The ladies' and men's sections have a degree of individuality, providing modern vanity style washbasins (H&C) and pre-set hot showers in individual cubicles (stools, no divider and non-slip floor). A separate en-suite unit provides for disabled visitors and also includes a baby bath and changing table. A new utility room has three dishwashing sinks and a laundry sinks (H&C), three washing machines and two dryers, plus tourist information. Telephone. Chemical toilet and waste water disposal are tucked away behind reception. A separate field with a 28 day licence has water points, two extra sinks (H&C) and two toilets, but it may put pressure on the main block when in use. Mountain bike hire and table tennis. Dog exercise field. Mrs Bradney holds a children's club once a week in high season. Reception stocks gas and basic necessities - baguettes can be ordered and helpful wardens will assist you to pitch. The site is in an area of Outstanding Natural Coastal Beauty, with Slapton Sands, Salcombe and Kingsbridge near and Dartmouth just a little further. It is an ideal area for walking, boating, diving, windsurfing and safe bathing Riding 4 miles, golf 8 miles. Two pubs are within one mile either way. Three cottages to let.

Charges 2000:
-- Per unit incl. 2 persons £7.00 - £9.00; tent incl. 2 persons £6.50; extra adult £2,00; child (3-12 yrs) £1.00; car, extra car or boat £1.00; dog £1.00; electricity £2.00.
-- Less £1.00 per pitch in low seasons.
-- Credit cards accepted

Open:
14 March - 15 November.

Address:
Stokenham,
nr. Kingsbridge,
South Devon TQ7 2LR.

Tel:
(01548) 580240.
FAX: (01548) 580875.

Reservations:
Made with 25% deposit; contact park.

Directions: From Kingsbridge on A379 Dartmouth road, go through Frogmore and Chillington to Carehouse Cross mini-roundabout at Stokenham. Turn right towards Beesands and follow camp signs for 1 mile. Site entrance is on right just past the post box - look out for the churns! Roads are a little narrow in places. O.S.GR: SX804417.

082 Moor View Touring Park, Modbury

Pleasant, maturing park with magnificent views of Dartmoor.

Moor View has a gently sloping position with terraced, individual, fairly level grass pitches connected by hard core roads with marvellous views across to the Dartmoor Tors. It provides 68 pitches of varying size, all with 10A electricity and 15 with hardstanding. Bushes and shrubs on the lower terraces are growing well, giving the park a more mature feel. A two acre field provides space for children and a dog walk, or for the odd rally. There is also a fenced play area on grass near a small river pool. The amenities are in one block near the entrance, not too far from the furthest pitches and providing a reception cum shop with basic food and some camping accessories. There is a comfortable TV room with tourist information, a games room with pool table, table tennis and video machines. Traditional type sanitary facilities have access from a courtyard area and are kept clean, providing all necessary facilities with hot water, including a laundry room, covered dishwashing sinks and chemical disposal. Takeaway in season, to order (6.30-7.30 pm). Public phone. Golf 5 miles, riding and fishing 6 miles. A local country pub is within walking distance, the small town of Modbury is 3 miles. Burgh Island and Bigbury Bay are near, Dartmoor is within striking distance. This is a park in a lovely corner of Devon, with enthusiastic owners, Alan and Julia Marshall. A member of the Countryside Discovery group.

Charges 2000:
-- Per pitch incl. 2 adults £8.00 - £10.00; extra adult £2.00; child (3-14 yrs) £1.50; small tent less £1.00; dog free; electricity (10A) £1.75; water hook-up 50p.
-- Credit cards accepted.

Open:
Mid-April - mid-October

Address:
California Cross,
nr. Modbury,
Ivybridge,
Devon PL21 0SG

Tel:
(01548) 821485.

Reservations:
Made with £10 deposit.

Directions: On A38 from Exeter, pass exit for A385 (Totnes) and continue for a further 2 miles. Just past Woodpecker Inn leave the A38 at Wrangaton Cross, signed Ermington, Modbury and Yealmpton. Turn left and follow straight on at crossroads (Kitterford Cross) signed Modbury, Loddiswell, Kingsbridge for 3 miles to California Cross. Leave garage on left and follow towards Modbury (B3207). Park is ½ mile on left. O.S.GR: SX705533.

083 Camping and Caravanning Club Site Slapton, nr. Kingsbridge

Well kept site overlooking the sea and freshwater nature reserve, close to Dartmouth; motorcaravans, trailer-tents or tents only.

Slapton is a charming village with tiny lanes and cottages, a shop and two historic pubs, one dominated by the ruined tower of an old monastery. The village (unsuitable for camping traffic) is about half a mile inland from the shingle beach of Slapton Sands and the fresh water Ley which is administered as a nature reserve by the Field Studies Council. The Club site is situated on the road leading from the Sands, on a well kept meadow overlooking the bay - the sea views are panoramic from most areas of the site, with shelter provided by some large bushes and the surrounding hedge. There are 126 grass pitches, some with a slight slope; electricity (16A) is available for 48 (including 11 with hardstanding). Motor-caravans, trailer tents and tents are accepted but planners only permit 8 caravan pitches which are kept for club members. The modern toilet block is central, can be heated and is kept very clean, providing toilets, washbasins (all in private cabins) and good, controllable free hot showers. A useful parent and child room is provided and a separate unit for disabled visitors (with key), plus dishwashing facilities, laundry sinks, washing machine and dryer (and outside lines), chemical disposal and a motorcaravan service point. Other than a small children's play area, there are no other on-site facilities but the village is a pleasant stroll and the milkman calls daily with bread, eggs, etc. A fish and chip van calls on Fridays and reception has sweets for children, a small library, telephone, gas and a freezer for ice blocks. Dog walk available. The Field Studies Centre arranges guided walks and short study courses on a wide variety of interests and can issue fishing permits for the Ley (perch and pike, of legendary size, in the summer months). Beach fishing is also popular. Riding ½ mile. This area was used for rehearsals for the WW2 Normandy landings, when the whole population was evacuated - there are memorials, including a tank in the village of Torcross. The quaint port of Dartmouth is 7 miles, Kingsbridge 8 miles and a variety of beaches and coves around the beautiful South Hams coastline are within easy reach.

Charges 2000:
-- Per adult £3.75 - £5.30; child (6-18 yrs) £1.65; non-member pitch fee £4.30; electricity £1.60 - £2.35.
-- VAT included.
-- Credit cards accepted.
Open:
March - October.
Address:
Middle Grounds, Slapton, Kingsbridge, Devon TQ7 1QW.
Tel:
(01548) 580538 (no calls after 8 pm).
Reservations:
Necessary and made with deposit; contact the wardens.

Directions: From A38 Exeter - Plymouth road, take A384 to Totnes. Just before town, turn right on A381 to Kingsbridge, then A379 through Stokenham and Torcross to Slapton Sands. Half way along the beach road turn left to Slapton village and site is 200 yds on right. Note: Avoid the very narrow Five Mile Lane from the A381 which is signed Slapton (just after a filling station) 6 miles from Kingsbridge. O.S.GR: SX825450.

085 Galmpton Touring Park, Galmpton, nr. Brixham

Quiet touring park close to Torbay, with wonderful views over the River Dart estuary.

Within a few miles of the lively amenities of Torbay, Galmpton Park lies peace-fully just outside the village of Galmpton, overlooking the beautiful Dart estuary just upstream of Dartmouth and Kingswear. Some 120 pitches, 60 marked for caravans, are arranged on a wide sweep of grassy, terraced meadow, each pitch with its own view of the river. Situated on the hillside, some parts quite a slope, but there are flatter areas (the owners will advise and assist). There are 95 electrical connections (10A) and 20 pitches are fully serviced. There is a separate tent field. American motorhomes are not accepted. A central, substantial looking sanitary block provides clean facilities including washbasins in flat surfaces with mirrors, with three private cabins, free hot showers, baby unit and hair care areas; also chemical disposal and a dishwashing room (free hot water) with a washing machine, dryer, iron and ironing board available. Milk, bread, papers and gas are available from reception. There is good adventure play equipment for children. The local pub is a five minute walk. Dogs (max. 2 per unit) are accepted at the owner's discretion and only outside the school summer holidays with an exercise area provided. Two holiday cottages to rent. Caravan storage. Galmpton is a quiet and simple park (with the gates closed 11.30 pm - 7.30 am) in a most picturesque setting, within easy reach of all the attractions of South Devon.

Charges 2000:
-- Per unit incl. 2 persons and awning £6.00 - £10.00, 'de-luxe' pitch plus £1.00 - £1.50; extra adult £2.00; extra child £1.00; electricity £1.70; extra car or boat £1.50; dog (off peak only) 50p.
-- Various discounts available.
-- Credit cards accepted.
-- VAT included.
Open:
Easter - 31 October.
Address:
Greenway Road, Galmpton, Brixham, Devon TQ5 0EP.
Tel:
(01803) 842066.
Reservations:
Made with £20 deposit p/week booked.

Directions: Take A380 Paignton ring road towards Brixham until junction with the Paignton - Brixham coast road. Turn right towards Brixham, then second right into Manor Vale Road. Continue through the village, past the school and site is 100 yds on the right. O.S.GR: SX885558.

Devon

084 Woodlands Leisure Park, Blackawton, nr. Dartmouth

Well planned touring site forming part of family run, countryside leisure park.

Woodlands is a surprise, a nice one - from the road you have no idea of just what is hidden away deep in the Devon countryside. To achieve this, there has been sympathetic development of farm and woodland to provide a leisure centre, open to the public and with a range of activities and entertainment appealing to all ages. Children (and many energetic parents too!) are kept amused for hours by a variety of imaginative adventure play equipment or amazing water toboggan runs and 'Arctic Coasters' hidden amongst the trees and many farm animals, birds and boats, while those more peacefully inclined can follow woodland walks around the attractive ponds. A Falconry Centre gives opportunities to watch displays (or for the birds to watch you!) There is plenty of play equipment for younger children too, including an indoor play barn with a circus theme. Opened for the millennium, the 'Empire of the Sea Dragon', a new two million pounds indoor play centre, has provided marvellous wet weather facilities - said to be the biggest indoor venture in the UK.

With two nights stay, campers on the touring park are admitted free of charge to the leisure park. The camping and caravan site, overlooking woodland and part of the leisure park, takes 220 units on two sloping, grassy fields, one original, the other newly developed. These have been fully terraced to provide groups of four to eight flat, very spacious pitches, 90% with electrical connections (10A) and a shared water tap, drain and rubbish bin. The level terraces are divided by young hedging and shrubs that are growing nicely in the original field. Two modern, heated toilet blocks are well maintained and kept very clean, providing free hot water in pre-set showers and washbasins (with dividers and curtains). An excellent provision in the new, smart toilet block includes private bathrooms (coin-operated, 20p) and seven family shower cubicles. Each block is fitted with hair dryers, a well equipped laundry room, dishwashing area and a freezer for ice packs. There are also baby changing facilities. A fully equipped TV and games room is to be found above the new block. Dogs are accepted on the campsite but not in the leisure park (kennels available). The leisure park café, with an outdoor rose terrace, provides good value meals and cream teas with entertainment (music, Morris men, etc.) at busy times, and a takeaway service for campers. The opening hours of the café and adjoining gift shop, where gas and a few basic food supplies are kept, vary according to season and demand. A popular park, early reservation is advisable. The charming town of Dartmouth and the South Hams beaches are near. Fishing 3 miles, golf ½ mile, riding 5 miles. Caravan storage.

Directions: From A38 at Buckfastleigh, take A384 to Totnes. Before town centre turn right on A381 Kingsbridge road. After Halwell turn left at Totnes Cross, on A3122 to Dartmouth. Park is on right after 2½ miles. O.S.GR: SX825456.

Charges 2000:
-- Per unit, incl. 2 persons £7.50 - £13.95; extra person (over 2 yrs) £2.75; awning or extra small pup tent £2.50; large tent or trailer tent (120 sq.ft. plus) plus £2.00; extra car, boat or trailer £1.00; dog £2.50; electricity £1.95.
-- Free entry to leisure park for stays 2 nights or more.
-- VAT included.
-- Credit cards accepted.

Open:
1 April - 4 November.

Address:
Blackawton,
Totnes,
Devon TQ9 7DQ.

Tel:
(01803) 712598.
FAX: (01803) 712680.
E-mail: bookings@ woodlands-leisure-park.co.uk.

Reservations:
Accepted for min. 3 nights with £35 deposit, except July/Aug. when min. 7 days and £50 deposit. Balance in full 21 days before arrival.

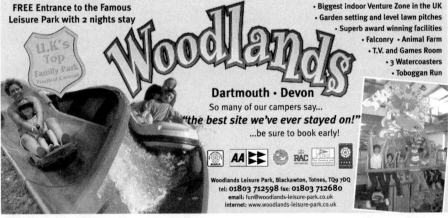

FREE Entrance to the Famous Leisure Park with 2 nights stay

U.K's Top Family Park Practical Caravan

Dartmouth • Devon

So many of our campers say...
"the best site we've ever stayed on!"
...be sure to book early!

• Biggest Indoor Venture Zone in the UK
• Garden setting and level lawn pitches
• Superb award winning facilities
• Falconry • Animal Farm
• T.V. and Games Room
• 3 Watercoasters
• Toboggan Run

AA ▶▶ RAC

Woodlands Leisure Park, Blackawton, Totnes, TQ9 7DQ
tel: 01803 712598 fax: 01803 712680
email: fun@woodlands-leisure-park.co.uk
internet: www.woodlands-leisure-park.co.uk

087 Beverley Holidays, Paignton

see colour advert
between pages 32/33

Popular Torbay park with holiday homes, many facilities and entertainment.

Beverley Park is a quality holiday centre, attractively landscaped and with views over Torbay. With pools and a large dance hall, with bars, entertainment, etc, all run in an efficient and orderly manner. The holiday caravan park has 197 caravan holiday homes and 23 lodges, mainly around the central complex. The 189 touring pitches are in the lower areas of the park, all reasonably sheltered, some with views across the bay and some on slightly sloping ground. All pitches have 16A electricity (15 m cable), 38 have hardstanding, 21 are fully serviced. Tents are accepted and a limited number of tent pitches have electricity. The park has a long season and reservations are essential for caravans. American motorhomes are accepted (max. 20 ft). The toilet blocks, adjacent to the pitches, are good (particularly the new ones) and, although they can receive heavy use and need regular attention, they are well maintained and heated. Showers and washbasins have free hot water, baths are on payment. There is a unit for disabled visitors and facilities for babies, water points around the park, recycling bins, laundry, gas supplies, chemical disposal and motorcaravan service facilities. Large general shop, 'express diner', garden bar and takeaway service (all Easter - 28 Oct). Dance hall with bars - entertainment at Easter and from early May in the Starlight bar. There are indoor and outdoor pools, each one heated and supervised. The adult pools are generous in size and the Oasis fitness centre provides a steam room, jacuzzi, sun bed, fitness room, etc. Activities include tennis, crazy golf, playground, nature trail and an amusement centre with pool, table tennis and amusement machines. Fishing, bicycle hire, riding and golf all within 2 miles. The park is in the heart of residential Torbay, with views across the bay, and sandy beaches under a mile. A minibus service runs to Paignton. No dogs are accepted. This park has lots to offer and is well run. A member of the Best of British group. Bellamy gold.

Directions: Park is south of Paignton in Goodrington Road between A379 coast road and B3203 ring road and is well signed on both. O.S.GR: SX882584.

Charges 2000:
-- Per unit incl. 2 persons: serviced pitch £11.00 - £22.00, electric pitch £9.00 - £20.00; tent £7.00 - £18.00, with electricity plus £2.00; extra adult £4.00, child (4-14 yrs) £3.00; awning or extra pup tent £3.00.
-- Max. 6 persons per reservation.
-- VAT included.
-- Credit cards accepted.

Open:
28 February - 21 Nov; tents 1 April - 31 Oct.

Address:
Goodrington Road, Paignton, Devon TQ4 7JE.

Tel:
(01803) 843887.
FAX: (01803) 845427.
E-mail: enquiries@ beverley-holidays.co.uk.

Reservations:
Made with £25 deposit (7, 14 or 21 days 17/7- 3/9, min. 2 nights all other times); balance payable more than 28 days before arrival.

086 Ramslade Touring Park, Stoke Gabriel, Paignton

Well kept, quiet, quality park in attractive rural location, 3 miles from sea at Paignton.

Personally run by the owners, Ramslade is a smaller, rural park with country views and provides a quiet, peaceful alternative to the many larger holiday parks in and around Paignton itself. A member of the Caravan Club's 'managed under contract' scheme, non-members are also very welcome. The attractively landscaped, neat park takes 135 touring units of all types. Pitches are arranged in two areas planted with maturing trees and some attractive flowering cherries. The larger area slopes towards the centre of the park but has been gently terraced and most pitches are level or very slightly sloping. Tarmac roads give good access and all but two pitches have electricity. There are 34 'all-service' pitches with shared picnic tables, 7 hardstandings for motorcaravans, 2 fully serviced hardstandings for RVs and a drive-on service area for caravans and motorcaravans. No groundsheets are allowed in awnings; inner tents to be lifted daily. A renovated lime kiln provides an ideal place for semi-communal barbecues. The well maintained central toilet block is heated in cool weather. Hot water is free for the washbasins (some cabins) and the plentiful showers. There is a make-up area for ladies and hair dryers, with a baby bathroom and washing-up sinks (free hot water) in a covered area at the rear of the block. Facilities for disabled visitors, a laundry room with free irons and microwave and a super luxury, family bathroom (£2). Recycling bins are provided and four chemical disposal points are enclosed in gazebo form. Small shop (Easter - mid Sept). TV room and games room with pool and table tennis. An adventure play area is set away from the pitches, plus a small, central area for younger children next to a splash pool with fountain feature, jacuzzi (from Spr. B.H.) and a paved area for parents to relax (it is walled with a locking gate). Weather station with daily forecasts. No dogs are accepted in the peak six weeks. No cycling, skateboarding or rollerblading. Indoor and outdoor caravan storage with servicing. Fishing or bicycle hire 3 miles, golf 4 miles. Large RVs are welcome. A member of the Best of British group. Bellamy gold.

Directions: Park is south of A385 (Paignton - Totnes) and is well signed. Turn off A385 to south alongside Parkers Arms pub (½ mile west of Paignton ring road), then follow road for 1½ miles. O.S.GR: SX857583.

Charges 2000:
-- Per unit incl. 2 persons and awning: standard pitch £8.80 - £13.80; electricity £1.50 - £2.25; water and drain services 50p - £2.00; extra adult £3.25 - £4.00; child (5-16 yrs) £1.10 - £1.20; extra car or boat £1.00.
-- Credit cards accepted.
-- VAT included.

Open:
30 March - 27 October.

Address:
Paignton Road, Stoke Gabriel, Paignton, Devon TQ9 6QB.

Tel:
(01803) 782575.
FAX: (01803) 782828.
E-mail: ramslade@ compuserve.com.

Reservations:
Any length stay, £15 deposit per week booked.

088 Dornafield, Two Mile Oak, Newton Abbot

Family run, rural touring park with all modern facilities including luxury pitches.

The entrance to Dornafield leads into the charming old courtyard of a 14th Century farmhouse giving a mellow feeling that is complemented by the warm welcome from the Dewhirst family. The reception, shop, tourist information/ ecology room have been sympathetically converted from farm outbuildings, with the games room from the old milking parlour, complete with stalls. Once booked in, you may continue down the lane (in spring overlooked by a tree covered bank and alive with wild flowers) to the Buttermeadow, a tranquil valley providing 75 individual, numbered pitches on flat grass, separated by grassy ridges and in some places, wild rose hedges. You pass the walled Orchard area, secluded and cosy for tents. Or take the road up the hill and reach Blackrock Copse, the development of large luxury pitches with all facilities including a chemical disposal point for each pitch and TV connections, very cleverly concealed and 38 with hardstanding. All electricity points are 10A. Whilst carefully designed, the environment has been kept natural. Both Buttermeadow and Blackrock have super woodland adventure play areas, well maintained and with Wendy houses. Perhaps the finest features of the park are the toilet blocks. The original one in Buttermeadow is good, heated, with vanity style units, some washbasins in cubicles and comfortable roomy showers, but the new block up the hill could be said to be 'state of the art' with under-floor heating and a heat recovery system. It is stylish yet warm providing everything for your comfort including a large, stylish clock! Both blocks have facilities for disabled visitors and babies, laundry rooms and covered washing up areas. They are bright, cheerful and spotlessly clean. Dogs have two exercise areas and walks from the site. Dornafield is a member of the Caravan Club's 'managed under contract' scheme, with both members and non-members made welcome. Gas supplies. All year caravan storage. All-weather hard tennis court. Games room with table tennis. The local inn is within half a mile. Fishing 2½ miles, golf 1 mile. Dornafield's rural situation is delightful and, being away from the coast and without evening activities, it is a haven for those seeking a quiet, restful holiday. A park that is well worth consideration. Bellamy Bronze.

Directions: Park is northwest of A381 Newton Abbot - Totnes road. Leave A381 at Two Mile Oak Inn, opposite garage, and turn left at crossroads after about ½ mile. Entrance is on the right. O.S.GR: SX848683.

Charges 2000:
-- Per pitch £1.50 - £4.50; adult £3.25 - £4.10; child (5-16 yrs) £1.10 - £1.50; awning free - £1.00; pup tent or porch awning free - 50p; tents over 100 sq.ft. charged awning rate; full services £1.00 - £1.50 (£2.25 outside 19/4-2/10); extra car or trailer £1.00; dog £1.00.
-- Credit cards accepted.
-- VAT included.

Open:
18 March - 1 November.

Address:
Two Mile Oak,
Newton Abbot,
Devon TQ12 6DD.

Tel:
(01803) 812732.
FAX: (01803) 812032.
E-mail: enquiries@
dornafield.com.

Reservations:
Any length, £10 p.w. low season, £25 p/week high season.

091 Ross Park, Ipplepen, nr. Newton Abbot

Excellent quality, friendly park in attractive landscaped surroundings.

Ross Park has to be seen to appreciate the amazing floral displays with their dramatic colours, that are a feature of the park. These are complemented by the variety of shrubs used to form hedging for most of the 110 pitches providing your own special plot, very much as on the continent. For those who prefer the more open style, a small area is left unhedged. There are views over the surrounding countryside but as the foliage has developed these are not quite as extensive but there is more protection on a windy day. The owners, Mark and Helen Lowe strive to provide quality facilities and maintain standards, and this is reflected in the awards they have won. There are nice personal touches, as seen in the utility room with beautiful photographs of the countryside and suggestions for visits cross-referenced to a map, or the impressive, heated conservatory with yet more named exotic and colourful plants. Seating is provided here as it is directly linked to the New Barn that provides a comfortable lounge, mezzanine bar with bar snacks and a restaurant with a la carte menu (all April - end Oct, plus Xmas and New Year). The touring area is divided into bays or groups by the hedging and shrubs and provides 110 pitches all with electricity (10/16A), 82 with a hard surface and some made larger with a gravel area. The main toilet facilities by the New Barn open from under a veranda style roof, colourful with hanging baskets. They comprise six well equipped, heated en-suite units, one with baby facilities, one suitable for disabled people. At the rear are further separate shower, washbasin and toilet facilities, all well equipped. Below the New Barn are more toilets and washbasins in a well kept, heated 'portacabin' style unit. Hot water is free and shaver points and hairdryers provided. Fully equipped laundry room and utility room providing dishwashing sinks, a freezer and battery charging. Chemical disposal, motorcaravan service point and recycling bins. Games room, table tennis, snooker table and billiards room. Comfortable reception with shop area and gas supplies. Tourist information chalet with herbs for your barbecue nearby. A 7-acre recreation area has bowling and croquet and a well equipped adventure playground for older children. An orchard area alive with daffodils in the spring and a conservation area with information on wild flowers and butterflies and with extended views completes these environmentally considered amenities. Dogs have a variety of walks in fields and orchards and even have their own shower/ grooming facilities, hot water included! Dainton Park 18 hole golf course is adjacent. Fishing 3 miles, riding 1 mile. Winter caravan storage. A park well worth consideration. Bellamy gold.

Charges 2000:
-- Per unit incl. 2 persons £7.70 - £12.10; extra adult £3.25 - £3.75; child (3-16 yrs) £1.50 - £1.75; electricity (16A) £1.70 - £2.20.
-- Christmas packages available.
-- VAT included.
-- No credit cards.
Open:
All year except Jan. and first two weeks of Feb.
Address:
Park Hill Farm, Ipplepen, Newton Abbot, Devon TQ12 5TT.
Tel:
(01803) 812983.
E-mail: enquiries@ rossparkcaravanpark. co.uk.
Reservations:
Made with £20 deposit.

Directions: From A381 Newton Abbot - Totnes road, park is signed towards Woodland at Park Hill crossroads and Jet filling station. O.S.GR: SX845671.

090 Widdicombe Farm Tourist Park, Paignton

Well situated park on fringes of Torquay, yet with rural outlook.

Widdicombe Farm, just 3 miles from Torquay, offers 200 numbered pitches (156 for tourers). Electricity (10A) is available on 140 pitches and 10 are fully serviced. Surrounded by farmland, the pitches are on gently sloping grass terraces giving a very rural feel. Trees and shrubs have been planted and there are tarmac access roads. A few pitches are fairly close to the A380 and there may be some traffic noise. Touring areas are separated into sections for families, couples or tents and some hardstandings are available. On site are a shop and the 'Poppy' restaurant providing evening meals, breakfasts, cream teas and takeaway (both Easter - mid Oct). A large comfortable bar offers family entertainment and opposite the bar is a 'do it yourself' barbecue area with large gas barbecues, patio area and seating (£2 per session). Games room with video games and pool tables, children's play area and a recreation field for ball games. There are three sanitary blocks - the original heated block near reception and fully equipped, and two newer blocks, one at the top of the site with provision for disabled visitors and another in the lower section (toilets and washbasins only). Baby room, dishwashing under cover, chemical disposal and a small laundry. The proprietors live on site. Caravan holiday homes for hire (3). Dogs are permitted in the touring section (no dangerous breeds). Fishing, bicycle hire, riding and golf, all within 2 miles. Caravan storage.

Charges 2000:
-- Per unit incl. 2 persons £6.00 - £10.00; extra adult £2.00 - £2.50; child (3-16 yrs) £1.00 - £1.50; awning, extra car or dog £1.00 - £1.50; electricity (10A) £1.80.
-- Credit cards accepted.
Open:
March - November.
Address:
The Ring Road, Compton, Paignton, Devon TQ3 1ST.
Tel:
(01803) 558325.
FAX: (01803) 559526.
Reservations:
Advised for July/Aug. (min. 4 days) and made with deposit (£20 per week) and fee (£2).

Directions: From Newton Abbot take A380 south for approx. 5 miles; site is well signed off this road. O.S.GR: SX874641.

Devon

092 Finlake Holiday Park, Chudleigh

Large, lively park, with entertainment complex and leisure facilities, open all year.

This extensive 130 acre park on the edge of Dartmoor has been purpose built as a modern touring park and leisure complex. Approached by a long, sweeping drive, with views up to the moor, the park is on well landscaped, undulating ground surrounded by woodland. There are 318 flat numbered pitches in two main areas, with some terracing on the higher parts. The pitches in the area around the central complex may well be affected by noise from the bars, etc. - for a quieter place, ask for a pitch further away (Lakeside or Deer Park). The pitches are of varying size, all with hardstanding and electricity (10A), 51 with water also. A separate, enclosed field is retained for tents and there is a special area for dog owners, with dog walks available. The five modern toilet blocks set around the park are being progressively refurbished and extended. Heated and of good quality, they have washbasins set in flat surfaces and free, pre-set hot showers, family shower rooms, bathrooms for ladies, suitable toilet/washrooms for disabled people and washing-up sinks outside, under cover. The facilities can come under pressure at peak times. A state-of-the-art 'portacabin' style unit with electricity was to be delivered for the tent field just after our visit. There are additional facilities in the pool complex. Chemical disposal and motorcaravan service points. Also open to the public, the park offers extensive leisure activities including a 9-hole pitch and putt course, two fishing lakes, fitness track, tennis courts, quad bikes and track for children and walks in the woodland around the park with pony riding at a centre 100 m. from the entrance. The modern, attractively designed, central complex provides three bars around a pool terrace, two with entertainment and one with a restaurant. There is a lively, free organised entertainment programme over a long season (out of season only one bar is open). A fitness suite (small charge, open all year) has a beauty treatment room and qualified instructors. Indoor and outdoor pools (with slide) are supervised in high season but are also easily observed from the bar areas and terrace. The Lakeside Bar, open in high season and for adults only, overlooks the fishing lake. Supermarket (Easter-Oct, limited opening early and late season). Gas supplies. Fully equipped launderette. There are two tennis courts and 'Quads for Kids'. Riding centre is adjacent. Bicycle hire 6 miles, golf 3 miles. For rent are 50 caravan holiday homes and, well hidden in woodland, 41 luxury log cabins. A torch would be useful. Caravan storage all year.

Charges 2000:
-- Per unit incl. 2 persons: caravan, trailer tent or motorcaravan £7.50 - £16.50; electricity £1.80; tent £5.50 - £12.00; extra person (from 3 yrs) £1.50 - £2.50; water and drainage £1.00 - £2.00; awning free; pup tent £1.00 - £2.00; dog £1.00 - £2.00; extra car £1.00 - £2.00.
-- Special themed weekends - details from park.
-- Bookings from young groups not accepted.
-- VAT included.
-- Credit cards accepted.

Open:
All year.

Address:
Chudleigh,
Devon TQ13 0EJ.

Tel:
(01626) 853833.
FAX: (01626) 854031.

Reservations:
Made with 25% deposit, balance 28 days before arrival.

see colour advert between pages 32/33

Directions: Park is signed on A38 dual-carriageway; take exit for Chudleigh Knighton, Kingsteignton, Teign Valley. O.S.GR: SX850778.

093 Ashburton Caravan Park, Ashburton

Small secluded park with new, enthusiastic owners; for tents and motorcaravans only.

The 4 acres of Ashburton Park nestle in a hidden valley below Dartmoor, bordered by mature woodland. The Ashburn, a shallow stream with rocky pools, evenly divides and screens the 2 acres of holiday homes from the two acre camping area. Sheltered and south facing, the park is a tranquil retreat but for the energetic a half mile steep uphill walk brings you to the moor or 1½ miles by Devon lanes to Ashburton village. There are 35 level or gently sloping pitches, 8 with electricity (16A), either side of a tarmac road which culminates in a small field area. First class sanitary facilities provide free hot showers, washbasins in cabins for ladies and a toilet/washbasin for disabled visitors (baby bath available). Washing machine and dryer, free spin dryer and iron. The unit also has a public phone and chemical disposal facilities. Reception provides gas, a freezer pack service, tourist information, maps and walks and a daily weather report. Each visitor receives a copy of the 'Dartmoor Visitor', the paper supplied by the Dartmoor National Park authorities - the campsite is actually within the boundaries of the Park. Shops, banks, post office, a small heated pool and pubs, etc. are in Ashburton, a pleasant walk away by the river. There are limited bus services to Newton Abbot, Exeter or Plymouth. Maps may be borrowed with walks. Bicycle hire 1 mile, riding and golf 3 miles. Dogs (limited breeds only) are welcomed if exercised off the park. Torches would be useful. A well maintained, tranquil small park for nature lovers.

Charges 2000:
-- Per unit incl. 1 person £4.00, 2 persons £7.50 - £10.00; extra person (over 1 yr) £1.50 - £2.25; dog 70p; electricity £1.80.
-- No credit cards.

Open:
Easter - mid October.

Address:
Waterleat,
Ashburton,
Devon TQ13 7HU.

Tel:
(01364) 652552.
FAX: as phone.

Reservations:
Made for min. 3 nights with £15 deposit.

Directions: In centre of Ashburton turn northwest into North Street. As built-up area thins out bear right before bridge following signs for 'Waterleat' (tent symbol) for approx. 1½ miles. Park is on the left. O.S.GR: SX752721.

094 Holmans Wood Caravan and Camping Park, Chudleigh

Neat, attractive family touring park adjacent to main Exeter - Plymouth road.

Close to the main A38 Exeter - Plymouth road, with easy access, this attractive, peaceful park makes a sheltered base for touring south Devon and Dartmoor. The hedged park is arranged on well kept grass surrounding a shallow depression, the floor of which makes a safe, grassy play area for children. Many attractive trees have been planted and the park is decorated with flowers. In two main areas, the 115 level pitches, 109 with electrical hook-ups (10A), are accessed by tarmac roads. There are 70 with hardstanding, electricity, TV aerial hook up, water and drainage. Grassy areas are provided for tents. The single toilet block is of good quality with washbasins set in flat surfaces, roomy, fully controllable free hot showers, a dishwashing room, laundry room, chemical disposal and facilities for babies and disabled visitors. The reception building at the entrance also houses a small licensed shop (with gas). Adventure play equipment is provided for children, with badminton and tennis nets and an extra meadow for recreation. Public telephone. Tourist information and advice. A pub/restaurant is nearby in Chudleigh village. Beaches or Dartmoor are 7 miles and Haldon Forest for walks is 2 miles. Sunday market at Exeter Racecourse 2 miles. Fishing 1 mile, golf or riding 4 miles. There may be some traffic noise on pitches to the west of the park. Caravan storage available. This is a pleasant, well run park and with no other on-site amenities would suit couples or families who prefer a peaceful stay.

Charges 2000:
-- Per unit incl. 2 persons £6.39 - £8.85, deluxe pitch £7.75 - £10.35; extra adult £1.65 - £2.20; child (4-14 yrs) £1.35 - £1.65; awning or child's tent £1.65; porch awning 90p; dog 85p; extra car or boat £1.05; electricity £2.00.
-- Credit cards accepted.
-- VAT included.
Open:
Mid-March - end Oct.
Address:
Chudleigh,
Devon TQ13 0DZ.
Tel:
(01626) 853785.
FAX: (01626) 854707.
Reservations:
Any length, £30 deposit per week.

Directions: From Exeter on A38 Plymouth road, ½ mile after the racecourse and just after a garage, take Chudleigh exit (signed). Park is immediately on the left. From Plymouth turn off A38 for Chudleigh/Teign Valley, then right for Chudleigh. Continue through the town and park is 1 mile. O.S.GR: SX882811.

095 The River Dart Country Park, Ashburton

Good quality, family touring site in country park on Dartmoor, with many outdoor activities for families.

With its mature park and woodland, once part of a Victorian estate, this interesting and unusual park could appeal to many, particularly those with children. Very close to Dartmoor, in the beautiful Dart valley, the park is open to the general public on payment. It features a variety of unusual adventure play equipment (eg. giant spider's web) arranged amongst and below the trees, 'Lilliput Land' for toddlers, woodland streams and a lake with raft for swimming and inflatables, fly fishing and marked nature and forest trails - all free to campers except fishing. It can become busy at weekends and school holidays. Supervised courses in caving, canoeing, archery or climbing are also arranged in school holiday periods (contact the park for details). The camping and caravanning area is in the more open parkland overlooking the woods and is mainly on a slight slope with some shade from mature trees. There are now 170 individual pitches of very reasonable size, marked by lines on the grass with 85 electrical connections (10A). The original toilet block for campers is of good quality and can be heated. There is free hot water in the washbasins (in cubicles with flat surface, hook and mirror, plus hair dryers), in the good hot showers and the washing-up sinks. Also provided are a baby changing room, a shower for disabled visitors, chemical disposal and a launderette and freezer. A second block has been added to serve the 50 newer pitches, fully equipped and including a separate unit for disabled visitors (access by key) and for ladies, washbasins in cubicles. Motorcaravan service point. Shop (all season). Restaurant and adjoining snack bar with takeaway (July/Aug). There is a small, heated swimming pool with lifeguard (50p per person) and tennis courts. Bar (July/Aug, plus Easter and B.Hs) with TV and games room with pool and amusement machines. Some self catering accommodation for rent. The entire estate is kept really clean and tidy. Dogs (max. two per pitch) are allowed on leads. American motorhomes are only accepted in dry periods (no hardstandings). Bicycle hire or riding 4 miles, golf 6 miles.

Charges 2000:
-- Per adult £4.75 - £6.50; child (over 3 yrs) £3.95 - £5.15; dog £1.00; electricity £1.85.
-- VAT included.
-- Credit cards accepted.
Open:
1 April - mid September.
Address:
Holne Park,
Ashburton,
Devon TQ13 7NP.
Tel:
(01364) 652511.
FAX: (01364) 652020.
Reservations:
Low or mid season, any length with £3 fee; high season (strongly recommended), £20 deposit plus £3 fee for 7 days or less; £40 + £3 for longer.

`Camping Cheque'

see colour advert between pages 32/33

Directions: Signed from the A38 at Peartree junction, park is about 2 miles west of Ashburton, on road to Two Bridges. Note: disregard advisory signs stating 'no caravans' as access to the park is prior to narrow bridge. O.S.GR: SX734701.

Devon

096 Parker's Farm Holiday Park, nr. Ashburton

Modern touring site on working farm at the foot of Dartmoor, close to A38.

Well situated with fine views towards the moor, Parker's Farm shows the trappings of a working farm. Close inspection reveals a unique chance to experience Devon country life at first hand, with pigs, sheep, goats, calves and rabbits, etc. in pens to feed and touch or the milking to get involved with. The Parker family have added a family bar (open Whitsun - mid Sept) and games room with table tennis and pool, an indoor play and TV area, a large outdoor play area, trampolines around the park, made-safe farm implements and tractors. The bar area provides entertainment during the season (quiz night, bingo, guitar player) and fills the gap created by the closure of the local pub and a restaurant provides good value meals. Farm walks are tremendously popular and take place four evenings a week in high season, on request at other times. The 100 touring pitches, with electricity (12A), are set directly above the farm buildings on terraces giving broad, flat groups of pitches, all with good views across the valley (to the A38 which may give some road noise). Hardstandings are available. Young trees and hedges have been planted and are maturing nicely on the lower terraces. There are two shower and toilet blocks. Modern, clean and tiled throughout, they provide good facilities with free hot water, a family shower room and baby bathroom, plus an en-suite for disabled visitors, dishwashing, laundry and chemical disposal facilities. A small shop is next to reception (open Whitsun - mid Sept). Dogs are welcome on leads with 400 acres for walks (the most we have seen on a site, but remember the Countryside Code). Public phone. American motorhomes accepted by prior arrangement. Rallies welcome. Caravan storage. Holiday homes and barn conversion cottages for hire. A camping barn will be ready for the 2001 season. Bicycle hire 5 miles, golf 4 miles, riding 5 miles. Parker's Farm will suit those who don't seek the sophisticated amenities of more developed parks and a warm welcome awaits - in the words of one camper, 'You come here and feel you belong'. Bellamy silver.

Directions: From Exeter on A38, 26 miles from Plymouth, turn left at Alston Cross signed 'Woodland Denbury ½ mile'. Site is ¼ mile. O.S.GR: SX757702.

Charges 2000:
-- Per unit incl. 2 persons £5.50 - £9.50; extra adult £1.30; child (3-15 yrs) £1.20; awning £1.30; pup tent £1.20; electricity £1.80; dog 60p.
-- VAT included.
-- Credit cards accepted.

Open:
Easter - 31 October.

Address:
Higher Mead Farm, Ashburton, Newton Abbot, Devon TQ13 7LJ.

Tel:
(01364) 652598.
FAX: (01364) 654004.
E-mail: parkersfarm@btconnect.com.

Reservations:
Made with £10 deposit

098 Lemonford Caravan Park, Bickington, nr. Newton Abbot

Attractive, family run park nestling in river valley, close to Dartmoor.

Lemonford has the look and atmosphere of the 'cultivated' caravan park. Well mown grass and trimmed, smart hedges bordered by the pretty River Lemon create the tranquil, attractive atmosphere the owners work hard to maintain. Despite its quite close proximity to the main road, this is a peaceful and relaxing site for all ages and families on the southern edge of the National Park, some 3 miles from both Ashburton and Newton Abbot. There are 96 touring pitches (62 with 10A electricity, 40 with hardstanding) on well kept, level grass and grouped in four areas according to whether they are to be used by families, couples or individuals. Some 14 holiday homes in a separate area and a cottage are for rent. The single, modern sanitary block is tiled, can be heated and has free, roomy, pre-set hot showers, free hairdryers and washbasins. Ladies have some private cabins, plus a bathroom (£1 payment). Hot water is free to the dishwashing area which is under cover. Amenities include a reception area and shop, gas, laundry facilities and clothes drying area, ice pack service, a children's play area, putting green, public phone, dog exercise area and a chalet with tourist information. Well located for excursions, the site provides discount vouchers for many nearby tourist attractions. Two good pubs are within walking distance and there is a leisure pool in Newton Abbot. Fishing 4 miles, riding and bicycle hire 3 miles, golf 2 miles. No commercial vehicles are accepted.

Directions: Turn off A38 Exeter - Plymouth road at A382 (Drumbridges) exit signed Newton Abbot, Bovey Tracey, Mortonhampstead. At roundabout take third exit to Bickington. Continue for 1 mile to Toby Jug Inn in the village and park is on left at the bottom of the hill. O.S.GR: SX793723.

Charges 2001:
-- Per unit incl. 2 persons £5.00 - £9.00; extra person £1.50; child (3-15) £1.10; awning £1.00; electricity £1.70; dog 70p.
-- Special low season offers.
-- VAT included.
-- No credit cards.

Open:
Mid March - 31 October.

Address:
Bickington, Newton Abbot, Devon TQ12 6JR.

Tel:
(01626) 821242.
FAX: as phone.
E-mail: lemonford@dartmoor.co.uk.

Reservations:
Advised for July/Aug. and made with £15 deposit (min. 3 nights Jul/Aug).

Alan Rogers' Discount

Low season discounts; contact park

Parkers Farm Holiday Park

Enjoy a relaxing holiday on a 400 acre real working
farm on the edge of Dartmoor National Park.
Barn converted cottages and holiday caravans and
a level, terraced touring site with fully tiled and
spotlessly clean shower and toilet blocks. ALL FREE.
Park Shop. Restaurant. Take Away. Family Bar.
A warm welcome awaits you.

Phone resident owners: Roger or Rhona.
Tel: 01364 652598. Fax: 01364 654004.
E-mail: parkersfarm@btconnect.com www.parkersfarm.co.uk
Higher Mead Farm, Ashburton,
Newton Abbot, S. Devon TQ13 7LJ   **AA** ►►►► **RAC**

SILVER
Int. Caravan & Camping 99
Gold Award for Quality & Service
Practical Caravan Top 100 Parks 1998

---

077 Clifford Bridge Park, Clifford, nr. Drewsteignton

Riverside touring park in beautiful, country location within the Dartmoor National Park.

This 8 acre park provides peace and tranquillity within the National Park and 3
miles from the nearest village with any facilities. In a wooded valley on the banks
of the River Teign, it can only be approached on narrow lanes (single track for the
last mile), but is a good base with plenty to do for those who like country pursuits
'away from it all'. Fingle Bridge is 3½ miles and Castle Drogo (National Trust) 5
miles. The site is licensed for 24 touring caravans or motorcaravans and 40 tents.
Pitches are of a good size on a flat grassy meadow, mainly around the perimeter
with some backing onto the river. Plenty of grassy space is left free for recreation
and there is a free swimming pool (54 x 24 ft. open 1/5-1/9, heated from Spr.
B.H). There are 3 hardstandings and 25 electrical connections (6A). The toilet
block, near the entrance to the park, is not large or modern but is satisfactory and
kept clean, with free hot water in the smallish washbasins and showers. Hand and
hair dryers. Chemical disposal. An adjacent 'portacabin' style unit provides extra
facilities in high season. Dishwashing sinks are outside, under cover. The farm
outbuildings house a shop (Spr. B.H - 1 Sept), gas supplies, games room with pool
table, amusement machine and tourist information, and a small laundry room
around a courtyard. Public phone. There are first class walks from the site and
game fishing is available on permit. Riding or golf 6 miles, bicycle hire 3 miles.
Bellamy silver.

Directions: To avoid much single-track road approach via the A30, turning off 11
miles west of Exeter to Cheriton Bishop. Left there (at Old Thatch Inn), 2 miles
to crossroads where right for Clifford Bridge, 1 mile of single track, over crossroads and bridge and left to park. O.S.GR: SX782897.

Charges 2001:
-- Per unit incl. 2 persons
£7.40 - £12.60; small
motorcaravan £6.60 -
£10.70; backpacker or
cyclist £2.50- £3.50 per
person; extra person
£2.50 - £3.50; child 8-16
yrs free - £2.50, 4-7 yrs
free - £1.75; awning
£1.60; extra pup tent free
- £1.00; dog free - 50p;
electricity £1.80.
-- No credit cards.
-- VAT included.

Open:
Easter - 30 September

Address:
Clifford, Drewsteignton,
Devon, EX6 6QE.

Tel:
(01647) 24226.
FAX: (01647) 24116.
E-mail: info@
clifford-bridge.co.uk.

Reservations:
Advised for school
holidays; made for any
length with £20 deposit.

Riverside and Forest Holidays
OS REF. SX782897

Attractive, small and level family-run park, in a Dartmoor National
Park woodland valley. Bordered by the River Teign, with just 24
touring pitches and 40 camping pitches. 5 acres set in an area of
outstanding natural beauty, this is a holiday setting you won't forget.

Magnificent walks along woodland tracks - up stream through the
Teign Gorge to Fingle Bridge or Castle Drogo (NT) - or down stream
through Dunsford Nature Reserve.

Heated swimming pool • Small shop • Electric
hook-ups • Flush toilets & free showers • Fly
fishing on Park • Golf at nearby
Moretonhampstead

AA 3 PENNANT FAMILY PARK. QUALITY ★★ ★ GRADED
RAC - DAVID BELLAMY SILVER AWARD

Free colour brochure: Clifford Bridge Park,
Nr. Drewsteignton, Devon EX6 6QE
Tel: 01647 24226 Fax: 01647 24116
Web: www.ukparks.co.uk/cliffordbridge

Devon

078 Dartmoor View Holiday Park, Whiddon Down, nr. Okehampton

Attractive park on north Dartmoor touring route with easy access.

With easy access from the A30 road, this peaceful park has been much improved by the friendly new owners. It is bordered by mature trees and hedges and has a well tended look with pretty flower beds around. There are 72 flat, grassy touring pitches (8 hardstandings) of which 50 have electricity (16A) and 14 have water and waste water too. The heated sanitary facilities are well-maintained with three unisex cabins and free push-button showers. Outside are chemical disposal facilities and a dog walk area. Near the entrance is a laundry and campers' kitchen, plus the Family Bar (1/4-1/10) with entertainment some evenings in season, TV and games rooms. Reception and the licensed shop are together here. Children have some good quality play equipment and there is a heated outdoor swimming pool (10 x 5 m) with children's pool, fenced with paved surrounds (1/6-15/9) and a small 9 hole putting green. No kite flying is permitted. Public phone. First aid caravan. Caravan storage available. Fishing or riding 5 miles, golf 3 miles. The site is close to the Dartmoor 'letter-boxing' area.

Directions: On A30 dual-carriageway at the Merrymeet roundabout, take the Whiddon Down road. Park is ½ mile on the right. O.S.GR: SX685928.

Charges 2000:
-- Per unit, incl. 2 persons £6.75 - £9.50; small one person tent £4.75 - £6.75; extra person £1.95; child (3-11 yrs) £1.40; dog £1.00; electricity £2.25; all service pitch £3.90; hardstanding plus £1.00; awning or pup tent £1.00.
-- VAT included.
-- Credit cards accepted.

Open:
March - November.

Address:
Whiddon Down,
Okehampton,
Devon EX20 2QL.

Tel:
(01647) 231545.
FAX: (01647) 231654.
E-mail: anyone@
dartmoorview.co.uk.

Reservations:
Any length, with deposit;
£25 p/week or £4 p/night.

105 Springfield Holiday Park, Tedburn St. Mary, nr. Exeter

Quietly situated park with marvellous rural views, all facilities and holiday homes to let.

Well situated to explore both Dartmoor and Exmoor, yet easily accessible, Springfield has room for 88 units on its 9 acres, mainly on level, grass terraces with views across the Devon countryside. Over 50 of these have 10A electricity. There are some seasonal units and 19 caravan holiday homes which are to be found at the lower part of the park (5 to hire). The reception cum shop is on the right as you drop down into the park and gravel access roads radiate out from here along the terraces and link up at the bottom where a new family 'terrace bar' has been built (open Easter, then May - Sept evenings and Sunday lunch) with a grass terrace making the most of the rural views. Good value meals are also provided to eat in or takeaway, even cream teas and the odd musical evening. Near reception is a small heated swimming pool, naturally sheltered (unsupervised). Children's play area and games room. Two toilet blocks of older design provide washbasins with curtains, pre-set showers (20p external meter) with curtain and stool, a family bathroom and baby changing facilities. Washing up and laundry sinks (H&C), three washing machines and two dryers, plus two chemical toilet disposal points. In all, it is a satisfactory provision which may be a little stretched when the field below the terrace bar is being used for camping. Martin and Eileen Johnson, the owners, are keen to help everyone enjoy their stay and can provide plenty of local information on Dartmoor walks and where to find the best fishing lakes, etc. Fishing 6 miles, bicycle hire 8 miles, riding 10 miles, golf 2 miles. They encourage local produce in the licensed shop which is quite well stocked. Gas supplies. Dog walk. A new bridge on the A30 provides much easier access to the site and to Dartmoor.

Directions: From M5 junction 31 take A30 towards Okehampton. Springfield is signed at the third exit where a new bridge has been built. Turn right at the round-about and follow Springfield signs and site is on the left O.S.GR: SX788936.

Charges 2000:
-- Per caravan or motor-caravan £8.00 - £10.00; tent £7.50 - £9.00;, acc. to season and size; walker or cyclist £5.00 - £6.00; extra person (over 3 yrs) £1.50; full or half awning, pup tent £1.00; dog £1.00; extra car, boat or trailer £1.50; electricity £1.80.

Open:
15 March - 15 November.

Address:
Tedburn Road,
Tedburn St. Mary,
Exeter,
Devon EX6 6EW.

Tel:
(01647) 24242.
FAX: (01647) 24131.

Reservations:
Made with deposit (£20 per unit per week or £5 per night with electricity).

46

106 Yeatheridge Farm Caravan Park, East Worlington, nr. Crediton

Friendly, family park with riding, fishing lakes, indoor pools and country walks.

Yeatheridge is a 200-acre farm, of which 9 acres has been developed over many years into an attractive touring park. With splendid views of the local hills and Dartmoor away to the south, and Exmoor easily accessible to the north, you can explore three woodland walks ranging from 1 to 2½ miles and the banks of the River Dalch. There are two deep coarse fishing lakes (bring your own rod), the top one offering family fishing and the lower one for serious fishing (age 14 or over) which are free of charge, as are the very popular heated indoor swimming pools and toddlers pool. These are open for long hours, the water slide has shorter hours, as it requires supervision. Horse riding is available on site (best to bring your own hat) with short rides for £1.80 and hour-long park rides for £7.00. The ponies and goats are popular with adults and children alike. For the children there is a fenced play area with a fort for under 10's (with parental supervision), a football field, TV room, pool table and, in one of the farm buildings, table tennis tables and skittles. The Club Bar has very good value drinks and a fish and chip van is on site, open Friday, Saturday and Tuesday evenings. The shop is open long hours and is also good value with local produce. The touring area was very neat and tidy during our stay in late August and, although the park was almost full, it did not feel crowded, as units are sited around the perimeter or back onto hedges, leaving open central areas. The 104 numbered, grass pitches are flat, gently sloping or on terraces and appeared sufficiently large, 80 with electricity (10A). A maximum of 24 pitches are for caravan holiday homes, with 3 site owned units for hire. The central sanitary facility, with free, very hot water and cabins for ladies, showed signs of heavy use (particularly the rather fierce push-button showers). For 2001, this may be alleviated by the addition of a new building by the pools. This will also house a new reception and shop. There are facilities for dishwashing (hot water 10p) and chemical disposal. The owners, Geoff and Liz, try very hard to make everyone feel at home.

Charges 2000:
-- Per unit incl. 2 persons £6.50 - £8.70; extra person over 4 yrs free - £1.70; awning or pup tent free - £1.70; extra car 50p; dog - first two 50p, extra dog £2.00; electricity £1.90.
-- Credit cards accepted.
-- VAT included.

Open:
April - September.

Address:
East Worlington, Crediton, Devon EX17 4TN.

Tel:
(01884) 860330

Reservations:
Advised for Bank and school holidays and made with £35 deposit; contact park.

Directions: Park is off B3042 Witheridge - Chawleigh (not in East Worlington). From M5 take exit 27 onto A361 to Tiverton. Turn left onto A396 for ½ mile then right on B3137 almost to Witheridge, then left on B3042 for 3 miles to site, well-signed down concrete roadway on left. O.S.GR: SS771112.

075 Minnows Camping and Caravan Park, Sampford Peverell

Small, neat, rural park with pleasant views close to M5 motorway near Tiverton.

Minnows is an attractive park with views across the Devon countryside, separated from the Grand Western canal by hedging, yet easily accessible from the M5 and suitable as an ideal touring centre for Devon and Somerset or simply for breaking a long journey. Part of the Caravan Club's 'managed under contract' scheme, non-members are also very welcome. Open for nine months of the year, it provides 45 level pitches all with 16A electricity. Of these, 37 are all weather (grass and gravel), including 3 fully serviced for motorcaravans. A further 3½ acres have been added to the park providing space for more and larger pitches, a children's playground and a large field for ball games. The heated toilet block is well maintained with modern facilities and constant hot water. There are facilities for disabled visitors, a baby bath on request, chemical disposal, covered dishwashing sinks and one for laundry, plus a spin dryer and washing machine. Motorcaravan service point. Gas available. Newspaper delivery can be arranged. Excellent tourist information provided. Public telephone. The village of Sampford Peverell, with pub and general store, is only a ½ mile walk via the towpath, with Tiverton 7½ miles. In fact, there are 12 miles of level walking on the towpath. The site is on the Sustran cycle route (3). Tiverton Parkway station (BR) is 1 mile and buses run past to Wellington, Taunton and Tiverton. Golf driving range near, full course 4 miles; riding 6 miles. Coarse fishing permits for the canal are available from reception. A horse-drawn barge makes trips on the winding 11 miles of the canal. Site gates closed 9 pm. and locked 11 pm.- 7.30 am. All year caravan storage.

Charges 2001:
-- Per caravan, motor-caravan or trailer tent £3.00; small tent and car £2.00; adult £2.60 - £3.90; child (5-16 yrs) £1.10 - £1.20; dog free; awning free; breathable groundsheets on grass, extra tent or extra car £1.00; electricity £1.50 - £2.25; serviced pitch plus £2.00.
-- Credit cards accepted for £10 or over.

Open:
5 March - 12 November.

Address:
Sampford Peverell, nr. Tiverton. Devon EX16 7EN.

Tel:
(01884) 821770.
FAX: as phone.

Reservations:
Made with £10 deposit.

Directions: From M5 junction 27 take A361 signed Tiverton. After about 600 yds leave on the first exit signed Sampford Peverell. After about 200 yds turn right at roundabout and cross bridge over A361 to a second roundabout. Go straight ahead and park is immediately ahead. From North Devon on A361 go to M5 junction 27 and return back up the A361 as above. O.S.GR: ST042148.

47

Devon

072 Easewell Farm Holiday Park, Mortehoe, nr. Woolacombe

Attractively situated, family run park with golf course, overlooking Bristol Channel.

Easewell Farm is near to the sandy beaches of Woolacombe and is a family run site run with families in mind. This is a traditional touring park which during the day is a hive of activity, but the nights are quiet and peaceful. The largest of the camping fields is sloping with superb views across the headland to the sea. The two smaller fields are terraced and one area has hardstandings. Together they provide 250 pitches, 90 with electricity connections (15A) and 20 with TV and water connections also. The central toilet block can be heated and is continually upgraded. Washbasins (with soap and hand dryers) are set in vanity style units, two in the ladies having extending hoses for hair washing, controllable showers (no dividers) are free and there is a small area with baby bath facilities, hairdryers, mirrors and seats. Dishwashing sinks are under cover with free hot water and the laundry has sinks, machines, dryers and irons. All these facilities are arranged around the farmhouse area and include a very well equipped unit for disabled people with everything in one large room including a hairdryer. Chemical disposal and motorcaravan service point. The shop is well stocked (gas available), there is a takeaway and restaurant and an attractive bar with patio overlooking a small duck pond. A small heated indoor swimming pool is well used, as are games and TV rooms. The well equipped, fenced play area has a bark chipping base. A very well maintained 9 hole golf course is popular and has reduced fees for campers. A huge redundant farm buildings has been put to excellent use - divided into three areas, it provides table tennis and pool, a skittle alley and two lanes of flat green bowling with changing rooms. In high season only one dog per pitch is allowed - they have an enormous exercise field to run in. Fishing or riding 1 mile, bicycle hire 3 miles. Walks to the local village and along the coastal path are easy from the site and a bus to Ilfracombe and Barnstaple stops 100 yds. from the entrance.

Charges 2000:
-- Per caravan incl. 2 persons £7.00 - £11.00; tent or motorcaravan incl. 2 persons £6.50 - £9.00; extra person incl. children £1.50; extra car £1.00; electricity £2.00; 'supersite' incl. electricity plus £4.00; awning or pup tent free.
-- VAT included.
-- Credit cards accepted.
Open:
Easter - 30 September.
Address:
Mortehoe,
Woolacombe,
N. Devon EX34 7EH.
Tel:
(01271) 870225.
FAX: as phone.
Reservations:
Made with £20 deposit per week booked.

Directions: From Barnstaple, take A361 Ilfracombe road through Braunton. Turn left at Mullacott Cross roundabout on B3343 to Woolacombe, turning right after 2-3 miles to Mortehoe. Park is on right before village. O.S.GR: SS465455.

073 Twitchen Parc, Mortehoe, nr. Woolacombe

Holiday park with touring areas and family entertainment, close to superb beaches.

Set in the grounds of an attractive Edwardian country house, Twitchen Park is now under the same ownership as Woolacombe Bay. Its main concern lies in holiday caravans and flats, although it also provides marked pitches for tourers at the top of the park, with some views over the rolling hills to the sea. They include 155 pitches with 16A electricity, 50 with tarmac hardstanding, mostly arranged around oval access roads in hedged areas. A further 50 non-electric pitches are behind in two open, unmarked fields which are sloping. There are two sanitary blocks, the larger one of an unusual design with different levels and rather narrow corridors. Both provide free, pre-set, hot showers (with stool and hook, but rather small), washbasins in rows and WCs. Dishwashing facilities are under cover outside each block and there are laundry facilities in each also, plus a good launderette at the central complex. A new toilet block is planned for 2001 in the same style as the one at Woolacombe Bay. American motorhomes are accepted (up to 30 ft). A smart, modern entertainment complex incorporates a licensed club and family lounge with snacks, restaurant, adults only bar, teenage disco room, and cartoon lounge, together with games rooms for table tennis, pool, snooker and arcade games, with entertainment for both adults and children, day and evening. Shop and takeaway. Outside is a swimming pool (heated mid-May - mid-Sept) and paddling pool. An excellent indoor pool has changing rooms, a sauna, children's paddling pool with fountain and a viewing area. With a super children's adventure play area (on bark) completing the facilities, Twitchen is very popular for families with children. If they become bored, there are always the excellent beaches nearby with a footpath down to the sea. All the facilities of the Golden Coast and Woolacombe Bay parcs are free, with a courtesy bus running regularly between the three parcs and to the beach. Bellamy gold.

Charges 2000:
-- Per caravan or motor-caravan incl. electricity £11.50 - £25.95; high season per week only: per pitch incl. electricity 27/5-3/6 £125, 15/7-26/8 £225.
-- Tent pitches: per adult £3.95 - £10.65; child (5-15 yrs) £1.95 - £5.35.
-- Dog £10 per week.
-- Special offers available.
-- VAT included.
-- Credit cards accepted.
Open:
1 April/Easter - end Oct.
Address:
Woolacombe,
N. Devon EX34 7ES.
Tel:
(01271) 870343.
FAX: (01271) 870089.
E-mail: goodtimes@ woolcombe-bay.co.uk.
Reservations:
Made with deposit (£2 per pitch per night).

Directions: From Barnstaple take A361 towards Ilfracombe and through Braunton. Turn left at Mullacott Cross roundabout towards Woolacombe and then right towards Mortehoe. Park is on the left before village. O.S.GR: SS466456.

071 Hidden Valley Touring Park, West Down, Ilfracombe

Delightful, family run park in countryside between Barnstaple and Ilfracombe.

Aptly named, this award winning park has been carefully developed in keeping with its lovely setting. In the valley beside a small stream and lake (with ducks), it is most attractive and also convenient for resorts, beaches and the surrounding countryside. The new owners, Martin and Dawn Fletcher, are continuing to run the park to the same high standards. The original part of the park has 74 good-size level pitches on three sheltered terraces. All have hardstanding, electricity (16A) and TV connections (leads for hire), with a water point between each pitch. Kingfisher Meadow, a little way from the main facilities and reached by a tarmac road, provides a further 60 pitches on grass (so suitable for tents), all with electricity, water, waste water and TV hook-ups. Two modern sanitary blocks (one heated), are tiled and have non-slip floors. One for each area, they provide free hot showers, some washbasins in cubicles, some en-suite with toilets in the Kingfisher Meadow block, hand and hairdryers (free), WCs, baby room, laundry facilities, and dishwashing under cover, plus facilities for disabled people. There are supplementary clean 'portacabin' style facilities in the original area. Chemical disposal and motorcaravan service facilities. Two good adventure play areas have wooden equipment and safe bark surfaces (one near a fast flowing stream). Small shop with off-licence, takeaway, a lounge bar and a good value, family restaurant serving meals in attractive surroundings, plus a games room. Dogs are accepted (max. 2 or by arrangement) with an exercise field. Caravan storage. Gas supplies. Public phone. Fishing or golf 2 miles, bicycle hire 4 miles, riding 5 miles. A park for those seeking good quality facilities in very attractive, natural surroundings, without too many man-made distractions - apart from some slight traffic noise during day time, it provides a really peaceful setting. Bellamy gold.

Charges 2001:
-- Per unit incl. 2 persons £5.00 - £13.00; extra person over 5 yrs £1.00; extra tent £1.00; extra car or boat free - £1.00; dog free - £1.00; electricity (16A) £1.75 - £2.00.
-- VAT included.
-- Credit cards accepted.
Open:
All year.
Address:
West Down,
Ilfracombe,
N. Devon EX34 8NU.
Tel:
(01271) 813837.
FAX: (01271) 814041.
E-mail: hvp@aol.com.
Reservations:
Accepted with £25 deposit.

see colour advert between pages 64/65

Directions: Park is on A361 Barnstaple - Ilfracombe road, 3½ miles after Braunton. O.S.GR: SS499408.

107 Woolacombe Bay Holiday Village, Woolacombe

Holiday park overlooking the Bay with facilities for camping - tents or trailer tents only.

Woolacombe Bay, and its sister site Golden Coast nearby, are well known holiday parks providing a range of accommodation from caravan holiday homes to chalets and apartments, with many amenities including pools, restaurants and bars, and a wide range of entertainment. A new camping section has been developed at the Woolacombe Bay park, whereby touring visitors can enjoy all the activities and entertainment of both parks. Partly terraced out of the hillside and partly on the hilltop with some existing pine trees but many more trees planted for landscaping, the site has magnificent views out across the bay. A super new central toilet block has excellent facilities, including en-suite shower and washrooms and separate toilets; also with a sauna and steam room - unusual but nice. Separate dishwashing and laundry rooms, plus a unit for disabled visitors. Marked and numbered pitches are provided on grass for 146 tents, 94 with electricity (10/16A). All should be level, having been terraced where necessary and they are connected by gravel roads. Water and refuse points are well spaced. Some up and down walking is needed for the toilet block. There are indoor (heated) and outdoor pools with flumes and slides, sauna, gym, tennis courts to mention just a few of the facilities, including supermarkets, on both sites. A bus service runs between the parks and the beach in the high season, although there is a path to the beach from the site. Both parks have entertainment programmes and children's clubs and Woolacombe Bay also boasts a health spa and beauty suite. Fishing or riding 1 mile. Dogs are welcome here and at the newly acquired Twitchen Parc. Bellamy gold.

Charges 2000:
-- Per adult £3.95 - £10.65; child (5-15 yrs) £1.95 - £5.35.
-- Dog £10 per week.
-- Credit cards accepted.
-- VAT included.
Open:
Easter - end October.
Address:
Woolacombe Bay
Holiday Village,
Sandy Lane,
Woolacombe,
Devon EX34 7AH.
Tel:
(01271) 870343.
FAX: (01271) 870089.
E-mail: goodtimes@
woolacombe-bay.co.uk.
Reservations:
Advised for peak season.

see colour advert between pages 32/33

Directions: Take A361 Barnstaple - Ilfracombe road through Braunton. Turn left at Mullacott Cross roundabout towards Woolacombe then right towards Mortehoe. Park is on left before village. O.S.GR: SS463445.

Devon

069 Stowford Farm Meadows, Combe Martin, nr. Ilfracombe

Large, popular family run farm park with much to do, set in North Devon valley.

Stowford Farm dates from the 15th century and is set in 450 acres of rolling countryside all of which is available for recreation and walking. With a nice spacious feel and a village-like atmosphere, this large touring park has been developed in the fields and farm buildings surrounding the attractive old farmhouse. There are 570 pitches for all units on four slightly sloping meadows. Unseparated, the numbered and marked pitches are accessed by tarmac or hardcore roadways, most have electricity (10A) and there are well placed water points. Awnings are free in low seasons if breathable groundsheets are used, and cheaper in high season. The four identical toilet blocks have their own personal cleaners and are kept very clean. Providing good, functional facilities, hot water is free to the washbasins, which are in rows and set in flat surfaces, and to the dishwashing sinks. Showers are on payment and each block has laundry facilities including irons and boards. The old farm buildings have been converted into a well stocked shop (holiday goods, gas and camping accessories) and a good value takeaway service with a restaurant area. An impressive reception area has toilet facilities adjacent that include private washrooms and facilities for disabled visitors. The original stables have become the Old Stable Bars, refurbished to a high standard and entertainment in high season include barn dances, discos, karaoke and other musical evenings. A barn houses a good, 22 x 10 m. swimming pool (heated Easter - Oct) at a small charge (75p) and the park has its own riding stables. Other activities include an 18-hole pitch and putt golf course, games room (with pool tables, table tennis and amusement machines), snooker room, crazy golf, bicycle hire, 'kiddies kar' track (all charged for) and a large children's play area. Children will also be entertained by the under cover mini-zoo (Petorama) where they can handle many sorts of animals (on payment). Games and activities are organised in high season. Dogs are welcome in one section (max. 2 per pitch) with a dog exercise area. Public phones and tourist information at reception. Fishing and boat launching 4 miles. Summer parking and winter caravan storage. In low season some facilities may only open for limited hours. Stowford provides plenty to keep families occupied without leaving the park, including a woodland walk. It is also a friendly, countryside base for exploring the North Devon coast and Exmoor.

Charges 2000:
-- Per unit and car incl. 2 persons £4.60 - £9.60; extra person (over 5 yrs) free - £2.00; awning with groundsheet £2.00 - £2.50, without free - £1.50; extra car or small tent £2.00; dog 60p - £1.50.
-- Reduced fees for over-50s low and mid seasons.
-- VAT included.
-- Credit cards accepted.

Open:
Easter - end October.

Address:
Combe Martin,
Ilfracombe,
N. Devon EX34 0PW.

Tel:
(01271) 882476.
FAX: (01271) 883053.
E-mail: enquiries@stowford.co.uk.

Reservations:
Any length, deposit £2 per night, £12 per week, £20 per fortnight. Balance due 28 days before arrival.

see colour advert between pages 64/65

Directions: From Barnstaple take A39 towards Lynton. After 1 mile turn left on B3230. Turn right at garage on A3123 and park is 1½ miles on the right. O.S.GR: SS560427.

070 Greenacres Touring Caravan Park, Bratton Fleming

Neat, quiet, small park on edge of Exmoor near Barnstaple; no tents.

A nice compact, rural park on the edge of Exmoor, Greenacres is managed and run alongside, but separately from, the working farm owned by the family. Drive through the farm access to the park (clearly signed) - you need to go back and call at the house to book in. There are 30 good sized pitches (no tents taken), well drained with connecting gravel paths to the road - in theory you can get to your unit without stepping on the grass; 22 electric hook-ups (16A). The top area is level, the lower part next to the beech woods is semi-terraced to provide six hardstandings and some hedged places. There are marvellous views outside the beech hedge which shelters the site. The toilet block, in the centre of the horseshoe layout has been well designed. It has vanity style washbasins with plenty of room, showers (1M, 1F) on payment (20p) and an en-suite room for disabled visitors. A laundry room, with spin dryer, iron and board, and dishwashing room, both have free hot water to sinks. Chemical disposal. Gas supplies. Tourist information hut. An area for children with net and swings is separated by a Devon bank from the 2 acre dog field. Fishing 3 miles, riding 5 miles, golf 12 miles. To the west of Exmoor, the park is very suitable for the coast at Ilfracombe and Combe Martin, or for exploring the moor. The family has opened up a woodland walk across the fields to a secluded valley picnic area beside a stream to take advantage of the marvellous views and surroundings.

Charges 2000:
-- Per unit incl. 2 persons £4.00 - £7.50; extra person 50p - £1.00; child (under 7 yrs) free; awning free - £1.50; dog free; electricity £1.50.
-- Less 10% for stays over 10 days.
-- No credit cards.
-- VAT included.

Open:
Easter/1 April - 31 Oct.

Address:
Bratton Fleming,
Barnstaple,
Devon EX31 4SG.

Tel:
(01598) 763334.

Reservations:
Made with £5 deposit - contact park.

Directions: From North Devon link road (M5, exit 27) turn north at South Molton on A399. Continue for 9 miles, past turn for Exmoor Steam Centre and on to Stowford Cross. Turn left towards Exmoor Zoo Park and Greenacres is on the left. O.S.GR: SS663404.

109 Peppermint Park, Dawlish, nr. Exeter

Family run touring park close to Exeter and large, sandy beaches.

First impressions of this extensive park are perhaps a lack of ambience. However this is quickly dispelled by the friendly reception, plenty of flowers and the constructive way the large pitches have been incorporated into the slightly sloping ground. There are 250 pitches, each with electricity connections (10A), and there at least another 60 hook-ups available for tent campers. Tarmac roads thread through the site giving easy access to all areas, each pitch being marked and numbered. Two modern sanitary blocks provide open style washbasins and free pre-set hot showers. They are kept in spotless condition and can be heated. Two units (WC, washbasin and shower) are provided for disabled visitors. Other facilities include a fully equipped baby room, laundry (washing machines, dryers and free irons) and dishwashing. Two chemical disposal points are clearly marked at each block and there are adequate water taps and refuse facilities. A shop stocking the usual foods and gas is open end May - end Aug, as are the restaurant, bar and takeaway. During low season, visitors to Peppermint Park can avail themselves of full facilities at the adjacent sister site (Golden Sands), which include a large indoor pool. From late May to late August, Peppermint Park's own pool complex is open and this includes a water slide in the larger pool. Also within the park are a children's playground, field for ball games and a small coarse fishing lake (£2.50 for adult day ticket). Nightly entertainment is staged in the Peppermint Club in high season and at Golden Sands at other times. This site's 'jewel in the crown' is the walking distance (700 yds) to the large, safe beaches of Dawlish Warren and its pleasure complex, ideal for families. A passenger ferry operates from Starcross (2 miles) across the estuary to Exmouth in high season. Dawlish Warren nature reserve is adjacent and includes an 18 hole golf course. Caravan holiday homes are to rent in self-contained paddocks to the south of the park. Bellamy silver.

Directions: From M5 junction 30 take A379 Dawlish road. After passing through Starcross (7 miles) turn left to Dawlish Warren just before Dawlish. Continue for 1½ miles down hill and park is on left in 300 yds. O.S. GR: SX978788.

Charges guide:
-- Per unit incl. all persons £5.50 - £11.00; tent incl. 2 persons and car £5.50 - £9.00; extra adult £1.00 - £2.20; child (2-13 yrs) £1.00 - £2.00; awning or pup tent £1.00 - £2.20; electricity £2.00; dog £1.00 - £2.00.
-- Credit cards accepted.
-- VAT included.
Open:
15 April - 28 October.
Address:
Warren Road,
Dawlish Warren,
Dawlish,
Devon EX7 0PQ
Tel:
01626 863436.
Reservations:
Made with £15 deposit (Sat. - Sat. only 24 July - 28 Aug).

101 Lady's Mile Touring and Camping Park, Dawlish

Popular, spacious, family touring park under a mile from the beach, with indoor and outdoor pools, and a range of leisure facilities.

A large, open park that caters well for children, Lady's Mile has extensive grassy fields (with some trees for shade), in addition to the main, landscaped camping area which is arranged in broad terraces. In July and August caravans and tents normally go in separate sections, at other times they are grouped together in the main part. The park has 486 pitches, mostly marked by lines but with nothing between them, and 450 with electrical connections (10A). It is a 20 minute walk to a good sandy beach at Dawlish Warren and also has its own good sized, free outdoor swimming pool with 200 ft. plus slide, children's pool and a paved surround (May-Oct), plus a super heated indoor pool (20 x 10 m.) with 100 ft. flume and separate paddling pool (both with lifeguards). In spite of its size, the park is popular over a long season, with reservation necessary. There are four toilet blocks, of various ages and styles, well spaced around the main areas of the park. They are of a good standard, with free hot water and, with an additional shower block (with some basins also), there should be an adequate provision overall. Facilities for disabled people and four family bathrooms (50p). Dishwashing sinks are under cover with free hot water. Two launderettes. Mini-market and fish and chip takeaway (both Easter - mid Sept). A large, attractive bar complex, with a family area overlooking the indoor pool, has food available and entertainment. A spacious games room is below including pool tables and video games, and a new separate disco and bar. A sloping recreation field is ideal for kite flying and a large fenced children's adventure playground has a safe, sand surface. Nine hole golf course on site (free but with small charge for hire of clubs) and multi-sports pitch. Tarmac area at reception for late arrivals. Dog walk. Public phones and post box. Holiday accommodation and mobile homes to rent. Winter caravan storage. Riding and bicycle hire 1 mile, fishing 3 miles.

Directions: Park is 1 mile north of Dawlish with access off the A379 (Exeter - Teignmouth) road. O.S. GR: SX969778.

Charges 2000:
-- Per unit incl. 2 adults £7.00 - £12.00; 2-man tent (no car) £6.00 - £10.00; awning or child's tent £1.20 - £2.50; extra adult £1.20 - £2.50; child (2-14 yrs) £1.20 - £2.50; boat or extra car £1.00 - £2.50; dog £1.00 - £2.00; electricity £2.00.
-- Low season special offers and OAP discount.
-- VAT included.
-- Credit cards accepted
Open:
13 March - 31 October.
Address:
Dawlish,
Devon EX7 0LX.
Tel:
(01626) 863411.
FAX: (01626) 888689.
E-mail:
info@ladysmile.co.uk.
Reservations:
Made for Sat to Sat only in peak seasons, with £15 deposit.

see colour advert between pages 64/65

Devon

097 Cofton Country Holiday Park, Starcross, nr. Dawlish

Large touring park with coarse fishing, swimming pools, bar and beautiful country views.

About 1½ miles from a sandy beach at Dawlish Warren this popular, family site takes over 400 touring units on a variety of fields and meadows. Although not individually marked, there is never a feeling of overcrowding. The smaller, more mature fields, including a pleasant old orchard for tents only, are well terraced. While there are terraces on most of the slopes of the larger, more open fields, there are still some quite steep gradients to climb. There are some 300 electrical connections (10A). One area has 62 park-owned, upgraded holiday homes to rent, including a special one for disabled visitors. There are five attractive holiday cottages on the park, plus three others a short drive away in secluded countryside and six holiday apartments (available all year). A well designed, central complex overlooking the pool and decorated with flowers and hanging baskets, houses reception, a shop and off-licence and a bar lounge, the 'Cofton Swan', where bar meals are usually available (all Easter - 30 Sept). A family room and bar are on the first floor of this building and there is an outdoor terrace and some light entertainment in season. The adjacent supervised kidney-shaped heated pool (overall length 100 ft. open Spr. B.H - mid Sept), with paddling pool and slide, has lots of grassy space for sunbathing. Other facilities include a fish and chip shop with breakfast also available, two launderettes and a games room (busy in high season). A small, but good, adventure playground is in an elevated position in the woods overlooking the swimming pools and two other well equipped play areas. Coarse fishing is available in three lakes on the park (from £16.50 per rod for 7 days, discount for senior citizens outside July) and there is a woodland trail towards Dawlish Warren. Sanitary facilities consist of three blocks, one on each side of the road dividing the park for the touring pitches and the third near the holiday home area. The newest, at the top of the larger fields is first rate, with laundry and facilities for disabled visitors and babies. The blocks have free hot water throughout, well equipped and controllable showers, basins set in rows in flat surfaces with two in cubicles, hair dryers, and dishwashing facilities under cover. In addition four 'portacabin' style units with basic toilet facilities are provided for the peak season. Chemical disposal. Gas available. Public phones. Post box. Ice pack hire service. Golf 3 miles. Winter caravan storage. Bellamy gold.

Charges 2000:
-- Per unit incl. 2 persons £6.50 - £11.00; extra adult £1.30 - £2.60; child (2-13 yrs) £1.10 - £2.40; awning or child's tent £1.30 - £2.60; boat, dog or extra car £1.10 - £2.40; electricity £2.00.
-- Small discount for Senior Citizens excl. July/Aug.
-- VAT included.
-- Credit cards accepted.

Open:
Easter - 31 October.

Address:
Starcross, nr. Dawlish, Devon EX6 8RP.

Tel:
(01626) 890111.
FAX: (01626) 891572.
E-mail: enquiries@cofton-holidays-devon.co.uk.

Reservations:
Made for min. 3 nights, 4 nights in peak season with £20 deposit.

see colour advert between pages 64/65

Directions: Access to the park is off the A379 road 3 miles north of Dawlish, just after Cockwood harbour village. O.S.GR: SX965797.

108 Coast View Holiday Park, Shaldon, nr. Teignmouth

Family run holiday park with magnificent views over Lyme Bay.

On the coast road between Teignmouth and Torquay, this park has a section of caravan holiday homes and chalets. However, the touring area of 100 pitches is quite separate. On terraced grass, some pitches are part sloping. There are 20 electricity connections (16A). At present, due to recent reconstruction of the park, there is little or no shelter but as the site is terraced into the hillside, there is adequate protection from the prevailing southwest winds. The new sanitary block is spacious with free hot showers and open washbasins, and it includes a baby room. Dishwashing and laundry facilities are separate and there are two chemical disposal points. To the right of the park entrance is an attractive indoor swimming pool, children's pool and an entertainment area comprising a clubroom with bar (bar meals and snacks), takeaway, TV room and games room. A licensed shop also stocks gas. All these facilities are open all season. Entertainment is organised each night and also activities in the mornings for children, who also have an adventure playground and indoor soft play area. The park is convenient for the beach (1½ miles) and the coastal footpath is adjacent. Torbay is 5 miles. A bus service stops at the gates. Fishing or golf 1 mile, riding 3 miles. Good for holiday-makers of all ages, this park offers superb views with excellent facilities.

Charges guide:
-- Per caravan incl. up to 8 persons £7.00 - £16.00; motorcaravan or tent (up to 8 persons) £7.00 - £14.00; tent incl. 2 persons £6.00 - £8.00; electricity £1.75; dog free - £3.00.
-- 7th night free if pre-booked and paid.

Open:
28 March - 30 October.

Address:
Torquay Road, Shaldon, Teignmouth, Devon TQ14 0BG.

Tel:
(01626) 872392.
FAX: (01626) 872719.

Reservations:
Contact park.

Directions: From A380 Exeter - Newton Abbot road, take A381 to Teignmouth. In town turn right over Shaldon Bridge on B3199 for Torquay. Park is on right in approx. 1½ miles. O.S.GR: SX932714.

100 Forest Glade Int. Caravan and Camping Park, nr. Cullompton

Country park with small swimming pool and some holiday homes.

Set in the Blackdown Hills (designated an area of outstanding natural beauty), Forest Glade is owned and run by the Wellard family, deep in mid-Devon away from the hectic life on the coast. A sheltered site set amongst woodland with extensive walking without using your car, there are 80 touring pitches, 70 of which have 16A electricity connections and 24 hardstanding. The pitches are all level, mostly backing onto the forest, and there is also a rally field. There is one main toilet block, heated in cold weather and with free hot water in washbasins (some in cubicles), showers and washing up sinks. There is a new laundry with washing machines and dryers. Extra facilities of `portacabin' style with toilets, washbasins and showers are at the swimming pool, but these are only available when the pool is open. This is a small heated, covered pool (from 6 April) with a paddling pool and a patio area outside. Other amenities include an adventure playground, games room with table tennis, video games and two pool tables, plus an all weather tennis court and a new sauna. The shop (open all season) is quite well stocked including gas and locally made bread and pastries and there is a takeaway (open evenings except Sunday). Chemical disposal and motorcaravan service facilities. Mobile homes to rent. Caravan storage available. Public phone. Dogs are accepted and the surrounding forest makes this a dog lovers paradise. Fishing or riding 1½ miles, golf 6 miles, bicycle hire 5 miles. Touring caravans must book in advance and the easiest route for them will be explained then (phone bookings accepted). Although set in the country, the beaches of East Devon are a fairly easy drive away. A member of the Best of British group. Bellamy silver.

Directions: Park is 5½ miles from M5 exit 28. Take A373 for 3 miles, turning left at camp sign towards Sheldon. Park is on left after approx. 2½ miles. This access is not suitable for touring caravans owing to a steep hill - phone park for alternative route details. O.S.GR: ST101073.

Charges 2001:
-- Per unit incl. 2 adults £6.25 - £11.75; child (5-9 yrs) £1.00 ; student (10 yrs - end of study) £2.00; awning free; backpacker or cyclist £2.50 per person; dog 50p; electricity £1.90.
-- VAT included.
-- Credit cards accepted.
Open:
23 March - 28 October.
Address:
Cullompton,
Devon EX15 2DT.
Tel:
(01404) 841381.
FAX: (01404) 841593.
E-mail:
forestglade@cwcom.net.
Reservations:
Any length with deposit of £4 p/day or £20 p/wk, (£15 for B.H. w/ends). Essential for B.Hs and school holidays.

see colour advert between pages 64/65

Alan Rogers' Discount

 Less £1 p/night on mid or high season rates

110 Webbers Farm Caravan & Camping Park, Woodbury

Family run park in rural, non-commercialised setting near Exmouth.

Over the past twenty years this park has been gradually enlarged from an initial open field site to one that can boast modern facilities, yet retaining its essentially rural character. The 115 marked pitches are large, on grass, with the majority level and a few gently sloping. There are 100 electricity connections (10A). Three modern sanitary blocks provide free hot showers and in the newest block (built in '99), full bathroom facilities (£1). There is a baby room and two units for disabled visitors (WC, shower and washbasin). Hot water is free throughout and the usual dishwashing and laundry facilities are provided. Unusual in terms of number, are seven chemical disposal points, located at each water point (and adequately separated). Amenities on the park include a new reception, a small shop (limited cold food only), a children's play area, a games field and two dog walks. Gas is available. Caravan storage. Although essentially a farm site, there is no problem with animal noise - this is a sheep farm and children are encouraged to participate in a hands-on experience. Only raised barbecues are permitted. Woodbury village is within walking distance with an excellent pub/restaurant, post office, etc. A short drive takes you to the two miles of glorious sand at Exmouth, with Woodbury Common (excellent heathland walks) just over a mile away. Exeter is 6 miles. Fishing or golf 2 miles; riding 5 miles; bicycle hire or boat launching 10 miles. This is a mature, friendly and modern park in a lovely situation. A member of the Countryside Discovery group. Bellamy silver.

Charges 2000:
-- Per pitch incl. 2 persons £7.50 - £10.30; extra person (over 5 yrs) £1.90; awning or extra tent £1.20; electricity £2.00; dog free.
-- Credit cards accepted.
Open:
Easter - 7 October.
Address:
Castle Lane,
Woodbury,
Exeter,
Devon EX5 1EA.
Tel:
(01395) 232276.
FAX: (01395) 233389.
E-mail: reception@ webbersfarm.co.uk.
Reservations:
Essential for peak periods and made with £20 deposit.

Directions: Leave M5 at junction 30 and follow A376 Exmouth road. At second roundabout take B317a (Budleigh Salterton and Woodbury). In village centre follow brown signs to park on right. O.S.GR: SY017874.

102 Oakdown Touring and Holiday Home Park, Weston, Sidmouth

Award winning, exceptionally well kept and environmentally conscious park.

Always a neat and tidy park, we continue to note developments at Oakdown under the special care, guidance and attention of Mr and Mrs Franks, who now provide one of the most comfortable, well equipped and attractively laid out family parks we know, complete with welcoming staff who help pitch your unit (and live on site). The park has a spacious, uncrowded feel with large pitches semi-screened in small bays or groves and edged with trees. There is a marvellous range of trees (all 70 types are named) providing variety, privacy and home for wildlife. A circular concrete road links the 120 pitches, all of which have electricity (16A), 26 with water, waste water and drainage and 90 with hardstanding. The central amenity block with piped music provides good, fully tiled, heated sanitary facilities, all well maintained. These include controllable showers, washbasins set in flat surfaces (one private cabin for ladies) and sinks for dishwashing, all with free hot water, hairdryers and shaver points. Two unisex family bathrooms (with bath, shower, toilet, washbasin and coin operated entry) also double as useful units for disabled people. There are laundry facilities, plus free use of a freezer and a microwave. Tourist information is provided on a wall board, together with the history of the park. This is interesting as it was within the boundaries of a secret wartime radar station which accounts for the very solid construction of the amenity block. TV room. Other services include a motorcaravan service point for fresh and waste water, chemical disposal, recycling point (glass, paper, cans), public phones and a fax service. A well equipped, grass based children's play area with adventure style equipment and play castle is in the centre of the park. No cycling, skate-boarding or kite flying is permitted. Dogs are accepted but not certain breeds. An interesting footpath edged with wild flowers leads through the fields to the nearby Donkey Sanctuary and one can walk further to the beach and sea (2 miles, steep in parts). There are, in fact, over 113 varieties of wild flower to be seen and 45 varieties of wild bird. A family of Lesser Spotted woodpeckers have caused interest and skylarks and goldfinches are regular visitors. Badgers also visit (after 10.30 pm), and trees and bushes have been planted to encourage butterflies and more birds. It is the care of and attention to all things natural that makes this park rather special. The 'reed bed' development is progressing well and is now complete with a bird-hide. Adjoining the touring park is Oak Grove, with 46 holiday homes, 16 for hire (under the same ownership). Riding 6 miles, golf 2 miles. Secure, alarmed caravan storage facilities, also closed circuit TV. A member of the Best of British group. Bellamy gold.

Charges 2000:
-- Per unit incl. 2 persons: standard pitch £7.50 - £11.30; super pitch (incl. water and drainage services and awning) £11.20 - £15.10; extra person (5 yrs and over) £1.75; dog £1.00; awning £1.70; porch awning £1.00; child's pup tent £1.00; extra car (by arrangement) £1.75; electricity £2.10.
-- Less 70p for senior citizens in low season.
-- VAT included.
-- Credit cards accepted.

Open:
28 March - 1 November.

Address:
Weston,
Sidmouth,
Devon EX10 0PH.

Tel:
(01297) 680387.
FAX: (01297) 680541.
E-mail: oakdown@
btinternet.com.

Reservations:
Made with £20 p/w deposit, min. 3 days at B.Hs. and 3/4 Aug. (Sidmouth Folk Festival).

see colour advert between pages 64/65

Directions: Turn off A3052 (Colyford - Sidford) road to south 2½ miles east of junction with A375 and park is on left. O.S.GR: SY167902.

137 Burrowhayes Farm Caravan & Camping Site, West Luccombe

Delightful park with riding stables on site, on the edge of Exmoor near Porlock.

The stone packhorse bridge over Horner Water beside the farm entrance sets the tone of this park, which the Dascombe family have created over the last thirty years having previously farmed the land. The farm buildings have been converted into riding stables with escorted rides available (from 7/4). Mature trees, neat grass, partly sloping with marvellous views, or level nearer the clear, bubbling river, allows for 20 caravan holiday homes in their own area, 66 tents and 54 touring caravans or motorhomes. Electrical hook-ups are available (10A). The sanitary facilities, in the reception and stable block area, are well maintained providing free hot showers with curtain, vanity style washbasins, a fully equipped laundry room with baby changing unit, and indoor dishwashing. A well stocked shop doubles with reception (from 1/4; 08.30-18.00 in the main season). With walking, birdwatching, plenty of wild life to observe, pretty Exmoor villages and Lorna Doone country nearby there is much to do, not forgetting Minehead, 5 miles, and the local pub only 20 minutes walk. Children can play in the stream or explore the woods at the top of the site. Limited trout fishing is available in Horner Water (NT permit) alongside the park. Bicycle hire or golf 5 miles.

Charges 2000:
-- Per unit incl. 1 or 2 persons £6.00 - £8.00; extra person £2.25 - £2.50; child (3-15 yrs) £1.00 - £1.25; 1-man tent £4.00 - £5.00; awning £1.00; porch awning 75p; extra car or pup tent 50p; electricity £1.75.
-- Credit cards accepted.

Open:
15 March - 31 October.

Address:
West Luccombe,
Porlock, Minehead,
Somerset TA24 8HT.

Tel:
(01643) 862463.

Reservations:
Made with £10 deposit per pitch.

Directions: From A39, 5 miles west of Minehead, take first left past Allerford to Horner and West Luccombe. Site is on right after ¼ mile. O.S.GR: SS897460.

146 Lakeside Touring Caravan Park, Exebridge, nr. Dulverton

Attractively situated park with hillside views, for caravans or motorcaravans only.

Lakeside is a modern park in a rural situation with panoramic views across the valley to wooded hills (especially colourful in the autumn) and within walking distance of the small village of Exebridge. The sloping, neatly mown grass field provides 50 spacious pitches, all with 15A electricity and 9 with hardstanding. Everyone is shown to their pitch and a 'pitching service' is available if required. Water and rubbish bin points are central. The top of the next field provides room for ball games, whilst the rest grows naturally. While the grass and wild flowers are growing, paths are mown to provide a 1¼ mile dog walk. Below the main field is the modern, heated, very well equipped toilet block which is light and airy with roomy showers, vanity washbasins (H&C) and chemical disposal. A separate room, also heated, has one dishwashing and laundry sink, washing machine and dryer, also a small freezer and a good supply of tourist information. An unusual, very nice and useful feature is the 'Starlight Express' - an old, but rather splendid railway carriage which has been adapted as a small licensed restaurant with tables in individual compartments overlooking the lake (open Tues.-Sat. evenings and for Sunday lunches). The menu, although not extensive, is rather special, but if your pocket is suffering you can always have a bar snack or takeaway. You can also walk beside the fishing lake (tickets from the local garage) to the local pub which has riverside gardens. The village shop (also the garage) makes another pleasant walk for the morning papers and milk. The owners say this is a site for 'relaxing, reading, sleeping or fishing!' and it certainly is peaceful with perhaps buzzards overhead. Exmoor awaits to be explored - Tarr Steps, Dunkery Beacon, Wimbleball Lake (ideal for fishing or walking) and Doone Valley. Riding 1 mile, golf 10 miles. Winter caravan storage. A member of the Countryside Discovery group.

Directions: From M5 junction 27 take A361 towards Barnstaple. At the first roundabout turn right on A396 for Dulverton. Turn left at next roundabout by the Exeter Inn. After 2 miles at the Black Cat, there is an unusual junction - taking care go straight on, still on A396 signed Dulverton. Site is 3 miles further on the left, just past Exebridge village sign. O.S.GR: SS932242.

Charges 2000:
-- Per unit incl. 2 adults £7.00 - £9.50; extra adult £2.50; child (3-16 yrs) £2.00; full awning, pup tent or extra vehicle £1.00; porch awning 75p; dog £1.00; electricity £1.90.
-- VAT included.
-- No credit cards.

Open:
1 March - 31 October.

Address:
Higher Grants, Exebridge, Dulverton, Somerset TA22 9BE.

Tel:
(01398) 324068. FAX: as phone.

Reservations:
Made with deposit (£2 p/night, min. £10); contact park.

136 Halse Farm Touring Caravan and Camping Park, Winsford

Small park near Minehead, adjacent to moor on Exmoor.

A really rural park with beautiful, moorland views, you may be lucky here and glimpse the red deer across the valley or be able to see Exmoor ponies and foals graze outside the main gate on one of the highest points on Exmoor Two open, neatly cut fields which are level at the top back onto traditional hedging and slope gently to the middle and bottom where wild flowers predominate. One provides electricity points (10A) and is used for motorcaravans and caravans, the other is for tents. The central, heated toilet block is of good quality. Well equipped and maintained, it has free hot water, showers and hairdryers, a toilet, washbasin and shower for visitors with disabilities, washing machine, dryer and iron, chemical disposal facilities, telephone and tourist information. There is no reception - you leave your unit by the toilet block and walk down to the farm kitchen to book in (gas available). Play equipment. The pretty village of Winsford is 1 mile (footpath from farm) with a post office, shop, pub and restaurant. Mrs Brown has encapsulated maps available (at a small cost) detailing six walks of varying distances, starting and finishing at the farm. Also available is a list of the wild birds, flowers, etc. to be found on the site. Fishing 4 miles, bicycle hire 5 miles, riding 2 miles. Tarr Steps and Barle Valley only 3 miles. A member of the Countryside Discovery group. Bellamy gold.

Directions: Turn off A396 Tiverton - Minehead road for Winsford (site signed). In Winsford village turn left in front of the Royal Oak (not over ford) and keep on uphill for 1 mile (go slowly round the sharp bend at the bottom). Cross cattle grid onto moor and turn immediately left to farm. Caravans should avoid Dulverton - keep to the A396 from Bridgetown (signed). O.S.GR: SS898342.

Charges 2001:
-- Per unit incl. 2 adults £6.00 - £8.00; 1 person tent and car £3.00 - £4.00; extra adult £2.00 - £3.00; child 0-5 yrs 50p, 5-16 yrs £1.00 - £1.50; extra vehicle £1.00; awning £1.00; electricity £1.70 - £1.85.
-- Less 10% for 7 days paid in advance 10 days before arrival.
-- No credit cards.

Open:
25 March - 29 October.

Address:
Winsford, Minehead, Somerset TA24 7JL.

Tel:
(01643) 851259. FAX: (01643) 851592. E-mail: ar@ halsefarm.co.uk.

Reservations:
Made with £10 deposit.

Somerset

138 Blue Anchor Park, Blue Anchor, nr. Minehead

Beach-side site, for caravans and motorvans only, with views across Bristol Channel.

Although mainly a holiday park, with 300 caravan holiday homes, Blue Anchor nevertheless offers good facilities for 103 touring units. Trailer tents are accepted but not other tents (other than pup tents with a touring booking). Virtually in a separate touring area, the level pitches all have hardstanding and 16A electricity. Facilities on the park include a good sized, irregularly shaped indoor swimming pool with an area for small children, complete with a mushroom shaped fountain. With views of the sea from the pool, it is heated and supervised. There is crazy golf, an excellent, attractive children's play area in the copse and a small supermarket/shop with coffee shop (open 8 am - 9 pm in high season, less at other times). Sanitary facilities provide large, free hot showers (with push-button), vanity style washbasins, dishwashing and laundry sinks under cover, a fully equipped launderette and chemical disposal facilities, in a single, modern block serving just the touring area. Although not actually within the park itself, there are both restaurants and takeaway food facilities within easy walking distance. Riding 5 miles, golf 4½ miles. The park's situation, directly across the small road from the beach, is unusual and gives some beautiful views across the Bristol Channel to South Wales. Dunster Castle, Exmoor, the Quantocks and Minehead are close and the West Somerset Steam Railway runs along one side of the park. No dogs are taken. American motorhomes are accepted (max. 36 ft). Part of the Hoburne Group.

Directions: From M5 junction 25, take A358 signed Minehead. After approx. 12 miles turn left onto A39 at Williton. After 4 miles turn right onto B3191 at Carhampton signed Blue Anchor. Park is 1½ miles on right. O.S.GR: ST025434.

Charges 2000:
-- Per unit, incl. up to 6 persons, electricity and awning £6.50 - £16.00; extra pup tent £3.00.
-- Weekend breaks available.
-- VAT included.
-- Credit cards accepted.

Open:
1 March - 31 October.

Address:
Blue Anchor Bay, nr. Minehead, Somerset TA24 6JT.

Tel:
(01643) 821360.
FAX: (01643) 821572.
E-mail: enquiries@ hoburne.co.uk.

Reservations:
For stays of 1-6 days, payment required in full at time of booking; for 7 nights or more £50 deposit. Min. bookings at B.Hs.

152 Waterrow Touring Park, Wiveliscombe, nr. Taunton

Peaceful park for adults only in lovely surroundings, open all year.

Tony and Anne Taylor have enthusiastically developed Waterrow into a charming, landscaped touring park by the river Tone in a pretty part of South Somerset. Nestling in a little sheltered valley, it is very peaceful here and convenient for an overnight stop (just over 30 minutes from M5 jct 25) or as a base for exploring nearby Exmoor and the Blackdown Hills. There are 45 touring pitches, 9 of which are on level hardstanding (2 doubles in the centre with flower beds around). The remainder are on flat or gently sloping grass with little shade as yet but with bushes and trees planned. Just over half have electrical connections (16A) and spring and mains water are available. Converted barns have been put to good use, housing local tourist information, a public phone, a small library, nature and conservation notes and diary and a visual record of the park's development. Also in here are the nicely fitted out and very clean heated 'portacabin' style units, one each for men and ladies, with open washbasins and controllable, free fairly small showers, with hand and hair dryers, also free. Dishwashing and laundry facilities are behind. Basic grocery provisions are available in reception and you may order jacket potatoes before lunchtime for the evening for just 60p. Further down the park, below the touring area, wide steps lead to the 'nature reserve', which is in fact a Country Wildlife Site, where you can find the recently constructed Otter Holt, go fly fishing for wild brown trout, take a riverside walk or just relax and watch the birds. There is a dog walk and the Taylors will even 'dog sit' for you if you are visiting somewhere your pet is not allowed. The Rock Inn is a short walk and provides good value meals and real ales, with Wiveliscombe and its shops just three miles away. TV aerial points are being installed and barbecues are allowed (no open fires). Bicycle hire 10 miles. Coarse fishing 5 miles. With secure caravan storage available, a 'store and stay' system is becoming increasingly popular. Bellamy gold.

Directions: From M5 exit 25 take A358 (signed Minehead) round Taunton for 4 miles, then at Staplegrove onto the B3227 for 11.5 miles to Wiveliscombe where straight over at lights towards Waterrow (still on B3227). Park is on left shortly after the Rock Inn. O.S.GR: ST053251.

Charges 2000:
-- Per unit incl. 2 persons (adults only 18 years and over) £7.00 - £8.50; extra adult £1.50; electricity £2.00; awning/pup tent £1.00; dog 50p; rallies by arrangement.

Open:
All year.

Address:
Wiveliscombe, Taunton, Somerset TA4 2AZ.

Tel:
(01984) 623464.
FAX: (01984) 624280.
E-mail: taylor@water-rowpark.u-net.com.

Reservations:
Advised for B.Hs and high season.

135 Quantock Orchard Caravan Park, Crowcombe, nr. Williton

Small, attractive, well cared for park with heated pool.

The old adage 'small is beautiful' certainly fits Quantock Orchard, nestling at the foot of the Quantocks in quiet countryside, yet close to many of the attractions of the area. Crowcombe Station on the West Somerset Steam Railway is only a short walk. The Brendon and Exmoor hills, Minehead, Dunster Castle and Taunton are within 10-15 miles. The park has been most attractively developed by the owners, Mr and Mrs Biggs. Mature apple trees, recently planted trees, shrubs and pretty flower beds with a nice use of heathers, make a very pleasant environment. Accessed by gravel roadways are 54 touring caravan pitches, part separated by growing shrubs and hedging, and 20 for tents. Of various sizes, 55 have 10A electrical hook ups, 20 with hardstanding, 4 have TV hook-up and 2 are fully serviced (one large with patio and TV). Only 'air-flo' style groundsheets are permitted on grass pitches. The central, heated sanitary block with its clock tower complements the surroundings, has some nice touches and is very well maintained. Hot water is free to ample vanity style washbasins (including three in cubicles for ladies) and free hot showers with good screens. An excellent family bathroom and separate mother and baby room are both well equipped. Good dishwashing provision, a microwave, laundry facilities and a state-of-the-art chemical disposal unit. Other facilities include a games room, Sky TV, fenced safe based children's play area and a heated swimming pool, walled with paved sunbathing surrounds (40 x 20 ft; open May - Sept). A new leisure suite provides a sauna, steam room, jacuzzi, spa, mini-gym and conservatory rest area with tea and coffee machine (membership optional; children must be accompanied). Four purpose built barbecues and picnic tables are set in the central grass area. Mountain bikes, some with buggies for children, may be hired, especially useful with the Quantocks on the doorstep. The well stocked licensed shop includes caravan and camping accessories and tourist information is in the TV room. A fish and chip van visits (twice weekly in summer). B&B is possible. The Carew Arms serving meals is within walking distance in the mellow village of Crowcombe. Caravan storage Oct. - March.

Directions: Park is west off A358 road (Taunton - Minehead), about 1 mile south of Crowcombe village. O.S.GR: ST140363.

Charges 2000:
-- Per unit incl. 2 adults and children under 3 yrs £7.00 - £10.45; medium or small tent £6.90 - £8.95; extra adult £2.50; child 3-5 yrs 75p, 5-16 yrs £1.75; child's pup tent with caravan £1.00; electricity £2.00 - £2.20; backpacker or cyclist £3.30 - £4.20 per person.
-- Winter weekend special rates.
-- VAT included.

Open:
All year.

Address:
Flaxpool,
Crowcombe,
Taunton,
Somerset TA4 4AW.

Tel:
(01984) 618618.
FAX: as phone.
E-mail: qocp@
flaxpool.freeserve.co.uk.

Reservations:
Made with £10 per week deposit, per booking (non-returnable).

Somerset

148 Home Farm Holiday Park and Country Club, Burnham-on-Sea

Large, well run park with a wide range of facilities.

Home Farm is impressive - neatly and attractively laid out covering 44 acres, well organised and professionally run. Over 600 pitches (including privately owned holiday homes) are regularly laid out on level mown grass. They are all clearly marked, accessed by tarmac roads and divided into various sections, for example an area for those with pets or a tenting area, etc. Including 183 pitches with hardstanding, there are 20 serviced pitches for motorhomes with water and grey water drainage. Electrical connections (16A) are available everywhere (fewer in the tenting area) with plenty of water points in all the sections, but one central refuse area. Toilet blocks, five in total, are good, heated and well situated for all parts of the park. Free hot showers in the newest block are family size minus dividers, there are vanity style washbasins and also some bathrooms (key with £5 deposit). A baby changing room is in one block, dishwashing facilities are under cover at two blocks and a very well equipped laundry room is in the block nearest the pool. Chemical disposal facilities and a dog shower! A large, modern pool with paved surrounds and a paddling section is neatly walled and overlooked by a pool-side terraced restaurant and takeaway (open B.Hs, weekends and high season). A sun-bed is also provided. Other facilities include a shop with general groceries, camping accessories and camping gaz. Reception holds a good supply of tourist information. There is a well equipped playground and a children's club for 4-10 year olds runs in the school holidays, with amusement machines and pool tables for those interested. The club house (with free membership) is a feature of the site providing carvery meals, a range of entertainment, a function room, wide screen TV, an attractive conservatory and outside barbecue area. Other on site amenities include fishing and boating lakes (paddle and bumper boats to hire), BMX and go-karting tracks and a five-a-side football pitch. It is a level site with facilities for disabled visitors. In all, it is an excellent provision and Burnham-on-Sea is only a mile away - there is a footpath from the site but you must cross the railway line. With Berrow Sands and Brean Down there is over seven miles of beach to choose from!

Charges 2000:
-- Per pitch incl. 2 persons, electricity and awning £7.50 - £16.50; extra person over 10 yrs £2.50 - £4.50, 4-9 yrs £1.50 - £3.00; extra car or small tent £2.50 - £4.00; dog £1.00 - £2.00; hardstanding £2.00 - £3.00.
-- Club membership free.
-- Security barrier card £2 (£1 refundable).
-- Special breaks available.
-- VAT included.
-- Credit cards accepted.

Open:
All year.

Address:
Edithmead, Burnham-on-Sea, Somerset TA9 4HD.

Tel:
(01278) 788888.
FAX: (01278) 780113.
E-mail:
homefarmholidaypark
@compuserve.com.

Reservations:
Contact park for details.

Directions: Home Farm is ¼ mile from M5 junction 22 and the A38. It is signed from the B3140 into Burnham-on-Sea. O.S.GR: ST327493.

153 Slimeridge Farm Touring Park, Uphill, Weston-super-Mare

Small beach-side site overlooking Weston Bay.

This attractive small touring site is next to the beach in Uphill village at the southern end of Weston Bay. There are 50 pitches (a few taken on seasonal lets), on level grass with electricity (10A) available, separated from the beach by stone walling. The view across the bay is quite something, with Brean Down and Steep Holm Island standing out. However it is worth noting that, because of its situation close to the beach, the site could be affected by the tide in extreme adverse weather conditions. You book in at the warden's caravan and a circular tarmac roadway connects the marked and numbered pitches which are allocated by the wardens. There are five hardstandings for motorhomes. A modern toilet block with electronic code entry system is well equipped and includes en-suite shower facilities that are also provided for handicapped visitors. Laundry room with washing machine, drier, and washing up sinks. A good chemical disposal unit is used for waste water also. A post office, general stores and pubs are all within close walking distance. Note: golfers have right of way to cross the park as the golf course is split by the site. Weston-super-Mare with all its leisure activities and entertainment is 2 miles, Cheddar Gorge, Wooky Hole and Glastonbury are within easy driving distance. Three farm cottages are to let. The park is under the same ownership as no. 148, Home Farm Holiday Park, a much larger site at Burnham-on-Sea with a wide range of facilities and entertainment. Slimeridge guests are entitled to free membership of Home Farm Country Club and free use of its swimming pool.

Charges 2000:
-- Per unit incl. 2 adults, electricity and awning £5.50 - £13.50; extra adult £1.50 - £3.50; child (4-9 yrs) £1.00 - £2.00; extra car or small tent £2.00; dog 50p - £1.50.
-- Min. stay 2 nights at B.Hs.
-- Credit cards accepted.

Open:
March to October

Address:
Links Road, Uphill, Weston-super-Mare, BS23 4XY.

Tel:
(01934) 641641
E-mail:
homefarmholidaypark
@compuserve.com

Reservations:
Made with deposit of £5 p/night; no refunds given.

Directions: Site is south of Weston-super-Mare. From A370 follow sign for Uphill village and beach. O.S.GR: ST312585.

149 Greenacres Camping, North Wootton, nr. Shepton Mallet

Rural site in Somerset countryside for tents, trailer tents and motorcaravans only.

Hidden away below the Mendips and almost at the start of the 'Levels', Greenacres is a simple green site - a haven of peace and quiet. The grass is neatly trimmed over the 4.5 acres and hedged with mature trees, though there is a view of Glastonbury Tor in one direction and of Barrow Hill in the other. Thirty perimeter pitches are well spaced and allow central space for ball games, whilst the narrower neck end is ideal for 'adults only' and bird watchers. Wild life abounds. The central wooden toilet block is simple but perfectly acceptable, with free hot showers accessed direct from the outside and with H&C water to washbasins, two dishwashing sinks and two laundry sinks (there is a spin dryer); all is kept nice and clean. Some children's play equipment with a caravan to use as a play house completes the provision on site but across the lane (gate is always keep shut), at the owner's bungalow where the office is situated, you can find a fridge, freezer, library, tourist information and bicycle hire. Batteries may be charged or borrowed and you may find the 'Turf Rider' which tows the cart used to give children an evening ride (a speciality of the park). In North Wootton itself, ¾ mile walk, is a large pub/restaurant and a vineyard. Fishing and riding are available nearby. There are many nearby attractions should you tire of the peace and quiet, such as Wookey Hole, Cheddar Caves and Gorge, Longleat, the beautiful small city of Wells (with leisure centre), Clarks Village, etc. You can cycle into both Wells and Glastonbury using Sustran Route 3. Dogs are not accepted.

Charges 2001:
-- Per adult £5.00; child (4-16 yrs) £1.50.
-- No credit cards.
Open:
March - October incl. plus Carnival Fortnight in Nov.
Address:
Barrow Lane, North Wootton, nr. Shepton Mallet, Somerset BA4 4HL.
Tel:
(01749) 890497.
E-mail: harvie.greenlands@talk21.com.
Reservations:
Made with £2 deposit.

Directions: From A39 Glastonbury - Wells road turn east at Brownes Garden Centre and follow camping signs. From A361 Glastonbury - Shepton Mallet road follow camp signs from Pilton or Steanbow. O.S.GR: ST553416.

154 Batcombe Vale Caravan and Camping Park, nr. Bruton

Delightful small park in rural situation with magnificent views and coarse fishing.

Set in a secluded valley with fields gently rising around it, contented black and white cows grazing with watchful buzzards cruising the thermals above and views across the distant hills, this is just a very special place. Home to Donald and Mary Sage, Batcombe Vale House is a mellow, attractive building covered with wisteria to one side of the valley overlooking the lakes and the 'wild' landscape of the valley. Different trees and shrubs have been skilfully placed to enhance the natural environment providing a range of colour and shape. It is actually designated an 'area of outstanding natural beauty' and there are 120 acres around the valley where you are welcome to wander and picnic in the fields, a haven for wild flowers, birds and butterflies. For those who fish, two of the lakes have carp and tench up to 18 lbs but you must have a current licence. As you descend slowly down the narrow entrance drive you see the 30 pitches, attractively set and terraced where necessary, in an oval with the lakes, one after another, below. The grass is neatly cut, the pitches level, marked and numbered, 16 provided with 16A electricity. The grass is left natural around the pitches and pathways mown where needed. The small rustic toilet block covered in honeysuckle meets all your needs. There is hot water for showers and washbasins, with a dishwashing sink in both the ladies' and the men's sides - no discrimination, but the men have the chemical disposal! There is also a public phone and tourist information and some useful folders on where to eat and what to visit, etc. Three water points are conveniently positioned, a bin area with plastic bags provided and a freezer thoughtfully and neatly placed under cover. When, and if, you tire of the views and the fishing there is a range of circular walks from the site or you can potter about in one of the three small rowing boats - free gentle exercise provided care is taken. One dog per pitch is welcome (no dangerous breeds) but they must respect the local wild life. Groundsheet awnings must be lifted daily. There are many places to visit nearby, from Glastonbury with the Tor, to Cheddar Gorge and the Caves. This is a marvellous site and it is a privilege to be able to share and enjoy it with the Sage family. It is also possible to book B&B at the House. Bruton for shops, etc. is only 2 miles, with launderettes at Shepton or Frome. Caravan storage.

Charges 2000:
-- Per unit incl. 2 adults £9.00; extra adult £3.00; child 8-18 yrs £3.00, 4-8 yrs £2.00; full awning £1.00; extra car or adult tent £1.00; electricity £1.50; dog £1.00.
-- Coarse fishing (up to 20 lbs) adults £3 p/day (child £1.50) or £2 p/day times length of stay.
-- No commercial vehicles or motorcycle 'packs' - family groups only.
Open:
Easter - September.
Address:
Batcombe Vale, Shepton Mallet, Somerset BA4 6BW.
Tel:
(01749) 830246.
E-mail: DonaldSage @compuserve.com.
Reservations:
Only essential for B.Hs and school holidays; made with £5 deposit and £1 fee (min. 2 nights).

Directions: Bruton is south of Shepton Mallet and Frome but north of Wincanton where the A359 intersects the B3081. Site is 2 miles north of Bruton (signed in town). The road is narrow in places but an easier way for caravans is clearly signed. O.S.GR: ST681379.

Somerset

139 The Old Oaks Touring Park, Wick, nr. Glastonbury

Excellent family park with extra large pitches in a rural situation.

Tucked below and hidden from the 'Tor', The Old Oaks has a lovely secluded setting with views across to the Mendips. Developed on a working farm over the last 10 years, there are 40 spacious pitches in a series of paddocks, most with 10A electricity and 18 with hardstanding; four are fully serviced (including sewage). Mainly backing on to hedges, they are attractively arranged, interspersed with shrubs and flowers in a circular development or terraced with increasing views. A quiet orchard area or a separated hedged paddock for camping and a larger field with chemical disposal facilities and plenty of space for ball games complete the provision. Mature trees and hedging combine with the mellow farm buildings to give a sense of timelessness, tranquillity and peace. The heated toilet block, converted from the old stables, is of excellent quality with fully equipped showers, some washbasins in cubicles, the others vanity style, and two new family rooms (shower, toilet and basin). It is nicely tiled and finished, with free hot water except for the bathroom (£1). Disabled visitors are provided with a toilet and basin, together with a shower, toilet and basin next door, with level access. A baby room, well equipped laundry room and covered dishwashing complete the block which is neatly paved outside and has digital security locks (a public footpath from the Tor passes through the farm). Chemical disposal and motorcaravan service facilities are provided, plus two recycling points, a freezer for ice packs (free) and a useful dog wash. An interesting development features reed beds to deal with waste water, a traditional method, now coming into its own again as we have seen at Oakdown Touring Park (no. 102). The reception/shop is modern, yet in keeping, providing tourist information and basic supplies including off licence (limited hours). The fishing pond (coarse) costs £2 per half day for adults, £1 per child. Whether you fish or not, the pond is worth a visit with its view of the Tor or just to see the ducks and the chickens on your way there. Bicycle hire from park, riding 5 miles and golf 6 miles. Market day is Tuesday. In an area steeped in history and legend, this is a very well equipped and maintained park which should meet the needs of the discerning family camper or caravanner. A new member of the Best of British group. Bellamy gold.

Charges 2001:
-- Per unit incl. 2 adults £7.00 - £10.00; extra adult £3.00; child (3-15 yrs) £2.00; awning with breathing groundsheet only £1.00; porch awning 50p; dog 50p - 75p electricity £1.75; `all service pitch £1.00 (free to disabled badge holders).
-- Walker, cyclist or single person less 75p per pitch.
-- Reduction for O.A.Ps excl. school and Bank holidays.
-- Credit cards accepted.
-- VAT included.

Open:
1 March - 31 October.

Address:
Wick Farm,
Wick, Glastonbury,
Somerset BA6 8JS.

Tel:
(01458) 831437.
FAX: (01458) 833238.
E-mail:
info@theoldoaks.co.uk.

Reservations:
Recommended for high season and made with £15 deposit.

Directions: Park is north off A361 Shepton Mallet - Glastonbury road, 2 miles from Glastonbury. Take unclassified road signed Wick for approx. 1 mile and the park is on the left. O.S.GR: ST521394.

140 The Isle of Avalon Touring Caravan Park, Glastonbury

Well planned, modern park with excellent facilities, 10 minutes walk from town centre.

This pleasant, modern park, owned by Mike and Sharon Webb, has a friendly atmosphere. Developed on flat, grassy ground, the park has been landscaped, part with trees and shrubs, part open, to provide 70 individual pitches. Well spaced out and connected by hard roads, they have hardstanding with adjacent grass for awning and electrical points (5/10A). A further 50 tent spaces are on the adjoining, level field. Water and refuse points are well spaced around and attractively surrounded by trees and shrubs. All units are personally seen to their pitches. The single, excellent, tiled toilet block is comfortable and spacious, and can be heated. It provides large, controllable hot showers, washbasins in cubicles for women and excellent units for disabled visitors (plus ramps to the shop and reception). There is a large laundry room and dishwashing area, plus chemical toilet and motorcaravan disposal point. American motorhomes are welcome. A well stocked shop with some camping accessories and reception with gas and tourist information is at the entrance with a well cared for, attractive and spacious feel. The top corner of the tenting field is left clear as a play area for children and parents and bicycle hire is available on site. Riding or golf 2 miles, fishing 200 yds. Glastonbury centre, with shops, restaurants and cafés, and the Abbey are a short walk and there are indoor and outdoor swimming pools at Street. The nearby town of Street is famous for its shoes and the 'Clark's Village' development with many factory outlets for well known high street names. Dogs are accepted (but by prior arrangement only on tent pitches). Winter caravan storage.

Charges 2000:
-- Per unit £4.95 - £5.95 (American style motorhomes +£1.00); adult £1.95; child (3-14 yrs) £1.50; awning £1.50; pup tent £1.75; electricity £1.85; dog £1.00; extra car £1.00.
-- VAT included.
-- No credit cards.

Open:
All year.

Address:
Godney Road,
Glastonbury,
Somerset BA6 9AF.

Tel:
(01458) 833618.
FAX: as phone.

Reservations:
Any length with £10 deposit.

Directions: Park is on west side of the town bypass (A39), just off B3151 (Wedmore Road) with good signs from the bypass. O.S.GR: ST495397.

141 Broadway House Holiday Caravan and Camping Park, Cheddar

Family owned, characterful touring park with some holiday caravans and activities for all ages, beside Cheddar Gorge.

An interesting and well maintained park offering a range of facilities on continental lines, Broadway has been developed by the Moore family with 'T.L.C.' over 30 years. On a gently sloping area at the foot of the Mendips, the park takes 250 touring units of all types. From the entrance, after the neat caravan holiday home area, a series of touring areas graduates upwards, culminating in a tent and overflow rally field. The central access avenue is lined by trees with the groups of pitches on either side separated by ranch style fencing or hedging and landscaped with trees and shrubs and interesting bygones. Most pitches have electricity(16A) and 30 have water and drainage. This park aims to cater for the normal active family - single sex groups are actively discouraged. The large, purpose built, tiled toilet block at the start of the touring area has a good provision of showers, with seat and hooks, vanity style washbasins and eight private cabins. Behind it are 10 family shower units with shower, bidet and washbasin, two of which are 'disabled friendly'. Extra facilities with bathroom (coin operated) and a unit for disabled visitors are near reception, with a 'portacabin' type unit (no showers) in the top tenting field. Other facilities include a babies' room, coin operated hairdryers, washing up sinks and a well equipped launderette. There is a secluded, walled, heated pool (60 x 25 ft) and children's pool (open Easter - Sept; unsupervised) with grass sunbathing area and shade from silver birches. The range of activities organised from the park is wide and includes abseiling, canoeing, hill-walking, archery, shooting, caving, mountain biking (bicycles for hire on site), windsurfing can also be arranged and there is a dry ski slope nearby. Fishing ½ and 5 miles. On site is an adventure playground, football field, indoor table tennis, barbecue area, target golf, boules pitch, skateboard ramp, croquet, games/amusements room, family room and large screen TV and tourist information room. Dogs (not dangerous breeds) have an exercise field. Two animal enclosures have a variety of interesting animals and Sonny the parrot is a character with a history! A nature trail leads from the park (and 'pixie walk') - Cheddar Wood is a site of special scientific interest. The shop has a range of goods and there is a bar and café with a reasonably priced menu at peak periods. Motorcaravan service point. Electronic barrier security. This is really a park to be experienced - there is always something to see and do and everything is well signed. Bellamy gold.

Charges guide:
-- Per adult £2.00 - £4.00; child (3-14 yrs) £1.00 - £2.00; caravan or tent and car £1.00 - £6.00; motorhome area, car £1.00 - £2.50; premier pitch (incl. 3 services) plus £2.00; electricity (16A) £1.50; awning, pup tent or extra car free - £1.00; dog £1.00, 2 small dogs £1.50.
-- Special discounts for longer stays and for O.A.P.s.
-- Min. charge £3.50.
-- VAT included.
-- Credit cards accepted (5% surcharge).

Open:
1 March - 30 November.

Address:
Cheddar,
Somerset BS27 3DB.

Tel:
(01934) 742610.
FAX: (01934) 744950.
E-mail: enquiries@
broadwayhouse.uk.com.

Reservations:
Advisable in high season, with £5 deposit per night.

Directions: Park entrance is on the A371 towards Axbridge, about 1 mile northwest of Cheddar. O.S.GR: ST449547.

142 Southfork Caravan Park, Parrett Works, nr. Martock

Personally run small park in pretty surroundings.

Don't be put off by the address, which is historic - it was once a 17th century flax mill, now no more. Mr and Mrs Metcalfe own and run this excellent, modern site (30 pitches on grass with gravel access road, 20 with 10A electricity) just outside the lovely village of Martock. This orderly, quiet park is on two acres of flat, tree lined meadow near the River Parrett. All the expected facilities are close to the entrance. Most things are available, including an NCC approved caravan repair centre (closed Xmas/New Year). The heated, well maintained, tiled toilet block has free hot water to the washbasins and showers and there is a laundry with public phone, and chemical disposal. Children's play area. Shop and limited off licence (also not Xmas/New Year) with a good supply of tourist information, gas supplies and comprehensive camping and caravan spares and accessories. As the owners live on the premises, the well drained park is open all year. Fishing is available (and licences) on the River Parrett a few yards from the park. Golf 3 miles. Despite the rural setting, the A303 trunk road is just ten minutes away. This area of South Somerset contains so much of interest, including gardens, historic houses and sites, the Fleet Air Arm Museum, Haynes Motor Museum and Cricket St Thomas Wildlife Park. Information about access to many cycle routes and numerous walks, including the Parrett Trail, is available from reception. Three caravan holiday homes are for hire.

Charges 2000:
-- Per unit incl. 2 persons £6.00 - £9.00; extra person £1.00, child under 5 free; awning 50p - £1.00; dog 50p; electricity £1.80 - £2.30.
-- Credit cards accepted.

Open:
All year.

Address:
Parrett Works, Martock, Somerset TA12 6AE.

Tel:
(01935) 825661.
FAX: (01935) 825122.
E-mail: southfork.
caravans@virgin.net.

Reservations:
Advisable for B.Hs. and peak season and made with £10 deposit.

Alan Rogers' Discount

Less £1 p/night
(max. 7)

Directions: From A303 between Ilchester and Ilminster take signs for South Petherton or Martock; park is mid-way on the road between the two villages (follow signs). O.S.GR: ST447187.

Somerset

150 Long Hazel International Caravan & Camping Park, Sparkford

Neat, small site near Yeovil, well situated to explore Somerset.

Pamela and Alan Walton, who live at the park, are really enthusiastic about their park in the Somerset village of Sparkford and will make you most welcome. With neat and level grass, attractive beech hedging, silver birches and many newly planted trees, the park has a comfortable feel and provides 69 touring pitches for all types of units, 20 with hardstanding (with more planned). There are 48 electrical hook-ups (16A) and again more are planned. The heated toilet block is kept immaculate and provides well equipped free hot showers, washbasins (H&C), separate washing up sinks (H&C) and chemical disposal. Motorcaravan discharge point. Well planned en-suite facilities are available for visitors with disabilities, with level, easily accessible pitches. A laundry is planned. Play equipment is centrally situated and a badminton net, bowls green and a 9-hole putting green are available. The entrance has been widened for easier access. Gas is available from reception. There is a post office/shop in the village selling bread baked on the premises and the Sparkford Inn provides good food. Sparkford is also home to the famous Haynes Motor Museum (½ mile), the most interested in the history of the world's motor industry, and the Fleet Air Arm Museum is near at Yeovilton (3 miles). You will also find several National Trust properties and gardens in the area and the park is the midway site for the Leland Trail. Riding or fishing 8 miles, golf 5 miles. Three holiday caravans to let. Note: the park edges the A303 bypass; although it is well hedged, there could be road noise at times in some areas of the park.

Charges 2001:
-- Per unit incl. 2 persons £10.00; extra person (over 5 yrs) £1.50 - £2.00; awning £2.00 - £2.50; extra vehicle £1.00; extra single tent £6.00; electricity £2.00 - £2.50.

Open:
1 March - 31 December.

Address:
Sparkford,
Yeovil,
Somerset BA22 7JH.

Tel:
(01963) 440002.

FAX: as phone.

Reservations:
Contact park.

Directions: From Yeovil direction on A303 take road into village of Sparkford and park is signed on the left 100 yds before the Inn. O.S.GR: ST604263.

143 Mendip Heights Camping and Caravan Park, Priddy, nr. Wells

Well kept, family run park in the peaceful Mendip Hills.

Historic Priddy is the highest village in the Mendips and is famed for its annual Sheep Fair in August. Nearby are extensive Roman lead-workings, Bronze Age burial mounds, the Priddy Circle and access to Swildons Hole, one of the popular cave systems in the Mendips. The park is half a mile from the village with tranquil views across the Mendip fields characterised by dry stone walling. It has a simple charm with field margins left natural to encourage wildlife and nest boxes in the mature trees edging the three fields which comprise the site. They provide space for 92 units on mostly level short grass with 21 electric hook-ups (8 at 10A,13 at 16A) and 8 with hardstanding available. The toilet block, although of older design, is bright and cheerful, spotlessly clean and heated, with well equipped showers (coin operated), open washbasins (H&C) and a baby changing area. Chemical disposal facilities are separately situated. Separate dishwashing and laundry facilities are fully equipped and well maintained. There are water points in each field. The reception/shop doubles as the village shop and is therefore open all season selling groceries, calor gas, etc. with an off licence and tourist information. Wendy house and table tennis for children. A range of activities can also be arranged covering canoeing, abseiling, archery, caving, mountain biking and others, with equipment provided. Free guided walks are also usually available at 2 pm. on Sundays during B.Hs and the summer holidays. The park is also on the Padstow-Bristol Sustran Route 3. Fishing 6 miles, riding 2 miles, Two traditional village pubs with very different characters stand by the village green within walking distance (½ mile). Other than all that activity, places like Cheddar Gorge, Wookey Hole, Glastonbury with the Tor, Wells, Bath and Weston-super-Mare are all within a 20 mile radius. Holiday caravan to rent (6 berth). Caravan storage. A member of the Countryside Discovery group. Bellamy gold.

Charges 2000:
-- Per adult £3.25 - £3.95; child (3-15 yrs) £1.30; electricity £1.80.
-- No charge for awning, extra car or pets.
-- No credit cards.

Open:
1 March - 15 November.

Address:
Priddy,
nr. Wells,
Somerset BA5 3BP.

Tel:
(01749) 870241.
FAX: (01749) 870368.
E-mail: enquiries@
mendipheights.co.uk.

Reservations:
Made with £10 deposit (min. 3 nights for electricity at B.Hs).

Directions: From M5 exit 21 (Weston-super-Mare) take A371 to Banwell. Turn left on A368, right on B3134 and right on B3135. After 2 miles turn left at camp sign. From M4 westbound exit 18, A46 to Bath, then A4 towards Bristol. Take A39 for Wells and right at Green Ore traffic lights on B3135; after 5 miles turn left at camp sign. From Shepton Mallet, follow A37 north to junction of B3135 and turn left. Continue on B3135 to traffic lights at Green Ore. Straight on and after 5 miles turn left at camp sign. O.S.GR: ST522518.

Somerset

151 Bath Chew Valley Caravan Park, Bishop Sutton, nr. Bath

Adults only, small, secluded garden site for caravans, motorhomes and trailer tents only.

Chew Valley is run with much tender love and care by Ray and Val Belton. The result is that you pitch on neat lawns amongst colourful beds of flowers and shrubs with your car tucked away on the car park, providing a tranquil and restful atmosphere. The park will particularly appeal to garden lovers and has actually been featured on BBC TV's Gardeners' World. A very nice touch is the small nursery 'Gone to Pot' where Val (the garden expert) does all her growing and where those staying on site can purchase some of the plants found on the park. The same care and attention is evident in all the facilities. The sanitary block is attractively wallpapered giving a 'home from home' feel, also heated with cubicled washbasins and the other fittings that make life comfortable. Two separate en-suite units ensure that there is an adequate provision for the 31 large pitches. Six pitches have neatly planned hardstanding and Ray will place your van for you levelling it if necessary. No groundsheets are allowed. A useful utility room is for dish or hand washing with spin drier and washing machine for service washes only. Chemical disposal and refuse points and two water points are all clearly marked, neat and well maintained including reception where a warm welcome awaits. Tourist information and a small library with coffee are next door. Animals are welcome with a dog walk provided. The village is only 100 yds up the road with a general store, newsagent, two pubs and a post office. Supermarkets are within 15 minutes drive. Chew Valley lake is a walk of about half a mile with trout fishing available and Blagdon lake is popular for birdwatching. Golf 1 mile, riding 8 miles. Bristol and Bath are within an easy distance and Cheddar Gorge or Longleat make excellent days out. This park only accepts adults. A Best of British group member. Bellamy gold.

Charges 2000:
-- Per pitch incl. 2 persons, electricity, awning, pets and TV hook-up £13.00 - £15.00.
-- No credit cards.

Open: All year.

Address: Ham Lane, Bishop Sutton, North Somerset BS39 5TZ.

Tel: (01275) 332127. FAX: (01275) 332664. E-mail: enquiries@ chewvalley.co.uk.

Reservation: Advisable for B.Hs.

Directions: From Bath direction on A368 turn right opposite the Red Lion pub. Road appears a little narrow but continue past a small track to the left (50 yds) for a further 50 yds. Park entrance appears on your left with neat, clear entrance (recently improved). O.S.GR: ST584599.

144 Baltic Wharf Caravan Club Site, Bristol

Excellent, small, city centre site, open all year, operated by the Caravan Club.

This gem of a little site in Bristol's re-developed dockland is well laid out and maintained with access via a lockable gate to the Baltic Wharf dockside. It is screened from the road by a high wall with a boatyard on one side and residential apartments on the other, and is well designed with a good use of trees. The view across the dock towards Clifton village and Bristol is unique and you can even glimpse the suspension bridge (lit up at night - quite effective). The 58 pitches are accessed by a circular tarmac road - the central nine are on grass (these are not used in the winter), the rest on stone chippings and ideal for all year round use (steel pegs are provided). All are supplied with 16A electricity. Two neat bin compounds have waste and fresh water points and a motorcaravan service point. The toilet block (coded access) is heated for winter use and provides good clean facilities including controllable showers and, for ladies, washbasins in cubicles well equipped with hooks, mirrors, etc. Good new facilities are provided for disabled visitors, plus toilets for the walking disabled and showers in the main block. Dishwashing under cover, good fully equipped laundry room and enclosed chemical toilet disposal. Overall, it is an excellent provision and there is also a tourist information room and a public phone (card or cash). The helpful wardens live on the site and a small general store with off licence and newsagent is 200 yds. Dogs are welcome but there is no dog walk. It is a 30 minute walk to the city centre, a ferry is available (weekends only in winter) or a regular bus service (every 30 mins, 7.30 am.- 6 pm). An extra ferry runs from the SS Great Britain. TV reception is poor but a booster may be hired for 55p per night. Golf 2 miles. The Sustran cycle route 3 ends here. This is a popular site so advance booking is necessary. Arrive by 8 pm.

Charges 2000:
-- Per pitch £6.00 - £7.00; person £3.25 - £4.00; child (5-16 yrs) £1.10 - £1.20; electricity £1.45 - £2.20.
-- Credit cards accepted.

Open: All year.

Address: Cumberland Road, Bristol BS1 6XG.

Tel: 0117 926 8030 (8 am. - 8 pm. only).

Reservations: Always advised, essential in high seasons, and made with £5 deposit; contact the Wardens with SAE for confirmation.

Directions: Easiest access is to follow signs for Historic Harbour and SS Great Britain. Site is just west of SS Great Britain, on the right behind a high wall - look carefully for the club sign (no brown signs to follow). O.S.GR: ST572718.

63

Somerset / Wiltshire

145 Bath Marina and Caravan Park, Bath

Good, purpose-designed touring park for caravans and motorhomes only.

Under the same ownership as the next door Marina, this a useful, well run park for visiting historic Bath or Bristol. A park-and-ride facility for Bath is outside the entrance, and the Bath - Bristol cycle path near. It provides 89 pitches for caravans or motorcaravans (no tents). With concrete hardstanding and 16A electricity, they are pleasantly interspersed with flowering trees and bushes. One 'super' pitch next to the toilet block has full services (electricity, water, drain and TV aerial). A reader tells us that TV reception is not good. The two heated toilet blocks (with digital entry) have free hot water, showers (lacking shelf space but with hooks and stools outside), vanity style washbasins in semi cubicles and hair dryers. Each block has dishwashing sinks outside, under cover and chemical disposal. There is a unit for disabled people and a laundry room. The reception/shop (for essentials and gas) has tourist information as well as necessities for the Marina. A gate gives access to the 'Boathouse', a bar with bar snacks and a terrace fronting the river. Children's play park next door. Public phone (card). Fishing on site, bicycle hire, riding, golf, boat launching within 2 miles. A useful park.

Charges 2000:
-- Per pitch £9.00; adult £2.00; child (5-15 yrs) £1.00; electricity (16A) £2.00; awning free; extra car £1.00; dog free.
-- Winter special (1/11-28/2): £12 per unit inclusive.
-- VAT included.
-- Credit cards accepted.

Open:
All year.

Address:
Brassmill Lane,
Bath BA1 3JT.

Tel:
(01225) 424301 or 428778.

FAX: as phone.

Reservations:
Any length with £10 deposit.

Directions: From M4 exit 18 take A46 for Bath for 8 miles to A4 T-junction. Turn right (signs for Bath city centre) to traffic lights at A36 intersection. Turn left on A36 signed Bristol. After 2 miles after Little Chef on right, turn right at traffic lights crossing over river. Immediately right next to Murco petrol station into Brassmill Lane. Park is 100 yds on right. O.S.GR: ST720655.

166 Piccadilly Caravan Park, Lacock, Chippenham

Attractive, small, quiet park, family owned and run.

Piccadilly is set in open countryside close to several attractions in northern Wessex, notably Longleat, Bath, Salisbury Plain, Stourhead, and Lacock itself. The park is neat and tidy and the landscaped shrubs and trees are maturing, giving the impression of three separate areas. There are 40 well spaced, clearly marked pitches, 11 with hardstanding. Electricity (10A) is available on 34 pitches. The one toilet block is well maintained with free controllable hot showers in large cubicles, with excellent seat, and washbasins with ample shelving, hooks and mirrors, shaving sockets and hairdryers. It should be adequate for peak period use and can be heated in cool weather. There is a dishwashing area, a laundry room with baby changing facilities and chemical disposal point. Public phone. Limited gas supplies and papers to order. Bark-based children's playground and a large, grass ball area. Fishing 1 mile, bicycle hire 6 miles, riding 4 miles, golf 3 miles. Bus service from Lacock village to Chippenham.

Charges 2001:
-- Per unit incl. 2 persons £8.50; extra person over 5 yrs £1.00; electricity £1.50.
-- VAT included.
-- No credit cards.

Open:
Easter/1 April - October.

Address:
Folly Lane West,
Lacock, Chippenham,
Wiltshire SN15 2LP.

Tel:
(01249) 730260.

Reservations:
Any length; deposit of 1 nights fee.

Directions: Park signed west off A350 Chippenham - Melksham (turn to Gastard with caravan symbol) by Lacock village. 300 yds. to park. O.S.GR: ST911682.

168 Plough Lane Caravan Site, Kington Langley, nr. Chippenham

Quality touring site in north Wiltshire, for adults only.

Opening for its first season in '98, this is a good example of a well designed modern touring site. The 35 pitches are half hardstanding, half grass and all have electricity (16A). Access roads are gravel and the borders are stocked with newly planted shrubs and trees. The sanitary building is heated, spacious, light and airy, and has all the usual facilities including roomy showers, washbasins (some in cubicles), with a hairdressing area for ladies. A room for disabled visitors has WC, washbasin and a pre-mix hot shower, with ramped access. Hot water is free. Dishwashing sinks are under cover at the front of the building, and the laundry has two further dishwashing sinks, laundry sinks, a free spin dryer, a washing machine and dryer and ironing. Chemical disposal. Public telephone kiosk. Tourist information is available in reception. Local facilities include a supermarket, two public houses, and two garages - both of which stock gas. Golf less than 1 mile. For adults only, this is an ideal base for visiting Bath, Westonbirt Arboretum and the many attractive villages of north Wiltshire and south Gloucestershire.

Charges 2001:
-- Per unit incl. 2 adults and electricity £11.00; extra adult £3.00.
-- VAT included.
-- No credit cards.

Open:
1 March - 4 November.

Address:
Plough Lane, Kington Langley, nr. Chippenham, Wiltshire SN15 5PS.

Tel:
(01249) 750795.

FAX: as phone.

E-mail: ploughlane@lineone.net.

Reservations:
Made with £10 deposit..

Directions: From M4 junction 17 turn south on A350 for 2 miles, then left at traffic lights where site is signed. From Chippenham head north on A350 (towards M4), approaching traffic lights (signed for site and Kington Langley) you will need the right hand lane. O.S.GR: ST915765.

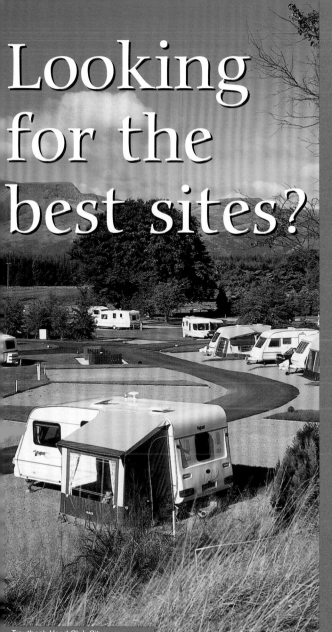

Looking for the best sites?

Troutbeck Head Club Site near

Here's what our visitors say

"A beautiful unspoiled site – one night 'en route' was transformed into 10 days of delight by helpful and knowledgeable Wardens"

Grummore, Scottish Highlands

"What a gem of a site – well kept, with birds, views and walks. What more could we ask for – we'll be back"

Dockray Meadow, Lake District

"Excellent site, very well run and ideally suited for visiting York. Would recommend to friends"

Rowntree Park, York

"This is our first time with The Club – if all sites are as good, we're in for a real treat"

See for yourself...

Our FREE 72-page 'Site Collection 2001' brochure, features over 200 quality Club Sites in the UK and Ireland. All welcome tourer and motor caravanners and trailer tenters and many are open to non-members and tent campers.

For your copy call us free on

0800 521161

Or write to The Caravan Club, Dept DC, FREEPOST, East Grinstead, West Sussex RH19 1ZB

Please quote ref ARG2

Brochure publication date end November 2000.

So much more to enjoy

www.caravanclub.co.uk

Hidden Valley Touring & Camping Park

Nr Ilfracombe, N. Devon EX34 8NU   Tel.: 01271 813837

1992-2000

AA - *Best Campsite in the South West 1997/98*

www.hiddenvalleypark.com

Oakdown

SIDMOUTH'S MULTI AWARD WINNING TOURING & HOLIDAY HOME PARK

Welcome to Oakdown, Regency Sidmouth's only 5★, multi award winning Park. Set within the beautiful East Devon Heritage Coast, Oakdown is level, sheltered and landscaped into groves to give privacy, with floral displays to delight you. Our award winning heated amenities include aids for the disabled. Enjoy our Field Trail to the world famous Donkey Sanctuary.
Free colour brochure with pleasure.

Tel. 01297 680387 Fax. 01297 680541
E Mail: oakdown@btinternet.com
Website: www.bestcaravanpark.co.uk

OAKDOWN TOURING & HOLIDAY HOME PARK

Weston, Sidmouth, Devon EX10 0PH

International Caravan & Camping Park

FOREST GLADE HOLIDAY PARK, CULLOMPTON, DEVON EX15 2DT

A small country estate surrounded by forest in which deer roam. Situated in an area of outstanding natural beauty.
Large, flat, sheltered camping/touring pitches
Modern facilities building, luxury 2/6 berth full service holiday homes, also self contained flat for 2 persons.

COUNTRY HOLIDAY PARK

Shop, Take Away Food, Tennis Court, Adventure Play Area, Games Room, Electric Hook-up Points. Riding Forest & Hill Walks, Gliding, Fishing & Golf are all nearby. Freedom for the children, peace for the adults. Central for touring S.W. Easy access coast and moors.
Motor caravans welcome.
Facilities for the Disabled.
Dogs welcome.
Tourers please book in advance.

FREE COLOUR BROCHURE
Tel: (01404) 841381
(Evgs to 8pm)
Fax: (01404) 841593
www.forestglade.mcmail.com
email: forestglade@cwcom.net

FREE Indoor Heated Pool

Wareham Forest Tourist Park

**OPEN
ALL
YEAR** For further details and free coloured brochure write or phone: Tel/Fax: (01929) 551393.
Peter & Pam Savage, Wareham Forest Tourist Park, North Trigon, Wareham, Dorset BH20 7NZ.
www.wareham-forest.co.uk email holiday@wareham-forest.co.uk. Credit cards accepted

170 Camping and Caravanning Club Site Devizes, Seend, Melksham

Modern touring site close to Caen Hill Locks on Kennet and Avon Canal, open all year.

First opened in 1998, this newly constructed site, occupies a level field with gravel roads and centrally located facilities. It is also adjacent to the Kennet and Avon Canal (opened in 1810, and recently extensively restored), and the towpath now provides a traffic-free route passing the Caen Hill flight of 29 locks into Devizes (4 miles). In the other direction the towpath runs towards Melksham (also 4 miles). The site has 50 hardstanding and 45 grass pitches, 75 with electricity (16A). A modern, heated toilet block provides spacious hot showers, washbasins in cubicles, laundry, chemical disposal point, dishwashing room, and a mother and baby room. Facilities for disabled visitors are in a suite (with alarm system) by reception, and there is a little playground on a rubber safety base. Reception opens 09.00-10.30 and 16.30-17.30, and stocks basic foods and drinks, snacks and gas supplies, fishing licences, cycle passes for the canal towpath and local tourist information. Motorcaravan services are in the late arrivals parking area. The site is central for visiting many places of interest including the stone circles at Stonehenge and Avebury. A more unusual outing is to Sandridge Farm, renowned for its speciality bacons, hams and sausages. The farm shop is open from 9-5 daily, and from May to Sept. visitors can see the pigs and piglets (admission free - wellies advisable). The Vale of Pewsey cycle route can be accessed from the canal towpath to the east of Devizes, and runs for 41 miles between Great Bedwyn and Corsham. Museums in the area include Calne Motor Museum. Wiltshire has a large number of 'free' attractions including Arn Hill Nature Reserve, Barton Farm Country Park, Battlesbury Hill, Smallbrook Meadows and Southwick Country Park.

Charges 2000:
-- Per adult: £4.80-5.30; child £1.65; pitch fee (non-members) £4.30; electricity £1.60 - 2.35.
-- VAT included.
-- Credit Cards accepted.
Open:
All year.
Address:
Spout Lane, Seend, Melksham, Wiltshire SN12 6RN.
Tel:
(01380) 828839 (not after 8.00 pm).
Reservations:
Recommended for B.Hs and peak season. Contact site for details.

Directions: From Devizes take A361 westbound, and ½ mile before Seend village, take A365 towards Melksham. Cross canal bridge, take next left by 'Three Magpies' and the site entrance is on your right. Approaching from the M4 junction 17, use A350 to Melksham and A365 to the site. O.S.GR: ST 951619.

169 Longleat Caravan Club Site, Longleat, Warminster

Rural park in amazing situation for caravans, motorcaravans and trailer tents only.

What a magnificent situation in which to find a caravan park, amidst all the wonders of the Longleat Estate including the Elizabethan House, Safari Park, the collection of mazes (including the world's largest), not to mention Doctor Who and the Daleks and the Adventure castle! These are just some of the attractions to be found here to suit all ages amidst a beautiful rural parkland setting. Visitors can roam the woodlands (leaflets are available on a range of walks) and enjoy the views, watch the wildlife and marvel at the azaleas, bluebells, etc. according to the season or listen to the occupants of the Safari Park. The site itself, well managed by Caravan Club wardens, is situated in 10 acres of lightly wooded, level grassland within walking distance of the house and gardens. There are 150 spacious pitches, a few with gravel hardstanding for motorhomes, connected by circular tarmac roads and with 16A electricity available on all, including the late arrivals area. The centrally situated, heated toilet block is well equipped with curtained wash cubicles for ladies, non-slip bases to controllable showers and a vanity section with shelf, mirrors and hairdryers. A separate laundry room, covered dishwashing, chemical toilet disposal and motorcaravan service point are provided. Water points and re-cycling bins are neatly walled with low night lighting. Children's play area and dogs welcome on a lead. The office is manned 8.30 am - 6 pm and stocks basic food items. Papers can be ordered, gas is available and a nice touch is a paperback exchange library. A fresh fruit and vegetable van drives around the site and a fish and chip van calls. A separate wooden chalet houses tourist information but the wardens will help you to get the best out of your stay at Longleat.

Charges 2000:
-- Per pitch £6.00 - £7.00; adult £2.60 - £4.00; child (5-16 yrs) £1.10 - £1.20; electricity £1.45 - £2.20; extra car, boat or trailer £1.00.
Open:
31 March - 30 October.
Address:
Warminster, Wiltshire BA12 7NL.
Tel:
(01985) 844663.
FAX: (01985) 844964.
Reservations:
Advisable for B.Hs and school holidays and made with £5 deposit.

Directions: The main entrance to Longleat which caravans must use is signed from the A362 Frome - Warminster road near to where it joins the A36 Warminster bypass. Turn into the estate and follow Longleat House route through the toll booths for 2 miles then follow caravan club signs for 1 mile. There are shorter ways to leave the site. O.S.GR: ST806434.

Wiltshire / West Dorset

167 Alderbury Caravan and Camping Park, Whaddon, nr. Salisbury

Village touring park, convenient for visiting Salisbury and the New Forest.

At the southern end of Alderbury/Whaddon village, this recently developed park is on level ground, with a gravel access road to the 39 numbered pitches; 26 have electricity (16A). The park has some mature trees for shade, plus younger trees, shrubs and flowers. Developments continue with 7 hardstandings, extra chemical disposal and waste water points, site lighting, more shrubs and trees, and a rally field. The centrally located toilet block is practical, clean and well maintained. It provides hot showers in cubicles with curtain and seat, washbasins set in vanity units, WCs, a separate unit for disabled visitors, a dishwashing sink also in a separate room and chemical disposal. Hot water is free throughout and there are water points around the site. The village shop and post office, a pub serving meals, public phone and a bus stop are within easy level walking distance of the entrance. There are hourly bus services to Salisbury, Southampton and Romsey. Good coarse fishing is available within 1 mile and the country lanes around the area are good for cycling and walking. Fishing 1 mile, bicycle hire 3 miles, riding 2 miles, golf 5 miles. Salisbury Museum, the Cathedral and its Close are all well worth a visit. There is some road noise, most noticeable at the far end of the park.

Charges 2000:
-- Per unit incl. 2 adults £7.50; extra adult £2.00; child (under 14 yrs) £1.00; awning £1.00; electricity £1.90.
-- No credit cards.
-- VAT included.
Open:
All year.
Address:
Southampton Road, Whaddon, Salisbury, Wiltshire SP5 3HB.
Tel:
(01722) 710125.
Reservations:
Write or phone park for details.

Directions: From Salisbury take A36 towards Southampton and, after 3 miles (at far end of the dual carriageway section), turn left at sign to Alderbury and Whaddon, then right, over bridge, and left for park entrance. From Southampton on A36 towards Salisbury, continue past the A27 (Romsey) junction and over Pepperbox Hill. At end of downhill straight, left onto slip road marked Alderbury, park is signed. O.S.GR: SU198263.

181 Newlands Caravan Park, Charmouth, nr. Lyme Regis

Family park with wide range of facilities including indoor and outdoor pools.

This family owned park, run with care, occupies a prominent position beside the road into Charmouth village with marvellous views southwards to the hills across the valley. By nature of the terrain the pitches, in two fields, are terraced to provide over 200 well spaced for touring units, some seasonal, and 86 caravan holiday homes, 50 for hire. The tenting field of mainly sloping grass also has super views towards the sea and Lyme Regis. Electric hook ups (10A) are provided on 144 pitches and 30 of these have hardstanding, water and waste water. Six of these are special 'Millennium' pitches with a washing machine and dryer for individual use. Other accommodation on the park includes 9 new, smart pine lodges, 15 apartments and 12 motel rooms (double and family). The lower toilet block is modern and light with roomy showers, WCs and vanity style washbasins, and has an adjoining washing up area. The other block is traditional in design with rather psychedelic tiles, but it is heated, clean, neat and tidy. A laundry room adjoins, plus dishwashing sinks (under cover) and two chemical disposal points. Reception, the well stocked shop (March-Nov), a licensed club bar (limited hours Nov - March), restaurant (open evenings 6-9 pm. March - Nov) including takeaway, and swimming pools are located in a modern building to one side of the wide tarmac entrance. Membership of the club is automatic and the bar is open every evening and lunch times to suit. A range of family entertainment includes a children's club during school holidays with Dino Dan (the dinosaur). Out of the main season opening hours of the various facilities may vary. A 9 pin bowling alley can be hired at £5 per half hour. The smaller indoor pool and jacuzzi is open all year (limited hours Nov - March). The adjacent outdoor pool and paddling pool is walled, paved and sheltered and the outside entrance is key coded; neither are supervised. Both pools are heated, the indoor one is charged for. A super large children's play area in the field below the tenting field is open dawn to dusk! I was tempted to try the maypole swing and bobsleigh ride. This is a comfortable site for families with the beach and village within easy walking distance and for those who enjoy some evening and family activity. Fishing 1 mile, riding 3 miles, golf 2 miles. Charmouth is also known for its fossil finds and its connection with Jane Austen. Bellamy silver.

Charges 2000:
-- Per pitch incl. up to 6 persons and awning £8.00 - £17.00, serviced pitch £16.00 - £24.00; extra pup tent £3.00; dog (max. 2) £1.00; electricity £2.00.
-- Only one van or tent per pitch.
-- VAT included.
-- Credit cards accepted.
Open:
All year.
Address:
Charmouth, Dorset DT6 6RB.
Tel:
(01297) 560259.
FAX: (01297) 560787.
E-mail: enq@ newlandsholidays.co.uk.
Reservations:
Made with £30 deposit per week.

`Camping Cheque'

see colour advert between pages 64/65

Directions: Approaching from Bridport leave A35 at first sign for Charmouth at start of the bypass and site almost directly on your left. O.S.GR: SY373935.

176 Wood Farm Caravan Park, Charmouth, nr. Lyme Regis

Excellent family run park maintained to a high standard for all units, with indoor pool.

Wood Farm is a very well kept park on the western side of Charmouth beside the A35 (some road noise may be expected), and only a mile or two from Lyme Regis and its beaches. Part of the Caravan Club's 'managed under contract' scheme (non-members are also very welcome). On sloping, well landscaped ground, it has open views across the countryside. There are 216 pitches for touring units of which 180 are neat, level all-weather pitches with hardstanding, electricity (10A) and TV connections, and provision for awnings. These are divided by neat, box-like leylandii hedging which has almost become a feature of the park. Water hook-ups are also available. One grassy terraced field takes about 25 tents and there are 80 caravan holiday homes in their own areas. American motorhomes are not accepted. Four good, modern toilet blocks can be heated and provide free hot water to washbasins (some in curtained cubicles for ladies), well equipped, pre-set hot showers and covered dishwashing sinks. The lower block is excellent, providing roomy, well equipped showers, wash cubicles, toilets and en-suite facilities for disabled people. Chemical disposal facilities are in each block. One block has a baby care unit and laundry sinks with a spin dryer. All visitors are offered temporary membership to the good heated indoor swimming pool (27 x 54 ft.) on payment of £1.50 per session. A recreation hall provides a snooker room and family games area with table tennis, also an outdoor tennis court. Laundry room by the pool, shop by reception, and a children's play field (equipment on safety surface). Bikes can be ridden on site, but helmets must be worn. A fish and chip van opens 2-4 times a week (acc. to season). Dogs are accepted and there is an enclosed 2 acre dog field. A small coarse fishing lake (carp, rudd, roach, tench) is adjacent - day and weekly tickets (rod licence required, also available from park). Golf 1 mile, beaches and shops ¾ and 2 miles. Motorcaravan service point. Caravan holiday homes to rent and two bed S.C. accommodation for visitors with disabilities. A member of the Best of British group. Bellamy silver.

Charges 2000:
-- Per unit incl. side awning £1.50 - £5.50; adult £3.25 - £4.00; child (5-16 yrs) £1.20; electricity (10A) £2.00 - £2.25; mains water pitch £1.00; dog, extra car, trailer or pup tent £1.00.
-- Special senior citizens low season discounts.
-- Credit cards accepted.
-- VAT included.

Open:
30 March - 27 October.

Address:
Axminster Road, Charmouth, Dorset DT6 6BT.

Tel:
(01297) 560697. FAX: as phone. E-mail: holidays@ woodfarm.co.uk.

Reservations:
Made with £30 deposit (non-returnable), min. 5 nights in high season, 3 nights other times.

Directions: Park is ½ mile west of Charmouth village with access near round-about at junction of A35 with A3052 (Lyme Regis) road. O.S.GR: SY356940.

173 Monkton Wylde Farm Touring Caravan Park, nr. Charmouth

Small, relaxed, family run park attached to a working farm.

Opened in 1991 by Simon and Joanna Kewley as part of a working sheep farm, Monkton Wylde is maturing nicely. Planting of flowering shrubs and trees continues (hydrangea and lavender) making an attractive, peaceful park. A wood-land walk has been created in 80 acres of the beautiful countryside surrounding the park. An abundance of mature trees around the perimeter provide shade and plenty of space between the 60 pitches gives a feeling of spaciousness. Most pitches have 16A electricity and around 25 have hardstanding. The modern, well maintained sanitary block has a fully equipped family room including baby changing facilities and is also accessible by wheelchair. Individual showers with folding screen are very spacious, there are vanity style washbasins and all hot water is free. A small laundry has a washing machine and tumble dryer, washing up is under cover and chemical disposal facilities are provided. On site facilities are limited but an area at the top of the park has been turned into a children's play area, with a good area for ball games, climbing frame, trampoline, etc. Bread, milk and papers may be obtained in the main season. There is no reception as such, however a wooden chalet near the entrance provides information regarding pitch vacancies and the owners or the resident wardens (high season) are never far away. The gate is locked at 11 pm. A separate paddock along the lane has been set aside as a dog walk. Caravan storage available. Fishing or riding 2 miles, bicycle hire, golf and boat launching 3 miles. Shops and local pubs are within a mile and Charmouth and Lyme Regis are only 3 miles (buses leave from just along the road to both towns). A separate new site has been developed next to the existing park for Camping and Caravanning Club members, managed by the Club.

Charges 2001:
-- Per unit incl. 2 adults £6.50 - £11.50; extra adult £1.50; child (5-16 yrs) 50p - £1.00; electricity £2.00; dog free - 75p; pup tent free - £1.00; no extra charge for awnings, 2nd car, boats or visitors.
-- No credit cards.
-- VAT included.

Open:
26 March - 31 October.

Address:
Monkton Wylde Farm, Charmouth, Dorset DT6 6DB.

Tel:
(01297) 34525. Warden (May - Sept) (01297) 631131. FAX: (01297) 33594.

Reservations:
Made with deposit of £3 per night booked.

Directions: Park is signed on A35 between Charmouth and Axminster, approx. 1½ miles west of Charmouth. Turn right at Greenway Head (B3165 signed Marshwood) and park is 600 yds on the left past new Club site. Don't go to Monkton Wylde hamlet - the road is very steep. O.S.GR: SY329966.

Dorset

174 Golden Cap Holiday Park, Chideock, nr. Bridport

Good beach-side touring park with holiday caravans in beautiful rural situation.

Golden Cap, named after the adjacent highest cliff in southern England which overlooks Lyme Bay, is only 150 yards from a shingle beach at Seatown and is surrounded by National Trust countryside and the Heritage Coastline. The park is arranged over several fields on the valley floor, sloping down gently towards the sea. It is in two main areas, having once been two parks, each separated into fields with marvellous views around and providing 108 tourist pitches, all with electricity and 28 with hardstandings with drainaway, electricity and gravelled awning area, and an extra sloping tent field for peak season (torch useful). There are 211 caravan holiday homes in their own areas. American motorhomes are not accepted. The main toilet block is modern and of very good quality, with free hot water in the washbasins and spacious shower cubicles (some with toilet and washbasin), good facilities for visitors with disabilities (Radar key) and a baby care room. There are two other smaller blocks around the park, plus a laundry room, motorcaravan service point and chemical disposal facilities. Gas is available. Useful and well stocked shop (8 am - 6 pm, or 9 pm in high season) and a takeaway service each evening in peak season. Caravan sales information and tourist information rooms. A pub with food service is close. The most attractive indoor swimming pool at Highlands End (under the same ownership) is 3 miles away and open for campers on payment. Public telephone. Dogs are accepted (poop-scoops provided). Beaches, sea fishing, boat launching, riding, fossil hunting and good walks are near, with access to the coastal path. A well run park and a member of the Best of British group. Bellamy gold.

Directions: Turn off A35 road at Chideock, (a bigger village with shops and restaurants) 3 miles west of Bridport, at sign to Seatown opposite church. Park is less than 1 mile down narrow lane. O.S.GR: SY423919.

Charges 2001:
-- Per unit incl. 2 persons and awning £8.00 - £12.50; extra adult £2.75 - £3.00; child (4-17 yrs) £1.25 - £1.50; dog £1.25 - £1.50; extra car £1.00; electricity £1.75 - £2.00; all service pitch (hardstanding, water and drainage, excl. electricity) plus £1.50.
-- VAT included.
-- Credit cards accepted.

Open:
20 March - 1 November.

Address:
Park: Seatown, Chideock, nr. Bridport; Booking: West Dorset Leisure Holidays, Eype, Bridport, Dorset DT6 6AR.

Tel:
(01308) 422139.
FAX: (01308) 425672.
E-mail: highlands
@wdlh.co.uk.

Reservations:
Essential in high season and made with £20 deposit (min. 4 days in high season).

175 Highlands End Farm Holiday Park, Eype, nr. Bridport

Good, well kept park on cliffs by sea, with holiday caravan and touring sections.

On slightly sloping ground with superb open views, both coastal and inland, Highlands End is quietly situated on the Dorset Heritage Coastline. With access to the coastal path, a path in front of the park runs along the cliff top and then leads down to a shingle beach a little further along. There are 180 caravan holiday homes which are mostly privately occupied but 17 are for letting. The 195 touring pitches are in two areas nearest to the sea - one has to travel through the holiday homes to reach them. All have electricity (10A) and 45 also offer water, drainage, hardstanding and a gravel awning area. A further area is used for tents in high season. The two toilet blocks near the tourist sections are excellent and well maintained (like the rest of the park) and can be heated. They provide washbasins (some in cubicles with toilets), large, comfortable, free hot showers, covered washing-up sinks and a dishwashing room. There is a laundry room, en-suite facilities for disabled visitors, a baby care room and chemical disposal points, plus water points around and a motorcaravan service point. A modern, attractive building houses a lounge bar, good value restaurant with takeaway facility, family room and games room (open Spr. B.H.- late Sept.) with some musical evenings in high season. The park's amenities include an excellent, air-conditioned indoor heated swimming pool with attendant (20 x 9 m. and charged £2 per session, £1 for children), a gym room, sun beds, steam room and sauna, a tennis court (all charged), tourist information room, and a good children's adventure playground. A well stocked shop is beside reception (opening times vary with the season), including gas supplies. Public phones. The owners have a long time interest in the fire brigade and an historic fire engine (1936 Leyland Pump Escape) along with memorabilia make an interesting display in the bar. Dogs are accepted (poop-scoops provided). The park was used to film scenes for Nick Berry's TV series based on nearby West Bay harbour. A well run park and a member of the Best of British group. Bellamy silver.

Directions: Follow Bridport bypass on A35 around the town and park is signed to south (Eype turning), down narrow lane. O.S.GR: SY452914.

Charges 2001:
-- Per unit incl. 2 persons and awning £8.00 - £12.50; extra adult £2.75 - £3.00; child (4-17 yrs) £1.25 - £1.50; dog £1.25 - £1.50; extra car £1.00; electricity £1.75 - £2.00; all service pitch (hardstanding, water and drainage, excl. electricity) plus £1.50.
-- VAT included.
-- Credit cards accepted.

Open:
20 March - 1 November.

Address:
West Dorset Leisure Holidays, Eype, nr. Bridport, Dorset DT6 6AR.

Tel:
(01308) 422139.
FAX: (01308) 425672.
E-mail: highlands
@wdlh.co.uk.

Reservations:
Essential in high season and made with £20 deposit (min. 4 days in high season).

see colour advert between pages 64/65

178 Freshwater Beach Holiday Park, Burton Bradstock, Bridport

Busy holiday and touring park with direct access to private beach.

Family run parks for families with direct access to a beach are rare in Britain and this one has the added advantage of being in beautiful coastal countryside in West Dorset. It is an ideal situation to explore the 'Hidden County' and the resort of Weymouth (17 miles) and is next to the sea and a beach of fine pebbles, sheltered from the wind by pebble banks. The River Bride edges the park and joins the sea here. Approached by a fairly steep access road, the park itself is on level, open ground. The 500 plus touring pitches, over 300 with 10A electricity, are on an open, undulating grass field connected by tarmac or hard-core roads. Caravan pitches (10 x 11 m.) are now marked, evenly spaced in lines. Some tent pitches are in the main field, with others well spaced around the edge of a sloping extra field. In separate areas there are 230 caravan holiday homes, plus 60 for hire. This lively holiday park has an extensive range of facilities which include a good value licensed restaurant (weekends only in late season; closed Mondays all season) and three bars with an evening entertainment programme in season. A range of daytime entertainment caters for all ages - don't miss the donkey derby! Also a good value supermarket and takeaway, plus a launderette. Activities include a heated and supervised outdoor swimming pool and children's pool (15/5-30/10) with swimming and diving lessons available, an adventure play area, pets corner, bicycle hire and pony trekking (own stables on site). A golf course is adjacent, fishing is possible from the Chesil Bank and there is a good connection to footpaths to the attractive, thatched village of Burton Bradstock or West Bay. Sanitary facilities are in two fully refurbished blocks, plus another with wash-basins and toilets only, all with free hot water. They are a good provision for a busy beach park. The main blocks have facilities for disabled people (Radar key), chemical disposal and a baby care room (key system), and cleaning and mainte-nance seem good. Laundry and washing up sinks cope well at peak times. The overall impression is of a large, busy holiday park with a friendly reception and happy atmosphere. Bellamy bronze.

Directions: Park is immediately west of the village of Burton Bradstock, on the Weymouth - Bridport coast road (B3157). O.S.GR: SY980898.

Charges 2000:
-- Per unit incl. up to 6 persons, car and awning £8.50 - £19.00; extra person £2.00; electricity £2.00; small tent incl. 2 persons walking or cycling £6.50 - £11.50; dog £2.50; extra car or boat £2.00.
-- Single sex groups not admitted.
-- VAT included.
-- Credit cards accepted.
Open:
19 March - 7 November.
Address:
Burton Bradstock,
nr. Bridport,
Dorset DT6 4PT.
Tel:
(01308) 897317.
FAX: (01308) 897336.
E-mail: enquiries
@fbhp.co.uk.
Reservations:
Made for min. 1 week with £20 deposit p/week, plus £1 fee. Short break reservations available - ring for details.

see colour advert
between pages 64/65

177 Binghams Farm Touring Caravan Park, Melplash, nr. Bridport

Small, purpose built park in rural Brit Valley location, open all year for adults only.

Binghams has a pleasant situation two miles from the market town of Bridport, with views seaward towards West Bay and inland across Beaminster Downs and Pilsdon Hill. The park provides an area of individual pitches with 10A electricity and over 40 hardstandings, nicely landscaped with shrubs and trees growing between the pitches, plus an open sloping field overlooking the valley with 20 electric hook-ups. The good heated toilet block, reception and games room (with table tennis) have been sympathetically converted from the original farm buildings with an upstairs lounge bar, games room, table tennis and pool table. The toilet blocks, with under floor heating for winter use and free hot water, provide well fitted, tiled, curtained showers, vanity style washbasins, hairdryers and a separate, fully equipped room for the less able with ramped access. There is a laundry room and a chemical disposal point, with gas available. The entrance to the park is neatly tarmaced and resident peacocks, ducks and chickens provide interest. Public telephone. A cottage has been converted into two flats to let. Winter caravan storage. Sea fishing and golf 3 miles, bicycle hire and riding 5 miles. A path has been provided to the river which links with the main footpaths for Bridport (20 minutes) or local hostelries. Limited bus service on the main road. The Brit Valley is an unspoilt area of West Dorset with an ancient heritage and coastal West Bay is only a couple of miles.

Directions: At main roundabout on A35 road, on east side of Bridport, take A3066 towards Beaminster. Watch for site entrance after approx. 2 miles on the left. O.S.GR: SY482963.

Charges 2001:
-- Per pitch incl. 2 persons and awning £8.00 - £12.00; extra adult £2.00; dog £1.00; electricity (10A) £2.00.
-- Adults only.
-- No credit cards.
-- VAT included.
Open:
All year.
Address:
Melplash,
nr. Bridport,
Dorset DT6 3TT.
Tel:
(01308) 488234.
FAX: as phone.
E-mail: binghamsfarm
@hotmail.com.
Reservations:
Made with £25 non-returnable deposit per week or part.

Dorset

180 East Fleet Farm Touring Park, Chickerell, Weymouth

Genuine touring park, attractively situated on the coast by the Fleet.

East Fleet Farm has a marvellous situation on part level, part gently sloping meadows leading to the shores of the Fleet, with views across to the famous Chesil Bank with the sea beyond. The Fleet is a lagoon renowned for its wildlife and popular with bird watchers. The park itself has been developed within the confines of a 300-acre working dairy and arable farm and is maturing nicely as bushes and trees grow. The 270 pitches are a comfortable size so there is no feeling of crowding. Of these, 97 are level and marked with 10A electricity, 25 also having hardstanding. The central sanitary block is built in natural stone and provides adequate rather than luxurious facilities with washbasins, coin-operated showers (one heated), shaver points, hairdryers, under cover washing up (H&C) and fully equipped laundry room with a self-contained unit for disabled people off it. Extra toilets and a bathroom are beside the bar. This is in a converted barn and has a terrace complete with views over the Fleet (high season and B.Hs). It also provides bar meals and a games room with pool table. Reception plus shop with basic groceries, bread, papers and gas, etc. opens longer in high season. A public phone and children's play area complete the provision but, remember, elsewhere this is a working farm. The busy resort of Weymouth with its safe bathing beaches and watersports facilities is only 3 miles (bicycle hire and boat launching possible). Riding or golf 2 miles. Bus service from the top of the lane (approx. ½ mile). Abbotsbury Swannery and Gardens are near. Bellamy silver.

Directions: Park is signed from B3157 Weymouth - Bridport road, 2 miles west of Weymouth. The narrow, uneven approach road is by the army camp on the southern side of the B3157. O.S.GR: SY639798.

Charges guide:
-- Per unit incl. 2 persons £4.50 - £10.00; extra adult £1.00 - £2.50; child (5-16 yrs) 25p - 50p; awning free - £1.75; extra car, large boat £2.50; dog 25p - 75p; electricity (10A) £1.75 - £2.25.
-- Senior citizen discount in June (10%).
-- VAT included.
-- Credit cards accepted.
Open:
15 March - 31 October.
Address:
Chickerell,
Weymouth,
Dorset DT3 4DW.
Tel:
(01305) 785768.
E-mail: camping@ eastfleet.abel.co.uk
Reservations:
Write with £20 deposit.

East Fleet Farm
Touring Park
Chickerell, Weymouth Tel: (01305) 785768
www.eastfleet.co.uk

★★★
TOURING PARK

- ● Electric Hook-ups
- ● Showers
- ● Bathroom
- ● H/C Water
- ● Shop

Peaceful and spacious park on the shores of the Fleet overlooking Chesil Bank and the sea, in an area of outstanding natural beauty
Telephone for brochure

- ● 'Old Barn' family bar & restaurant
- ● Games Room
- ● Children's Play Area
- ● Toilets
- ● Laundry

201 Sandyholme Holiday Park, Owermoigne, nr. Dorchester

Tranquil, family run park near pretty Dorset village.

Sandyholme is a peaceful haven providing 44 holiday homes (privately owned or to hire) and 40 pitches for touring units on level, short grass fields with one corner lightly wooded. The next door field is operated by a local farmer on a 28 day licence with use of the park's facilities (extra facilities opened in high season ensure no problems). Two toilet blocks, although of older design, are bright and well maintained, with vanity style washbasins, pre-set showers (20p) and laundry facilities in both, dishwashing sinks (10p) and chemical disposal. The Holme Club (free membership) is open every evening at B.Hs during April and May, then mid-July to mid Sept. It has a cosy bar and patio, and a good bar menu. Games room with pool table and amusement machines. The shop/reception stocks basic necessities including papers and gas. A good, fenced, safe-based adventure play area is next to a rather special duck pond with an amazing variety of ducks from all over the world. There is a pleasant walk with seats around the pond (an electric fence keeps the foxes at bay!) Fishing is available on an adjacent farm, bicycle hire or golf 5 miles, riding 6 miles. There are walks and cycling direct from the site or in Puddletown and Wareham Forests, or along the coastal path. Lulworth Cove and Durdle Door are near. Bellamy silver.

Directions: On A352 Wareham - Dorchester road going west, watch for short dual carriageway before Weymouth roundabout. Turn north through Owermoigne village and park is on the left (signed) in approx. ¼ mile. O.S.GR: SY768863.

Charges 2000:
-- Per pitch incl. all persons £6.50 - £12.00; dog £1.00 p/n or £5 p/w; electricity £2.00.
-- Credit cards accepted.
-- VAT included.
Open:
Easter/1April - 31 Oct.
Address:
Moreton Road,
Owermoigne,
Dorchester DT2 8HZ.
Tel:
(01305) 852677.
FAX: (01305) 854677.
Reservations:
Made with £20 deposit with SAE for receipt.

Alan Rogers' Discount

Less 50p p/night
-3 nights or more

Dorset

Southern Tourist Board

East Dorset, Hampshire, Isle of Wight, South Wiltshire, Oxfordshire, Berkshire and Buckinghamshire

40 Chamberlayne Road, Eastleigh, Hampshire SO50 5JH
Tel: 023 8062 5505 Fax: 023 8062 0010
E-mail: stbinfo@bta.org.uk
Internet: http://www.visitbritain.com/southern-england

The Southern Tourist Board covers three distinctive areas:

The **South Coast** comprises Weymouth and Portland with its safe sandy beach and the Isle of Portland joined to the mainland by the unique Chesil beach, and Swanage with the famous Studland beach and Purbeck hills. The cosmopolitan resort of Bournemouth, with its seven miles of golden sand, and the New Forest renowned for its trees and ponies, with its famous yachting havens of Lymington and Buckler's Hard. The Isle of Wight is just a short ferry trip across the Solent and offers a wealth of activities for all ages with a mild and sunny climate. Day trips to France are possible from Portsmouth, the flagship of Maritime England and now the home of the 'Mary Rose', also Southampton, with its maritime connections including the 'Titanic' and the International Boat Show.

Rural **Southern England** comprises green rolling hills and scenic wooded valleys covering North and West Wiltshire, parts of Dorset, Hampshire, Kennet and Avon Canal country and the New Forest and the Test Valley. Worthy of mention is the beautiful medieval city of Salisbury with its inspirational Cathedral and Close, and Winchester, ancient capital of the Kingdom of Wessex.

Thames and Chilterns, dominated by the River Thames, its tributaries and the Chiltern Hills offers a mix of internationally famous cities and sporting events, royal pomp and traditional English village life. Buckinghamshire inspired John Betjeman and John Milton finished 'Paradise Lost' in his cottage at Chalfont St. Giles. Benjamin Disraeli, the 19th Century Prime Minister came from near High Wycombe and the scenic village of Great Missenden was home to the great children's story teller Roald Dahl. The Oxfordshire Cotswolds has picturesque villages, the regal splendour of Blenheim Palace and market towns such as Chipping Norton. Berkshire is within 50 miles of London and is well known for its racing connections, and Royal connections at Windsor and Eton.

202 Ulwell Cottage Caravan Park, Ulwell, Swanage

Family run holiday park with indoor pool and wide range of facilities for families.

Nestling under the Purbeck Hills in this unique corner of Dorset on the edge of Swanage, Ulwell Cottage provides for a range of needs. A good proportion of the park is taken by caravan holiday homes (140), but an attractive, undulating area accessed by tarmac roads is given over to 77 numbered touring pitches, with 68 electric hook-ups (16A) and 18 hardstandings, 8 of which are serviced. The mixture of level and sloping pitches, interspersed with trees and shrubs, is quite pretty. The sanitary block serving the touring section is modern and cheerful with bright yellow doors, and can be heated. It is supplemented by an older block in the holiday home section. They are well equipped, with vanity style wash-basins, pre-set showers with dividers, laundry room and baby washing sinks in the lower block, dishwashing under cover and chemical disposal. The colourful entrance area is home to the Village Inn with a courtyard adjoining the heated, supervised indoor pool complex (both open all year and open to the public), well stocked shop for gas, etc. (Easter - mid-Sept) and modern reception. The inn provides bar snacks and a restaurant with a family room. Takeaway (June-Sept). Amusement arcade, playing fields and play areas with a long slide and boat. Public telephone. Bicycle hire or riding 2 miles, fishing 1 mile, golf 1 mile. The hill above the touring area, Nine Barrow Down, is a Site of Special Scientific Interest for butterflies overlooking Round Down. It is possible to walk to Corfe Castle this way. With Brownsea Island, Studland Bay, Corfe village and the Swanage Railway, Ulwell Cottage makes a marvellous centre for holidays. Bellamy silver.

Directions: From A351 Wareham - Swanage road, turn on B3351 Studland road just before Corfe Castle, follow signs to right for Swanage and drop down to Ulwell. O.S.GR: SZ019809.

Charges 2000:
-- Per unit incl. up to 6 persons £12.00 - £23.00, with electricity £12.00 - £25.00, fully serviced with hardstanding £13.50 - £26.50; extra tent, car or boat £1.50.
-- Less £2.00 for 2 people only, less £1.00 for 3.
-- VAT included.
-- Credit cards accepted.

Open:
All year except 8 Jan - 28 Feb.

Address:
Ulwell, Swanage, Dorset BH19 3DG.

Tel:
(01929) 422823.
FAX: (01929) 421500.
E-mail: enq@ulwell cottagepark.co.uk.

Reservations:
Made with 25% deposit; Sat.- Sat. only in high season.

see colour advert between pages 64/65

71

203 Wareham Forest Tourist Park, nr. Wareham

see colour advert
between pages 64/65

Well run park in forest setting with swimming pool.

A peacefully located, spacious park in an unspoilt corner of Dorset, this site becomes very busy in high season. Developed to high standards by the present owners, it provides formal pitching, with or without hardstanding, for caravans or natural pitches for tents in pine wood or open field. Drainage appears satisfactory. The setting in Wareham Forest is attractive offering space for 200 units, 102 with hardstanding and all with electricity. There are 8 luxury pitches on hardstanding with water, drainage, TV aerial, dustbin and light (available 1/3-31/10 only). A cafeteria for breakfasts, etc. (open in the main season) looks out over a patio-terrace onto the free, open-air swimming pool, which can be heated (60 x 20 ft; open all day in peak season), with a surrounding grass sunbathing area. There is a small shop with off-licence and gas (limited hours) and a busy games room with video machines next door. The two well maintained toilet blocks are spacious and of a good standard and have some washbasins in cubicles for ladies with free hot water, plus adjustable showers on payment. The block used in the winter months is centrally heated. There are facilities for disabled people, well equipped laundry rooms, deep sinks for washing up (free hot water), chemical disposal and a motor-caravan service point. A large children's adventure play area is on sand and grass. Forest walks. Fishing 5 miles, bicycle hire or golf 3 miles, riding 8 miles. In high season a bus service to and from Wareham leaves the site six times daily. The park is well situated to explore the Dorset coast and Thomas Hardy country. All year caravan storage. Entrance closed 11 pm. - 7 am. Resident wardens on site.

Directions: Park is north of Wareham between Wareham and Bere Regis, located off the A35 road. O.S.GR: SY899903.

Charges 2000:
-- Per pitch: standard £3.50 - £6.00, serviced £6.00 - £8.00; adult £1.80
- £3.00; child (2-14 yrs) £1.00 - £2.00; awning, boat, trailer, extra car 50p - £1.00; dog 50p - £1.50; electricity £2.00 - £2.25.
-- Couples/families only.
-- Discount for OAPs in low season.
-- VAT included.
-- Credit cards accepted.
Open:
All year.
Address:
North Trigon, Wareham, Dorset BH20 7NZ.
Tel/Fax:
(01929) 551393.
E-mail: holiday@ wareham-forest.co.uk.
Reservations:
Made with £25 non-returnable deposit and £2 admin. fee, balance 28 days before arrival.

WAREHAM FOREST TOURIST PARK

Resident owners Peter and Pam Savage

Enjoy the peace and tranquillity of Wareham Forest, developed to the highest standards and comparable with the best in Europe
HEATED SWIMMING POOL ✦ CHILDREN'S POOL ✦ Fully serviced pitches
✦ Children's adventure playground ✦ Indoor games room ✦ Shop ✦ Off Sales ✦ Snackbar
✦ Takeaway foods ✦ Disabled facilities ✦ Discount rates for S/Cits early and late season
All year Storage Facilities ✦ Direct access to forest walks

WAREHAM FOREST TOURIST PARK

Situated mid-way between Wareham and Bere Regis (off A35), an ideal base for exploring this unspoilt corner of Dorset, with over 60 miles of coastline offering sandy beaches and sheltered coves.

OPEN ALL YEAR   CREDIT CARDS ACCEPTED

For further details and free coloured brochure write or phone: Peter & Pam Savage, Wareham Forest Tourist Park, North Trigon, Wareham, Dorset BH20 7NZ
Tel/Fax: (01929) 551393   www.wareham-forest.co.uk   holiday@wareham-forest.co.uk

---

204 Manor Farm Caravan Park, Wareham

Small, rural park near the Purbecks beside a working farm.

David and Gillian Topp own and carefully run this small, simple park which is set in a hedged, level field, now semi-broken up by newly planted evergreens. It provides 50 level, well spaced pitches, 30 for touring units, with 43 electrical connections (16A), on neatly cut grass. The toilet block (key system) is at the top of the field and is timber clad, adequate inside with all necessary facilities and kept very clean. Hot showers (no divider) are metered (20p). A toilet for disabled people is in the men's room, and there is a sink for washing up and one for laundry with spin dryer (all 20p), plus chemical disposal facilities. An 'original' recycling point is to be found next door for rubbish. An ice pack service and gas exchange are provided and there is a site shop. Sturdy children's play unit. East Stoke village has a pub, Wool is 2 miles with a pub and shops, Wareham and Swanage are near. Fishing, bicycle hire, boat launching, riding all 3 miles, golf 4 miles. Public telephone. Caravan storage. Dogs are accepted at the discretion of the owner.

Directions: Off A352 Wareham - Wool road, turn into lane by church, over manned level crossing and park is ½ mile on right. From B3070 turn right signed East Stoke, then right signed Manor Farm and site is on left. O.S.GR: SY872867.

Charges 2000:
-- Per unit incl. 2 persons £7.50 - £9.50; extra adult £2.00; child (3-13 yrs) £1.20; dog £1.25; electricity (16A) £2.10.
-- No groups, singles, motorcycles or rallies.
-- No credit cards.
Open:
April - 30 September.
Address:
1 Manor Farm Cottage, East Stoke, Wareham, Dorset BH20 6AW.
Tel:
(01929) 462870.
Reservations:
Made with £20 deposit.

205 Rowlands-Wait Touring Park, Bere Regis

Pretty, rural site with good facilities and views.

Bernard and Linda Hammick have worked hard to make Rowlands-Wait into a most attractive park catering for all types of humans and units! The top of the park, edged by mature woods (full of bluebells in spring) is a haven for tents (and squirrels) with marvellous views and providing 30 places in three descending fields. The rest of the park is a little more formal, and nearer to the central toilet block, but most pitches back on to hedging or trees and they are generally level. The toilet block is purpose built and well equipped, with free hot water except for the showers (10p, 3-4 minutes). There is a laundry room, covered dishwashing area, recycling bins and chemical disposal. Reception and a new shop (high season) provide milk, papers and basic essentials and a freezer for ice packs. The village, a 10 minute walk, has shops, two pubs, etc. plus a bus service for Dorchester and Poole. A play area for little ones with miniature assault course and castle is well placed near reception and there is a games room with pool table, table tennis and table football behind the sanitary block and crazy golf. Public phone. Bring your own bikes or bicycle hire can be arranged and there are many walks available from the park and information on wildlife. A torch is useful. Fishing 5 miles, golf 3 miles, riding 9 miles. A warm welcome awaits, particularly for those new to camping and caravanning. A reader reports the park as "very friendly and relaxed, with few rules". The park takes bookings for groups or for rallies all year. No charge is made for dogs in winter. A member of the Country-side Discovery group. Bellamy gold.

Directions: Park is south of Bere Regis, just off the road to Wool, well signed from A35/A31 roundabout. O.S.GR: SY842933.

Charges 2000:
-- Per unit incl. 2 persons £6.10 - £9.10; adult £1.40 - £1.90; child (under 16 yrs) 90p; awning, pup tent, extra car, boat or trailer free - £1.00; electricity (10A) £2.00; dog free - 60p.
-- Credit cards accepted.
Open:
16 March - 31 October, and winter by arrangement.
Address:
Rye Hill, Bere Regis, Dorset BH20 7LP.
Tel:
(01929) 472727.
FAX: as phone.
E-mail: ar@ rowlandswait.co.uk.
Reservations:
Made with £15 deposit per week.

Alan Rogers' Discount

 Less 50p p/night

206 Wilksworth Farm Caravan Park, Wimborne Minster

Spacious, quiet park with heated outdoor pool, for families.

Wilksworth Farm has a lovely rural situation just outside Wimborne and around 10 miles from the beaches between Poole and Bournemouth. With its duck pond at the entrance, it is a quiet, well designed park on good quality ground with fairly level grass and with some views. It takes 65 caravans (awning groundsheets up in daytime) and 25 tents mainly on grass but with some hardstandings. All pitches have electrical connections, 10 with water and drainage also. There are also some 77 privately owned and self contained caravan holiday homes. The central toilet block, converted from an original farm barn, is of good quality and well maintained (heated); it should be ample for these numbers. The ladies' part has been completely refurbished (the men's to be ready for 2001) and now provides a family bathroom and a shower room for disabled visitors, with under-floor heating throughout. Hot water is free to showers and washbasins. There are toilet facilities for disabled visitors, a shower/bath for children and a baby changing point, three covered, outside washing-up sinks and a laundry room with telephone. Amenities include a heated 40 x 20 ft. swimming pool (unsupervised, but fenced and gated, open May - Sept) with a small children's pool with paved surround, reception cum shop (basics only, limited hours, Easter - 30 Sept), gas supplies, barbecue, BMX track, golf practice net and two tennis courts, one full and one short course size. Football ground and excellent children's adventure section. Dog exercise paddock. Games room with table tennis, pool, some games machines, etc. Freezer for ice packs. A new coffee shop (unlicensed), attractively designed in keeping with the listed buildings, adjoins the games room, with a full menu and takeaway service (open weekends and B.Hs only outside the main season). Golf, fishing and riding 3 miles. Tower Park leisure and entertainment centre is 6 miles, Kingston Lacy (NT) 3 miles and Wimborne town centre (with its Minster) 1 mile. Winter caravan storage.

Directions: Park is 1 mile north of Wimborne, west off the B3078 road to Cranborne. O.S.GR: SU010019.

Charges guide:
-- Per pitch incl. 2 adults £6.00 - £12.00; child (3-16 yrs) £1.00 July, Aug. & Spr. B.H - other times one free with each adult; dog £1.00; extra adult £2.00; boat, extra car or pup tent £1.00; electricity £2.00; full services £1.00.
-- VAT included.
-- No credit cards.
Open:
1 March - 30 October.
Address:
Cranborne Road, Wimborne, Dorset BH21 4HW.
Tel:
(01202) 885467.
FAX: as phone.
Reservations:
Advised for July/Aug. and B.Hs. Made with payment in full at booking or £20 per week deposit; balance more than 28 days beforehand (min. 5 days at B.Hs).

Dorset

208 Merley Court Touring Park, Wimborne Minster

Quality family run park with excellent amenities and heated outdoor pool.

Merley Court must be one of the best examples today of a family touring park and is a credit to the Wright family. It is a well planned, attractively landscaped park, run with consistent care and attention to very high standards. The latest addition is the Leisure Garden, an historic walled garden (the Grade II listed walls date back to the 18th century) formerly part of the Merley House estate, the design and construction of which was overseen by John Nash. With flower collections, rock garden and sunken garden lovingly tended by Mrs Wright, it offers space for picnics and recreation facilities including croquet, crazy golf, petanque, badminton, volleyball and basketball or perhaps just an evening stroll.

The touring area has 160 pitches for all types of unit, all with 16A electricity, on clearly marked neat lawns interspersed with a variety of shrubs, palms and plants and the odd ornamental urn. This provision includes 11 neat all-service pitches with water, waste water and satellite TV connection. Some attractive tent pitches nestle in a small wooded valley with woodland walks and a dog walk, complete with the graves of past doggie friends. The three heated toilet blocks are well designed and of good quality, with free hot water in washbasins with shelf and mirror, two with pre-set well equipped showers. There are separate facilities for disabled visitors and for babies, excellent dishwashing and laundry facilities, chemical disposal and a motorcaravan service point. A large, well appointed indoor games room with pool tables and a family room adjoin the club complex with lounge bar, where meals are available (limited hours in low and mid seasons). The complex is well furnished and the family room opens out onto a spacious and attractive sheltered patio, which leads through to the paved, walled pool area. The pool (30 x 20 ft) with children's section is open mid May - Sept. Other amenities include an all-weather tennis court, outdoor table tennis and two good children's playgrounds. An enlarged shop in the Leisure Gardens carries gas and caravan accessories and there is a useful takeaway with café facility (all reduced hours in low season). A tourist information centre and two public phones complete the wide range of facilities, all well maintained. The park is only 6 miles from Poole, 8 from Bournemouth. Tower Park leisure and entertainment centre is nearby, Kingston Lacy House, Knoll Gardens and Brownsea Island are also near. Fishing, bicycle hire, riding and golf all within 5 miles. Dogs are not accepted in high season (14/7-31/8). Caravan storage (all year). Conference/meeting venue available in the Orangery within the Leisure Garden. A member of the Best of British group. Bellamy silver.

Directions: Park is signed at an exit from A31/A349 roundabout on the Wimborne bypass. O.S.GR: ST008984.

Charges 2000:
-- Per standard pitch (caravan, small tent or motorcaravan - no awning) incl. 2 persons £7.00 - £12.00, all service pitch (excl. electricity) £9.50 - £14.50; extra adult £3.00; child (3-13 yrs) £2.00; awning (no tent as well as awning) £1.00; dog (outside 14/7-31/8) £1.00; extra car/boat (on car park) £1.00; electricity (16A) £2.00.
-- Min. 5 nights Easter, 7 nights Spr B.H. and high season.
-- Less 10% for senior citizens in low season (excl. B.Hs).
-- Credit cards accepted.
-- VAT included.

Open:
All year except 8 Jan - 28 Feb.

Address:
Merley, Wimborne, nr. Poole, Dorset BH21 3AA.

Tel:
(01202) 881488.
FAX: (01202) 881484.
E-mail: holidays @merley-court.co.uk.

Reservations:
Made with deposit (£35 p/w), balance due 28 days before arrival.

209 Whitemead Caravan Park, Wool, nr. Wareham

Pleasant, small, family run park between Dorchester and Wareham.

The Church family are continuing to make various improvements to this rather pleasant little park which is within walking distance of the village of Wool. Providing 95 numbered pitches on flat grass sloping gently north and orchard-like in parts, it is very natural with open views over the Frome Valley water meadows. They are well spaced and mostly back onto hedges or fences. There are 65 electrical connections for tourers (10A) and no caravan holiday homes. The single, comfortably sized toilet block provides free hot water both in the washbasins, set in flat surfaces, and the pre-set hot showers (with adjustable flow in ladies) and a baby room which doubles as a facility for disabled visitors. Also provided are a washing machine, spin and tumble dryers and chemical disposal facilities. A small shop (limited hours) doubles as reception and gas is available. There is an information room, a children's playground with sand or grass base and a public phone. A fish and chip van calls three nights weekly in high season. The Ship Inn is 300 m. The park is 4½ miles from the nearest beach at Lulworth and is handily placed for many attractions in this part of Dorset (train services and limited bus service close). Riding or golf 3 miles. Caravan storage available. Possibly some rail noise.

Directions: Turn off main A352 on eastern edge of Wool, just north of level crossing, onto East Burton road. Site is 300 m. on right. O.S.GR: SY841871.

Charges 2000:
-- Per caravan, tent or motorcaravan £4.25 - £8.25; person over 5 yrs £1.00; awning or tent (over 15 x 15) £1.00 - £1.50; dog 75p; electricity £2.00.
-- No credit cards.
-- VAT included.

Open:
20 March - 31 October.

Address:
East Burton Road, Wool, Dorset BH20 6HG.

Tel/Fax:
(01929) 462241.
E-mail: nadinechurch @aol.com.

Reservations:
Made with £15 deposit, min. 3 nights at B.Hs.

207 The Inside Park Caravan & Camping Park, nr. Blandford Forum

Small, family run, rural park ideal for touring Dorset.

The Inside Park is set in the grounds of an 18th century country house which burned down in 1941. Family owned and carefully managed alongside a dairy and arable farm, it is a must for those interested in local history or arboriculture and is a haven for wildlife and birds. The reception/toilet block and games room block are respectively the coach house and stables of the old house. The 9-acre camping field, a little distant, lies in a sheltered, gently sloping dry valley containing superb tree specimens - notably cedars, with walnuts in one part - and a dog graveyard dating back to the early 1700s under a large Cedar of Lebanon. In total there are 125 spacious pitches, 90 with electricity (10A) and some in wooded glades. The six acres adjoining are the old pleasure gardens of the house where campers can walk and exercise dogs in the former garden, now mostly overgrown and providing what must be one of the largest children's campsite adventure-lands in the UK. The toilet block houses comfortably sized showers (pre-set, push button type with curtain), washbasins (some in cubicles) and toilets, all with free hot water and non-slip floors. A room for use by disabled visitors or mothers and babies has been added, plus dishwashing sinks. A laundry room is in the same block. Chemical toilet disposal and recycling bins are provided. Spacious games room with pool tables, table tennis, etc. and a tourist information section. Safe based children's adventure play area with trampolines and organised farm tours. Shop with basics, gas and camping provisions (open limited periods out of main season). Public telephone. No vehicle access to the park is allowed after 10.30 pm. (separate late arrivals area and car park). Day kennelling facilities for dogs. Winter caravan storage. The market town of Blandford with its leisure and swimming centre (temporary membership for Inside Park guests) is 2 miles and the area is excellent for walking and cycling (test your fitness on a 5 mile mountain bike course). Fishing and riding 2 miles, golf 3 miles. Extensive walking routes are marked through the farm and woodland, with a guide showing points of interest available in the shop. Bellamy bronze.

Directions: Park is about 2 miles southwest of Blandford and is signed from roundabout junction of A354 and A350 roads. If approaching from the Shaftesbury direction, do not go into Blandford but follow the bypass to the last roundabout and follow camp signs. O.S.GR: ST864045.

Charges 2000:
-- Per pitch £3.00 - £4.80; adult £2.50 - £3.00; child (5-16 yrs) free - £1.10; dog 60p - 90p; electricity £2.25; tent light free - £1.00.
-- VAT included.
-- Credit cards accepted.
Open:
Easter - 31 October.
Address:
Blandford Forum, Dorset DT11 9AD.
Tel:
(01258) 453719.
FAX: (01258) 459921.
E-mail: inspark @aol.com.
Reservations:
Essential for B.Hs and high season; made with £10 deposit (min. 4 nights 13 July - 1 Sept).

Dorset

210 Sandford Holiday Park, Holton Heath, nr. Poole

Pleasant, well run park with many first-class amenities near popular coastal areas; holiday caravans and large touring section.

Sandford Park has a large permanent section with 248 static holiday homes and lodges. However, the touring sections can accommodate 460 units of any type, mainly on individual pitches, on level grass with mature hedging in the main area, all with 10A electrical connections. Early booking is advisable. The main toilet block in the touring area provides facilities for disabled visitors and a baby room. It is supplemented by the former main block and subsidiary 'portacabin' style units in the touring and static areas (one a bath block). Hot water is free in the washbasins, set vanity-style in flat surfaces, and in the pre-set showers (under pressure at peak times). Plenty of water points around. Sandford is a large, very busy holiday park with a wide range of entertainment. The clubhouse (free membership) is spacious with dance floor, bar and seating area, and caters for different tastes and age groups. There is also a large air-conditioned ballroom for entertainment and dancing. Both are open over a long season. There is a variety of bars, restaurants (book in busy periods) and simple hot meals, breakfasts and takeaway elsewhere in peak season. The heated outdoor swimming pool (25 m. long, open May-Oct. and supervised) and a very large play pool (0-2 ft.) with a sandy beach, ideal for children, are attractively situated with a snack bar, terraced area and super kart track. An impressive, heated and supervised indoor pool is a nice addition, also a separate soft indoor play area for children (open April - Oct and Christmas, also supervised). Other amenities include a large supermarket and other shops, including well stocked camping accessory shop (all open peak season only), a large launderette, ladies' hairdresser and TV lounges. On site are a children's playground, two tennis courts, mountain bike hire, table tennis, two short mat bowling greens (outdoor) and a large crazy golf course. Public phones. The many activities include riding lessons at the stables on site. Fishing 9 miles. Dogs or pets are permitted in the touring section from 2 Sept. onwards with a dog walk provided. Bellamy silver.

Directions: Park is just west off A351 (Wareham - Poole) road at Holton Heath. O.S.GR: SY940913.

Charges 2000:
-- Per pitch free - £6.25, acc. to season; adult £4.45; child (3-13 yrs) £1.50 - £2.65; extra car free - £1.50; awning free; electricity £2.75; 'super hook-up' (16A electricity, TV, water) £4.50; dog (1 only, after 2 Sept) £2.50; boat and trailer £1.50 - £2.00; visitor £3.95, child £1.75.
-- Special offers and special interest weeks.
-- VAT included.
-- Credit cards accepted.

Open:
Easter - January incl.

Address:
Holton Heath, nr. Poole, Dorset BH16 6JZ.

Tel:
(01202) 631600.
E-mail: bookings@ weststarholidays.co.uk.

Reservations:
Early booking advisable (min. 3 days); contact park.

see colour advert opposite page 65

211 Pear Tree Touring Park, Organford, nr. Poole

Neat, well cared for, family run park catering for families and couples only.

Pear Tree is obviously the pride and joy of its owners, Mr and Mrs Broome, and this clearly shows. Set in 7½ acres, with mature tress and views across to Wareham Forest, the 125 good sized, grassy pitches are separated into areas by high hedges and shrubs. There are 120 pitches with 10A electricity, 43 with full services (water, waste water and electricity) of which 14 have hardstanding. The main heated sanitary block is opened by key and has vanity style washbasins and controllable showers (coin operated, hot water 20p throughout), with a baby changing unit and two WCs for disabled visitors. All is kept spotlessly clean. Also here is a `state of the art' chemical disposal point. Another small block with washbasins and WCs only, is near the tent area, which is a lovely secluded spot with many mature trees. Reception and a small shop supplying milk, bread, gas and other basics is at the park entrance where the gates (with key) are closed at 9 pm. (no late arrivals area, so book in before 9 pm). Public telephone and tourist information. Motorcaravan service point. Only breathable groundsheets are permitted with awnings. Dogs are only accepted outside July/Aug. and there is a bridle path extending into Wareham Forest for exercise. A large, fenced children's play field is at the top of the park with swings, climbing frame, trampolines and ball games area. There is no restaurant but a fish and chip van calls three times weekly in high season and the Clay Pipe Inn is just 500 m. away. Also 500 m. a coarse fishing lake (day tickets from reception) and bicycle hire. Riding 5 miles, golf 2 miles. A bus service stops nearby for Wareham (2½ miles) or Poole (8 miles). All year caravan or boat storage available.

Directions: Park is just west off A351 (Wareham - Poole) road at Holton Heath near Sandford Park. O.S.GR: SY940915.

Charges 2001:
-- Per unit incl. 2 persons £7.50 - £10.00; extra adult £3.00; child (3-14 yrs) £1.50; extra tent £2.50; awning free; dog (not July/Aug) £2.00; extra car or boat £3.00; electricity (10A) £2.20 - £2.50.
-- Security key deposit £10 (refundable).
-- VAT included.
-- Credit cards accepted.

Open:
Easter - mid October.

Address:
Organford Road, Holton Heath, Poole, Dorset BH16 6LA.

Tel:
(01202) 622434.
FAX: (01202) 631985.
E-mail: info@ visitpeartree.co.uk.

Reservations:
Made for min. 4 nights with £25 deposit.

76

212 Hoburne Park, Christchurch

Well kept holiday and touring site with many amenities; for caravans and motorcaravans only, with holiday homes section.

This well kept and tidy park, with a range of good quality amenities, is conveniently situated for Bournemouth or the New Forest. There are 71 level, grass touring pitches (for caravans or motorcaravans only), all with 16A electricity and some with individual water supply and hardstanding, in a separated hedged, neatly grassed field. The park also caters for 376 caravan holiday homes for hire. The amenities include an outdoor pool, with both paved and grass sunbathing areas, children's pool and an attractive indoor leisure pool with sauna, spa bath, solarium and steam rooms. We are impressed with the number of lifeguards on duty and the attendance to safety here and at other Hoburne parks. A large reception/club area (air-conditioned) incorporates a restaurant, snack bar, takeaway, well furnished bar with terrace, video games room and snooker room forming part of the indoor complex. A large adventure play area with play castle is near this main complex together with hard court tennis, crazy golf and a field area with goal posts. There is an organised programme of entertainment for adults and children in the season. A well stocked shop and launderette complete the facilities. Modern sanitary facilities are centrally situated, with free hot showers, hairdryers, baby changing units and chemical disposal, with additional facilities attached to the main building. Many large sites have a somewhat frenzied atmosphere in the high season. This one can be busy but the atmosphere is pleasantly quiet and relaxed. No tents, trailer tents or pup tents are permitted. Dogs and pets are not accepted. American motorhomes accepted in limited numbers up to 30 ft. A security barrier operates (with card). Fishing or golf 3 miles, bicycle hire or boat slipway 2 miles, riding 6 miles. A well managed park, the flag flier of the Hoburne group.

Directions: Park is signed (left) from roundabout about 2 miles east of Christchurch on the A337. From Lyndhurst, travel south on A35 to junction with A337 - turn left on A337 then left again at the first roundabout. O.S.GR: SZ169928.

Charges 2000:
-- Per unit, incl. electricity and awning (up to 3 x 9m.) £11.00 - £25.00.
-- Weekly rates and special weekend breaks.
-- VAT included.
-- Credit cards accepted.

Open:
March - October.

Address:
Hoburne Lane, Christchurch, Dorset BH23 4HU.

Tel:
(01425) 273379. FAX: (01425) 270705. E-mail: enquiries@ hoburne.co.uk.

Reservations:
Made with payment in full (6 days or less) or £50 deposit; min. periods 4 nights for B.Hs, 7 nights mid July - end Aug.

214 Mount Pleasant Touring Park, Christchurch, nr. Bournemouth

Neat tidy park on edge of New Forest, within 3 miles of Bournemouth centre.

Mount Pleasant is a surprisingly pretty, 'rural' park for its situation near Bournemouth. Under new ownership, the numbered pitches are on mostly level, sandy grass with circular connecting tarmac roads, neatly fenced and interspersed with pine trees, rhododendron bushes and newly planted evergreens, etc. In total there are 175 pitches for all types of units, 87 of them marked and with 10A electricity, with a separate, more open and sloping area for tents. Two good, purpose built, modern toilet blocks are heated, well maintained and fully tiled, with vanity style washbasins with free hot water (some washbasins in cubicles), adjustable hot water to free, well equipped roomy showers. There is a toddler room, separate, en-suite unit for disabled visitors, a laundry room and a can recycling unit. A good basic shop and information area in reception and a mobile takeaway, open all season (closed afternoons), is very popular, especially for breakfast! Mountain bike hire can be arranged. Fishing 2 miles, boat launching facilities 4 miles. Fenced adventure play area and direct access to the forest for dog walking, etc. A card operated security barrier is at the entrance. Bournemouth is around 10 minutes by car (depending on the traffic), Tesco hypermarket, 7 minutes. Dry ski centre within ½ mile with bars and restaurants. The nearest bus service is 2 miles. Barbecues are allowed. Due to its situation between Bournemouth airport and the A338 dual-carriageway there may be road or aircraft noise. Despite this, it is a very popular, well run park.

Directions: From A338 Ringwood-Bournemouth road, take B3073 in direction of Hurn airport. Follow camp signs at first mini roundabout onto Matchams Lane. O.S.GR: SZ129987.

Charges 2000:
-- Per unit incl. up to 2 persons £7.50 - £12.00; small tent £5.50 - £9.50; extra person (over 4 yrs) £1.00 - £2.00; extra car, boat or trailer £1.50 - £2.00; dog £1.00 - £1.50; electricity (10A) £2.00.
-- Credit cards accepted.

Open:
1 March - 31 October, (try phoning for winter stays).

Address:
Matchams Lane, Hurn, Christchurch, Dorset BH23 6AW.

Tel:
(01202) 475474. FAX: as phone. E-mail: enq@mount-pleasant-cc.co.uk.

Reservations:
Made with £30 deposit (non-refundable).

Dorset / Hampshire

213 Grove Farm Meadow Holiday Park, Christchurch

Quiet, traditional park with holiday vans, with small provision for touring caravans.

The grass flood bank separating the River Stour from this park provides an attractive walkway. The river bank has been kept natural and is well populated by a ducks and a swan family and early in the season they parade their young through the park. There are just under 200 caravan holiday homes (118 privately owned, 77 for hire), regularly sited in rows. For touring units 44 level grass pitches, all with 15A electricity, are clearly numbered, backing on to fencing or hedging and accessed by tarmac roads. Some are fully serviced (with hardstanding, shingle base for awnings and chemical disposal), the other grass pitches sharing service points. The sanitary block is tiled and provides vanity style washbasins, free hot showers with a bathroom for each sex (50p), a separate toilet and washbasin with ramp access for visitors with disabilities, and a baby changing room. Dishwashing sinks, together with spin dryer, iron and board and a washing line are provided, with a launderette near reception. Games room with pool table and video games, a play area is beside the river bank. There is a good, well stocked shop, 8-8 in high season but limited hours in early March and late Oct. The impressive modern reception has good tourist information. Fishing is possible and bicycle hire can be arranged. Nearby is a 9 hole golf course (pay as you play) and the Littledown Centre, said to be the south coast's premier leisure facility. Bournemouth is 10 minutes by car, Christchurch 5. No dogs or other pets are accepted.

Directions: From A388 (Ringwood - Bournemouth) take B3073 for Christchurch. Turn right at the first roundabout and then third right. O.S.GR: SZ136946.

Charges 2000:
-- Per 'luxury' pitch incl. 2 persons, 10A electricity and awning £9.00 - £18.00, large or standard pitch (no awnings) £6.00 - £16.00; extra person over 5 yrs £1.00 - £2.00.
-- VAT included.
-- Credit cards accepted.
Open:
1 March - 31 October.
Address:
Stour Way, Christchurch, Dorset BH23 2PQ.
Tel:
(01202) 483597.
FAX: (01202) 483878.
E-mail: enquiries@ meadowbank-hols. demon.co.uk.
Reservations:
Made for Sat-Sat or Sun-Sun in high season, min. 3 nights at other times, with £30 deposit.

231 Hollands Wood Camping and Caravanning Site, Brockenhurst

Spacious, level Forestry Commission site in the heart of the New Forest.

Hollands Wood is a large 168 acre secluded site in a natural woodland setting (mainly oak) with an abundance of wild-life, including the famous New Forest ponies. The site is arranged informally with 600 unmarked pitches but it is stipu- lated that there must be at least 20 feet between each unit. There are no electrical connections and possible traffic noise from the A337 which runs alongside one boundary. One area is designated dog free. Two large utilitarian toilet blocks (and a third smaller, older one) have free hot showers, open washbasins, free hairdryer, razor points, two laundry rooms with washing machines and dryers, water points, chemical disposal, facilities for disabled people and baby changing surfaces. These facilites are under pressure at peak times. There is no shop, but the site is only about ½ mile from Brockenhurst village with shops for supplies and gas, etc, plus trains and buses. No barbecues in dry weather. Barrier closed 23.30 - 07.30 hrs. Public phones. Torches essential. Motorcaravan service point. It can get very busy and we include the smaller Ashurst site as an alternative.

Directions: Site entrance is on east side of A337 Lyndhurst - Lymington road, half a mile north of Brockenhurst. O.S.GR: SU303038.

Charges 2000:
-- Per unit incl. up to 4 persons £7.00 - £13.20; extra person (over 5 yrs) £1.00; extra car, trailer or pup tent £3.80.
-- Credit cards accepted
Open:
23 March - 26 September.
Reservations:
Necessary for B.Hs and peak times (min. 3 nights with £30 deposit).
Contact (at all times): Forest Holidays, 231 Corstorphine Road, Edinburgh EH12 7AT.
Tel: (0131) 314 6505. E-mail: fe.holidays@ forestry.gov.uk.

227 Oakdene Forest Park, St. Leonards, nr. Ringwood

Woodland park with range of facilities, under new ownership.

Set in 55 acres of park and woodland, with direct access to the Avon Forest and near the New Forest, Oakdene provides caravan holiday homes to let or 149 pitches for all types of touring unit. These pitches are numbered, many with electricity connections (10A). Sanitary facilities include free hot showers, a launderette and dishwashing sinks. Free membership is provided for the Leisure and Country Club that offers a bar, buffet and a range of entertainment. A super new indoor swimming pool with a flume and an outdoor pool have been built. Also provided are crazy golf, a children's adventure play area, the Squirrel's Kids Club, bicycle hire and a shop. Very popular is the Forest Edge Stables where it is possible to ride straight into the forest with rides for beginners or experienced riders. Oakdene is now under the same ownership as Shorefield Country Park at Milford on Sea and massive investment is being carried out (as can be seen by the pools) and future plans aim to provide the quality and standard of facilities and entertainment found at Shorefield and Lytton Lawn (no. 228).

Directions: Park access leads off the main A31 westbound carriageway about 2½ miles west of Ringwood. O.S.GR: SU101016.

Charges 2000:
-- Per pitch incl. electricity and water £5.10 - £21.00, without services £3.30 - £20.00.
-- Min. stays at B.Hs.
-- VAT included.
-- Credit cards accepted.
Open:
All year except January.
Address:
St. Leonards, Ringwood, Hampshire BH24 2RZ.
Tel:
(01202) 875422.
Reservations:
All bookings are handled by Shorefield Country Parks - see no. 228.

230 Ashurst Caravan and Camping Site, Ashurst, nr. Lyndhurst

Attractive Forestry Commission site on the fringe of the New Forest.

A smaller site than Hollands Wood (23 acres), Ashurst is set in a mixture of oak woodland and grass and heathland which is open to the grazing animals of the Forest. Of the 280 pitches, 180 have been gravelled to provide semi-hardstanding; otherwise you pitch where you like, applying the 20 ft. rule on ground that can be uneven. There are no electricity connections. Some noise must be expected from the adjacent railway line - the station is just five minutes walk away. The single central sanitary block is fairly basic, but provides everything necessary, including hairdryers, a well equipped unit for visitors with disabilities (key required) and a good laundry room. It appears to be well maintained but could be under pressure when the site is full. Within easy access of all pitches are 8 water points and there are chemical disposal and motorcaravan service points. Reception is run by the very helpful site managers. There is a late arrivals area and separate car-parking area for those arriving or returning after the gate has closed (11.30 pm). A nearby pub is accessible by footpath across an adjacent field and shops and local buses are within a five minute walk. Guided forest walks are organised during the main season. A local garage sells gas. Public telephone. A torch is useful. Barbecues are not permitted in dry weather. No dogs are accepted at this site.

Charges 2000:
-- Per unit incl. up to 4 persons £6.20 - £12.00; extra person (over 5 yrs) £1.00; extra car, trailer or pup tent £3.50.
-- Credit cards accepted
Open:
23 March - 26 September.
Reservations:
Necessary for B.Hs and peak times (min. 3 nights with £30 deposit). Contact (at all times): Forest Holidays, Forestry Commission, 231 Corstorphine Road, Edinburgh EH12 7AT. Tel: (0131) 314 6505. E-mail: fe.holidays@ forestry.gov.uk.

Directions: Site is 2 miles east of Lyndhurst, set back from the A35 Southampton - Bournemouth road, 5 miles southwest of Southampton. O.S.GR: SU332102.

234 Shamba Touring Park, St Leonards, nr. Ringwood

Friendly, family run park with outdoor pool on Dorset/Hampshire borders.

The Gray family have been gradually upgrading Shamba over the last few years and it is developing into a comfortable park with good sized, well drained pitches (150 in total, all with 10A electricity). Most of the amenities are good including a well stocked shop and a cosy bar offering bar snacks, takeaway and a small family room, heated and with a pool table. At the rear is an open terrace area overlooking the heated outdoor pool, which is very popular with children and carefully fenced. Also popular is a large play area and a games room with video games and table football. The owners have a young family and seem to be aware of their needs, even down to providing a small child's toilet and basins in the toilet blocks. The showers, in a separate heated block, are controllable with seat and divider. The rest of the provision is adequate but is a little dated; however, it is kept clean and provides free hot water, make-up area for ladies, Belfast sink for the baby, covered dishwashing sinks (H&C), plus a laundry sink, two washing machines and two dryers, and chemical disposal facilities. This is the area where improvements are planned. The Grays live on site and have created a relaxed, pleasant atmosphere. Bournemouth with its beaches is 8 miles, Ringwood 2½ miles and the Moors Valley Country Park 1 mile. Riding stables and a fishing lake are 500 yds. Note: site is near the A31 so there could be some road noise.

Charges guide:
-- Per pitch incl. up to 6 persons £8.00 - £12.00; extra person £1.00 - £2.00; electricity £2.00; dog free - £1.50.
Open:
1 March - 31 October
Address:
Ringwood Road, St Leonards, Ringwood, Hampshire BH24 2SB.
Tel:
(01202) 873302.
Reservations:
Made with non-returnable deposit of £25.

Directions: Site is signed directly off the A31 Ringwood - Wimborne Road, 400 yds. down a small lane. Approaching from the east, after passing Little Chef, you will need to go round the next roundabout back on yourself, then immediately left down lane. O.S.GR: SU104026.

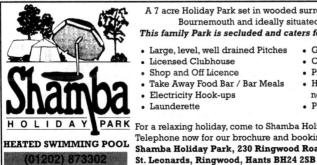

A 7 acre Holiday Park set in wooded surroundings some 8 miles from Bournemouth and ideally situated for the New Forest.
This family Park is secluded and caters for discerning holidaymakers

- Large, level, well drained Pitches
- Licensed Clubhouse
- Shop and Off Licence
- Take Away Food Bar / Bar Meals
- Electricity Hook-ups
- Launderette

- Games Room
- Children's Playground
- Pre-bookable Pitches
- Horse Riding, Fishing & Sailing nearby
- Plus Winter Storage

HOLIDAY PARK For a relaxing holiday, come to Shamba Holiday Park. Telephone now for our brochure and booking form.
HEATED SWIMMING POOL
(01202) 873302
Shamba Holiday Park, 230 Ringwood Road, St. Leonards, Ringwood, Hants BH24 2SB

Hampshire

225 Bashley Park, New Milton

Pleasant park with large section for caravans or motorcaravans, with swimming pools and evening entertainment.

A well run park with many holiday homes (380, including some for hire), Bashley Park also has a very sizeable tourist section and can take 420 touring units (tents, trailer tents and pup tents are not accepted). Spread over three flat meadows plus a woodland area complete with visiting squirrels, pitches are all marked out, individual ones with electricity. A number are now separated by fences and growing hedges, and with hardstanding - a nice development. Groundsheets must be lifted daily. The four toilet blocks, one central to each area, are well constructed buildings, fully tiled with modern fittings. Two have been refurbished in cheerful yellow and blue with washbasins in cabins. They have free hot water throughout and push-button, pre-set showers (no dividers, but shower heads are set fairly low). Set in pleasant park-like surroundings not far from beaches, Bournemouth and the New Forest, the site has a good clubhouse with excellent facilities overlooking an 18 m. circular outdoor swimming pool (heated mid-May - mid-Sept) and 18 m. children's paddling pool, a sensible size and fun with its geysers and beach effect. An impressive indoor pool complex houses a water flume, sauna, spa bath and steam room. There is evening entertainment (also for children) in the club with live or taped music Spring B.H. to mid-Sept; it has a ballroom, large lounges and bars, restaurant, simple hot food takeaway all day, TV room. Also a video arcade and games room with two full-size snooker tables, plus three pool tables spread among other rooms and a children's club. Very well equipped children's play area, crazy golf, nine hole, 'par 3' golf course on site, bicycle hire and three tennis courts. Fishing or riding 1 mile. Shop (mid-May to end Sept). Launderette. Up to 6 American motorhomes accepted (40 ft. max). One dog or pet is allowed per unit. A popular park with lots going on, part of the Hoburne group.

Charges 2000:
-- Per unit incl. all persons and electricity £10.00 - £25.00; multi service pitch £10.50 - £30.00; pet (1 only) £2.00.
-- Weekend breaks available.
-- VAT included.
-- Credit cards accepted.
Open:
28 February - 31 October.
Address:
Sway Road,
New Milton,
Hampshire BH25 5QR.
Tel:
(01425) 612340.
FAX: (01425) 632732.
E-mail: enquiries@ hoburne.co.uk.
Reservations:
Necessary for peak season and made for any length: 1-6 nights with payment in full at booking; 7+ nights, £50 p/w. deposit, balance 3 weeks before arrival.

Directions: Park is on the B3055 about ¼ mile east of the crossroads with the B3058 in Bashley village. O.S.GR: SZ246969.

226 Camping International, St Leonards, nr. Ringwood

Well kept, lively, family managed touring park with small heated pool, close to New Forest and Bournemouth.

Now incorporating Redcote Holiday Park, Camping International has a neat, compact appearance and closer inspection of the facilities confirms that everything is orderly, clean, and well cared for. The flat, grassy terrain is divided into two parts. The first, which is the original Camping International, comprises 80 numbered pitches, quite close together, all with electricity and 30 with gravel area for awnings. This is the more lively part with a central bar, pool and children's adventure play area, shop, reception and tourist information. The second part, formerly Redcote, is the quieter area taking 125 units on a flat, grassy meadow with some hardstanding and does not accept dogs. A games room has five pool tables, table tennis, amusement machines and under-fives playroom. To one side is a fully fenced ball game area. Both parts have fully equipped sanitary facilities with hot showers on meters. The block in the second part is larger and both functional with plenty of toilets including one for mother and child. Both have facilities for babies, covered dishwashing facilities (H&C), laundry rooms and chemical disposal. Motorcaravan service point. The 'Old Trout' pub has a pleasant licensed bar, family room, TV and video room and a patio overlooks the children's adventure play area and neatly paved small pool (1 m. deep) and paddling pool. There are restaurant and takeaway facilities (all 1/6-30/9 and B.Hs) and a well stocked shop with camping accessories (all season). Public phones. Secure caravan storage. Fishing, golf or bicycle hire 2 miles, riding ½ mile. The park is well situated to tour the New Forest, Bournemouth, Beaulieu, etc. and is essentially a park for families. It is also very popular, particularly with visitors from the continent, so reservation is advisable for July/Aug. Possible road noise from the A31 on some pitches.

Charges 2001:
-- Per unit incl. 2 persons £8.50 - £12.80; extra person (4 yrs and over) £1.60 - £1.80; awning or extra car £1.80 - £2.10; dog £1.50 - £1.90; electricity £2.60.
-- Less 20% for OAPs.
-- VAT included.
-- Credit cards accepted.
Open:
1 March - 31 October.
Address:
229 Ringwood Road,
St Leonards,
nr. Ringwood,
Hants BH24 2SD.
Tel:
(01202) 872817 or 872742.
FAX: (01202) 893986.
E-mail: campint@ global.co.uk.
Reservations:
Made with £40 deposit.

Directions: Park is off main A31 road to south at second roundabout travelling west from Ringwood (3 miles). Turn off at camp signs. O.S.GR: SU106024.

229 Sandy Balls Holiday Centre, Godshill, Fordingbridge

Amazing holiday park with excellent range of facilities for all types of touring unit and with holiday homes and lodges to hire.

Sandy Balls must be one of the oldest 'camp sites' in the UK, celebrating its 75th anniversary in 1995. Ernest Westlake, grandfather of the present owners and an educationalist and idealist, bought the ancient woodland overlooking the Avon Valley in 1919 to save it from the axe and today, while the majestic oaks, beeches, Scots pine and larch have matured, new facilities have been designed to be in sympathy with the setting. Sandy Balls is now an award winning park, high above the sweep of the Avon River and protected as a nature reserve. There is much to discover in the history of the park, such as how it came to get its name, the significance of the organisation founded by Ernest Westlake ('The Order of Woodcraft Chivalry') and his commitment to life-long learning. Perhaps visit Good Friday Hill and try to absorb the atmosphere and some of the thinking behind the development of Sandy Balls to what it is today, deserving of the entry which it has maintained in these guides for over 30 years.

It continues to be a very well run and progressive park set within 120 acres and with a wide range of leisure facilities developed around a 'village' centre. Open all year, it covers an extensive area in a series of fields which include terrain of different types: light woodland with 186 caravan and chalet holiday homes (many for rent), and some tent areas with unmarked pitches, tourist units for the most part on open meadows, and some general parts including woodland not used for camping. They include 256 'all service' pitches for touring units with electrical connections (10-16A), water, drainaway and TV connection - site satellite dish, on concrete or gravel with gravel hardstanding for awnings (steel pegs can be provided if required). In winter only 50 pitches are available.

There are four modern toilet blocks (three very modern, with under-floor heating) and one of `portacabin' type which remains as overflow in the tenting field (28 day). One block has a bath in each section (M&F) and all have washbasins in cubicles. Hot water is free and showers are of the pre-mixed type. The blocks are spacious and airy and should be adequate for peak season, with 'Northfield' having been added to provide extra, good quality facilities. Toilets for disabled visitors and baby changing facilities are provided in at least two blocks. Excellent launderette plus washing machines in all the toilet blocks. Chemical disposal, motorcaravan service point and recycling stations - look for the green coloured sheds. The central area with the park's facilities is pleasantly laid out and designed to blend with the forest surroundings. There is a large indoor heated swimming pool (66 x 30 ft) and a solar heated outdoor pool (25/5-30/8) with lifeguards and free at all times (in high season, sessions are timed according to demand). Other facilities include a well equipped fitness gym, jacuzzi spa bath, steam room, toning tables, sauna and solarium and dance studios. There is a Spar supermarket with its own bakery, a takeaway service and a licensed pub complete with bar, family room, with wide screen and patio area and with entertainment every evening in high season. Vlencio's pizzeria has a bar/grill for eating in or takeaway. The park also owns the Fighting Cocks pub, ¼ mile away. Games room with pool and table tennis, children's adventure playgrounds and two other play areas for younger children are provided, plus a soft play area for 2-5 year olds. Bicycle hire, petanque, archery, orienteering, hot air balloon rides along the Avon valley. The park has ites own riding stables. River fishing on permit. Tourist information. Gift shop. Telephones. The park has recently won a 'Good Lighting Award' from the British Astronomical Association for the design of its lighting which enables visitors to better appreciate the night sky; a new and unusual award for a park to win. Sandy Balls provides a range of all-round family entertainment, including a woodland leisure trail where wild animals and birds can be observed in their natural surroundings, as well as the New Forest on your doorstep, and even clay-modelling tuition and story telling for the children. Dogs are only allowed on certain fields. An ideal park for families and couples. Bellamy gold.

Directions: Park is northwest off B3078 (Fordingbridge - Cadnam) just west of Godshill village, and about 1½ miles east of Fordingbridge. O.S.GR: SU168147.

Charges 2001:
-- Serviced pitch weekends and high season £17.00, mid-week £12.75; non-serviced pitch weekends and high season £15.00; mid-week 11.25.
-- Mid and high seasons only: adult £1.50 - £3.50, young adult (12-17 yrs) £1.25 - £2.00, child (3-11 yrs) 75p - £1.50; additional car or m/cycle 50p; dog 75p - £1.25.
-- VAT included.
-- Credit cards accepted.
Open:
All year.
Address:
Sandy Balls Estate, Godshill, Fordingbridge, Hampshire SP6 2JY.
Tel:
(01425) 653042.
FAX: (01425) 653067.
E-mail: post@sandy-balls.co.uk.
Reservations:
Made with deposit and compulsory cancellation insurance - contact park for details.

see colour advert between pages 96/97

Hampshire

235 Red Shoot Camping Park, Linwood, nr. Ringwood

Rural retreat in the heart of the New Forest.

On three acres of open, slightly sloping, level grass-land, this site has panoramic views of the surrounding countryside and forest, and is very popular in high season. There are around 130 good sized pitches, 45 with electric hook-ups (16A), served by a circular gravel roadway. There is no site lighting so a torch would be useful. The sanitary facilities are fairly modern, well maintained, practical but not luxurious. They include push-button hot showers, dishwashing sinks under cover and chemical disposal, with free hot water throughout. The laundry has washing machine, dryers and a spin dryer, plus a baby bath facilitity, and there is a good unit for disabled visitors. A well stocked shop provides fresh and frozen foods, camping equipment and gas, wine and beer, toys and gifts plus maps and guides. Also on site is a fenced adventure style playground on a bark safety base, mountain bike and tandem hire. The adjacent Red Shoot Inn (under separate ownership) serves hot or cold meals and brews its own real ales - Forest Gold and Tom's Tipple. There are ample opportunities for walking, cycling and naturalist pursuits, nearby Ringwood has a market on Wednesday. Local attractions include watersports at the New Forest Water Park near Ringwood, a Doll Museum in Fordingbridge, cider making in Burley, and Breamore House just north of Fordingbridge. An extensive range of tourist information brochures is kept.

Directions: From A338 about 1.75 miles north of Ringwood, turn east (signed Linwood, Moyles Court). Follow signs over a staggered cross-roads and continue straight on for another 1.75 miles to Red Shoot Inn. O.S.GR: SU188095.

Charges 2000:
-- Per adult £3.75; child 5-14 yrs £2.20, 0-4 yrs 95p; car £1.10; m/cycle £1.10; day visitor 50p; electricity £2.20; awning £1.40; extra pup tent (by prior arrangement) £3.50; dog 65p.
-- VAT not included.
-- Min. stays at B.Hs.
-- Less 20% in low seasons (min. 3 nights).

Open:
1 March - 31 October.

Address:
Linwood, nr. Ringwood, Hampshire BH24 3QT.

Tel:
(01425) 473789/478940.
FAX: (01425) 471558.

Reservations:
Advised for w/ends, B.Hs and peak season (school holidays) and made with £15 deposit per week or part week.

228 Lytton Lawn Touring Park, Lymington

Modern, well equipped park with access to leisure complex, near Milford on Sea.

Lytton Lawn is the touring arm of Shorefield Country Park, a holiday home park and leisure centre. Situated 2½ miles from Shorefield itself, campers and caravanners staying at Lytton Lawn are entitled to free membership of the Leisure Club. The comprehensive facilities at Shorefield are of a very good standard and are mostly free (extra charges are made for certain activities). They comprise a very attractive indoor pool (20 m. heated), solarium, sauna, spa bath and steam room, dance studios and two all weather tennis courts, open all year with fully trained attendants. There are outdoor pools, crazy golf (Easter - Sept). restaurant facilities including a bistro (Easter - 2 Nov) and a range of entertainment and activity programmes, fitness classes and treatments, all well managed and organised. Lytton Lawn provides 133 marked pitches, including 43 'premier' pitches (hardstanding, 16A electricity, pitch light, water and waste water outlet) in a hedged area of natural grass. This section, with its heated toilet block, is open for a longer season. The rest of the pitches, all with electrical connections (tenters note), are in the adjoining, but separate, gently sloping field, edged with mature trees and hedges and with a further toilet block. Access roads are either tarmac or gravel. Both areas have purpose built, modern toilet blocks which are fully tiled, heated and well fitted, with free hot water, vanity style washbasins and showers with dressing area. Dishwashing, washing machine and dryer, plus chemical disposal in each block. Baby changing facilities in one block and facilities for disabled visitors (Radar key). There is a simple shop (Easter - end Oct), with a supermarket and takeaway (main season) at Shorefield. The fenced children's play area is small but there is also a fairly large, hedged field with goal posts. Barbecues are allowed. Only one dog per pitch is accepted. Public phones. The village pub is a 10 minute walk. The New Forest, Isle of Wight, Bournemouth, Southampton and the beach at Milford on Sea are near, as are golf, riding, coarse fishing (all within 3 miles), sailing, windsurfing and boat launching facilities (1½ miles).

Directions: From M27 follow signs for Lyndhurst and Lymington on the A337. Continue towards New Milton and Lytton Lawn is signed at Everton; Shorefield is signed at Downton. O.S.GR: SZ293937.

Charges 2000:
-- Per 'premier' pitch incl. all persons, electricity, water, drainage and TV connection £10.50 - £23.00; basic pitch incl. electricity £8.00 - £21.00; pup tent or awning free, together £2.50; dog (1 only) £2.50; extra car £3.50.
-- Less 40% Mon - Thurs in certain periods.
-- Min. weekly charge at busy times.
-- Credit cards accepted.
-- VAT included.

Open:
All year except 4 Jan - 9 Feb.

Address:
Shorefield Holidays Ltd, Shorefield Road, Milford on Sea, nr. Lymington, Hampshire SO41 0LH.

Tel:
(01590) 648331.
FAX: (01590) 645610.
E-mail: holidays@ shorefield.co.uk.

Reservations:
Made with deposit and cancellation insurance - contact park for details.

see colour advert opposite page 97

232 Camping and Caravanning Club Site Chichester, Southbourne

Small, well kept touring park near the Hampshire/Sussex coast.

This is a neat park, just to the west of Chichester and north of Bosham harbour. Formerly an orchard, it is rectangular in shape with 60 pitches on flat, well mown lawns on either side of gravel roads. All pitches have 16A electricity, 32 with level hardstanding. Situated on the main A259 road, although the new A27 bypass takes most of the through traffic, there may be some traffic noise in some parts (not busy at night). The site has a security barrier. Opposite the park are orchards through which paths lead to the seashore and the location is ideal for touring this part of the south coast or inland. The well designed, brick built sanitary block is of first class quality. Fully tiled and heated in cool weather, there is free hot water in washbasins set in flat units, showers and sinks, with facilities for people with disabilities (access by key). Washing machines and dryers are provided, plus a chemical disposal point. No ball games are permitted on the park. Gas available. There are shops, restaurants and pubs within easy walking distance in the nearby village and the park is on a main bus route. Fishing or golf 5 miles, riding 6 miles. Dogs can be walked in the lane opposite the entrance. Unfortunately there is no overnight area for late arrivals; the gates are shut between 11 pm. and 7 am. with no parking outside. An excellent caravan shop is near. Chichester has a leisure centre and market day is Wednesday. Also nearby are Bignor Roman villa, Apuldram Roses and the Weald and Downland open-air museum

Charges 2000:
-- Per adult £4.80 - £5.30; child (6-18 yrs) £1.65; non-member pitch fee £4.30; electricity £1.60 - £2.35.
-- VAT included.
-- Credit cards accepted.
Open:
7 February - 26 Nov.
Address:
Main Road,
Southbourne,
Hampshire PO10 8JH.
Tel:
(01243) 373202
(no calls after 8 pm).
Reservations:
Necessary and made with deposit (min. 2 nights); contact the wardens.

Directions: Park is on main A259 Chichester - Havant road at Southbourne, 750 yards west of Chichester Caravans. O.S.GR: SU774056.

245 The Orchards Holiday Caravan Park, Newbridge, nr. Yarmouth

Peaceful, spacious family park, well kept and with indoor and outdoor pools.

In a village situation in the quieter western part of the island, The Orchards is a busy and lively family holiday park combining 63 holiday caravans (in a separate area) with a neat touring area. Run personally by the proprietor, it provides a pleasant, comfortable base from which to explore, about 4 miles from the beaches and from Yarmouth. A pool complex provides a medium size, heated swimming pool and children's pool (late May - early Sept) with a grass sunbathing area, supplemented by a supervised irregularly shaped indoor pool with spa pool (on payment, open all year), attractively glass walled with terrace and café bar for relaxing - a nice addition. About 175 marked pitches are arranged on gently sloping meadow, broken up by apple trees, mature hedges and fences. All have electricity and 45 have hardstanding, including 5 with water hook up and drain (more planned). Sanitary facilities are provided by three blocks of varying age and size which together should be an ample provision. Hot water is free for the washbasins (some with shelf, others set in flat surfaces and a few in private cabins), for controllable hot showers and for dishwashing. There are also baths on payment and toilet facilities for disabled visitors (a hardstanding pitch close by can be reserved). Free irons and hairdryers (10p) are thoughtfully provided, with full laundry facilities. There are facilities for chemical disposal, a motorcaravan service point, ice pack and battery charging services and gas supplies. The large reception provides useful tourist information and there is a well stocked shop and takeaway service (mid-March - Oct, limited opening at quiet times). Dog walk area. A meetings room (up to 50 persons) is suitable for small rallies. Activities available are football pitch, exercise stations, pool, table tennis, TV and amusements rooms (there is no evening entertainment on site). Coarse fishing on site (no closed season). Bicycle hire, boat launching 4 miles, riding 1 mile. Walks from the park. Membership is available for the village social club and a small discount at Freshwater golf course (4 miles) - ask at reception. Golfing and walking holidays available. Limited caravan storage available. Part of the Caravan Club's 'managed under contract' scheme, non-members are also very welcome, the park is also a member of the Best of British group. Bellamy gold.

Charges 2000:
-- Per unit incl. 2 adults £7.75 - £11.25; extra adult £3.25 - £5.00; child £1.45 - £3.15; awning free; pup tent £1.50; electricity (16A) £2.15 - £2.95; dog 50p - £1.20; no pitch fee for hikers or cyclists; all-service pitch plus £3.15.
-- Packages incl. ferry travel available - ring park for best deal.
-- VAT included.
-- Credit cards accepted.
Open:
All year
excl. 3 Jan - 17 Feb.
Address:
Newbridge,
Yarmouth,
I.O.W. PO41 0TS.
Tel:
(01983) 531331 or 531350.
FAX: (01983) 531666.
E-mail: info@orchards-holiday-park.co.uk.
Reservations:
Made for min. 5 days with £30 p/wk deposit.

see colour advert between pages 96/97

Directions: Park is in Newbridge village, signed north from B3401 (Yarmouth - Newport) road. O.S.GR: SZ412878.

Isle of Wight

The island is a popular destination with a certain old world charm, combining coast and countryside activities and scenery with a mild, sunny climate and a network of footpaths and bridleways. It has a wide range of tourist attractions and sports facilities. Ferry companies offer mid-week discount packages for touring caravan owners. We found that most of the park owners are knowledgeable about deals and we suggest you contact the parks and let them arrange the most economical crossing.

Red Funnel Ferries

As the original cross-Solent operator, Red Funnel celebrated 135 years of running a ferry service between Southampton and Cowes with the introduction of three super modern car ferries. The new ships have been fitted out to a very high standard and we were very impressed with the on-board facilities which include a shop, bar, restaurant, seating areas and sun deck. Each vessel is able to carry up to 140 cars and there are 19 sailings a day in high season. The crossing time is 55 minutes.

see colour advert
between pages 96/97

244 Adgestone Camping Park, nr. Sandown

Well run and maintained touring park with swimming pool, popular with families.

Nestling at the foot of Brading Down, near the Adgestone Vineyard and with pleasant views across the valley, Adgestone provides a relaxed holiday atmosphere for families, complementing the attractions of nearby beaches and amenities at Sandown and Shanklin. About 200 marked pitches of average size, some slightly sloping, are divided into groups by tidy bar-rail fences, hedges and many attractive, ornamental trees. All pitches have electricity hook-ups (10/16A). A further group of pitches can be found close to the banks of the small River Yar on the park's perimeter, where you can take a peaceful stroll or go fishing. There are no caravan holiday homes. Two, low, neat sanitary blocks offer very clean facilities with free hot water to controllable showers and washbasins with some in private cabins also providing three en-suite family shower rooms, three toddler/baby care areas with baby baths and full facilities for disabled visitors. Fully equipped launderette, also hair care areas with hairdryers and sockets. Amenities on the park include floodlit swimming and paddling pools, heated from mid-May, but open earlier for brave swimmers, with a sheltered, grass sunbathing area, beautifully kept with colourful flower displays, as there are elsewhere on the park. Two sturdy, fenced children's adventure playgrounds (grass based) with a Tudor style playhouse for the little ones. Table tennis room, petanque court, volleyball, badminton and a football pitch with goal posts. Good sized fenced and hedged dog exercise field. Barbecues allowed and are available for hire from reception. Two public phones and post box. Ice pack and battery charging services and tourist information. Well stocked, licensed shop with wide range of camping and caravan accessories - in fact it is the island's main stockist. Good value takeaway (limited opening before Whit B.H). There is a small, private fishing lake and access to walks and bridleways on the Downs behind the park. One mile to bus route and pub.

As we go to press, we understand that the Camping and Caravanning Club have purchased this park and will operate it for 2001. The park will continue to be open to non-members.

Directions: The park is signed only from the A3055 at Lake (a place) between Sandown and Shanklin. Leave A3055 just west of railway bridge, by Manor House pub. 1 mile to park. O.S.GR: SZ590855.

Charges 2000:
-- Per adult £4.50 - £6.00;
child (3-15 yrs) £2.25 -
£3.50; dog £1.50;
electricity £2.20; extra
car £1.50; pup tent or
awning free.
-- Off peak concessions
for the over 50s.
-- Ferry packages
available - park will help
get best deal.
-- Good behaviour
deposit required for
young persons.
-- VAT included.
-- Credit cards accepted.
Open:
Easter - end September.
Address:
Adgestone,
nr. Sandown,
I.O.W. PO36 0HL.
Tel:
(01983) 403432/403989.
FAX: (01983) 404955.
Reservations:
Deposit £5 per night
booked on standard tariff;
balance payable on
arrival.

247 Southland Camping Park, Newchurch, nr. Sandown

Quiet, well run touring park 3 miles from popular resorts.

Southland was opened in 1981 in the grounds of a former nursery and has matured nicely with many attractive shrubs and trees. In the peaceful country setting of the Arreton valley, it is a sheltered park with 120 large, level pitches backing on to and separated by hedging. Comfortable and spacious, all have electricity (10/16A) and some water points. A modern building houses reception and the shop, with tourist information. The excellent, well maintained toilet block has been extended recently. The ladies' is now very modern, being light and airy, with washbasins in spacious cubicles, low level washbasins for children, push-button hot showers, three basin and shower cubicles, and a hairdressing area. The men's gains extra space and more of all the facilities. There is a bathroom (on payment), baby room, a good unit for disabled people, and two new family shower rooms which are also suitable for the disabled. A rustic building houses laundry and dishwashing sinks (H&C) and there are plentiful water points, chemical disposal and a motorcaravan service point. A quiet, well kept park, a fenced children's play area is in the top corner and dog walks are provided (more than one dog per pitch by prior arrangement only). Only raised barbecues are permitted. Nearby Arreton and Newchurch have craft shops and in August there is the National Garlic Festival. Sandown and Shanklin are 3 miles, the beach at Lake, 2½ miles. A main bus route stops at the top of the road, two pubs are within walking distance and there is direct access to walks and bridleways. The park has arranged concessions at the Heights Sports Centre for visitors. Fishing ½ mile, riding 2 miles, bicycle hire or golf 3 miles. A member of the Countryside Discovery group. Bellamy gold.

Directions: Park is signed from A3055/6 Newport-Sandown road, southeast of Arreton. O.S.GR: SZ557847.

Charges 2001:
-- Per adult £3.60 - £5.50; child (3-15 yrs) £1.65 - £3.00; electricity £2.00; dog £1.10.
-- Packages incl. ferry travel available.
-- Special low season offers.
-- VAT included
-- Credit cards accepted.
Open:
Easter - end September.
Address:
Newchurch,
Sandown,
IOW PO36 0LZ
Tel:
(01983) 865385.
FAX: (01983) 867663.
E-mail: info@
southland.co.uk.
Reservations:
Made for any length with £30 deposit per pitch, per week (or part week).

248 Appuldurcombe Gardens Caravan and Camping Park, Wroxall

Pleasant, family park with heated outdoor pool, with some holiday caravans.

This well kept little park would be a pleasant spot for a stay on the Isle of Wight. Quietly situated in a village and once part of the grounds of Appuldurcombe House, it is a little back from the sea - Ventnor beach 2½ miles and Shanklin 3 - with distant views and good walks nearby. It has a good, sheltered, heated swimming pool (60 x 25 ft), with underwater floodlighting, (Spr. BH.- end Aug) and an attractive bar and lounge, with dance floor, beside the pool, where there is limited entertainment at Spr. B.H. and school holidays. It is therefore quite a lively park - there are also 40 holiday caravans for hire in the attractive, old walled garden and two 8-bed flats. The 100 marked touring pitches, 46 with electricity (10A), are arranged on either side of gravel access roads on a slightly sloping grassy meadow. A further field with a pond is available for recreation, with goal posts, and a little stream flows past the reception block. Two small sanitary units serve the site. The older unit, now very dated, is behind reception and to one side of the touring field. The other unit, more recently refurbished, is close to the pool in the old walled garden. Washbasins are set in flat surfaces, showers are free, there are dishwashing sinks and facilities for disabled visitors. Small shop (in school holiday periods, otherwise limited). Fishing, bicycle hire, riding, golf and boat launching facilites are within 3 miles. The park can be peaceful and quiet in early and late season, whilst being busily active in high season.

Directions: From A3020 Newport - Sandown road turn right on Shanklin road. Follow through Godshill to Whiteley Bank roundabout and turn right for Wroxall. Continue for 1 mile past Donkey Sanctuary and site is to right in village - watch for sign. The entrance to the site access lane is off a narrow road on a blind bend and the access lane itself is too narrow for two units to pass (unguarded stream on one side and corners with jutting out walls). O.S.GR: SZ548803.

Charges 2000:
-- Per adult £2.95 - £4.85; child (3-13 yrs) £2.00; pitch free - £1.75; dog 50p or £3.00 per week; awning free; electricity £2.00.
-- Credit cards accepted.
-- VAT included.
Open:
1 April - 31 October.
Address:
Wroxall,
nr. Ventnor,
I.O.W. PO38 3EP.
Tel:
(01983) 852597.
FAX: (01983) 856225.
E-mail: appuldurcombe @freeuk.com.
Reservations:
Made with £10 non-refundable deposit per week booked.

see colour advert between pages 96/97

Isle of Wight

249 Kite Hill Farm Caravan and Camping Park, Wootton Bridge

Traditional touring site on northern side of island, near Fishbourne.

Kite Hill Farm is set in a designated area of outstanding natural beauty, its elevated position above the old mill pond of Wootton Creek where you may find kingfishers and herons. In the woods below the site you might catch a glimpse of the island's other famous inhabitant - the red squirrel. The 50 unmarked pitches are on a large gently sloping field, with 48 electric hook-ups (10A). There is a small children's playground plus a very large area for ball games, etc. (kite flying is not allowed due to light overhead power cables). The nicely tiled modern sanitary unit has WCs, washbasins and controllable, high pressure showers, a room with dishwashing and laundry sinks, washing machines and dryer, a fully equipped room for disabled persons and chemical disposal. Ironing facilities and gas are available from reception. Torches would be useful. Wootton Bridge village has a fish and chip shop, plus a mini-market which is open long hours, and several supermarkets are only ten minutes away by car. Fishing, riding and golf, all within 3 miles. Bus stop close (every 15 minutes to most parts of the island). The Firestone Copse, managed by the Forestry Commission, is near with walking trails and wildlife. Nearby attractions include the Steam Railway, Butterfly World, Brickfields Horse Country, Robin Hill Theme Park, and Haseley Manor - the island's oldest manor.

Charges 2001:
-- Per adult £3.00 - £3.50;
child (5-15 yrs) £1.50 -
£2.10; electricity £2.00;
dog free.
-- VAT included.
Open:
All year.
Address:
Firestone Copse Road,
Wootton Bridge,
Ryde,
I.O.W. PO33 4LE.
Tel:
(01983) 882543.
Reservations:
Advisable for B.Hs and
peak season, made with
£15 p/week deposit.

Directions: From A3054 (Newport - Ryde road), just east of Wootton Bridge, half way up hill (where site is signed) turn right into lane, site entrance is 250 yds. on right. O.S.GR: SZ550918.

250 Heathfield Farm Camping, Freshwater

Quiet family camping site, with views over the Solent.

Heathfield is a pleasant contrast to many of the other sites on the island, in that it is a 'no frills' sort of place, very popular with tenters, cyclists and small camper vans. Despite its name, it is no longer a working farm. The large, open meadow provides 60 large, level pitches, 30 with electricity (10A), and a very large open area for non-electric pitches. The main sanitary unit is housed in a modern, ingeniously customised, 'portacabin' type unit which provides WCs, washbasins (one cubicle for ladies) and showers - these are slightly different in that they have two pushbutton controls, one for pre-mixed hot water, the other for cold only (provided at the special request of some of the regular customers). To the side of this unit are covered laundry and dishwashing sinks. A second smaller unit has WCs and washbasins only. Further facilities include a baby room, a red telephone kiosk, recycling bins, chemical disposal and a motorcaravan service point by the entrance. Also here is a late arrivals and parking area on grass. A play field for ball games also has two picnic tables and two barbecues provided. There is no shop as you are only eight minutes walk from the centre of Freshwater, but Gaz and an ice pack service are provided. Nearby Ivylands Holiday Park is under the same ownership and the laundry facilities there may be used by Heathfield campers. No commercial vehicles are accepted and the gate is locked 22.30-07.00. The site overlooks Colwell Bay and across the Solent towards Milford-on-Sea and Hurst Castle. It is ideal for visiting attractions on the western side of the island including Totland and Freshwater Bays, The Needles and Old Battery, Compton Down, and Mottistone Manor Garden. The Military road which runs from Freshwater Bay to St Catherine's Point gives spectacular coastal views. Bellamy gold.

Charges guide:
-- Per adult £3.00 - £3.50;
child (3-15 yrs) £1.25 -
£1.75; extra car 50p; dog
50p; electricity £1.75.
-- VAT included.
-- No credit cards.
Open:
1 May - 30 September.
Address:
Ivylands Holiday Park,
The Broadway,
Totland Bay,
I.O.W. PO39 0AN.
Tel:
(01983) 756756.
FAX: (01983) 752480.
Reservations:
Advisable for B.Hs and
peak season; contact site.

Directions: From A3054 north of Totland and Colwell turn into Heathfield Road where site is signed. The site entrance is on right after a short distance. O.S.GR: SZ334878.

257 Lincoln Farm Park, Standlake, nr. Witney

Family run park with indoor leisure facilities in quiet, rural position.

From its immaculately tended grounds and quality facilities, to the efficient and friendly staff, this park is a credit to its owner. Situated in a small, quiet village it is well set back and screened by mature trees, with wide gravel roads, hedged enclosures, attractive brick pathways and good lighting. All 90 numbered, level touring pitches are generously sized and have electrical connections (10/16A), 75 with gravel hardstanding and adjacent grass for awnings, and 22 fully serviced (fresh and waste water, electricity and TV). The two toilet blocks are of notable quality, from Cotswold stone exteriors and colourful hanging baskets, to tiled and pine clad interiors, with background music and enormous plant displays. Showers (sensibly sized and designed), washbasins in cubicles, WCs, hairdryers, ample shelf space and heating make them a pleasure to use. A well equipped, separate unit for disabled people is adjacent to a specially reserved pitch with direct access. Two family bathrooms (incorporating baby bath and changing facilities) complete the sanitary amenities. Everything is well maintained and exceptionally clean. Each block also contains a laundry room, dishwashing sinks under cover (more throughout the site), freezers, fridges and microwaves; the latter being welcome provision for campers. Other amenities include a small shop, with basic supplies, telephone box, information kiosk, outdoor chess/draughts, putting green and sizeable adventure play area (bark chipping and rubber base), motorcaravan service point, chemical disposal and battery charging. Although only a relatively small site its leisure facilities are quite outstanding. One indoor swimming pool is always appreciated, but two (30' x 15' and 40' x 20') plus a toddlers' pool, spa pools, saunas, steam room, sun bed and a fitness suite really offer something rather special. Charges for all of these are modest, and outside of the open sessions everything can be hired privately by the hour. Dogs welcome (2 per pitch) with allocated walks. Fishing (lake and river) 300 yds - 5 miles, riding centre and water sports nearby, plus Oxford and the Cotswolds conveniently close. A member of the Best of British group.

Charges 2000:
-- Per unit incl. 2 persons £10.95 - £12.95; extra adult £2.25; child (5-14 yrs) £1.25; full awning (no groundsheets) £1.25, porch awning 75p; electricity £2.25 - £2.50; `super' pitch (excl. electricity) £4.00; extra pup tent £1.25; dog 60p.
-- Low season offers.
-- VAT included.
-- Credit cards accepted.

Open:
1 February - 18 Nov.

Address:
High Street, Standlake, nr. Witney, Oxon OX8 7RH.

Tel:
(01865) 300239.

Reservations:
Made with £15 non-returnable deposit.

Directions: Take A415 Witney - Abingdon road and turn into Standlake High Street by garage; park is 300 yds on the right. O.S.GR: SP396029.

260 Barnstones Caravan and Camping Park, Great Bourton

Small, tidy park, 3 miles from Banbury, open all year.

This small, neat park provides an excellent point from which to explore the Cotswolds, Oxford and Stratford-upon-Avon. The 49 level pitches all have gravel hardstanding with a grass area for awnings (no groundsheets allowed) and 10A electricity; 20 of these are fully serviced. Shrubs, flowers and a central gravel road convey a tidy impression throughout and the low level lighting is subtle but effective. The newly upgraded toilet block is small, but it can be heated and is quite adequate for the number of people it serves. It houses vanity style washbasins, WCs and adjustable unisex showers, all with free hot water. There is chemical disposal and a separate dishwashing and laundry room. The small, fenced play area for children (grass and bark chipping base) is adjacent to the entrance road. A fenced dog walk and rally field is near the main road, so some traffic noise is to be expected. All arrivals are required to report to the warden's caravan at the park entrance. Gas is available but no on-site shop - the nearest village is 1 mile, a supermarket 3 miles and a pub 150 yds. Fishing, bicycle hire, golf and riding, all within 3 miles.

Charges 2000:
-- Per unit incl. 2 persons £5.50; extra person 5-12 yrs 50p, over 12 yrs £1.00; 1-man tent £3.50; awning 50p - £1.00; electricity £1.50; fully serviced pitch incl. electricity £8.50.
-- OAPs less 50p per night.
-- No credit cards.

Open:
All year.

Address:
Great Bourton, nr. Banbury, Oxfordshire OX17 1QU.

Tel:
(01295) 750289.

Reservations:
Contact park.

Directions: From M40 take exit 11 for Banbury. Turn off following signs for Chipping Norton, straight on at two small roundabouts. At third roundabout turn right on A423 signed Southam and in 2½ miles turn right signed Great Bourton, Site entrance is 100 yds on right. O.S.GR: SP455454.

Alan Rogers' Discount

Less 50p p/night per pitch all year

Oxfordshire

258 Cotswold View Caravan and Camping Site, Charlbury

Well run family site with good facilities in quiet location.

On the edge of the Cotswolds and surrounded by fine views, this site offers a warm welcome. It successfully combines a working farm, touring site and self catering country cottages. Wide gravel or tarmac roads ensure easy access to all of the pitches in the 10-acre touring area. A second toilet block, together with the original, very well maintained block, provide excellent facilities for the expanded site which now has 125 all-electric pitches (10A). The newly developed area will naturally take some time to mature, but the work has been undertaken to a high standard throughout and the owner is justifiably proud of this latest development. All of the facilities are free (except baths, 50p) and washbasins in cubicles, showers with ample changing space, two family rooms, hairdryers, razor points, soft piped music, central heating and full length mirrors show careful attention to detail. Both blocks have good units for disabled people. There are baby changing facilities, a laundry room, freezers for ice packs and dishwashing sinks under cover (free hot water). Plenty of fresh and waste water points and a motorcaravan service point complete the amenities. The small reception also serves as a shop that is licensed and sells freshly baked bread, home-made cakes and eggs from their own hens. Farmhouse breakfasts (ordered the night before) are served in the farmhouse itself. The farm's animals (sheep, hens, pigs, rabbits, ducks, goats, ponies and a donkey) add great interest to one's stay. Well defined and maintained trails around the enclosures enable the animals to be safely observed, whilst additional trails and woodland plantations provide more walking opportunities, particularly for dogs who can be allowed off the lead. Children have a central, sheltered grassed area in which to play and a games room with table tennis, pool table and football table. A hard tennis court, outdoor chess and bicycle hire are available and there is a skittle alley is for hire. American motorhomes accepted. B&B is offered at the farmhouse. Fishing 1 mile, riding 10 miles, golf 7 miles. Convenient for touring the Cotswolds, there is also a good train service for day trips to London.

Charges 2000:
-- Per unit incl. 2 persons £8.00 - £11.00; extra adult £1.75; child (5-16 yrs) £1.00; electricity £2.00; dog free.
-- VAT included.
Open:
Easter - 31 October.
Address:
Enstone Road,
Charlbury,
Oxfordshire OX7 3JH.
Tel:
(01608) 810314.
FAX: (01608) 811891.
E-mail: cotswilview@
cotswoldview.f9.co.uk.
Reservations:
Advisable for B.H.s and peak season.

Directions: From A44 Oxford - Stratford-on-Avon road, take B4022 to Charlbury, just south of Enstone. Park is 2 miles on left. O.S.GR: SP365210.

262 Wysdom Touring Park Caravan Site, Burford

Very small garden-like site only a few minutes walk from Burford town centre.

You will have to go a long way before you find anything else remotely like this site! The land is owned by Burford School and the enterprising caretaker and his wife, caravanners themselves, suggested that they create this wonderful place to raise money for the school (hence cheques payable to Burford School). It is really like putting your caravan or motorcaravan (no tents permitted) into their own private garden. The 19 pitches are separated from each other by hedges, all have electricity hook-ups (16A) and a picnic table and some have their own tap. The small sanitary building offers all you need including chemical disposal, although with only one shower per sex, whilst it meets statistical requirements there may be a queue at times. When we visited, the site was a true riot of colour. The town of Burford is yards away with its famous shop lined hill full of antique shops, old coaching inns and all those 'interesting' shops it is so much fun rooting about in. The site is immediately next to Burford Golf Club and, for those interested, you can walk from your caravan to the first tee. A great location for exploring the Cotswolds, Burford calls itself the 'Gateway to the Cotswolds'. There is a narrow turn into the site off the school drive and this site is not therefore considered suitable for large motorhomes.

Charges 2001:
-- Per unit incl. 2 persons and electricity £7.00 - £8.00; extra person £1.50; dog in excess of one 50p.
-- No credit cards.
Open:
All year.
Address:
The Bungalow,
Burford School,
Burford,
Oxfordshire OX18 4JG.
Tel:
(01993) 823207.
Reservations:
Contact park.

Directions: From roundabout on A40 at Burford, take A361 and site is a few yards on the right signed Burford School. Once on school drive watch for narrow entrance to site on right in about 100 yards. O.S.GR: SP249117.

261 Bo Peep Farm Caravan Park, Adderbury, nr. Banbury

Peaceful, friendly park in rural setting with extensive walks and good views.

Set amongst 85 acres of farmland and woodland, there is an air of spacious informality about this park and it blends perfectly with the views surrounding it. Part of the Caravan Club's 'managed under contact' scheme, non-members are also very welcome. All of the 82 numbered, grass pitches are large, have 16A electricity and, with the exception of eight that slope gently, are otherwise quite level. Gravel roads connect the various areas, such as Poppy Field, The Paddocks and The Warren, with reasonable shelter provided by hedges and trees. Pitches are mostly set around the perimeters, leaving central areas free for a liberal sprinkling of picnic tables. A separate 4 acre field is reserved for tents. The original toilet block, not modern but heated, clean and fresh has been supplemented by a larger, purpose-built unit, equally clean and heated. There are ample showers (with seat, hooks and changing space), vanity style washbasins, WCs and hairdryers. A small shop stocks gas and basic supplies, information centre (with maps, leaflets, sample menus from local pubs, etc). Other facilities include chemical disposal, a motorcaravan service point, caravan cleaning area and telephone, with undercover dishwashing sinks, laundry rooms and low level lighting. Children are welcome but there is no play area. A network of walks around the site, including the pleasant river walk, has wide, well-kept paths and is being continually extended; bench seats and waste bins are provided. Dogs are also welcome on these walks, even without a lead. A 15 acre field has recently been acquired which can be used for recreation and, in the longer term, a lake is planned, plus the reclaiming of farmland to redevelop as woodland and more walks, a clear indication that owners Andrew and Margaret Hodge seek to improve an unusual site even further. Fishing (apply to office). Next door is a golf course. Banbury is just 3 miles, the famous Blenheim Palace 6. Great day trips to Stratford upon Avon, Warwick and its castle and even Silverstone can be entertained from this base. Caravan storage.

Directions: Adderbury village is on the A4260 Banbury - Oxford road. At traffic lights in Adderbury turn on B4100 signed Aynho; park is clearly signed, ½ mile on the right (½ mile drive). O.S.GR: SP482353.

Charges 2001:
-- Per adult £3.90; child (over 5 yrs) £1.20; pitch (non-member) £4.00; electricity £1.50.
-- Tent campers: per adult £4.00; child £1.20.
-- No credit cards.
Open:
16 March - 1 November.
Address:
Aynho Road,
Adderbury,
Banbury,
Oxfordshire OX17 3NP.
Tel:
(01295) 810605.
FAX: as phone.
E-mail: warden@
bo-peep.co.uk.
Reservations:
Advised and made with
£10 deposit.

269 Wellington Country Park, Riseley, nr. Reading

Quiet, wooded touring site within popular country park.

The Wellington Country Park is open to all on payment of an entry fee (entry for campers included in pitch fee) and many visit it for a day out. It contains a boating and fishing lake, a large adventure playground and other activities for children, nature trails, deer park, fitness course, crazy golf, narrow-gauge railway, animal farm and a dairy museum. Within the 350 acre park, the camping site is set in a woodland area. It has 70 pitches, 18 with hardstanding and 42 with electricity (10A). There are several individual pitches and some small groups all within woodland clearings which gives a very rustic and casual feel. It is a very pleasant setting and we found it quite nostalgic, the site being of the older and more traditional style of camping found frequently some 20 years ago. Once the Country Park closes at 5.30 pm. all is very quiet. There is limited site lighting and a torch is advised. Access is through a locked gate (deposit for key) and you must make advance arrangements if you plan to arrive after 5.30 pm when the main park shop closes. However, there is a late arrivals field at the entrance, although this has no sanitation at all. We did have reservations about the standard of the sanitary facilities, but the ladies' have been completely refitted for 2000 and we understand that the men's will have similar treatment for 2001. This work will bring the standards up greatly, with comfortable facilities including washbasins in cubicles and well equipped showers with good dry areas. Free hot water is plentiful, three pre-set showers in each section are adequate, there are good dishwashing sinks, an ample laundry and chemical disposal. A small shop stocks basics (from 1/5; no gas) with very limited hours. Public phones are at the sanitary block and near reception. Riding nearby. This site is just 30 minutes drive from Legoland and Windsor. The park remains simple and we feel that it is a very special place and recommended for those who prefer the quiet and simple style of camping.

Directions: Park is signed at Riseley, off A32/A33 road between Reading and Basingstoke, and from M4. It is 4 miles south of M4 exit 11 and 7 miles north of M3 exit 5. O.S.GR: SU727628.

Charges 2001:
-- Per unit incl. up to 2 adults and 2 children £13.00 for Fri, Sat and Sunday nights, B.Hs and high season; Mon - Thursday off-peak £7.50; extra adult £1.50; child £1.00; dog free; electricity £1.75.
-- Fee includes fishing permit for ONE person.
-- VAT included.
-- Credit cards accepted.
Open:
1 March - 31 October.
Address:
Riseley,
nr. Reading,
Berkshire RG7 1SP.
Tel:
(0118) 9326444.
FAX: (0118) 9326445.
Reservations:
Made with £13 non-returnable deposit (min 2 nights July/Aug. or 3 nights at B.Hs).

Buckinghamshire / Surrey

275 Highclere Farm Country Touring Park, Seer Green

Useful country park near Beaconsfield for London or Legoland.

Only 25 miles from London and 10 from Legoland and Windsor, this is a peaceful park that backs onto fields and woodland. Developed around a working chicken farm, there are also sheep, horses and a pot-bellied pig to provide that country feel. There are 60 level grass pitches, most with 10A electricity and gravel hardstanding, the rest being reserved for tents. The heated sanitary facilities have been converted from a chicken house and offer large showers (20p), roomy toilets, washbasins with room for wash bags, etc, hairdryers (20p); all is very clean and cosy. A unit with toilet and washbasin is provided for disabled people. A laundry room has washing machine, dryer, spin dryer and iron, plus washing up and laundry sinks. Converted chicken houses also form the basis for the excellent en-suite bed and breakfast facilities. The atmosphere is friendly, but informal, with reception doubling as a small shop that can supply all types and sizes of fresh laid eggs. A fenced children's play area plus a footpath are at the top of the site. Fishing 8 miles, bicycle hire 3 miles, riding or golf within 1 mile. A bus service to Uxbridge passes the site, London is 35 minutes by train, whilst Windsor Castle and Thorpe Park are also within easy reach. A member of the Countryside Discovery group.

Directions: From M40 take exit 2, then follow A40 towards London. Take first left for Seer Green, then follow site signs. O.S.GR: SU977927.

Charges 2001:
-- Per unit £10.00 - £12.00; tent £8.00 - £12.00; extra pup tent £1.00; electricity £2.00; awning, dog or extra car free.
-- Credit cards accepted (min. £20).
-- VAT included.
Open:
All year except February.
Address:
Newbarn Lane,
Seer Green, Beaconsfield,
Buckinghamshire
HP9 2QZ.
Tel:
(01494) 874505.
FAX: (01494) 875238.
Reservations:
Contact park.

281 Camping and Caravanning Club Site, Chertsey

Splendidly located site on banks of the River Thames.

This is an old-established site (1926), a flagship for the Club, which is only a few minutes walk from the shops and amenities of Chertsey. In the summer, lovely flower displays greet you as you drive in - an indication of a well cared for site. There are 204 numbered pitches in total (for all types of unit), 100 with 16A electricity and 33 with hardstanding. They are either in open, field-like areas, beside the river creek or in little nooks and corners, which avoids the regularity of some sites. Squirrels, rabbits and ducks abound and mature trees and plants create a pretty site, with views across the water and towards Chertsey bridge, although unfortunately there is some road noise and, depending on flight paths, aircraft noise. The main toilet block is centrally situated next to the recreation hall with table tennis. The other is at the entrance in the same building as reception and the shop. They are well equipped with free hot water, washbasins in cabins, hairdryers and laundry and dishwashing rooms. Separate facilities are approached via a ramp for wheelchair users. There is an area for hanging clothes out, a chemical disposal point and a motorcaravan service point. A good, under cover tourist information area is next to reception, again suitable for disabled people, plus a children's play area on bark and short dog walk areas. Shop (well stocked with essentials and gas) open 8-11 am. and 4-6 pm. Public telephone. The rail station for London is at Chertsey or Weybridge. Fishing is possible (£1 per day, NRA licence needed). Canoeing can be arranged (Chertsey is the main base of the Club's canoe section). The river can flood but the site has a well established warning system and will not allow camping near the river when floods are expected. Torches are necessary. Caravan storage.

Directions: Suggested: from M25 use junction 11. Turn left at roundabout on A317 towards Shepperton and continue to second set of traffic lights. Turn right then almost immediately left watching for green Club camp sign just before Chertsey bridge; the opening is narrow. O.S.GR: TQ052667.

Charges 2000:
-- Per adult £4.80 - £5.30; child (6-18 yrs) £1.65; non-member pitch fee £4.30; electricity £1.60 - £2.35.
-- VAT included.
-- Credit cards accepted.
Open:
All year.
Address:
Bridge Road,
Chertsey,
Surrey KT16 8JX.
Tel:
(01932) 562405.
(no calls after 8 pm).
Reservations:
Necessary and made with deposit; contact the wardens.

South East England Tourist Board

East Sussex, West Sussex, Surrey and Kent
The Old Brew House, Warwick Park,
Tunbridge Wells, Kent TN2 5TU
Tel: (01892) 540766 Fax: (01892) 511008
E-mail: enquiries@seetb.org.uk
Internet: http://www.southeastengland.uk.com

The four counties of Kent, East and West Sussex and Surrey provide the warmest of welcomes for all our visitors. With over 270 miles of coastline, plenty of open spaces, attractive countryside and evidence of our historic past round every corner; there's something for everyone to enjoy.

For visitors enjoying history and heritage, there's a real feast of interesting, cultural places to visit - famous castles such as Dover Castle overlooking the English Channel and Leeds Castle, sometimes known as 'the loveliest castle in the world', historic cathedrals at Canterbury, Rochester and Chichester and homes belonging to Sir Winston Churchill and author, Rudyard Kipling being just a few examples of the many heritage attractions on offer.

All types of architecture can be enjoyed in towns like Rye, Guildford and Arundel alongside modern facilities for shopping, leisure and sporting activities, many of which are undercover for all-year-round enjoyment. Dedicated shoppers may like to visit the new Bluewater complex near Dartford – the largest in Europe. Antique hunters will enjoy Petworth, Tenterden or the well-loved Brighton Lanes for the individual and unusual. There are also factory outlets in Dover and Ashford.

The South East also has many theatres providing entertainment to suit all tastes. Brighton's Theatre Royal and the Chichester Festival Theatre are just two that preview London runs with all-star casts and many of the larger venues play host to major pop and orchestral concerts, opera and ballet.

The region, though, is definitely not all hustle and bustle - there are wide open spaces and hundreds of footpaths and scenic viewpoints for the walker and cyclist to appreciate. The North and South Downs rolling hills straddle the region, with many parts of the South Downs following the Sussex coastline. Long-distance footpaths run along the top of these hills and provide spectacular walking countryside, picnic areas or just places for a gentle stroll.

Hundreds of interesting events take place in South East England throughout the year. Sporting venues such as the world-famous Brands Hatch motor-racing circuit, Hickstead Showjumping Course and Wentworth Golf Course provide a variety of spectator sports. Many events - country fayres, sheep fairs and pageants for example - are based on old historic customs and traditions and others, like Broadstairs' annual Dickens Festivals are fascinating occasions with plenty of opportunity for visitors and local residents to participate and be transported back to a different age through a variety of events and performances.

282 Camping and Caravanning Club Site Horsley, East Horsley

Pretty site with small lake and good facilities.

London and all the sights are only 40 minutes away by train but Horsley is a delightful, quiet unspoilt site with a good duck and goose population on its part lily covered lake (unfenced). It provides 130 pitches, of which 70 have 16A electrical connections; 29 are all weather pitches (most with electricity). Seventeen of the pitches are around the bank of the lake, the rest further back in three hedged, grass fields with mostly level ground but with some slope in places. There is a range of mature trees and a woodland dog walk area (may be muddy). The soil is clay based so rain tends to settle - sluice gates remove extra water from the lake area when rain is heavy. There are two purpose built, heated toilet blocks, one part of the entrance building which includes reception. Fittings and design are good, with free hot water, well equipped showers, hairdryers, some washbasins in cabins, Belfast sink and parent and child room with vanity style basin, toilet and wide surface area. There are also well designed facilities for disabled people, a chemical disposal point and new drying areas. A recreation hall with TV and table tennis (bring your own bats) is sometimes used for bingo. Children's play area. Basic provisions, gas and books are kept in reception. Shops and the station are 1 mile, pubs 1½-2 miles. Fishing is possible from May (£3 per day, NRA licence required). Golf 1½ miles, riding 2 miles. Resident wardens will make you comfortable and the R.H.S. gardens at Wisley are close by.

Charges 2000:
-- Per adult £3.75 - £5.30; child (6-16 yrs) £1.65; non-member pitch fee £4.30; electricity £1.60 - £2.35.
-- Credit cards accepted.
-- VAT included.

Open:
March - October.

Address:
Ockham Road North, East Horsley, Surrey KT24 6PE.

Tel:
(01483) 283273 (no calls after 8 pm)

Reservations:
Necessary and made with deposit; contact the wardens.

Directions: From M25 exit 10, go 2½-3 miles towards Guildford and take first left on B2039 to Ockham and East Horsley. Continue through Ockham towards East Horsley. Site is on right; watch carefully for small club sign. O.S.GR: TQ083552.

Sussex

289 White Rose Touring Park, Wick, nr. Littlehampton

Small, well organised park close to West Sussex seaside resorts.

Situated about midway between the imposing castle at Arundel and the beaches of Littlehampton, White Rose makes an excellent base from which to enjoy the many attractions of this popular district. Watersports centres, race courses, beaches, historical and cultural interests, downland walks and the resorts of Bognor and Brighton are within easy reach. There are 140 pitches available for tourists, 88 with electricity (10/16A). The flat grassy meadow is surrounded by trees and divided into two areas. The first part has individually hedged pitches, as on the continent, on either side of concrete access roads, with electricity hook-ups and shared water/waste water connections. The second area includes 14 'super' pitches (each having electricity, fresh and waste water and sewage connections, TV aerial socket and night light), full sized pitches with no electricity, plus special pitches for small tents and small motorcaravans. The central toilet block is fully tiled with free hot water in washbasins set in flat units and showers with hot water controlled by push-button taps. Two washrooms are provided for disabled people (key from reception). Chemical disposal point. Reception has a few basic supplies and gas available; a supermarket is ¼ mile away. Fishing, boat launching, bicycle hire, riding and golf within 2 miles. Special dog walking area and a central play area for children. A busy road runs along one side of the park and road noise could be disturbing in the early mornings during the week to a few pitches.

Directions: Take A284 Littlehampton road from A27 just to the east of Arundel station, pass the campsite behind the pub at this junction and park is signed along on the left. O.S.GR: TQ026041.

Charges 2000:
-- Per pitch incl. unit, car and up to 4 people: super pitch £16.00, fully serviced pitch (electric, water, drain) £14.00, no services £12.00; extra person £2.50; extra car £2.00.
-- Trailed boats by prior arrangement only.
-- Reductions for 1 week or 1 month outside 10 July - 31 Aug.
-- Credit cards accepted.

Open:
All year except 14 Jan - 15 March.

Address:
Mill Lane, Wick, W. Sussex BN17 7PH

Tel:
(01903) 716176.
FAX: (01903) 732671.

Reservations:
Made with deposit of 1 nights fee p/week reserved.

288 Raylands Caravan Park, Southwater, nr. Horsham

Spacious park with excellent facilities in rural environment.

A pleasant, reasonably priced park (owned by Roundstone Caravans at Southwater), deep in the heart of the Sussex countryside, Raylands is well maintained and thoughtfully landscaped. The 65 caravan holiday homes occupy an area of their own and touring units use marked, numbered pitches on gently sloping grass meadows separated into smaller areas by trees and hard access roads, with electricity (15A) available to 50 of the 65 pitches. The park manager seems to have engendered a friendly atmosphere and is willing to advise on the very numerous attractions the locality has to offer. London and Brighton are easily reached by rail from nearby Horsham and the region abounds with places of historical, cultural and sporting interests. The clubhouse (weekends only in low season) has snacks and good value full meals at weekends (to early Sept) with a special bar/dining room for non-smokers and children's games room with pool, table tennis, video games and TV. An adult's games room has pool, darts and a small library. The single toilet block (unheated) is centrally situated and is a modern building of good quality with free hot water in the basins and hot showers on payment. There are separate en-suite facilities for disabled visitors, a laundry room with washing machine, dryer, a dishwashing sink with free hot water and chemical disposal facilities. There is no shop on site but a supermarket and other shops are under 2 miles. Public telephone. Large dog exercise field complete with seats at the far end and another large field for children's ball games. Tennis court. Swimming pool 3 miles. Fishing, bicycle hire riding and golf, all 2 miles. Some road noise from the A24.

Directions: Leave A24 Worthing - London road for Southwater and follow signs for approx. 2 miles on narrow lanes to park. O.S.GR: TQ170265.

Charges 2000:
-- Per pitch incl. 2 persons £9.00; extra person 50p; hiker or cyclist tent, 1 person £6.00 - £9.00; electricity £1.50.
-- Credit cards accepted.

Open:
1 March - 31 October.

Address:
Jackrells Lane, Southwater, Sussex. RH13 7DH.

Tel:
(01403) 731822.
FAX: (01403) 732828.

Reservations:
Essential for BHs, advisable for peak season, with £10 deposit.

294 Honeybridge Park, Dial Post, nr. Horsham

Touring park in the South Downs area.

Honeybridge's owners, Jeff and Val Burrows, continue to develop this 15 acre park which now has around 100 pitches, including 40 with gravel hardstanding and 86 with electric hook-ups (16A). There are plans for more electric hook-ups and to increase the number of individually hedged places (until now these have usually been taken by longer stay units). The other pitches are on slightly sloping grass with little to separate them. The reception building houses a small shop, and the park provides a discount voucher pack for local attractions on booking in. The sanitary unit can be heated in cool weather and provides all modern facilities including some washbasins in cubicles and push-button hot showers. There is a unit for disabled persons, dishwashing and laundry sinks, a washing machine and dryer, plus a motorcaravan service point. A large wooden, adventure-style play area is on grass well away from the pitches, and simple family entertainment is organised on special occasions. A games room has darts, table tennis and board games, TV and tourist information. This site is ideal for visiting the South Downs with its many attractive villages. A pub, restaurant and tea shop are in Dial Post. Billingshurst and Horsham are both 8 miles. Fishing 1 mile, golf or riding 10 miles. The barrier (card access) is locked 11.30 pm - 7 am. Bellamy silver.

Directions: Two miles south of junction of A24 and A272 at Dial Post, turn east by Old Barn Nurseries. Follow signs to site (½ mile). O.S.GR: TQ150190.

Charges 2000
-- Per pitch £2.50; adult £2.50 - £3.50; child (5-14 yrs) £1.00; 2 man small tent (incl. pitch fee) £7.50; electricity £2.00; extra car £1.00; dog free.
-- VAT included.
-- Credit cards accepted.
Open:
All year.
Address:
Honeybridge Lane, Dial Post, West Sussex RH13 8NX.
Tel/Fax:
(01403) 710923.
E-mail: enquiries@ honeybridgepark-free-online.co.uk.
Reservations:
Made with £10 p/night deposit (June-Aug).

295 Washington Caravan and Camping Park, Washington

Unusual site with superb equestrian facilities, near Worthing.

A campsite with a bias towards tenting families, there are only 21 hardstanding pitches for caravans or motorcaravans, and a large gently sloping grassy field with enough space for 80 tents. The 23 electric hook-ups (16A) are on meters (50p). The sanitary facilities are in a heated chalet style building and are of an excellent standard, including spacious shower rooms (on payment), and indoor dishwashing and laundry facilities. No shop but eggs, bread, butter and milk can be obtained from reception. There is some road noise from the A24. The latest development is an equestrian centre adjacent to the campsite, including an Olympic standard floodlit arena, a small children's pony arena, stabling and paddock facilities. Excellent riding opportunities on the bridle paths of the South Downs Way. Local attractions (all with free admission, check opening times) include Highdown Chalk Gardens at Worthing, Nutbourne Vineyard near Pulborough, and Steyning Museum. Eating out options include the local pub and a nearby restaurant.

Directions: Site entrance is just east of the junction of A24 and A283 roads at Washington, 6 miles north of Worthing. O.S.GR: TQ125130.

Charges 2000:
-- Per caravan or motor-van incl. 2 persons £9.00; extra person £3.00; electricity 50p meter.
-- Per tent £2.00; person £3.00; car or m/cycle £1.00.
Open:
All year.
Address:
London Rd, Washington, West Sussex RH20 4AJ.
Tel:
(01903) 892869.
FAX: (01903) 893252.
Reservations:
Contact site for details.

290 Horam Manor Touring Park, Horam, nr. Eastbourne

Secluded rural park in the heart of the Sussex countryside.

The touring park is part of, but under separate management from, Horam Manor which has a farm museum, nature trail (free for campers) and Merrydown Winery. The 90 pitches, 52 with electricity, are on two open meadows joined by a tarmac/gravel road. The field nearer reception is undulating, the second field is flatter but slopes - levelling blocks are needed for motorcaravans. Pitches are of generous size, those with electricity being numbered and marked, the rest not. The park, back from the main Eastbourne to Tunbridge Wells road, is a haven of peace and tranquillity. The modern, well built sanitary block at the entrance to the larger field has free hot water in washbasins (set in flat surfaces), showers, laundry and washing up sinks. A family room (key access) has shower, washbasin and toilet and is suitable for disabled visitors. Washing machine. Chemical disposal. Gas available. No shop but the village is close, with supermarkets in Heathfield, 3 miles. Two inns are within walking distance and the Barn cafe at the Farm Centre serves drinks and snacks (10 am. - 5 pm). The Craft Centre has some interesting exhibits and riding stables. The nature trail has walks from ½ -1½ hours in length (written guide available). Fishing is available in 10 lakes on the estate (adults £3). Bicycle hire and golf within 1 mile. Dogs are accepted (max. 2 per unit).

Directions: Entrance is signed at the recreation ground at southern edge of Horam village. O.S.GR: TQ577169.

Charges 2000:
-- Per unit incl. 2 adults and 2 children (under 18 yrs) £11.85; extra adult £3.50; extra child 95p; electricity £1.85; extended awning £2.50; dogs (max 2) free.
-- No credit cards.
-- VAT included.
Open:
1 March - 31 October.
Address:
Horam, nr. Heathfield, E. Sussex TN21 0YD.
Tel:
(01435) 813662.
E-mail: horam.manor @virgin.net.
Reservations:
Telephone or write to park.

Sussex

293 Sheepcote Valley Caravan Club Site, Brighton

Excellent site in quiet location within boundary of popular resort.

Brighton is without doubt the South of England's most popular seaside resort and now that the Caravan Club has taken over and modernised the Sheepcote Valley Site, there is a first class base from which to enjoy the many and diverse attractions both in the town and this area of the south coast. The site occupies a quiet situation in an almost fully enclosed valley in the South Downs, a mile north of the town's interesting Marina which has a superstore and good variety of shops and restaurants. It is adjacent to extensive recreation grounds and the centre of Brighton is only two miles away with a bus service from the entry road. A wide tarmac road winds its way through the site from reception, with pitches on either side, leading to terraces with grass pitches on the lower slopes of the valley. With a total of 249 pitches, 169 have electricity (16A), 82 have hardstanding and 13 have water, drainage and TV sockets. Two grass terraces are for tents and these have hard parking near as a low fence prevents cars being taken onto the camping areas. Although there are a number of trees, many of these are young so do not provide shade as yet. Flower beds add to the attractiveness of the site. Two well built, brick, heated sanitary blocks have excellent facilities including free hot water in washbasins (all in private cabins), showers and sinks. In the main season a `portacabin' type building provides additional services near the tent places. There is a well equipped room for wheel chair users, another one for walking disabled and two baby and toddler wash rooms. Other facilities include washing machines, dryers, iron and spin dryer, a motorcaravan service point, chemical toilet disposal points and a children's play area with safety base. Gas is available. The site fully lives up to the very high standards expected from the Caravan Club and provides a first class venue both for a quiet holiday and as a base from which to explore this interesting and historic town and delightful Sussex downland countryside either by car or on foot. A wide variety of tourist attractions is displayed in reception. Non-members are welcome.

Charges 2000:
-- Per pitch (non members) £6.00 - £7.00; person £3.25 - £4.00; child (5-16 yrs) £1.10 - £1.20; electricity £1.45 - £2.20.
-- VAT included.
-- Credit cards accepted.
Open:
All year.
Address:
East Brighton Park, Brighton, Sussex BN2 5TS.
Tel:
(01273) 626546.
FAX: (01273) 682600.
Reservations:
Advised for high season with £5 deposit.

Directions: Site is in eastern part of Brighton and well signed from A259 coast road opposite the Marina through to site entrance. O.S.GR: TQ341043.

292 Bay View Caravan and Camping Park, Pevensey Bay

Friendly beach-side park for couples and families only.

The Adams family have developed Bay View with care over the last few years, a fact which is obvious as soon as you arrive and see the tidy state of everything. There are 3½ acres of mainly flat grass with gravel access roads and a low bank on three sides giving some shelter if it is windy. Careful use of fencing adds to the attractiveness, whilst also keeping the rabbits off the flowers. The 49 pitches (80 sq.m, all with 10/16A electricity and 10 with hardstanding) are neatly marked out by numbered posts, while 5 caravan holiday homes for hire are at the back of the park. There are plenty of water and waste water points. A well made, fenced children's play area on a bark surface has adventure equipment (10 years and under) and is very popular. The centrally placed sanitary facilities are housed in a very well maintained 'portacabin' style building which will be heated when necessary. Hot water is free to the washbasins, dishwashing and laundry sinks and on payment (20p) for the showers. There are chemical disposal and motorcaravan services and a laundry room has a washing machine, dryer, spin dryer, iron and board, plus tourist information. Reception is combined with a well stocked shop which is good value and open long hours (the owners live next to it). Gas available. A large overflow field opposite the entrance with small 'portacabin' style sanitary facilities is for use in the peak season. At other times this space may be used for games. Apart from all the attractions of Sussex, from this very pleasant park you may swim, fish, windsurf, sail or just enjoy the view. Bicycle hire 1 mile, golf 2 miles. Winter caravan storage available. A new marina complex is under construction nearby. Bellamy gold.

Charges 2001:
-- Per caravan, motor-caravan or trailer/family tent £3.10 - £5.30; 2 person tent £2.65 - £2.80; adult £2.20 - £2.50; child (2-16 yrs) £1.55 - £1.70; awning £1.55 - £1.70; dog 60p - £1.00; electricity £2.00.
-- VAT included.
-- Couple and families only; no commercial vehicles, large vans or pick-ups.
-- No credit cards.
Open:
Easter/1 April - October.
Address:
Old Martello Road, Pevensey Bay, East Sussex BN24 6DX.
Tel:
(01323) 768688.
FAX: (01323) 769637.
E-mail: bayviewcara-vanpark@tesco.net.
Reservations:
Made with deposit (£25).

Directions: Park is about 1 mile west of Pevensey Bay and 2 miles east of East-bourne, off the A259 Pevensey Bay road. O.S.GR: TQ648028.

296 Crazy Lane Tourist Park, Sedlescombe, nr. Battle

Small touring park in '1066' country, ideal for couples.

Formerly known as Whydown Farm Tourist Park, this peaceful, traditional style two acre park has just 36 pitches arranged on grassy terraces, all with electric hook-ups (5/10A). It may be best to phone to make sure space is available before travelling long distances. The tiny, but well maintained sanitary unit has coloured fittings and towel rails and includes controllable hot showers (on payment), laundry facilities with a washing machine and dryer, plus dishwashing sinks, and a suite for disabled persons. A new reception and shop was added recently. Local attractions include the very pretty village of Sedlescombe, two steam railways, an organic vineyard, Rye with its quaint cobbled streets and of course Battle itself.

Directions: From A21, 100 yards south of junction with B2244 (to Sedlescombe) turn into Crazy Lane, where site is signed. O.S.GR: TQ782170.

Alan Rogers' Discount
Stay 7 nights, pay for 6, in low season

Charges 2000:
-- Per unit incl. 2 adults £7.75 - £9.00; electricity £2.00.
Open: March - October
Address: Crazy Lane, Sedlescombe, nr. Battle, East Sussex TN33 0QT.
Tel: (01424) 870147.
E-mail: info@crazylane.co.uk.
Reservations: Contact site for details.

309 Black Horse Farm Caravan Club Site, Densole, nr. Folkestone

Well organised park near Channel Ports and Tunnel.

This neat, tidy and attractive 6 acre park, owned by the Caravan Club, is situated amidst farming country in the village of Densole on the Downs just 4 miles north of Folkestone, 8 northeast of Dover and 11 south of Canterbury. This makes it ideal for a night stop travelling to or from the continent, or a base for visiting the many attractions of this part of southeast England. Accessed directly from the A260, the tarmac entrance road leads past reception towards the top field which has gravel hardstanding pitches with a grass area for awnings (possibly some road noise), past hedging to the smaller middle area with 8 hardstandings, then to the large bottom field which has been redeveloped to give 104 large pitches, all with electricity (16A). A late arrivals area and pitches for 'one-nighters' are located in the top field. A new area for tents and summer use should be ready for 2001. The carefully thought out and well constructed toilet blocks, one below reception and the other at the far end of the site, have washbasins set in flat surfaces (in cabins with curtains), good sized shower compartments, a baby room and facilities for disabled visitors, laundry and washing-up facilities, all with free hot water and well heated in cool weather. Chemical disposal, motorcaravan service facilities and gas supplies. Opposite the entrance is a general store and newsagent and within 100 m, a pub and filling station. Riding 1 mile, golf or fishing 5 miles.

Directions: Directly by the A260 Folkestone - Canterbury road, 2 miles north of junction with A20. Follow signs for Canterbury. O.S.GR: TR211418.

Charges 2000:
-- Per adult £4.00; child (5-17 yrs) £1.20; pitch (non-member) £6.00 - £8.00; electricity £1.50 - £2.25.
-- VAT included.
-- Credit cards accepted.
Open: All year.
Address: 385 Canterbury Road, Densole, Folkestone, Kent CT18 7BG.
Tel: (01303) 892665 (not after 8 pm.).
Reservations: Advised at all times - write to or phone the Warden.

310 Hawthorn Farm Caravan and Camping Site, Martin Mill, Dover

Large, relaxed park close to Dover, useful for continental ferries.

Hawthorn Farm, set in 27 acres, is an extensive park taking 224 touring units of any type on several large meadows which could accommodate far more, plus 157 privately owned caravan holiday homes in their own areas. Campers not requiring electricity choose their own spot, most staying near the two toilet blocks leaving the farthest fields to those liking solitude. There are 120 pitches with electricity (10/16A), 46 of which are large pitches separated by hedges, the remainder in glades either side of tarmac roads. The heated sanitary blocks are well tiled and good quality, providing free hot water to washbasins set in flat surfaces, roomy pre-set showers with seat and screen, plus covered dishwashing and laundry sinks. Chemical disposal, motorcaravan service and a launderette. Breakfast and other snacks are served at the shop (closed 31/10) and a pub is nearby. This is a well run, relaxed park with plenty of room and mature hedging and trees making an attractive environment. A torch would be useful. Riding ½ mile, golf 3 miles, bicycle hire, fishing and boat launching 4 miles. Caravan storage available. Being only 4 miles from Dover docks, it is a very useful park for those using the ferries and is popular with continental visitors. Close to the sea at St Margaret's Bay, it is a fairly quiet situation apart from some rail noise (no trains 23.30 - 05.30). Gates close at 8 pm. A member of the Best of British group. Bellamy silver.

Directions: Park is north of the A258 road (Dover - Deal), with signs to park and Martin Mill where you turn off about 4 miles from Dover. O.S.GR: TR341464.

Charges 2000:
-- Per car, caravan/tent incl. 2 persons £9.00 - £12.00; extra adult £2.00 - £2.50; child (7-16 yrs) £1.50 - £2.00; hikers and bikers (2 man tent) less £2.00; dog £1.00; electricity £2.00.
-- Credit cards accepted.
-- VAT included.
Open: 1 March - 30 November or mid-December by arrangement.
Address: Martin Mill, Dover, Kent CT15 5LA.
Tel: (01304) 852658.
FAX: (01304) 853417.
Reservations: Contact park for details.

Kent

306 Yew Tree Caravan Park, Petham, nr. Canterbury

Tranquil country site with swimming pool.

Yew Tree Park, a small site, is located in the heart of the Kent countryside overlooking the Chartham Downs. Just 5 miles south of Canterbury and 8 miles north of the M20, it is ideally placed either to explore the delights of the ancient city or the many attractions of eastern and coastal Kent. Its nearness to the channel ports also makes it useful for a night stop on the way to, or on return from, the continent. If catching a late evening ferry you may remain on site after 12 noon for a small payment. Apart from the peaceful environment, the main feature of the park is the swimming pool (60 x 30 ft. open June-Sept) which is surrounded by caravan holiday homes and apartments, but is available to all campers. There are 45 pitches for tourers and tents, 20 with electricity (10A), marked on mainly level grass either side of the entrance road, the remainder unmarked on a rather attractive, sloping area which is left natural with trees and bushes creating cosy little recesses in which to pitch. The main brick-built sanitary blocks (one for each sex) are behind reception. They can be heated and each has four washbasins (warm water from a single tap), four toilets and four showers (on payment), with two more toilets on the edge of the camping area. Recently added is a toilet/ shower room for families or disabled visitors. Clothes and dishwashing facilities are provided, plus a washing machine, dryer and iron and chemical disposal. Shop (from April) and gas supplies. This neat, tidy, well cared for park that resident proprietors, Derek and Dee Zanders, have created makes an excellent base away from the hurly-burly of life where you can enjoy the rural scenery and also have the opportunity for walking, riding, visiting local places of interest or for cross-Channel excursions. Riding 4 miles, golf 6 miles. The County cricket ground is 4 miles. Tourist information. Dogs are not accepted. Torches useful.

Directions: Park is on B2068 Canterbury-Folkestone road. From south, take exit 11 from the M20. From Canterbury, ignore signs to Petham and Waltham on B2068 and continue towards Folkestone. From either direction, turn into road beside the Chequers Inn, turn left into park and follow road to owners' house/ reception. O.S.GR: TR138507.

Charges 2000:
-- First two adults £3.00 - £4.00 per person; extra adult £2.00 - £3.00; child 2-11 yrs 75p - £1.10, 12-16 yrs £1.00 - £1.60; caravan or trailer tent £2.00 - £3.50; motor-caravan £1.30 - £3.00; tent £1.00 - £2.50; extra car £1.00; electricity (deposit required) £1.75 - £2.00.
-- VAT included.
-- Credit cards accepted.

Open:
March - October.

Address:
Stone Street, Petham, Kent CT4 5PL.

Tel:
(01227) 700306. FAX: as phone. E-mail: yewtreepark @dialstart.net.

Reservations:
Made with deposit of £5 per night.

Alan Rogers' Discount

Less 10% in low season

307 Camping and Caravanning Club Site, Canterbury

Ideal site for touring northern Kent or as a stop-over for the ferry or the Tunnel.

Situated just off the A257 Sandwich road, about 1½ miles from the centre of Canterbury, this site is an ideal base for exploring Canterbury and the north Kent coast, as well as being a good stop-over to and from the Dover ferries, and the Folkestone Channel Tunnel terminal. There are 208 pitches, 87 with electricity hook-ups (16A) and, except at the very height of the season, you are likely to find a pitch, although not necessarily with electricity. Most of the pitches are on well kept grass with hundreds of saplings planted, but there are also 24 pitches with hardstanding. Some pitches do slope so blocks are advised. A good sized over-night area for late arrivals can be reached even when the barriers are down. Two modern, heated toilet blocks, the main one also with a laundry room plus a room for washing dishes, an outside vegetable preparation area, chemical disposal point and recycling bins. Not far from the second block is a motorcaravan service point where chemical toilets may also be emptied. Reception stocks a small range of essential foods, milk, papers and gas, and there is an excellent tourist information room next door. Not far from reception is a children's play area with equipment on bark chippings. The site is adjacent to Bekepond nature reserve and within walking distance of Howletts Zoo. Golf adjacent, bicycle hire 2 miles. Although the busy A257 is close, there is minimal noise from the traffic. Note: power lines cross the site.

Directions: From A2 take Canterbury exit and follow signs for Sandwich - A257. After passing Howe military barracks turn right into Bekesbourne Lane opposite golf course. O.S. GR: TR173575.

Charges 2000:
-- Per adult £3.75 - £5.30; child (6-18 yrs) £1.65; non-member pitch fee £4.30; electricity £1.60 - £2.35.
-- VAT included.
-- Credit cards accepted.

Open:
All year.

Address:
Bekesbourne Lane, Canterbury, Kent CT3 4AB.

Tel:
(01227) 463216 (no calls after 8 pm).

Reservations:
Necessary and made with deposit; contact the wardens.

South Coast
& New Forest

With two high quality
destinations to choose from,
Shorefield Country Parks
offers you the best
of both worlds
in touring
locations

LYTTON LAWN

Set in beautiful natural parkland close to Milford beach and the historic New Forest with views to the Isle of Wight. Peaceful, unspoilt and relaxing. Electricity hook-up, showers, laundrette, shop, 'Premier Pitches' and a children's area. Optional Leisure Club facilities 2¹/₂ miles away, at Shorefield.

OAKDENE
FOREST PARK

Over 55 acres of beautiful parkland giving direct access to the Avon Forest, and only 9 miles from Bournemouth's sandy beaches. New indoor and outdoor pools, sauna, steam room, spa bath, flume, gym, riding stables, adventure playground, club with entertainment, cafeteria, takeaway, general store and launderette.

SHOREFIELD
HOLIDAYS LIMITED

RALLIES WELCOME AT BOTH SITES

For further details telephone
01590 648331 Ref. A.R.

ENGLAND FOR EXCELLENCE
THE ENGLISH TOURIST BOARD
AWARDS FOR TOURISM

Oakdene Forest Park, St. Leonards, Ringwood, Hants BH24 2RZ
Lytton Lawn, Lymore Lane, Milford on Sea, Hants SO41 0TX
e-mail: holidays@shorefield.co.uk   **www.shorefield.co.uk**

305 Pine Lodge Touring Park, Bearsted, nr. Maidstone

Useful park near main London - Folkestone - Dover M20 motorway.

Set in the heart of Kent, near Leeds Castle and central for the historical and scenic attractions of this county, this park is on a slight slope, the rectangular field surrounded by rolling hills, farmland and trees. A gravel, one-way road circles the site with pitches set against hedges around the perimeter and around a figure of eight in the centre with picnic areas. Trees have been planted but these at present are for decoration and will take a while to grow enough to provide shade. Of the 100 pitches, 85 have electricity (10A), several have hardstanding and 2 are serviced. Water points, fenced central refuse, motorcaravan services, chemical disposal and waste water area. Access from the A20 road is wide but there may be background traffic noise. The new, good sanitary facilities are situated at the entrance to the park and include vanity style washbasins (free hot water), metered showers (token), laundry and washing up facilities, plus a shower and toilet room for disabled visitors. Basic supplies and gas are available from reception which also has tourist information. Fishing 3 miles, riding 2 miles, golf 1 mile. Local shops 1 mile (Bearsted) or 3½ miles (Maidstone). The park is very convenient for events staged at Leeds Castle and is a useful overnight stop between London and the channel ports. Small children's play area in a corner of the site, well away from the entrance. No dogs are admitted.

Charges 2000:
-- Per unit incl. 2 adults £9.00 - £11.00; extra adult £2.00; child (3-14 yrs) £1.00; electricity £1.50 - £2.25; awning or cyclists please enquire.
-- Credit cards accepted.

Open:
All year.

Address:
A20 Ashford Road, Hollingbourne, nr Maidstone, Kent ME17 1XH.

Tel:
(01622) 730018. FAX: (01622) 734498.

Reservations:
Contact park.

Directions: From M20 junction 8, at A20 roundabout, turn towards Bearsted and Maidstone and park is about ½ mile on the left. O.S.GR: TQ808548.

312 Gate House Wood Touring Park, Wrotham Heath

Sheltered park within easy reach of Brands Hatch.

This park, which opened for its first season in '98, has been created in a former quarry where all the pitches are on well drained grass. A spacious paved entrance with a new reception building and well stocked shop, leads on to the park itself. The 60 pitches are level and open with a few small trees, four water and fire points, two brick built barbecue units, and 40 electric hook-ups (10A). A children's playground has swings, seesaw and a slide all set on a safety base, and the entire site is enclosed by grassy banks on three sides, with a wild flower walk around the top. The comprehensive sanitary facilities are smart and well maintained, including open washbasins and push-button hot showers, with a well equipped family room, which is also fully designed for disabled people. The laundry and dishwashing room is at one end of the modern heated building, and there is free hot water throughout. Local attractions include Brands Hatch Circuit, the International Karting Circuit at Buckmore Park, and the nearby Country Park at West Malling. Within walking distance of the park are three pubs and a Cantonese restaurant. Trains run to London Victoria from Borough Green (2½ miles). No dogs or other pets, commercial vehicles or caravans/motorcaravans greater than 25' overall are admitted.

Charges 2000:
-- Per unit incl. 2 adults £8.00 - £9.50; hiker's tent (incl. 2 adults) £6.00 - £7.00; extra adult £1.50; child (3-12 yrs) £1.00; awning £1.00; extra car £1.00; electricity £1.70 - £2.20.
-- VAT included.

Open:
1 April - end October.

Address:
Ford Lane, Wrotham Heath, Sevenoaks, Kent TN15 7SD.

Tel:
(01732) 843062.

Reservations:
Made with deposit (£5 for 3 days, £10 over 3 days or £10 p/week for longer stays).

Directions: From M26 junction 2a, take A20 eastwards towards Wrotham Heath and Maidstone. Just past junction with A25, and opposite the Royal Oak pub, turn left into Ford Lane, and park is immediately on left. O.S.GR: TQ630580.

Kent

303 Tanner Farm Touring Caravan and Camping Park, Marden

Quality park in quiet, spacious, rural setting.

Developed as part of a family working farm, Tanner Farm is recognised as a top class park. This is the heart of the Weald of Kent with orchards, hop gardens, lovely countryside and delightful small villages. The owners are much concerned with conserving the natural beauty of the environment and visitors are welcome to walk around the farm and see the Shire horses at work. The park extends over 15 acres, most of which is level and part a gentle slope. The grass meadowland has been semi-landscaped by planting saplings, etc. which units back onto (the owners don't wish to regiment pitches into rows). Places are numbered but not marked, allowing plenty of space between units which, with large open areas, gives a pleasant, comfortable atmosphere. There are 100 pitches, all with 16A electricity, 13 with hardstanding, 4 with water tap and 1 with waste water point also. The farm drive links the park with the B2079 and a group of refurbished oast houses (listed heritage buildings) with a duck pond in front, along with rare pigs, pygmy goats, lambs, etc. make a focal point. The traditional farm building on the right at the entrance houses a small shop (opening hours and stock limited in winter) and reception. Gas is supplied. The two heated sanitary units are well tiled and given a most pleasant appearance with interior flower arrangements, hanging baskets and flower beds. Hot water is free for the washbasins (private cubicles in both units), which have mirrors and shaver points, in the showers and in the dishwashing sinks. There are purpose built facilities for disabled visitors, a small launderette, chemical disposal and motorcaravan service point. A bathroom (£1 token) and baby facilities have been added in the newer block (this block is closed Nov - Easter). Small children's play area with swings and adventure climbing frame and fishing on site (on payment). Dogs are accepted on leads with paths for exercise. There is good lighting around the park, but a torch may be useful. The friendly management advise on local attractions, shops and pubs. There are many National Trust attractions in the area (Sissinghurst, Scotney Castle, Bodiam Castle), riding and golf within 6 miles, leisure centres and sailing facilities near and good shopping facilities at Maidstone and Tunbridge Wells. Caravan storage all year. The park is a member of the Caravan Club's 'managed under contract' scheme although non-members are also very welcome. Early reservation is advised at this popular park.

Directions: Park is 2½ miles south of Marden on B2079 towards Goudhurst. O.S.GR: TQ732417.

Charges 2000:
-- Per pitch £3.00; adult £2.60 - £3.90; child £1.10 - £1.20; 2-man tent plus car (all incl.) £8.00 - £8.50, plus bicycles £5.50 - £6.00; electricity £1.50 - £2.25; all service pitch +£2.00.
-- Only one car per pitch permitted.
-- VAT included.
-- Credit cards accepted.

Open:
All year.

Address:
Goudhurst Road, Marden, Kent TN12 9ND.

Tel:
(01622) 832399.
FAX: (01622) 832472.
E-mail: tannerfarmpark @cs.com.

Reservations:
Essential for high season and B.Hs, recommended for other times. Made with deposit (£5 for 1-3 nights; £10 over 3 nights and B.Hs).

311 Quex Caravan Park, Birchington, nr. Margate

Peaceful site in a secluded location; no tents accepted.

This park does not accept tents and, although there are a fair number of privately owned holiday homes, they do not intrude on the touring area which is in a sheltered glade under tall trees. There are 60 touring pitches with 48 electric hook-ups (16A) and a well equipped central sanitary unit. This is in a chalet style building with all the usual facilities including free controllable hot showers, dishwashing sinks under cover at the rear, and a laundry room with sink, washing machine and dryer. When we visited there was no heating, but this has now been added. There is a well stocked shop on site, although there are many supermarkets close by, and reception can provide you with a map of the local area. Local attractions include Quex House and gardens, the model village and motor museum at Ramsgate, while in the seaside resort of Margate you can walk through 1,000 years of history at the Caves, or visit the Hollywood Bowl. Fishing, golf or riding 3 miles. More than one dog per pitch is accepted by prior arrangement only. A member of the Best of British group. Bellamy silver.

Directions: From roundabout at junction of A28 and A299, take A28 east towards Birchington and Margate. At Birchington carry straight on at roundabout by church, then take next right, then right again, and left at mini roundabout. Site is on right in ½ mile (well signed). O.S.GR: TR320685.

Charges 2000:
-- Per unit incl. 2 adults £9.00 - £12.00; extra adult £2.00 - £2.50; child (5-16 yrs) £1.50 - £2.00; dog £1.00; electricity £2.00.
-- Less 10% for 4 nights booked (and paid for on arrival).
-- VAT included.

Open:
7 March - 7 November.

Address:
Park Road, Birchington, nr. Margate, Kent CT7 0BL.

Tel:
(01843) 841273.
FAX: as phone.

Reservations:
Contact site for details.

TANNER FARM
TOURING CARAVAN & CAMPING
PARK
Goudhurst Road, Marden, Kent TN12 9ND
Tel: **01622 832399** Fax: **01622 832472**
e-mail: tannerfarmpark@cs.com www.tannerfarmpark.co.uk
Attractively landscaped, peaceful Touring Park set in the centre of 150 acre idyllic Weald family farm.
Spotless facilities. Central for a wealth of attractions, including our own Shire Horses.
★ Open All Year ★ 100 Electric Touring Pitches ★ Centrally Heated Toilet Blocks ★ Free showers
★ Dogs Welcome on Leads ★ Children's Play Area ★ Shop/Gas Supplies
★ Launderette ★ Hard Standings ★ Disabled Facilities

304 Broadhembury Caravan and Camping Park, Ashford

Small, pleasant touring park with some holiday homes, near to Folkestone and ferries.

In quiet countryside just outside Ashford, this well landscaped, sheltered park takes 65 touring units of any type, plus 25 caravan holiday homes (5 for hire). All pitches are on level, neatly cut grass backing onto hedges, 50 have electrical connections (10A), 4 are fully serviced and have 16A electricity, 8 have double hardstanding plus a grass area for an awning. The park is friendly and popular and often becomes full in the main season, with a good proportion of continental visitors, so reservation is advisable. The single small toilet block is kept very clean, can be heated in cool weather and has free hot water to washbasins (with shelf and mirror) and showers. Alongside is a campers' kitchen, fully enclosed with dishwashing sinks, plus a microwave, fridge and freezer, all free of charge. There is a small laundry room, chemical disposal and motorcaravan service point. Other facilities include a TV and pool room, games room with table tennis, two children's playgrounds (grass or wood-chip bases) and play field away from the touring area, public phone and a dog exercise field. Security arrangements are excellent - the gates are closed at 11 pm. in high season with coded entry. The new reception building at the park entrance also contains a well stocked shop and comprehensive tourist information. Up to two dogs per pitch are accepted. Fishing ½ mile, bicycle hire or riding 2 miles and golf 1 mile. For those who would like a trip to France, the International Railway Terminal is at Ashford (Paris in 2 hours) - take your passport. A member of the Best of British group.

Directions: From M20 exit 10 on A2070, after 2 miles follow sign for Kingsnorth. Turn left at second crossroads in Kingsnorth village. O.S.GR: TR010382.

Charges 2000:
-- Per unit incl. 2 persons £10.00 - £13.00; extra adult £2.20; child (5-16 yrs) £1.80; extra car £2.20; electricity (10A) £2.20; one awning or pup tent included; 'super' pitch plus £6.00.
-- Less 10% outside July/Aug. for bookings of 7 nights or more.
-- VAT included.
-- Credit cards accepted.

Open:
All year.

Address:
Steeds Lane, Kingsnorth, Ashford, Kent TN26 1NQ.

Tel/Fax:
(01233) 620859.

E-mail: holidays@broadhembury.co.uk.

Reservations:
Essential for B.Hs and peak season; made with £5 per night deposit (min. 3 nights at Easter or Spr. B.H). Balance 21 days before arrival for B.Hs, on arrival at other times.

Important London Events

January
International Boat Show, Earl's Court.
March
Ideal Home Exhibition. Earls Court.
April
London Marathon.
May
Chelsea Flower Show. Chelsea Royal Hospital.
June
Beating the Retreat. Horse Guard's Parade
Trooping the Colour. Queen's official Birthday.
Starts at Buckingham Palace.
Biggin Hill International Air Fair

June/July
Wimbledon Lawn Tennis Championship
August
B.H. Weekend- Notting Hill Carnival. Europe's largest outdoor festival.
October
Annual Full Tidal Closure. Lifting of the Thames Flood Barrier
November
London to Brighton Veteran Car Run
December
Olympia International Showjumping Championships

London

London Tourist Board & Convention Bureau

Glen House, Stag Place,
Victoria, London SW1E 5LT
Tel: 0171 932 2000 Fax: 0171 932 0222
Internet: www.LondonTown.com.

London is the largest city in Europe, covering some 610 square miles with a population of nearly seven million.

However, the centre is fairly compact and covers the financial district called 'The City', the entertainment and shopping area known as 'The West End' and Westminster, seat of Parliament and home of royalty.

London's wealthiest neighbourhoods, such as Knightsbridge, Kensington and Chelsea, lie to the west. East of the city is the culturally intriguing East End and the ambitious Docklands development and further down-river, historical Greenwich.

For information on West End shows, visit the web site: www.officiallondontheatre.co.uk

For more details about London's restaurants visit the web site: www.eatlondon.net

For information on shopping visit: www.shop-london.net.

Experience the London Eye: www.ba.londoneye.com. The world's highest observation wheel sweeps the London skyline at an incredible 450 feet. Thirty-two high tech capsules carrying up to 25 passengers each, offer unique and breathtaking views of London, day and night.

327 Crystal Palace Caravan Club Site, Crystal Palace, London

Busy but friendly site with easy access for central London attractions.

The Caravan Club's site at Crystal Palace in south London provides easy access to the city centre and all its many attractions. A pleasant and efficiently run site, it is arranged in terraces overlooking the ruins of the old Crystal Palace, its park and National Sports Centre. It is surprisingly quiet given its location (with the possible exception of regular police sirens and over-flying aircraft). In peak season it is even busier than Abbey Wood with many overseas visitors and advance booking is always necessary. However, as most of the pitches are on gravel hardstanding, it is particularly useful for out of season stays. There are places for 84 caravans or motorcaravans, all with electricity connections (16A). Tents are placed on the site's well mown lawns at the top of the site near reception. In summer an overflow area across the approach road (with portacabin style sanitary facilities) takes further tents or small motorcaravans. The single toilet block can be heated in cool weather and has free hot water in the washbasins (with shelf and mirror, curtained for ladies) and controllable showers, a WC and washbasin for disabled visitors and a laundry room. Washing up sinks and neat rubbish bins are outside, under cover. Chemical disposal and motorcaravan service facilities. Gas is available from reception where there is plenty of tourist information (travel cards for sale). Shops, pubs, etc. are ¼ mile away. Many buses stop outside the site, including services to central London. The Crystal Palace park is extensive and provides open spaces for strolls or picnics and plenty of activities for children. The Sports Centre has two swimming pools, tennis and squash courts and gym facilities, with national events in a variety of sports to watch at certain times. The park and the Sports Centre are due for substantial redevelopment and when this begins access will obviously be restricted. An area at the site entrance should be used for arrivals after 10.30 pm.- the pitch areas have a coded security barrier.

Charges 2000:
-- Per pitch £6.50 - £9.00; adult £3.25 - £4.00; child (5-16 yrs) £1.10 - £1.20; electricity £2.20 - £1.45.
-- Caravan Club members pay less.
-- Tent campers - apply to site.
-- VAT included.
-- Credit cards accepted.
Open:
All year.
Address:
Crystal Palace Parade, London SE19 1UF.
Tel:
(020) 8778 7155. (08.00-20.00 hrs).
FAX: (020) 8676 0980.
Reservations:
Essential at all times and made with £5 deposit - contact site.

Directions: On A205 South Circular road travelling east, pass Dulwich College and Golf Course on right (avoid College Road - width restriction), turn right at traffic lights (Harvester pub on left). Within ¼ mile at traffic lights turn right into Sydenham Hill; in 350 yds at roundabout turn left (still Sydenham Hill). Site entrance is 1 mile opposite mini-roundabouts (take care on these). Travelling west on A205 South Circular, immediately after passing under Catford railway bridge, keep left onto A212 signed Crystal Palace. After 2¾ miles site entrance is on left at top of Westwood Hill before two mini-roundabouts. O.S.GR: TQ341724.

321 Lee Valley Caravan Park, Dobbs Weir, Hoddesdon

Pleasant park north of London in Lee Valley Park.

Stretching for 23 miles along the Lee Valley and covering 10,000 acres from Ware to the east end of London, Lee Valley Park is administered by the Lee Valley Regional Park Authority. Extensive development of the Park into a leisure area now means it offers a wide variety of outdoor and sporting pursuits, including riding, water sports, golf, cycle tracks and places of interest. Set between Hoddesdon, Broxbourne and Nazeing, and under the same management as Lee Valley Campsite, this park is situated in the far north of the complex. The touring section consists of a large, open, well mown meadow with space for 100 units (36 with 10A electricity) and is quite separate from 100 caravan holiday homes. There is no shade in the touring area, but tall trees surrounding the site offer adequate shelter, and it has a neat, tidy and well cared for appearance. The single, heated sanitary block (access by key) has been recently refurbished and is of good quality with free hot water to the open washbasins and shower cubicles. Other facilities include a baby room, laundry, rotary clothes dryers and good en-suite facilities for disabled visitors. There is no shop on site, but a free bus service to a nearby super-store is offered three times a week, and there is a bar/restaurant just 100 yards from the entrance. Some fishing is possible from the canal towpath that runs past the site, with further opportunities nearby and a swimming pool is just 2 miles away. Trains run from Broxbourne (about 2 miles) to London, with the journey taking about 30 minutes. Dobbs Weir industrial estate and garden centres are near, although surrounding trees screen out noise and create some privacy.

Directions: Take exit 25 from M25 and then north on A10 for 4 miles; take the Hoddesdon exit, turn left at second roundabout following signs for Dobbs Weir and park is on the right within 1 mile. O.S. GR: TL383082.

Charges 2000:
-- Per adult £5.20; child (3-16 yrs) £2.10; electricity £2.25.
-- Min charge £7.10 (but not backpackers).
-- VAT included.
-- Credit cards accepted.
-- Check out time 5 pm.
Open:
March - 31 October.
Address:
Charlton Meadows, Essex Road, Dobbs Weir, Hoddeson, Hertfordshire EN11 OAS.
Tel:
(01992) 462090.
FAX (01992) 462090.
E-mail: info@ leevalleypark.org.uk
Reservations:
Made with £5 deposit - write to park for reservation form. (For information contact PO Box 88, Enfield, Middlesex: tel: 01992 700766).

see colour advert between pages 128/129

325 Lee Valley Campsite, Chingford, North London

Friendly and well run park, conveniently placed for visits to the London area.

This site provides an excellent base from which to visit the capital, having both easy access to the M25 and excellent public transport links into the centre of London. Close to Epping Forest and in the heart of the Lee Valley there is much to enjoy in the surrounding area; from walking and cycling, to golf, fishing and riding. With capacity for 200 units of all types the site is mostly level, with several bush sheltered avenues and plenty of trees throughout. There are 20 pitches with tarmac hardstanding and 100 with electricity (10A). Of the three toilet blocks (one of which is heated), two have been refurbished in readiness for this year. All, however, are more than adequate and clean, with free hot water to washbasins and controllable showers. There is also a well equipped room for disabled visitors. Clothes and dishwashing facilities are provided, plus washing machines, dryers, rotary clothes lines, irons and chemical disposal. Well stocked shop, gas available. Children's playground, but no other on-site amenities; although those staying here are often out visiting London. Two local buses stop by the site at fairly frequent intervals in season, with another alternative, and equally good service, every 20 minutes to Walthamstow underground station just 500 yds away. Alternatively you can park at South Woodford or Chingford stations and go by train.

Directions: From M25 exit 26 (Waltham Abbey) from where site is signed take A112 towards Chingford and site is about 3 miles on right. It can also be approached on A112 from the North Circular Road. O.S. GR: TQ378970.

Charges 2001:
-- Per adult £5.40; child (under 16 yrs) £2.40; electricity £2.25.
-- Min charge £7.80 per unit/night.
-- VAT included.
-- Credit cards accepted.
Open:
Easter - 27 October.
Address:
Stewardstone Road, Chingford, London E4 7RA.
Tel:
0181 529 5689.
FAX: 0181 559 4070.
E-mail: scs@ leevalleypark.org.uk
Reservations:
any length up to 14 days with £5 deposit. (For information contact PO Box 88, Enfield, Middx; tel: 01992 700766).

Lee Valley Cycle Circuit Campsite

This site is set in 40 acres of parkland, only 4 miles from the Tower of London and with views of the Millennium Dome. It is a short bus ride to the nearest Underground station for easy access to central London. The adjacent Cycle Circuit offers bicycle hire on an off-road 1.6 km. circuit and is opposite a nature reserve.

Directions: Site is a short distance from Eastway/Ruckholt Road directly linked to the A102M. Follow signs for Spitalfields Market or camping signs.

Address: Quartermile Lane, Layton, London E15 2EN. Tel: 020 8534 6085. FAX: 020 8536 0959.

London / Essex

326 Abbey Wood Caravan and Camping Site, Abbey Wood

Quietly situated Caravan Club site in S.E. London with rail links to the city centre.

This site is run by the Caravan Club and there are reductions for their members. It is one of the nearest sites to London and it becomes very full and crowded in the summer months with campers of many nationalities. Reservations are made for all units except tents and are very advisable for July/Aug. and B.Hs. Tent campers, for whom there is a special railed area, with cars parked separately, must take their chance. Stays are limited to a maximum of 14 days. Although within a built-up area, this grassy site is in a quiet and pleasant setting with many mature trees. Most parts, especially those for caravans, are sloping but many of the 360 pitches are levelled. A curving line of gravel hardstandings is available for 14 motorcaravans. The three traditional type toilet blocks, all heated in cool weather, have free hot water in the washbasins (with shelf and mirror, curtained for ladies), mostly controllable showers, washing-up sinks and laundry room. Chemical disposal and motorcaravan service facilities. There is not much on-site activity but nearly all those staying here want to visit London. There is a train service every 15 minutes from Abbey Wood station (5 mins walk) to either Charing Cross or Cannon Street. Bread, milk and cold drinks are available from the office in high season. Gas is available. A good travel and information centre (open 8.30- 11 am) can provide tickets for travel and attractions. Children's playground with sand base. Golf 4 miles. Sports centre at Crook Log, 1 mile. The Royal Observatory and the Thames Barrier are nearby. Dogs are accepted on leads. A car park at the entrance has electrical connections for late arrivals (after 10.30 pm). Security could be a problem - be aware.

Charges 2000:
-- Per pitch £6.00 - £8.50; adult £3.25 - £4.00; child (5-16 yrs) £1.10 - £1.20; electricity £2.20 - £1.45; extra car £1.00.
-- Caravan Club members pay less.
-- Tent campers - apply to site.
-- VAT included.
-- Credit cards accepted.

Open:
All year.

Address:
Federation Road, Abbey Wood, London SE2 0LS.

Tel:
010 8311 1465 (08.00-20.00 hrs). FAX: 010 8311 7708.

Reservations:
Essential for Easter, Spring B.H. July/Aug with £5 deposit.

Directions: From east on M2/A2 or from central London: on A2 turn off at A221 junction (third exit off the A2) into Danson Road (signed Bexleyheath, Welling and Sidcup). Follow sign Bexleyheath to Crook Log (A207 junction); at traffic lights turn right and immediately left into Brampton Road. In 1½ miles at traffic lights turn left into Bostal Road (A206); in ¾ mile at traffic lights turn right into Basildon Road (B213). In 300 yds turn right into McLeod Road, in about ½ mile at roundabout turn right into Knee Hill; in 100 yds turn right (second right) into Federation Road. Site on left in 50 yds. From M25, north, west or south approach: leave at junction 2 onto A2 (signed London), then as above. Note: route is well signed with International caravan and camping signs. O.S.GR: TQ472785.

330 The Grange Country Park, East Bergholt, nr. Colchester

Pleasant well tended all year park with heated pool and high season entertainment.

Set in the heart of Constable country, this neat 11 acre park is under new ownership. It offers 120 pitches, many with electrical connections (16A). All are on flat grass with well lit, tarmac roads throughout the site. There are 41 fully serviced 'executive' pitches, a separate area for tents and 52 privately owned caravan holiday homes including seven for hire. In addition to a communal barbecue point, many pitches also have their own facilities (equipment can be hired from reception). Three modern heated sanitary blocks with good, clean facilities have free hot water. There is an en-suite unit for disabled visitors and two laundry rooms. A range of amenities includes a 60 x 30 ft. outdoor, heated swimming pool plus children's paddling pool (open Whitsun - 7 Sept and super-vised during high season), with snack bar, grass seating area, sauna and solarium. There is also a bar and restaurant, offering reasonably priced meals and enter-tainment in high season, with games and TV room and a small children's play area on grass and matting. Well stocked shop (April - Sept, limited hours out of peak season) Single groups, motorbikes and commercial vehicles are not accepted. Dogs are permitted (max. 2, no dangerous breeds) and a dog walk and nature trail are offered. Limited facilities available during winter (Nov - March).

Charges 2000:
-- Per unit incl. 2 adults £9.00 - £13.00; premier pitch incl. 2 adults, electricity, awning £14.00 - £18.00; extra adult £1.50 - £2.50; child (3-14) £1.00 - £2.00; electricity £2.25 - £2.50; dog £0.50 - £1.00.
-- Less 10% for stays over 10 nights.
-- VAT included.

Open:
All year except 4 Jan. - 1 Feb.

Address:
East Bergholt, Colchester, Essex CO7 6UX.

Tel:
(01206) 298567/298912. FAX: (01206) 298770. E-mail: enquiries@ grangecountrypark.co.uk

Reservations:
Made with £10 deposit and £2 fee.

Directions: Park is between Ipswich (8 miles) and Colchester (10 miles). Follow signs for East Bergholt from the A12 (4 miles). O.S.GR: TL097352.

East of England Tourist Board

Essex, Suffolk, Norfolk, Cambridgeshire, Hertfordshire and Bedfordshire

Toppesfield Hall, Hadleigh, Suffolk IP7 5DM
Tel: (01473) 822922 FAX (01473) 823063
E-mail: eastofenglandtouristboard@compuserve.com
Internet: http://www.visitbritain.com/east-of-england

Covering the seven counties of **Cambridgeshire, Essex, Hertfordshire, Bedfordshire, Norfolk, Suffolk** and **Lincolnshire**. The region as a whole is characterised by a bracing windswept climate, prairie-like fields of wheat, sugar-beet and rape and no significant industrial centres. The legacy of the medieval wool trade when the region was the best-off and most populated in England is evident in the rich array of parish churches, often faced in flint and sometimes thatched, and the handsome market towns.

The region as a whole is characterised by a bracing Windswept climate, prairie-like fields of wheat, sugar-beet and rape and no significant industrial centres. The legacy of the medieval wool trade when the region was the best-off and most populated in England is evident in the rich array of parish churches, often faced in flint and sometimes thatched, and the handsome market towns.

Norfolk is best experienced in the quiet resorts, bird reserves, dunes and sand marshes of the north coast. The Broads have a charm of their own. Norwich is a city on a human scale, and well worth a visit

The Fens of **Cambridgeshire** are absolutely flat, criss-crossed by drainage canals installed by Dutch engineers in the 17th century and the peat rich soil makes this one of England's most fertile agricultural areas. Ely cathedral is not to be missed nor the college courts and 'backs' at Cambridge where the punt (a flat-bottomed boat propelled by a long pole) is the traditional form of transport.

Suffolk's undulating country has been immortalised by John Constable. Lavenham is one of the best preserved villages with timbered halls, and houses covered in ornamental plaster work. Suffolk's charming coast is part reed-fringed, part heath-topped, with small time soothing resorts. Aldeburgh and the 'Maltings' hold one of the most prestigious festivals of Music and Arts, founded by the famous British composer, Benjamin Britten.

The Roman town of Colchester is the principle reason for visiting **Essex**, perhaps the least attractive of the counties.

Hatfield House in **Hertfordshire** is one of England's finest stately homes and more grand country houses can be found in **Bedfordshire**.

---

333 Moat Barn Touring Caravan Park, Woodbridge

Small, tranquil site, ideal for touring and cyclists.

Mike Allen opened this small, new family run touring park in April 2000. It provides just 20 level pitches, all with electricity hook-ups (10A). As yet, the hedges have not matured, but the pitches are spacious. A new sanitary block provides two each of washbasins, showers and WCs for each sex. Showers are free and controllable, there are non-slip floor tiles, hair and hand dryers are provided and the facilities can be heated. A separate unit houses a dishwashing sink with free hot water. A laundry and shop are planned for 2001, Dogs are welcome on leads. All this goes to make this park a very pleasant place to use as a base. Walkers and cyclists will enjoy this location - the park is on the Suffolk Heritage Cycle Route, and also the Hull - Harwich National Cycle Route. Moat Barn also offers bed and breakfast.

Directions: From Ipswich on A12 to Lowestoft, after Hasketon roundabout take first left signed Bredfield. At village pump turn right and follow road past public house and church. Continue through S-bends and, after 200 yards, site entrance is on left, just after farm buildings. From Lowestoft, take right turn to Bredfield just before Hasketon roundabout, then as above. O.S.GR: TM270537.

Charges 2000:
-- Per unit incl. 2 adults £9.00; extra car £1.00; electricity £1.50.
-- VAT included.

Open:
April - October.

Address:
Dallinghoo Road, Bredfield, Woodbridge, Suffolk IP13 6BD.

Tel:
(01473) 737520.

Reservations:
Advised, especially for B.Hs.

Suffolk / Norfolk

331 Low House Touring Caravan Centre, Foxhall, nr. Ipswich

Small tranquil touring park, open all year; tents accepted subject to space.

Set in 3½ acres, this beautiful garden site has 30 pitches, all with electrical connections (most 16A, but some 10A) and an abundance of trees, shrubs and flowers. In two sections, you drive through one field (the rally field) to reach the more secluded, sheltered garden area. We understand from the owner that there are 90 different varieties of trees on site, and an ornamental tree walk can be followed around the edge of the park. Pitches back onto trees, offering plenty of shade and the opportunity to observe a range of wildlife. The rally field has a more open aspect, but is still well sheltered and tranquil. Tents are accepted only if space is available. Reception and the office are in the cottage and there is a modern, heated sanitary block which is spotlessly clean with hot showers (50p). There are chemical disposal facilities, but no dishwashing sinks. No on-site provision facilities but a supermarket is 2 miles (towards Ipswich), frozen goods can be stored and Calor gas is available. A good bus service to Ipswich stops just outside the site. A small children's adventure play area is on grass and bark chipping base, with the added attraction of a pets corner, with rabbits and ornamental fowl. Public phone. A torch would be useful. The enthusiastic and helpful owner, John Booth, has made arrangements for site residents to join the Civil Service club which is 5 minutes walk, with a bar, good value meals and a sports centre. There is also a pub in Bucklesham village (1½ miles) and other good pubs nearby. Golf 2 miles. The centre lies between Felixstowe (8 miles) and Ipswich (5 miles) and would be a useful stopover for the Felixstowe port or Harwich.

Charges 2000:
--Per unit incl. 2 adults and children £6.50; adult (over 16 yrs) £2.00; awning no charge (but please lift groundsheets); extra car 50p; electricity (16A) £1.50 - £2.25 (1/10-5/4).
-- No commercial vehicles.
-- No credit cards or Eurocheques.
Open:
All year.
Address:
Bucklesham Road, Foxhall, nr. Ipswich, Suffolk IP10 0AU.
Tel:
(01473) 659437.
FAX: (01473) 659880.
E-mail: john.e.booth @talk21.com.
Reservations:
Advanced booking advised - phone any time.

Directions: Turn off A14 (was A45) Ipswich ring road (south) via slip road onto A1156 (signed Ipswich East). Follow road over bridge which crosses over the A45 and almost immediately turn right (no sign). After ½ mile turn right again (signed Bucklesham) and site is on left after ¼ mile. O.S.GR: TM225423.

348 Little Lakeland Caravan Park, Wortwell, nr. Harleston

Traditional, mature little site with own fishing lake.

This peaceful hideaway is tucked behind the houses and gardens that border the village main street. There are 58 pitches with a number of caravan holiday homes and long stay units, but there should always be around 22 places for tourers. The pitches are mostly individual with mature hedges and trees separating them. A modern, heated sanitary unit is well tiled and has washbasins in vanity style units (all in cubicles for ladies, one for men), and spacious, controllable showers. Hot water is free throughout. The laundry has a washing machine, dryer, spin dryer and ironing facilities. A well equipped room for disabled visitors also has facilities for baby changing. A further unit (also heated) by reception provides a shower, WC and basin per sex and is used mostly in the colder months. There is a small children's play area, and a library of paperback books in the summerhouse. Reception stocks gas and some basic essentials. Recycling bins. Fishing in the lake is free for campers, max. 4 rods per unit. Riding 6 miles, golf 4 miles. The village has a post office and general store, a pub and garage. Places to visit nearby include The Cider Place at Ilketshall St Lawrence, The Otter Trust at Earsham, and there are numerous local way-marked walks around Wortwell and nearby Harleston which also has a market every Wednesday. A member of the Countryside Discovery group. Bellamy silver.

Charges 2001:
-- Per unit incl. 2 adults £7.80 - £9.80; extra adult £2.00; child (4-16 yrs.) £1.00; electricity (10A max) £1.60; extra vehicle £1.00.
-- VAT included.
-- No credit cards.
Open:
15 March - 31 October.
Address:
Wortwell, Harleston, Norfolk IP20 0EL.
Tel:
(01986) 788646.
FAX: as phone.
E-mail: information @littlelakeland.co.uk
Reservations:
Advisable for B.Hs and peak season; made with £20 deposit or full fee if less.

Directions: Approaching from Diss, leave A143 at roundabout signed Wortwell. Continue to village, pass 'The Bell' public house then a garage on the right, after which turn right at first bungalow (Little Lakeland Lodge) watching carefully for signs. Site is down lane, 250 yards on right. O.S.GR: TM270850.

351 Liffens Holiday Park, Burgh Castle, nr. Great Yarmouth

Long established family holiday site with outdoor pool.

This popular family holiday park is in a semi-rural location, but within easy reach of Great Yarmouth. On site there is an area with 109 privately owned caravan holiday homes, plus 35 site owned units for rent. A separate grassy open area provides around 150 touring pitches, some slightly sloping, with only 100 having electrical hook-ups (16A), plus 2 fully serviced pitches. Two sanitary units of differing ages provide clean but fairly standard facilities with pre-set hot showers, open style washbasins, a unit for disabled persons, a baby room, and dishwashing sinks. All hot water is free. The laundry is located in a separate older unit and has washing machines, dryers, spinners and irons. There are chemical disposal and motorcaravan service points, and gas is available. Other facilities include a large restaurant/bar that has club style entertainment in season, and a takeaway service (noon-7pm) and overlooks a heated outdoor swimming pool (60 x 30 ft; open 29/5-10/9). Campers can also use the indoor pool and other facilities at Liffens Welcome Holiday Centre close by. The excellent children's playground and a fenced hard surfaced multi-court for ball games are far enough from the pitches to preserve peace and quiet. The site also operates a post office/shop which is adjacent to the site, and a regular bus service runs from here to Great Yarmouth. Golf 2 miles, fishing ¼ mile. The remains of a Roman fortress border the site.

Directions: At junction of A12 and A143 at roundabout south of Great Yarmouth take Burgh Road westwards, straight over at next roundabout, then second left into Butt lane. Site is on right. Avoid width restricted road closer to Great Yarmouth. O.S.GR: TM490050.

Charges 2001:
-- Per unit incl. 4 persons £8.00 - £15.00; extra person free - £2.00; fully serviced pitch plus £4.00; awning £1.50 - £2.00; extra pup tent £5.00; electricity £3.00; dog (one only) £2.00.
-- Special offer breaks available.
-- Credit cards accepted.
-- VAT included.

Open:
2 April - 30 October.

Address:
Burgh Castle,
Great Yarmouth,
Norfolk NR31 9QB.

Tel:
(01493) 780357.
FAX: (01493) 782383.

Reservations:
Essential for high season and made with £20 p/week deposit.

Norfolk

339 The Dower House Touring Park, Thetford Forest

Peaceful park in a woodland setting.

Situated in 20 acres of Britain's largest woodland forest on the Suffolk and Norfolk borders, the Dower House provides quiet woodland walks (you may be asked to 'donate' a walk) and cycle ways, with an abundance of wildlife. It is also an ideal centre from which to explore Breckland. The present owners acquired the park some years ago and have worked hard to upgrade the facilities, yet without compromising its natural features. There is provision for 60 tents and 100 vans on unmarked, fairly level, open grass with some mature oaks, in four field areas surrounded by forest, with the Dower House in the centre. Electrical hook-ups (10-16A) are available on three fields with wheel hardstandings on one. Six pitches for visitors with mobility problems are linked by a path to the main facilities. A smallish swimming pool (only 1.1 m. deep, late May - early Sept), with a paddling pool alongside, is near the house. The Dower House, as well as being the home of the owners, houses a pleasant bar that has been extended and which also serves bar food (weekends only in low season) and a takeaway. TV and quiet rooms (no games machines). A pleasant patio area is used for special feature weekends (e.g. Morris dancing, Star Gazers and Swinging 60s). A licensed shop doubles as reception and opens in the season, on request at other times. There are two toilet blocks – a small, refurbished one near the entrance, and a larger one with free hot water in the row of washbasins with mirrors, shaver points and a baby room. A separate building houses the showers (5 for each sex, 20p) and a unit for disabled people. Dishwashing room, including a lower sink for children or disabled people. Laundry room with washing machine and dryer. Chemical disposal. Gas supplies. Caravan storage available. Public phone. Information room. A torch is necessary as there is no site lighting. Fishing nearby (1½ miles). Very large, open air market at Snetterton motor racing circuit (2-3 miles) on Sundays. Bellamy gold.

Directions: From A11 (Thetford - Norwich) road follow signs to east Harling and park is signed. Turn right at the church and right at T junction; park is on right. From A1066 Thetford-Garboldisham road follow signs for East Harling and park is on left after passing Forestry Commission site. Follow unmade road for approx. 1 mile driving slowly past the Gamekeepers cottage. O.S GR: TL969853.

Charges 2000:
-- Per unit incl. 2 persons £8.50 - £10.80; extra adult 55p - £1.75; extra child 45p - 95p; hikers or cyclists (2 persons) incl. tent £6.50 - £8.80; electricity £2.25 - £2.50; visitor £1.25 - £2.50 per car; dog or awning free.
-- Credit cards accepted.

Open:
17 March - 1 October.

Address:
Thetford Forest,
East Harling,
Norfolk NR16 2SE.

Tel:
(01953) 717314.
FAX: (01953) 717843.
E-mail: info@
dowerhouse.co.uk.

Reservations:
Accepted by phone; deposit of £10 required for electricity.

349 The Grange Touring Park, Ormesby St Margaret, Gt Yarmouth

Very appealing and well appointed, family touring site.

The overall appearance of this site is that of a garden, with many hanging baskets, flower beds, bluebells and daffodils under the trees in spring, and all carefully tended by the resident wardens. Of the 70 level grassy pitches, 62 have electricity (5A) and all are arranged around tarmac access roads. The modern stylish sanitary building is exceptionally well appointed, beautifully tiled and spotlessly clean, housing all the usual facilities including a baby changing room in the ladies' and with free hot water throughout. The laundry room has a washing machine, dryer and a mangle (very popular we were told), and washing lines are provided at the rear of the building. Other facilities include children's swings, a mobile shop calls daily in high season and gas is available from reception. Next to the campsite is The Grange itself - a free house offering a wide range of meals, beers and real ale, plus children's play equipment (open all year). The site owner also has a holiday campsite at Hemsby (4 miles) with its own wide sandy beach, which guests at The Grange are welcome to use. Fishing 4 miles, golf 3 miles. Local attractions include Caister Castle and Motor Museum, Norfolk Rare Breed Centre, Yarmouth greyhound stadium and ten pin bowling.

Directions: Site is north of Great Yarmouth and east of Ormesby St Margaret, just south of the roundabout where the B1159 road joins the A149. O.S.GR: TG515140.

Charges 2000:
-- Per unit incl. 4 persons £6.50 - £11.00; extra adult £2.00; awning £2.00; electricity £1.50; extra car or boat £2.00; first dog free, extra dog by arrangement £2.00.
-- Credit cards accepted.
-- VAT included.

Open:
20 March - 26 September.

Address:
Yarmouth Road,
Ormesby St Margaret,
Great Yarmouth,
Norfolk NR29 3QG.

Tel:
(01493) 730306.
FAX: (01493) 730188.

Reservations:
Advisable for B.Hs (min. 3 nights), school holidays and peak season and made with deposit (£10 for under 7 days or £20 per week).

338 Clippesby Holidays, Clippesby, nr. Acle

An unusual park in the grounds of a private estate where one can wander at will, Clippesby offers the choice of pitching in shady secluded woodland or on more open parkland with mature colourful trees and shrubs on gently sloping lawns. All 100 pitches are well spaced and clearly numbered (70 have 10A electricity). Hardstanding is available in the car parking area. Three timbered toilet blocks are well placed, with heating, free hot water in washbasins (some private cabins), ten showers in total including two in the Pinewoods block which are large enough to take a family. Showers are free but hot water for dishwashing is charged (20p) - the park is not on mains services. However, the real pleasure of Clippesby is the friendly welcome from the family who live in the single storey Hall and the opportunity to enjoy the mature gardens and facilities. These include a sunken grass tennis court, a small heated swimming pool with mellowed flagstone patio area behind the Hall, the timber adventure playground, putting and recreation greens. The Muskett Arms (evenings only in low season), with attractive and comfortable family bar and a sheltered courtyard outside, provides evening meals, music nights and other family entertainment, again individual in design. Clippesby Stores and Café provides for basic needs, a coffee bar for lunches and teas, a craft shop, and equipment hire including board games. All fascinating and open from end-May, 9 am.-5 pm. in the main season. Facilities also include chemical disposal, a washing machine and dryer, gas supplies and bicycle hire. Remember a torch and wellington boots - the environment is very natural and is deliberately kept that way. Dogs have a dog walk (max. 1 per pitch). Reservations are advised for peak periods and visitors return year after year. For those who want to take granny, there are 23 cottages around the park for hire, all in keeping with the environment (in use all year). Sunday evening services are held in the beautiful Saxon church on the estate. Children can roam at will, and in safety, and parents can unwind in this comfortable park, never mind all the attractions of the Broads and Great Yarmouth on your doorstep and only the peacocks to disturb you! Pony rides for children (6-11 yrs) on the park. Riding 3 miles, golf 5 miles, fishing 2 miles. Bellamy gold.

Directions: Park is signed off B1152 road about a mile north of the junction with A1064, 2 miles south of the junction with A419. O.S. GR: TG423145.

Charges 2001:
-- Per unit incl. 2 adults £8.60 - £15.75; unit 22 ft. or over plus £2.00 in high season; extra adult or visitor £1.50 - £2.00; child or student (over 3 yrs) 50p - 75p; awning £1.00 - £2.00; extra car £1.00 - £2.50 (free on car park); pup tent or boat trailer 45p - 95p; dog £1.00 - £2.00; electricity £2.00 (£3.00 at Easter; 20 m. lead required).
-- VAT included.
-- Credit cards accepted.

Open:
Easter w/end, then
4 May - 23 September.

Address:
Clippesby Hall,
Clippesby,
Norfolk NR29 3BL.

Tel:
(01493) 367800.
FAX: (01493) 367809.
E-mail: holidays@clippesby.co.uk.

Reservations:
Made with deposit (£20 per week or part week).

Alan Rogers' Discount

Less 50p per unit, per night

Norfolk

350 Woodhill Park, East Runton, nr. Cromer

Seaside site with good views and traditional atmosphere.

Situated on the cliff top, on a large gently sloping open grassy field, are 113 marked touring pitches, all with electricity (16A), many of which have wonderful views over the surrounding countryside. A small number of holiday homes which are located nearer to the cliff edge unfortunately have the best sea views, although perhaps at times a little bracing! The three sanitary units (the newest of which is part of the reception building) provide a more than adequate supply of WCs and washbasins, but could be a little short of showers at peak times. There is, however, free hot water throughout, a laundry with washing machines and dryer (iron available from reception), a fully equipped unit for disabled persons and chemical disposal facilities. A very well stocked mini-market had a good range of beers, wines and magazines, alongside the usual groceries, toys and sweets, plus gas exchange. There is a good adventure playground for the children, plenty of space for ball games and new crazy golf. A 9 hole golf course is adjacent to the site. Bicycle hire nearby. Although the site is fenced there is access to the cliff top path, a possible hazard for small children. Attractions nearby include 'Karttrax' at Cromer (go-karting), boat trips to see the seals off Blakeney Point, the Shire Horse Centre at West Runton, the North Norfolk Steam Railway, and at Sheringham you can find a fun pool complex with wave machine. Bellamy silver.

Charges guide:
-- Per unit £6.25 - £7.00; small pitch (non-electric) £4.35 - £5.20; adult £1.17 - £1.45; child 60p - 80p; electricity £1.25; multi-service pitch plus £2.20 - 2.70; dog 80p.
-- VAT included.

Open:
20 March - 31 October.

Address:
Cromer Road, East Runton, Cromer, Norfolk NR27 9PX.

Tel:
(01263) 512242.

FAX: (01263) 515326.

Reservations:
Accepted for min. 3 nights with £15 p/week non returnable booking fee.

Directions: Site is beside the A149 coast road between East and West Runton. O.S.GR: TG190420.

340 The Old Brick Kilns Caravan & Camping Park, Barney

Tranquil, rural site on split levels with good quality facilities, near Fakenham.

This family run park, owned by Alan and Pam Greenhalgh, has been developed on the site of an old brick kiln resulting in land on varying levels. It provides areas of pitches (eg. the Dell, the Orchard) which have been well drained and grassed over. Banks around the park and trees provide shelter, home for a variety of wildlife with a wide range of trees and shrubs. There are new garden areas, including a butterfly garden, and a central conservation pond is the main feature. There are 60 pitches, all with electricity (10/16A) and semi hardstanding. Drinking water is supplied by a 285 ft. bore and excellent, roofed service areas provide water and waste disposal. Toilet facilities are very good with under floor heating, washbasins in curtained cubicles, free hot water, hand and hair dryers. There are facilities for babies and disabled people (unisex), a laundry room and dishwashing (H&C), chemical disposal. A small toilet block at the furthest end and motorcaravan services complete the provision. Amenities include a large, comfortable bar area and à la carte restaurant, open selected evenings and weekends. Patio area outside with barbecue. TV room, an information centre, table tennis, bicycle hire, giant chess and mini library. The reception area also provides a shop and gas is available. The children's play area is fenced, with bark surface. Telephone. Dogs are accepted on leads with a dog walk provided. Winter caravan storage available. B&B is also available. Gas barbecues for hire. Fishing on site, riding 6 miles, golf 5 or 8 miles. A friendly, helpful atmosphere prevails and as the park is 8 miles from the coast, it is ideally situated to explore North Norfolk. A member of the Best of British group. Bellamy gold.

Charges 2001:
-- Per pitch £5.25 - £7.75; adult £2.00; child 4-15 yrs £1.00 - £1.50, 0-3 yrs 50p - 75p; awning free; extra pup tent £1.00 - £1.50; extra car on pitch £1.50 - £2.50; dog (max. 2) free; visitor £1.00; electricity £2.00.
-- VAT included.
-- Credit cards accepted.

Open:
All year
excl. 7 Jan - 20 Feb.

Address:
Little Barney Lane, Barney, Fakenham, Norfolk NR21 0NL.

Tel:
(01328) 878305.

FAX: (01328) 878948.

E-mail: enquire@ old-brick-kilns.co.uk.

Reservations:
Advised and made with £15 deposit (non-refundable).

Directions: From Fakenham take A148 Cromer road. After 6 miles, fork right on B1354 Aylsham road and in 300 yds, turn right, signed Barney, and then first left along a narrow country lane with passing places, for ¾ mile. O.S.GR: TG004332.

Travelling to France this year?
Book your site with the experts
Call **01892 55 98 98**

Low cost ferries
guaranteed!

343 Kelling Heath Holiday Park, Weybourne, nr. Sheringham

Spacious, heathland park with a range of amenities overlooking north Norfolk coast.

Kelling Heath is a holiday park set in a 250-acre estate in a designated area of outstanding natural beauty. The 384 caravan holiday homes (36 to let, the rest privately owned) and the 300 touring pitches blend easily into the part-wooded, part-open heathland. A wide range of on-site facilities, including a club complex, fitness centre and nature trail, provide activities for all ages. The touring area is quiet and peaceful, away from the facilities, on fairly level grass amid pine trees and open heathland with gorse and heather. It has 246 marked pitches with electrical hook-ups (16A) and a further 54 unmarked pitches. Three toilet blocks serve the site, the most modern of which is heated with a glazed conservatory that provides covered access all year to disabled people, baby changing and dishwashing and laundry sinks. All blocks provide free pre-set hot showers, washbasins (a few in private cubicles), an excellent supply of toilets, chemical disposal, baby bath and in season, a nappy disposal service. There are washing machines (3), tumble dryers (2) and irons from reception (with £20 deposit). The central reception area, between the statics and the tourers, has been attractively paved and pedestrianised with village stores, bar and bandstand. 'The Forge', a complex comprising an entertainment bar, an adults only bar and family room provides a comprehensive range of entertainment and amusements all season. Opened last year, 'Fitness Express' is a new development that offers an indoor swimming pool (19 x 9 m), spa pool, sauna, steam rooms and gym with fully trained staff (membership is available on either daily or weekly basis). An adventure playground with assault course is near, as is the nature trail. Other facilities include two hard tennis courts, a small outdoor, heated fun pool (main season only), sports field, play areas (some rather hidden from the pitches) and a small lake for free fishing (permit holders only). Well stocked supermarket and takeaway. Gas is available. Torch useful. A range of information is available on places to visit and the North Norfolk steam railway has a halt within walking distance, giving access to Cromer. Bellamy gold.

Charges 2000:
--Per unit £10.75 - £15.45; pitch with electricity £12.75 - £17.45; extra person (under 16 yrs.) free - £1.95; extra car or pup tent free - £2.00; dog (max. 2) £1.50
-- Min 7 day stay in high season.
-- No single sex groups.
-- Credit cards accepted.
Open:
19 March - 16 December.
Address:
Weybourne, Sheringham, Norfolk NR25 7HW.
Tel:
(01263) 588181.
FAX: (01263) 588599.
E-mail: info@ kellingheath.co.uk.
Reservations: Necessary for July/Aug. on a weekly basis with £30 booking remittance.

Directions: Park is signed on A148 Holt - Cromer road, between High Kelling and Bodham. On A149 Sheringham road turn right at the church in Weybourne. O.S GR: TG117418.

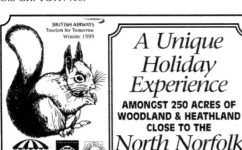

Norfolk

346 The Garden Caravan Site, Barmer Hall, Syderstone

Imaginative touring site in an enclosed, south facing, walled garden.

This newly developed site has 30 spacious marked pitches, all on gently sloping grass in the most attractive setting behind the Hall itself. There are 30 electrical connections (16A), each with a TV hook-up as reception is variable, possibly due to the high wall and woodland surrounding the site. However, this does mean that the site is peaceful and a little sun-trap, a haven from the busy world outside. Attractive mature trees, shrubs and climbers provide shade at various times of the day. Reception is housed in a small kiosk (not always manned, so pitch yourself and pay later). There is no shop, but gas, ices, soft drinks and free range fresh eggs are usually available. The sanitary facilities are in a new building (heated when necessary) providing the usual facilities with extremely spacious hot showers, free hot water throughout, dishwashing sinks under cover at one end of the building and chemical disposal. The site is not far from Sandringham, and there are plenty of peaceful lanes to explore on your bicycle or take a woodland walk from the little door in the wall at the rear of the site. Maybe visit Norfolk Lavender, Langham Glass or the Thursford Collection of steam engines, mechanical organs and Wurlitzer fame. The North Norfolk coast and beaches, numerous golf courses and bird sanctuaries are all within easy reach. Bicycle hire 4 miles, riding 6 miles, golf 10 miles.

Directions: About.4 miles west of Fakenham turn off A148, taking B1454 northwards and turning to Barmer Hall after a further 4 miles, where site is signed - the road is marked 'unsuitable for motor vehicles' but ignore this and follow past and behind the Hall and farm buildings. O.S.GR: TF810330.

Charges 2000:
-- Per adult £4.00; child £1.50; electricity £2.00; TV aerial hook-up 50p.
-- VAT included.
-- No credit cards.

Open:
1 March - 1 November.

Address:
Barmer Hall,
Syderstone, Kings Lynn,
Norfolk PE31 8SR.

Tel:
(01485) 578220 (house)
or 578178 (site).
FAX: (01485) 578178.

Reservations:
Advised for B.Hs and peak season; contact site for details.

Alan Rogers' Discount

Less 10% for
adults in June

344 Gatton Waters Lakeside Touring Site, Hillington

Peaceful park set round fishing lakes, for adults only, near Sandringham.

Developed around two fishing lakes (formerly stone quarries), Gatton Waters has a pleasant open aspect. The reception/bar, which is housed in an old Norfolk barn, provides a friendly welcome, an open fire and serves real ale (closed Tuesdays). Evening meals and Sunday lunches are served (weekends only out of main season and not October). The 60 caravan (all with electric hook ups) and 30 tent pitches are set further away, around the lakes and quite a number are occupied by seasonal caravans. However, there is room for those seeking either to fish (day tickets available) or for a quiet base to visit Sandringham (2.2 miles) or the north Norfolk coast (8 miles). Everything is kept as natural as possible and skylarks, pheasants, ospreys and leverets are frequently to be seen, in addition to the many types of ducks, etc. on the lakes. Two new toilet blocks can be heated and provide free hot water, vanity style washbasins, push-button showers and dishwashing facilities. Extra facilities are near reception. Chemical disposal, motorcaravan services and battery charging available. Dogs are welcome on leads. Caravan storage. Riding or golf 8 miles. In keeping with the natural, relaxed atmosphere of the site the owners made the decision to go 'adult only' in '98, and have been encouraged by the positive response they have received. Only people over 18 years are accepted.

Directions: From Kings Lynn follow A148 Cromer road. Site is signed after sign to West Newton, but before sign to Sandringham and village of Hillington (all to the left). O.S.GR: TF705255.

Charges 2001:
-- Per unit incl. 2 persons: caravan or trailer tent £5.00 - £9.00; tent incl. 2 persons £4.00 - £9.00; extra person £1.00; electricity £1.75 - £2.00.

Open:
April - 1 October.

Address:
Hillington,
nr. Sandringham,
Kings Lynn,
Norfolk PE31 6BJ.

Tel:
(01485) 600643.
E-mail: gatton.waters
@virgin.net.

Reservations:
Advisable during peak periods and made for min. 3 days at B.Hs.

342 Two Mills Touring Park, North Walsham

Small, sheltered and secluded park but for adults only.

Two Mills is a quiet site situated in the bowl of a former quarry and is therefore a real sun trap, both secluded and sheltered. The park is neatly maintained with natural areas, varied trees, wild flowers and birds. It is a good centre from which to explore the north Norfolk coast, the Broads or for visiting Norwich and a footpath from the park joins the Weavers Way. Including five 'panorama' pitches (with patio area, water and waste water drainage), there are 54 level, marked pitches for tourers, 30 all weather gravel, three with hardstanding and 18 grass. All are generously sized and have electricity (10/16A). A small, secluded area is reserved for tents. The central, very well maintained, heated and clean toilet block has free hot water in curtained showers and washbasins (some in cabins), en-suite facilities for disabled people, laundry and dishwashing rooms and chemical disposal. There is a small shop with tourist information and a community room with TV and tea and coffee facilities. The town is a 20 minute walk. Dogs are accepted by arrangement (several breeds not welcome) with kennels and a dog walk provided. No plastic groundsheets. Public phone. Ice service. There is a hotel/pub across the road and a fish and chip van calls every Thursday evening. Fishing, golf or riding 5 miles, bicycle hire 1½ miles and the coast is 5 miles. Only adults are accepted. A new member of the Best of British group. Bellamy gold.

Directions: Approach from southeast on A149 and watch for caravan sign approx. 1½ miles before North Walsham (also signed White Horse Common). The road runs parallel to the A149; site is on right after 1¼ miles. O.S.GR: TG292287.

Charges 2001:
-- Per unit incl. 2 adults £7.50 - £10.50; panorama pitch £87.50 - £112.00 per week; extra person £2.50; awning £1.00 - £1.50; dog 50p; electricity £2.00.
-- Credit cards accepted.
Open:
All year except 4 Jan - 28 Feb.
Address:
Scarborough Hill, North Walsham, Norfolk NR28 9NA.
Tel:
(01692) 405829. FAX: as phone. E-mail: enquiries@ twomills.co.uk.
Reservations:
Made with £10 deposit; balance payable on arrival.

345 Little Haven Caravan and Camping Park, Erpingham

Secluded and pretty, touring site for adults only.

Within easy reach of the coast and the Broads, this is an attractive and peaceful little site with excellent facilities. The 24 grassy pitches, all with electricity (16A), are arranged around the outside of a gravel access road, with a central lawn and decorative pergola, neat little garden and seating area. The well maintained sanitary unit is heated and provides modern facilities including spacious hot showers and two covered dishwashing and laundry sinks at one end of the building, with free hot water throughout. There is no shop, but gas is available on site. Two pubs serving food and traditional ales are within walking distance. An ideal base for cycling, walking, horse riding, or just relaxing, the Weavers Way footpath is within half a mile of the site, whilst a riding stables and craft centre are at nearby Alby. Also close by is magnificent Blickling Hall with its superb state rooms, gardens and park, or a short drive takes you to the historic market town of Aylsham. Note: this site is unsuitable for American motorhomes. Only adults and accompanied children over 14 years are accepted.

Directions: From A140 Cromer - Norwich road, going south towards Aylsham and 3 miles south of Roughton, past Horseshoes pub and Alby crafts, take first right signed Erpingham 2 miles. Site is 175 yards on right. O.S.GR: TG190320.

Charges 2000:
-- Per unit incl. 2 adults £7.50 - £9.00; extra adult £3.00; awning 50p-£1.00; electricity £1.50 - £2.00.
-- No credit cards.
-- VAT included.
Open:
1 March - 31 October.
Address:
The Street, Erpingham, Norwich, Norfolk NR11 7QD.
Tel/Fax:
(01263) 768959. E-mail: john@bass. freeserve.co.uk.
Reservations:
Advisable for B.Hs and peak season and made without deposit.

347 Breckland Meadows Touring Park, Swaffham

Small touring park within walking distance of historic market town.

This is a pleasant little park which would make a good base to explore the local area. The 45 pitches are on fairly level, neat grass, all with electricity (16A). There may be some road noise at times but newly planted trees should reduce this as they mature. Adjacent to the site is the Swaefas Way, a seven mile circular walk which links to the more well known Peddars Way. The toilet block has been completely refurbished and is neat, clean and heated when necessary. It provides all the usual facilities, a separate toilet and washbasin unit for disabled visitors, outside covered washing up facilities and chemical disposal. Gas is available. Fishing 5 miles, riding 4 miles, golf 2 miles. Local attractions include Cockley Cley Medieval Iceni Village and Saxon Church, Castle Acre Priory, Oxburgh Hall and the Thursford Collection of steam engines, mechanical organs and Wurlitzer fame. Swaffham (½ mile), a historic market town has a popular Saturday market.

Directions: Park is just west of Swaffham on the old A47, approx. ½ mile from town centre. O.S.GR: TF820080.

Charges 2000:
-- Per unit incl. 2 adults £5.00 - £8.00; extra adult £1.00; child (5-15 yrs) 50p; electricity £2.00.
-- Credit cards accepted.
Open:
1 March - November.
Address:
Lynn Road, Swaffham, Norfolk PE37 7PT.
Tel:
(01760) 721246. FAX: (01760) 725994. E-mail: info@breckland-meadows.co.uk.
Reservations:
Essential for B.Hs and advised for peak season.

111

Cambridgeshire

355 Old Manor Caravan Park, Grafham

Clean, peaceful and friendly park, situated near large reservoir.

This small, attractive park is under the new ownership of David and Christine Howes, who plan to upgrade and improve the site, but without compromising its natural charm or background. The old white cottage was once occupied by Oliver Cromwell's family and the grounds formed part of their garden. Even today the horse pond and part of the moat still remain. A tarmac road serves the 80 numbered grass pitches (69 with 10A electrical connections, with more planned shortly). Privacy and shade is provided by varied and plentiful trees and hedges throughout the six acre, level grounds. The park is neat and carefully maintained, with ample service points for water and refuse. The single, tiled toilet block is thoughtfully planned and exceptionally clean. Hot water is controllable, whilst all showers and washbasins are in generously sized cubicles. Laundry and dish-washing rooms, similarly tiled and clean, are further complemented by a new parent and baby room, plus a free freezer for ice blocks and food storage. Basic provisions are available from reception (1/3-31/10), with the nearest shops being at West Perry or Buckden (5 and 3 miles respectively). Leisure facilities comprise a large playground, with bark chipping base and a large, heated outdoor pool (small extra charge; unsupervised). Sailing, fishing, bicycle hire, nature trails and bird watching can be found at nearby Grafham Water. Cambridge, The Imperial War Museum at Duxford, Woburn Abbey and the Shuttleworth Collection at Old Warden are nearby too. Public phone and post box provided; dogs are welcome on leads, but must be exercised off-site.

Charges 2001:
-- Per unit incl. 2 adults £10.00 - £12.00; extra person £2.50 - £3.00; child (5-15 yrs) £1.20 - £1.50; extra car or boat £1.20 - £1.50; dog (max. 2) £1.00; electricity £2.00 (£10 per week).
-- Credit cards accepted

Open:
All year (reduced facilities Nov-Feb incl).

Address:
Church Road, Grafham, Huntingdon, Cambs. PE28 0BB.

Tel:
(01480) 810264.
FAX: (01480) 819099.
E-mail: camping@old-manor.freeserve.co.uk

Reservations:
Made with £10 non-returnable deposit (min 3 nights at B.Hs)

Directions: Leave A1 at Buckden roundabout and follow B661 towards Grafham Water for approx. half a mile. Turn right towards the village of Grafham following camping signs. From A14 at Ellington, turn off and follow camping signs. O.S GR: TL160 680.

Alan Rogers' Discount

 One night free for one week booked

358 Ferry Meadows Caravan Club Site, Peterborough

Family holiday site in extensive country park.

Only 3 miles from Peterborough and closer still to the East of England Showground, Ferry Meadows occupies 30 acres of the much larger Nene Country Park. The meadows, lakes and woodlands provide ample opportunities to sample the numerous facilities on offer, more of which later. Open all year, the site provides 254 pitches in total, 160 grass pitches on one side of the park and 94 gravel hardstandings on the newer side, just across the road. Privacy, shade and character are assured by the abundance of trees, bushes and shrubs that are part of the park as a whole. All pitches have electricity (16A) and tents are accepted on the grassed section of the site. Two modern, heated toilet blocks are of the usual good Club standard, with free, controllable showers, curtained washbasins, hand and hair dryers and en-suite facilities for disabled visitors. Each section has dishwashing sinks under cover, as well as a laundry room with sinks, washing machine, dryer and ironing board. There are chemical disposal facilities, numerous points for waste and drinking water, plus a motorcaravan service point and a barrier system to prevent unauthorised access. Families with children may prefer the grass section, from where they can keep a watchful eye on the well-equipped children's play area. The site office stocks basic provisions (nearest shops 1½ miles) and there is a room devoted to tourist information and ideas on where to go. Returning to the Country Park, it covers over 500 acres within which are miles of walks and cycle ways, horse routes, lakes for coarse fishing, sailing and windsurfing, a wetland nature reserve, archery field, two golf courses and a miniature railway. Well laid out for the disabled visitor, free wheelchair hire is available on request. Also passing within nostalgic earshot and yielding the occasional tempting aroma of bygone eras is the Nene Valley Steam Railway, complete with Thomas the Tank Engine. Other attractions include Spalding Flower Festival and Burghley Park.

Charges 2000:
-- Per adult £2.00 - £4.00; child £1.10 - £1.20; non-member pitch fee £6.00 - £7.00; electricity £1.45 - £2.20.
-- Credit cards accepted

Open:
All year.

Address:
Ham Lane, Peterborough PE2 5UU.

Tel:
(01733) 233526.

Reservations:
Essential for B.Hs, July/Aug and all w/ends.

Directions: From A1 south, do not turn onto A1139, but turn left at next junction (signed Showground, Chesterton, Alwalton). At T-junction turn left on A605, continue straight at three roundabouts, following signs for Nene Park to site in Ham Lane. O.S.GR: TL151975.

356 Highfield Farm Touring Park, Comberton, nr. Cambridge

Quality, peaceful and very well kept, family run park.

Situated five miles from Cambridge, this eight acre park is set in a delightfully quiet touring location. Family run, the welcome is always warm and the facilities of superior quality. Divided into five enclosures by hedges and conifers, there are also shady glades for those who wish to retreat even further; plus one enclosure is reserved for those without children. Offering 60 numbered pitches for caravans or motorcaravans, and 60 for tents, personal space is further enhanced by the fact that the centre of each enclosure is left free. All pitches have 10A electricity, 50 have gravel hardstanding, and most are level. Three, heated toilet blocks provide more than adequate coverage. The original block offers controllable showers on payment, free hot water to washbasins and an additional set of unisex showers. The other two blocks (fully tiled) provide a combination of showers on payment (10p), free hot water to washbasins, some open plan, others in cubicles, and ample toilets; all of which are outstandingly clean and well maintained. There is no dedicated provision for disabled visitors, although one block has extra wide doors and easy access. The laundry has washing machines, tumble dryers, spin dryer, iron, board and sinks. Hot water is free to 10 covered dishwashing sinks spaced throughout the site, there are good chemical disposal facilities and a motorcaravan service point is provided. A spacious baby changing room has now been added to the facilities. Basic provisions are available from reception and there are nearby shops and pubs. Two play areas (swings and tree house) plus two sizeable areas for football, kite flying or merely running. Bicycle hire available from site. Fishing 3½ miles, golf 2 miles. A small kiosk offers tourist information about area and there is a public phone and post box. A good dog walk is provided, which can be extended to a pleasant 1½ mile walk, with seats, around the site perimeter. Gates closed midnight to 7.30 am. A member of the Best of British group.

Directions: Park is 5 miles southwest of Cambridge city centre near eastern edge of Comberton village. From M11 take exit 12, the A 603 towards Sandy and right after ½ mile on B1046 to Comberton. From A428 turn south at Hardwick roundabout and follow international camping signs to Comberton. O.S GR: TL391571.

Charges 2001:
-- Per caravan or large tent incl. 2 persons £7.75 - £9.00; motorcaravan or small tent £7.50 - £8.50; m/cyclist tent £6.50 - £7.50; hiker/cyclist tent £6.50 - £7.25; extra adult £2.00; child (5-16 yrs) £1.50; awning/pup tent £1.00; porch awning 50p; electricity £1.75.
-- No credit cards.
-- VAT included.

Open:
23 March - 31 October.

Address:
Long Road, Comberton, Cambridge, CB3 7DG.

Tel:
01223 262308
FAX: as phone.

Reservations:
Made for any length with £10 deposit and 50p fee.

see colour advert between pages 128/129

Alan Rogers' Discount

Less 10% for senior citizens, 3 or more nights in low season

376 Tallington Lakes Caravan and Camping, Tallington, Stamford

Modern touring site and holiday park, with dry ski slope and range of watersports.

This large, 160-acre site spreads around a series of lakes which provides for many watersport activities including water-ski (slalom and jump courses), jet-ski, sailing (sailboards and dinghies), and angling. Also on site is a tennis court, and a dry-ski and snowboard centre. The touring campsite has recently been brought up to date and now has around 120 pitches, of which 66 have electric hook-ups (10A), and 11 are on hardstandings. Major roads are tarmac, with gravel roads around the pitches, but the small hedges and shrubs separating the pitches are new and will need time to mature. At one end of the site is a small, well fenced, children's adventure style playground (5-12 yrs) on a sand base. At the other end of the site is the newly built, heated sanitary unit which opened in early 2000. This provides WCs, vanity style washbasins and roomy showers, facilities for babies, small children and disabled visitors, plus a room with dishwashing sinks. A laundry, and additional WCs and showers (also used by the water skiers) are situated at the end of the bar and restaurant building by the lakeside. An excellent motorcaravan service point has facilities for chemical disposal, fresh and waste water, and a drive-over drain. The complex also has a good number of permanent holiday homes and there are also some units for rent. Local places of interest are Stamford Museum, Burghley House, Sacrewell Farm and Country Centre and the Nene Valley Railway. NOTE: The key-card for the sanitary unit and barrier has a £10 refundable deposit.

Directions: From A16, midway between Stamford and Market Deeping, just east of the railway crossing at Tallington, turn north into Barholm Road and site entrance is on the right. (site is signed). O.S.GR: TF 085090.

Charges 2000:
-- Per adult: £1.50; motorcaravan £6.00; caravan £6.00; awning £1.50; tent £4.50; pup tent £1.50; extra car £1.50; dog £1.00 (max. 2 dogs per unit); electricity £1.50.
-- VAT included.

Open:
1 March - 31 January.

Address:
Barholm Road, Tallington, Stamford, Lincolnshire PE9 4RJ.

Tel:
(01778) 347000.
FAX: (01778) 346213.
E-mail: info@ tallingtonlakes.com

Reservations:
Accepted with full payment, contact site for details.

Lincolnshire

Heart of England Tourist Board

Lincolnshire, Derbyshire, Nottinghamshire, Staffordshire, Leicestershire, Northamptonshire, West Midlands, Warwickshire, Gloucestershire, Worcestershire, Shropshire and Herefordshire

Larkhill Road, Worcester WR5 2EZ
Tel: (01905) 761100 Fax: (01905) 763450
or Premier House, 15 Wheeler Gate, Nottingham NG1 2NA
Tel: (0115) 959 8383 Fax: (0115) 959 8686
Internet: www.visitbritain.com/heart-of-england

This central area of England, bordering Wales on the west, Lincolnshire on the east and with Birmingham, at its heart covers:

Derbyshire – The Peak District is ideal for leisure and activity holidays, with spectacular crags, dales and moorland. There are ample opportunties for walking, cycling or the more daring challenges of rock climbing, gliding or hang-gliding.

Staffordshire – Stunning countryside and moorlands, combine with Britain's number one theme park, Alton Towers. Stoke on Trent, the birthplace of British ceramics, is where Josiah Wedgwood, Sir Henry Doulton and Josiah Spode worked their magic transforming base clay to objects of beauty. Visitor centres and factory shops tell their story.

Nottinghamshire – Nottingham Castle above the city presides over a modern vibrant city and nearby Sherwood Forest is still alive with tales of Robin Hood and his merry men.

Leicestershire – Home to the pork pie of Melton Mowbury fame and Stilton cheese.

Rutland – England's smallest county, just 20 miles across. Rutland Water is a Mecca for watersports.

Northamptonshire – Known as the county of 'spires and squires', Kings and Queens of England used to hunt in Rockingham Forest but today its royal connection is centred on Althorp the resting place of Diana, Princess of Wales. It is also home to Silverstone, Britain's Formula 1 Grand Prix circuit.

Lincolnshire – From the gently rolling landscape of the Lincolnshire Wolds and dramatic open landscape of the Fens, to the cathedral and antique shops in Lincoln, traditional seaside resorts and the network of tranquil waterways. There is a huge variety in the setting of vast skies and unforgettable sunsets.

Warwickshire – Shakespeare Country, birthplace of the world's greatest playwright and home of the Earls of Warwick. Warwick castle must be the finest mediaeval castle in England.

Birmingham – one of the UK's most important cities and a leading international centre.

Worcestershire – Ranks as one of England's most attractive counties. Home to Malvern Water, Worcestershire Sauce and the Morgan sports car.

Shropshire and **Herefordshire** – Where England meets Wales and a mix of heritage and history brought to life in Ellis Peters' Brother Cadfeal series, the medieval whodunits based on Shrews-bury. Herefordshire is the home of cider and timber framed buildings are a feature.

Gloucestershire – From the Cotswold hills and villages, the Forest of Dean, the Wye valley to Regency Cheltenham with its world standard festivals of literature, jazz and famous for its horse racing not to mention the art of chasing a Double Gloucestershire cheese down a hill!

366 Walesby Woodlands Caravan Park, nr. Market Rasen

Family owned, small, pleasant touring park near the Wolds.

This park is surrounded by mature Forestry Commission woodland and is therefore very peaceful and sheltered. About 1½ miles distant is the small town of Market Rasen, but further afield and within easy driving distance, are Lincoln, the Wolds and the coast. There are 64 well spaced pitches, 61 with 10A electricity, marked out on a single, mainly flat, grassy field sectioned by double rows of trees and divided by a central gravel track. The one toilet block, operated by key, has fully tiled surfaces and toilet facilities for disabled people. Hot water is free to pre-set showers (curtain screen, seat, hook but no shelf), vanity style washbasins with ample mirrors, hooks etc. and outside, covered, dishwashing sinks. Chemical disposal facilities. The same block also houses a laundry room and a small shop with an information section (all season). Battery charging and gas are available. A children's play area is on grass to one end of the site (no kite flying - overhead wires). Fishing 3 miles, riding 2 miles, golf 1½ miles. Winter caravan storage. The Viking Way passes through Walesby and there are many other shorter walks in the forest and surrounding area.

Charges 2001:
-- Per unit incl. 2 persons £8.00; extra person £1.25; child (2-12 yrs) £1.00; awning or child's pup tent £1.25; electricity £2.00.
-- Credit cards accepted.
Open:
1 March - 31 October.
Address:
Walesby, Market Rasen, Lincolnshire LN8 3UN.
Tel:
(01673) 843285.
Reservations:
Any length, with deposit.

Directions: Park is northeast of, and signed from, the main approach roads to Market Rasen. O.S.GR: TF117907.

114

369 Bainland Country Park, Woodhall Spa, nr. Lincoln

Family park with many amenities including indoor pool.

Bainland has 150 spacious, level pitches in hedged bays, linked by circular roadways, forming circles and islands. Of these, 51 are `super' pitches with hardstanding for car and caravan, honeycombed for awning, individual water, drainage and chemical disposal, electricity and TV aerial hook-ups. The remainder of the pitches are either on gravel hardstandings or level grass, all with 16A electricity. There are 10 caravan holiday homes and 25 bungalows to hire. Two solid toilet blocks can be heated and are equipped for all basic necessities (except, perhaps, for showers in peak times), and in addition provide a baby care centre, unisex shower room for families, hair care room, family bathroom, fully equipped unit for disabled people, laundry room, chemical disposal, enclosed dishwashing and separate hand washing sinks. Maintenance can be variable. The park is also well equipped with bins, water points and motorcaravan service points. The friendly reception (08.00-22.00 hrs) is housed in a pleasant Swiss-style building adjacent to the shop (groceries, souvenirs and licensed, open March - Oct). Also here is the heated indoor pool and jacuzzi, etc. (under 16s must be accompanied by an adult). This is overlooked by the bistro (all year) and spacious bar area, which also overlooks the golf course and outdoor bowls area. A children's adventure play area has been created in a large hollow with a sand base in addition to a trampoline, crazy golf, croquet, TV and games room and soft play area. For adults there is an 18 hole, par 3 golf course, a tennis club with a year round floodlit tennis dome with 3-4 courts including badminton (the dome comes off in the summer). Note: the bar and bistro are open to the public; the great range of leisure activities, including the pool, are individually booked and paid for at reception. Barbecues, jazz, country and western evenings are organised. Bicycle hire on site. Fishing 3 miles, riding 6 miles. Bainland is 1½ miles from Woodhall Spa, with its old fashioned charm and Dambusters associations, yet deep in the heart of the Lincolnshire Wolds, surrounded by mature trees and with direct access to woods for walking dogs. Winter caravan storage. A member of the Best of British group.

Directions: Entrance to park is off B1191 Horncastle road just outside Woodhall Spa by derestriction sign. O.S.GR: TF214637.

Charges 2000:
-- Per unit incl. electricity and awning £9.00 - £14.00; serviced pitch £11.00 - £17.00; pup tent free - £3.00.
-- Firework display (min. 2 nights, 5/6 Nov) £25.00; serviced pitch £30.00.
-- Discounts for senior citizens.
-- VAT included.
-- Credit cards accepted

Open:
All year (in winter, super pitches only).

Address:
Horncastle Road, Woodhall Spa, Lincs LN10 6UX.

Tel:
(01526) 352903. FAX: (01526) 353730. E-mail: bookings @bainland.com.

Reservations:
Recommended and made for any length. Deposit at B.Hs. only (one night's fee).

see colour advert between pages 128/129

365 Cherry Tree Site, Sutton-on-Sea, nr. Mablethorpe

Small, well kept, good value park.

Cherry Tree is a good example of a small touring park. The grass is neatly trimmed and well drained, and is divided by evergreen hedging to site your unit against. Some hedges are well grown, the rest recently planted. Connected by a one-way circular gravel road, there are 60 good sized pitches all with 10A electricity. The brick built toilet block can be heated and is immaculately kept, providing vanity style washbasins and controllable hot showers (20p). A nice new en-suite unit for disabled visitors is a good addition. A combined dishwashing and laundry room complete with washing machine, spin dryer and tumble dryer, and outside, two water points, a chemical disposal point and a waste disposal area provide for all practical needs. There is also a neat reception, public telephone and a well fenced children's play area again on neat grass. Gas is available. Buses stop outside hourly, and a shop and pub are within 10 minutes walk. It is also possible to walk to the sea via the road. Tennis and bowls nearby, fishing 1½ miles, golf 1 mile, riding 4 miles. Mablethorpe beach is known for its sand yacht racing and Skegness, with all its popular attractions is just down the road. Dogs are welcome on leads if exercised off the park and, for campers, a very warm welcome awaits from Geoff and Margaret Murray.

Directions: Park is 1½ miles south of Sutton-on-Sea on A52 coast road to Skegness, with the entrance leading off a lay-by on the left. O.S.GR: TF518828.

Charges 2000:
-- Per unit incl. 2 persons £6.00 - £7.50; extra person 50p - 75p; awning 75p; electricity £1.75.
-- Min. stay 3 nights at B.Hs.
-- No credit cards.

Open:
3 March - 31 October

Address:
Huttoft Road, Sutton-on-Sea, Lincolnshire LN12 2RU.

Tel:
(01507) 441626. FAX: as phone. E-mail: murray. cherrytree@virgin.net.

Reservations:
Made with £20 deposit (non-returnable).

Lincolnshire

367 Lakeside Park, North Somercotes, nr. Louth

Large family park near coast with comprehensive entertainment (no tents).

With a splendid water feature at the entrance, good tarmac access roads and well tended grounds throughout, first impressions are most rewarding. Set in 47 acres of pine forest, this park is continually seeking to improve and develop the service it offers. The majority is occupied by 300 privately owned holiday homes, all proudly maintained, with the touring section in a separate 15 acre field, but furthest from the leisure areas and activities. Although rather open, a programme of long term landscaping has commenced, intended to impart more character to this area. The number of grass based touring pitches, all level and with 16A electricity has been reduced to 150, whilst hardstanding `super' pitches have been increased to 50. The original heated sanitary facilities, washbasins, showers and toilets, are augmented by another newer block so provision should be adequate (although showers are rather slow to drain and cleaning can be variable). Indoor dishwashing facilities and a launderette are nearby, with another launderette near the shop. Chemical disposal and motorcaravan service facilities. Two play areas in the touring section, plus an amusement arcade and games room near the leisure area. The outdoor pool remains popular (from July), although the heated indoor 'Tropicana' complex, with jacuzzi and sauna, is an outstanding facility and well worth the small charge (adult £2.20, child £1.50). Both pools are well maintained and supervised at all times. An impressive, new development, with family, cabaret room and stylish bar is the Waterfront Club, providing a varied entertainment programme all season. Bar meals and Sunday lunches available, with takeaway also (daily 12-2 and 6-11 except Sunday), plus a well stocked, licensed shop (from April). Visitors have free use of the large, 7 acre fishing lake. A new all-weather tennis court and a nine hole golf course (£5 per day) have been added. Riding 4 miles. Staff are friendly and helpful, with security barrier (£10 deposit) and night patrols. Gas available. Caravan storage. The nearest beach, at Mablethorpe, is 15 minutes by car, and Grimsby, Alford and Louth are also accessible. No tents are accepted.

Charges 2000:
-- Per unit incl. up to 5 persons, awning and electricity £7.00 - £17.00; `super' pitch plus £3.00; extra person £5.00; dog £1.00; extra car £2.00.
-- Min. stays at B.Hs.
-- VAT included.
-- Credit cards accepted.
Open:
March - end November.
Address:
North Somercotes, nr. Louth, Lincolnshire LN11 7RB.
Tel:
(01507) 358315 or 358428.
FAX: (01507) 358135.
E-mail: lakeside@ donamott.com.
Reservations:
Advised for B.Hs and main summer season with deposit (£5 per night booked, min. 3 nights for electricity at B.Hs).

Directions: Park is on A1031 road, 7 miles north of Mablethorpe towards Cleethorpes. O.S.GR: TF430960.

373 Skegness Sands Touring Site, Skegness

Modern, well appointed, touring site, adjacent to promenade and beach.

This very well organised touring site is actually part of a much larger caravan holiday home park, but it has its own entrance and, indeed, its own, more intimate character. There are 85 pitches, all level and with electricity (16A). Most are grass although there are now 32 gravel hardstandings, 4 of which are fully serviced. Site lighting is good throughout, there are regular security patrols and the vehicle entry gates are locked 11 pm - 6 am. The good quality, heated sanitary unit is fully tiled with washbasins in curtained cubicles and good adjustable hot showers, plus three family bathrooms comprising WC, washbasin and shower and a well equipped room for disabled people. Two dishwashing sinks are outside under cover, a laundry room has two washing machines and dryers and there are chemical disposal facilities. Hot water is free throughout. Tourist information is available in reception. A well stocked shop/post office is 200 yards. Gas supplies on site. Other amenities include a hairdressing salon and an indoor heated swimming pool (open end May - 30 Sept; adult £2, child £1.50) which is located in the 'static' area of the site. A small children's playground is on a grassy area towards the promenade. The gate to the promenade is kept locked at all times, campers getting a key. Pubs, fast food outlets and a supermarket are all within easy walking distance, and there is a 'hail and ride' bus service to Skegness and Ingoldmells at 200 m. Local attractions include Funcoast World, Fantasy Island, Hardys Animal Farm, a seal sanctuary, stock car racing, ten pin bowling and golf. The site is a member of the Caravan Club's 'managed under contract' scheme, members and non-members are all made very welcome.

Charges 2000:
-- Per adult £2.60 - £4.00; child (5-16 yrs) £1.10 - £1.20; non-member pitch fee £6.00 - £8.00; electricity £1.50 (summer) - £2.25 (winter); fully serviced pitch plus £3.00.
-- Credit cards accepted.
Open:
All year.
Address:
Winthorpe Avenue, Skegness, Lincolnshire PE25 1QZ.
Tel:
(01754) 761484.
Reservations:
Advised for B.Hs, school holidays and peak season; contact site.

Directions: Site is north of Skegness. Turn from the A52 opposite 'Garden City' public house into Winthorpe Avenue and site entrance is on the left at far end of road. O.S.GR: TF570640.

375 Foreman's Bridge Caravan Park, Sutton St James, nr. Spalding

Peaceful, comfortable, Fenland touring site.

Not only is Foreman's Bridge an extremely pleasant little park, but it also provides a good base from which to explore the Fens, including Spalding, famous for its annual flower festival. Fishing and cycling are also to be recommended, indeed bicycle hire and fishing licences are both available from the site. Arranged around a large, level and grassy meadow there are 40 pitches, 32 of which have electricity (10A) and 7 have gravel hardstanding. Fruit trees, flower beds, hanging baskets and planted troughs punctuate the site with bursts of vibrant colour. The modern sanitary unit provides spacious individual shower rooms with seats and wash-basins (showers on payment), and the thoughtful provision of soap, hand towels, tissues and pot pourri. Dishwashing sinks are in their own room, the laundry room has a washing machine, dryer and ironing facilities and the site recycles glass, aluminium and paper. There are chemical disposal and motorcaravan service points. Basic provisions and gas are available on site – the nearest shop is just two miles away. Seven site owned mobile homes are for rent, as well as two comfortable and well equipped cottages. The adjacent Fenland 'drain' is suitable for fishing, but could be a hazard for young children. Riding 8 miles, golf 5 miles. Winter caravan storage. Site barrier (£5 deposit for card). Bellamy silver.

Directions: From A17 Spalding - Kings Lynn road turn south on B1390 at Long Sutton towards Sutton St James for approx. 2 miles. Site entrance is on the left immediately after the bridge. O.S.GR: TF410198.

Charges 2000:
--Per unit incl. 2 adults £6.00; small 1 person tent £4.50; extra adult £2.00; child £1.00; awning £1.00; dog 50p; electricity £1.50.
-- No credit cards.
-- VAT included.

Open:
1 March - 30 November. (holiday cottages all year)

Address:
Sutton St James, Spalding, Lincolnshire PE21 0HU.

Tel:
(01945) 440346.
FAX: as phone.
E-mail: foremansbridge @btinternet.com.

Reservations:
Advisable for Flower Festival, B.Hs (min. 3 nights), and peak season; made with £10 deposit

370 Pilgrims Way Caravan and Camping Park, Fishtoft, nr. Boston

Excellent touring site, with cosy facilities, close to historic Boston.

Located in a rural setting this delightful, family run site is two miles from Boston and its famous church tower. There are 20 individual pitches of which 5 have hardstanding, whilst all have access to electricity (10A). Housed in a good quality conversion at one end of what was once a workshop, the sanitary facilities have been thoughtfully planned and are exceptionally clean and well maintained. Entry is by keypad and all of the usual facilities are provided, including well fitted, pre-set hot showers with seats and changing space, open washbasins in vanity units, dishwashing and laundry sinks, chemical disposal, plus an excellent fully equipped unit for disabled persons. Hot water is free throughout and there is a laundry with washing machine and dryer. Although there is no shop, gas is available on site and a mini-market, baker and fuel station are within 1 mile, a supermarket just 2 miles. Groundsheets, kite flying and ball games are not allowed and the site is not really suitable for American motorhomes. Local attractions include the 'Boston stump', the Pilgrim Fathers Memorial and Maud Foster Windmill, all in and around the town. Further afield is Heckington village and its unique eight sailed windmill (6 miles) and the Aviation Heritage Centre (12 miles). Boston market days are on Wednesdays and Saturdays and the town also has a fine marina, two sports and leisure centres (one with swimming pools) and there is a ten-pin bowling alley and a tennis centre. Golf, fishing, bicycle hire and riding within 2 miles.

Directions: From A52, 1 mile east of junction with A16, turn south by the 'Ball House' public house, continuing past the Boston Bowl towards Fishtoft, where the site is on your left. O.S.GR: TF360420.

Charges 2001:
-- Per unit incl. 2 persons £7.50; electricity £2.00; extra person or car £1.00.
-- VAT included.
-- No credit cards.

Open:
1 April/Easter - 30 Sept.

Address:
Church Green Road, Fishtoft, Boston, Lincolnshire PE21 0QY.

Tel:
(01205) 366646.
FAX: as phone.

Reservations:
Advised for B.Hs and peak season; contact park.

Derbyshire

385 Rivendale Caravan and Leisure Park, Alsop-en-le-Dale

New park in course of development in the Peak National Park near Ashbourne.

When we visited this new park at the invitation of the owners we were immediately struck by the size of the project they had taken on. The reception and shop building you first see on arrival has been carefully renovated and there is now a small cafe and a bar within this building (limited opening in low seasons). Moving into the park proper which is located in an old quarry, we were impressed by the continued effort since our last visit. There are 80 pitches completed, all with hardstanding and 16A electrical hook up. Set out in small groups with names such as 'Little Delving' or 'Crickhollow', each pitch is separated from its neighbour and some have a grass area. The sanitary facilities are first rate with under-floor, computer controlled central heating, free showers, washbasins (with cubicles for ladies), a good shower room for disabled visitors and chemical disposal. The touring park will eventually take up about 11 acres of the total land space of 37 and a newly levelled field will take caravans and tents with a limited number of electricity points. An environmental pond should be completed for 2001. The park is situated almost on The Tissington Trail offering walking and off road cycling and, with the Peak National Park on hand and towns such Ashbourne, Bakewell and even Buxton nearby, there is lots to do and see here. Riding 3 miles, fishing 5 miles, bicycle hire 2½ miles. The important thing to remember about this park is that it is new and needs to mature which will, of course, take time. It is a credit to the owners who deserve congratulations for providing such an excellent park.

Directions: Park is by A515 Buxton - Ashbourne road at Alsop-en-le-Dale, about 7 miles north of Ashbourne. O.S.GR: SK161566.

Charges 2000:
-- Per pitch incl. 2 adults £6.20 - £8.20; pitch with water connection plus £2.70; extra adult £1.00; child (4-15 yrs) 50p; awning £1.50; extra car £1.00; dog 50p; electricity £2.20.
-- Credit cards accepted.
-- VAT included.

Open:
All year excl. February.

Address:
Buxton Road, Alsop-en-le-Dale, Ashbourne, Derbyshire DE6 1QU.

Tel:
(01332) 843000.
FAX: (01332) 842311.

E-mail:
rivendale@fsmail.net

Reservations:
Made with £10 deposit; contact park.

`Camping Cheque'

A peaceful 37 acre park with a superb, south-facing, sheltered pitching area in a natural sun-trap. Ideal for cycling and rambling in the surrounding Peak District with lots to see and do close by - from sailing at Carsington Water - to a day out at Chatsworth and Alton Towers.

Rivendale

In The Peak District

Tel: 01332 843000 or 01335 310311
Fax: 01332 842311 rivendale@fsmail.net

Convenient for Chatsworth, Alton Towers, Dovedale, Hartington, Bakewell, Ashbourne.

GOLD

For lists of parks which offer facilities on site for
FISHING, GOLF, HORSE RIDING, BICYCLE HIRE
or BOAT LAUNCHING see pages 238 - 240

382 Darwin Forest Country Park, Darley Moor, Two Dales

Well maintained park for caravans and motorhomes in heart of the Derbyshire Dales, near Matlock, with indoor pool.

Between Matlock and Bakewell, this park, as its name implies, is set amongst 44 acres of mixed woodland close to the Peak District National Park. A large proportion of the park is given over to pine lodges for holiday letting but it also provides 50 touring pitches. All with hardstanding and electric hook-up (10A), they are clearly defined with hedging or open fencing in level grass bays amongst the pines - the unspoilt woodland is home to a variety of birds and wildlife. The modern toilet block is tiled and well equipped, providing free hot showers, washbasins in cabins, free hairdryers, a full unit for disabled people, laundry room and covered washing up area. The pleasant Forester's Inn provides meals and a beer garden. A small shop has basics and Calor gas. Other amenities include a children's adventure play area on bark, separate games room with pool tables, tennis court and short-tennis and minigolf. The heated, indoor swimming pool (40 x 20 ft.) has a railed off children's section, spectator area and terrace, with good changing and shower facilities (see charges below). Fishing 2 miles, bicycle hire 8 miles, riding 2 miles, golf 4 miles. This is a useful park from which to explore the picturesque towns and villages of the Peak District - 4 miles from Chatsworth House, 40 minutes from Alton Towers. The Peak District Steam Railway currently operates a two mile section from Darley Dale to Matlock Riverside. Bellamy gold.

Directions: Park is best approached via the A632 Chesterfield - Matlock road. North of Matlock take the B5057 signed Darley Dale and park is on the right before descending into the village of Two Dales. O.S.GR: SK287633.

Charges 2000:
-- Per unit incl. all persons: Fri. and Sat. £12.00, other nights £10.00 - £12.00, acc. to season; awning £2.00; electricity £2.00 - £2.50.
-- Swimming pool charges: adult £1.00 - £2.50, child (4-14 yrs) 50p - £1.50.
-- VAT included.
-- Credit cards accepted.

Open:
March - October.

Address:
Darwin Moor, Two Dales, Matlock, Derbyshire DE4 5LN.

Tel:
(01629) 732428.
FAX: (01629) 735015.
E-mail: admin@ darwinforest.co.uk.

Reservations:
Advised and made with deposit; contact park.

The Perfect Setting For Your Caravan Holiday in in the heart of the Derbyshire Peak District

FOR A FREE BROCHURE CALL 01629 732428

383 The Firs Farm, Nether Heage, Ambergate, nr. Belper

Neat and tidy park with views over the Derwent Valley.

We were impressed with the facilities and helpful attitude of the owners at Firs Farm. The views across and along the wooded Derwent Valley are marvellous and the owners have thoughtfully provided a picnic terrace with tables. Pitches further back have pleasant flowers and shrubs to compensate for the lack of a front line position for the view. There are 60 large, level pitches for touring units, all with 10A electricity and about 50% with gravel hardstanding. The attractive toilet block to one side of the park, with a veranda and set in its own garden featuring flowering cherries, is heated, double glazed and curtained! Spotlessly clean, it provides modern fittings including washbasins in cubicles and controllable showers with stools. Under the veranda are washing up sinks, a public phone, tourist information and a seat - very pleasant. Chemical disposal point. A sauna is also provided (£5 charge). No laundry facilities, but a launderette is at Belper (1½ miles) with shops, etc. A pub is a half mile walk, with other restaurants within driving distance. Fishing 1 mile, riding 1½ miles, golf 5 miles, bicycle hire 7 miles. Caravan storage available.

Directions: From A6 road, ¼ mile north of Belper, turn right into Broadholme Lane and follow signs.O.S.GR: SK354504.

Charges 2000:
-- Per unit incl. 2 persons £8.00; extra person £2.00; awning or pup tent £1.50; electricity (10A) £1.75.
-- No credit cards.

Open:
All year.

Address:
Crich Lane, Nether Heage, Ambergate, Belper, Derbyshire DE56 2JH.

Tel:
(01773) 852913.

Reservations:
Essential for B.Hs and peak season; contact park.

Derbyshire

380 Highfields Camping and Caravan Park, nr. Ashbourne

Quiet, spacious park in Peak District National Park.

The Redfern family run Highfields, which is set on high, flat ground in the Peak District National Park with marvellous views. It takes 50 touring units and 50 seasonal vans in open, hedged fields accessed by tarmac roads, with an area for tents, another for vans with concrete slabs for jockey wheels and an area for adults only. There are 8 hardstandings and 89 electrical connections (16A), with 55 privately owned caravan holiday homes in separate fields. The main toilet block is kept locked (deposit for key) and is well maintained. Hot water is free to the washbasins, but metered to laundry and dishwashing sinks, and to the showers. A baby bath and chemical disposal are provided. A smaller block is in the far static field and further sanitary facilities are provided adjacent to the new rally room. All blocks are heated when necessary. There is a shop for basics and gas, a children's playground, bicycle hire and a dog exercise field. A room, complete with in-built barbecue, table and chairs, is available for hire. Public phone. An indoor, heated swimming pool is open all season (restricted times if the park is not very full), with a small charge (90p per session). Although not supervised at all times, the pool is monitored from reception by closed circuit TV. Fishing 3 miles, golf 5 miles, riding 2 miles, boat launching 5 miles. Pub and restaurant close. People frequently venture off the site to enjoy the Peak District - Dovedale and Ilam are only a mile or two's distance by footpath and the Tissington Trail with access to the High Peak Trail passes by the park. American motorhomes are accepted. Winter caravan storage.

Charges 2000:
-- Per unit incl. 2 persons £10.00; extra adult £1.50; child (under 16 yrs) 75p; electricity (16A) £2.50.
-- Credit cards accepted.
-- VAT included.

Open:
1 March - 31 October.

Address:
Fenny Bentley,
nr. Ashbourne,
Derbyshire DE6 1LE.

Tel:
(01335) 350228.
FAX: (01335) 350253.

Reservations:
Made with payment of one night's fee; min. stay at B.Hs - 3 nights.

Directions: Park is west off A515 Buxton - Ashbourne road, just north of Fenny Bentley village (take care at sharp turn to site road when approaching from Ashbourne). O.S.GR: SK170510.

384 Lime Tree Park, Buxton

Select park with high quality modern facilities in convenient, edge of town location.

This park is a very good base for touring the Peak District. A new sanitary building serves the caravan/motorcaravan area, complete with patio and pergola frontage, together with the refitted original unit which serves the tenting area, provide ample facilities for all. Both units are heated, attractively tiled and have top quality fittings including brass taps. They provide WCs, washbasins, both open and in cubicles, controllable showers with dividers, shelf and seats, a baby room with the very latest design of baby bath, and a family room with facilities for disabled people. Dishwashing sinks are outside under cover and there are chemical disposal points, motorcaravan service area and good lighting. A washing machine and dryer are in the laundry room, hot water is free throughout. The 99 touring pitches, of which 64 have access to electricity (10A), are on the two upper terraces which have the best views but are slightly more exposed until the new plantings mature. Below are areas set aside for late arrivals and the caravan holiday homes (26 privately owned and 10 for rent). There is a small shop with gas and basics, public telephone and a new, extended children's playground with grass and rubber safety base. A games/TV room is alongside reception. The nearest pub serving food is just around the corner and Buxton town centre is a comfortable stroll away. Fishing, bicycle hire, riding and golf, all within 5 miles. Alton Towers is 22 miles. A new member of the Best of British group.

Charges 2000:
-- Per unit incl. 2 adults £8.00 - £10.00; extra adult £1.50; extra child (5-15 yrs) 75p; hiker, cyclist or m/cyclist £3.50 - £4.00; awning £1.50; dog 50p; extra car £1.00; electricity £2.00.
-- Credit cards accepted.
-- VAT included.

Open:
1 March - 31 October

Address:
Dukes Drive, Buxton,
Derbyshire SK17 9RP.

Tel:
(01298) 22988.

Reservations:
Made with £10 deposit; contact park for details.

Directions: From Buxton take A515 (Ashbourne) road south, turning sharp left into Dukes Drive after the hospital on the outskirts of the town, under the railway viaduct, and site is on right. O.S.GR: SK069725.

Nottinghamshire

394 Smeaton's Lakes Touring Caravan Park, South Muskham

New touring site, popular with fishermen, near Newark-on-Trent.

This site is really here for fishermen, with tarmac access roads and a modern building housing reception and the sanitary facilities, it is set in 82 acres with three fishing lakes and river fishing. Reception keeps gas, soft drinks, dairy produce, sweets, crisps, etc. and newspapers can be ordered. The sanitary facilities (with keypad access) are heated, with open style washbasins, pre-set hot showers, free hot water throughout and a good unit for disabled people, but no laundry room. There are 45 pitches on grass, 14 with hardstanding and 40 electrical connections (16A), with a separate rally field for 100 units. The lakes and river provide good sport and include coarse, carp and pike lakes, with on site concessions. This site is probably the best choice for visiting events at nearby Newark Showground, or Newark town (1 mile) with its castle, the Millgate Folk Museum, and the Air Museum. Newark has a Flea market (Mon. and Thurs), a fruit, vegetable and general market (Wed, Fri and Sat), and a car boot sale (Sun). A bus stop is at the end of the entry lane and buses run into Newark every hour until 10 pm. The site is also central for visiting Southwell Cathedral, Lincoln with its castle and cathedral and Nottingham with its Lace Hall, Castle or Caves.

Directions: Site lies on A6065 west of the town, south of junction of A616 towards Ollerton (well signed). O.S.GR: SK792558.

Charges 2000:
-- Per unit incl. 2 adults £7.50 - £8.50; extra adult £1.00 - £1.50; children (over 5 yrs) 75p - £1.00; electricity £2.00 - £2.50.
-- VAT included.
-- No credit cards.
Open: All year.
Address: Great North Road, South Muskham, Newark-on-Trent, Nottinghamshire NG23 6ED
Tel: (01636) 605088 or 673250.
Reservations: Contact site.

395 Orchard Park Touring Caravan and Camping Park, Tuxford

Rural family run site, created in old fruit orchard.

This well established site is in a quiet location and has 65 pitches. There are also 23 hardstandings, most of which were occupied by longer stay or seasonal units at the time of our visit. All pitches have access to electricity (10A). Reception is at the owners' house and includes a small shop with basic essentials and gas, more services (some open to 10 pm) are in the village (½ mile). The specially designed sanitary unit (with piped music) has the usual facilities including spacious pre-mixed hot showers, a well equipped room for disabled persons and free hot water throughout. The laundry has washing machines, dryer and sinks and there are two dishwashing sinks outside. At the far end of the park is a children's play area with swings, slide etc. and a nature walk with wild flowers, birds and butterflies. Local attractions include Tuxford Windmill, Sundown Adventureland kiddies theme park, Laxton Medieval village and Victorian Times, with its working horse drawn carriage driving centre, at nearby Kirton.

Directions: From the A1 turn onto A6075 towards Lincoln, continue through village to eastern outskirts, turning right towards High Marnham. Site is on right ½ mile after railway bridge (well signed in village). O.S.GR: SK750710.

Charges guide:
-- Per unit incl. 2 adults £7.00 - £7.50; extra adult £1.00; child (4-15 yrs) 50p; electricity £1.50.
-- Credit cards accepted.
-- VAT included.
Open: March - October
Address: Marnham Road, Tuxford, Nottinghamshire NG22 0PY.
Tel: (01777) 870228.
Reservations: Advised for B.Hs (min. 3 nights) and peak season with £10 deposit.

392 Riverside Caravan Park, Worksop

Town centre touring site adjacent to county cricket ground.

An excellent, attractive and surprisingly peaceful site, Riverside is within easy walking distance of the town centre precinct and shops. The Chesterfield Canal runs close to the northern side of the site offering delightful tow-path walks or fishing and, for those who cannot resist the thwack of leather on willow, this site is ideal. Of the 60 marked level pitches, 50 are on gravel hardstanding, some separated by trees and low rails, and all with electricity (10A). The modern sanitary unit near reception can be heated and has all the usual facilities, although showers are on payment (20p). There is no laundry, but a launderette is close in the town. Activities available locally include squash, flat or crown green bowling, bicycle hire and campers are also very welcome at the Cricket Ground clubhouse. Worksop provides well for golfers with three courses in the area. One of the town's most interesting buildings, the medieval Priory Gatehouse, is open free of charge, market days are Wednesday, Friday and Saturday. This site is also a good base for exploring Creswell Craggs, Clumber Park, the Dukeries Cycle Trail, and Rufford Mill Craft Centre and Country Park.

Directions: Easiest approach is from roundabout west of the town (A57) - third roundabout from the A1, junction of A57/A60. Turn into Newcastle Avenue, then left into Stubbing Lane, right into Central Avenue, left into Cricket Ground, follow through to camping site (well signed). O.S.GR: SK580790.

Charges 2001:
-- Per adult £3.50 - £3.75; child (5-16 yrs) £1.30; electricity £1.60 - £2.00.
-- No credit cards.
-- VAT included.
Open: All year.
Address: Central Avenue, Worksop, Nottinghamshire S80 1ER.
Tel: (01909) 474118.
Reservations: Advised for B.Hs, peak season and weekends, with £5 deposit.

Staffordshire

396 Silvertrees Caravan Park, Rugeley

Small, peaceful park in light woodland for caravans and motorhomes only.

Silvertrees, as its name suggests, is in a beautifully wooded setting with many silver birches on the edge of Cannock Chase. In the evenings the deer roam down the little valley in which the site is situated and there is evidence of much more animal and bird life - the park is actually designated a Site of Special Scientific Interest (SSSI). Of the older style, it comprises three paddock areas with 50 mobile homes (most privately owned, 10 to hire), plus 50 touring pitches on gently sloping grass. Double paving stones for the main wheels mark each pitch - chocks would be useful. All pitches have 16A electrical connections. The small, heated toilet block provides vanity style washbasins (H&C), two showers each for men and women (20p) with shared changing area, laundry and dishwashing sink, and a washing machine and dryer. It could be under pressure at B.Hs. Chemical disposal facilities. A small, unheated fun pool (3 ft deep, open April - Sept) is to be found in the valley bottom - a real sun trap. Amenities include a good tennis court, adventure play area, ball field and a comfortable games room with table tennis, video games, TV and an unusual ceiling. The park is set in 20 acres of woodland so there is plenty to do on site, never mind the natural heathland of the Chase. Helpful wardens and the owners live on site. There is a little library in reception and much useful tourist information in the games room. Gas supplies. Most dogs are accepted (not certain breeds). Barbecues must be raised off the ground. Fishing 1 mile, riding 6 miles, golf 3 miles. Supermarket 2 miles. Bus service outside park. A pub with food is within walking distance. Alton Towers is nearby. A member of the Countryside Discovery group.

Directions: Park is 2 miles from Rugeley just off the Penkridge - Rugeley road. It is signed from Rugeley off the A51. O.S.GR: SK014173.

Charges 2000:
-- Per pitch incl. 2 persons and electricity £7.00 - £9.00; extra person £1.00; awning £2.00.
-- Credit cards accepted (+3%).
-- VAT included.

Open:
April - October.

Address:
Stafford Brook Road,
Penkridge Bank,
Rugeley,
Staffordshire
WS15 2TX.

Tel:
(01889) 582185.
FAX: as phone.

Reservations:
Made with £20 deposit and essential at B.Hs. (when min. 3 nights).

397 Glencote Caravan Park, Cheddleton, nr. Leek

Pleasant, family run park, 3 miles south of market town, at entrance to Churnet Valley.

A 6-acre park, Glencote has 60 numbered pitches set on flat grass, 50 of which have patio style hardstandings, with a tarmac, curved central access road. All pitches have electrical connections (10A) and a dedicated water supply. Attractive flower-beds and trees make a very pleasant environment. The good, modern toilet block is centrally situated and can be heated. Facilities include free, controllable showers, vanity style washbasins (one private cabin for ladies), hair dryer, razor points and mirrors, a small laundry room, two dishwashing sinks under cover (free hot water) and chemical disposal. Gas is available. An attractive, sunken children's play area, on grass and bark with an abundance of shrubs and flowers, sits alongside the small (fenced) coarse fishing pool, together with a new barbecue area with a tented cover. Dogs are accepted (max. 2 per unit). In the village of Cheddleton, ½ mile away, is a small supermarket and a post office. A variety of inns are within easy walking distance - the Boat Inn beside the canal is very good value. Attractions nearby include a renovated Flint Mill powered by two giant water wheels and Cheddleton railway centre. The Churnet Valley, an Area of Outstanding Natural Beauty is good for walking, the Staffordshire Way is also near. For the more energetic, canoeing and hang gliding opportunities are close. Riding 10 miles, bicycle hire 5 miles, golf 4 miles. Alton Towers is 10 miles (you may leave your unit on site after 3 pm. for an additional £2 charge).

Directions: Park is signed off A520 Leek - Stone road, 3½ miles south of Leek on northern edge of Cheddleton Village. O.S.GR: SJ982524.

Charges 2000:
-- Per unit incl. 2 persons £9.00; child (under 16 yrs) £1.50; extra adult £2.00; pup tent or extra car £1.00; electricity (10A) £1.80.
-- For each 7 nights booked, one night free (except electricity).
-- Min. 3 nights at B.Hs.
-- Credit cards accepted.
-- VAT included.

Open:
Easter - end October.

Address:
Station Road,
Cheddleton,
nr. Leek,
Staffodshire
ST13 7EE.

Tel:
(01538) 360745.
FAX: (01538) 361788.

Reservations:
Advised for peak season asnd made with deposit of £18 (2 nights) or £25 (over 2 nights).

410 Cotswold Hoburne, South Cerney, Cirencester

Good touring park with holiday caravans and a variety of watersports amenities close.

Since the park is adjacent to the Cotswold Water Park, those staying will have easy access to the varied watersports there which include sailboarding and water ski-ing. On the park itself there is a lake with pedaloes and canoes for hire. Its wide range of other amenities include an outdoor (44 x 22 ft) heated swimming pool (open Whitsun - early September) and an impressive, large indoor leisure complex including pool with flume, spa bath, sauna, steam room (all free) and sun bed. There are 300 well marked touring pitches for any type of unit, all with hardstanding (only fairly level) and grass surround for awning or tent. Of good size but with nothing between them, all have electrical connections (some need long leads). Also 150 holiday units, mainly for letting. Six toilet blocks are all quite small but are clean and well maintained. Hot water is free in the washbasins and pre-set showers. Baby changing facilities. Basic facilities for visitors with disabilities are to be found in the clubhouse, but are locked at night. The site has heavy weekend trade. The large clubhouse has a big general lounge with giant TV screen, entertainment at times, food service (or food bar in lounge), big games room and a lounge bar which overlooks the outdoor pool and lake with a patio. Supermarket. Launderette. Activities include a football field, tennis courts, a good quality adventure playground with bark base and crazy golf. Fishing lake (permits from reception). No dogs or pets are accepted. Part of the Hoburne group.

Directions: Three miles from Cirencester on A419, turn right towards Cotswold Water Park at new roundabout on bypass onto B4696. Take second right and follow signs. O.S.GR: SU055957.

Charges 2000:
-- Touring pitch incl. electricity £9.00 - £23.00; pup tent £3.00.
-- Weekly rates or week-end breaks available.
-- VAT included.
-- Credit cards accepted.
Open:
March - 31 October.
Address:
Broadway Lane,
South Cerney,
Cirencester,
Glos. GL7 5UQ.
Tel:
(01285) 860216.
FAX: (01285) 862106.
E-mail: enquiries@
hoburne.co.uk.
Reservations:
Bookings of 1-6 nights payable in full at time of reservation; caravans with £50 deposit for 1 week. Min. 4 nights booking at B.Hs.

411 Tewkesbury Caravan Club Site, Tewkesbury

Attractive site in a beautiful part of the country.

There are two important reasons why the Caravan Club site at Tewkesbury is so popular: firstly, it is within five minutes walk of the town centre and is overlooked by the Norman Abbey, the focal point of the town and secondly, it is a good base for exploring the eastern end of the Cotswolds as well as some of the country's most delightful towns. Gloucester, Cheltenham, Stow-on-the-Wold, Bourton-on-the-Water, Chipping Norton and Broadway are just a few that immediately spring to mind. The Malvern hills are also within driving distance. The site, which accepts non-members and campers with tents, covers nine acres and has 170 pitches reached by tarmac roads. All are on grass, but some slope so blocks are essential, and all have electric hook-ups (16A). There are three toilet blocks, although the one in the reception building has no showers. One block has facilities for disabled visitors and two have laundry rooms. All the blocks are built and maintained to the Club's usual high standards and can be heated. Chemical disposal and motorcaravan service facilities are provided. The entrance to the site is locked at night but there is a late arrivals area just outside it. The reception sells basic supplies and gas, and food shops, restaurants, pubs, etc. are all within easy walking distance. Adjoining reception is a tourist information room and a dog walk is provided in the adjacent field. Fishing 400 yds, riding 5 miles, golf 1 mile. Although one of the largest sites operated by the Caravan Club, Tewkesbury's popularity is such that booking is essential at B.H.s and during the period June to August. A further factor contributing to its popularity must be the friendly and helpful wardens.

Charges 2000:
-- Non-member pitch fee £7.00; adult £4.00; child (5-17 yrs) £1.10 - £1.20; awning free; electricity £2.20 - £1.45.
-- Credit cards accepted.
Open:
April - October.
Address:
Gander Lane,
Tewkesbury,
Gloucestershire
GL20 5PG.
Tel:
(01684) 294035
(8 am. - 8 pm. except emergencies).
Reservations:
Accepted and are essential all B.Hs. and June-Aug.

Directions: From all directions follow signs for town centre and head for the Abbey which is easily distinguished. Turn by the Abbey into Gander Lane, follow down passing two car parks to site at end of the lane. O.S.GR: SO894324.

Gloucestershire

412 Briarfields Caravan and Camping, Cheltenham

Park close to M5 for night stop or for visiting the Cotswolds and local towns.

Newly planted saplings (in addition to the mature trees already here) and 3,000 rosewall bushes will mature to enhance the overall appearance and security of this developing park. Just a mile from the M5, a short entrance drive leads from the B4063 to the 75 flat, grassy pitches. Over 50 have hardstanding and can take motorhomes up to 38 ft. Set around the tarmac access road and in the central area, all have electricity (16A) and are well lit. The heated sanitary building (coded security locks) has washbasins in cabins, curtained showers with shared undressing area and excellent facilities for disabled visitors, plus a large laundry and dishwashing room. Motorcaravan service point. Just across the road, in the owner's holiday home park, is a well stocked, licensed mini market. A pub, a short walk away, offers meals and a children's garden. Cheltenham Racecourse is 4 miles and there is a golf course open to all just a few minutes up the road. Some road noise is to be expected. Caravan storage.

Charges 2000:
-- Per unit £6.50;
hardstanding £1.00;
electricity £1.90.
-- Credit cards accepted.
Open:
All year.
Address:
Gloucester Road,
Cheltenham,
Gloucestershire
GL51 0SX.
Tel:
(01242) 235324.
Mobile: 0836-274440.
FAX: as phone.
Reservations:
Advised at times of race
meetings; contact park.

Directions: From M5 exit 11 take A40 towards Cheltenham. In ½ mile turn left on B4063 Gloucester road and park entrance is shortly on the left at motel. Via Cheltenham take signs for M5 and look for B4063 as above. O.S.GR: SO922220.

413 Moreton-in-Marsh Caravan Club Site, Moreton-in-Marsh

Well located, all year site in the heart of the Cotswolds.

This excellent, busy, but rural, tree-surrounded site offers everything one would hope for from a camping holiday. Only 250 yards from the town, there is plenty of choice for food and pubs. The site has 180 pitches, all with electricity, 120 with hardstanding and most offering TV sockets. The two toilet blocks offer spacious showers, washbasins in cabins, hair and hand dryers with facilities in each block for the walking disabled (4 inch step). There is an excellent en-suite room for disabled visitors in another building and a large laundry. Milk, bread, papers and ice-cream are available from reception. A large play field provides a climbing frame with bark base and space for football, volleyball, boules and crazy golf. Kite flying is not allowed because of low power cables. Moreton-in-Marsh is famous for its Tuesday street market and is always a busy town, being only a few miles from the pretty villages of Bourton-on-the-Water and Stow-on-the-Wold, which are just two of the interesting villages worthy of a visit in this lovely area.

Charges 2000:
-- Per unit £7.50 - £15.00.
Open:
All year.
Address:
Bourton Road,
Moreton-in-Marsh,
Gloucestershire
GL56 0BT.
Tel:
(01608) 650519.
Reservations:
Contact site.

Directions: From Evesham on A44, site on left after Bourton-on-the-Hill village, 150 yards before town sign. From Moreton-in-Marsh take A44 towards Evesham and site is on right, 150 yards past Wellington museum. O.S.GR: SP200323.

414 Camping and Caravanning Club Site Winchcombe, Alderton

Quiet site, close to Tewkesbury and Cotswolds attractions, with small fishing lake.

This is a popular site in a rural location, where some of the pitches surround a small fishing lake and others are in a more recently developed area, with open views over the countryside. In total there are 80 pitches, 58 with electric hook-ups (10A) and 42 with gravel hardstandings. The reception building flanks a small gravel courtyard car park and late arrivals area approached from a tarmac drive. This building also houses the laundry with washing machine and dryer, and a well equipped unit for disabled people. Gas is stocked. The main, heated sanitary unit, kept very clean and tidy by the wardens, has controllable hot showers, vanity style washbasins and WCs, with dishwashing sinks and a chemical disposal point under cover outside. To the rear of the site is a small, 'portacabin' style sanitary unit (also heated) with additional WCs, washbasins and dishwashing sinks. A large games room with a bowling alley, table tennis and a pool table, supplement the outdoor children's small play area. For the adults there are several pubs and restaurants in the area, and on Saturdays between 5-6 pm. you will find a fish and chip van in the car park. Places to visit include Gloucester Docks and the National Waterways Museum, whilst south of Gloucester are Owlpen Manor near Uley, and Painswick Rococo Garden. The Wildfowl and Wetlands Trust at Slimbridge, first opened in 1946 by Sir Peter Scott is well worth a visit.

Charges 2000:
-- Per adult: £3.75 - 5.30;
child £1.65; non-member
pitch fee £4.30;
electricity £1.60 - 2.35.
-- VAT included.
Open:
16 March - 15 January.
Address:
Brooklands Farm,
Alderton,
nr. Tewkesbury
GL20 8NX.
Tel:
(01242) 620259
(not after 8.00 pm).
Reservations:
Contact site for details.

Directions: From M5 exit 9, take A46 Evesham road for 3 miles to Toddington roundabout, then B4077 towards Stow-on-the-Wold, for a further 3 miles to the site entrance. Ignore signs for Alderton village. O.S.GR: SP 007324.

407 Somers Wood Caravan and Camping Park, Meriden

Useful park in light pine woods near the N.E.C. for adults only, open all year.

Somers Wood, although near Birmingham, is attractively situated and edged by pine woods., with views of the adjacent 16 hole golf course (including driving range) and coarse fishing lake; both these are available for customer's use. Log buildings blend comfortably into their surroundings providing reception, with the owners' home at the entrance and for the separate sanitary facilities. An oval, gravel road provides access to the 48 large pitches, 42 of which have 10A electricity. In winter drainage may be a problem, although there are 30 pitches with hardstanding. The central, heated sanitary facilities provide free hot showers and vanity style washbasins with plenty of mirrors. Two dishwashing sinks with hot water are on the veranda area to one side of the block, with a laundry service available at reception. Refuse areas, water taps and a simple chemical disposal point (short hose) complete the facilities. There is a supply of tourist information in reception and a public phone. This is a very useful park for those visiting the NEC, and for certain shows such as the National Boat, Caravan and Leisure Show in February, it can be busy, although at other times it is quiet and peaceful. Local shops and a restaurant are less than 1 mile and visitors are also welcome to use the bar and restaurant at the golf club. Only adults are accepted.

Directions: From M42 junction 6 (NEC) take A45 towards Coventry. Almost immediately, on left-hand side, take A452 signed Leamington. Turn right at roundabout on A452 then turn left into Hampton Lane at the next roundabout, signed Stonesbridge Golf Centre and site is signed with golf and fishing centres on the left. O.S.GR: SP228819.

Charges 2000:
-- Per pitch incl. 2 persons £10.00; 1-man tent £6.00; extra adult £2.00; full awning £1.00, orch awning 50p; extra car £1.00; electricity £2.50.
-- No credit cards.
-- VAT included.

Open:
All year.

Address:
Somers Road, Meriden, N. Warwickshire CV7 7PL.

Tel:
(01676) 522978.
FAX: as phone.
E-mail: enquiries@ somerswood.co.uk.

Reservations:
Advised for B.Hs and certain NEC exhibitions; made with deposit of £3 per night booked.

390 Bosworth Water Trust, Market Bosworth

Water Sports Centre with touring site adjacent.

Essentially designed for the water sports enthusiast, the camping area at Bosworth has 80 pitches on mostly level grass with electricity (5A) available to 31. The good quality, heated sanitary facilities in the main building are designed more for the watersports users, with communal showers and changing area, however the adjacent small `portacabin' style unit does have conventional separate shower cubicles. This unit may be replaced in the future, as the current facilities could be slightly over-stretched during peak times. Reception serves a good range of snacks, soft drinks, ices, etc. Gas is available and chemical disposal facilities. This RYA recognised centre offers a range of watersports - dinghy and board sailing, canoeing, rowing and fishing (swimming is not advised in the lake). Tuition is available for all watersports activities, lifejackets and wet suits can be hired, and there is a 'Kids Club' every Saturday (call site for brochure). On arrival you will need £2 to operate the Centre's entrance barrier. Riding 1 mile, golf ½ mile. Local attractions include Snibston Discovery Park, Twycross Zoo, Mallory Park motor racing circuit, steam trains and the battlefields.

Directions: Site is off B585 about 1 mile west of Market Bosworth. O.S.GR: SK370020.

Charges 2000:
-- Per unit incl. all persons £8.00; pup tent £2.00; awning £1.00; extra car £1.00; electricity £2.00.
-- Fishing and lake fees: 50% discount for campers.
-- VAT included.
-- No credit cards.

Open:
All year.

Address:
Market Bosworth, Nuneaton, Warwickshire CV13 6PD.

Tel/Fax:
(01455) 291876.

Reservations:
Advised at B.Hs, school holidays and peak season.

For a list of parks which are open all year - see page 235

Worcestershire

CARAVAN PARK — HOLIDAY CENTRE

- ESTABLISHED FAMILY-RUN PARK
- LOCATED IN THE VALE OF EVESHAM
- TOURERS WELCOME
- ELECTRIC AND MULTISERVICE HOOK-UPS AVAILABLE
- LICENSED CLUB SERVING MEALS
- HEATED OUTDOOR SWIMMING POOL
- SHOP
- LAUNDRY

HONEYBOURNE, EVESHAM, WORCS. WR11 5QG

Tel: EVESHAM (01386) 830744

404 Camping and Caravanning Club Site Clent Hills, Romsley

Surprisingly pretty and tranquil site close to Birmingham and motorways.

This site, conveniently close to Birmingham and only a couple of miles or so off the M5/M42 intersection, is a real surprise in terms of being quiet and peaceful and very pretty with good views. Its only disadvantage is that it is on sloping ground, but the present, very helpful wardens are happy to assist in pitching anyone who has a problem in getting level (mainly motorcaravanners); in fact, there are some level pitches and these are all earmarked for motorcaravans. The 118 pitches are all of a good size, 47 with electrical connections (10A). There are 14 with hardstanding (more to be added in the future). The central sanitary block can be heated and provides the latest facilities, including hot showers, washbasins in cabins, hairdryers, baby room and a toilet and shower for disabled people. It was spotless when seen in high season. A washing machine, dryer and ironing facilities are available, plus a chemical disposal point. The modern reception building with excellent tourist information, gas, arrivals area and larger car parking area are at the entrance. A small children's play area has a rubber safety surface. Fishing 3 miles, riding 1 mile. Caravan storage. Generally this is a well run and attractive site, very usefully situated.

Directions: From M5 junction 4 take A491, branch right to Romsley on B4551 and watch for site signs in Romsley village by shops. Site is on left. O.S.GR: SO955795.

Charges 2000:
-- Per adult £3.75 - £5.30; child (6-18 yrs) £1.65; non-member pitch fee £4.30; electricity £1.60 - £2.35.
-- VAT included.
-- Credit cards accepted.

Open:
March - October.

Address:
Fieldhouse Lane, Romsley, Halesowen, West Midlands B62 0NH.

Tel:
(01562) 710015 (no calls after 8 pm).

Reservations:
Necessary and made with deposit; contact the wardens.

419 Kingsgreen Caravan Park, Berrow, nr. Malvern

Friendly, comfortable farm site, with good facilities and views of the Malvern hills.

In an attractive rural location, this site is ideal for adults who like the quiet life, so there are no amusements for children. The surrounding countryside is ideal for walking or cycling, and the small, fenced fishing lake on the site is well stocked (£3 per day). There are 45 level, grass and gravel pitches, all with electricity (16A), plus an additional area for tents. Some old orchard trees provide a little shade in parts. Modern sanitary facilities (key on deposit) provide good hot showers with changing area, curtain and seat (token from reception, 25p), WCs, washbasins in flat surfaces, plus a separate unit for disabled people (WC and washbasin). Dishwashing sinks are under cover at the rear of the building and there is a chemical disposal point. A recent and excellent addition is a small laundry with washing machine, dryer, sink and iron and board (all metered). Gas and barbecue fuels are available and a milkman calls daily with milk, eggs, bread, soft drinks, etc. The nearest shop and pub are 1½ miles. The site is 7 miles from the market town of Ledbury with its half timbered buildings and within easy driving distance of Malvern, the Three Counties showground, Cotswolds, Forest of Dean or Tewkesbury with its 12th century Abbey. Bicycle hire 2 miles, riding 3 miles, golf 5 miles.

Directions: From M50 junction 2, take A417 towards Gloucester, then first left, where site is signed, also signed the Malverns, back over the motorway. Site is 2 miles from the M50. O.S.GR: SO767338.

Charges 2000:
-- Per unit incl. 2 adults £6.00; tent incl. 2 adults £5.00 - £6.00, acc. to size; extra person over 2 yrs £1.00; dog 50p; awning £1.00; electricity £1.50.
-- No credit cards.
-- VAT not included.

Open:
1 March - 31 October.

Address:
Kingsgreen, Berrow, Malvern, Worcestershire WR13 6AQ.

Tel:
(01531) 650272. FAX: as phone.

Reservations:
Essential for peak season and B.Hs. - contact site.

418 Ranch Caravan Park, Honeybourne, nr. Evesham

Popular touring park in 50 acres for caravans only, close to the Cotswolds.

The Vale of Evesham is noted for being a sheltered area growing fruit and other produce from early spring through to late autumn. Ranch lies not far from both Evesham and Broadway in quiet country surroundings, and is also only half an hour's drive from Stratford-on-Avon. A free swimming pool (55 x 30 ft.) with slide is open and heated June - Sept. The park takes 120 touring units - caravans, motorcaravans or trailer tents but not other tents - on flat, partly undulating, hedged meadows with well mown grass and a spacious feel. Pitches are not marked but the staff site units. There are around 100 electrical connections (10A) and 8 fully serviced pitches (electricity, TV, water and sewer connections). There are 169 caravan holiday homes in their own section (4 to rent). Two very well appointed, modern sanitary blocks, with free hot water to washbasins and hot showers on payment, make a good provision. Self-service shop (mornings only early and late seasons). Gas is available. The comfortable clubhouse (weekends only in early and late season) offers a wide range of value for money meals and entertainment is arranged at B.H. weekends and Saturdays in school holidays. A small games room has TV (incl. Sky), video machines and pool table. Children's playground. Laundry room. Fishing 2 miles, bicycle hire 4 miles, and riding stables close. American motorhomes not accepted. Caravan storage. Reservation for peak weeks and B.Hs. is advisable. Bellamy silver.

Directions: From A46 Evesham take B4035 towards Chipping Campden. After Badsey and Bretforton follow signs for Honeybourne down unclassified road (Ryknild Street, Roman road). Park is through village on left by station. O.S.GR: SP112444.

Charges 2000:
-- Per unit incl. 2 adults £7.50 - £12.50; extra person (over 5) free - £1.75; awning free - £1.50; extra car free - £1.00; electricity £2.50; full services £2.50; dog free - £1.75.
-- One free night for every 7 booked.
-- VAT included.
-- Credit cards accepted.

Open:
1 March - 30 November.

Address:
Honeybourne,
nr. Evesham,
Worcestershire
WR11 5QG.

Tel:
(01386) 830744.
FAX: (01386) 833503.

Reservations:
Made with £5 per night deposit and essential for B.Hs. (when min. 3 days).

421 Lickhill Manor Caravan Park, Stourport-on-Severn

Well managed touring or holiday site in attractive parkland setting on outskirts of town.

This park is within easy walking distance (15 minutes) of the town centre via a footpath along the River Severn which lies a short distance below the site. There are opportunities for fishing and boating. The touring field has 90 marked, level, grassy pitches accessed via gravel roadways, all with electricity (10/16A). The 124 holiday homes, well screened from the touring area amongst tree lined avenues, are not visually intrusive, and there is a separate rally field. There is an extended children's playground and the site has recently created wildlife ponds and planted over 1,000 native trees and shrubs. A second sanitary building was added in '98 to serve the touring pitches. This heated building provides sparkling modern facilities including a comprehensively equipped suite for disabled guests that also double as a family washroom with facilities for babies. There are roomy showers with good seats and plenty of hooks, a good number of washbasins and WCs, plus chemical disposal and motorcaravan service points. This, together with the older unit at the other end of the park, now provides a good supply of all facilities. Gas is available on site. With its new sanitary block, roads, landscaping and friendly welcoming staff, this park promises to mature into one of the best in the area. Stourport is a lively bustling town with some splendid public parks, amusements and sports facilities. Riding 1 mile, bicycle hire 3 miles, Six golf courses within 5 miles. A small parade of shops and the nearest pub are 10 minutes walk. Kidderminster, the Forestry Commission Visitor Centre at Bewdley, the Severn Valley Railway and West Midland Safari Park are a short drive from the site. Bellamy silver.

Directions: From centre of Stourport take B4195 northwest towards Bewdley. After 1 mile turn left at crossroads (traffic lights), into Lickhill Road North where site is signed. O.S.GR: SO790730.

Charges 2000:
-- Per caravan or motorcaravan £6.00 - £9.25; small tent £6.00; large tent £8.25; awning £1.50; extra car, trailer or boat £1.00; electricity £2.00.
-- Weekly rates available.
-- VAT included.
-- Credit cards accepted.

Open:
All year.

Address:
Stourport-on-Severn,
Worcestershire
DY13 8RL.

Tel:
(01299) 871041.
FAX: (01299) 824998.
E-mail: enquiries@
lickhillmanor.co.uk.

Reservations:
Recommended for B.Hs. and peak season; contact park.

Worcestershire / Herefordshire

420 The Boyce Caravan Park, Stanford Bishop, nr. Worcester

Very peaceful site on rolling downland, with distant views of the Malvern Hills.

Within its 17 acres The Boyce has 20 touring pitches and 140 permanent caravan holiday homes. The relatively new landscaping and screening is maturing and electrical connections (10A) are available throughout. The modern sanitary unit, built to serve the touring section, can be heated and provides WCs, open, vanity-style washbasins, controllable hot showers with curtain and seat (10p for 4 mins), and a hairdressing area. A utility room houses dishwashing and laundry sinks, a washing machine, dryer, iron, and a freezer for campers' use. There is a chemical disposal point and gas is available. There is a fenced and gated playground for smaller children, plus plenty of open space for ball games (no cycling on the park). The adjacent disused railway line is now the dog walk (dogs accepted by arrangement, no dangerous breeds). Coarse fishing is available across a meadow, and the area is rich in wildlife. Nearby Shortwood Farm has Jacob sheep, cider making, sheep shearing and a farm trail, and at the Pig Pen you can handle the piglets (wellingtons recommended). The new reception building offers good tourist information including maps of local walks. The local pub is 500 yards and serves meals including breakfast. Horse riding 5 miles and several golf courses in the area. Bromyard with its shops and restaurants is 4 miles, and the cathedral cities of Hereford and Worcester are within easy driving distance.

Directions: From A44 (Worcester - Leominster), turn on B4220 1 mile east of Bromyard. After 1½ miles, turn opposite Herefordshire House inn (signed Linley Green), site is 500 m. and signed. O.S.GR: SO698527.

Charges 2000:
-- Per unit incl. 2 adults £7.50; extra person over 5 yrs £1.00; extra car £1.00; 1-man tent £4.00; awning/pup tent £1.50; electricity £1.50.
-- No tent pitches at B.H. weekends.
-- VAT included.
-- No credit cards.
Open:
1 March - 31 October.
Address:
Stanford Bishop,
Bringsty,
nr. Worcester
WR6 5UB.
Tel:
(01885) 483439
(evenings).
Reservations:
Made with deposit of one night's fee; contact park for details.

432 Broadmeadow Caravan and Camping Park, Ross-on-Wye

Modern, spacious site, convenient for town with open views and own fishing lake.

The approach to this site is unusual, but persevere and you will find one of the best laid out, immaculately maintained sites with the very highest quality facilities. A recently constructed level site, it offers 150 large pitches on open grass, and is especially good for tents. It has excellent illumination and two superb modern sanitary buildings with free hot water throughout. Each includes push-button showers with dividers and seats, washbasins, hairdryers, baby changing rooms, family bathrooms each with WC, basin and bath, and a comprehensive unit for disabled visitors with alarm and handrails. A dishwashing room with separate vegetable preparation sinks, laundry with sinks, washing machine, dryer, iron (tokens from reception) plus chemical disposal, are also provided at each building. A keypad entry system is used on all external doors. Each set of four pitches has a service post with water, drain, electricity points (16A) and site lighting, and is within view of the clock-tower on one of the sanitary buildings. There is a small fenced playground and a well fenced fishing lake (coarse fishing £5 per day). The town centre is within easy walking distance and the supermarket is 200 yards. Although the A40 relief road is at the eastern end of the site, the traffic noise should not be too intrusive (but tenters be aware). Bicycle hire in town, riding 8 miles, golf 3 miles. This is a good base for touring Herefordshire, the Wye Valley or the Forest of Dean.

Directions: From A40 relief road turn into Ross at roundabout, take first right into industrial estate, then right in ½ mile, before Safeway supermarket, where site is signed. O.S.GR: SO610240.

Charges 2000:
-- Per pitch £5.50 - £6.50; adult £2.25; child (6-14 yrs) £1.75; awning or pup tent £1.75; extra car £1.75; dog £1.00; electricity £2.25.
-- VAT included.
-- Credit cards accepted.
Open:
Easter/1 April - 31 Oct.
Address:
Broadmeadow,
Ross-on-Wye,
Herefordshire HR9 7BH.
Tel:
(01989) 768076.
FAX (01989) 566030.
Reservations:
Made with £10 deposit; contact park.

For lists of parks which offer facilities on site for FISHING, GOLF, HORSE RIDING, BICYCLE HIRE or BOAT LAUNCHING see pages 238 - 240

Perfectly Placed for the
City of London
and the countryside of Hertfordshire and Essex

There are plenty of camping and caravan sites to choose from in Lee Valley Regional Park. All sites have modern facilities, offer value for money and are located in pleasant surroundings with their own local leisure attractions.

Lee Valley Leisure Centre Campsite, Picketts Lock, Edmonton, North London
Only 34 mins from the West End. The site also boasts a large leisure centre, 18 hole golf course and 12 screen UCI cinema.
Tel: 020 8803 6900
Fax: 020 8884 4975

Lee Valley Campsite, Chingford, London
Situated on the edge of Epping Forest and close to the historic town of Waltham Abbey, this site is easily accessible from the M25 and just 42 minutes from the West End by public transport.
Tel: 020 8529 5689
Fax: 020 8559 4070

Lee Valley Caravan Park, Dobbs Weir, Hoddesdon, Herts
Enjoy the peace and tranquillity of this riverside site with good fishing, walking and boating nearby. Get to the West End by train and tube in under an hour.
Tel/Fax: 01992 462090

Lee Valley Cycle Circuit Campsite, Leyton, East London
Set in 40 acres of open parkland, this site is only 4 miles from the Tower of London.
Tel: 020 8534 6085
Fax: 020 8536 0959

For more information, call our Information Centre on 01992 702200 or find us on the web at:
www.leevalleypark.org.uk

Lee Valley Park

Highfield Farm Touring Park

A warm welcome awaits you at our popular award winning Park with its excellent facilities, set in peaceful farming countryside. It is close to the historic University City of Cambridge, The Imperial War Museum, Duxford and ideally suited for touring East Anglia.

Please write or phone for colour brochure
Comberton, Cambridge CB3 7DG Tel/Fax: 01223 262308

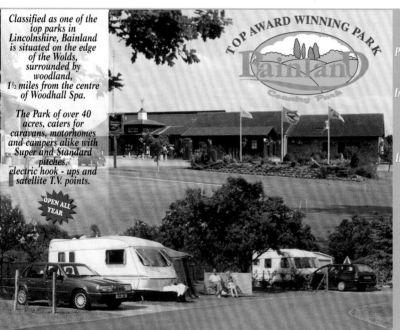

Classified as one of the top parks in Lincolnshire, Bainland is situated on the edge of the Wolds, surrounded by woodland, 1½ miles from the centre of Woodhall Spa.

The Park of over 40 acres, caters for caravans, motorhomes and campers alike with Super and Standard pitches, electric hook - ups and satellite T.V. points.

OPEN ALL YEAR

TOP AWARD WINNING PARK

Bainland Country Park

18 hole Par 3 Golf Course
Practice Putting Green
All weather Bowling Green
Indoor/Outdoor Tennis
Crazy Golf
Trampoline
Table Tennis
Indoor Swimming Pool
Childrens Adventure Playground

Sauna
Jacuzzi
Sunbeds

Childrens 'Poachers Den' soft playroom
Bar
Restaurant
Rallies Welcome

Horncastle Road, Woodhall Spa, Lincolnshire, LN10 6UX   Tel: Woodhall Spa (01526) 352903

430 Poston Mill Park, Peterchurch, Golden Valley

Pleasant, neat park in farmland, a mile from Peterchurch in heart of the Golden Valley.

Poston Mill Park offers 82 touring pitches set on level grass, with some very pleasant pitches near the River Dore, with mature trees and conifers surrounding the perimeter. All pitches have electricity, water and TV connections (leads to hire), and 35 have waste water and sewage outlets. There are also 83 caravan holiday homes (3 to rent). There is one central sanitary block with a smaller block near the holiday home area. They are of reasonably modern construction, tiled with controllable showers (free) and mainly semi-open washbasins. Also a unit for disabled people (toilet and basin only), baby room, chemical disposal and motorcaravan service point. A small, well equipped laundry houses a campers' fridge and a freezer for ice packs. Within the park's 33 acres activities include a pleasant, large children's play area on grass with pitch and putt, tennis court, petanque, croquet, bicycle hire, golf driving range, a football pitch and a games room with snooker and darts. An attractive walk along one side of the park, edging the river (fishing available), follows the line of the old Golden Valley railway and there is a footpath from the site over the fields. Next to the park is the 'The Mill' restaurant for lunches, evening meals and takeaway. The restaurant also has a TV room and sells bread and milk. Gas is available. Peterchurch village is 1 mile. Bicycle hire. Riding 3 miles. American motorhomes are welcome. Winter caravan storage. A member of the Best of British group.

Directions: Park is 1 mile SE of Peterchurch on the B4348. O.S.GR: SO356371.

Charges 2000:
-- Per unit incl. 2 adults £7.50 - £10.00; family tent incl. 2 persons £8.50 - £11.00, 1 man tent £4.75 - £6.75; extra person £1.00; child (3-10 yrs) 50p; dog 50p; electricity £2.00.
-- Min. at B.Hs. 5 nights.
-- Credit cards accepted.
Open:
All year.
Address:
Peterchurch, Golden Valley, Herefordshire HR2 0SF.
Tel:
(01981) 550225.
FAX: (01981) 550885.
E-mail: enquiries@ poston-mill.co.uk.
Reservations:
Made with £10 deposit, min. 5 nights for B.Hs.

431 Luck's All Caravan and Camping Park, Mordiford, Hereford

Spacious site beside the River Wye, with good countryside views, canoeing and fishing.

Set in around 9½ acres on the bank of the river Wye, Luck's All has 80 large, well spaced and level touring pitches, of which 41 have electricity (10/16A). A small, unfenced playground and a large grassy area for children's games are provided. The river is open to the site but lifebelts and safety messages are in evidence. Canoes are for hire (or bring your own) and fishing permits are obtainable from the local tackle shop. The site shop has basic supplies and gas, plus home-made cakes - a mini-market is within 1½ miles. The main sanitary facilities are housed in a new building which provides WCs, open washbasins, showers (20p) with curtains and seats, and a separate unit for disabled visitors with ramped entrance, WC, washbasin, shower and hand-dryer. Dishwashing sinks and chemical disposal. A smaller, older unit near the entrance provides extra facilities for peak periods, also a laundry room with sink, washing machine, dryer and ironing. Local places worthy of a visit are the Cider Museum and King Offa Distillery in Hereford, Belmont Abbey and Queenswood Country Park. Golf 5 miles, bicycle hire 9 miles. Caravan storage. A member of the Countryside Discovery group.

Directions: Between Mordiford and Fownhope, 5 miles southeast of Hereford on B4224, the park is well signed. O.S.GR: SO571355.

Charges 2000:
-- Per unit incl. 2 adults £7.00 - £7.50; 2-man tent £6.00 - £6.50; extra person over 5 yrs £1.00; dog 75p; awning £1.00 - £1.25; electricity £2.00.
-- Credit cards accepted.
-- VAT included.
Open:
Easter/1 April - 31 Oct.
Address:
Luck's All, Mordiford, Hereford HR1 4LP.
Tel:
(01432) 870213.
Reservations:
Essential for B.Hs. and peak season and made with £15 deposit.

442 Severn Gorge Park, Tweedale, nr. Telford

Mature park in woodland setting, ideal for visiting the Ironbridge Museums.

With 16 acres, this touring park has 110 pitches including a few seasonal tourers, 40 hardstanding pitches and 60 electricity hook ups (10/16A). A small development of park homes is under construction on one side of the park. The sanitary buildings can be heated and provide comprehensive facilities with free showers, facilities for disabled visitors and a baby room, plus a dishwashing conservatory leading to an ample laundry (8 am.- 9 pm). Chemical disposal and motorcaravan services. A small shop opens 8.30 am - 5.30 pm and gas is available. Amenities include a small play area, a large field nearby with a three hole pitch and putt and a small lake (unfenced) stocked for fishing. Kite flying is discouraged because of nearby overhead cables. There could be some road noise from the A442 which runs down one boundary. A pub is 10 minutes away serving meals until 9 pm. The main local attraction has to be the Ironbridge Museums. Hawkstone Park is very popular. Golf 1 mile, riding 3 miles. Caravan storage.

Directions: From M54 junction 4 follow signs (A442) onto the A442 signed Kidderminster. Take slip road signed Bridgnorth to next roundabout, turn right and pick up park signs. O.S.GR: SJ704052.

Charges 2000:
-- Per unit £3.50 - £4.00; adult £2.50 - £3.00; child (5-15 yrs) £1.00 - £1.25; awning £1.00; dog (max 2) £1.00; electricity £2.25 - £2.50.
-- VAT included.
-- Credit cards accepted.
Open:
All year.
Address:
Bridgnorth Road, Tweedale, Telford, Shropshire TF7 4JB.
Tel/Fax:
(01952) 684789.
Reservations:
Contact park for details.

129

Shropshire

438 Fernwood Caravan Park, Lyneal, nr. Ellesmere

Quiet, pretty park in semi-woodland near Welsh border, for caravans and motorhomes.

Fernwood is set in a lovely area known as the Shropshire 'Lake District' - the mere at Ellesmere is the largest of nine meres - and the picturesque Shropshire Union Canal is only a few minutes walk. The park itself, with its floral landscaping, the setting and the attention to detail, all of a very high standard, with planted and natural vegetation blending harmoniously, is a real oasis of calm and rural tranquillity. In addition to 165 caravan holiday homes, used normally only by their owners, the park takes 60 caravans, motorcaravans or trailer tents, but not other tents in several well cut, grassy enclosures (plus 25 seasonal long stay). Some are in light woodland, others in more open, but still relatively sheltered situations. All 60 pitches have electricity (10A). One area is set aside for units with adults only. Siting is carried out by the management and there is always generous spacing, even when the site is full. The refurbished sanitary block for tourers can be heated and has free hot water to washbasins (with good shelves) and pre-set hot showers, a unit for disabled people, but no dishwashing sinks. There are water points, chemical disposal and motorcaravan service points. A tiled laundry room is near the shop, and adjacent are ladies and mens WCs. Other facilities include the small shop, which doubles as reception (open from 1 April, sometimes limited hours). There is a coarse fishing lake, 40 acres of woodland for walking and a children's play area on grass. Public phone. Bellamy gold.

Directions: Park is just northeast of Lyneal village, signed southwest off the B5063 Ellesmere - Wem road, about 1½ miles from junction of the B5063 with the A495. O.S.GR: SJ453338.

Charges 2000:
-- Per unit incl. electricity £10.00 - £14.00; awning free - £1.60; extra car free - £1.00.
-- One night free for every 7 booked in advance.
-- VAT included.
-- Credit cards accepted.

Open:
1 March - 30 November.

Address:
Lyneal, nr. Ellesmere, Shropshire SY12 0QF.

Tel:
(01948) 710221.
FAX: (01948) 710324.
E-mail: fernwood@caravanpark37.fsnet.co.uk.

Reservations:
Necessary for peak season and B.Hs (min. 3 nights) with deposit of £5 per night.

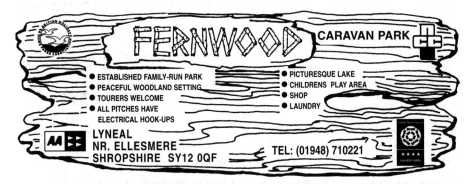

FERNWOOD CARAVAN PARK

- ESTABLISHED FAMILY-RUN PARK
- PEACEFUL WOODLAND SETTING
- TOURERS WELCOME
- ALL PITCHES HAVE ELECTRICAL HOOK-UPS
- PICTURESQUE LAKE
- CHILDRENS PLAY AREA
- SHOP
- LAUNDRY

LYNEAL
NR. ELLESMERE
SHROPSHIRE SY12 0QF

TEL: (01948) 710221

439 Westbrook Park, Little Hereford, nr. Ludlow

Older style, peaceful orchard park beside the River Teme.

Bordering the River Teme, this 45 pitch, all-touring park is of the older style, but does retain the simplicity and tranquillity lost on so many other developed parks. The pitches are well spaced and level, and there are several available with hardstanding. All have electricity connections (but only 6A) and TV aerial hook-ups. The timber-clad sanitary block houses roomy, curtained showers (20p for 5 mins) which are perhaps beginning to show their age – and certainly their vintage – but they are clean and they do work. There is a simple laundry room with washing machine, dryer and sinks (hot water 10p). We have been reporting a fine timber-clad reception as being due for two years now, but it is still in its flat-pack state in a barn, so who knows for 2001? Bicycles are not permitted on this park. There are lovely riverside walks and fishing is available (£3 per day). Simple play equipment is sited on grass at the entrance, but Gert and Daisy the Shetland ponies are perhaps the children's favourites. This is a simple, unpretentious park, situated near the lovely market towns of Tenbury Wells, Leominster and Ludlow. Caravan 'storage and use' available.

Directions: From A49 Ludlow - Leominster road turn east at Woofferton onto the A456 signed Tenbury Wells, Kidderminster. After 2 miles turn right just before the bridge over river and the Temeside Inn. Park is down the lane on the left. O.S.GR: SO547679.

Charges 2000:
-- Per unit incl. 2 adults £7.50 - £10.00; trailer or family tent £8.50 - £11.00; one man tent £4.75 - £6.75; extra person over 10 yrs £1.00, 3-10 yrs 50p; awning £1.50; dog 50p; electricity £1.75.
-- Min. B.H. stay 3 nights.

Open:
All year.

Address:
Little Hereford, Ludlow, Shropshire SY8 4AU.

Tel:
(01584) 711280.
FAX: (01584) 711460.

Reservations:
Recommended for B.Hs (min. 3 nights) and made with £10 deposit.

440 Stanmore Hall Touring Park, Bridgnorth

Good quality park overlooking lake in the Severn Valley.

Situated in the former grounds of Stanmore Hall, this site's huge lily pond, fine mature trees and beautifully manicured lawns give a mark of quality. Open views take precedence over maximising the number of units per square metre, with the result that all pitches are generously sized. In addition, caravans can be orientated in any direction the owner wishes, thus breaking the feeling of regimentation. There are 131 pitches, all with 16A electricity, 30 of which are hardstanding 'super pitches' with TV connections. A limited number of 'standard' hardstanding pitches are available, but the majority are on grass. Some pitches are reserved for adult only use (21 years). Access and internal roads are all tarmac surfaced; site lighting is adequate and reassuring. Reception is located within the shop which is licensed and well stocked (open all year) – there are even caravan accessories and repair items. The adjacent conservatory and patio overlook the lake, accommodating everything from humbler ducks to the resident peacocks who strut proudly around their domain. Access to the centrally heated sanitary block is by key. Washbasins in private cubicles, abundant hot water, hairdryers, and a room for disabled people (which includes equipment for baby care), demonstrate thoughtful design. Its laundry facilities comprise two sinks, a washing machine, tumble dryer and spin dryer. Chemical disposal and motorcaravan service points. Limited, bark based children's play area. Overall the facilities are excellent and the cleanliness outstanding. But there's something else too; this is a peaceful site with personality. Little wonder it needs advance booking and people keep returning to enjoy its atmosphere. Open all year round, there are even groups who spend Christmas and New Year at Stanmore Hall. The Severn Valley is full of interest – Bridgnorth nearby, the Clee Hills and Ironbridge Gorge Museum are just a few suggestions. Fishing at Bridgnorth (1½ miles), golf 2 miles. Dogs are welcome, but with a limit of two per unit. The site is a member of the Caravan Club's managed under contract scheme but non-members are also very welcome.

Directions: Site is 1½ miles from Bridgnorth on the A458 (signed Stourbridge). O.S.GR: SO742923.

Charges 2000:
-- Per pitch £3.80 - £4.20; adult £3.40 - £4.20; child £1.45 - £1.60; awning or pup tent £1.00; dog (max. 2) 75p; extra car or trailer £1.20; electricity £2.00 - £2.75; full services £2.50 - £3.00.
-- Credit cards accepted.
Open: All year.
Address: Stourbridge Road, Bridgnorth, Shropshire WV15 6DT.
Tel: (01746) 761761. FAX: (01746) 768069. E-mail: stanmore@morris-leisure.co.uk.
Reservations: Advisable and made with £10 deposit.

443 Oxon Hall Touring Park, Shrewsbury

Purpose-built park, brilliantly situated for a visit to Shrewsbury . . and more.

This park is under the same ownership as Stanmore Hall (see above) and has been developed from a green field site by an experienced park operator to a very high standard. When we first made contact a couple of years ago, the place felt a little bleak, but nature has done its bit and on our latest visit, a much greater feeling of maturity existed. The sanitary facilities here are first rate with washbasins in cubicles, ample showers, baby room, facilities for disabled visitors, dishwashing room and laundry, all situated at the entrance in a centrally heated building which also houses reception and the shop – even if they are a hike from some of the pitches. Of the 130 pitches, half are all weather, full service pitches (fresh and waste water facilities, TV hook-up), the others being either grass or with hardstanding. An area is set aside as an 'adults only' section. All pitches have 16A electricity hook-ups. Ample water points are scattered around the park and at each of these there are waste water and chemical disposal points, together with bins and fire extinguishers. A motorcaravan service point is provided and there are some extra long hardstandings for American motorhomes. Entry to the park is controlled by electronic barriers. Dogs are welcome (max. 2 per pitch). Virtually adjacent to the park is the Oxon 'park and ride' which makes a trip into Shrewsbury (some 2 miles) very simple. Golf, riding and fishing are available nearby, and the famous Ironbridge Gorge Museum and the mysteries of the Welsh Borders are all easy day trips from this excellent base. Bellamy silver.

Directions: From junction of A5 and A458, west of Shrewsbury, follow signs for Oxon 'park and ride'. Park signed just ½ mile from junction. O.S.GR: SJ455138.

Charges 2000:
-- Per unit £3.80 - £4.20; adult £3.40 - £4.20; child (5-15 yrs) £1.45 - £1.60; awning or pup tent £1.00; extra car or trailer £1.20; dog (max. 2) 75p; supplement for 'super' pitch £2.50 - £3.00.
-- Credit cards accepted.
Open: All year.
Address: Welshpool Road, Shrewsbury, Shropshire SY3 5FB.
Tel: (01743) 340868. FAX: (01743) 340869. E-mail: oxon@morris-leisure.co.uk.
Reservations: Made with £10 deposit.

441 Beaconsfield Farm Touring Caravan Park, nr. Shrewsbury

Purpose designed park just north of historic market town; adults only in peak season.

A neat stone entrance and a tarmac drive of half a mile through open fields lead to this park, with security barrier in operation. Neatly laid out in a rural situation, with a well stocked trout fishing lake and a small coarse pool forming the main feature, the ground has been levelled and grassed to provide 60 well spaced pitches, 25 'de-luxe' hardstanding pitches with 16A electricity connections, and with 10A hook-ups to other pitches. The park is well lit with a circular tarmac access road and two brick built refuse, water and chemical disposal areas. A large timber chalet building with tiled Canadian maple roof provides reception and heated sanitary facilities. An indoor heated pool, available throughout the year, has two daily open sessions (adult £2.50, child £1) and may be hired privately at other times (£3 and £1, min. £10 per hour). Adjacent to reception and the pool is the coffee shop, open during reception hours. Toilet facilities (£2 key deposit) are of excellent quality, as is everything featured on the park. They have curtained, roomy, pre-set showers, vanity style washbasins (H&C), mirrors, free hairdryers, washing up room, also with washing machine, dryer, free irons and boards. Motorcaravan service point. There is no children's play area, but a central grass area can be used for ball games and new for 2000 is a snooker room in a purpose built log building that will eventually incorporate a bistro. Also, for 2001, is a bowling rink - free use, but woods are available to hire for those without such essential caravanning kit. Only two dogs per unit are accepted. Last arrivals 7 pm. (8 pm. Fridays). Golf 3 miles. Limousins and pedigree Suffolk sheep graze in neighbouring fields and a 'park and ride' scheme operates nearby for those interested in Shrewsbury and its medieval past, bought to life by the Brother Cadfael novels. This is a top class park, maturing by the year. It is now an adults only touring park (25 yrs) from 5 July - 25 August. A member of the Best of British and the Countryside Discovery groups.

Charges 2001:
-- Per grass pitch incl. unit and 2 persons £8.50 - £10.50; de-luxe pitch £10.50 - £12.50; extra adult £3.00; child (3-14 yrs) £2.00; awning or child's tent £1.50; extra car or boat £1.00; dog (max. 2) 75p; electricity £2.00.
-- No credit cards.

Open:
All year.

Address:
Battlefield,
Shrewsbury,
Shropshire SY4 4AA.

Tel:
(01939) 210370 or 210399.

FAX: (01939) 210349.

E-mail:
mail@beaconsfield-farm.co.uk.

Reservations:
Recommended for B.Hs and July/Aug. and made with £20 deposit.

Directions: Site is north of Shrewsbury and off the A49 Whitchurch road just before the village of Hadnall. Turn opposite the New Inn at brown camping sign towards Astley and park entrance is 400 m. on right. O.S.GR: SJ523196.

451 Thorpe Hall Caravan and Camping Site, Rudston, Bridlington

Pleasant touring park, west of Bridlington.

This small park in the grounds of Thorpe Hall, just outside the village of Rudston and 4½ miles from the sea at Bridlington is enthusiastically managed by Jayne Chatterton. It is set on flat grass, largely enclosed by the old kitchen garden wall. The 90 pitches are numbered and well spaced with 78 electrical hook-ups (16A) and TV connections. A separate area takes tents and there are no caravan holiday homes. There is always a chance of finding space, though it is best to book for B.H.s and peak weeks. The solid, central toilet block can be heated and has free hot water in the washbasins, with shelf and mirror, and showers with turn-on tap. Ladies have three washbasins in private cabins and a bath. There are hair drying facilities, a well equipped unit for disabled visitors with a bath, a launderette, covered dishwashing sinks and chemical disposal. Small shop with gas, essentials and local produce with adjacent patio. Public phone. Games room with two pool tables, table football and table tennis, tourist information area and satellite TV room. Five acre games field and children's play area on grass and sand. Dog walk. Information sheets on a range of local walks are available and Thorpe Hall Gardens are open to park visitors between 1-4 pm. There is a footpath to the village with a shop, post office, garage, a pub serving bar meals and a new restaurant, plus a twice weekly bus service to Bridlington. The site's own coarse fishing lake is now open nearby. Bicycle hire, golf and boat launching at Bridlington (4½ miles), riding 2 miles. A member of the Countryside Discovery group. Bellamy gold.

Charges 2000:
-- Per unit incl. all persons £5.95 - £11.45; tent field £4.95 - £10.30; extra car £1.00; electricity (16A) £2.00.
-- Less 10% on booked stays of 7 days or over.
-- No credit cards.
-- VAT included.

Open:
1 March - 31 October.

Address:
Rudston,
Driffield,
East Yorkshire
YO25 4JE.

Tel:
(01262) 420393.
FAX: (01262) 420588.
E-mail: caravansite@
thorpehall.co.uk.

Reservations:
Made with advance payment (min. 4 nights at Spr. B.H).

Directions: Site is by the B1253 road, 4½ miles from Bridlington, on east side of Rudston. O.S.GR: TA105676.

Yorkshire Tourist Board

North, South, East and West Yorkshire

312 Tadcaster Road, York YO24 1GS

Tel: (01904) 707961 Fax: (01904) 701414

E-mail: info@ytb.org.uk

Internet: http://www.yorkshirevisitor.com

Yorkshire, vast and beautiful, the land of the White Rose was once a kingdom in its own right and its people are proud of its heritage; their welcome warm if their character is a little blunt.

Today more than 1,000 square miles of Yorkshire are protected as National Parks, Areas of Outstanding Natural Beauty and Heritage Coast and visitors are encouraged to park the car and 'go green'. Guided walks, way-marked paths and bridleways all explore deepest Yorkshire. The latest long distance challenge is the 240 km. Trans-Pennine Trail from Liverpool to Hull - part of a new Euro 'superpath'!

North Yorkshire offers the Yorkshire Dales and the North York Moors, with ruined abbeys and castles on both fringes of which magnificent Fountains Abbey, now a World Heritage site is the best known also Castle Howard of 'Brideshead Revisited' fame.

The gentle spa town of Harrogate with its antique shops, tea-rooms and colourful gardens is now an important conference centre.

Harewood House, six miles to the south is one of the finest mansions in England.

Ancient streets, buildings and museums make York one of England's most fascinating cities. Explore the Shambles or walk the medieval walls for much of their 2¼ mile length. The Jorvik Viking Centre is a popular experience involving travelling back in time through the history of York to a Viking Age, brought to life with the aid of sound effects and smells.

West and **South Yorkshire** are largely industrial, the charm of their cities - Leeds, Bradford and Sheffield depends mainly on their Victorian industrial legacy. Today Bradford's top attraction is the National Museum of Photography, Film and Television, free and very popular with children. Haworth is however on the literary trail as the home of the Bronte sisters.

One must not forget the coast line, the traditional resorts of Scarborough, Bridlington, Filey and timeless fishing harbours such as Whitby and Robin Hood's Bay.

However perhaps our knowledge of Yorkshire today is coloured by the TV series such as 'The Last of the Summer Wine', 'All Creatures Great and Small', 'Heartbeat' and 'Emmerdale'.

454 St Helens in the Park, Wykeham, nr. Scarborough

Spacious, high quality touring park with views.

St Helens is set within 30 acres of parkland and the 250 mainly level pitches have a spacious feel. The 52 pitches with hardstanding are used by seasonal lets in the summer months but are available for tourers in winter. Electrical hook-ups (10A) are available on 240 pitches, also in the late arrivals area. Set on a hillside (hence the views), the park's buildings are built in local stone and all is maintained to a high standard. The four heated toilet blocks are well equipped, two having been extended and refurbished recently. They have free hot water, washbasins, both vanity style and in cabins, large, pre-set showers and baby baths. A new unit for disabled visitors is of a very high standard. Everything is clean and well maintained and all four blocks have dishwashing sinks under cover. A good laundry room is next to the well stocked shop (Mar-Oct). Located centrally are a small games room with pool table and amusement machines and a takeaway cabin providing simple meals on certain evenings each week during busy periods. There is also a telephone chalet containing a large selection of tourist information. The adventure playground set on bark is part of a three acre area set aside for children with goal posts and a mountain bike track. Dogs are accepted with a large, well-cut field to run in. The Downe Arms, a short stroll away, is known for its good food and it occasionally runs family discos in high season. Nearby Wykeham Lakes offer fishing (trout and coarse), scuba diving, windsurfing and sailing (in your own boat). Scarborough is only 5 miles with its beaches and summer shows.

Directions: Park access road leads off the A170 (Pickering - Scarborough) road in Wykeham village 2 miles west of junction with B1262. O.S.GR: SE963835.

Charges 2000:
-- Per unit incl. 2 persons £7.40 - £9.40; extra person (over 3 yrs) £1.00; awning £1.80; porch awning £1.30; pup tent £6.00; dog 50p; electricity £2.10.
-- VAT included.
-- Credit cards accepted.

Open:
All year excl. 15 Jan. - 13 Feb. (reduced facilities Nov-Feb).

Address:
Wykeham, Scarborough, N. Yorks YO13 9QD.

Tel:
(01723) 862771.
FAX: as phone.
E-mail: caravans@ wykeham.co.uk.

Reservations:
Made with £10 deposit (min. 4 nights for Spr. and Aug. B.Hs).

Yorkshire

452 Flower of May Holiday Park, Lebberston, Scarborough

Large, family owned park with indoor pools.

Flower of May is a large park for both touring caravans and caravan holiday homes situated on the cliff tops, 4½ miles from Scarborough and 2½ miles from Filey. There is a cliff walk to the beach but it is only suitable for the reasonably active - there is an easier walk down from a car park one mile away. The entrance to the park is very colourful and the reception office is light and airy. Leisure facilities are grouped around reception. The indoor pool has areas for both adults and children, a water flume and jacuzzi. In the same building are two squash courts, 10 pin bowling, table tennis and amusement machines. The leisure centre is also open to the public (concessionary rates for campers) but during the high season it is only available to local regulars and the caravanners and campers on the park. There is also a pay and play golf course (£5 a round). The park is licensed for 300 touring units and 184 caravan holiday homes (45 to hire, the remainder privately owned). The touring pitches are pretty level, arranged in wide avenues mainly on grass and divided by shrubs. There are 210 with electricity (5A), including 50 'star pitches' with water and drainage also. The three toilet blocks have all been refurbished in a light and colourful style, fully tiled with washbasins in both cabins and vanity style. Roomy showers are pre-set with free hot water, plus baby rooms, facilities for disabled visitors and chemical disposal. A well stocked and licensed shop (closes end Sept) is near the leisure centre, as is the laundry room. Amenities include two modern bar lounges, one for families and one for adults only, with discos in season, a games room with TV, large adventure playground with safety base, and a café plus takeaway fish and chips. The Plough Inn near the park entrance offers a good bar meal. There is a dog exercise area, but numbers and breeds are limited (one per pitch) and not allowed at all at B.Hs and the six week summer holiday. Fishing, boat slipway or riding 2 miles, bicycle hire 4 miles. Flower of May also owns Riverside Meadows at Ripon.

Charges 2000:
-- Per unit incl. up to 4 persons £7.00 - £11.50; awning £2.00; extra person (over 3 yrs) £2.00; extra car (on car park only) £2.00; dog (see text) £1.00; electricity £2.00; `star' pitch £4.00 extra.
-- 10% discount on pitch fee for weekly bookings.
-- No credit cards.
-- VAT included.

Open:
Easter - 31 October.

Address:
Lebberston Cliff,
Scarborough,
N. Yorks YO11 3NU.

Tel:
(01723) 584311.

Reservations:
Made with £20 deposit per week and £1 booking fee (Sat.-Sat. only for Spr. B.H. and 13/7-31/8).

see colour advert opposite page 129

Directions: Park is signed from roundabout at junction of A165 and B1261 from where it is 600 yds. O.S.GR: TA088836.

477 Rosedale Caravan and Camping Park, Rosedale Abbey

Well situated park below Rosedale Moor, near Pickering.

In a beautiful location, on the edge of a popular village, here is a campsite that is highly suitable for walkers. The surrounding hillsides are a maze of public footpaths and these and nearby Cropton Forest can all be reached without using your car. The site itself has a wide entrance on the edge of the village and, due to it being within the National Park, all the buildings are in the local stone and in keeping with the area. Reception provides maps and a small selection of camping accessories, plus gas supplies. The entrance barrier is controlled by card (£5 deposit). The site is reasonably level, with 200 pitches, a few with hardstanding and with 28 electricity connections (10A). One field is for tents only, there are some caravan holiday homes (private) and seasonal touring pitches in their own areas, with the remainder for touring caravans and motorcaravans. The majority have superb views of the surrounding hills. Amenities include a games room with pool and video games and a large play area has space for ball games. The toilet blocks are due to be refurbished for the 2001 season, together with laundry and dishwashing sinks. Dogs are accepted with a good dog walk provided. The village has a general store with daily papers, a post office, bakery, pubs and a restaurant. There is a glass blower at the village blacksmiths. In summer the Dales bus runs through the village, connecting several of the popular villages. A nine hole golf course, set on a picturesque hillside is 500 yards away. The 13 mile Rosedale circuit follows the route of the old iron-ore railway, giving magnificent views and reminders of bygone industries. The Ryedale Folk Museum at Hutton-le-Hole is 3½ miles and the whole area has numerous other attractions.

Charges 2000:
-- Per unit £6.50 - £11.50, acc. to type and season; hiker's tent (1 person) £3.00 - £5.00; extra person (over 5 yrs) £1.00; awning £2.00; extra car £1.00; electricity £2.00.
-- No credit cards.

Open:
31 March - 31 October.

Address:
Rosedale Abbey,
Pickering,
North Yorkshire
YO18 8SA.

Tel:
(01751) 417272.

Reservations:
Contact site.

see colour advert opposite page 129

Directions: Rosedale is signed from the A170, 2 miles west of Pickering. Site is in village of Rosedale Abbey, 8 miles north of the A170. O.S.GR: SE725958.

473 Far Grange Park, Skipsea, nr. Driffield

Large family site with something for everyone.

Far Grange is a very well maintained holiday park which will especially appeal to families. A comprehensive leisure centre is located at the park entrance, well away from the touring pitches. The indoor pool, fitness suite, sauna and solarium (with charges) are excellent facilities with lifeguards who are happy to give assistance to swimmers with disabilities if needed. This area also includes bars with shows, cabaret acts and dancing (adults only). A family room provides games and shows for children and discos for teenagers. These rooms are tastefully decorated and furnished, making a pleasant, relaxing environment. There are also facilities for pool, snooker, darts and a TV room (children to be accompanied). Bar meals are served in the evenings and also Sunday lunches. Outside is an attractive patio area. The park grounds are extensive with plenty of room for team games, tennis, a fitness trail for young and old, an excellent adventure playground with a skateboard ramp, and a play area for younger children (both with rubber safety bases). Adjacent (but not owned by the park) is golf, pitch and putt and bowls. Across the road from the entrance, is the park's own country park with fishing and wildfowl lake, visitor centre and a dipping pond for youngsters. It is an idyllic place to get away for a walk and a picnic. In the central reception area is a well stocked supermarket (with gas), takeaway, amusement arcade and a well appointed laundry. The tiled toilet blocks are heated in low season and provide showers, some washbasins in cabins, baths and mother and baby rooms, also a bathroom for wheelchair users. These facilities are clean and well maintained. The 130 touring pitches all have electrical hook-up (10A) and include 66 `super' pitches (these available for long weekends all winter). The cliffs here are high and in summer a steel stairway is put in place to give access to the long beach. This is a large, popular site with many caravan holiday homes and seasonal tourers, but with lots of space and plenty to do whatever the weather. Bellamy gold.

Charges 2000:
-- Per unit incl. 2 persons £11.00 - £14.00, 3 persons £11.00 - £15.00, 4 persons £11.00 - £16.00; `super' pitch £16.00 - £19.00; extra person (3 yrs and over), dog, car or small tent all £1.00.
-- Min. charge for Easter £55.
-- Less 10% for booked stays over 7 days excl. March and Oct.
-- VAT included.
Open:
1 March - 31 October.
Address:
Skipsea, Driffield, East Yorkshire YO25 8SY.
Tel:
(01262) 468293 or 468248.
FAX: (01262) 468648.
Reservations:
Made with £20 per week deposit (min. 7 days B.Hs and high season).

Directions: From A165 (Bridlington - Beverley) take B1242 Skipsea road. Park is on seaward side of this road, 1½ miles south of Skipsea. O.S.GR: TA186530.

453 Northcliffe Holiday Park, High Hawsker, nr. Whitby

Very high quality, family park with splendid sea views.

Within the North Yorkshire Moors National Park, Northcliffe caters for 170 caravan holiday homes as well as tourers, although they are entirely separate. The park is modern, well planned and attractive, the very friendly owners keeping everything neat and tidy - the toilet facilities are especially good. Totally refurbished and extended in '99, the block is heated in early and late seasons and uses a coded number pad entry system. Fully tiled, there are free hot showers, some washbasins in cabins, good facilities for babies and for disabled visitors. There is also a dishwashing room, a well equipped laundry and chemical disposal. When we visited everything was spotless. A well stocked shop (with gas) incorporates an attractive tea-room with a good range of reasonably priced food to eat in or takeaway (8 am - 8 pm in high season, mornings and evenings in low season, from 1 April). Two play areas have good quality fittings with safety bases, and are both fenced. There is lots of grass for team games and an indoor room with pool table and amusement machines. The 30 touring pitches are a good size, all with electrical hook-up, and 16 of them fully serviced. These 16 have 16A electricity, the rest have 10A. Many trees and flowering bushes have been planted to provide wind breaks. The park is situated on the Heritage Coast and one can walk the Cleveland Way into Whitby or to Robin Hood's Bay. Available at reception are leaflets on walks and countryside notes (75p and produced by the park). Fishing 4 miles, riding 10 miles, golf 4 or 6 miles. Whitby and Scarborough with their sandy beaches are within easy reach as are the moors. York is about an hour away. Dogs are not accepted. A member of the Best of British group. Bellamy gold.

Charges 2000:
-- Per unit incl. awning and up to 6 persons in 1 family £6.00 - £11.00; pitch incl. 10A electricity £8.00 - £13.00; 'super' pitch with 16A electricity £9.00 - £15.00; backpacker (no car) £3.00 - £4.00 per person; extra person, pup tent or extra car £3.00 - £4.00.
-- Less 10% if 7 nights booked.
-- Credit cards accepted (surcharge).
-- VAT included.
Open:
14 March - 31 October.
Address:
High Hawsker, nr. Whitby, N. Yorks YO22 4LL.
Tel:
(01947) 880477.
FAX: (01947) 880972.
E-mail: enquiries@ northcliffe.com.
Reservations:
Made with deposit and fee, min. 2-6 nights acc. to pitch type and season; contact park for details.

Directions: Three miles south of Whitby on A171 (Scarborough) road turn left onto the B1447 signed High Hawsker and Robin Hood's Bay. Go through Hawsker village and continue on Robin Hood's Bay road. At top of hill turn left onto private road - go on ½ mile towards sea. O.S.GR: NZ936080.

458 Foxholme Touring Caravan and Camping Park, Helmsley

Well shaded touring park at Harome for caravans and a few tents.

Foxholme is an unusual park with only 60 pitches for caravans and a small field for a few tents. Nearly all the pitches are individual ones in clearings in the quite dense coniferous plantation. The trees give a lot of shade and quite a lot of privacy (manoeuvring may be difficult on some of the pitches). All pitches have electricity (6A, a few need long leads) and six places have hardstanding. Some picnic tables are provided. The toilet block is of good quality, built in local stone, with all washbasins in private cubicles and free hot showers. Also part of this building is a laundry room with washing machine and sinks and a washing up room (H&C). Two further small blocks provide WCs only in other parts of the park. There are two chemical disposal points and a motorcaravan service point. The site is managed by a warden and his wife with reception usually open 9 am. - 9 pm. with an hour for lunch. Very basic provisions are kept. Public phone. The park is set in quiet countryside and would be a good base for touring, being within striking distance of the moors, the coast and York. There are no on site activities but the indoor pool at the Pheasant Hotel in Harome may be used by campers (£3 per session). The nearest shops are at Helmsley and Kirkbymoorside, both about 4 miles away, where there is also bicycle hire. Riding and golf also 4 miles. Caravan storage available. There is lighting, but a torch would be useful.

Charges 2001:
-- Per unit £7.00 - £7.50; awning £1.50; extra car 60p; electricity £2.00.
-- No credit cards.
-- VAT included.
Open:
Easter - 31 October.
Address:
Harome,
Helmsley,
North Yorkshire
YO62 5JG.
Tel:
(01439) 770416, 771241 or 771696.
FAX: (01439) 771744.
Reservations:
Made for any dates with £10 deposit.

Directions: Turn south off the A170 between adjoining villages of Beadlam (to west) and Nawton (to east) at sign to Ryedale School, then 1 mile to park on left (passing another park on right). From east ignore first camp sign at turning before Nawton. From west turn right ¼ mile east of Helmsley, signed Harome, turn left at church, go through village and follow camp signs. O.S.GR: SE661831.

FOXHOLME TOURING CARAVAN PARK

HAROME, HELMSLEY, NORTH YORKSHIRE YO62 5JG
Telephone: (01439) 771241, 770416 or 771696   Fax: (01439) 771744

AA 3 PENNANT - CARAVAN CLUB APPROVED - CAMPING CLUB APPROVED

A quiet, rural site for touring vans, motor caravans and some tents. All pitches in well sheltered clearings in the 6 acres of 39 year old woodland. All weather roads; Some hardstandings; Luxury toilet block graded excellent by the A.A. Washbasins in cubicles; H&C showers; Laundry room; Small shop; Gas exchange; Mains electric hook-ups available.

BEAUTIFUL COUNTRYSIDE, CLOSE TO THE NORTH YORK MOORS NATIONAL PARK
Please send stamp for brochure to G.C. Binks

---

460 Vale of Pickering Caravan Park, Allerston, nr. Pickering

Well designed, neat and tidy, family owned park.

Vale of Pickering is a level park edged by grassy banks and, although over the 12 or so years that the site has been developing these have been partly hidden by foliage, trees and attractive flower beds, they do give shelter from the wind. The owners, who are local farmers, have put a lot of thought into planning the site. There are 130 pitches, 75 of which are for touring units, all with electrical connections (10A). The refurbished, tiled toilet block is well maintained, providing washbasins (some in cabins), coin-operated (20p) showers with curtains, hooks, shelves and mirrors, and also a bath. A separate toilet and washbasin are provided for visitors with disabilities. Other facilities include chemical disposal facilities, motorcaravan service point, a launderette, dishwashing sinks (2p for hot water) and a microwave oven. A well stocked, licensed shop also stocks a few caravan accessories and gas (open according to demand in low season). Tourist information is provided in a separate wooden chalet. A local pub is at Yedingham, 1½ miles. Fishing 1 mile, bicycle hire and riding 3 miles, golf 5 miles. There is a good play area with safety bases and a playing field for football, etc. Dogs are accepted with a good dog walk provided. Bellamy silver.

Charges 2000:
-- Per unit incl. 2 adults and 2 children (under 12 yrs) £6.50 - £9.25; extra person £1.00; awning £1.50; electricity £2.00; large tent plus £1.50; hardstanding 50p; 2 dogs free, extra dog £1.00.
-- No credit cards.
-- VAT included.
Open:
14 March - 31 October.
Address:
Carr House Farm,
Allerston, N. Yorks,
YO18 7PQ.
Tel:
(01723) 859280.
FAX: (01723) 850060.
Reservations:
Made with £10 deposit (min. 3 nights at B.Hs with £20 deposit).

Directions: Park is 1 mile off the main A170 (Scarborough - Helmsley) road at the village of Allerston. O.S.GR: SE879808.

455 Cayton Village Caravan Park, Cayton, nr. Scarborough

Quiet, spacious touring park close to the attractions of Scarborough.

Cayton Village Caravan Park can only be described as a gem. Just three miles from the hustle and bustle of Scarborough, it is a peaceful, attractive haven. Originally just a flat field with caravans around the perimeter, four years of hard work, a lot of time and even more expense has produced a park which is very pleasing to the eye and of which the owner, Carol, can be justly proud. The entrance is a mass of flowers and the late arrivals area has electrical hook-ups, very handy because the gates are locked at night and anyone leaving early is also expected to use it so as not to disturb others. Reception and the shop are side by side, both open 8.30 am. to 8 pm. Reception has quantities of tourist information, and the shop stocks a very comprehensive range including gas and caravan spares. The three toilet blocks (with key code locks) are heated, with very high quality tiling and fittings. Hot water is free, there are hand dryers and hair dryers, and washbasins are in vanity units. Some showers are pre-set, others controllable and there are also two family shower rooms, a family bathroom, baby changing facilities and chemical disposal. The 200 pitches, 160 are for touring units, are numbered and everyone is taken to their pitch. There are 170 with electricity and 18 'super' pitches. An adventure playground with safeyy surface has been added. Dogs are accepted on leads and a superb dog walk is provided (an enormous well mown field, floodlit at night). A short walk across a field takes you to Cayton Village which has a popular pub providing excellent meals, a shop/post office and a church. A regular bus service passes the gate to Scarborough or Filey. The North York Moors are a short distance away, as is the Forestry Commission's Dalby Forest Drive with its scenic drive, mountain bike trails and way-marked walks. The steam railway at Pickering is a big attraction. Fishing and bicycle hire ½ mile, riding 4 miles, golf 3 miles. Bellamy silver.

Charges 2000:
-- Per unit incl. 4 persons £6.00 - £9.50; extra adult £1.50; child £1.00; awning £2.00; dog £1.00; electricity £2.00.
-- Low season 7 nights for price of 6.
-- Credit cards accepted.
-- VAT included.
Open:
Easter - 1 October.
Address:
D23 Mill Lane, Cayton Bay, Scarborough, North Yorkshire YO11 3NN.
Tel:
(01723) 583171 (winter (01904) 624630).
Reservations:
Are advised and made for min. 3 nights (4 at B.Hs) with £20 deposit.

Directions: From A64 Malton - Scarborough road turn right at roundabout (with MacDonalds and pub) signed B1261 Filey. Follow signs for Cayton. In Cayton Village take 2nd left after Blacksmiths Arms down Mill Lane (at brown caravan site sign); park is 200 yds. From roundabout to park 2¼ miles. From A165 turn inland at Cayton Bay traffic lights to park in ½ mile on right. O.S.GR: TA057837.

474 Jasmine Park, Snainton, nr. Scarborough

Quiet, well manicured park in the Vale of Pickering.

This is an area of North Yorkshire that is very popular so although we have other parks nearby, we feel there is room for another. Jasmine is a very attractive, well manicured park with owners who go to much trouble to produce masses of plants to give a very colourful entrance. Set in the Vale of Pickering, the park is level, well drained and protected by a coniferous hedge. The 106 pitches (54 for touring units) are on grass, with electricity connections (10A) for all caravans and some tents. The sanitary block is kept very clean and provides adjustable, free hot showers and a large room for families or disabled visitors containing a bath, shower, WC and washbasin (access by key). A laundry room has dishwashing sinks, washing machine, dryer and iron (hot water metered). Chemical disposal and motorcaravan point. There is no play equipment for children, although a field is provided for football, etc. Dogs are welcome but there is no dog walk. Masses of tourist information is provided in a log cabin and the owners are only too happy to advise. A licensed shop sells essentials and gas. The market town of Pickering and the seaside town of Scarborough are both 8 miles. Many local attractions are within easy reach, including Castle Howard, Dalby Forest, Sledmere House, Nunington Hall, Goathland (the setting for ITV's 'Heartbeat') and the North York Moors Railway. Closer to the park are facilities for riding (2 miles), fishing or golf (6 miles), bowls, also quiet lanes for cycling. There are 11 privately owned log cabins on the park, plus some seasonal tourers and a caravan holiday home for hire. This is a quiet, peaceful park for a restful holiday. A member of the Countryside Discovery group. Bellamy gold.

Charges 2000:
-- Per unit incl. 2 persons £6.50 - £10.00; extra adult £1.00; child (6-13 yrs) 75p; awning or tent over 150 sq.ft. £1.50; extra car £1.00; electricity £2.00.
-- Min. stay at Easter 4 nights, other B.Hs 3 nights.
Open:
1 March - 31 December.
Address:
Cross Lane, Snainton, Scarborough, N. Yorks YO13 9BE.
Tel:
(01723) 859240, FAX: as phone.
E-mail: info@ jasminepark.co.uk.
Reservations:
Made with £10 deposit and S.A.E.

Directions: Snainton is on the A170 Pickering - Scarborough road and the park is signed at eastern end of the village. Follow Brakers Lane to park on left after 1 mile. O.S.GR: SE928813.

Yorkshire

456 Golden Square Caravan and Camping Park, Oswaldkirk

Popular, high quality, family owned touring park, near Helmsley.

Mr and Mrs Armstrong are local farmers who have worked hard to turn an old quarry into a very attractive caravan park with a number of levelled bays that have superb views over the Vale of Pickering. The 130 pitches are not separated but they do have markers set into the ground and mainly back onto grass banks. In very dry weather the ground can be hard, steel pegs would be needed (even in wet weather the park is well drained). All pitches have electrical connections (10A), 24 have drainage and 6 are 'deluxe' pitches (with waste water, sewage, electricity, water and TV aerial connection). The two heated toilet blocks are of excellent quality, with washbasins in vanity units (some private cabins) with free hot water. Showers are pre-set and metered (token) and the heated bathroom (token) also houses baby changing facilities. Both ladies' and men's blocks have full facilities for disabled visitors. Dishwashing sinks are under cover and the laundry provides washing machines, dryers, a spin dryer and iron and board. All these amenities are made attractive by the care Mrs Armstrong takes in providing plants and flower arrangements. Chemical disposal and motorcaravan service point. The tourist information room also houses a microwave and an extra iron and board. The licensed shop is very well stocked, selling home-made fresh bread and cakes, dairy produce, fresh vegetables and groceries, newspapers, gas and gifts. Two excellent play areas allow the tiny tots to be kept separate from older children. Games field and a barn with table tennis and pool table. Bicycle hire on site. Visitors may have membership of the Ampleforth College sports centre, with its indoor pool, tennis and gym, etc. Riding 2 miles, golf 3 miles, fishing 5 miles. The area abounds with footpaths and three well known long distance footpaths are near. Dog owners are well catered for with two or three enormous fields for exercising alongside the park. Nearby Helmsley and Ampleforth have shops and pubs with food. All year caravan storage and seasonal pitches. Bellamy gold.

Charges 2000:
-- Per unit incl. 2 persons and all children up to 10 yrs £6.50 - £9.50; extra person (10 yrs or over) £1.00; full awning £1.40; porch awning £1.00; extra car £1.00; electricity £2.00; hikers/bikers £3.00 - £3.50 per person; `deluxe' pitch £15.00 - £20.00, all incl.
-- No credit cards.
-- VAT included.

Open:
1 March - 31 October.

Address:
Oswaldkirk,
York YO62 5YQ.

Tel:
(01439) 788269.
FAX: (01439) 788236.
E-mail: barbara@golden-squarecaravanpark.com.

Reservations:
Essential for B.Hs and made with £10 deposit (£20 for B.Hs).

Directions: Park is on the Helmsley - Ampleforth road on the 'caravan route' which avoids the banned Sutton Bank on the A170 Thirsk - Helmsley road. Turn off B1257 to west at camp sign by Golden Square Farm, 1 mile south of junction with A170. O.S.GR: SE605797.

464 Goose Wood Caravan Park, Sutton-on-the-Forest, York

Family owned park in natural woodland setting 6 miles from York, for caravans and motorcaravans only.

Goose Wood provides a quiet, relaxed atmosphere from which to explore York itself or the surrounding Yorkshire Dales, Wolds or Moors. Under new ownership, the park has a well kept air and rural atmosphere, with 75 well spaced and marked pitches on level grass, all with electricity (16A) and 75 with paved hardstanding and patio pitch. No tents are accepted. The excellent toilet block, modern and well maintained, provides good facilities including free showers (four minute push-button which also operates the light and is located outside cubicle), a bathroom (£1) and hairdryers. A separate unit provides four extra toilets and washbasins, and coin-operated washing up sinks. A motorcaravan service point, chemical disposal, laundry room, small shop (with gas supplies) and a public phone complete the practical facilities supporting the needs of the discerning visitor. For children, there is a 'super plus' adventure playground in the trees at one side of the park and, for adults, a small coarse fishing lake (unfenced) and attractive, natural woodland for walking, plus a large scale chess set. Dogs are welcome on a lead (max. two per pitch), to be exercised in nearby woodland. The park is popular with families in high season when it can be busy at weekends. A 'park and ride' scheme for York operates from nearby all year, six days a week or there is a local bus every two hours, six days a week. The park is 1¼ miles from Sutton village and only 7 miles from 'Water World' a new water leisure centre with pool, slides, wave machines, etc. Riding or golf 1 mile. A member of the Best of British group.

Charges 2000:
-- Per unit incl. 1 or 2 persons and car £8.50 - £10.50; extra person £1.00; awning (no groundsheet), extra pup tent (1 only) or extra car £1.00; electricity (16A) £2.50; hardstanding free.
-- Credit cards accepted.
-- VAT included.

Open:
1 March - 31 October.

Address:
Sutton-on-the-Forest,
York YO61 1ET,

Tel:
(01347) 810829.
FAX: (01347) 811498.

Reservations:
Made with £20 deposit (min. 3 nights at B.Hs).

Directions: Park is 6 miles north of York; from the A1237 York outer ring-road take the B1363 for Sutton-on-the-Forest and Stillington, taking the first right after the Haxby and Wigginton junction and follow park signs. O.S.GR: SE595636.

Alan Rogers' Discount

Less £1 p/night

138

Regional `Loo of the Year' winner
7 times between 1988-1999
North Yorks Moors National Park

CARAVAN &

Helmsley 2 miles, Ampleforth 1 mile. Secluded site surrounded by open countryside and woodland with magnificent views. Luxury heated toilet block and bathroom. Electric hook-ups. Shop. Launderette. Covered washing up sinks. Indoor and

OSWALDKIRK YORK
Tel: 01439 788269
Fax: 01439 788236
barbara@goldensquarecaravanpark.com
www.goldensquarecaravanpark.com

outdoor play areas. Indoor sports centre nearby. Dogs welcome with walks available. **Deluxe all service pitches.** Storage compound. Seasonal pitches.

462 Rawcliffe Manor Caravan Park, Rawcliffe, York

Very good quality, neat touring park close to the city of York.

Don't be put off by the road down to Rawcliffe Manor - admittedly it is not a very nice ride, past an industrial estate and new houses, but you will be rewarded. The park itself comes as a very pleasant surprise. The 120 touring pitches are on flat, very well manicured grass with some tarmac and concrete hardstandings. Originally in the middle of the countryside, the park is now surrounded by houses and a shopping centre. However, the hedges have grown so there is no feeling of being overshadowed. Over the years much money has gone into updating and redesigning the facilities. There are hedged bays, flower beds and all the pitches are fully serviced, giving 10A electricity, satellite TV, water and drainage connections. American motorhomes can be catered for, mainly in the quieter periods (contact park for details). Being a city site, Rawcliffe naturally gets very busy. There are two modern toilet blocks (opened by security codes and heated in winter). Tastefully tiled, they have free hot water in fully controllable showers and washbasins (some in cabins, others vanity style), baby baths, hair dryers and excellent facilities for disabled visitors. Both blocks have laundry rooms with washing machines, dryers, spin dryers and irons. Chemical disposal and motorcaravan service point. Gas is available. The clubhouse at the entrance has a large bar and lounge, with bar meals, takeaway service and a separate restaurant. Open all year, this can be used by the general public. Entertainment is organised frequently in the bar in high season and a games room for both adults and children with pool tables, etc. opens out onto a well equipped children's play area (bark safety base) where barbecues are held in high season. Foreign visitors make full use of a boules pitch. This is not really a suitable site for dogs being surrounded by houses as it is, but they are accepted and there is a small dog walk. A very short walk takes you to an 'out of town' shopping centre, with a 12 screen cinema and 10 pin bowling, also a park and ride bus into York. Also near is the local park with tennis courts, and a cycle route is adjacent. Golf 1 mile, riding 3 miles.

Directions: Park is ½ mile off A19 York - Thirsk road at A1237 junction (York side) with the new northern bypass. O.S.GR: SE583552.

Charges 2000:
-- Per unit incl. 2 persons £9.00 - £11.50; small camper van less £1.00; small tent (no car) incl. 2 persons £6.00 - £7.00, 1 person £4.00 - £5.00; extra adult £2.00; child (5-15 yrs) £1.50; awning (grass friendly) £1.20; extra car £2.00; electricity £2.00 (plus 80p Dec-Feb); satellite TV £1.00 - £1.20; m/cycle £1.50; dog £1.00.
-- Less 10% in low season for senior citizens.
-- VAT included.
-- Credit cards accepted.
Open:
All year.
Address:
Manor Lane,
Shipton Road,
York YO30 5TZ.
Tel:
(01904) 624422.
FAX: (01904) 640845.
Reservations:
Made with deposit (£10 p/night for up to two nights, £25 for three nights or more) plus £1 fee; min. 3 nights at B.Hs.

Yorkshire

463 Ripley Caravan Park, Ripley

Spacious, family run touring park with heated indoor pool.

Peter and Valerie House are the resident owners of Ripley Park, an 18 acre grass park accommodating 130 units. On fairly level grass, undulating in parts, with 130 electrical connections (10A) and 10 hardstandings, some pitches are marked, others carefully spaced (allowing the grass to recover) and all connected by a circular gravel road. Recent developments include electric hook-ups, water points and refuse areas for tents and 2,000 trees have been planted. The park has a fairly open field like aspect, with growing trees and a small pond (lake) with ducks providing an attractive feature. The central, attractively designed toilet block provides push-button hot showers, washbasins in curtained cubicles, baby bath and a separate unit with a shower for disabled people. It can be heated and has been extended to provide extra, smart facilities for both male and female. Small laundry, washing up sinks under cover, chemical disposal and motorcaravan service point. The leisure block beside the entrance with the reception and shop (with gas), offers a games room with colour TV, nursery playroom and a heated indoor pool (50p per person) and sauna. Adventure play equipment and football area. Dog walk (max. two dogs per unit unless by prior arrangement). Winter caravan storage. The park is at the gateway to the Yorkshire Dales National Park and almost midway between the spa town of Harrogate and historic Knaresborough. The village of Ripley, dominated by its castle, is within walking distance. Fishing, riding or golf 3 miles. Bus service 150 yds. Bellamy silver.

Directions: Four miles north of Harrogate, site is 150 yds. down Knaresborough B6165 road from its roundabout junction with the A61. O.S.GR: SE291601.

Charges 2000:
-- Per unit incl. 2 adults £6.95 - £8.50; extra adult £2.00; child (5-18 yrs) £1.00; small tent incl. 2 persons, no vehicle £5.00; awning £1.50; porch awning, child's pup tent or extra car £1.00; electricity £1.95; water and drainage £2.00.
-- Max. per family unit £11.50.
-- VAT included.

Open:
Easter - 31 October.

Address:
Ripley,
Harrogate,
Yorks HG3 3AU.

Tel:
(01423) 770050.
FAX: as phone.

Reservations:
Made with £10 deposit, min. 3 nights at B.Hs.

Ripley Caravan Park
where the country and enjoyment comes naturally...

This luxury touring caravan park in the beautiful North Yorkshire countryside is within easy reach of Ripley Castle and village and only ten minutes north of Harrogate. First class facilities include indoor heated swimming pool, sauna, games room, nursery playroom, children's playground and play area. There is a shop, laundry, telephone, electric hook-up points and amenities for the disabled.

Special offers on minimum seven nights stay in low season.

For further information: -
Peter & Valerie House, Ripley Caravan Park
Ripley, Harrogate, HG3 3AU
Tel: (01423) 770050   *Dogs permitted*

  RAC
SILVER

465 Fangfoss Old Station Caravan Park, Fangfoss, nr. York

Small, rural, family run park at the foot of the Yorkshire Wolds.

The Station House and platform give this site character, its rural situation amongst rolling farmland gives it peace and quietness and its owners, a friendly welcome and clean and comfortable facilities. The grassed over track and sidings provide hardstanding and, with the adjacent fairly level grass field, give a total of 75 marked pitches, all with 10A electricity and 18 with hardstanding. A modern, centrally situated toilet block provides free adjustable hot showers, vanity style washbasins (two in cubicles for ladies). A separate wooden utility block 'The Wendy House' provides covered washing up sinks and a laundry sink with free hot water and a food preparation bar (useful for tenters). There is no washing machine but a laundry service is offered. Chemical disposal. Reception carries food essentials with an off-licence facility, gas and tourist information. Some play equipment on grass, public telephone, central refuse area and six water points. York is 10 miles (with 'park and ride'), Hull 28 miles and the Yorkshire Wolds 5 miles. There are nearby market towns and a variety of pubs and restaurants within a 6 mile radius. Fangfoss is 1 mile, Pocklington 4 miles, with sports facilities, etc. Fishing, bicycle hire, riding and golf within 4 miles. This area will encourage walkers and cyclists. Winter caravan storage.

Directions: On A166 York - Bridlington road, park is clearly signed at Stamford Bridge, on right just after crossing the river. Using A1079 York - Hull road, follow signs at Wilberfoss for 1½ miles (in a northerly direction). O.S.GR: SE748527.

Charges 2000:
-- Per unit incl. up to 4 persons £7.70 - £12.50, acc. to season and unit; 2-man tent £6.00; awning £1.00 - £3.00; extra person £1.00; extra car £1.50; electricity £2.00.
-- Credit cards accepted.

Open:
1 March - 31 October.

Address:
Fangfoss,
York YO41 5QB.

Tel:
(01759) 380491.
E-mail: fangfoss
@pi2000.co.uk.

Reservations:
Made with £20 deposit.

140

471 Rudding Holiday Park, Follifoot, Harrogate

Touring park set in quiet, mature parkland, with swimming pool and golf course.

The extensive part wooded, part open grounds of Rudding Park are very attractive, peaceful and well laid out. One camping area is sloping but terraces provide level pitches and further pitches are in the very sheltered old walled garden. All 141 pitches have electricity (10-16A) and 17 'super pitches' are fully serviced with satellite TV connections. Some pitches are let on a seasonal basis and a separate area contains 52 owner occupied caravan holiday homes and pine chalets. The two tiled toilet blocks are of a good standard, centrally heated and well maintained. They may be under pressure when the park is full when cleaning may be variable. All hot water is free, there are some washbasins in cabins, pre-set showers (button by door), soap and hand dryers, a baby room and bathroom and ladies have free hairdryers. A laundry room at each block has washing machines, dryers, sinks, irons and boards and disabled people have well appointed facilities. Chemical disposal and motorcaravan service point. A heated outdoor swimming pool with sunbathing areas (Spr. B.H. - early Sept) is supervised at all times (extra charge). The well stocked, self-service shop is open all season (sometimes limited hours). Gas supplies. On the outer edge of the park is an 18 hole golf course and driving range, together with the 'Inn in the Park', a bar and restaurant open twice daily during B.Hs and school holidays, otherwise only weekends. Adventure playground on bark chippings, football pitch, games room and minigolf. Bicycle hire on site. Caravan storage. Buses pass the gate hourly to Harrogate and Knaresborough. Fishing 2 miles, riding 1 mile. York is less than an hour. An attractive park with something for all the family. Bellamy silver.

Directions: Park is 3 miles south of Harrogate clearly signed between the A658 and A661 roads. O.S.GR: SE333528.

Charges 2000:
-- Per pitch £9.50 - £13.00; awning £1.00 - £2.00; electricity £2.50; `supersite' incl. awning and electricity £16.50 - £21.50; 2-man tent £7.00 - £8.50; extra car £1.00; dog (on lead) free.
-- Special offers - contact park.
-- VAT included.
-- Credit cards accepted
Open:
17 March - 5 November.
Address:
Follifoot, Harrogate, North Yorkshire HG3 1JH.
Tel:
(01423) 870439.
FAX: (01423) 870859.
E-mail: hpreception @rudding-park.co.uk.
Reservations:
Made with full advance payment (essential for B.H. w/ends).

TOURING CARAVANS and Family Camping

Award winning holiday park - your gateway to the Yorkshire Dales

RUDDING
holiday PARK

● Heated swimming pool & children's paddling pool
● Licensed bar serving meals ● Free showers
● Children's playground ● Games room and bicycle hire ● Laundrette ● Park lighting
● Electrical hook-up points ● 18 hole pay & play golf course plus floodlit driving range

SUPERSITES: These individual pitches have a hard standing for touring caravans, 16 amp electricity, water, direct drainage, TV and satellite hook-up and a picnic table. *Please send for free illustrated brochure:*

Rudding Holiday Park, Follifoot, Harrogate HG3 1JH. Tel: 01423 870439 Fax: 01423 870859

469 Constable Burton Hall Caravan Park, nr. Leyburn

Tranquil park in beautiful Wensleydale for caravans and motorcaravans only.

This is a park where the emphasis is on peace and quiet, the wardens working to provide a relaxing environment. Being in the grounds of the Hall, it has a spacious, park-like feel to it. On part level, part sloping, well trimmed grass, the 120 pitches (40 for touring units) are of a good size and all have electrical connections (10A). The two sanitary blocks, built of local stone and blending in with the surroundings, have been refurbished, are well tiled, kept immaculately clean, and can be heated. Washbasins are in vanity style and the showers are controllable and free. The former deer barn has been adapted for use as a laundry room, tourist information room and extra washrooms with basins for both men and women. The park is ideally placed for visiting the Northern Dales. The gardens of the Hall are open to the public, with a collection of maples and terraced gardens developed by Mrs Vida Burton. There is no shop on site but nearby Leyburn will provide all your needs. Opposite the park entrance is the Wyvill Arms for bar meals. Public telephone. Gas supplies. Chemical disposal. Ball games are not permitted on site. Fishing, riding or golf within 4 miles. Gates closed 10 pm - 8 am.

Directions: Park is by the A684 between Bedale and Leyburn, ½ mile from the village of Constable Burton on the Leyburn side. O.S.GR: SE152907.

Charges 2000:
-- Per unit incl. 2 persons £7.50 - £10.00; extra adult £2.00; child 75p; awning £1.80; extra car 50p; electricity £2.00.
-- No credit cards.
-- VAT included.
Open:
Late March - 31 October.
Address:
Constable Burton Hall, nr. Leyburn, N. Yorks DL8 5LJ.
Tel:
(01677) 450428.
FAX: (01677) 450622.
Reservations:
Made with deposit (£20 for B.Hs. £5 other times).

Yorkshire

476 Riverside Meadows Country Caravan Park, Ripon

Busy park only a short walk from Ripon.

Riverside Meadows has a new name and new owners who have lots of experience in the caravan park world. All the facilities are being upgraded and brought up to their demanding standards. This is a rural park, although the approach to it belies that fact. The short approach from the main road passes a row of houses and a factory, but once they are passed, the park opens up before you and you are once again back in the countryside. There are plenty of caravan holiday homes but they are, on the whole, quite separate from the touring units. The pitches, practically all with electrical hook-ups, are mainly on gently sloping grass with just a few hardstandings. A meadow separates the park from the River Ure, a favourite place for strolling and fishing (licences available) The tiled toilet block is new, with large, pre-set hot showers and washbasins set in vanity units. A baby room, dishwashing room, a fully fitted shower room for disabled visitors and a chemical disposal point are provided. There are laundry facilities. A new shop, reception, a bar with snacks and a games room are planned. A good dog walk is provided (max. 2 dogs per unit) which can be extended to a two mile round walk. There is a golf course within a mile and the delightful market town (city) of Ripon with its ancient cathedral is only 15 minutes walk. Close to Ripon is the Lightwater Valley theme park, and a little further are Fountains Abbey, Harrogate, Knaresborough, the Yorkshire Dales and Thirsk with its market and the new James Herriot centre. There is lots to see and do on and off the park for both families and couples.

Charges 2000:
-- Per unit incl. 4 persons £7.00 - £11.00; extra person £2.00; awning or extra car £2.00; dog (max. 2) £1.00; electricity £2.00.
-- No credit cards.
Open:
Easter - 31 October.
Address:
Ure Bank Top,
Ripon, North Yorkshire
HG4 1JD.
Tel:
(01765) 602964.
Reservations:
Made for min. 3 nights with £20 per week deposit.

see colour advert opposite page 129

Directions: At most northern roundabout on the Ripon bypass (A61), turn onto the A6108 signed Ripon, Masham and Leyburn. Go straight on at mini-roundabout and park is signed. O.S.GR: SE317727.

475 Howgill Lodge Caravan and Camping Park, Barden, nr. Skipton

Small, traditional, family site, set in the heart of the Dales.

Arranged on a sloping hillside, the terraced pitches at Howgill Lodge have fantastic views. It is a small park catering for the needs of walkers, tourers and the people who like to just relax. The whole area is a haven for both experienced walkers or the casual rambler, without having to move your car. All the pitches at the upper part of the park are on hardstanding and have electricity connections (10A), the lower ones are mainly on grass (30 in total). Picnic tables and chairs are provided. The sanitary facilities, which can be heated, are at the entrance, close to reception, with dishwashing sinks outside, under cover. Showers are large and adjustable (on payment). The laundry room is fully equipped with washing machine, dryer and iron and four unisex showers are also located here. Outdoor washing lines are provided. A small block housing WCs, with another one planned, are lower down the site for the convenience of tent campers. Reception also houses the small shop which sells most of the basics including fresh foods. A dog walk is provided; there is no children's play area. Fishing licences are available from reception. Part of the farmhouse has been tastefully converted into a licensed restaurant, open six days a week (noon - 6 pm) in season, weekends only in winter. B&B is offered and there are 4 caravan holiday homes for rent (no pets). Skipton, an agricultural market town, is only 8 miles and the well known Bolton Abbey, with its beautiful riverside walks is only 3 miles. Pretty villages abound in the area, all with attractive inns and nearby Embsay has the Dales Railway with steam trains. This very pleasant park, with clean facilities, has a very relaxing feel to it. A member of the Countryside Discovery group. Bellamy gold.

Charges 2001:
-- Per unit incl. 2 persons £9.50, incl. family £11.50; tent or motor-caravan £9.00 or £11.00; awning or extra car £2.00; hiker £3.30.
-- VAT included.
Open:
1 April - 31 October.
Address:
Barden,
Skipton,
N. Yorks BD23 6DJ.
Tel:
(01756) 720655.
Reservations:
Made with £10 deposit.

Directions: Turn off A59 Skipton - Harrogate road at roundabout onto B6100 Bolton Abbey, Burnsall road. Three miles past Bolton Abbey at Barden Towers, bear right signed Appletreewick and Pateley Bridge. This road is fairly narrow for 1¼ miles (passing places). Park signed on right at phone box. O.S.GR: SE055582.

468 Street Head Caravan Park, Newbiggin, nr. Leyburn

Small, rural park with marvellous views.

Street Head is a no frills, simple site next door to the local hostelry. There are 50 privately owned holiday homes arranged over two areas, while a separate, fairly level, hedged field with a circular gravel road provides 25 pitches for touring units. Each has hardstanding and 10A electricity. A further separate sloping field is for tents. At the entrance in traditional, stone buildings are reception and the sanitary facilities. These provide metered hot showers (20p), free hot water to washbasins, but metered for washing up sinks, washing machine and dryer, plus chemical disposal. Public telephone. Basic essentials and gas are held in reception (very limited hours). However, Thoralby village (¼ mile) has a PO/general store and West Burton (1½ miles) is pretty with a pub and shops. Bar snacks are served next door at the Street Head Inn. Aysgarth Falls are 1½ miles. Local markets at Hawes and Leyburn. Bicycle hire ½ mile, fishing 4 miles. Caravan storage.

Charges guide:
-- Per unit £9.00; hiker's tent £8.00; awning £2.00; electricity £2.00.
-- No credit cards.
Open:
1 March - end October.
Address:
Newbiggin, Bishopdale, Leyburn, North Yorkshire DL8 3TE.
Tel:
(01969) 663472 or 663571.
Reservations:
Advised at B.Hs; contact site.

Directions: From A684 going west take B6160 to Kettlewell after Swinithwaite. Continue to Newbiggin past turn to West Burton (park is on right beside road). O.S.GR: SD998862.

470 Nostell Priory Holiday Park, Nostell, nr. Wakefield

Attractive, quiet woodland park.

A tranquil, secluded park within the estate of Nostell Priory, this site provides 60 touring pitches, all with electrical connections (5A), in a grassy, flat and sheltered area edged with mature trees. There is a hardstanding area suitable for motorcaravans, plus 80 caravan holiday homes in a separate area (5 for hire). Amenities are designed to blend into the environment in rustic wood, including the sanitary block which, although older in style, is very clean and well maintained. Accessed by key, it has free, roomy showers, vanity style washbasins and a separate room for dishwashing (free hot water) and laundry with two washing machines and a dryer (opening times on the door). Chemical disposal and motorcaravan service facilities are provided. There is a children's play area (no ball games on the site). Milk and papers can be ordered at reception, the nearest shops are 2 miles. Nostell Priory with its collection of Chippendale furniture and attractive gardens is well worth a visit. The Dales, York and the Peak District are all an easy drive away. A fishing lake is within the grounds, with golf and watersports locally (details in reception). Golf 5 miles, boat launching 8 miles. The park is very well cared for and the natural environment is encouraged so there is an abundance of birds and wildlife. Dogs are accepted (max. 2). A rally field is adjacent to the site. Buses pass the end of the drive (½ mile long).

Charges 2000:
-- Per unit incl. 2 persons £8.00 - £8.50; extra person (over 7 yrs) £1.00; extra vehicle £1.25; porch awning £1.00; awning (no pup tents) £1.25; electricity (5A) £1.25; dog (max. 2) £1.00.
-- No units over 21'6".
-- VAT included.
Open:
1 April - 30 September.
Address:
Nostell, Wakefield, W. Yorks WF4 1QD.
Tel:
(01924) 863938.
FAX: (01924) 862226.
Reservations:
Advised and made with £5 deposit and 50p booking fee (min. 2 nights).

Directions: Entrance is off A638 (Wakefield - Doncaster), 5 miles southeast of Wakefield. Follow drive for ½ mile with rose nursery on left. O.S.GR: SE394181.

461 Moorside Caravan Park, Strensall, nr. York

Adults only park with a neat and tidy appearance.

Strensall is only a few miles from York, one of England's most attractive cities and Moorside will provide a peaceful haven after a day's sightseeing. It will impress you with its pretty fishing lake, masses of flowers and the quietness (except for the odd passing daytime train). There are 57 marked pitches on neat well trimmed grass, most with electricity (5/10A) and 18 with paved hardstanding. The purpose built toilet block can be heated and houses immaculately kept facilities with very spacious showers and washbasins in cubicles for ladies. One WC is suitable for use by visitors with disabilities. Fully equipped laundry room, also housing a public phone, washing up area and chemical disposal. Reception has books to borrow and tourist information. The whole park is very well maintained and is a very pleasant environment. The small lake is well stocked for coarse fishing (£2 charge) and the pitches bordering the lake are the most popular. Dogs are accepted (poop scoops provided) and there is a good dog walk off site. York golf course is almost opposite the site entrance and Strensall village with shops and places to eat is less than a mile. Caravan storage. No children (under 16) are accepted.

Charges 2000:
-- Per unit incl. 2 persons £6.50 - £9.00; extra person £2.00; awning £1.00; hardstanding 50p; electricity £1.50.
-- No credit cards.
Open:
March - end October.
Address:
Lords Moor Lane, Strensall, York Y032 5XJ.
Tel:
(01904) 491208 or 491851.
Reservations:
Contact park.

Directions: From A1237 York outer ring road, follow Flaxton road. The park entrance is on the left past signs to Strensall village and York Golf Club. O.S.GR: SE647614.

Yorkshire

467 Wood Nook Caravan Park, Threshfield, Skipton

Small, family run, rural park in the heart of Wharfedale, popular for walking holidays.

The access road to Wood Nook is narrow for a short distance, but you will find it is well worth this slight inconvenience. Set in the Yorkshire Dales National Park, the site includes six acres of woodland with quite rare flora and wildlife. Reception is in the farmhouse, the small licensed shop is also here (from Easter, gas and basics only). Farm buildings have been converted to provide modern, neat sanitary facilities which can be heated, are well maintained and kept very clean (opened by key). Washbasins are in cubicles for ladies, there are hairdryers and the showers (in another building) are roomy, tiled and coin operated. The laundry has a washing machine, dryer, spin dryer and iron, with clothes lines available. Dishwashing sinks are outside but under cover. Chemical disposal and motor-caravan service points. A wooden chalet provides tourist information. The gently sloping fields have gravel roads and provide 25 pitches with gravel hardstanding. All have electricity (10A, long leads may be required) and there are water and chemical disposal points. There is also room for 24 tents and the park also has 10 caravan holiday homes to let. A small, attractive children's play area with good quality equipment is on top of a small hill, between the touring fields and farm-house buildings. The Thompson family are very friendly, trying always to have time for a chat, although Wood Nook is still a working farm producing beef cattle. Dogs are accepted (but not cats) with a good area provided for walking. American motorhomes are taken by prior arrangement. The Old Hall Inn at Threshfield offers bar food and there is a leisure centre with swimming pool nearby. Fishing or bicycle hire 2 miles, riding 3 miles, golf 9 miles. The park itself adjoins the fells, with direct access from the top of the site. A visit to the nearby village of Grassington is a must, with its cobbled main street and quaint gift shops. All in all, this is a peaceful park from which to explore the Yorkshire Dales. Bellamy gold.

Charges 2001:
-- Per adult £2.30; child 3-15 yrs 95p, 16-17 yrs as part of a family unit £1.50; pitch incl. car £5.00; awning £1.00; hiker/cyclist £4.00; electricity £2.00.
-- Credit cards accepted.
Open:
1 March - 31 October.
Address:
Skirethorns, Threshfield, Skipton, N. Yorks, BD23 5NU.
Tel:
(01756) 752412.
FAX: as phone.
E-mail: enquiries@wood-nook.demon.co.uk.
Reservations:
Necessary for high season and B.H.s with £10 deposit.

Directions: From Skipton take B6265 to Threshfield, then B6160. After 50 yds turn left into Skirethorns Lane and follow signs for 600 yds, up narrow lane then 300 yds. O.S.GR: SD974641.

466 Woodhouse Farm Caravan & Camping Park, Winksley, nr. Ripon

Secluded family park on former working farm.

This unsophisticated park is only 6 miles from Ripon and about 4 miles from the World Heritage site of Fountains Abbey. It is a very rural park with a spacious feel and various pitching areas tucked away in woodland or around the edges of hedged fields with the centres left clear for children. There are hard roads and most of the 160 pitches have 16A electricity, 50 also with hardstanding. The farm buildings at the entrance house reception and a shop plus some of the sanitary facilities. These are supplemented by a separate block nearer the pitches which includes unisex showers (20p) that are roomy with shelf, curtain, etc. and open direct to the outside. Clean and functional, there is free hot water to vanity style washbasins (some in cabins) and for covered dishwashing sinks. A well equipped laundry is in the main building and there are chemical disposal and motorcaravan services. There are 56 acres in total, 17½ devoted to the site and 20 acres of woodland for walks, etc. with a good area where dogs can run free. The 2½ acre fishing lake (day tickets from reception) is a big attraction and provides a pleasant area for picnics or walks. Children have a games room, table tennis, pool table and TV, and play equipment with rubber bases is placed at strategic points around the park. Riding 3 miles, golf 6 miles. The Yorkshire Dales of Nidderdale, Wharfe-dale, Wensleydale and Swaledale are all within easy reach and there are numerous villages around with attractive country inns supplying both food and drinks. The small historic city of Ripon has a beautiful cathedral. Woodhouse Farm is a quiet, secluded location from which many excursions can be made. As in most parts of the Dales, the peace is occasionally disturbed by passing jets, but happily not very often. Caravan storage.

Charges 2000:
-- Per caravan and car or motorcaravan incl. 2 persons £7.50; tent £7.00; cyclist or hiker with tent £4.00; extra person (over 5 yrs) 75p; awning, pup tent £2.00; extra car £1.00 (on visitors car park); electricity £2.00.
-- Plus £1 on hook-up pitches at B.Hs.
-- Credit cards accepted.
-- VAT included.
Open:
1 March - 31 October.
Address:
Winksley, nr. Ripon, North Yorkshire HG4 3PG.
Tel:
(01765) 658309.
FAX: (01765) 658882.
E-mail: woodhouse.farm@talk21.com.
Reservations:
Contact park.

Directions: From Ripon take Fountains Abbey - Pateley Bridge road (B6265). After approx. 3½ miles turn right to Grantley and then follow campsite signs for further 1-2 miles. O.S.GR: SE241715.

472 Knight Stainforth Hall Caravan and Camping Park, nr. Settle

Traditional campsite in the Ribble Valley with outstanding scenery.

This park is located in the heart of the Yorkshire Dales and the whole area is a paradise for hill-walking, fishing and pot-holing. The camping area is on slightly sloping grass, sheltered by mature woodland in a very attractive setting. There are 100 touring pitches, 50 with electricity (10A) and 10 with hardstanding. A separate area houses 60 privately owned caravan holiday homes. Buildings near the farmhouse provide reception, a games/TV room and a shop (with basics). The sanitary facilities are in converted stone barns. One houses pre-mixed hot showers plus a room with dishwashing sinks, the other building providing WCs and washbasins, including three curtained cubicles for ladies, plus a laundry room (with washing machine and dryers) and chemical disposal. The facilities are practical rather than luxurious, but there is heating and a good supply of free hot water throughout. A gate leads from the bottom of the camping field giving access to the river bank where the Ribble bubbles over small waterfalls and rocks and whirls around deep pools where, we are told, campers do swim in warm weather. This is not fenced and children should be supervised, although it is a super location for a family picnic. Fishing permits and licences are available from reception and one can fish for trout (or salmon when available). A partially fenced children's playground is on site. Settle is only 2 miles away, as is Giggleswick and its well known school. Train buffs will want to travel on the Settle-Carlisle railway over the famous Ribblehead Viaduct. The magic of the Dales National Park is on the doorstep and just off the A65 to the west of Settle at Felzor is the Dales Falconry and Conservation Centre. Bicycle hire on site, riding or golf 3 miles. Security barrier at entrance (£10 deposit). Bellamy silver.

Charges 2000:
-- Per unit incl. 2 adults £8.75; extra adult £2.50; extra child (5-16 yrs) £1.50; backpacker £3.90; extra vehicle £1.00; electricity £1.75.
-- Weekly rate: 7 nights for the price of 6.
-- Deposit for amenity block key £2.
-- VAT included.
-- Credit cards accepted.
Open:
1 March - 31 October.
Address:
Little Stainforth, Settle, North Yorkshire BD24 0DP.
Tel:
(01729) 822200.
FAX: (01729) 823387.
E-mail: info@knight-stainforth.co.uk.
Reservations:
Write or phone for details.

Directions: From Settle town centre, drive west towards Giggleswick. Ignore turn to Stainforth/Horton and after 200 yards turn right into Stackhouse Lane (signed Knight Stainforth). After 2 miles turn right at crossroads. O.S.GR: SD815671.

North West Tourist Board

Cheshire, Lancashire, Merseyside, Greater Manchester
and the High Peaks of Derbyshire

Swan House, Swan Meadow Road,
Wigan Pier, Wigan WN3 5BB
Tel: (01942) 821222 Fax: (01942) 820002

The North West Tourist Board includes the counties of Cheshire, Greater Manchester, Lancashire and Merseyside, and the High Peak District of Derbyshire.

The north of England expresses itself in a scale and sternness not found in the south of the country, with some magnificent scenery. However, the area suffers from the legacy of the cotton industry and the effects of the Industrial Revolution.

Merseyside with Manchester and Liverpool was at the heart of the cotton business, expanded rapidly and then experienced economic decline. Now **Greater Manchester** is England's second largest urban area, boasting a very vibrant night life and, with Liverpool, brings together one of the most innovative music and arts scenes in Britain. Liverpool's once thriving docks are now clustered with museums and each pub, restaurant and corner claim a Beatles connection.

Cheshire has distinctive timber framed houses best seen in Chester, which is also a Roman city well worth visiting. Again much of the region was, and is still, industrial; cotton mills can be visited at Style.

The most well known resorts are **Lancashire's** Blackpool and Morecambe, still with a fairly strong working class flavour developed from the past. Brash and cheerful Blackpool with its three piers and dominated by the Tower, still attracts many visitors who go, not only to visit the Pleasure Beach with its 140 rides, but to see the famous 'illuminations' in September and October. Morecambe is more family orientated

The **Peak District** National Park wedged between industrial giants like Manchester, Sheffield, Nottingham and Stoke on Trent, serves as a play-ground to 17 million urban neighbours and receives over 26 million visitors a year.

528 Abbey Farm Caravan Park, Ormskirk

Quiet, well equipped, family park beside Abbey ruins with views over open farmland.

This is an ideal base for a longer stay with plenty of interest in the local area, including Ormskirk parish church, unusual for having both a tower and a spire. Market days are on Thursday and Saturday. The park is divided into small paddocks, one of which is for 44 privately owned seasonal units, one for tents, the others for touring units, plus a rally field for special events. The 60 touring pitches, all with electricity (10 or 16A), are on neatly mown level grass, separated by small shrubs and colourful flower borders. Some mature trees provide shade in parts. Children have a whole field to themselves, with a small adventure playground and space for ball games. There is a farm walk and a fishing lake is on site for the exclusive use of customers (£2 per rod, per day). A little well stocked shop shares space with reception, with a butcher calling twice weekly. The main sanitary building which is modern, heated and spotless, provides WCs, washbasins, controllable hot showers with curtain and seat, hand-dryer and hairdryer, plus a dual purpose family bathroom, which includes facilities for disabled people. A second smaller unit has WCs and washbasins, but there are plans to develop this into individual shower/WC/washbasin cubicles for the 2001 season. Hot water is free throughout. Dishwashing sinks are under cover at both units and a laundry room has washing machine, dryer, spinner, ironing board and airing cupboard. There is a small free lending library, with a good stock of tourist information. The site organises two events annually - a barbecue in early June and a Bonfire Night in November. Wigan Pier, the British Commercial Vehicle Museum, Aintree for the Grand National, the annual Beatles Festival or Southport Flower Show and Martin Mere Nature reserve are some of the attractions within easy reach. A member of the Countryside Discovery group.

Directions: From M6 junction 27 take A5209 (Parbold) road. After 5 miles turn left (just before garage) onto B5240, and then first right into Hob Cross Lane, following signs to site. O.S.GR: SD433099.

Charges 2000:
-- Per unit incl. 2 adults standard pitch £7.75 - £10.75, serviced pitch £10.75 - £12.00; extra adult £1.75; child (5-15 yrs) £1.00; small tent £5.00 - £6.50; hiker's tent incl. 1 adult £3.50 - £4.50; porch awning 50p, standard awning £1.00 - £1.50; extra car/trailer 50p; electricity £1.50 - £2.00.
-- Less 10% for 7 nights booked on or before arrival.
-- VAT included.
-- Credit cards accepted.

Open:
All year.

Address:
Dark Lane, Ormskirk, Lancashire L40 5TX.

Tel:
(01695) 572686.
FAX: as phone.

Reservations:
Essential for high season or B.Hs. Min charge 3 nights for B.Hs. + £10 deposit. Write or phone park for details.

529 Royal Umpire Caravan Park, Croston, nr. Preston

Spacious park near coast and M6 motorway for overnight stops or longer stays.

Royal Umpire is under the family ownership of Frank and Dot Rowe, who took over the running of this well-established park ready for the '99 season. The entrance to the park is a large grass area leading to the security barrier with the shop and reception immediately to the left, and slightly ahead, an unusual sunken garden area that is a pleasing feature. Comprising 58 acres, the park has 200 pitches, almost all with 10A electricity, but a few with 16A. About 75% of the pitches have gravel hardstanding, some with TV and water connections. Tarmac and gravel roads connect the various pitch areas. The two tiled toilet blocks, one beside reception, are excellent with well equipped showers, free hot water, and are an excellent feature of the park. There are fully equipped laundry and dishwashing sinks, very good facilities for disabled visitors which are shared with baby facilities (entrance with key, £5 deposit) and a good first aid room. Chemical disposal and motorcaravan services. Among the general facilities are a licensed shop, large indoor recreation area, somewhat rugged, but effective, with table tennis, pool and various games, and an adventure playground. A field area is used for ball games and a leisure area with outdoor draughts and other games. Dog walk. A short walk takes you to the nearby river for fishing, there is riding 2 miles away. There is a field for rallies. A good choice of pubs serving bar or restaurant meals nearby. Gates closed 11 pm. - 7 am. A member of the Best of British group.

Directions: From north use M6 exit 28 joining A49 going south (parallel to M6) for 2 miles. Then right across M6 on A581 to Croston (approx. 4 miles). From the south use M6 exit 27 onto A5209 but immediately right on B5250 and follow towards Eccleston, joining A581 at Newtown (approx. 5 miles). Site is clearly signed with wide entrance east of Croston. O.S.GR: SD505189.

Charges 2000:
-- Per grass pitch incl. 2 persons, electricity and awning £8.20 - £12.70, hardstanding pitch £9.20 - £13.70, `Royal' pitch £11.20 - £15.90, `Super Royal' £12.20 - £17.00; extra adult £2.50; extra child (5-16 yrs) £1.70; dog free.
-- Less 10% for 7 nights pre-booked.
-- Mid-week stays less.
-- VAT included.
-- Credit cards accepted.
Open: All year.
Address: Southport Road, Croston, nr. Preston, Lancs PR5 7JB.
Tel: (01772) 600257. FAX: (01772) 600662.
Reservations: Made with £5 per night deposit and £1 fee.

see colour advert between pages 160/161

531 Pipers Height Caravan and Camping Park, Peel, nr. Blackpool

Family site in open country with modern facilities, clubroom, bar and restaurant.

Only 4 miles south of Blackpool, this well-run, value-for-money park is a useful alternative to the larger holiday sites nearer to town, and is also convenient for visiting Lytham St Anne's with its attractive gardens. There are 140 pitches with electricity (10A) on concrete hardstandings and a further grassy area for tents which also has a small adventure type playground in one corner. Unlike many sites in this area, there are only 28 holiday homes at Pipers Height. Due to its rather flat and exposed location it can be windy at times, even with two grassy dividing banks topped with small trees and shrubs, and there are no dividing hedges between the pitches. The modern sanitary unit, which can be heated, provides WCs, washbasins in vanity units, hot showers with curtain and seat, with a separate unit for disabled visitors and a chemical disposal point. All hot water is free. A refundable deposit is payable for the amenity building key and barrier card £4. There are dishwashing sinks and a laundry with washing machine and dryer. The main building houses the reception which controls the entry barrier, a small shop stocking basic supplies and gas (open mid-peak season), and a games room with pool table and TV. The large club room/lounge with bar and restaurant is open evenings in peak season and weekends at other times, providing disco or cabaret entertainment during peak season. Hourly bus service to Blackpool. Riding 1 mile, golf 3 miles. Family groups are encouraged at this well-run park. Commercial vehicles are not accepted.

Charges 2000:
-- Per unit incl. up to 4 adults £11.00; extra adult £2.00; child (3-12 yrs) £1.00; extra car £2.00; awning £1.50; electricity £1.50.
-- Reduced rates for low season.
-- VAT included.
-- No credit cards.
Open: 1 March - 30 November.
Address: Peel Road, Peel, Blackpool, Lancashire FY4 5JT.
Tel: (01253) 763767.
Reservations: Essential for B.Hs, peak season and the illuminations (Sept/Oct) and made with £10 deposit.

Directions: From M6 junction 32 take M55 towards Blackpool. Leave at junction 4, taking first left off roundabout, straight on at second roundabout, then right at traffic lights into Peel Road, where site is signed. O.S.GR: SD355327.

Lancashire

530 Kneps Farm Holiday Park, Thornton Cleveleys, nr. Blackpool

Well established park with top class modern facilities, adjacent to Wyre Country Park.

This well managed park is still operated by the family who opened it in 1967, and it makes an excellent base from which to explore the area. A card operated barrier system flanks the reception building which also houses the well stocked shop. The small, fenced children's playground is nearby. The 70 marked and numbered touring pitches are generally on hardstandings with electricity (10A) available to most, and all are accessed from tarmac roads. There are also some grassy pitches and a separate area with 80 caravan holiday homes (78 privately owned, 2 for rent). The excellent, large, centrally heated sanitary building has a main hallway accessed from either end and is decorated with troughs of artificial plants. It is warm and inviting and has free hot water throughout. Along one side are ten individual family bathrooms, each providing a WC, basin and bath/shower. To the other side are separate toilet facilities with electric hand-wash units for men and women, a very well equipped room for disabled visitors, notice boards and a haircare/shaving centre. The building has external access to dishwashing sinks, combined baby care/first aid room, laundry room with washing machines, dryers, spinner and ironing facility, and a chemical disposal point. Dogs are accepted (max. 2 per unit). A path leads through a gate at the back of the site into the Wyre Country Park. Just down the lane is a public slip-way and the Wyreside Ecology Centre. A list and map are provided of local services and amenities, including pubs, restaurants, takeaway, etc. Other local attractions include Marsh Mill Village with a restored windmill, the Freeport Shopping and Leisure village at nearby Fleetwood (discount shopping), and several bird-watching sites around the estuary and country park. Fishing ½ mile, golf 2½ miles. Bellamy gold.

Charges 2000:
-- Per unit incl. 2 adults and 2 children £11.00 - £14.50; adult couple £9.00 - £11.50; single adult £7.00 - £8.50; extra adult £2.00 - £3.00; extra child £1.00 - £1.50; electricity £1.75 - £2.25.
-- Special Senior Citizen rates.
-- Refundable deposit for barrier card and amenity unit key £10.
-- VAT included.
-- Credit cards accepted.
Open:
1 March - 15 November.
Address:
River Road, Stanah, Thornton-Cleveleys, Lancashire FY5 5LR.
Tel:
(01253) 823632.
FAX (01253) 863967.
Reservations:
Essential for B.Hs. and peak season and illuminations, and made with £10 deposit.

Directions: From M55 junction 3, take A585 towards Fleetwood. Turn right at traffic lights by Shell station (for Thornton-Cleveleys), straight across next traffic lights, then right at the next roundabout by River Wyre Hotel. After one mile (past school) turn right at mini-roundabout into Stanah Road, continue across second mini-roundabout and eventually into River Road with site entrance ahead of you. O.S.GR: SD350430.

536 Willowbank Touring Park, Ainsdale, Southport

New park, still under development, beautifully situated for Sefton Coast and Southport.

Willowbank was only in its fourth season when we visited, and things take time and money. The touring park is situated on the edge of sand dunes amongst mature, wind swept trees, The purpose built, heated toilet block is developed to a high standard, with full tiling throughout, offering compact but adequate, free, pre-set showers. Although there are plenty of washbasins, the design did not provide for private cubicles (the management are aware of this shortcoming and hope to provide one cubicle per sex in due course, which would be an improvement). There is a small dishwashing room, also a laundry with washing machine and dryer. There is an excellent bathroom for visitors with disabilities. Entrance to the touring field is controlled by a barrier, with a pass-key issued at the excellent reception building which doubles as a sales office for the substantial static development that is underway at the same site. The owner/operators, Mike and Janet, are very well supported on the touring side by Norman and Christine Roberts who have considerable experience in managing touring parks and have encouraged the development of the touring pitches. Already there is a good block of 12 gravel hardstanding pitches with more planned for the 2001 season. Eventually the park will have 99 pitches, but presently only 54 are developed, all with 16A electricity. The park does not accept motorhomes longer than 27 feet. There could be a little noise at times from the nearby main road. Beaches and sand dunes are everywhere, the famous Martin Mere, the very special town of Southport and the hallowed Royal Birkdale are just down the road. A young park, being enthusiastically developed. Bellamy silver.

Charges 2000:
-- Per unit incl. 2 adults: standard pitch £7.50 - £10.50; serviced pitch £9.50 - £12.50; extra adult £2.00; child (5-16 yrs) £1.50; dog 50p; extra car or boat £1.00; backpacker/cyclist £3.50.
-- VAT included.
-- Credit cards accepted.
Open:
All year
excl. 11 Jan - 28 Feb.
Address:
Coastal Road, Ainsdale, Southport, Lancashire PR8 3ST.
Tel:
(01704) 571566.
FAX: as phone.
E-mail: willowbankcp@yahoo.com.
Reservations:
Made with £5 deposit and £1 fee; contact park.

Directions: Park is 4 miles south of Southport. From A565 in Ainsdale turn into Coastal road by traffic lights 1½ miles south of town centre. O.S.GR: SD308108.

532 Bridge House Marina and Caravan Park, Nateby, Garstang

Small, friendly park on bank of Lancaster Canal, close to M6; for caravans, motorcaravans and trailer tents only.

A simple little park making a good stopover close to the M6 and A6, Bridge House is also only 12 miles from Morecambe and 15 from Blackpool. Adjacent to the Marina (with joint reception/shop) and the Lancaster Canal, the park has 50 pitches on flat grass, all marked but with nothing between them; giving a pleasant open feel about the place. Caravans, motorcaravans and trailer tents are taken, but not other tents, with 32 hardstandings and 37 16A electrical connections (note: no groundsheets). It can become full, especially at B.Hs. The heated, tiled toilet block is older in style, with washbasins set in flat surfaces, well spaced out with free hot showers, hairdryer, dishwashing room (free hot water) and laundry room with washing machine and dryer, plus hot water (10p). Shop with provisions, gas and boat accessories. Public phone. Limited children's play equipment but a large grass play area. No other on-site amenities but pub with meals and shops quite close. Boat slipway on site, fishing nearby, golf 1½miles. Dogs are permitted (on leads) with a pleasant exercise area on the old railway line behind the site. Caravan storage.

Directions: Garstang is on the A6 between exits 32 and 33 of the M6. Follow A6 Garstang bypass and turn off west by The Flag pub. After 20 yds turn right into Nateby crossing lane. O.S.GR: SD483458.

Charges 2000:
-- Per unit incl. 2 persons £8.00; extras adult £1.00; awning £1.50; electricity £1.50.
-- VAT included.
-- Credit cards accepted.
Open:
All year except 5 Jan - 28 Feb.
Address:
Nateby, Garstang, nr. Preston, Lancs PR3 0JJ.
Tel:
(01995) 603207.
FAX: (01995) 601612.
Reservations:
Made for any length without deposit.

535 Holgates Caravan Park, Silverdale, nr. Carnforth

Attractive site in craggy, part-wooded, hillside location, with views over Morecambe Bay.

This is a very high quality park in an outstanding location. It takes 70 touring units, with 339 privately owned caravan holiday homes and 11 to rent located in woodland away from the tourist pitches. There are just 5 grassy pitches for tents and the remaining 65 large touring pitches, all with electricity (16A), free TV connection, individual drainage and water points are on gravel hardstandings. Two modern, heated, sanitary buildings are built from local stone and have top quality fittings, providing push-button hot showers and private cubicles with WC and washbasin. Dishwashing sinks and chemical disposal points are at each unit. There is excellent separate provision for disabled visitors at one unit, with a reserved pitch and parking bay adjacent. Hot water is free throughout. The main complex with reception and entrance barrier has recently been redeveloped. It provides a well stocked supermarket, boutique, launderette, games room with pool table and video games, lounge bar, restaurant with good value meals and a terrace with views over the bay, plus a new heated indoor swimming pool (17 x 17 m) with a spa pool, steam room and sauna (all free to campers, no unaccompanied under 10s). There are good changing rooms, a baby room and lockers and a lifeguard on duty. Children have a choice of two adventure playgrounds and plenty of space for ball games. Everything is completed to the highest standards. Also on site is a small but challenging golf course (75p per person). Facilities are limited mid-week in January and early February. Opportunities for riding, cycling, walking and fishing all within 7 miles. Morecambe or Lancaster are just 12 miles and Kendal is 15 miles. Admission restrictions include no unaccompanied under 18's or single sex groups, no dangerous breeds of dog or commercial vehicles. Minimum stays apply for B.H. weekends (contact park). Bellamy gold.

Directions: From traffic lights in centre of Carnforth take road to Silverdale under low bridge (12' 9"). After 1 mile turn left signed Silverdale and after 2½ miles over a level crossing carry on and then turn right at T junction. Follow the Holgates signs from here watching for left fork followed by right fork (narrow roads). O.S.GR: SD460755.

Charges 2000:
-- Per unit incl. 2 adults and 2 children £10.00 - £19.50; extra adult £4.00; extra child (5-17 yrs) £2.00; awning/pup tent £2.00; electricity (16A) £2.50.
-- VAT included.
-- Credit cards accepted.
Open:
All year except 5 Nov. - 21 Dec.
Address:
Middlebarrow Plain, Cove Road, Silverdale, Carnforth, Lancashire LA5 0SH.
Tel:
(01524) 701508.
FAX: (01524) 701580.
E-mail: caravan@holgates.co.uk.
Reservations:
Essential for B.Hs and peak season; made with £10 deposit for 1 or 2 nights, £20 for longer.

Cumbria

Cumbria Tourist Board

Ashleigh, Holly Road, Windermere LA23 2AQ
Tel: (015394) 44444 Fax: (015394) 44041
E-mail: mail@cumbria-tourist-board.co.uk
Internet: http://www.gocumbria.co.uk

From the tallest mountain in England to the deepest lake, from the country's steepest roads to the world's biggest liar – Cumbria has a lot to offer and it is no surprise so many visitors return year after year. The heart of the county is the Lake District National Park, well known for the dramatic scenery of mountains and lakes which inspired the lake poets including William Wordsworth and formed the setting for Beatrix Potter's many characters.

Each valley and lake has its own character and charm from powerboats on Windermere to sailing boats on Derwentwater, from the rolling hills east of Coniston Water to the rugged drama of Ullswater's surrounding mountains. While the Lake District is well known, there are also many quiet, undiscovered areas including the wild moors of the north Pennines and the peaceful green Eden Valley.

In the north, the city of Carlisle still bears of the marks of a turbulent history. Tullie House Museum & Art Gallery, highlights that violent past from the Romans and the Border Reivers to the present day.

The contrasts of Cumbria are best seen in the west where the Lakeland fells drop down to a long and varied coastline. There are many undiscovered and quiet corners from Ennerdale and Eskdale to the sandstone cliffs of St Bees Head, part of a designated Heritage Coast. The Georgian town of Whitehaven was once Britain's third largest port and is now undergoing its renaissance and developing as a major new tourism centre.

The southern coast of Cumbria – the Lake District Peninsulas – were recent winners of the English Holiday Destination of the Year largely due to its spectacular scenery and the mildest climate in the North. This corner of the county has its fun side too with Ulverston not only being home to the world's only Laurel and Hardy Museum but also the birthplace of Quakerism and pole vaulting.

Compact and accessible, Cumbria is a region which can offer something for every taste with many undiscovered and quiet corners waiting to be explored. It is no surprise that National Geographic Traveller Magazine listed the county as one of 50 places in the world which had to be seen in a lifetime.

552 Skelwith Fold Caravan Park, Ambleside

Spacious, family owned park in southern Lake District for caravans, motorcaravans and trailer tents.

Skelwith Fold was developed in the extensive grounds of a country estate taking advantage of the wealth of mature trees and shrubs. The 300 privately owned caravan holiday homes and 150 touring pitches are absorbed into this unspoilt natural environment, sharing it with red squirrels and other wildlife in several discreet areas branching off the central, mile long main driveway. Touring pitches are on gravel hardstanding and metal pegs will be necessary for awnings. Electric hook-ups (10A) and basic amenities are available in all areas. Eight toilet blocks, well situated to serve all areas, provide free hot showers and all usual facilities including laundry, drying and ironing rooms. There is a well stocked, licensed self-service shop, together with a store for gas, battery charging and caravan spares and accessories. Public phones. Whilst there is an adventure playground, most youngsters and indeed their parents will find endless pleasure exploring over 90 acres of wild woodland and, if early risers, it is possible to see deer, foxes, etc. taking their breakfast in the almost hidden tarn deep in the woods. It is a fascinating site where you feel at home with nature at any time of the year, but it is particularly beautiful in the spring with wild daffodils, bluebells and later rhododendrons and azaleas. There is a family recreation area with picnic tables and goal posts in the Lower Glade area of the park. Reservation is essential for July, August and B.Hs. It is 1½ miles to Ambleside village and pubs within walking distance. Bellamy gold.

Charges guide:
-- Per caravan or trailer tent £10.00; motorcaravan £9.50 (both + £1.00 in August); awning £2.50; extra car or boat £4.00; electricity £1.50 (or £1.75 before 1 May, after 30 Sept).
-- Discounts for weekly or monthly stays.
-- Credit cards accepted.
-- VAT included.

Open:
1 March - 15 November.

Address:
Ambleside,
Cumbria LA22 0HX.

Tel:
(015394) 32277.
FAX: (015394) 34344.

Reservations:
Essential for July/Aug and B.Hs. and made for min. 3 days with £10 deposit.

Directions: From Ambleside take A593 towards Coniston. Pass through Clappergate and on the far outskirts watch for B5286 to Hawkshead on the left. Park is clearly signed approx. 1 mile down this road on the right. O.S.GR: NY358028.

553 Walls Caravan and Camping Park, Ravenglass

Small, neat, well equipped park in west Cumbria.

Set in 5 acres of existing woodland amongst a variety of mature trees, Walls was once part of the large Pennington Estate. It has space for 25 touring units on hardstanding pitches with a grass verge for awnings (plus 25 seasonal units). A circular gravel road provides access and all pitches have electrical hook-ups (10A). A small grass area at the top and back of the park provides an attractive spot for 10 tents overlooking fields. An attractively designed central courtyard complex includes the owner's home, reception with tourist information, 'shop' (only a few basic necessities, plus gas) and a good modern toilet block with all the usual amenities and H&C water throughout. This is very well kept and has a comfortable feeling often missing in British campsite toilet blocks. There is also a laundry room, with washing machine, tumble and spin dryers, iron and board and a separate room with dishwashing facilities and further tourist information. Chemical disposal facilities and motorcaravan service point. Public teleophone. All is excellently maintained by Keith and Stephanie Bridges, who have used the site since it was first developed and now own it and provide a very warm welcome. Dogs are accepted but must be exercised off the park and 'poop-scoops' used. Fishing and bicycle hire 3 miles, boat launching 1½ miles, golf 6 miles. It is a useful site for all sorts of walking - estuary, river or fell - or to explore the Cumbria coast with its Roman connections, the western Lake District or to enjoy the Ravenglass and Eskdale Miniature Railway. The small village of Raven-glass, a single, cottage lined street, is within walking distance, has a pub and holds a Charter Fair in June. A daily bus service runs from Whitehaven to Barrow calling at Ravenglass, or there are trains from the local station to Carlisle and Barrow.

Directions: Park is just off A595 (between Egremont and Millom) on road into village of Ravenglass. O.S.GR: SD096965.

Charges 2001:
-- Per caravan, frame or trailer tent incl. 2 adults £9.00, motorcaravan £8.50; medium tent (2 persons) £8.00; small tent (1 person) £3.50; extra person £1.00; child under 16 yrs free; awning, extra car or dog 50p; electricity £1.50.
-- No credit cards.

Open:
1 March - 31 October.

Address:
Ravenglass,
Cumbria CA18 1SR.

Tel:
(01229) 717250.
E-mail: wallscaravanpark
@ravenglass98.
freeserve.co.uk.

Reservations:
Contact park.

561 Waterfoot Caravan Park, Pooley Bridge

Quiet family park for caravans and motorcaravans only.

Waterfoot is set in 22 acres of partially wooded land, developed in the fifties from a private estate. The 126 private caravan holiday homes are quite separate from the 57 touring pitches. Lake Ullswater is only about 400 yds away and a half mile stroll through bluebell woods brings you to the village of Pooley Bridge. Here are a post office/general store, hotels and restaurants. Waterfoot's touring pitches are arranged very informally in a large clearing. Most are level, there are some hard-standings and all have 10A electricity. Several of the pitches are long enough for American RVs, although there is quite a tight corner leading into the main touring area. The heated toilet block is close and contains some vanity style washbasins with others in large cubicles which also contain free adjustable showers. These are activated by a button on the wall outside the cubicle and give five minutes showering time. A hairdressing area has mirrors, shelves and free hair dryers. The dishwashing room is large, light and airy with free hot water and the laundry has a washing machine, dryer and spin dryer, plus a free iron. In a separate building is chemical disposal. A large fenced field with play equipment to suit all ages and goal posts for football is close to the pitches. A small shop sells basics, gas and newspapers. The bar (with strictly enforced, separate family room) opens week-end evenings in low season and every evening in high season. This is in a large, imposing mansion which has been in the past a family home then a golf hotel. Dogs are accepted with a small dog walk provided and there are public footpaths straight from the park. Fishing close, boat slipway or riding 1½ miles, golf 5 miles.The regular lake steamer service calls at Pooley Bridge, the Ullswater yacht club is only 10 minutes drive and the market town of Penrith is 5 miles. The historic house and gardens of Dalemain is a short walk. Bellamy gold.

Directions: From M6 junction 40, take A66 signed Keswick. After ½ mile at roundabout take A592 signed Ullswater and site is on right after 4 miles. O.S.GR: NY460245.

Charges 2000:
-- Per unit £12.00, with electricity £14.00.
-- VAT included.
-- No credit cards.

Open:
1 March - 31 October.

Address:
Pooley Bridge,
Penrith,
Cumbria CA11 0JF.

Tel:
(017684) 86302.
FAX (017684) 86728.

Reservations:
Essential for B.Hs and summer holidays; contact the Warden.

Cumbria

555 Limefitt Park, Windermere

Well managed and popular Lake District park.

Limefitt Park is owned and run by the Whiteley family (who also own Fallbarrow Park) and is centrally situated for the southern lakes. It has fine views and walks, with the beck running alongside. With various active pursuits nearby and some evening entertainment, it is very well managed and is for families or couples (no organised groups of young people). There are 85 pitches with hardstanding for touring caravans or motorcaravans (of which 20 are seasonal). Each has electricity (10A), fresh water tap and waste water point. Cars are parked at an angle on hardstanding in front of each pitch. There are 80 additional pitches for tents, or more caravans and motorcaravans on flat or slightly sloping grass with some terracing and shade provided by trees. The ground by the beck has been developed for 45 log cabins (for private sale) and there are 20 caravan holiday homes (9 for hire). The sanitary facilities consist of one large, central block for the tenting area and a smaller block for the caravan area, accessed by combination locks. Both are of excellent quality with modern fittings including oval washbasins with mixer taps, flat surfaces, mirrors and side lighting. Hot water for the washbasins, showers, covered washing up and vegetable preparation areas is free. Part of one building is dedicated to three toddlers' rooms with half-size bath and changing facilities. Amenities include a well stocked supermarket, licensed bar lounge with real ales, bar meals and weekly entertainment (both all season), and a takeaway. Also provided are a campers' kitchen (metered), gas supplies, launderette and motorcaravan service point. Sporting activities include walking and fishing, and many local facilities, including bicycle hire, can be booked from the park. Riding 3 miles, golf 5 miles. Games room with many machines. Away from the camping area is a play field and adventure playground on grass by the river and a small beach area with picnic tables. American motorhomes, dogs, boats, single persons, groups and rallies are not accepted; to quote, "in order to preserve Limefitt's unique atmosphere and provide restful nights ... we accept families and couples only." The park is popular throughout the season so advanced reservation is recommended.

Charges 2001:
-- Per unit incl. 2 persons, electricity and TV hook-up £9.50 - £13.00; tent £9.50 - £13.00; extra adult £2.00 - £2.50; child (2-14 yrs) £1.00 - £1.25; awning, pup tent, trailer or 2nd car £2.00 - £2.50.
-- Max. charge 1 family per pitch £11.50 - £15.50 (excl. supplements).
-- Prices are higher for stays not booked in advance.
-- VAT included.
-- Credit cards accepted.

Open:
31 March - 27 October.

Address:
Windermere,
Cumbria LA23 1PA.

Tel:
(015394) 32300 ext. 49.
FAX: (015394) 32848.

Reservations:
Made with full payment at time of booking; cancellation insurance available.

'Camping Cheque'

see colour advert between pages 160/161

Directions: Limefitt Park lies 2½ miles north up the A592 from its junction with the A591 north of Windermere. O.S.GR: NY416030.

560 Pennine View Caravan and Camping Park, Kirkby Stephen

Small, well managed touring site, suitable for night halts or longer breaks.

Pennine View was opened in 1990 and is built on reclaimed land from a former railway goods yard. This super park has a very attractive rockery at the entrance and the whole site is very neat, tidy and well maintained. All very level, numbered pitches with gravel hardstandings are arranged around the perimeter, with grass pitches in the centre. The pitches are of a good size (some being especially large) and are all are supplied with electric hook-ups (16A). One end of the park adjoins the River Eden with steps leading down from the site to huge projecting stone slabs on the river bank (good for sunbathing). There are trout but a licence is needed for fishing. The modern toilet block is built of local stone and is accessed by a digital keypad (as is the telephone box). There are individual wash cubicles and spacious free showers. Hair dryers are metered (20p) but sockets are available for visitors' own equipment. A deep sink is provided to bath the baby, and both ladies and men have a large unit for disabled visitors with toilet, wash-basin, shower, grab handles and shaver points. Well equipped laundry room with washing machine, dryer, spin dryer and iron. Washing up sinks with free hot water are outside but under cover. There is no shop but gas is sold in reception and the hotel nearby offers bar meals and takeaway pizzas. Kirkby Stephen is 1 mile and, although only a small town, its shops should fill most needs. Dogs are accepted (exercised off site). Large American motorhomes cannot be catered for.

Charges 2000:
-- Per adult £3.60 - £3.80; child (4-15 yrs) £1.40; pitch £1.00 - £2.00; extra car £1.00; electricity £1.50 - £2.00; cyclist or backpacker £3.60 - £4.00 per person.
-- VAT included.

Open:
1 March - 31 October.

Address:
Station Road,
Kirkby Stephen,
Cumbria CA17 4SZ.

Tel:
(017683) 71717.

Reservations:
Made with £5 deposit; min. 3 days Easter and B.Hs..

Directions: Park is on the A685 on the southerly outskirts of Kirkby Stephen (just under a mile from the town centre). Turn left at small site sign opposite the Croglin Castle hotel. Site is 50 yds on right. O.S. GR: NY772075.

152

556 Sykeside Camping Park, Patterdale, nr. Penrith

Touring park in attractive Lake District location for tents and 6-8 small motorcaravans.

This small, family owned site, set in the northern lakes area (just ¼ mile from Brotherswater Lake) and surrounded by fells, is ideal for active holidays with walking or climbing on high hills. It would also be useful for a touring holiday being a little away from the busiest areas. The park is licensed to take 80 tents which could include 6-8 small motorcaravans, but definitely no caravans, on flat grass in the valley floor. Pitches are not marked and campers arrange themselves. There are 16 electrical connections (5/10A). The stone-built building, an original barn, near the entrance just 200 yards from the field, houses all the facilities, including the washing and toilet block which has washbasins with free hot water (one private cubicle in ladies' and make-up section) and hot showers (20p); a little basic but clean and functional - updating is planned. There is no chemical disposal point although the owner plans to construct one near the toilet block. Small launderette and dishwashing room. The self-service shop with camping equipment, gas and an ice-pack service, doubles as reception. Public telephone. A cosy, licensed bar and restaurant serves breakfast (8.15-10 am) and evening meals during peak periods (6-9 pm, bar open 5-11 pm). Bunkhouse accommodation is provided for 30 persons in various groupings. As well as fell and hill walking, fishing is available nearby. Bicycle hire 3 miles, riding 8 miles, golf 10 miles. Reservation is essential in peak seasons. The family also own the Brotherswater Inn, 200 yards from the site overlooking the fells which is open all day including meals and has rooms to let.

Directions: On west side of A592 road about 2 miles south of Patterdale, which lies at the southwestern end of Ullswater - entrance is just behind the Brotherswater Inn. (Note: the road is narrow and hilly, and unsuitable for touring caravans and large motorhomes). O.S.GR: NY396005.

Charges 2000:
-- Per adult £2.00 - £2.50; child (4-14 yrs) £1.30 - £1.50; car or m/cycle £2.00 - £2.50; motorcaravan, tent or awning £2.00 - £2.50; dog £1.00; electricity £1.50.
-- Min. charge for motorcaravan £5 per night.
-- VAT included.
-- Credit cards accepted.

Open:
All year.

Address:
Brotherswater, Patterdale, Penrith, Cumbria CA11 0NZ.

Tel:
(017684) 82239.
FAX: (017684) 82558.

Reservations:
Made with £10 per pitch deposit (not possible to book electric hook-up) with balance on arrival. Easter or Spr. B.H. - min. booking, 3 and 4 days respectively.

Sykeside
CAMPING PARK

Brotherswater, Patterdale, Penrith,
Cumbria CA11 0NZ
Tel. 017684 82299 Fax. 017684 82558
Site no. 556

and Bunkhouse Accommodation

Cumbria

554 Fallbarrow Park, Bowness, Windermere

Quality park with Lake Windermere frontage, for caravans and motorcaravans only.

Fallbarrow Park is most attractively situated alongside Lake Windermere with a lake frontage of about 600 yards; one can stroll among the lawns and gardens near the lake. The park is owned and managed by its founders, the Whiteley family, who are committed to caring for the countryside and raise funds for the District Tourism and Conservation Partnership. The major part of the park is occupied by approximately 270 seasonal holiday homes, with about 80 for letting and the remainder privately owned. In the 'Lake' area (not actually by the lake, but some pitches have lake views), there are 38 fenced or hedged touring pitches, all with hardstanding, fresh and waste water points, electric hook-up (10/16A) and TV aerial connection. Fallbarrow Park is very popular and reservations are essential for June - Sept. and B.Hs. American motorhomes are accepted by arrangement. There is a motorcaravan service point and the site is well lit. Two excellent toilet blocks serve the touring sections (access by combination locks). With top quality fittings and heating when required, they provide vanity style washbasins, free controllable showers, make up and hairdressing areas and a baby washroom. There are dishwashing sinks and a very well equipped laundry which also houses a freezer. The Boathouse pub has a spacious and comfortable lounge with bar meals and snacks, a separate restaurant section with varied menu and table service, and an attractive outdoor terrace. TV lounge with occasional entertainment and a large games room with pool table and games machines. Gas is available at the well stocked supermarket. Public telephones. Dogs are accepted (only one per booking) with an exercise area provided. Reception is smart and comfortable, with lots of tourist information. New pet area. The site has a boat park with winter storage and two launching ramps and three jetties can cater for craft up to 18 ft in length. Fishing on site. Bicycle hire 1 mile, riding 2 miles, golf 3 miles. The centre of Bowness is only a short walk and facilities for pony trekking and numerous visitor attractions are close. Bellamy gold.

Charges 2000:
-- Per unit inclusive:
Glade pitch £11.35 - £15.95, Lake pitch £13.25 - £18.65; awning £2.95 - £4.00; boat (max 18 ft.) £10.00; car-top dinghy £5.00; sailboard or canoe £2.00; second car £2.50.
-- VAT included.
-- Credit cards accepted.
Open:
10 March - 4 November.
Address:
Rayrigg Road,
Windermere,
Cumbria LA23 3DL.
Tel:
(015394) 44422, ext. 49.
FAX: (015394) 88736.
Reservations:
Made for 3 nights min. (7 at Spring B.H.). Payment in full at time of booking.

Directions: Park is beside the A592 road just north of Bowness town centre. O.S.GR: SD401971.

557 Wild Rose Park, Appleby-in-Westmorland

Well organised, neat family park in the Eden Valley with excellent facilities and holiday homes.

The entrance to Wild Rose is very inviting with its well mown grass, trim borders and colourful flower displays. The first impression is of well maintained facilities and the feeling that nothing but the best will do. This is reflected throughout the park and each year the owners find something new to provide or something to upgrade. There are three touring areas, two with their own warden to ensure that everything is always spick and span. The top areas have been upgraded to provide neat, level, fully serviced pitches. Separated by hedges (plus a small fence until the hedge grows), many have views. The lower touring area on a slightly sloping field caters for both tents and caravans. Next to this are six individual 'super' pitches fenced or hedged with full services, some with patio, barbecue, picnic table, grass area and satellite TV connections. Privately owned caravan holiday homes occupy their own areas and do not intrude. The final touring field is for 60 tents, gently sloping with an oval road linked to the large field or ball game area with its special viewpoint. Three toilet blocks (two heated) are of excellent quality, well maintained and kept spotlessly clean. Nothing has been forgotten - washbasins are mainly in private cubicles, showers are free and there are hair washing basins, hairdryers, baby baths and bottle warmers, soap and hand dryers, plus full facilities for disabled visitors, a laundry with washing lines and drying rooms, and chemical disposal. The kidney shaped outdoor pool has a landscaped sunbathing area with sunbeds, tables and chairs. Heated mid-May - mid-Sept and open 10 am.- 10 pm, this is a popular, free attraction. The shop is well stocked and the licensed restaurant (with takeaway) has a conservatory/coffee lounge (all 1/4-5/11). Sunday lunches are very popular. Amenities for children include a well kept, fenced play area with safety bases, an indoor playroom for under fives, a games room with table tennis and video games for older children and two TV rooms, one with a cinema style screen. Bicycle hire, BMX track, half court tennis and a field for ball games on site. Dogs are accepted (excluding certain breeds) with a small dog walk. A 'state of the art' entrance barrier and intercom (pass from reception with deposit) deters unwanted guests. Wild Rose has a fully deserved, excellent reputation, which the owners strive to maintain and improve. Nothing is overlooked from recycling bins, electric dust carts to keep the noise down, 'sac-o-matic' special bags in the dog walk and cycle racks placed around the park. Motorcaravan service point. Gas available. Caravan storage. In a peaceful rural situation, the Yorkshire Dales and the Lake District are within easy reach and there are many public footpaths in the area. Fishing, golf or riding within 4 miles. A member of the Best of British group. Bellamy gold.

Directions: Park is signed south off B6260 road 1½ miles southwest of Appleby. Follow signs to park, in the direction of Ormside. O.S.GR: NY697165.

Charges 2000:
-- Per unit incl. 2 persons: standard pitch £7.60 - £12.90; super pitch £12.50 - £25.00; walker or cyclist £3.00; extra person (over 4 yrs) £1.60; awning, extra car, toilet or pup tent £1.90; electricity summer £2.00, winter £2.50; dog 50p.
-- 10% discount for 7 nights or more.
-- Special winter or long-stay rates.
-- VAT included.
-- Credit cards accepted.
Open:
All year.
Address:
Ormside, Appleby-in-Westmorland, Cumbria CA16 6EJ.
Tel:
(017683) 51077.
FAX: (017683) 52551.
E-mail: mail@ wildrose.co.uk.
Reservations:
Essential for B.Hs and July/Aug; made with deposit of £5 per night + £2 fee, remainder on arrival. Min. 3 nights at B.Hs.

559 Westmorland Caravan Site, Tebay, nr. Penrith

Ideal stopover on the M6, for caravans and motorcaravans only.

This caravan park is the ideal stopover for anyone heading either north or south, near the M6 motorway, but far enough away for the traffic noise not to be too disturbing. The 77 level pitches are on gravel and divided into bays of about six or seven units (41 for touring units, 34 seasonal and 7 for caravan holiday homes). All touring pitches have electricity (10/16A). The bays are backed by grassy banks alive with rabbits and birds - a long list in the office describes the large variety of birds to be seen on the site. The heated toilet block is kept very clean. Showers are pre-set and coin operated (10p), all other hot water is free, there are sinks for clothes and dishwashing, a laundry with washing machine, spin dryer, dryer and iron and two chemical disposal points. The site has no shop (although reception sells gas) but there are shops, restaurants and a bar five minutes walk away at the motorway service area (awarded 'Best Motorway Service Station in England 2000'). The site is well lit and there is a late arrivals area. Dogs are accepted with a good walk around the perimeter of the site.

Directions: From the M6, just north of junction 38, exit for Tebay Services (site signed). Site is accessible from the services travelling north or south. O.S.GR: NY607060.

Charges 2000:
-- Per unit £8.50 - £9.50; awning £1.00 - £1.50; electricity £1.85.
-- OAPs less £1.00.
-- Discount on hotel and café meals.
-- VAT included.
-- No credit cards.
Open:
Mid-March - end Oct.
Address:
Orton, Penrith, Cumbria CA10 3SB.
Tel:
(015396) 24511.
FAX: as phone.
Reservations:
Advised for B.Hs and July/Aug; contact park.

Cumbria

551 The Larches Caravan Park, Mealsgate, nr. Carlisle

Peaceful, quality, family run park with excellent sanitary facilities, for adults only.

Mealsgate and The Larches lie on the Carlisle - Cockermouth road, a little removed from the hectic centre of the Lakes, yet with easy access to it (and good views towards it) and to other attractions nearby - the Western Borders, Northumberland, etc. The park takes 73 touring units of any type with 100 privately owned holiday leisure homes. Touring pitches are in different grassy areas with tall, mature trees, shrubs and accompanying wildlife. Some are sloping and irregular, others on marked hardstandings, with electricity (10A), water and waste water connections. The sanitary facilities, in two purpose designed blocks, are of good quality providing en-suite facilities for both sexes. Washbasins for ladies are in cubicles, those for men are set in flat surfaces. The showers (with curtains) are controllable. A separate unit for disabled visitors that can be heated is in one block. Chemical disposal facilities. A well stocked self-service shop, includes gas, camping accessories and off-licence, with events in the surrounding district each day displayed prominently in the window. Amenities include table tennis, TV room in a summer-house, camping kitchen with metered power to cooker, microwave and breakfast bar, laundry room and a telephone. A small indoor, heated swimming pool has been added (small charge). Caravan storage. On arrival everyone is loaned very comprehensive tourist information brochures. Fishing 8 miles, bicycle hire 7 miles, riding 10 miles, golf 3½ miles. There are bus routes to Carlisle and Keswick, walks from the park and good restaurants nearby. The Elliotts provide a warm welcome at this peaceful, well organised park, which is an ideal haven for couples - only adult visitors are accepted.

Charges 2001:
-- Per unit incl. 2 adults £8.00 - £10.00; backpacker £4.00 - £5.00; extra person, awning or car £1.00; electricity £2.00.
-- Discounts for senior citizens and bookings over 7 nights.
-- VAT included.
-- No credit cards.
Open:
1 March - 31 October.
Address:
Mealsgate, Wigton, Cumbria CA7 1LQ.
Tel:
(016973) 71379.
FAX: (016973) 71782.
Reservations:
Made with £1 per night deposit, balance on arrival.

Directions: Park entrance is south off A595 (Carlisle - Cockermouth) road just southwest of Mealsgate. O.S.GR: NY206415.

THE LARCHES
Caravan Park

Mealsgate, Cumbria Tel: (016973) 71379

Adults Only

The Larches, where a warm and friendly welcome awaits you on this family-run Park, offering not only the tranquillity of a quiet rural setting but also the kind of facilities which offer a relaxed and refreshing holiday. The toilet block houses suites of beautifully tiled rooms, each complete with shower, toilet, hairdrier, shower point and vanity unit. A unisex unit for disabled persons is also available with plenty of space for a wheelchair and a helper if necessary. The well stocked shop supplies everything from food to camping accessories. Small indoor heated swimming pool (small charge). The park provides an ideal touring base.

ADAC

562 Cove Camping Park, Watermillock, nr. Penrith

Quiet, peaceful park with views over Lake Ullswater.

Under new ownership, Cove is a delightful small site, some pitches having great views over Lake Ullswater. A separate area behind the camping field holds 38 privately owned holiday homes (1 for hire). The grass is well trimmed and the site is well lit. The tiled toilet blocks are immaculate and are heated in cooler months, providing adjustable showers, some washbasins in cabins and, for ladies, a hairdressing area and a baby changing unit. Dividing the ladies' and men's facilities is a foyer containing a freezer (free), coffee machine and tourist information. The laundry has a washing machine, dryer and an iron, there are washing up sinks in a separate area and chemical disposal. Gas supplies. At the top of the park are 17 level pitches with electricity and one hardstanding suitable for touring units. The rest of the site is quite sloping. Small, grass play area. Fishing 1½ miles, riding 3 miles, golf 6 miles, bicycle hire 7 miles (will deliver). There are two large fields for exercising dogs. A shop is nearby. The park is well situated for walking, boating, fishing and pony trekking. The road from the A592 is narrow, but a self imposed one way system is generally adhered to and the warden will advise.

Charges 2000:
-- Per person (over 3 yrs) £1.80 - £1.90; caravan, motorcaravan or larger tent £3.60 - £3.80; pup tent or awning £1.80 - £1.90; car, boat or m/cycle £1.80 - £1.90; dog 50p.
-- No credit cards.
Open:
Easter - 31 October.
Address:
Ullswater, Watermillock, nr. Penrith, Cumbria CA11 0LS.
Tel:
(017684) 86549.
FAX: as phone.
Reservations:
Made with deposit (caravans or motorcaravans £10, tents £5).

Directions: From A66 Penrith - Keswick road, take A592 south, signed Ullswater. Turn right at Brackenrigg Inn (site signed) and follow road uphill for about 1½ miles to park on left. This road is narrow so if you have a larger unit, phone the park for advice about an alternative route. O.S.GR: NY431236.

Northumbria Tourist Board

Northumberland, Durham, Tyne and Wear and Teeside
Aykley Heads, Durham DH1 5UX
Tel: (0191) 375 3000 Fax: (0191) 386 0899
E-mail: enquiries@ntb.org.uk
Internet: http://www.visitnorthumbria.com

Northumbria covers the counties of **Northumberland, Durham, Tyne and Wear** and the **Teeside** area. Even before the Victorians invented tourism travellers were drawn to this vast empty area between England's industrial belt and the rugged wilderness of Scotland, bisected by the Pennine Mountains and the start of the Pennine Way. Proud castles, glorious coastline and unspoilt countryside, with a spirit of history and a buzzing modern life - that's Northumbria today.

The Pennine Way was the country's first official long-distance path and still the longest (268 miles), stretching from the Peak National Park to the border. Northumberland borders Scotland and is an ancient rugged area dotted with forts from its passionate past when the Scottish raiding parties ventured south.

The 400 square mile Northumberland National Park stretches south from the now peaceful Cheviot Hills near the border, through the Simonside Hills, to the crags of Whin Sill, where it engulfs part of Hadrian's Wall. When the Romans ruled, this line marked the northern limit of their Empire. The surviving sections of this 73 mile long fortification must be the most impressive legacy of

Roman rule. The best part, popular for walking, is along the crest of Whin Sill crags around Housteads fort, the most complete fort on the wall.

The coastline is not to be forgotten, deserted white sandy beaches, majestic castles, including Bamburgh and islands. Lindisfarne known for its links with St Cuthbert and early Christianity and the Farnes, remembered locally through the daring of Grace Darling, now a bird sanctuary.

The small city of **Durham** has a more historical feel, dominated by England's greatest Norman Cathedral. Surrounded on three side by the river Wear, with cobbled medieval streets and restricted car access it is a popular with tourists. For hundreds of years Durham was a quasi-regal state called a 'palatinate' with its own currency, arms and courts with the governors and prince bishops living in the castle, divided from the cathedral by Palace Green. Today it is all part of the university, the third oldest after Oxford and Cambridge in England.

The North East was a coal-producing and shipbuilding area and proud of its heritage but the high-tech industries have moved in, watched over by the 'Angel of the North'.

576 Percy Wood Caravan Park, Swarland, nr. Morpeth

Well equipped, quality woodland site, open 11 months of the year.

Percy Wood provides excellent, modern facilities whilst still maintaining the feel of camping in woodland. A lot of thought and effort has gone into developing a park which blends with its natural surroundings. There are 60 level touring pitches, all with electrical connections (10A), of which 20 have hardstanding and full services. A grass tent field with 5A electricity has a more open aspect with views. The central sanitary block is of wooden construction (heated) and in consequence blends in naturally with the woodland surroundings. It is very well equipped with controllable showers, open, vanity style washbasins, free hot water throughout, dishwashing under cover, a laundry room, baby room and chemical disposal and motorcaravan service facilities. Reception provides basic necessities including gas and local tourist information. The village store and post office are just ½ mile away and local pubs and a restaurant are within a mile. Children's play area, outdoor table tennis and games room with two pool tables and video games. Six caravan holiday homes for hire (plus over 60 privately owned). Dogs are accepted on leads (but not certain breeds). On the boundary of the park is an 18 hole golf course, with a bar and restaurant, and membership can be arranged. Fishing 1½ miles. This is an excellent area for rambling, walking and for nature lovers generally. The park is only 4 miles from Throughton Wood and on the bus route for Alnwick and Rothbury. Druridge Bay Country Park is near (lake visitor centre, good for watersports). Bellamy silver.

Directions: Park is 2 miles west of the A1 (only signed northbound), 3 miles from the A697. It is 12 miles north of Morpeth and 7 miles south of Alnwick. Site is signed at the northern end of Longframlington on the A697. O.S.GR: NU160042.

Charges 2000:
-- Per unit incl. 2 persons, awning and 10A electricity £8.50 - £10.00; fully serviced pitch in July/Aug plus £1.50; camping field incl. 2 persons and 5A electricity £8.00; extra person (over 5 yrs) £1.00; dog 50p; extra car £1.00.
-- Credit cards accepted.

Open:
All year except February.

Address:
Swarland, Morpeth, Northumberland NE65 9JW.

Tel:
(01670) 787649.
FAX: (01670) 787034.
E-mail: enquiries@percy wood.freeserve.co.uk.

Reservations:
Made with 10% non-refundable deposit (min. £10).

Northumberland

577 Dunstan Hill Camping and Caravanning Club Site, nr. Alnwick

Peaceful site within a mile of one of Northumberland's golden beaches.

Northumberland is not very well blessed with good campsites, so we are pleased to feature Dunstan Hill. Off a quiet lane between Embleton and Craster this is a rural site with a tree belt to shelter it from the north wind and access to the beach by a level footpath through the fields, across the golf course and past the ruins of Dunstanburgh Castle. This is 1-1½ miles by car. With gravel access roads, the site has 150 level, well spaced pitches, 78 with 16A electricity hook-ups. The two sanitary blocks have some washbasins in cubicles, free controllable showers, hairdryers and a washroom for children with deep sinks. The fully equipped suite for disabled visitors is in one block, the laundry is in the other block. Chemical disposal point. All is very clean and well maintained. Reception is located in a new building and is manned by very helpful wardens. It also contains the small shop which has gas and basic provisions. Bread and milk can be ordered and a mobile shop and the paper man visit. A tourist information room, a small children's play area and a dog walk are provided, with a large area for outside parking and late arrivals at the entrance. Torches are useful. This is a wonderful area to visit, with its unspoilt beaches and the whole area is steeped in history with Holy Island, the Farne Islands, Bamburgh, Dunstanburgh, Walkworth and Alnwick castles. Buses pass the site entrance. Fishing 1½ miles, riding 8 miles. There are good eating places near.

Charges 2000:
-- Per adult £3.75 - £5.30; child (6-18 yrs) £1.65; non-member pitch fee £4.30; electricity £1.60 - £2.35.
-- VAT included.
-- Credit cards accepted.
Open:
March - October.
Address:
Dunstan Hill, Dunstan, Alnwick, Northumberland NE66 3TQ.
Tel:
(01665) 576310, (no calls after 8 pm).
Reservations:
Necessary and made with deposit; contact the wardens.

Directions: From A1 just north of Alnwick take B1340 or B6347 (further north) for Embleton. Site is signed in Embleton village - avoid signs to Dunstanburgh Castle and follow those for Craster. Site is (south) on the left after approx. ½ mile. O.S.GR: NU236214.

575 Waren Caravan and Camping Park, Bamburgh

Spacious family park with touring area, holiday homes and good sea views.

Developed from 100 acres of undulating private heath and woodland, Waren Park is a large family site with marvellous views. A large area for caravan holiday homes (for hire), is separate from a self contained 4-acre touring area, enclosed by sheltering banks. This provides 170 reasonably level pitches, 100 with electrical connections (10A). The old toilet block is still in use providing basic facilities including free hot showers and baby changing equipment. The addition of a new block is very welcome, with excellent provision for disabled visitors, baby mats, bathroom and four self-contained rooms with shower, WC and wash-basin. Hopefully the old block will be refurbished soon. Further facilities include a laundry room, dishwashing sinks with free hot water, chemical disposal and a new motorcaravan service point. Amenities on the static site are for all to use and include a licensed shop, games room and a children's play park (there is a small one in the touring area). The bar serves meals and has an attractive terrace overlooking the outdoor heated swimming pools (June - Sept). There are playing fields and dog walks. Golf, birdwatching and riding are nearby. As well as the spacious grounds to wander in, there is much to see nearby from historic castles, the Farne Islands to the Cheviot Hills and miles of sandy beaches. Bellamy silver.

Charges 2001:
-- Per unit incl. 2 persons £8.00 - £13.50; extra person (over 5 yrs) £1.00; 1-man tent £5.00 - £10.00; boat or awning £1.50; dog £1.00; electricity £2.00.
-- Credit cards accepted.
-- VAT included.
Open:
Easter/1 April - end Oct.
Address:
Waren Mill, Bamburgh, NE70 7EE.
Tel:
(01668) 214366.
FAX: (01668) 214224.
E-mail: meadowhead-parks@aol.com.
Reservations:
Advised for high season. Deposit 1 night's charge.

Directions: Follow B1342 from the A1 to Waren Mill towards Bamburgh. After Budle Bay turn right and follow signs. O.S.GR: NU154342.

580 Ord House Country Park, East Ord, nr. Berwick-upon-Tweed

Holiday home park with well equipped touring area.

Ord House is 40-acre park for 200 privately owned holiday homes and 75 touring caravan and tent pitches. The whole park has a very well cared for appearance, with well mown grass and colourful arrays of flowering bushes. The touring pitches, all with electricity (10A), are in small sections, from the secluded, walled orchard to the more open areas nearer the toilet blocks. The walled garden provides 19 hardstanding pitches, each with electricity, water and drainage and separated by flowering shrubs and camomile lawns. The main, modern sanitary building is heated, is of excellent quality and cleanliness and is very well maintained. It provides free hot showers and two excellent large family bathrooms (with two showers, a bath, WC and washbasin). There are two rooms for disabled visitors, dishwashing sinks, chemical disposal and a motorcaravan service point. At the entrance to the park is an area with a few pitches suitable for wheelchair users and close by is a small sanitary unit with WCs and showers plus a large, unisex, well appointed unit (Radar key). The whole site is 'wheelchair friendly' with good access to the airy reception and the well stocked accessory shop. Behind reception is a large, well equipped laundry. Ord House itself, an 18th century mansion, has been tastefully converted to provide a bar, lounge bar and family room with reasonably priced meals in each (closed two days each week Nov - March). Although there are many caravan holiday homes on the park, they are not overwhelming and their presence does mean that other amenities can remain open all season. These include a popular 6-hole golf practise area, bicycle hire, crazy golf, table tennis, draughts and a children's play area which has a bark base. Tourist information is available in reception. Gas supplies. A post office stores is 50 yards from the entrance and a leisure centre with a pool has opened 15 minutes walk away. Fishing 1½ miles, riding 8 miles, golf 2 miles. Dogs are accepted by prior arrangement only. No commercial vehicles are accepted. Sea fishing can be booked in Berwick. A member of the Best of British group. Bellamy gold.

Directions: From the A1 Berwick bypass take East Ord exit and follow signs. O.S.GR: NT982515.

Charges 2001:
-- Per unit incl. up to 4 people £9.50 - £13.25; extra adult £2.25; child (6-15 yrs) £1.50; awning £2.25; electricity £2.25; dog £1.50; extra car, boat and trailer by prior arrangement.
-- 1-man tent less £3.00, 2-man less £2.00.
-- Discounts for longer stays.
-- Credit cards accepted.

Open:
All year.

Address:
Ord House, East Ord, Berwick-upon-Tweed, Northumberland TD15 2NS.

Tel:
(01289) 305288. FAX: (01289) 330832. E-mail: enquiries@ ordhouse.co.uk.

Reservations:
Advisable at all times, essential in high seasons (min. 3 nights at B.Hs) - contact park for details.

see colour advert opposite page 161

578 Brown Rigg Caravan & Camping Park, Bellingham, nr. Hexham

Interesting, developing park in the heart of Northumberland.

Bellingham is tucked away amidst heather clad moors in the North Tyne valley, just below the Scottish Borders on the edge of the Northumberland National Park - 'full of history, myth and legend', to quote from the Bellingham town guide. John Mowatt went to school here and has returned with his wife and family to establish Brown Rigg in part of the grounds of his old school. The park provides 70 pitches, 26 with electricity (10/16A), for all types of unit on a level grass field between the moor and the road. Reception with shop, the games room and the sanitary facilities have all been converted from the former wooden school dormitory buildings with a central courtyard area and are rather distinctive. Ladies' facilities are finished in pine and provide washbasins in cubicles, controllable showers on payment (10p), free hairdryer and a baby bath can be provided. The men's have been tiled. In total, it is a good provision, cleverly adapted and well maintained and is operated on a key system. There is a washing machine and dryer, free iron and board, laundry and dishwashing sinks with free hot water, chemical disposal and motorcaravan service point. Reception provides tourist information and basic food supplies, gas and battery charging. There is a games room with pool and table tennis, a TV room, public phone and a children's play area. A tea shop and craft centre are planned. Bellingham is ½ mile away and an 18 hole golf course has been opened recently. Fishing or golf within 1 mile, bicycle hire 7 miles, boat launching 7 miles, riding 10 miles. The Pennine Way passes the entrance and Kielder Water is 9 miles to the west, as is Hadrian's Wall to the south.

Directions: Park is on the B6320, south of Bellingham. O.S.GR: NY835826.

Charges 2001:
--Per unit incl. 2 adults £8.00 - £9.50; 2-man tent £7.00 - £8.50; 1-man tent £4.00 - £4.50; child's pup tent £2.00; extra adult £1.50 - £2.00; child (6-14 yrs) £1.00; awning £1.00; one dog free, others 50p; electricity £1.50 - £2.00.
-- No credit cards.

Open:
Easter - 31 October.

Address:
Bellingham, nr. Hexham, Northumberland NE48 2JY.

Tel:
(01434) 220175. FAX: as phone. E-mail: enquiries@ northumberland caravanparks.com.

Reservations:
Made with £10 deposit for bookings.

536 Fallowfield Dene Caravan & Camping Park, Acomb, Hexham

Neat and tidy, family park in secluded location close to Hadrian's Wall.

Although only 2½ miles from Hexham, Fallowfield Dene is very secluded, situated in mature woodland at the end of a no-through road. Set in woodland glades, each with a Roman name, are 113 seasonal pitches and 37 touring pitches, mostly with 10A electricity. The neat and tidy entrance is very colourful with reception, a small shop and a public phone in a log cabin. The brick built sanitary blocks (one for each sex) are central and heated in cool weather. Well tiled and kept very clean, each has free, adjustable showers, washbasins in cabins and free hairdryers. A separate, fully equipped room is provided for disabled people and a laundry room with washing machine, spin dryer and dishwashing sinks. Chemical disposal and motorcaravan service points are at the block also. There is no play area or games field, but the surrounding woods are a children's paradise. Dogs are welcome with a walk provided. Fallowfield Dene is a network of tracks and there are footpaths from the site entrance. The site is a haven for wildlife with red squirrels, foxes and badgers to be seen. A small shop provides necessities, including gas, with supermarkets and other shops at Hexham or Corbridge. A good restaurant is five minutes walk. Hadrian's Wall is only a mile away, with Roman forts such as Housteads Fort and Chesters, being great attractions. In fact the whole area abounds with well preserved Roman remains. Hexham has its Border History museum, housed in the oldest purpose-built gaol in England, where one can learn about the Border Reivers. Bicycle hire can be arranged with advice on routes to use to explore the area. This site has a very friendly atmosphere that we noticed as soon as we arrived.

Charges 2000:
-- Per adult £2,50 - £3.00; child (5-17 yrs) £1.25 - £1.50; car and caravan or trailer tent, or motor caravan £3.00 - £4.00; tent £2.50 - £3.00; car £1.25; m/cycle £1.00; awning 50p - £1.00; dog 50p; electricity £1.75.
-- Barrier card £5 deposit.
Open:
1 April - 31 October.
Address:
Acomb,
Hexham,
Northumberland
NE46 4RP.
Tel:
(01434) 603553.
FAX: (01434) 601252.
Reservations:
Made with deposit (£5 for one night, £10 for two or more); min. 3 nights at B.Hs.

Directions: From A69 Newcastle - Carlisle road, take A6079 north signed Bellingham and Rothbury. At village of Acomb, site is signed to right. Follow site signs for approx. 1½ miles. The last ½ mile is single track with passing places. O.S.GR: NY938676.

574 White Water Caravan Club Site, Tees Barrage, Stockton-on-Tees

Modern Club site with easy access to leisure and retail centres, open all year.

Being part of the multi-million pound development at the Tees Barrage, this pleasantly landscaped club site caters for all tastes, especially water sports enthusiasts. The recently opened Tees Barrage has transformed eleven miles of the Tees, providing clean, non-tidal water for many activities. The adjoining White Water Course (Britain's largest purpose-built canoe course) provides facilities for both advanced and beginner canoeists, and hosts major national and international events. Families will also enjoy the retail and leisure park, just across the attractive barrage bridge, with its 14-screen cinema, 10-pin bowling, shops and fast food outlets. Close to the site are wetlands that provide a home for a variety of birds. Within a 40 minute drive are the North Yorkshire Moors and the Hartlepool Historic Quay. The site itself provides 117 pitches set in bays and hedged with bushes, all with electricity connections. There are 21 fully serviced pitches (fresh water and waste disposal) on hardstandings. Water points are well placed around the site, with a chemical disposal and motorcaravan service point at the central, heated toilet block. This is a high quality amenity with free hot water, adjustable showers, washbasins in cubicles, baby changing facilities and a well appointed unit for disabled visitors. Washing up sinks and a laundry room are here also. Children are provided with a play area on fine gravel and there is a club room with a pool table for wet weather. The site is well lit, with a security barrier. A supermarket is within six minutes, and a hotel near the entrance.

Charges 2000:
-- Per pitch £6.00; adult £2.60 - £3.25; child (5-16 yrs) £1.10; extra car, boat or trailer £1.00;
electricity £1.50 (31/3-2/10) or £2.25.
-- Tent campers apply to site.
-- Credit cards accepted.
Open:
All year.
Address:
Tees Barrage A66,
Thornaby,
Stockton-on-Tees
TS18 2QW.
Tel:
(01642) 634880.
Reservations:
Contact site by phone or in writing. Made with £5 deposit.

Directions: From A1(M) take A66 for Darlington and follow until you pick up signs for Teeside Retail Park and the Tees Barrage. Cross railway bridge and the Barrage bridge, then first right to site on left in ¼ mile. O.S.GR: NZ463194.

THE **LOW** COST **LOW** SEASON HOLIDAY SOLUTION

Looking for a Go-As-You-Please holiday?

Looking for low season prices but high season quality?

Looking for rock bottom ferry prices?

Enjoy **HUGE** Ferry Savings

Ferry-inclusive prices

from

£**239**

per party

- 10 Camping Cheques
- Return Dover-Calais crossing for car and up to 5 passengers

answer.

Camping Cheques offer a choice of nearly 200 of Europe's finest sites – all at an incredible fixed price of just £7.95 per night for pitch + 2 adults. That's a saving of up to 50% off normal site tariffs. What's more they guarantee fully open services (and a cheerful welcome!) throughout the low season.

For a **FREE** colour brochure

01892 55 98 55

We're waiting to hear from you

www.campingcheque.co.uk

ABTA
W1610

Ord House
Country Park

**Pride of Northumbria Caravan Park
of the Year 1997 / 98 / 99 / 00**

An Award Winning Park situated in North
Northumberland's "Secret Kingdom" about two
miles from the Scottish Border.

Tourers, Motor Homes and Tents welcome.
Luxury Heated Toilets and Shower Facilities.
Country Pub with Bar, Lounge and Family
Room. Play Area and 6 Hole Practice Golf
Course. Superb Caravan and Camping
Accessory Shop.

East Ord, Berwick-upon-Tweed,
Northumberland, TD15 2NS
Tel: 01289 305288
Fax: 01289 330832
www.ordhouse.co.uk
email: enquiries@ordhouse.co.uk

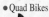

Co. Durham

571 Doe Park Touring Caravan Park, Cotherstone, Barnard Castle

Peaceful site in the old mould with character, ideal for couples (no tents).

This is Hannah Hauxwell country and the Dales, less frequented than other upland areas, provide wonderful walking country; indeed part of the Pennine Way runs near the site. The farm and park are close to where the River Balder joins the Tees at Cotherstone and the ancient oak wood beside the river is an SSSI (Site of Special Scientific Interest) for its insects and flowers, but is also a haven for bird-watchers. The park's reception is in a new log cabin at the entrance to the pitch area, although at quiet times you may be directed to the farmhouse, formerly Leadgard Hall. This is a mellow three storey, Grade II listed building with a history of its own. Mr and Mrs Lamb or son Stephen will make you very welcome and personally take you to your pitch. The camping fields have a lovely open aspect with wonderful views and the 70 pitches are spacious with well mown grass (all with 10A electricity, 20 with hardstanding). There are toilet facilities at the farmhouse, but the two newer blocks are closer to the pitches. Built in local stone, these are good quality, fully tiled facilities, with the newest one heated. There are washbasins in cabins, metered, adjustable showers (20p) and a really well appointed unisex unit for disabled visitors. There are dishwashing sinks and a small laundry, plus a new chemical disposal point. Although there is no play area, a large grass area in front of some of the pitches can be used for ball games. Eggs and milk are available from the farmhouse, plus gas supplies and battery charging. A bus service passes the park from Barnard Castle to Middleton and there is a local leisure centre with swimming pool (4 miles). The village of Cotherstone is ½ mile with post office and a restaurant with bar meals, a pleasant walk by road or river bank. River fishing on site, reservoirs 3 miles, bicycle hire or golf 4 miles, riding 2 miles. Dogs and pets are accepted by arrangement only.

Charges 2000:
-- Per car and caravan or trailer tent incl. 2 persons £6.50 - £7.50; motor-caravan £6.00 - £7.00; extra person (over 6 yrs) 80p; full awning or extra car £1.00; electricity £1.80 - £1.90.
-- VAT included.
Open:
1 March - 31 October.
Address:
Cotherstone, Barnard Castle, Co. Durham DL12 9UQ.
Tel:
(01833) 650302.
FAX: as phone.
Reservations:
Advised for high season and made with £10 deposit (send SAE); min. 4 days at B.Hs.

Directions: Follow B6277 from Barnard Castle in direction of Middleton in Teesdale. The farm is signed on the left just after Cotherstone village (there is no need to go into Barnard Castle). O.S.GR: NZ005204.

572 Camping and Caravanning Club Site Barnard Castle

Family site taking all types of unit including tents, also accepting non-members.

For those readers with tents who wish to visit this area, we have added this new Club site as unfortunately nearby Doe Park does not take tents. The Camping and Caravanning Club site at Barnard Castle was only opened in '96. Originally level farm fields, one side of the site is bordered by mature trees and 11,000 young trees and bushes have been planted so eventually it will become an even more attractive location. Most of the 94 pitches are on grass, 56 electrical hook-ups (16A) plus 12 hardstanding pitches which have a gravel base with room for both car and caravan and space for an awning on grass. Both the toilet block and reception (another large spacious room) are built of local stone and, true to the club's reputation, there is always a warm welcome on arrival. The centrally positioned toilet facil-ities are of good quality and kept spotlessly clean, the whole building having a feeling of spaciousness. Washbasins are in cubicles and the free, controllable showers are roomy. A large laundry has a washing machine, dryer, iron and sink with outside lines provided. Chemical disposal, dishwashing sinks, a baby room and a large, fully equipped unisex unit for visitors with disabilities are also here. Gas is available. Central children's play area with rubber safety base. Barnard Castle, an old town with its market cross still standing, is well worth a visit. The Bowes museum in the town is a French style chateau housing one of Britain's finest art collections. Raby Castle, near Staindrop, is a very impressive mediaeval castle, formerly the seat of the powerful Neville family. Durham has a castle and cathedral (both World Heritage Sites). High Force, England's highest waterfall is about 12 miles away, and the forest of Hamsterly about 16 miles. A riding centre is next to the site and a public footpath leads from the site to Barnard Castle, with a network of public footpaths in the area. Dogs are accepted with a dog walk provided. Fishing 4 miles, golf 2½ miles.

Charges 2000:
-- Per adult £3.75 - £5.30; child (6-18 yrs) £1.65; non-member pitch fee £4.30; electricity £1.60 - £2.35.
-- VAT included.
-- Credit cards accepted.
Open:
March - October.
Address:
Dockenflatts Lane, Lartington, Barnard Castle, Co. Durham DL12 9DG.
Tel:
(01833) 630228, (no calls after 8 pm).
Reservations:
Necessary and made with deposit; contact the wardens.

Directions: Follow B6277 from Barnard Castle (towards Middleton in Teesdale) for 1 mile to Lartington. Turn left at club sign into narrow lane with passing places to site entrance on left (no need to go into Barnard Castle). O.S.GR: NZ025168.

WALES

Wales Tourist Board

Brunel House, 2 Fitzalan Road, Cardiff CF24 0UY

Tel: 029 2049 9909

E-mail: info@tourism.wales.gov.uk

Internet: http://www.visitwales.com

Invigorating. Natural. Rejuvenating. Relaxing. Wales can be all of these things. And much more…

Wales is a compact country with an endless variety of landscape and terrain. Its mountains and lakes, rivers and valleys, coast and country can offer you a break from the pressures of everyday living; Wales has all the benefits of a relaxing escape without any of the disadvantages attributed to travelling long distances.

With a population of just under three million, Wales is a small country with plenty of spirit. It is currently experiencing the most exciting period in its recent history, having in the last few years seen the opening of the National Assembly and hosted the European Summit and Rugby World Cup.

Few parts of the world can claim such a varied landscape in such a small land area; only in Wales can you go from mountains as dramatic as those in Snowdonia to beautiful golden beaches in no time at all. Only in Wales is it but a short journey from city centre to undulating countryside, from inland waterfalls and lakes to coastal cliffs and islands.

Add to this one of Europe's richest cultures, a thriving arts scene, the unique lyrical Welsh language and a wealth of history spanning many centuries and an image emerges of a nation which has much to offer.

Wales' capital, Cardiff, is Europe's youngest, and one of its fastest growing, cities. Many exciting projects are giving the city an air of dynamism and newfound confidence. The barrage in Cardiff Bay is complete and projects such as the new building for the National Assembly and the Wales Millennium Centre are under way. Pride of place goes to Wales' new national stadium – the Millennium Stadium – which has a retractable roof and a 72,500 capacity. Located in the heart of the city, it creates a unique atmosphere during sporting and non-sporting events.

Wales' biggest asset is undoubtedly its countryside. Wales has three National Parks, making up almost a quarter of the country's total area. The dramatic towering mountain scenery of Snowdonia National Park in the north contrasts with the boulder-shaped bare hilltops of the Brecon Beacons in the south and the marine-based coastal beauty of the Pembrokeshire Coast in the west.

Wales also has five designated Areas of Outstanding Natural Beauty, namely the Gower Peninsula, the Wye Valley, the Lln Peninsula, the Anglesey Coast and the Clwydian Range.

An outdoor enthusiast's dream as it evidently is, Wales offers much more. There are many tourist attractions, such as the Great Little Trains, museums, theme and wildlife parks, country houses and estates and of courser more castles per square mile than any other country in Europe.

592 The Bridge Caravan Park and Camping Site, Dingestow

Quiet, family run park in village 4 miles from Monmouth.

The Bridge Caravan Park was established in 1979, being a working farm until a few years ago. Still in the hands of the Holmes family, it provides a peaceful haven bordered by the River Trothy and woodland on one side and by the farm buildings and church on the other. Over half the park is taken up by seasonal long stay pitches. The touring area is to one side, edged by the river at a lower level. Neat, level grass accessed by a circular tarmac roadway provides 33 pitches for caravans and motorcaravans with electricity (10A) and 16 hardstandings. A further 20 places for tents are available, all with electricity (5A), and there are three holiday homes for hire. A pleasant, friendly atmosphere prevails. The purpose built, central toilet block is well maintained and now has a separate shower section, with metered showers in excellent cubicles with dry area, seat and hooks. A bathroom for disabled visitors has also been added here, but this does not have a shower. There is hot water to washbasins in cubicles and hairdryers. A fully equipped laundry and dishwashing room has free hot water. Gas is available on site. Nearby is a village shop and Post Office and there is a children's play area in the village also. A local pub offers good food a short walk away. River fishing is possible. Bicycle hire 6 miles, boat slipway 4 miles, golf 3 miles.

Charges 2001:
-- Per unit incl. 2 adults £8.00; extra adult £1.50; child (5-14 yrs) £1.00; awning £1.00; electricity 10A £2.00, 5A £1.50.
-- No credit cards.

Open:
Easter - 30 October.

Address:
Dingestow,
Monmouth,
Gwent NP25 4DY.

Tel:
(01600) 740241.

Reservations:
Contact park.

Directions: Park is signed off A40 road by junction with A449 (about 4½ miles from junction). O.S.GR: SO458099.

162

Tourism information for South and West Wales may also be obtained from:

Tourism South and West Wales, Charter Court, Enterprise Park, Swansea SA7 9DB
Tel: (01792) 781212 Fax: 01792 781300 E-mail: marketing@tsww.com

606 Caravan Club Tredegar House Country Park, Newport

Immaculate new site, ideally situated for breaking the journey or longer stays.

This newly developed Caravan Club site accommodates 82 caravans, all with 16A electricity hook-up and 40 with gravel hardstanding. A further grass area is allocated for 30 tents, with use limited to families and couples - no single sex groups are accepted. The sanitary block is of an excellent standard with a digital lock system. It provides showers and washbasins in cubicles, all with hooks, mirrors and seats, a bathroom for visitors with disabilities and a baby and toddler bathroom complete with small bath, toilet, washbasin and changing unit. The usual dishwashing, laundry and chemical disposal facilities are also here. Entry to and exit from the park are controlled by a barrier (card required). Calor gas can be purchased from the warden but no other facilities are considered necessary as a large supermarket is just three minutes away. The site itself is within the gardens and park of Tredegar House, a 17th century house and country park which is open to the public to discover what life was like 'above' and 'below' stairs. Newport is some 3 miles away and is a good shopping centre and Cardiff with its castle, shops and much more is only 9 miles. On site there is a well stocked tourist information centre for places of interest, places to eat, etc. Caravan Club policy is to charge non-members an extra £5 per night - or invite them to join, of course - so for those who choose not to join the Club and particularly for overseas visitors, site fees can be high if you are a larger group. Those affected by this policy may wish to consider staying at Cwmcarn Forest Drive Campsite (no. 593) where the charges could well be half that of this most excellent club site and is 15 minutes away.

Charges 2000:
-- Per pitch £6.00; adult £2.60 - £3.90; child (5-16 yrs) £1.10 - £1.20; electricity £1.45 (26/3-4/10) - £2.20.
-- Credit cards accepted.
-- VAT included.
Open:
All year.
Address:
Newport,
Gwent NP10 8TW.
Tel:
(01633) 815600.
FAX: (01633) 816372.
E-mail: cc92@
gofornet.co.uk
Reservations:
Advisable for peak season - contact the warden.

Directions: From M4 take exit 28 or from A48 junction with the M4 follow brown signs for Tredegar House. The caravan park is indicated to the left at the house entrance. O.S.GR: ST299855.

593 Cwmcarn Forest Drive Campsite, Cwmcarn, nr. Newport

Small, council owned park in a beautiful setting.

Set in a narrow, sheltered valley with magnificent wooded slopes (it's hard to believe it was once the site of the Cwmcarn Colliery), this park is not only central for the many attractions of this part of Wales, but there is now also much of the natural environment to enjoy including a small fishing lake. The seven mile forest drive (open daily in season) shares its Visitor Centre with the camp reception and has much to offer - bird watching, badger seeking, the Twmbarlwm ancient hill fort to visit with its magnificent views across the Severn to Somerset, Devon and Gloucestershire. Guided walks are available. The site has a slightly wild feel, but is stunningly located and has 40 well spaced, flat pitches (30 with 15A electric hook-ups, 3 with concrete hardstanding and with tarmac for the car) spread over three small fields between the Visitor Centre and the small lake (fishing permits available). There is one well equipped, heated toilet block (£5 deposit for key) including toilet facilities for disabled visitors, chemical disposal facilities, laundry with washing machine, dryer, iron and board, and a kitchen with two washing up sinks, small cooker and fridge (hot water free). Telephone. The Visitor Centre has a coffee shop open 1-5.30 pm. at weekends from Easter. A variety of shops, a leisure centre, pubs and takeaway food are available in the village ¾ mile away. Riding 2 miles, golf 6 miles. Pets are welcome under control. Wardens are on hand daily and the Visitor Centre and reception are manned 9 am - 5 pm. - arrive before then. Rallies can be accommodated.

Charges 1999:
-- Per unit £6.60 - £7.70; large tent £5.70 - £6.70; small ridge tent £4.20 - £5.30; electricity £2.00.
-- Credit cards accepted.
-- VAT included.
Open:
January - December.
Address:
The Warden, Cwmcarn Forest Drive Campsite,
Cwmcarn,
Crosskeys,
nr. Newport NP1 7FA.
Tel:
(01495) 272001.
Reservations:
No stated policy. 14 day max. stay.

Directions: Cwmcarn Forest Drive is well signed from junction 28 on M4. From the Midlands and the 'Heads of the Valleys' road (A465), take A467 south to Cwmcarn. O.S.GR: ST230935.

South Wales

594 Pembrey Country Park Caravan Club Site, Pembrey, Llanelli

Comfortable, quiet site with access to Pembrey Country Park and beach.

A sheltered peaceful park, this Caravan Club site provides 115 level grassy pitches, accessed by a semi-circular tarmac, one-way road and pleasantly interspersed with clumps of bushes and trees. All but 4 of the pitches have electric hook-ups (16A) and tents are taken providing there is room (steel tent or awning pegs may be needed). The heated sanitary block, well situated for all the pitches, is of the usual good Club standard with curtained washbasins, well equipped, controllable, free hot showers, hand and hair dryers and en-suite facilities for the handicapped (with key). A laundry room has two sinks (H&C) and a washing machine, dryer and ironing board, three dishwashing sinks are under cover, chemical disposal facilities, a motorcaravan service point, four neat service points for drinking water and waste water, plus two large rubbish bins. A small children's play area, giant draughts set and boules pitch are alongside a tarmac area near the reception, which also sells gas, toilet chemicals, bottled water, sweets and barbecue charcoal, and has a small library. However the real plus for this site is its proximity to the Country Park - access to this is free on foot direct from the site, or the Club has organised a special weekly car pass for £6.50. The Park covers 520 acres of grass and woodland, with 7 miles of soft sandy beaches, about a mile of which has a `Blue Flag' rating (dogs are limited to a special area). There are some 64 miles of walks and cycle ways, picnic and conservation areas, a wealth of birds and butterflies, pitch and putt, narrow gauge railway, a dry ski slope (excellent value) and toboggan run, plus an orienteering course, nature trails, and equestrian centre - all part of a really wonderful provision which is both quiet and safe for families. A small drawback could be some noise during the day from aircraft or from occasional meetings at the nearby Pembrey motor racing circuit (on the other hand, enthusiasts can watch the racing from the bicycle trail!) Plenty of family orientated pubs nearby serve good value meals and the Gower Peninsula is only 20 miles away.

Charges 2000:
-- Per pitch (non-member) £6.00 - £7.00; adult £2.60 - £4.00; child (5-16 yrs) £1.10 - £1.20; electricity £1.45 - £2.20.
-- Credit cards accepted.
Open:
All year except 5 Jan. - 26 March.
Address:
Pembrey, Llanelli, Carmarthenshire SA16 0EJ.
Tel:
(01554) 834369, (not after 8 pm).
Reservations:
Essential for July/Aug. and B.Hs; contact the Warden.

Directions: Leave M4 at junction 48 onto A4138. After 4 miles turn right onto A484 at roundabout signed Carmarthen. Continue for 7 miles to Pembrey. The Country Park is signed off the A484 in Pembrey village; site entrance is on right 100 yds before park gates. O.S.GR: SN415005.

596 Abermarlais Caravan Park, Llangadog, nr. Llandeilo

Sheltered park close to main holiday route, in natural setting.

Apart from the attractions of south or mid Wales for a stay, this family run park could also double as a useful transit stop for those en-route to Pembrokeshire. Up to 88 touring units are accommodated in one flattish, tapering 5-acre grass field edged by mature trees and a stream. Pitches are numbered, and generously spaced around the perimeter or on either side of a central, hedged spine at the wider end, with 42 electrical hook-ups (10A) and some hardstanding. Backpackers have a small, separate area. The park is set in a sheltered valley with a range of wildlife and 9 acres of woodland walks. There is also an old walled garden, with some pitches and lawns for softball games, which screens the park, both audibly and visibly, from the A40 road. However, the most sought after pitches are beside the stream, loved by children and a haven for wildlife. The one small toilet block is older in style, but it can be heated and is clean and adequate with free hot water to washbasins (shelf and mirror) and controllable showers. There are two external, covered washing-up sinks (free hot water), chemical disposal, but no laundry facilities - nearest about 5 miles away. Motorcaravan service point. A small shop doubles as reception and gas supplies are available. Play area with tennis and volleyball nets and play equipment. No other major on-site amenities and a torch would be useful. Little Chef restaurant near and pubs, etc. at Llangadog. Fishing 2 miles, riding 5 miles. Winter caravan storage.

Charges 2000:
-- Per pitch £4.50; adult £1.50; child (over 5 yrs) £1.00; awning 60p; electricity £1.75.
-- No credit cards.
Open:
14 March - 14 November.
Address:
Llangadog, nr. Llandeilo, Carmarthenshire SA19 9NG.
Tel:
(01550) 777868 or 777797.
Reservations:
Any length, with £5 deposit.

Directions: Park is on the A40, between the junctions with the A4069 and A482, between Llandovery and Llandeilo. O.S.GR: SN685295.

595 Afon Lodge Caravan Park, St. Clears, nr. Carmarthen

Small park in a peaceful, rural setting, personally run by new owners.

Formerly known as Parciau Bach Caravan Park, there are some narrow lanes to be negotiated to get here, but it is well worth it to enjoy its quality and peaceful setting. The 26 privately owned caravan holiday homes (and 5 site-owned for letting) are hidden in the wooded slopes at the back of the park - a haven for wild flowers and squirrels. The open field for tents is sloping, but now has individual terraced places with dividing shrub hedges (10 pitches) and a lower level, part terraced for 25 caravan pitches, all with electrical hook-ups (16A), 9 with hardstanding, water and TV connections. All are on neatly cut grass with views across the valley. A wooded stream area unfortunately does not belong to the park but further up on the park is a small wildlife pond. The owner's pine chalet home, sited on the slope between the touring field and the wooded area houses reception, a tourist information room and recently extended sanitary facilities with showers, toilets and washbasins with hairdryers. There is a laundry room here. Hot water is free and there are facilities for dishwashing and chemical disposal. Children have an adventure play unit and a pets corner. Shop at reception (limited hours, Easter - end Oct). Bar snacks and evening meals are available at the Parciau Bach Inn (weekends only in low seasons; separate ownership) situated above the site. Telephone. A haven of tranquility, even when we visited in peak season, if you tire of the rural atmosphere, Tenby is only 18 miles, with the 7 mile long Pendine Sands 6 miles away or to the north, the Preseli Mountains. Riding ½ mile, fishing 2 miles, golf 5 miles. Birdwatching opportunities abound. A member of the Countryside Discovery group.

Charges 2000:
-- Per unit £6.50 - £9.00; 2 person tent £5.00 - £7.50; awning £1.00; electricity £1.80; TV connection 50p.
-- No credit cards.
Open:
All year except 9 Jan. - 1 March.
Address:
Parciau Bach, St. Clears, Carmarthenshire SA33 4LG.
Tel:
(01994) 230647.
E-mail: yvonne@ afonlodge.fg.co.uk.
Reservations:
May be advisable for B.Hs; contact park for details.

Directions: From St Clears traffic lights, take road to Llanboidy forking right after 100 yds. Follow this road for almost 2 miles and turn right. After less than a mile turn right at small crossroads and park is on left. O.S.GR: SN298184.

597 Noble Court Holiday Caravan and Camping Park, Narberth

Family owned park with good facilities, centrally situated for southwest Wales.

The neat entrance sets the standard for Noble Court which is part caravan holiday homes (60) and part touring. Arranged over four hedged fields, each one at a slightly lower level, with an additional tenting field, the last has lovely views over the rural Welsh countryside. All 92 touring pitches have electricity, 25 on grass terraces with waste water connection, fresh water supply and 16A electricity, and the others mainly on gravel based hardstanding. An area is available for rallies. Gas is available. Well equipped sanitary facilities are in two similar, well equipped blocks and feature pine doors. They provide vanity style washbasins and reasonably sized showers with a movable shelf, and all hot water is free. There is a laundry, covered dishwashing sinks and chemical disposal. Facilities for disabled people with ramped access are in the lower block (access by key). Children have an adventure play area on bark and there is good access to a further 20 acres of rural land for walking. There is an excellent bar/restaurant, a new bistro, TV and games rooms, plus an outdoor heated pool (35 x 20 ft) with a beach effect and children's splash pool, nicely paved (from Spr. B.H). A new ½ acre coarse fishing lake is excellent with free use for campers. Noble Court is centrally situated for all that Pembrokeshire has to offer and is easily accessed from the A40. Bicycle hire 5 miles, riding 4 miles, golf 3 miles, boat launching 8 miles. The market town of Narberth is ½ mile. Only one dog per pitch is accepted.

Charges 2000:
-- Per unit incl. up to 4 persons with electricity £9.00 - £15.00; tent pitch incl. 2 persons £8.00; extra person £1.25; child (under 12 yrs) £1.00.
-- 2 night specials - contact park.
-- Credit cards accepted.
-- VAT included.
Open:
1 March - 30 November.
Address:
Redstone Road, Narberth, Pembrokeshire SA67 7ES.
Tel:
(01834) 861191.
FAX: (01834) 861484.
Reservations:
Recommended for electricity; contact park for details.

Directions: Going west on A40 ignore roundabout with sign to Narberth (A478) and continue to next junction signed Narberth (B4313) with camping sign. Site is ½ mile on the left and you come on it quite suddenly. O.S.GR: SN111158.

South Wales

607 Camping and Caravan Club Site, Rhandirmwyn, nr. Llandovery

Countryside site in a very scenic location

This is a popular site with those who like a peaceful life with no on-site entertainment, just fresh air and beautiful countryside. The site is only a short drive from the magnificent Llyn Brianne reservoir and close to the Dinas RSPB nature reserve, where a two mile trail runs through oak and alder woodland alongside the River Tywi and the wildlife includes many species of birds including red kites. The site is in a sheltered valley with 96 pitches on level grass, 50 electric hook-ups (16A), and 6 hardstandings. The heated sanitary block is kept very clean, with controllable hot showers, washbasins (some cubicles), WCs, dishwashing sinks and a laundry with a washing machine, dryer, and ironing. Chemical disposal point is in a small building near the site entrance, and there is a drive-over motorcaravan service point. The village is within walking distance although there is a fairly steep hill to negotiate (the return is much easier), and you can take a short cut through the woodland grove dedicated to John Lloyd, a former Chairman of the Club. The village has a Post Office stores and the Royal Oak Inn serves meals.

Directions: From centre of Llandovery take A485 towards Builth Wells, after a short distance turn left, signed Rhandirmwyn, continue for approx. 7 miles along country lanes. O.S.GR: SN779435.

Charges 2000:
-- Per adult £3.75 - £5.30; child (6-18 yrs) £1.65; non-member pitch fee £4.30; electricity £1.60 - £2.35.
Open:
March - October.
Address:
Rhandirmwyn,
Llandovery,
Carmarthenshire
SA20 0NT.
Tel:
(01550) 760257
(not after 8 pm).
Reservations:
Advised for high season and made with deposit; contact the wardens.

598 Moreton Farm Leisure Park, Saundersfoot

Well run park with modern facilities, 4 miles from Tenby.

Moreton Farm has been developed in a secluded valley, a 10-20 minute walk from Saundersfoot. It provides 20 caravan and 40 tent pitches on two sloping, neatly cut grass fields, with 12 pine holiday lodges and 4 cottages for letting, occupying another field. The site is approached under a railway bridge (height 10'9", width across the top 6'6", but with alternative access over the railway line for larger vehicles). There are a few trains during the day, none at night. The toilet block (heated) is light and airy, providing excellent facilities with pre-set hot showers (metered), vanity style washbasins (H&C) with soap and hand dryers, a ramp to a unit for disabled visitors with toilet and washbasin, a baby bath, dishwashing sinks and laundry facilities. A fenced, outside clothes drying area is provided. The small shop, part of reception, provides basics and gas. Telephone. Children's playground on bark and grass. An attractive lake at the bottom of the valley is home to ducks, geese and chickens (fishing no longer possible) - pride of place must go to 'Missy and her girls'! Fishing or riding 1 mile, bicycle hire 2 miles, golf 4 miles. Pembroke and Carew castles and a variety of attractions are close. This is a quiet family site. No dogs or pets are accepted.

Directions: From A477 Carmarthen - Pembroke road take A478 for Tenby at Kilgelly. Park is signed on left after 1½ miles. Watch carefully for sign and park is ½ mile up poorly made-up road and under bridge. O.S.GR: SN122047.

Charges 2000:
-- Per caravan £8.00 - £10.00; trailer tent or motorcaravan £7.00 - £9.00; tent £5.00 - £7.00; awning £1.50; electricity £2.00.
-- VAT included.
-- No credit cards.
Open:
1 March - 31 October.
Address:
Moreton, Saundersfoot, Pembs SA69 9EA.
Tel:
(01834) 812016.
FAX: (01834) 811890.
E-mail: moretonfarm
@btconnect.com.
Reservations:
Made with deposit (£20 p/wk caravans, £15 p/wk tents).

599 Freshwater East Caravan Club Site, nr. Pembroke

Park with excellent facilities, a few minutes from the beach.

This Caravan Club site in the Pembrokeshire Coast National Park is open to non-members (for all units). At the bottom of a hill, it has 126 mainly level, grassy pitches bounded by trees and with electrical hook-ups available. The heated toilet block is modern and in pristine condition with free, controllable showers, washbasins in cubicles, free hairdryers or sockets for your own. There are facilities for disabled visitors, a fully equipped laundry room, chemical disposal and a waste point for motorcaravans. Small play area. Gas supplies. Public phone. Shop ½ mile. The beach and the Pembroke Coastal Path are about a 5 minute walk. This is an excellent area for walking with magnificent cliff views and birdwatching. Fishing within 5 miles. You will find St. David's, the smallest cathedral city, well worth a visit. Note: booster aerial connections available at a small extra charge.

Directions: From the east on A477, fork left 1¼ miles past Milton onto A4075 Pembroke road. After 2 miles in Pembroke immediately (after railway bridge) turn sharp left at roundabout on A4139 Tenby road. In 1¾ miles in Lamphey turn right onto B4584 signed Freshwater East. In 1¾ miles turn right signed Stackpole and Trewent and after 400 yds at foot of hill, right into lane at Club sign. Note: do not tow to beach area. O.S.GR: SS015979.

Charges 2000:
-- Per pitch £6.00 - £7.00; adult £2.00 - £4.00; child (5-16 yrs) £1.10 - £1.20; extra car and trailer (in excess of 2 units) £1.00; electricity £1.45 - £2.20.
-- Credit cards accepted.
Open:
26 March - 1 November.
Address:
Freshwater East,
Lamphey, Pembroke
SA71 5NL.
Tel:
(01646) 672341,
not after 8 pm.
Reservations:
Write to or phone the Warden at site.

600 Gwaun Vale Holiday Touring Park, Llanychaer, Fishguard

Small park with marvellous views, very convenient for Fishguard and the ferries.

In a superb rural setting, with cows in the field behind and wonderful views across the countryside towards the sea, Gwaun Vale provides 28 pitches. On mainly level grass, with one terrace above another, connected by an oval, gravel and tarmac roadway, 10 pitches have hardstanding and 19 have electricity connections (10A). There are plenty of water points and several picnic tables. A useful little shop doubles as reception with a well presented display of tourist information and variety of books on local walks to buy or borrow. One can also borrow a barbecue, iron and board, a boules set, baby bath or videos! Plans are in hand for a new shop and tea rooms next season. The sanitary block, beside reception and to one side of the site is a little old fashioned. However, it is neat, clean and heated with mirrors, hooks and shelves. There are hot showers (20p, which could do with some improvement) and washbasins including one in the ladies' with a WC. A cheerful laundry room with sink, washing machine and dryer and two dish-washing sinks, is also well provided with tourist information. Chemical disposal facilities are outside. A play area is in a small sloping fenced field with adventure type equipment and a field for dogs next door complete with a useful seat - to watch dog and child! A pub serving bar meals is within easy walking distance. Fishing, bicycle hire and riding 2 miles. Golf 7 miles. Day trips to Ireland are possible, as well as windsurfing, boating and fishing trips, and the Pembroke coastal footpath is nearby. A 'must' to see is Wales' answer to the Bayeux Tapestry, a 100 ft. long tapestry on view in Fishguard (the French invaded Britain in 1797 and the tapestry, embroidered by 70 local women, gives a carefully researched account of this invasion and its defeat - full of life and humour).

Charges 2000:
-- Per unit incl. 1 or 2 persons £6.00 - £7.00, 3 or 4 persons £7.00 - £8.00, 5+ persons £8.00 - £1.50; awning, dog, extra car no charge.
-- No credit cards.

Open:
1 March - 31 October.

Address:
Llanychaer, Fishguard, Pembrokeshire SA65 9TA.

Tel:
(01348) 874698. FAX: (01348) 874000. E-mail: margaret. harries@talk21.com.

Reservations:
Advised for high season and B.Hs. and made with £10 deposit and 50p fee.

Directions: Park is on the right, 1½ miles from Fishguard; follow brown camping signs from centre. O.S.GR: SM977356.

608 Llwyngwair Manor Holiday Park, Newport, nr. Fishguard

Riverside hotel and caravan park on the Pembrokeshire coast.

A feeling of grandeur strikes you when you turn into the drive at Llwyngwair Manor. As you turn the corner and come over a small hill, there are neatly sited and cared for caravan holiday homes and soon the ivy-clad manor house comes into view. The Manor is run as an hotel, but this is also where you check in for the touring park which you will see signed to the left of the open area in front of the house (take it steady here - there are a lot of fairly serious speed humps). The touring park is behind the manor house and is laid out in two areas, the first with electricity hook-ups available on the right hand side. The far area is for those who book in advance and all pitches have electricity. These hook ups are only 5A each because of the limited supply coming to the whole park, so those with state of the art electric water and space heating will need to watch out because those trips will blow all the time. The new sanitary block is mid-way and equi-distant from both camping areas. It is of a good modern standard, with spacious showers with a good dry area but, rather disappointingly, no soap tray and only one small hook on which to hang everything to keep clothes dry whilst showering. Washbasins are in cubicles in the shower area and there are separate rooms with toilets which also have washbasins. A bathroom for disabled visitors is provided with excellent facilities, a family bathroom (key from the hotel) and chemical disposal facilities. The River Nevem runs through the park, down one side of the touring area so those with small children need to take care. On the other hand, fishermen should be overjoyed as it is claimed that salmon and sea trout swim up and down and you have ½ mile over which you are invited to fish. The hotel provides food and drink (bar 11 am. - midnight, food noon - 1.30 and 6 - 9.30 pm. but shorter hours on Sunday). All children must be out of the bar area by 9 pm. A tennis court, boules, snooker room and a TV lounge may be used by visitors. Apart from wonderful St Davids, the Dyfed Shire Horse and Leisure Farm and the Oakwood Coaster Country Park are popular with visitors and of course a day trip to Ireland can be taken by ferry from nearby Fishguard. There are lovely walks, beaches and the beautiful small town of Newport nearby.

Charges guide:
-- Per unit £9.00; awning £1.00; electricity £2.00.
-- Weekly rates available.
-- Credit cards accepted.

Open:
April - end September.

Address:
Newport, Pembrokeshire SA42 0LX.

Tel:
(01239) 820498.

Reservations:
Advised in high season and B.Hs; contact park.

Directions: Park entrance is off the A487, 1 mile east of Newport. O.S.GR: SN072391.

South Wales

603 Brynich Caravan Park, Brecon

Well kept, family run park with picturesque setting and super views towards the Brecon Beacons.

Brynich has been gradually developed over the years by Colin and Maureen Jones to a very high standard. Originally farmland near the Brecon bypass, there are now three hedged camping fields, neatly mown and level with tarmac roads and a mixture of hardwood trees and shrubs maturing nicely, providing for 130 touring units of all types with 108 electricity points (10/16A). Two modern toilet blocks, which can be heated, have free hot water throughout, well equipped showers, washbasins in cubicles, washing up sinks, a laundry room and chemical disposal points. Two fully equipped units for visitors with disabilities are in one block, one providing left handed toilet facilities, the other right handed (key system) and a baby unit including bath. A fridge, freezer and microwave are provided for visitors' use. In total it is an excellent provision. A nice addition in a sloping field leading down to a stream is an extensive dog walk on one side of the Brynich Brook and an adventure play area, reached by stepping stones, on the opposite side. The stream is shallow and an added attraction along with the play equipment. Seats have also been provided. For smaller children there is some play equipment near reception and there is a large recreation field for ball games. Reception and a well stocked shop (with gas) are housed in a recent building at the entrance. Motorcaravan service point. Within the Brecon Beacons National Park, this is a good area for hill walking and climbing. There are two golf courses and possibilities for watersports. A local pub serving 'pub grub' is within walking distance. Fishing or bicycle hire 1½ miles, riding 2 miles, golf 3 miles. Access to the towpath of the Brecon and Monmouthshire Canal is only 200 yds. Market days in Brecon on Tuesday and Friday. A member of the Best of British group.

Charges 2001:
-- Per unit incl. 2 persons £8.50 - £10.00, 1 person £6.50 - £8.00; extra adult £2.25 - £3.00; child (4-16 yrs) £1.25 - £1.75; backpacker £4.00 - £4.50; awning £1.50 - £1.75; electricity £2.00 - £2.25; dog 50p.
-- Credit cards accepted.

Open:
29 March - 31 October.

Address:
Brecon, Powys LD3 7SH.

Tel:
(01874) 623325.

FAX: as phone.

E-mail: brynich @aol.com.

Reservations:
Advisable for hook-ups at B.Hs. and made with £10 deposit.

see colour advert between pages 160/161

Directions: Park entrance is off A470 (Builth Wells) road, 250 yds. from junction with A40 (Abergavenny) road, 1 mile east of Brecon. O.S.GR: SO069278.

604 Pencelli Castle Caravan and Camping, Pencelli, nr. Brecon

Quality park with atmosphere and character amidst Brecon scenery.

This year-round site offers excellent facilities in peaceful, rural tranquillity. The owners, Liz and Gerwyn Rees, have retained the country charm but have added a new, all embracing range of luxury heated facilities which were completed in spring 2000. Forming part of its exceptional design are ample toilets, free showers, washbasins and private cubicles. There are two large fully equipped rooms for families or disabled visitors incorporating double showers, baby changing and bath facilities, all humorously decorated for the young at heart. There is a drying room with lockers (a must as this is walking country), an information and planning room, a laundry and an indoor dishwashing and food preparation room. Reception and a shop complete the new block. All rooms are spacious and potted plants and soft music are added niceties. A new field, the 'Orchard', incorporating 15 pitches with hardstanding, some fully serviced, has also been completed; together with the shrubs, fruit trees and stone cider mill, this is a wonderful facility. The 'Oaks' (20 caravans and tents) and the 'Meadow' (40 tents) with boot and bike wash, are bordered by majestic trees and the Monmouthshire and Brecon Canal, where gaily painted barges slip past. All fields are level with neatly mown grass and tarmac access roads. There is an excellent chemical disposal and motorcaravan service point (with washbasin, soap and hand dryer). Further new attractions are the rabbits, ducks and the red deer which enjoy being hand-fed by visitors. The historic manor house, dating back to 1583, is adjacent to arched barns that house an increasing collection of vintage farm machinery including carts and rare tractors. The Royal Oak inn with meals is 100 m. from the park. For mountain bikers and walkers, a path leaves the village to reach the top of the Brecon Beacons or there is an easy towpath ramble to Tal-y-Bont where there are pubs, tea rooms and a post office. Bicycle hire is available and buses pass regularly for Brecon, Abergavenny, etc. Regrettably no dogs are accepted.

Charges 2000:
-- Per caravan or motorcaravan incl.. 2 persons £9.00 - £9.50; extra adult £2.25 - £2.75; child (5-13 yrs) £1.50; awning £1.50; electricity £2.25.
-- Tents: per adult £4.50.
-- No credit cards.

Open:
All year.

Address:
Pencelli, Brecon, Powys LD3 7LX.

Tel:
(01874) 665451.

FAX: (01874) 665452.

E-mail: pencelli.castle @virgin.net.

Reservations:
Advised for peak season and B.Hs; contact site for details.

Directions: From A40 south after Brecon bypass take the B4558 at signs for Llanfrynach and later Pencelli; or if travelling north on A40, approach via Tal-y-Bont. Site at south end of Pencelli. O.S.GR: SO096248.

601 Cenarth Falls Holiday Park, Cenarth, Newcastle Emlyn

Excellent provision for tourers near the renowned Cenarth Falls.

The Davies family have developed an attractively landscaped, part wooded holiday home park with 80 privately owned units and 7 for hire. However, a neat well cared for, sheltered grassy area at the top of the park provides 30 touring pitches, 17 with sunken grass grid hardstanding and all with electricity (16A). Accessed via a semi-circular tarmac road, they enjoy views across the Teifi valley. An excellent, heated sanitary block complements this provision. Accessed by key, it uses a 'P.I.R.' system to control heating, lighting, water and air-freshener on entry - very efficient. Tiled with non-slip floors, both men and ladies have an en-suite family room (that doubles as provision for disabled visitors), an additional well equipped shower and also one washbasin in a roomy private cabin. There are plenty of mirrors, shelves, etc. A laundry room has two washing machines, two dryers and ironing facilities, for the use of the whole park. There are no laundry sinks, but two dishwashing sinks are under cover, neatly equipped with bowl and rack. There is easy ramped access, even to the chemical disposal unit. A state-of-the-art, electrically operated motorcaravan service point using the van's own pump system is most impressive. A welcoming reception doubles as a shop for essential groceries, newspapers and gas, while the 'Fisherman's Cove', a friendly little private bar (membership for all guests, weekends only March - May and Sept. onwards) serves good value, home cooked meals, together with some entertainment, especially at weekends. Children's play area and games room with pool table and video game machine. A sunken, kidney shaped heated pool with landscaped surrounds and sun-beds is very pleasant (mid-May - mid-Sept). Fiishing ¼ mile, bicycle hire 8 miles, riding 7 miles, golf 10 miles. A footpath leads to the village and the famous Cenarth Falls (with leaping salmon). The National Coracle Centre is worth a visit. A member of the Best of British group. Bellamy gold.

Directions: Follow A484 Cardigan - Newcastle Emlyn road and park is signed before Cenarth village. O.S.GR: SN265421.

Charges 2001:
-- Per unit incl. up to 4 people and a car £8.00 - £15.00; extra person £2.00; awning £2.00; extra pup tent (space permitting) £2.50; dog £1.00; electricity (16A) £2.00.
-- Credit cards accepted.
-- VAT included.
Open:
1 March - November.
Address:
Cenarth,
Newcastle Emlyn,
Ceredigion SA38 9JS.
Tel:
(01239) 710345.
FAX: (01239) 710344.
E-mail: enquiries@
cenarth-holipark.co.uk.
Reservations:
Made with 33% deposit;
contact park.

628 Aeron Coast Caravan Park, Aberaeron

Family park with wide range of recreational facilities, on west coast of Wales.

Although Aeron Coast has a high proportion of caravan holiday homes (150 privately owned), it provides for touring units of all types in two fields separated from the beach and sea by a high bank (although the best beach is on the south side of this traditional fishing village). Pitches are on level grass with all units regularly and well spaced in lines in traditional style. There are two toilet blocks, one of older design but now updated and part-tiled, the other completed for later. The new block offers excellent facilities, including large family showers with free hot water and facilities for disabled people and babies. Chemical disposal facilities are provided and a basic motorcaravan service point. The main attraction of the park is its excellent recreational provision, both in and out of doors. These include a heated kidney shaped pool (June - Sept) plus toddlers' pool (unsupervised) and paved, walled area good for sunbathing, tennis court and small half-court for youngsters, football and a sand pit. The indoor leisure area provides an under-5s' room with slide, etc, teenagers' only room with juke box, table tennis, pool and games machines, a large entertainment room and TV room. During high season these are looked after by two students who also arrange other activities such as tennis tournaments, rounders, 5-a-side football, treasure hunts, teenage discos or free films if the weather is poor. A club house and bar complete the amenities (from Easter, 12 -2 and from 7 pm). There is a family room with bar meals and takeaway available in school holidays periods. Reception keeps a wide range of tourist information and there is a shop at the petrol station at the entrance. Telephone. Only one dog per unit is accepted. Fishing and boat launching ½ mile, bicycle hire 6 miles, riding or golf 5 miles. A steam railway, craft centre, woollen mills and potteries can be visited locally.

Directions: Park is on northern outskirts of Aberaeron village with entrance on the right beside a Texaco petrol station - not too easily seen. O.S.GR: SN461633.

Charges 2001:
-- Per unit incl. 2 persons £8.00 - £11.00; extra person over 12 yrs £1.00, 2-12 yrs 50p; electricity £2.00.
-- Credit cards accepted.
Open:
1 March - 31 October.
Address:
North Road,
Aberaeron,
Ceredigion SA46 0JF.
Tel:
(01545) 570349.
Reservations:
Made with £10 deposit.

Alan Rogers' Discount

Less £1 p/night
excl. Bank &
school holidays

Mid Wales

Tourism information for Mid Wales may also be obtained from:

Mid Wales Tourism, Marketing Dept, The Station, Machynlleth SY20 8TG
Tel: 0800 273747 Fax: 01654 703855 E-mail: info@brilliantbreaks.demon.co.uk

630 Ocean View Caravan Park, Clarach Bay, Aberystwyth

Small, quiet holiday home park, with good provision for tourers and no entertainment.

The two, gently sloping, neatly cut grass fields for tourers at Ocean View have good views over Clarach Bay. There are 24 numbered touring pitches for all types of unit. All have electrical hook-ups (5/10A) and 10 also have hardstanding, TV, water and waste water. There are also 50 privately owned caravan holiday homes, plus 3 for hire, also 4 cottages. A neat clean sanitary block provides free hot showers and laundry facilities, as well as washbasins, mirrors, hooks, shaver points, hand-dryers, soap, dishwashing sinks and chemical disposal. The usual water and waste water points and refuse bins are provided. A football field, complete with goal posts, a dog walking area, picnic tables, public telephone and a small reception area (with gas supplies) complete the on-site facilities. Everything else, including bars and shops, is only 200 m. away beside the safe sand and pebble beach. This is sheltered by steep shale cliffs, along the top of which there are many walks enjoying magnificent views in the direction of both Borth and Aberystwyth. Golf 2 miles, riding 5 miles.

Directions: Clarach is signed west from A487 (Aberystwyth - Machynlleth) in village of Bow Street. Follow signs to beach and park. Access for caravans from Aberystwyth on the B4572 is difficult. O.S.GR: SN592842.

Charges 2000:
-- Per unit incl. 2 persons £6.50 - £9.50, 'de-luxe' pitch £8.50 - £11.00; extra person 50p - £1.00; awning free - £1.00; dog 75p; electricity 5A £1.50. 10A £2.00.
-- One night stay + £1.00.
-- Credit cards accepted.
-- VAT included.
Open:
April - October.
Address:
Clarach Bay, Aberystwyth Ceredigion SY23 3DT.
Tel:
(01970) 828425/623361.
FAX: (01970) 820215.
Reservations:
Made with £20 deposit.

632 Fforest Fields Caravan and Camping Park, nr. Builth Wells

Secluded 'different' park set on family hill farm in the heart of Radnorshire.

This truly rural park has glorious views of the surrounding hills and a distinctly family atmosphere. This is simple country camping and caravanning at its best, without man-made distractions or intrusions - a place to unwind and watch the stars. The facilities include 50 large pitches on level grass, with electrical connections (mostly 16A), on a spacious and peaceful, carefully landscaped field by a stream. The sanitary facilities are acceptable, if not especially luxurious, with free hot showers (with seat, curtain and hook), open washbasins with mirrors, razor points, baby bath and with dish and clothes washing facilities including washing machines and a dryer, chemical disposal and heating in cool weather. Milk, eggs and orange juice are sold in reception and gas, otherwise there are few other on-site facilities, but the village of Hundred House, one mile away, has a pub, village stores and post office. George and Kate, the enthusiastic owners, have opened up much of the farm for moderate or ample woodland and moorland trails which can be enjoyed with much wildlife to see. Indeed wildlife is actively encouraged with nesting boxes for owls, song-birds and bats, by leaving field margins un-mown to encourage small mammals and by yearly tree planting. Bellamy gold. A torch is useful. Fishing 3 miles, bicycle hire or golf 5 miles, riding 10 miles. George and Kate also run a para-gliding school where beginners are welcome.

Directions: Park is signed off A481 between Hundred House and Builth Wells. O.S.GR: SO098535.

Charges 2000:
-- Per caravan or trailer tent £7.50; motorcaravan or family tent £6.50; small tent £3.00 - £6.50; awning or child's tent £1.00; electricity £1.50.
-- No credit cards.
Open:
1 April - 6 November.
Address:
Hundred House, Builth Wells, Powys LD1 5RT.
Tel:
(01982) 570406.
FAX: (01982) 570444.
E-mail: fforestfields@ btinternet.com
Reservations:
Contact park.

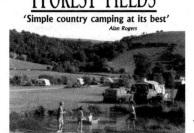

This delightful campsite is spacious, level and really peaceful. It nestles in a woodland bowl straddling a mountain stream in which children love to play. It has very clean modern toilets and free showers. There are no statics and no clubhouse. 16 amp electrics, laundry and plenty of space. Lovely walks direct from site and dogs are welcome. Reservations are free and no deposit required. Family run. Phone for brochure which will be sent by return. You'll wonder why you haven't been before!

01982 570406
www.fforestfields.co.uk

FFOREST FIELDS

'Simple country camping at its best'
Alan Rogers

- No statics
- No Clubhouse
- No Traffic Noise
- No Booking Deposit
- No Extras
- Excellent free facilities
- Family run
- 'A gem of a site'

★★★

RAC

AA

ENVIRONMENTAL AWARD

629 Glan-y-Mor Leisure Park, Clarach Bay, Aberystwyth

Busy, sea front, holiday-style park with many holiday homes and touring sections.

Glan-y-Mor has an enviable situation on this part of the Cambrian coast, on an attractive bay beside the beach, yet within easy reach of Aberystwyth. On a wet day you may not wish to go far with the comprehensive leisure centre on site - it has reduced entry for campers. Although the balance of pitches is very much in favour of holiday homes (3:1) which dominate the open park and bay, there are 60 touring pitches, 45 with electricity (10A) and 4 'super' pitches. They are rather pressed together in two sections on the lower part of the park. In high season, tents, tourers or motorcaravans can opt for space and fine views (but beware of winds) on a ridge of higher ground. An excellent, heated toilet block on the lower touring area has free hot water, dishwashing and a laundry, plus a WC for disabled people and chemical disposal. Motorcaravan services. A 'portacabin' type block is on the ridge. Further facilities for disabled people are at the leisure centre. This well equipped centre offers a heated, irregularly shaped pool, jacuzzi, solarium, sauna, steam room and gym. The complex houses reception, an amusement room, 10-pin bowling, bar, buffet bar and dance room (free entertainment nightly, Easter and May-Oct). Elsewhere are a supermarket, play area, designed with younger children in mind, and a large sports field. Reduced rates are available at local golf courses. Licensed restaurant and takeaway (from Easter). Freezer pack service and gas supplies. Winter caravan storage. No dogs are accepted on touring pitches during B.H. and school summer holiday periods. An ideal site for those seeking 'all the bells and whistles'! Bellamy bronze.

Directions: Clarach is signed west from the A487 (Aberystwyth - Machynlleth) in village of Bow Street. Follow signs over crossroads to beach and park. Access for caravans from Aberystwyth on B4572 is difficult. O.S.GR: SN580850.

Charges 2000:
-- Per unit incl. 2 persons £6.00 - £12.00; 'super' pitch £9.00 - £15.00; child free; extra person over 18 yrs £2.00; awning £3.00; electricity £2.00; dog (not 14/7-31/8) £2.00.
-- Club membership (not Leisure complex) incl.
-- VAT included.
-- Credit cards accepted.
Open:
1 March - 31 October.
Address:
Clarach Bay, Aberystwyth, Ceredigion SY23 3DT.
Tel:
(01970) 828900.
FAX: (01970) 828890.
E-mail: holidays-in-wales@sunbourne.co.uk.
Reservations:
Any length, with £20 deposit; balance 28 days before arrival.

EXCELLENT TOURING AND CAMPING FACILITIES ON TWO GREAT MID WALES SEASIDE HOLIDAY PARKS

Glan☆y☆Mor
LEISURE PARK
Clarach Bay
Nr Aberystwyth
SY23 3DT
Tel: 01970 828900

● Free hot showers
● Free washing-up facilities
● Flush toilets ● Electric hook-ups
● Facilities for the disabled
● Launderettes

Cambrian Coast
HOLIDAY PARK
Borth, Ceredigion
SY24 5JU
Tel: 01970 871233

Park facilities include: indoor swimming pools, licensed family clubrooms with nightly entertainment, children's play areas, junior clubrooms, shops, restaurants and take aways.

631 Disserth Caravan Park, Disserth, nr. Llandrindod Wells

Small, family owned riverside park with some caravan holiday homes.

In a secluded situation between the ancient church of Disserth and the Ithon river and sheltered by a wooded cliff formed by river action, yet with handy access to many attractions in mid-Wales, Disserth provides a good base for families with an outdoor disposition. Up to 40 caravans, motorcaravans and tents are taken on one meadow adjacent to the river made attractive with shrubs and trees, a beautiful setting. The pitches are marked and spacing is generous with electricity (10A) for all. The pride of the park is the homely restaurant/coffee shop with an upstairs bar serving real ales (weekends and at peak times). Nicely converted from an old barn, this provides a restful haven after a day out. Reasonably priced meals are served (7.30 - 9.30 pm). The toilet block provides free hot showers (3M, 3F) and, for ladies, a hair drying cubicle and 3 washbasins in cubicles. Laundry room, separate dishwashing sinks with hot water, and chemical disposal. These facilities are perhaps a little rustic for some but are adequate. Recycling bins. Other amenities include a small shop, information kiosk, public phone, private fishing and access to the river with a pebble beach. Bicycle hire 3 miles, riding 6 miles, golf 3 miles. Torch advised. Winter caravan storage. Two holiday homes to let, 17 privately owned. A member of the Countryside Discovery group. Bellamy gold.

Directions: Follow signs for park, either west off A483 at Howey, or east from B4358 around the eastern edge of Newbridge-on-Wye. O.S.GR: SO035585.

Charges 2000:
-- Per unit, incl. 2 adults £6.75 - £7.95; extra adult £1.95; child (3-15 yrs) £1.00; full awning 85p, porch 50p; electricity £1.95; single hiker and tent £4.95.
-- Credit cards accepted.
-- VAT included.
Open:
1 March - 31 October.
Address:
Disserth, Howey, Llandrindod Wells, Powys LD1 6NL.
Tel:
(01597) 860277.
FAX: as phone.
Reservations:
Made with £5 deposit (non-returnable).

Mid Wales

634 Penybont Touring and Camping Park, Bala

Small park close to lake and mountains.

This is a pretty little park with 92 pitches on level grass for caravans, on either flat or sloping grass for tents. Connected by circular gravel roadways, they are intermingled with trees, and tall trees edge the site. Gravelled strips are provided for cars and there are 34 electric hook-ups (16A). The sanitary block comprises roomy, pre-set showers with dividers and curtains, a good supply of well equipped washbasins (H&C) in cubicles with mirror, light and curtain for privacy, extra washbasins and hairdryers. Laundry facilities, in a separate room, and an en-suite unit for disabled visitors, which doubles as a baby room, are operated by key (£4 deposit). Outside a large covered area has a concrete floor and dishwashing sinks, bins and chemical disposal. It is a nice provision. Public phone, barbecues for hire, motorcaravan services and caravan storage. The park has a useful location being the closest park to Bala town, 100 yds from Bala Lake and 3 miles from the Welsh National White Water Centre, with Snowdonia on hand. Fishing 200 yds, boat launching, bicycle hire and golf ½ mile, riding 3 miles.

Directions: Park is ½ mile southeast of Bala village on the B4391. Bala is between Dolgellau and Corwen on the A494. O.S.GR: SH931349.

Charges guide:
-- Per unit incl. 2 persons £8.45 - £9.45; extra person (over 5 yrs), £2.00; awning £1.50 - £1.75; electricity £1.75.
-- VAT included.
-- No credit cards.
Open:
1 April - 31 October.
Address:
Llangynog Road, Bala, Gwynedd LL23 7PH.
Tel:
(01678) 520549.
FAX: (01678) 520006.
Reservations:
Made for exact dates with deposit of £10 per pitch.

636 Pen-y-Garth Caravan and Camping Park, Bala

Tranquil park set in a high valley; an ideal touring base.

An attractively located touring park, Pen-y-Garth has 63 pitches (35 with 10A electrical hook-ups) and two rally fields. Adjacent to the touring area are 54 caravan holiday homes, mainly privately owned (5 for hire). The main sanitary block offers free controllable showers. In addition to this block, there are two further men's and ladies' toilets and showers on payment (10p or 20p). All these facilities have been refurbished and redecorated, although a reader reports that maintenance can be variable in early season. There is a new dishwashing and food preparation room with free hot water, further facilities for dishwashing, a freezer for ice blocks, a laundry and a small games room for children. At reception the well stocked shop (Easter - end Sept) has gas and comprehensive tourist information. There is a good six acre recreation field opposite the park. Watersports are plentiful in this area with the National White Water Centre 5 miles away and Lake Bala and Lake Vyrnwy close. Portmeirion, Snowdonia, Bodnant Gardens and many of those little railways are easy day trips from this park. Fishing, bicycle hire, riding and golf, all within 3 miles. Dogs are accepted by prior arrangement.

Directions: Take B4391 from Bala and in 1 mile turn right uphill at sign. Park is 600 yds on right before road narrows. O.S.GR: SH940349.

Charges 2000:
-- Per unit incl. 2 persons £7.25 - £8.95; extra person (over 5 yrs) £1.75; awning £1.75; electricity £1.75.
-- Credit cards accepted.
Open:
1 March - 31 October.
Address:
Bala, Gwynedd LL23 7ES.
Tel:
(01678) 520485.
FAX: (01678) 520401.
E-mail: stay@ penygarth.co.uk.
Reservations:
Made with 25% deposit (min. 3 nights at B.Hs).

635 Barcdy Caravan and Camping Park, Talsarnau, nr. Harlech

Rurally situated park with good facilities and marvellous views.

Barcdy is partly in a sheltered vale, partly on a plateau top and partly in open fields edged by woods, with fells to the rear and views across the Lleyn peninsula in one direction and towards the Snowdon range in another. The Roberts family opened to their first visitors over 60 years ago, and they still welcome them today. The park provides level or sloping grass pitches, either secluded in the valley or enjoying the view from the plateau or the lower field. The 108 pitches include 38 for touring vans and 40 for tents, with or without 10A electricity (50 electricity points), plus 30 holiday homes (3 for hire). There are two toilet blocks, the one at the top of the valley open in high season only. Facilities include large, comfortable showers (with curtain and stool), that open to the outside except for one in each male and female sections. Hot water is free to the washbasins and dishwashing sinks, metered to the showers (20p). There is an excellent chemical disposal point. All is nicely built in the local stone. Shop (Spr. B.H, then mid July-end Aug) for essentials including gas. The grounds of the farm include 28 acres of open fields and oak woods and further up the hills are the two Tecwyn lakes for fishing or just to relax by and enjoy the views. Riding 4 miles, golf 4 or 6 miles. Harlech beach and the castle are only 4 miles, the Italianate village of Portmeirion is nearby. No dogs are accepted. A member of the Countryside Discovery group.

Directions: Park is just off the A496 between villages of Llandecwyn and Talsarnau, 4 miles north of Harlech. O.S.GR: SH622371.

Charges 2000:
-- Per unit incl. 2 persons £8.50 - £10.00; extra adult £3.00; child (up to 16 yrs) £1.00; awning free; electricity (10A) £1.95.
-- Credit cards accepted.
Open:
Easter - 31 October.
Address:
Talsarnau, nr. Harlech, Gwynedd LL47 6YG.
Tel:
(01766) 770736.
FAX: as phone.
E-mail: anwen@ barcdy.idps.co.uk.
Reservations:
Contact park.

637 Hendre Mynach Touring Caravan and Camping Park, Llanaber,

True family park, near Barmouth, between mountains and beach.

A neat and tidy park, colourful flowers and top rate facilities make an instant impression on arrival down the steep entrance to this park (help is available to get out if you are worried). There are two toilet blocks, one modern and one traditional, but both offering excellent facilities including spacious showers (20p) and washbasins in cubicles in the new block. Extra showers are provided in mobile units which are used in peak times and, although this is a large park, the facilities should cope well even when it is full. The 220 pitches are allocated in various areas, with substantial tenting areas identified. Twenty gravel hardstandings are available and around the park there are 120 electricity hook-ups (10A) and ample water points. An on-site shop is well stocked and incorporates a snack bar and takeaway (Easter - 1 Nov; 08.30 - 21.00 hrs. in peak times, less at quieter times). The quaint old seaside and fishing town of Barmouth is just ¾ mile away - a 15-20 minute walk along the prom. Here you will find 'everything'. The local pub offers a courtesy bus service from the park (19.30-22.00) and serves bar snacks, etc. The beach is only 100 yards away but a railway line runs between the park and the beach. This can be crossed at any of three points by pedestrian operated gates and this could be a worry for those with young children. Snowdonia National Park and mountain railway, the famous Ffestiniog railway, castles and lakes everywhere provide plenty to see and do - a classic park in a classic area.

Directions: Park is off the A496 road north of Barmouth in village of Llanaber with entrance down a steep drive. O.S.GR: SH608168.

Charges 2000:
-- Per caravan or large motorcaravan incl. 2 persons £8.00 - £13.00, 3 or 4 persons £10.00 - £14.50; electricity (10A) £2.00; tent or caravanette incl. 2 persons £7.00 - £10.00, 3 or 4 persons £8.00 - £12.00; extra adult £3.00; child (2-15 yrs) £1.00; first dog free, extra dog 50p.
-- Credit cards accepted.
Open:
All year excl. 10 Jan - 28 Feb.
Address:
Llanaber, Barmouth, Gwynedd LL42 1YR.
Tel:
(01341) 280262.
FAX: (01341) 280586.
E-mail: mynach@lineone.net.
Reservations:
Made with £20 deposit and £1.50 booking fee.

633 Daisy Bank Touring Caravan Park, Churchstoke

Pretty, tranquil adults only park in Camlad Valley with panoramic views, ideal base for walkers.

Attractively landscaped with 'old English' flower beds and many different trees and shrubs, this small park has been carefully developed by its previous owners (it was taken over by its present owners in August 2000). The Welsh hills to the north and the Shropshire hills to the south overlook the two fields of 20 pitches each. The field nearer to the road (perhaps a little noisy) is slightly sloping but there are hardstandings for motorcaravans, while the second field is more level. All pitches have 16A electricity, water and waste water drainage and TV hook up. The heated toilet block, cheerful with stencils, plants and music, provides roomy free showers, vanity style washbasins with free hot water and good mirrors. Covered washing up sinks (H&C) are at rear of block, but there are no laundry facilities (launderette at Churchstoke, 2 miles). There is a carefully screened refuse point with chemical disposal. Other amenities include brick built barbecues, a dog walk plus a small area for dogs to run free and a small putting green (free loan of clubs and balls). With many walks in the area, including Offa's Dyke, a series of walk leaflets is available centred on Bishop's Castle 3 miles away. Tourist information is provided and a public phone. Supermarket 2 miles and many eating places near. Bicycle hire, riding or fishing 3 miles. The owners will site your van for you and there is a late arrivals area with hook-up. A security bar at the entrance has to be lifted for motorcaravans. Gas is stocked. Winter caravan storage. Although technically in Wales, the park is 500 yds from the Shropshire border, an area rich in history.

Directions: Site is by the A489 road 2 miles east of Churchstoke in the direction of Craven Arms. O.S.GR: SO303929.

Charges 2000:
-- Per unit incl. 2 adults £7.50; extra person £1.50; awning £1.00; porch awning 50p; dog 50p; electricity £1.50 - £1.75; TV aerial hook-up free.
-- Adult only park.
-- No credit cards.
Open:
All year.
Address:
Churchstoke, Montgomeryshire, Powys SY15 6EB.
Tel:
(01588) 620471.
Reservations:
Contact park.

North Wales

Tourism information for North Wales may also be obtained from:

North Wales Tourism, 77 Conwy Road, Colwyn Bay LL29 7LN
Tel: 01492 531731 Fax: 01492 530059 E-mail: croeso@nwt.co.uk www.nwt.co.uk

658 Camping and Caravanning Club Site Llanystumdwy, Criccieth

Small, well maintained park with good facilities, overlooking mountains and sea.

One of the oldest Camping and Caravanning Club sites, Llanystumdwy is on sloping grass, but the wardens are very helpful and know their site and can advise on the most suitable pitch and even have a supply of chocks. There are 60 pitches in total (20 ft. spacing), 45 with 10A electricity, spaced over two hedged fields with mainly caravans in the top field, motorhomes and tents lower down. A purpose built toilet block to one side provides excellent, full facilities for the disabled including access ramp. Tiled and nicely finished with green fittings, it has free hot water (you can set your own temperature in the showers), one washbasin each in a cubicle for male and female and extra large sinks. Facilities for babies, hairdryers and laundry (taps with fitting for disabled people). Chemical disposal point, enclosed with bolt, and neat, fenced refuse points located about the park. Gas is available. A small dog walk is provided but main exercising should be off the park. Public telephone. A little library with a supply of tourist information is next to the small reception. A shop and pub are in the village and a bus leaves each hour from outside the site to Pwllheli or Porthmadog. This is a good base from which to explore the Lleyn peninsula or Snowdonia National Park. Portmeirion with its Italianate village is near. Riding or fishing ½ mile, golf 2½ miles.

Charges 2000:
-- Per adult £3.75 - £5.30; child (6-18 yrs) £1.65; non-member pitch fee £4.30; electricity £1.60 - £2.35.
-- VAT included.
-- Credit cards accepted.
Open:
April - October.
Address:
C&C Club Site, Tyddyn Sianel, Llanystumdwy, Criccieth, Gwynedd LL52 0LS.
Tel:
(01766) 522855.
(no calls after 8 pm).
Reservations:
Necessary and made with deposit - contact the wardens.

Directions: Follow the A497 from Criccieth west and take the second right to Llanystumdwy. Site is on the right. O.S.GR: SH469384.

659 Forestry Commission Caravan and Camping Site, Beddgelert

Well equipped Forestry Commission site in the heart of Snowdonia.

Set in a marvellous, natural, wooded environment on the slopes of Snowdon with abundant fauna and flora, tumbling streams and always something to watch from the cheeky squirrels to the smallest bird in Britain, this site is well equipped and well managed. Two fully equipped sanitary blocks clad in natural wood provide large, free hot showers (with good dry areas), washbasins and washing up sinks (both with H&C). There is laundry equipment in one block. A small unit provides extra washbasins and toilets in peak season and there is a toilet and washbasin for disabled visitors. The site provides 280 pitches - tents in a semi-wooded field area and caravans with numbered hardstandings amongst the trees with 10A electricity. Tents may pitch where they like in their areas leaving 6 m. between units. Metal tent pegs may be best (available from shop). There are plenty of water points, central refuse areas and two chemical disposal points are provided together with a motorcaravan emptying point. Reception is central, as is a well provisioned shop. Free maps of the forest walks are provided in reception and orienteering and fishing possible. A bus service stops at the top of the entrance lane (two hourly for Caernarfon and Porthmadog). A pub is within walking distance (¾ mile) and other eating places nearby. Bicycle hire within 500 yards in the forest. There is a well equipped children's adventure playground, but we wonder if it is used considering what nature has provided - water, trees, rocks, etc!

Charges 2000:
-- Per adult £3.40 - £4.60; child (5-14 yrs) £1.50 - £2.10; extra car, trailer or pup tent £2.50; electricity £2.10 - £2.30.
-- Less 20% all year for disabled guests and outside 7/7-28/8 for senior citizens.
-- Credit cards accepted.
Open:
All year.
Address:
Beddgelert Campsite, Beddgelert, Gwynedd LL55 4UU.
Tel:
(01766) 890288.
Reservations:
Necessary for B.Hs and peak times (min. 3 nights with £30 deposit).
Contact (at all times): Forest Holidays, Forestry Commission, 231 Corstorphine Road, Edinburgh EH12 7AT. Tel: (0131) 314 6505. E-mail: feholidays@ forestry.gov.uk.

Directions: Site is clearly signed to the left 1 mile north of Beddgelert on A4085 Caernarfon road. O.S.GR: SH578490.

660 Bryn Gloch Caravan and Camping Park, Betws Garmon

Well run and family owned touring park in the impressive Snowdonia area.

Bryn Gloch is a neat, well kept and quiet country park taking some 160 units on five flat, wide meadows, with 12 caravan holiday homes. There are tarmac roads and free areas are allowed in the middle for play. With 150 electrical connections (10A) available, there are 8 all weather pitches, 6 'super' pitches and 8 serviced pitches (shared). The sanitary arrangements have been extensively upgraded and the two original blocks are now of very commendable standard. A further, purpose built shower and toilet block has been added. The far field has been equipped with a 'portacabin' style unit containing all facilities, for use in peak season. There is free hot water in the washbasins (some private cabins) and in the pre-set showers and indoor washing-up sinks. An excellent building houses a family bathroom (£1 for hot water), baby changing room and complete facilities for visitors with disabilities (with coded access). Chemical disposal point. Fishing is possible on the river bordering the park with a barbecue and picnic area, adventure play area and field for ball games. Shop (1/3-30/10). A well equipped laundry and separate drying room, TV and games rooms with pool tables, amusement machines and tourist information are located in one complex by the reception; this building also houses an extra shower and toilet per sex. Other amenities include minigolf, a public phone and a car wash and motorcaravan service point. Riding 2½ miles, bicycle hire or golf 5 miles, as is Caernarfon with its famous castle. Bungalow and bunk type self catering accommodation can be rented.

Directions: Park is just beyond Waunfawr, 4½ miles southeast of Caernarfon on A4085 towards Beddgelert. Watch for signs and park entrance is opposite St Garmon church. O.S.GR: SH538578.

Charges 2000:
-- Per unit incl. 2 persons £9.00 (caravans over 18 ft. plus £1); extra adult £2.00; child (3-16 yrs) £1.50; awning or pup tent £1.50; dog 50p; electricity £2.50; 'super' pitch incl. electricity, etc. plus £5.50.
-- VAT included.
-- Credit cards accepted.
Open:
All year, limited facilities 1 Nov - 1 March.
Address:
Betws Garmon,
nr. Caernarfon,
Gwynedd LL54 7YY.
Tel:
(01286) 650216.
FAX: (01286) 650591.
E-mail: eurig@
easynet.co.uk.
Reservations:
Necessary for B.Hs. (min. 3 nights) with payment in full; other times in deposit of first night's fee.

661 Cadnant Valley Caravan Park, Caernarfon

Pretty town park 10 minutes walk from Caernarfon centre.

This is an older style, town centre park where the fairly steep road past reception leads you to a hidden, tree lined valley area with a little stream, complete with two bridges, which once fed the moat of the historic Caernarfon Castle. The shower and toilet blocks (with free hot water), whilst somewhat dated, are satisfactory and to one side of the site, which has 69 marked, level pitches (35 with 16A electricity and 5 hardstandings). You can choose a more secluded area across the stream, a more open, central grass area or a terraced pitch, depending on your unit. Cadnant's natural environment has been enhanced with plants, shrubs, picnic tables and stepping stone paths; even the play area blends in and provides solid, rustic equipment on safety matting. Fully equipped laundry room, under cover dishwashing (with H&C) and chemical disposal. Reception keeps gas and tourist information. A small supermarket is 100 yards but the main shops and restaurants are only a 5-6 minute walk and Caernarfon's leisure centre with swimming pool is 400 yds. Fishing 1 mile, riding and golf 2 miles, bicycle hire and boat launching ½ mile. Easily accessible by public transport are Bangor, Llanberis/Snowdon and Porthmadog. It is nice to find such a site within town centre walking distance, never mind the added attractions of this historic area of Wales. The park is, however, within the town and in an urban area so there may be odd extra noise. Dogs are welcome on a lead, small dog area provided.

Directions: Park is on A4086 Llanberis road. From town centre watch carefully for park entrance after second roundabout, opposite a school and just before the fire station. O.S.GR: SH488628.

Charges 2000:
-- Per unit incl. 2 persons £7.00 - £9.00, 1 person £5.50 - £7.50; 2-man tent and car £6.00 - £8.00; backpacker (no car) £4.00 - £5.00; extra adult £1.50; child (4-15 yrs) £1.00; dog or extra car 50p; electricity £2.00.
-- Credit cards accepted.
Open:
14 March - 31 October.
Address:
Llanberis Road,
Caernarfon,
Gwynedd LL55 2DF.
Tel:
(01286) 673196.
E-mail: camping@
cadnantvalley.co.uk.
Reservations:
Advised for high season and made with £10 deposit.

North Wales

664 Home Farm Caravan Park, Marianglas, Anglesey

Good quality site with excellent facilities for children.

A tarmac drive through an open field leads to this neatly laid out park, with caravan holiday homes to one side. Nestling below what was once a Celtic hill fort, later decimated as a quarry, it is edged with mature trees and farmland. There is a circular, tarmac access road for the 61 well spaced and numbered pitches, which include 9 fully serviced with electricity, water and waste water and a further 19 with electricity and water, All of these have hardstanding with 16A electricity; other pitches all have 10A supply. On neatly cut grass, some areas are slightly sloping, and there is a separate area for tents. Two purpose built toilet blocks, one part of the reception building, are of the same design, fully tiled and can be heated. They provide excellent roomy showers with curtains, vanity style washbasins (H&C), free hairdryer, soap and hand dryer, en-suite provision for people with disabilities (with key) and an excellent small bathroom for children with baby bath and curtain for privacy, a laundry room and good washing up facilities. Neat refuse, water and waste points, chemical disposal, motorcaravan point, and a public telephone complete the facilities. Reception provides basic essentials, gas and some caravan accessories, alongside tourist information. The 'piece de resistance' of this park must be the children's indoor play area, large super adventure play equipment, complete with tunnels, bridges on safe rubber matting, not to mention an outside fenced play area. TV and a pool table complete the provision, although there are fields available for sports, football, etc. and walking. Fishing or golf 2 miles, riding 8 miles. Various beaches, sandy or rocky, are within a mile. A member of the Best of British group. Bellamy silver.

Charges 2000:
-- Per unit incl. 2 persons £7.50 - £10.25, large or trailer tent £7.50 - £11.75; extra person (over 5 yrs) £1.50; extra car or boat £1.50 - £2.00; awning or extra pup tent £1.50; electricity £2.00; fully serviced pitch plus £2.50 - £3.50; dog free.
-- Credit cards accepted.
Open:
April - October.
Address:
Marianglas,
Isle of Anglesey,
North Wales LL73 8PH.
Tel:
(01248) 410614.
FAX: (01248) 410900.
E-mail: enq@homefarm-anglesey.co.uk.
Reservations:
Essential for peak season (min. 3 days at B.Hs) and made with £20 deposit.

Directions: From the Britannia Bridge take second exit left signed Benllech and Amlwch on the A5025. Two miles after Benllech keep left at roundabout and park entrance is approx. 300 yards on the left beyond church. O.S.GR: SH498850.

669 Bron-Y-Wendon Touring Caravan Park, Llanddulas, Colwyn Bay

Mature, 'non-seaside' type of park beside the sea.

Bron-Y-Wendon is right by the sea between Abergele and Colwyn Bay on the beautiful North Wales coast road. However, this is a quiet park which, by its own admission, is not really geared up for the family unit - there is no children's playground here, although there is a games room with table tennis and a separate TV room. On the day we visited there was wall-to-wall blue sky, a slight breeze and a fantastic blue sea - quite something. The site is manicured to the highest standards. Two sanitary blocks, both with heating, provide excellent facilities with men's and women's shower rooms separate from the toilets and washbasins. There are good facilities for disabled visitors, chemical disposal and a laundry with washing machines and dryers. The park caters for a large number of seasonal caravans on pitches with gravel bases which are kept very tidy. There are a further 65 grass based touring pitches, all with electrical hook ups (16A) and tarmac access roads. All pitches have coastal views and the sea and beach are just a short walk away. A mobile shop visits the park daily and gas is available on site. Very close by is the village of Llanddulas which has shops and several good pubs. Colwyn Bay, Conwy, Anglesey, Llandudno, Snowdonia and Chester are all within easy reach of the park, so there is lots to do. Having said how peaceful and quiet everything is (particularly for a seaside park in this area), there could be a little road noise from the adjacent A55 and during our visit a small train passed on the tracks between the park and the sea (just a few yards) and at night with little else going on it could be noticeable.

Charges 2000:
-- Per pitch £5.00 - £7.00; person £1.50; child (2-12 yrs) £1.00; awning £2.00; electricity (16A) £2.00.
-- VAT included.
-- Credit cards accepted.
Open:
21 March - 30 October.
Address:
Wern Road,
Llanddulas,
Colwyn Bay
LL22 8HG.
Tel:
(01492) 512903.
FAX: as phone.
E-mail:
bron-y-wendon@north-water-holidays.co.uk.
Reservations:
Made with £5 deposit; contact park.

Directions: From A55 Chester - Conwy road turn at Llanddulas junction (A547). Turn right opposite Shell garage and park is approx. ¼ mile, signed on coast side of the road. O.S.GR: SH903785.

665 Hunter's Hamlet Touring Caravan Park, nr. Abergele

Small, family owned, quality park with beautiful rural views (no tents).

The design, layout and facilities of this purpose built site are of a very high standard and the Hunter family are justifiably proud of the park, which is licensed for all units except tents (trailer tents allowed). On a gently sloping hillside providing panoramic views, one area provides 15 well spaced pitches with hard-standing and 10A electricity hook-ups, with access from a circular, hardcore road. A new area has been developed next to this of a similar design but with 8 pitches fully serviced by new tourer `superpitches' (water, waste water, sewerage, TV and electricity connections). Shrubs and bushes at various stages of growth enhance both areas. An excellent purpose built, heated sanitary block has fully tiled facilities including showers en-suite with toilets for both sexes, vanity style wash-basins and hairdryers. There are sinks for laundry and dishwashing (H&C), washing machine and dryer, iron and board, freezer and fridge. A family bath-room (metered) has been added, there are separate toilet and shower facilities for visitors with disabilities, plus chemical disposal and refuse points. A natural play area incorporating rustic adventure equipment set amongst mature beech trees with a small bubbling stream (supervised by the ducks) is a children's paradise. Table tennis and pool in a barn. Milk and papers can be ordered and the Hunters will do their best to meet your needs, even to survival rations! Public telephone. Only two dogs per unit allowed (not certain breeds in July/Aug. and B.Hs). Self catering flat available. All year caravan storage. Fishing or golf 2 miles, riding 10 miles. The park is well situated to tour Snowdonia and Anglesey and is within easy reach of Llandudno and Rhyl.

Charges 2001:
-- Per unit incl. 2 adults and 2 children: basic pitch £9.00 - £11.00, 'superpitch' (fully incl.) £16.00 - £19.00; extra person £2.00; awning £2.00; extra car £2.00; electricity (10A) £2.00.
-- Less £5 on weekly bookings.
-- Aug. B.H, plus £1.00.
-- Credit cards accepted.
Open:
21 March - 31 October.
Address:
Sirior Goch Farm, Betws-yn-Rhos, Abergele, LL22 8PL.
Tel:
(01745) 832237. FAX: as phone.
Reservations:
Made with £3 per night deposit (min. £10). B.H. bookings min. 4 nights.

Directions: From Abergele take A548 south for 2¾ miles; turn onto B5381 in direction of Betws-yn-Rhos and park is on left after ½ mile. To date there are no local authority caravan signs so watch carefully for the farm after turning - it can be identified by an artistically painted sign with the house and farm name: 'Sirior Goch Farm' and Hunter's Hamlet. O.S.GR: SH929736.

670 Ty Ucha Caravan Park, Llangollen

Quiet, family owned park in the Vale of Llangollen, for caravans and motorhomes only.

Only a mile from Llangollen, world famous for the Eisteddfod, Ty Ucha has a rather dramatic setting, nestling under its own mountain and with views across the valley to craggy Dinas Bran castle. It is a neat, ordered park, carefully managed by the owners, providing 40 pitches (30 with 10A electrical hook-up) well spaced round a large, grassy field with an open centre for a play area and a small paddock area. One side slopes gently and is bounded by a stream and wood. A path leads from here for various mountain walks, depending on your energy and ability. The single toilet block, although of 'portacabin' style, is clean and well maintained and can be heated. It provides two metered showers for each sex (a little cramped), small washbasins with free hot water, shelf and mirror, toilets and chemical disposal. A dishwashing sink with cold water is outside. There are no laundry facilities but there is a launderette in Llangollen. Gas is available. Games room with table tennis. Because of overhead cables, kite flying is forbidden; no bike riding either. The paddock area provides for those who prefer to be without the company of children or dogs. Late arrivals area. There is an hotel ½ mile away where reasonably priced meals are available. Fishing 1 mile, golf ½ mile. The Eisteddfod is an international festival of music and dance held for six days starting on the first Tuesday of the first full week in July every year - a very busy time for the area.

Charges 2001:
-- Per caravan incl. 2 persons £7.00, motor-caravan £6.50; extra person £1.00; awning (environmental ground-sheets) 50p - £1.00; electricity £2.00.
-- Reductions for OAPs for weekly stays.
-- No credit cards.
Open:
Easter - October.
Address:
Maesmawr Road, Llangollen, Denbighshire LL20 7PP.
Tel:
(01978) 860677.
Reservations:
Necessary for B.Hs. and Eisteddfod and made with £10 deposit; 3 days min. at B.H.s.

Directions: Park is signed off A5 road, 1 mile east of Llangollen (250 yds). O.S.GR: SJ228411.

Alan Rogers' Discount

Less 50p per unit, per night

North Wales

667 The Plassey Touring and Leisure Park, Eyton, nr. Wrexham

Spacious, rural 250-acre park in the Dee Valley, offering many activities.

The Plassey is not just a touring park but is also a leisure and craft centre with a friendly, busy atmosphere and pleasant environment. The Edwardian farm buildings have been tastefully converted to provide a restaurant, coffee shop, health, beauty and hair studio, small garden centre and 16 different craft and retail units, open all year to the public. Other amenities include a 9 hole golf course, fishing pools and countryside footpaths. Unusually there is also a small brewery on site, producing its own unique Plassey Bitter! The park itself is spacious with pitches around the outer edges of a series of fields forming circles. There are 120 pitches with electrical connections (16A) and 30 new serviced pitches (water, waste water. 16A electricity, lighting), plus two fields of seasonal caravans which will put pressure on the facilities. The original toilet facilities beside the entrance and under the clubhouse have been refurbished to a good standard. These are supplemented by a new heated block in the top field area with showers, toilets, a room for disabled visitors or families, individual washbasins cubicles, dishwashing and chemical disposal. There is a laundry and motorcaravan service point. The Tree Tops clubhouse, serving Plassey Bitter, overlooks the park and has a children's room (open March - Oct). A good adventure playground beside a small wood has equipment for smaller children on bark chippings (note: bicycles, skateboards or footballs are not allowed on the site). Badminton courts including an indoor one can be booked and there is an indoor, heated swimming pool with sun-bed and sauna (May - Sept, limited hours mid-week, 80p per hour). Shop (all season) and gas. Winter caravan storage. Riding or bicycle hire 5 miles. There is much to do and to look at in a rural setting at the Plassey but it is probably best enjoyed mid-week and avoiding the busy Bank Holidays. Certainly for peace and quiet, you should try and pitch away from reception, the clubhouse and arcade games.

Directions: Follow brown and cream signs (for The Plassey) from the A483 Chester - Oswestry bypass onto the B5426 and park is 2½ miles. Also signed from the A528 Marchwiel - Overton road. O.S.GR: SJ349452.

Charges 2000:
-- Per unit incl. 2 adults, 2 children, electricity and club membership £11.00 - £13.50; serviced pitch £3.00; extra person, dog or extra car £1.50; awning or pup tent £2.00.
-- Includes club membership, coarse fishing, badminton and table tennis (own racquets and bats required).
-- B.H. supplement £1 per night.
-- VAT included.
-- Credit cards accepted.

Open:
5 March - 7 November.

Address:
Eyton,
Wrexham LL13 0SP.

Tel:
(01978) 780277.
FAX: (01978) 780019.
E-mail: jbrookshaw
@aol.com.

Reservations:
Necessary for weekends, B.Hs and July/Aug. and made with £20 deposit.

Alan Rogers' Discount

Less 50p per unit, per night

668 James' Caravan Park, Ruabon, nr. Wrexham

All year site, easily accessible and with good facilities.

Open all year, this park has a heated toilet block and attractive, park-like surroundings with mature trees and neat, short grass. However, edged by two main roads it is subject to some road noise. The old farm buildings and owner's collection of original farm machinery, carefully restored and maintained, add interest to the park. The heated toilet block offers roomy showers (20p) with a useful rail to help those of advancing age with feet washing, curtain and shelf, vanity style washbasins with good mirrors and a hairdryer for ladies (20p). En-suite facilities for visitors with disabilities complete with special 'clos o mat' toilet! The park has over 40 pitches, some level and some on a slope, with informal siting giving either a view or shade. Electricity (6A) is available all over, although a long lead may be needed. Tourist information, free freezer for ice packs and a telephone are in the foyer of the toilet block. Chemical disposal and motor-caravan service point. Gas available. The village is a 10 minute walk with a Spar shop, fish and chips, a launderette and four pubs. Golf 3 miles. This is a useful park with easy access from the A483 Wrexham - Oswestry road.

Directions: Park is at junction of A483/A539 Llangollen road and is accessible from the west-bound A539. O.S.GR: SJ302434.

Charges 2000:
-- Per unit incl. 2 persons £7.00; extra person £1.00; awning £2.00; extra car £1.00; dog 50p; electricity £2.00.
-- No credit cards.

Open:
All year.

Address:
Ruabon,
Wrexham LL14 6DW.

Tel:
(01978) 820148.
FAX: as phone.
E-Mail: ray@carastay.
demon.co.uk.

Reservations:
Contact park for details.

Scottish Tourist Board

23 Ravelston Terrace, Edinburgh EH4 3TP
Tel: (0131) 332 2433 Fax: (0131) 315 4545
E-mail: inf@stb.gov.uk Internet: http://www.visitscotland.com

We have used the following Regional Tourist Areas to list our parks:
1. Scottish Lowlands   2. Heart of Scotland
3. Grampian   4. Highlands and Islands

Scotland provides superb opportunities to enjoy wild and grand scenery. It also offers towns and cities with a rich cultural life and over the centuries has had a disproportionately large impact on the world with many of its philosophers, scientists and inventors being responsible for the ideas on which we base our understanding of the world.

The area we identify as the **Scottish Lowlands** or Southern Scotland, covers Dumfries and Galloway, the Scottish Borders, Edinburgh and Lothians, Greater Glasgow and the Clyde valley. In Dumfries and Galloway lonely hills roll down to pastures and dark woods which give way to rich farmlands and a sunny south facing coast. The Borders is an area of tranquil villages, bustling textile towns and a wild coastline running north from Berwick-upon-Tweed. There are magnificent historic houses, great Border abbeys, working woollen mills and craft workshops. Sir Walter Scott, the famous Scottish writer, lived at Abbotsford near Melrose and is buried at Dryburgh Abbey. The Lothians, bordered by the sea waters of the Firth of Forth to the unspoiled Pentland Hills, has a beautiful coastline and rich countryside. Edinburgh is dealt with elsewhere as is Glasgow. Paisley is known for the Paisley shawl and Lanark for the enlightened industrialist Robert Owen whose Utopian ideas on workers welfare in his textile mills.

Heart of Scotland covering Loch Lomond, Stirling and the Trossachs, Perthshire, Angus, Dundee and the Kingdom of Fife. Here the Lowlands meet the mountains of the north and west and in old days all routes led to Stirling. Because of its strategic position whoever held Stirling Castle controlled the Scottish nation. The Trossachs with their heather-clad hills are the home of Rob Roy the folk hero. Fife boasts two ancient 'capitals'. Dunfermline, the seat of early Celtic kings and the final resting place of Robert the Bruce and St Andrews, the ecclesiastical capital, now a university town and the 'Home of Golf'.

Grampian includes the Grampian Highlands, Aberdeen and the North East Coast and is probably best known for Royal Deeside where Prince Albert built Balmoral Castle as a summer home for Queen Victoria and the Malt Whisky Trail. This is a signed route featuring seven whisky distilleries, each with excellent interpretation facilities for visitors.

The **Highlands and Islands** one of the last wildernesses in Europe, from the soaring beauty of Glencoe to the to the idyllic charm of the Isles, and from the crashing waves of the northern coastline to the silence of the windswept moors. Home to the Loch Ness Monster and the famous Fort William to Mallaig railway, one of the greatest railway journeys in the world.

701 Camping and Caravanning Club Site Culzean Castle, Maybole

Quiet family Club site with fantastic views, also taking non members.

Culzean Castle (pronounced Kullayne), with its grounds and 17 miles of footpaths, is next door to the Club site and visitors are given a pass to walk in the grounds (when open). The 18th century, cliff top castle is built on the site of a former ancient castle and its armoury exhibition is superb. Besides the woodland walks, adventure playground, deer park and aviary, there are three miles of rocky shore, small sandy beaches and stunning views of the Firth of Clyde. Events are staged at the castle over the season, including children's weeks, sheep-dog trials, bands, battle re-enactments and craft fairs. The campsite has 90 pitches, some level others slightly sloping, and 60 have electricity (10A). A few level pitches are suitable for motorcaravans and 20 pitches have hardstanding. American style motorhomes (less than 27 ft. only) should make prior arrangements. A small shop has very basic provisions. The very clean toilet blocks can be heated and provide washbasins (in cubicles and vanity style), free showers, dishwashing sinks with hot water, chemical disposal and a well equipped laundry with lines. A unit for disabled visitors is excellent. Maybole with shops, etc. is only 4 miles. Buses pass the gate. Golf or bicycle hire 4 miles, riding 2 miles, fishing 8 miles.

Charges 2000:
-- Per adult £3.75 - £5.30; child (6-18 yrs) £1.65; non-member pitch fee £4.30; electricity £1.60 - £2.35.
-- VAT included.
-- Credit cards accepted.
Open:
March - October.
Address:
Maybole, Strathclyde KA19 8JK.
Tel:
(01655) 760627, (no calls after 8 pm).
Reservations:
Advised for high season and made with deposit; contact the wardens.

Directions: From Maybole follow signs for Culzean Castle and Country Park, turning in town on B7023 which runs into the A719. Country Park entrance is clearly signed on right after 3¾ miles; entrance to caravan park is on the right in Country Park drive. O.S.GR: NS247103.

Lowlands

690 Seaward Caravan Park, Dhoon Bay, Kirkcudbright

Quality park in idyllic location overlooking Kirkcudbright Bay.

Seaward Caravan Park is little sister to the much larger Brighouse Bay Holiday Park 3½ miles away. Set in an idyllic location overlooking the bay, this park is suitable for all units. The terrain is slightly undulating, but most of the numbered pitches are flat and a good size. There are 35 pitches (18 hardstandings) designated for caravans and motorcaravans, a further 14 for tents, and 43 caravan holiday homes for hire. Electric hook-ups (16A) are on 32 of the touring pitches, 12 also serviced with water tap, waste water disposal, and TV socket. The principal toilet block is to the rear of the park and comprises toilets, open style washbasins (H&C), showers (with curtain and dressing area), ample mirrors, hooks, hand and hair dryers, and sockets. The laundry has washing machines, tumble dryer, spin-dryer, irons and deep sinks, and a dishwashing room with three sinks (H&C). Chemical disposal is in an enclosed section adjoining the building. Close by are two rooms with en-suite facilities suitable for campers with disabilities. A baby room and two more en-suite cubicles are being built. There is no motorcaravan service point but the manager can lift a manhole cover to empty waste water tanks. A central play area has a bark surface, outdoor chess, rocking horse, table tennis and picnic tables. Next to reception is an unsupervised heated outdoor swimming pool with sunbathing area. The reception/shop stocks a variety of provisions, books, gifts, gas, and tourist information. The remainder of this modern building features more toilets and excellent games room on the ground level, with a well stocked bar and TV/family room on the first floor. A toilet for wheelchair users is on both levels. Visitors can play golf on the park's par 3 nine-hole course (£3 per round) or watch others play while walking the dog around its perimeter. Facilities at Brighouse Bay Holiday Park are free to all campers. Beach and sea angling nearby, and Kirkcudbright is just 2½ miles away. This is a quiet park with excellent views ideally suited for relaxing or for touring the region.

Directions: Follow international camping signs from Kirkcudbright on A711. O.S.GR: NX680510.

Charges 2000:
-- Per unit incl. 2 adults £8.50 - £11.25; extra adult £1.60 - £1.70; child (4-15 yrs) £1.20 - £1.30; awning £1.70 - £1.80; extra car, porch awning or small tent £1.00; electricity £2.25 - £2.75; electric/TV aerial £2.85 - £3.20; dog £1.00.
-- Less 5-10% for bookings (not valid with some other discount schemes).
-- VAT included.
Open:
1 April - 31 October.
Address:
Dhoon Bay, Kirkcudbright, DG6 4TJ.
Tel:
(01557) 331079.
E-mail: info@ seaward-park.co.uk
Reservations:
Made with deposit of £25 per week booked, balance on arrival.

695 Brighouse Bay Holiday Park, Borgue, Kirkcudbright

Seaside park with exceptional all weather facilities.

Hidden away within 1,200 exclusive acres, on a quiet, unspoilt peninsula, this spacious family park is only some 200 yards through bluebell woods from a lovely sheltered bay. It has 120 self-contained holiday caravans of which about 30 are let. Over 90% of the 120 touring caravan pitches have electricity (16A), with hardstanding and some with water, drainage and TV aerial. The three tenting areas are on fairly flat, undulating ground and some pitches have electricity. The well maintained main toilet block is large with washbasins with shelf and free hot showers. It also has 10 unisex cabins with shower, basin and WC, and 12 with washbasin and WC, a launderette and covered dishwashing sinks. A second, excellent block next to the tent areas has en-suite shower rooms (one for disabled people) and bathroom, separate washing cubicles, free hot showers, baby room, laundry sinks, and covered dishwashing sinks. One section is heated in winter. Chemical disposal, motorcaravan service point and gas supplies. Leisure facilities include a golf and leisure club with 16.5 m. pool, water features, jacuzzi, steam room, fitness room, sun-bed, games room (all on payment), golf driving range and clubhouse bar and bistro. The 18 hole golf course extends onto the headland with superb views over the Irish Sea to the Isle of Man and Cumbria. These facilities are also open all year. The BHS approved pony trekking centre (April - Oct) offers slow hacks for the nervous or inexperienced or gallops on the beach for the more experienced. Other amenities include mountain bike hire, quad bikes, boating pond, 10 pin bowling, playgrounds, putting, new nature trails, coarse fishing ponds, sea angling and an all-tide slipway. Cottages, pine lodges, chalets and caravans to rent all year. Supermarket and takeaway. Caravan storage. A well run park of high standard. A member of the Best of British group. Bellamy gold.

Directions: From Kirkcudbright turn south off A755 onto B727 (to Borgue); after 4 miles Brighouse Bay is signed to south. From west take B727 to Borgue and beyond, turning south as above. Or follow Brighouse Bay signs off A75 just east of Gatehouse of Fleet. O.S.GR: NX630455.

Charges 2000:
-- Per unit incl. 2 persons £9.50 - £12.75; extra adult £2.00 - £2.20; child (4-15 yrs) £1.25 - £1.50; awning £1.00 - £2.00; electricity £2.75 - £2.25; electricity and TV hook-up £3.20 - £2.85; fully serviced pitch £4.20 - £3.95; dog £1.00.
-- Winter rate: from £12.50 incl. all pitch fees.
-- Up to 10% reduction for weekly bookings.
-- Credit cards accepted.
-- VAT included.
Open:
All year.
Address:
Brighouse Bay, Borgue, Kirkcudbright, Dumfries and Galloway DG6 4TS.
Tel:
(01557) 870267.
FAX: (01557) 870319.
E-mail: arogers@ brighouse-bay.co.uk
Reservations:
Made with £25 deposit.

`Camping Cheque'

see colour advert opposite page 161

180

693 Park of Brandedleys, Crocketford, nr. Dumfries

Good quality, friendly park providing a range of facilities including swimming pools.

Brandedleys is a first class park providing pitches for some 80 caravans and a limited number of tents, plus 27 self-contained holiday homes (12 of which, with two cottages and three chalets, are let) in three or four flat and variably sloping fields with tarred access roads. It has excellent facilities and amenities. Caravan pitches are on lawns or terraced hardstandings, many with a pleasant outlook across a loch. There are 80 electrical connections (10A), 21 pitches with water and drainage also, plus some 'premier' pitches with TV connection and picnic bench. The main centrally heated toilet block has been extensively modernised with clean, well appointed cubicled showers with toilet and washbasin (just one for men), in addition to the normally provided showers, washbasins and toilets, full length mirror, hand and hairdryers and a bathroom for disabled visitors. Also a laundry room, baby and hair care room, covered dishwashing sinks and chemical disposal. There is a second block of equal size and standard in the lower field with laundry and dishwashing facilities also. It is excellently equipped and maintained. A small, heated outdoor swimming pool is open when the weather is suitable and the heated indoor pool adjacent to the bar/restaurant is open all season with changing room (both pools free) and a sauna. Well stocked shop. Bar and licensed restaurant with full menu at reasonable prices, and open for lunch and dinner, with patio area overlooking Auchenreoch Loch. Takeaway food to order (18.00 - 21.30 hrs). All-weather tennis courts, outdoor badminton court and draught board. Games room with TV, table tennis, pool table and air-hockey table. Football pitch, putting and golf driving net. Small playground with grass base and adventure play area for older children by the pool. Dog exercise area. Public phone. Fishing (½ mile), golf, riding and pony trekking all nearby. Walks on open moors or forest and beautiful sandy beaches 12 miles away. A popular, quality park and a member of the Best of British group. Bellamy silver.

Charges 2001:
-- Per unit incl. 2 persons £9.00 - £15.00; extra adult £2.00; child (5-17 yrs) £1.50; awning £2.00; extra small tent £3.00; extra car £1.00; electricity £2.00; individual water/drainage £2.00; premier pitch £5.00; dog £1.00.
-- VAT included.
-- Credit cards accepted.

Open:
All year.

Address:
Crocketford, Dumfries, Dumfries and Galloway DG2 8RG.

Tel:
(01556) 690250.
FAX: (01556) 690681.

Reservations:
Recommended for peak dates and made with £20 deposit per pitch.

Directions: Park is 9 miles from Dumfries on the south side of the A75 Dumfries - Stranraer road, just west of the village of Crocketford. O.S.GR: NX830725.

694 Caldons Caravan and Camping Site, Galloway Forest Park

Truly peaceful Forestry Commission site ideal for exploring vast Forest Park.

The drawbacks first - Scotland is known for its midges and they love the combination of water and trees here (mid June - end Aug), so follow the site manager's advice on where to pitch (away from the trees) and use repellents. Secondly, the sanitary facilities, with the notable exception of the expensively refurbished ladies' toilets, are adequate rather than luxurious but are well maintained and clean with free hot water to the showers and washbasins. Facilities for disabled visitors are good. The benefits are a wonderfully quiet and relaxing streamside site, close to the loch with mountain views, and a perfect base for exploring this enormous 240 square mile Forest Park. The site has 160 large pitches, 50 with electricity (10A) and 15 with hardstanding. In several different areas, these offer shady, flat pitches or an open, sloping area. Situated in the beautiful Glen Trool, the Loch Trool Trail oak and pine woods are a naturalist's delight. The trail starts at the site and takes walkers on a 5 mile circuit of the Loch with spectacular loch views and passing Bruce's Stone, commemorating his first victory over the English in 1307 (this can also be reached by car). There are many other walks and drives into the moorland and rugged hills. At the site, children can play on the varied adventure equipment (on bark) or splash around in the Caldon Burn. Neither boating nor fishing is permitted in Loch Trool, but permits (from £6.50 for adults, £1.50 for children) for fishing elsewhere in the park are cheap for Scotland. In spring and early summer goats roam the site with their kids. Picnic benches, games rooms with table tennis and pool, and a rest room with drinks machine are provided. There is a shop for basic supplies, plus a launderette and dishwashing facilities. Access to the site makes it unsuitable for very large units. Dogs are accepted. Caravan storage. The village of Glentrool is 4 miles, with a pub at Bargrennan, 5 miles.

Charges 2000:
-- Per unit incl. up to 4 persons £6.00 - £7.50; extra person (over 5 yrs) £1.00; extra car, trailer or pup tent £2.50; electricity £2.10.
-- Less 20% all year for disabled guests and senior citizens.
-- VAT included.

Open:
25 March - 28 September.

Address:
Glentrool, Newton Stewart, Wigtownshire DG8 6SU.

Tel:
(01671) 840218, or out of season (0131) 314 6505.

Reservations:
Necessary for B.Hs and peak times; made for min. 3 nights with £30 deposit. Contact site when open or Forest Holidays, Forestry Commission, 231 Corstorphine Road, Edinburgh EH12 7AT. Tel: (0131) 314 6505. E-mail: fe.holidays@ forestry.gov.uk.

Directions: From A714 Newton Stewart - Girvan road turn east at Bargrennan and right just past Glentrool, following signs on single track forest road with passing places. O.S.GR: NX400790.

Lowlands

691 Hoddom Castle Caravan Park, Lockerbie

Attractive site in well landscaped, spacious park.

The oldest part of Hoddom Castle is a 16th century Borders Pele Tower, or fortified keep. This was extended to form a residence for a Lancashire cotton magnate, became a youth hostel and was then taken over by the army during WW2. Since then parts have been demolished but the original border keep still survives, unfortunately in a semi-derelict state. The site's bar and restaurant have been developed in the courtyard area from the coach houses and the main ladies' toilet block was the stables. The park is well laid out on mainly sloping ground with many mature and beautiful trees, originally part of an arboretum. The drive to the site is ¾ mile long with a one way system. Many of the 120 numbered pitches have good views of the castle and have gravel hardstandings with grass for awnings, most with electricity (10A). In front of the castle are flat fields for tents and caravans not needing electricity. The main toilet block can be heated and is very well appointed with washbasins in cubicles and free hot showers. A unit for disabled visitors provides a shower, WC, hairdryer, etc. The other two blocks are tiled and are kept very clean, with washbasins and WCs. Each block has dishwashing sinks and there is a well equipped laundry room at the castle. Behind the castle a building houses a chemical disposal point (washbasin and soap) and near this, a motorcaravan service point. Reception is combined with the licensed shop (with gas). Amenities include the comfortable bar lounge with family room and TV, the restaurant and takeaway (restricted opening outside high seasons) and a games room with pool tables, table tennis and video games. Large, grass play area, crazy golf, bicycle hire and mountain bike trail. The park's 9 hole golf course is in an attractive setting alongside the Annan river, where fishing is possible for salmon and trout (tickets available). Coarse fishing is also possible elsewhere on the estate. Guided walks are organised in high season. Tennis nearby. Caravan storage. A peaceful place from which to explore historic southwest Scotland.

Charges 2000:
-- Per unit incl. up to 4 persons £6.00 - £11.50; small tent incl. 1 or 2 persons £5.00 - £8.50; extra person £2.00; awning £2.00; electricity (10A) £2.00.
-- VAT included.
-- Credit cards accepted.

Open:
1 April - 25 October.

Address:
Hoddom,
Lockerbie,
Dumfriesshire
DG11 1AS.

Tel:
(01576) 300251.
FAX: (01576) 300757.

Reservations:
Necessary for July/Aug and B.Hs. Any length with deductible £5 deposit.

Directions: Leave A74M at junction 19 (Ecclefechan) and follow signs to park. Leave A75 at Annan juncion (west end of Annan by-pass) and follow signs. O.S.GR: NY155725.

692 Cressfield Caravan Park, Ecclefechan, nr. Lockerbie

Purpose designed, well run, modern park just north of the border, open all year.

Cressfield is close to main routes (A74M/M6) and is an ideal transit park, although the Solway Firth or Dumfries and Galloway tourist features are nearby. It has been developed in pleasant undulating countryside, next to the village of Ecclefechan, to a very high standard and is personally managed by the owner. The park provides 153 pitches of which 47 are available for touring units (hardstanding or grass), the remainder being taken up by holiday homes and seasonal vans. The park is pleasantly landscaped (trees are growing well) and the level pitches, mostly with hardstanding, are connected by tarmac or gravel roads and provided with 16A electric hook-ups. A good rally field is also fully equipped with electrical hook-ups. The modern, heated toilet block is central, operated on a key system and provides excellent facilities - free, well equipped showers, washbasins in cubicles, hairdryers (metered) and a bath is a welcome addition in the ladies' (20p). A toilet and washbasin, plus a separate shower area are provided for disabled visitors, plus shower seats, in both male and female sections. There is an excellent laundry room, a washing up area under cover, bin store, chemical disposal and a motorcaravan service point. Large dog exercise field and dog waste bins. Other amenities include a well equipped, fenced children's play area, 9 hole putting green and a sports field with goal posts (not in wet weather or Nov-March), tennis and badminton nets, netball posts, giant chess and draughts, plus boules. There is no shop but it is only ¼ mile from the village and adjacent to the park is an hotel for a drink or a meal. Gas is available on site. For the more active there are seven golf courses nearby, opportunities for coarse or game fishing, cycling, walking, birdwatching and historical Solway to explore. Boat launching 8 miles. Some road noise is possible.

Charges 2001:
-- Per unit incl. 2 adults £6.50 - £8.50; awning, extra car or small tent £1.00; extra adult £2.00; child (under 16 yrs) £1.00; car and small tent £6.50 - £7.00; walkers or cyclists with 2-man tent £5.00; electricity £2.00 - £2.50.
-- B.H.s - £2 extra per night, per unit.
-- No credit cards.
-- VAT included.

Open:
All year.

Address:
Ecclefechan, nr.
Lockerbie,
Dumfries and Galloway
DG11 3DR.

Tel:
(01576) 300702.
FAX: as phone.

Reservations:
Phone bookings accepted.

Directions: Approaching from north or south on A74(M) (10 miles north of Gretna, 5 miles south of Lockerbie) take exit 19 for Ecclefechan and follow B7076 for ½ mile to south side of village; park is signed. O.S.GR: NY196744.

Alan Rogers' Discount

Less 50p per unit, per night

182

HODDOM CASTLE CARAVAN PARK
10 minutes drive from A74M and A75
QUALITY FACILITIES AVAILABLE ON OR ADJACENT TO HODDOM CASTLE

QUAD BIKING, CLAY PIGEON SHOOTING AND THREE 18 HOLE GOLF COURSES ALL WITHIN 10 MILES	FISHING Exclusive beats for quality game and coarse fishing WALKING Nature trails, foot paths and ranger guided walks GOLF Our own nine hole course ENQUIRIES THE WARDEN, HODDOM CASTLE, HODDOM, LOCKERBIE DG11 1BE TEL: 01576 300251

Scottish TOURIST BOARD ★★★★★ HOLIDAY PARK 2000

Practical Caravan TOP 100 FAMILY PARKS 2000

AA BEST SCOTTISH CAMPSITE 1996/1997

Calor 2000 Best Park in Britain

702 Aird Donald Caravan Park, Stranraer

Tidy site suitable for night halt or longer.

Aird Donald makes a good stopping off place when travelling to and from the Irish ferries, but it is also useful for seeing the sights around Stranraer. The park comprises 12 acres surrounded by conifers, flowering trees and shrubs and the 300 yard drive is lit and lined with well trimmed conifers. There are grass areas for caravans or tents and hardstandings with electricity hook-up (these very handy for hardy winter tourers). A small play area caters for young children, but the local leisure centre is a walk away and caters for swimming, table tennis, gym, etc, and a theatre that hosts everything from country and western to opera. It also has bar facilities. The site has two toilet blocks; the old original one is very basic with free showers and this is open all the time. The other is new, modern and heated. Kept very clean with excellent, tiled facilities, this one is kept locked with a key deposit of £5 - we recommend you use this facility. It has two types of shower, an electric one which is metered (20p) and two others which are free (strange, because they are all excellent). Washbasins are in vanity units, ladies having one in a cubicle. A unit for visitors with disabilities has a washbasin and WC. Dishwashing sinks and a small laundry with sinks, dryer, twin-tub washing machine, an old fashioned mangle and clothes lines are provided. Chemical disposal and motorcaravan service facilities. The area has three world famous gardens to visit, numerous golf courses, fishing, riding and watersports.

Charges 2000:
-- Per unit incl. 2 adults, 1 child and electricity £10.40.
-- No credit cards.
Open:
All year.
Address:
London Road, Stranraer, Wigtownshire, DG9 8RN.
Tel:
(01776) 702025.
E-mail: aird@ mimman.u-net.com.
Reservations:
Contact park.

Directions: Enter Stranraer on A75 road. Watch for narrow site entrance on left entering town, opposite school. O.S.GR: NX075605.

703 Gibson Park Caravan Club Site, Melrose

Beautiful small park on town edge.

This is an ideal transit park, being so close to the A68, but is also a perfect base for exploring this Southern Scotland area or indeed a trip to Edinburgh, as this is only 35 miles away by car or one of the regular buses which run from the park entrance. On the edge of the little town of Melrose (5 minutes walk), shops, pubs and restaurants are all in easy reach. This small, three acre park has only 60 touring pitches plus, unusually, an extra 12 tent pitches (summer only) next to the adjacent rugby pitch. All touring pitches have electricity (16A) and TV connec-tions (otherwise a bad signal here), 51 have hardstanding and 10 are serviced with water and drainage. The park has a one way system on tarmac roads. The sanitary facilities are in a new building and are first rate with spacious showers, washbasins in cabins, centrally heated and fitted with faced boarding giving a pleasing finish. There are facilities for laundry and a separate room with shower and WC for disabled visitors. Motorcaravan service point. Gas is available. This is Sir Walter Scott country - visit Abbotsford House, his romantic mansion on the banks of the River Tweed. Melrose's Abbey ruins are believed to be the final resting place of Robert The Bruce and the starting place of St Cuthbert's Way. A new cross border 62 mile trail leads to Northumberland's Lindisfarne.

Charges 2000:
-- Per pitch £6.00 - £7.00; adult £3.90 - £4.00; child (5-16 yrs) £1.20; extra car, boat or trailer (in excess of 2 units) £1.00; electricity £1.45 (26/3-4/10) - £2.20; TV hook-up 55p (bring own cable); serviced pitch £1.00.
-- Tent pitches £6.90 - £12.50.
-- Credit cards accepted.
-- VAT included.
Open:
All year.
Address:
High Street, Melrose TD6 9RY.
Tel:
(01896) 822969.
FAX: (01896) 823641.
Reservations:
Made with £5 per night deposit - contact park.

Directions: Turn left off A68 Jedburgh - Lauder road at roundabout about 2½ miles past Newton St Boswell onto A6091 Galashiels road. In about 3¼ miles at roundabout turn right onto B6374 to Melrose. Site is on right at filling station opposite Rugby Club, just before entering town centre. O.S.GR: NT545340.

Lowlands

696 Crossburn Caravan Park, Peebles

Peaceful, friendly small park, suitable as a night stop.

Half a mile north of the town centre, Crossburn is on the south side of the A703 road. The entrance has a fairly steep slope down to reception and the shop selling basic food items and a large selection of camping accessories. Passing caravans for sale and holiday homes you might think that this is not the site for you, but persevere as the touring area is very pleasant, with attractive trees and bushes. Of 50 pitches, 46 have electricity (16A), 20 have hardstanding and 8 fully serviced. There is also a sheltered area for tents. There are two sanitary blocks, the smaller one (with heating) fairly basic, the other more modern with basins in cubicles, free hairdryers and spacious, controllable free showers. A campers' kitchen gives free use of an electric hot plate, kettle and fridge. Adjacent is a large games room with table tennis and games machines. The field behind the resident donkey has a 9-hole putting green. A good play area is on bark chippings and there is a dog walk along the side of the burn. Mountain bike hire. If you decide to stay longer, the area has many places to visit and things to do. From historic homes, abbeys, woodland walks, fishing, riding, golf and canoeing - it's all there. Edinburgh is only 40 minutes drive. Perhaps the night halt may turn into a longer visit.

Directions: Park is by the A703, ½ mile north of Peebles. O.S.GR: NT248417.

Charges 2000:
-- Per unit incl. 2 persons £8.50 - £10.00; serviced pitch +£2.00; extra person (5 yrs and over) £1.00; awning £2.00; hiker or cyclist plus tent £5.00; electricity £2.00.
-- Credit cards accepted.
Open:
Easter/1 April - end Oct.
Address:
Edinburgh Road, Peebles EH45 8ED.
Tel/Fax:
(01721) 720501.
E-mail: enquiries@crossburncaravans.co.uk.
Reservations:
Made with £14 deposit including £2 fee.

697 The Monks' Muir, Haddington, nr. Edinburgh

Small, relaxed, 'individual' park, open all year and handy for visiting Edinburgh.

The Monks' Muir is just back from the A1 (but the layout makes traffic noise minimal), a few minutes from Haddington, about 15 minutes by car, 20 minutes by rail (P&D) or an hour by bus from Edinburgh from just outside the site (parking in Edinburgh is not advised). It therefore provides a base from which to explore the city, to enjoy the golden beaches of East Lothian, discover the border country or just play golf! A continental style café cum delicatessen shop provides the atmosphere which sets the style of this park. The park has extensive development plans that will take some years to complete. As a result, with the steadily increasing number of static units, the touring area will initially decrease and be even further away from the toilet blocks. Eventually a new area is to be developed for touring, complete with a central toilet block. There are no marked pitches for about 40 units that are taken on mostly fairly level grass beyond a line of holiday homes. Finding your own place either side of the central gravel road amongst the odd tree contributes to the friendly, relaxed atmosphere. There are 35 electrical connections (12A) on an elongated strip of land between the fields, finishing with a natural play area for children. The main toilet block, a fair walk now from the touring pitches, provides toilets, free hot showers and washbasins. Outside washing-up sinks also have free hot water and a fully equipped laundry room also provides tourist information. A second smaller block nearer the touring units ensures an adequate provision. One block is closed in low season. Chemical disposal and motorcaravan services. Public phones. Boules and bicycle hire are on the park, fishing and golf within 2 miles. The Macfarlanes have planted thousands of trees and shrubs and there is a garden centre selling the kinds of plants used on the park. Caravan holiday homes for hire (10) and seasonal lets. Bellamy gold.

Directions: Park is on the north side of the A1, halfway between East Linton and Haddington. O.S.GR: NT 559762.

Charges 2001:
-- Per unit £7.50 - £8.30, large motorhome £10.80 - £12.00, 2 man tent and car £5.00 - £6.20; m/cyclist and tent £4.50 - £5.00, cyclist or walker and tent £2.00 - £3.00; each person (14 yrs or over) £1.85 - £1.95; child (0-13 yrs) free; full awning or pup tent free - £3.00 (July/Aug. only); dog free; electricity £1.80 - £2.20, acc. to season.
-- Less 10-20% for 7 day or more stays, plus a further 30% for over 60s pre-booked for over 7 days outside July/Aug.
-- Credit cards accepted.
Open:
All year.
Address:
Haddington, East Lothian EH41 3SB.
Tel:
(01620) 860340.
FAX: (01620) 861770.
E-mail:
d@monksmuir.com.
Reservations:
Made with £7 deposit and £3 booking fee.

698 Drum Mohr Caravan Park, Musselburgh, nr. Edinburgh

Family owned, attractively laid out touring park on east side of Edinburgh.

Although adjacent to built-up areas, this is a secluded, well kept modern park, conveniently situated for visits to Edinburgh, the Lothian and Borders regions. It has been carefully landscaped and there are many attractive plants, flowers and hedging. There are 120 individual pitches, 40 with hardstanding, for touring units of any type, well spaced out on gently sloping grass in groups of 12 or more, marked with white posts. There are electric hook-ups on 110 of them and 7 are fully serviced with water and waste water connections also. Free space is left for play and recreation. The two toilet blocks are clean, attractive, of ample size and can be heated. They have washbasins set in flat surfaces with free hot water in these and in the four external washing-up sinks, but hot water is on payment for the showers (outside the cubicle) and laundry sinks. Laundry facilities are in each block, chemical disposal and motorcaravan service point. There is a well stocked, licensed shop (gas available, bread and papers to order) and a children's play-ground on sand, but no other on-site activities. However, the town amenities are quite close, as is a golf course. Musselburgh centre is 1½ miles, Edinburgh 7, with a frequent bus service to the latter. A well run park, managed personally by the owner, Mr Melville. A member of the Best of British group.

Directions: From Edinburgh follow A1 signs for Berwick on Tweed for 6-7 miles. Turn for Wallyford and follow camp and Mining Museum signs. From south follow A1 taking junction after Tranent village (A199 Musselburgh) and follow signs. O.S.GR: NT371732.

Charges 2000:
-- Per unit incl. 2 persons £8.00 - £10.00; extra person (over 3 yrs) £1.50 - £2.00; extra pup tent £2.00; awning £1.00; electricity £2.00; fully serviced pitch incl. electricity + £6.00; extra car £1.00.
-- VAT included.
-- Credit cards accepted.
Open:
1 March - 31 October.
Address:
Levenhall, Musselburgh, East Lothian EH21 8JS.
Tel:
0131 665 6867.
FAX: 0131 653 6859.
E-mail: bookings@drummohr.org.
Reservations:
Made for any length with deposit of one night's charge plus £1 fee.

699 Mortonhall Caravan Park, Edinburgh

Attractive, large touring park in the mature grounds of Mortonhall mansion.

The Mortonhall park makes a good base to see the historic city of Edinburgh and buses to the City leave from the park entrance every ten minutes (parking in Edinburgh is not easy). Although only 4 miles from the city centre, Mortonhall is in quiet mature parkland, easy to find with access off the ring road. The park can accommodate 250 units mostly on numbered pitches on a slight slope with nothing to separate them but marked by jockey wheel points. There are over 170 places with electricity (10A), 16 with hardstanding, water and drainage as well, and many places for tents. Holiday caravans to let. The park is very popular but only part is reserved and tourists arriving early may find space. Two modern toilet blocks have free hot water in washbasins, showers and outside, uncovered dishwashing sinks. A third excellent, new facility at the top of the park has eight unisex units incorporating shower, washbasin and WC, with covered dishwashing sinks. The courtyard area provides further standard facilities and 'portacabin' type units are added for the high season to serve the large number of tents. There are facilities for disabled visitors, chemical disposal units, and a laundry room with washing machines and dryer. Shop. An attractive courtyard development houses a lounge bar and restaurant, open to all, with good value meals in pleasant surroundings. Games and TV rooms. Table tennis, play area on sand. Late arrivals area with hook-ups. Torches useful. Golf courses and driving range very near.

Directions: Park is well signed south of the city, 5 minutes from A720 city by-pass. Take Mortonhall exit from Straiton junction and follow camping signs. Entrance road is alongside Klondyke Garden Centre. O.S.GR: NT262686.

Charges 2001:
-- Per unit incl. 2 persons £9.00 - £13.25; extra person (5 yrs and over) £1.00; serviced pitch + £4.00; electricity £3.00; awning £2.50 - £5.00; porch awning £2.50; dog £1.00.
-- Credit cards accepted.
-- VAT included.
Open:
14 March - 31 October.
Address:
38 Mortonhall Gate, Frogston Road East, Edinburgh, East Lothian EH16 6TJ.
Tel:
0131 664 1533.
FAX: 0131 664 5387.
E-mail: enquiries@mortonhallcp.demon.co.uk.
Reservations:
Made with 1 night's charge plus £1.50 fee.

Mortonhall Caravan Park, Edinburgh

Country estate situated just 15 minutes from city centre and 5 minutes from the bypass. Parkland estate hosts premiere graded park. Luxury holiday homes (Thistle Award), touring and tenting pitches. Excellent amenities - modern toilet and shower block, restaurant and bar, shop, games room, TV room and laundry. An ideal base to see Edinburgh and Southern Scotland. Free colour brochure and tariff.

Mortonhall Caravan Park, Frogston Road East,
Edinburgh EH16 6TJ Tel: 0131-664 1533 Fax: 0131-664 5387
E-mail: enquiries@mortonhallcp.demon.co.uk

EDINBURGH SCOTLAND

MORTONHALL CARAVAN & CAMPING PARK

0131 664 1533

Lowlands

705 Edinburgh Caravan Club Site, Edinburgh

Large, well managed site to the north of Edinburgh on the Firth of Forth, open all year.

Situated as it is on the northern outskirts and within easy reach of the city of Edinburgh, this Caravan Club Site (open to non-members) provides an ideal base for touring. A bus (number 8A and 28A stop just outside the gates) takes you right into the centre of the city and within walking distance of many of its attractions. Enter the site through rather grand gates to find the visitors' car park and reception to the left. There are 150 large flat pitches (103 hardstandings, 12 with water tap and waste water disposal) with electricity (16A) and TV aerial, and provision for 50 tents in a separate field (hook-ups available). As bushes mature, there will be shade. Two heated sanitary blocks provide immaculately clean toilets, showers, washbasins in cubicles, hairdryer and hand dryer free of charge, and hand basins. There is also a heated room with toilet, shower, washbasin, hairdryer and handrails for campers with disabilities, plus a baby and toddler room with child-size facilities. Each block houses a chemical disposal point, dishwashing area, and a laundry with sinks, washing machine, tumble dryer, spin-dryer, and iron. Clothes lines are banned in summer so a drying room is provided. In the tent field is a covered cooking shelter, and there are bicycle stands close by. There is no shop, but campers can order milk, bread, and newspapers, or purchase ice cream and change gas cylinders at the reception. A tourist information centre is well stocked, there is a fenced play area for youngsters, and a dog walk in the only natural wood in Edinburgh (part of the site). The nearest hotel/restaurant is about ½ mile.

Charges 2000:
-- Per adult £3.90 - £4.00; child (5-16 yrs) £1.20; non-member pitch fee £1.00 - £3.00; electricity £1.50 - £2.25; extra car, boat or trailer £1.00; serviced pitch supplement £1.00.
-- Tent campers apply to site for details.
-- VAT included.

Open:
All year

Address:
Marine Drive,
Edinburgh EH4 5EN.

Tel:
0131 312 6874.

Reservations:
Made with £5 deposit, balance on arrival.

Directions: From A720 (signed City Bypass North), turn right at Gogar roundabout onto A8 and follow international camping signs. O.S.GR: 66:212768

704 Slatebarns Caravan Park, Roslin, nr. Edinburgh

Small, select park for city and country.

Slatebarns is a small, well groomed park, perfectly located for that trip to Edinburgh. It has only 30 pitches, all with electricity hook-ups (10A), some with hardstanding and some on grass (steel awning pegs useful). This recently developed park has a small purpose built toilet block with well equipped showers, washbasins in cubicles for ladies and an excellent separate provision for those with disabilities. Plentiful water points, waste water points, a practical motorcaravan service point and chemical disposal complete the facilities. The small reception office within this park provides tourist information. A public telephone is on hand and a good launderette with washing machine, dryer and spin dryer is impressive. Gas is available. Buses run from the village (five minutes' walk) regularly into Edinburgh (30 minute journey, 6 miles), although they are less frequent in the evening. In the village there are shops, pubs and hotels for all that you may need. Slatebarns is a small park with little on site for children or teenagers. Managed under contract for the Caravan Club, non-members are also very welcome. An ideal base to get away from the bustle after a full day in Edinburgh, or equally attractive as a touring base or country hideaway.

Charges guide:
-- Per pitch £1.00; adult £3.25 - £3.75; child £1.10; electricity £1.50 - £2.00 (Oct).

Open:
Easter - 31 October.

Address:
Slatebarns,
Roslin,
Mid Lothian EH25 9PU.

Tel:
0131 440 2192
(up to 8 pm).

Reservations:
Contact park for details.

Directions: From Straiton junction on A720 (Edinburgh bypass) go south on A701 signed Bilston, Penicuik. At roundabout in Bilston turn left on B7006 signed Roslin. After 1 mile continue over crossroads signed Rosslyn Chapel. Site entrance is immediately past Chapel. O.S.GR: NT275632.

Edinburgh

The capital, a World Heritage Centre and now the home of the Scottish Parliament, is one of the most beautiful cities in the world dominated by its castle. At the very heart is the Royal Mile where you can stroll through the centuries from Parliament Square, the magnificent 15th century St Giles' Cathedral and down to the Palace of Holyrood-house, the Queens's official Edinburgh residence. Further north of the city is the historic Port of Leith, with its restaurants, bistros and pubs and now home to HM Yacht Britannia and the future focus of Conran's Cruise Ship Terminal which promises to be architecturally spectacular. The most exciting developments yet include Sir Michael Hopkin's 'Dynamic Earth' exhibition – a huge tented structure at the foot of Arthur's Seat which describes the evolution of the planet, and the new Museum of Scotland where you can absorb the essence of Scottish architecture and material culture from beam engines to Bonnie Prince Charlie.

700 Strathclyde Country Park Caravan Site, Bothwell, Motherwell

Good touring site near Glasgow in Country Park with many amenities.

The 1,200 acre Country Park is a large green area less than 15 miles from the centre of Glasgow and is suitable for both overnight or period stays (max. 14 days). The very well kept park, open to all, has a large water sports centre offering sailing, water skiing, windsurfing, canoeing, rowing (all with craft for hire), a water bus, a selection of family `fun boats' and bicycle hire, plus Scotland's own theme park only ½ mile from the site. Also provided within the park are coarse fishing, nature trails, children's adventure play area, sandy beaches and an 18 hole golf course. The site has 100 numbered pitches for caravans, all with electricity (10A). Arranged in semicircular groups on flat grass they are served by made-up access roads and the site is well lit. There is also a camping field which holds 150 or more for special events. Four solidly built modern toilet blocks make a good provision, with free hot water to close together washbasins (shelf and mirror) and showers. Enclosed sinks for dishwashing or food preparation and launderette (irons from reception). Block 4 has facilities for visitors with disabilities, there are motorcaravan service and chemical disposal facilities. Gas is available and bread, milk and basics are kept in reception (shop 1 mile). Within the park are bar and restaurant facilities (100 yds). Children's play equipment on bark. Public phone. 24 hour security. American motorhomes accepted up to 22 ft. The site is close to the motorway so there may be some traffic noise.

Directions: Take exit 5 from M74 and follow sign for Strathclyde Country Park. Turn first left for site. O.S.GR: NS720584.

Charges 2001:
-- Per caravan pitch incl. 2 persons £8.20; awning £2.00; tent pitch (3 or 4 persons) £7.10; small ridge tent £3.70; extra adult £1.00; child 80p; electricity £2.30.
-- No credit cards.

Open:
April - mid October.

Address:
Information and enquiries: Strathclyde Country Park, 366 Hamilton Road, Motherwell ML1 3ED.

Tel:
(01698) 266155.
FAX: (01698) 252925.
E-mail: strathclydepark @northlan.gov.uk.

Reservations:
Made for any period with deposit of one night's fee.

724 Lomond Woods Holiday Park, Balloch

Good touring park south of Loch Lomond, open all year.

Almost, but not quite, on the banks of Loch Lomond (10 minutes or ¼ mile), this family owned, landscaped and well planned park is suitable for both transit or longer stays. Formerly known as Tullichewan Holiday Park, it takes 120 touring units, including 30 tents, on well spaced, numbered pitches on flat or gently sloping grass. Most have hardstandings, 106 have electrical connections (10A) and 8 have water and waste water too. The single heated toilet block has been totally refitted over the past two winters and is kept in an excellent state. It is large with plenty of WCs and basins, hot showers (some with WC), new baths, a shower room for disabled visitors and two baby baths. Water and refuse points are around the site, and there are covered dishwashing sinks, a launderette, chemical disposal and motorcaravan service points. A well stocked shop is combined with reception, and amenities include a games room with TV, table tennis, pool table and a children's playground on grass and bark. A leisure suite provides a sauna, sun-bed and spa-bath (on payment). Bicycle hire on site, fishing and boat launching ¼ mile, riding 4 miles, golf 5 miles. Watersport activities and boat trips are possible on Loch Lomond, with a new visitor attraction, 'Lomond Shores' opening nearby for 2001. There are rail and road connections to Glasgow. Dog walks - 'owners must be kept on leads at all times'. Public phone. Restaurants and bar meals in Balloch (5 mins). American motorhomes accepted with prior notice. Pine lodges and caravan holiday homes for letting. Caravan storage. This is a well run park with very helpful wardens and reception staff. A member of the Best of British group.

Directions: Turn off A82 road 17 miles northwest of Glasgow on A811 Stirling road. Site is in Balloch at southern end of Loch Lomond and is well signed. O.S.GR: NS389816.

Charges guide:
-- Per unit incl. up to 2 persons £10.00 - £12.00 (all persons in winter season £8.00); extra adult £1.50; child (3-12 yrs) £1.00; awning £1.50 - £2.00; electricity £2.00 - £2.50; fully serviced pitch with electricity £4.00 - £4.50; hikers (2 persons) £6.50 - £9.00.
-- VAT included.
-- Credit cards accepted.

Open:
All year except Nov; (reduced facilities Dec-March).

Address:
Tullichewan, Balloch, Loch Lomond G83 8QP.

Tel:
(01389) 755000.
FAX: (01389) 755563.
E-mail: lomondwoods@ holiday-parks.co.uk.

Reservations:
Any length with deposit of first night's charge and £2 fee.

see colour advert between pages 160/161

Glasgow

One of the most magnificent 19th century cities in Europe and now known as Scotland's style capital with its art deco brasseries, stylish shops and cultural centres boasting more than 30 art galleries and museums. Worth visiting is the new elegant Gallery of Modern Art in Queen Street and Charles Rennie Mackintosh's finest building - The Glasgow School of Art. Also interesting along the banks of the River Clyde is the restored Carlton Terrace and Glasgow's newest landmark, the Clyde Auditorium, popularly known as The 'Armadillo', due to its distinctive shape.

Heart of Scotland

723 Trossachs Holiday Park, Aberfoyle

Well run, friendly family park, ideal for exploring the Trossachs and Loch Lomond.

Nestling on the side of a hill 3 miles south of Aberfoyle, this is an excellent base for touring this famously beautiful area. Lochs Lomond, Ard, Venachar and others are within easy reach, as are the Queen Elizabeth Forest Park and, of course, the Trossachs. The park specialises in sales and hire of top class mountain bikes. A very neat and tidy park, there are 45 well laid out and marked pitches arranged on terraces with hardstanding. All have electricity and TV connections and most have water and drainage also. There are trees between the terraces and lovely views across the valley. A modern wooden building houses the sanitary facilities which offer a satisfactory supply of toilets, showers and washbasins, the ladies' area being rather larger, with two private cabins. The building also contains a laundry room and a large games room with TV and lots of seating. There are several items of play equipment on gravel. The park purchased the adjoining oak and bluebell woods in '97. A 'passport' scheme arranged with a local leisure centre (10 miles, 8 passes) provides facilities for swimming, sauna, solarium, badminton, tennis, windsurfing, etc. Nearby are opportunities for golfing, boat launching and fishing (3 miles). A well stocked shop (all season) and the bike shop are either side of reception, where you will receive a warm welcome from Joe and Hazel Norman. Luxury caravans (12) for hire in separate section. A new member of the Best of British group. Bellamy gold.

Directions: Park is 3 miles south of Aberfoyle on the A81 road, well signed. O.S.GR: NS544976.

Charges 2001:
-- Per unit incl. 2 persons £9.00 - £12.00; extra adult £2.00; child (2-14 yrs) £1.25; awning £1.50 - £2.00; small pup tent £3.00; electricity and TV connection, hardstanding pitch £2.00; all services £3.00.
-- VAT included.
-- Credit cards accepted.
Open:
1 March - 31 October.
Address:
Aberfoyle,
Stirling FK8 3SA.
Tel:
(01877) 382614 (24 hrs).
FAX: (01877) 382732.
E-mail: info@
trossachsholidays.co.uk.
Reservations:
Advised and made for min. 3 days with £15 deposit.

726 Ardgartan Caravan & Camping Site, Arrochar, nr. Tarbet

Forestry Commission site on banks of Loch Long with mountains all around.

Ardgartan, a rugged site in the Argyll Forest Park, is splendidly situated with lovely views of Loch Long and with lots of sightseeing and activity opportunities. At the northern end of the Cowal Peninsula, it is on a promontory on the shores of Loch Long, there is good sea fishing and facilities for launching small boats. The 160 touring pitches are in sections which are well divided by grass giving an uncrowded air. Most with hardstanding and marked by numbered posts, they are accessed from hard surface roads and 46 have electricity. There are additional grass areas for tents. The main sanitary block is opposite the reception and shop with two small others (one for each sex) close by for the busiest periods. It is a basic, but clean provision with facilities for disabled visitors and a launderette. These facilities may be quite stretched when the park is busy. Play equipment is provided (with bark surfaces) and barbecues are allowed. Arrochar village (2 miles) has fuel, general stores and a restaurant. Walking and climbing, as well as sea and river fishing (permits obtainable locally), are all available nearby. The site gate is locked 10.30 pm. - 7.30 am.

Directions: From A82 Glasgow - Crianlarich take A83 at Tarbet signed Arrochar and Cambletown. Site is 2 miles past Arrochar, with the entrance on a bend. O.S.GR: NN275030.

Charges 2000:
-- Per adult £2.90 - £4.10; child (5-14 yrs) £1.20 - £1.80; electricity £2.10; select pitch incl. electricity +£3.20.
-- Credit cards accepted.
Open:
23 March - 23 October.
Address:
Ardgartan, Arrochar, Dunbartonshire G83 7AR.
Tel:
(01301) 702293.
Reservations:
Contact site. Brochure requests: Forest Holidays, Forestry Commission, 231 Corstorphine Road, Edinburgh EH12 7AT. Tel: (0131) 314 6505. E-mail: fe.holidays@ forestry.gov.uk.

BLAIR CASTLE CARAVAN PARK

BLAIR ATHOLL, PERTHSHIRE PH18 5SR TEL: 01796 481263 FAX: 01796 481587

★ 32 Acre Park set amidst spectacular mountain scenery
★ Grass and hard-standing mains serviced pitches
★ Spacious park and recreation areas
★ Extensive woodland, hill and riverside walks
★ Heated amenity blocks
★ Indoor Games Room and Television Lounge
★ Scottish Tourist Board rated "Excellent"
★ Holder of "Thistle Award" for our hire caravan holiday homes
★ Situated in the grounds of the historic and elegant Blair Castle (open to public)
★ Pony trekking, golf, fishing, bowling, mountain bikes all available from the village of Blair Atholl (100 yards)

PLEASE WRITE OR TELEPHONE FOR OUR FREE COLOUR BROCHURE

727 Auchterarder Caravan Park, Nether Coul, Auchterarder

Small, family run park in sheltered position.

This is a charming small park, purpose designed and landscaped by the owners Stuart and Susie Robertson. It is conveniently situated for exploring central Scotland and the Highlands with many leisure activities close at hand, particularly golf, and within walking distance of the village (1 mile). The 21 original pitches, all with electricity (6A) and hardstanding, 12 with drainage also, are well spaced around the edge of the elongated, level grass park. Marked pitches with grass frontage back on to raised banks which are planted with trees. More pitches have been developed to one side of the park, along with a fishing pond (exclusively for campers) and woodland walk. A tarmac hold-over area at the entrance is for late arrivals (with electricity). A modern pine chalet, blending with the environment, is also at the entrance housing reception, a small shop with basic items (milk delivered daily), small library and excellent sanitary facilities with a key system and piped music. These include roomy toilets, controllable hot showers with dressing area, seat, shelf, hooks and vanity style washbasins with large mirrors. A toilet for disabled people is provided in both the male and female units. Laundry room with sink and washing machine - an iron can be provided as well. Under cover washing up with free hot water. Chemical disposal. Two secluded chalets (self catering) for hire and B&B. Public phones. A trout fishing pond has been added on the park. Golf 1 mile, bicycle hire or riding 6 miles. With plenty of outdoor pursuits locally, the historic cities of Perth and Stirling are less than half an hour's drive away. Caravan storage. There is easy access from the nearby A9 road which does create some background noise, although it is peaceful at night.

Directions: Park is between the A9 and A824 roads east of Auchterarder village, only ½ mile from the main road. It is reached by turning on to the B8062 (Dunning) road from the A824. O.S.GR: NN964138.

Charges guide:
-- Per unit incl. up to 4 persons £8.00; tent and vehicle from £6.00; extra person (over 5 yrs) £1.00; awning £1.00; porch awning 50p; electricity and drainage £1.50 - £2.50.
-- VAT included.
-- No credit cards.
Open:
All year.
Address:
Nether Coul,
Auchterarder,
Perthshire PH3 1ET.
Tel:
(01764) 663119.
FAX: as phone.
E-mail: nethercoul
@talk21.com.
Reservations:
Advisable July/Aug. and made with deposit of one night's charge and booking fee (£1). Bookings held until 5 pm. on day reserved.

730 Blair Castle Caravan Park, Blair Atholl

Well kept park in attractive, spacious setting with some holiday homes.

This attractive park is set in the grounds of Blair Castle, the traditional home of the Dukes of Atholl. The castle is open to the public, its 32 fully furnished rooms showing a picture of Scottish life from the 16th century to the present day. The caravan park has a wonderful feeling of spaciousness with a large central area left free for children's play or for general use. There is space for 283 touring units with 191 electricity connections (10A), 144 hardstandings and 42 fully serviced pitches with water and waste water facilities also. A motorcaravan service point is provided and American motorhomes are accepted (max. 30 ft or 5 tons). Caravan holiday homes, 85 privately owned and 28 for hire, in separate areas. The original sanitary building has been updated in parts but is only open at peak times. The four newer blocks can be heated and are of excellent quality with very high standards of cleanliness. They have large, free hot shower cubicles, some also incorporating WC and washbasin, and further cubicles with WC and washbasin. Three blocks have facilities for disabled visitors, one with WC and washbasin, the others with a bath also. There are baby changing mats, chemical disposal points and dishwashing sinks. A good launderette has washing machines, dryers, spin dryer and irons plus a separate drying room and outside lines. Gas is available. Near reception is a games room with pool, table tennis and table football, plus a TV room. Mountain bike hire, riding, golf and fishing within 1 mile and the castle grounds provide many walking trails. The village is within walking distance with hotels, shops, a water mill craft centre and folk museum. A quality park, quiet at night and well managed. Member of the Best of British group.

Directions: From A9 just north of Pitlochry take B8079 into Blair Atholl. Park is in grounds of Blair Castle, well signed. O.S.GR: NN868659.

Charges 2000:
-- Per unit with all persons £8.00 - £10.00; tent (no car) incl. 2 persons £6.50 - £8.50; extra person £1.00; child (5-12 yrs) 50p; awning or pup tent £1.50 - £2.00; dog (max. 2) 50p; electricity £1.50 - £2.00.
-- VAT included.
-- Credit cards accepted.
Open:
1 April - 30 October.
Address:
Blair Atholl,
Pitlochry,
Perthshire PH18 5SR.
Tel:
(01796) 481263.
FAX: (01796) 481587.
Reservations:
Made for any length with deposit of 1 night's charge + £2 booking fee except 15/7-15/8 when min. 3 nights and payment in full.

Heart of Scotland

728 Nether Craig Caravan Park, by Alyth, Blairgowrie

Very attractive, family run touring park in truly peaceful Glenisla.

Nether Craig is attractively designed and beautifully landscaped, with views across the Strathmore valley to the long range of the Sidlaw hills. The 40 large pitches are accessed from a circular, gravel road; 26 have hardstanding (for awnings too) and 10A electrical connections. The majority are level and there are 9 large tent pitches on flat grass. The central, modern, purpose built toilet block can be heated and provides free pre-set hot showers with dressing area, seat, shelf and hooks, vanity style washbasins and free hairdryers for both male and female. A complete unit for disabled visitors (entry by key) also includes a hairdryer. Chemical disposal. Separate sinks for dishwashing and clothes are provided in the laundry room with metered hot water, washing machine, dryer and iron, with a rotary clothes line outside near the dog walk. It is a good provision which is very well maintained. There is a personal welcome for all visitors at the attractive wooden chalet beside the entrance (with a slope for wheelchairs) which doubles as reception and shop providing the necessary essentials, gas and tourist information. Children have swings and other play equipment, plus a small football field opposite the entrance. A one mile circular woodland walk from the park has picnic benches and a leaflet guide is provided. Otherwise you can just enjoy the peace of the Angus Glens by hill walking, birdwatching, fishing or pony trekking. Three golf courses are within 4 miles. Alyth with its Arthurian connections is only 4 miles away and Glamis Castle, the childhood home of the Queen Mother, is nearby, as is the beautiful Glenshee and Braemar with its castle. Caravan storage.

Charges 2001:
-- Per unit incl. 2 persons £10.00 - £12.00; tent incl. 2 persons £6.00; extra person £1.00; electricity £1.80.
-- VAT included.
-- No credit cards.
Open:
15 March - 31 October.
Address:
By Alyth, Blairgowrie, Perthshire PH11 8HN.
Tel:
(01575) 560204.
FAX: (01575) 560315.
E-mail: nethercraig @lineone.net.
Reservations:
Advisable for main season - contact park.

Directions: From A926 Blairgowrie - Kirriemuir, at roundabout south of Alyth join B954 signed Glenisla. Follow caravan signs for 4 miles and turn right on unclassified road signed Nether Craig. The park is on left in ½ mile. O.S.GR: NO265528.

729 Craigtoun Meadows Holiday Park, St. Andrews

Attractively laid out park with individual pitches and good facilities; holiday homes to let.

Though outnumbered by caravan holiday homes, the touring section on this park is an important subsidiary. The facilities offered are both well designed and comprehensive with 70 units taken on gently sloping land. Caravans go on individual hardstandings with grass alongside for awnings on most pitches. All caravan pitches are equipped with electricity (16A), water and drainage and have been redesigned to increase size (130 sq.m.). There are 24 larger `patio' pitches with summer house, barbecue patio, picnic table and chairs, partially screened. Tents are taken on a grassy meadow at one end, also with electricity available. Only `breathable' type groundsheets to be used in awnings. The 157 caravan holiday homes stand round the outer parts of the site; 32 are owned and let by the park. An excellent, de-luxe, centrally heated sanitary building serves the touring area. All washbasins are in cabins and each toilet has its own basin. Showers are unisex, as are two bathrooms, there are hand and hair dryers, facilities for disabled people and babies, a dishwashing room and chemical disposal. All is free in this first-rate provision. Amenities on the park include a shop and an attractive little licensed restaurant (both restricted hours in low seasons) which also provides a takeaway service. There is a launderette, a games room and mini-gym, a well equipped children's playground and play field and 8 acres of woodland. Barbecue area. Public phone (card). All weather tennis court. Small information room. Dogs are accepted (good dog walk). Buses pass the entrance and Craigtoun park with boating pond and miniature railway, etc. is within walking distance. This is a well run park, only 2 miles from St Andrews with its golf courses and sandy beaches. Bellamy gold.

Charges 2000:
-- Per unit incl. 2 persons and electricity £13.50 - £20.00, 3-6 persons £14.50 - £21.00; backpacker's tent (1 person) £11.50.
-- Credit cards accepted.
-- VAT included.
Open:
1 March - 31 October.
Address:
Mount Melville, St. Andrews, Fife KY16 8PQ.
Tel:
(01334) 475959.
FAX: (01334) 476424.
E-mail: craigtoun @aol.com.
Reservations:
Advised for main season; any length with full payment at time of booking.

Directions: From M90 junction 8 take A91 to St. Andrews. Just after sign for Guardbridge (to left, A919), turn right at site sign and sign for 'Strathkinness, 1¾ miles'. Go through village, over crossroads at end of village, left at next crossroads, then ¾ mile to park. O.S.GR: NO482151.

731 Twenty Shilling Wood Caravan Park, Comrie, nr. Crieff

Secluded family park, taking caravans and motorcaravans only.

Everyone gets a warm welcome from the Lowe family when they arrive at Twenty Shilling. Set amongst 10.5 acres of wooded hillside, this unusual park has a few touring pitches plus a number of owner occupied caravan holiday homes. However, because of terracing and landscaping not many of them are visible and flowering trees and shrubs help to hide them. The lowest level is the entrance (controlled by an automatic barrier; £10 deposit for card) where there is a late arrivals area and visitor car park. The drive then rises to reception (there is no shop but rolls, milk and papers can be ordered here). Alongside is a games room with pool table and table tennis (both free). There is masses of tourist information in the lounge area which has comfortable seating and a well stocked library and where responsible parents can keep an eye on the children whilst they use the games equipment. The fenced adventure playground is on bark and for all ages. The 20 pitches are all level, on gravel with grass bays between them. All have electric hook-ups (10A) and, because of the poor TV reception, also have a free TV aerial hook up with lead provided. You will be escorted to your pitch and sited. The toilet blocks are of an older design but are kept very clean and bright, and have been refurbished to give some washbasins in cubicles and free, controllable showers in tiled, spacious cubicles. The dishwashing area leads into the laundry with washing machine, dryer, iron and clothes lines. Up to two dogs per pitch are accepted with a dog walk provided. Buses pass the gate. Comrie is 1 mile where most things can be purchased. Golf or fishing within 1 mile, riding or bicycle hire 6 miles. There are many walks in the area from strenuous Munros to a gentle stroll to the Devil's Cauldron waterfall. Glen Turret, Scotland's oldest distillery is at Crieff, 7 miles away, Auchingarrich Wildlife centre is 2½ miles, there are watersports at Loch Earn, 11 miles. Bellamy gold.

Charges 2000:
-- Per unit incl. 2 adults £8.00 - £10.50; extra person (over 5 yrs) £1.00; awning (rock pegs required) £1.00; electricity and TV hook-up £2.00.
-- Credit cards accepted.
Open:
23 March - 23 October.
Address:
Comrie,
Perthshire PH6 2JY.
Tel:
(01764) 670411.
FAX: as phone.
E-mail: alowe20
@aol.com.
Reservations:
Advised for B.Hs and July/Aug; made with £10 deposit.

Directions: Park is on north side of A85 Crieff - Lochearnmead road, about ¾ mile west of B827 junction, ½ mile west of Comrie. O.S.GR: NN762222.

732 Witches Craig Caravan Park, Blairlogie, nr. Stirling

Neat and tidy park, nestling under the Ochil Hills.

Witches Craig is a friendly park and the Stephen family take great pride in the fact that so many families return year after year. They take each visitor to their pitch to make sure that they are happy with it. All the 60 pitches have electrical hook-ups (10A) and 14 have hardstanding, 7 of which are enormous taking American style motorhomes easily. The whole site is reasonably level. The toilet and shower block is modern, can be heated and was very clean when we visited. There are vanity style washbasins and a cubicle with washbasin and WC for ladies. Showers are on payment, adjustable with a dividing curtain and room to dress. Soap, hand and hairdryers are provided for both men and women, plus a baby bath and mat. The unit for campers with disabilities is excellent. Laundry with washing machine, dryer and spin dryer and there are washing up sinks. Masses of tourist information is kept in reception, and bread, milk, drinks and papers are available daily (supermarket 2½ miles). The large play area is fenced and surrounded by flowering shrubs with all the equipment on grass or safety rubber, also a field for team games. The park covers 5 acres and there is a pleasant welcoming feel with everything well maintained and the grass beautifully manicured. Seven owner occupied residential park homes are very well kept and surrounded by flowering shrubs. Dogs are accepted with a good walk straight up into the hills from the back of the site. The area has a wealth of historic attractions, starting with the Wallace Monument which practically overlooks the park. Its 220 ft. tower dominates the surrounding area and the climb up its 246 steps gives spectacular views. Stirling is known as the 'Gateway to the Highlands' and its magnificent castle is world renowned. Within 10 miles there are castles, museums, cathedrals and parks. There are many walks from the site into the Ochil Hills. A leaflet of local walks is usually available in reception. Riding or bicycle hire 2 miles, fishing 3 miles, golf 1 mile. Buses stop at the park entrance. Being by the A91, there is some daytime road noise. Trees have been planted to try to minimise this but the further back onto the park you go, the less the traffic is heard.

Charges guide:
-- Per unit incl. 2 adults £9.20 - £10.20; extra adult £1.30; child (2-13 yrs) 80p; extra car £1.30; awning (no groundsheets) or extra small tent £1.80; electricity £1.80; walker with tent £3.95 - £4.95 per person.
-- VAT included.
-- No credit cards.
Open:
1 April - 31 October.
Address:
Blairlogie,
Stirling FK9 5PX.
Tel:
(01786) 474947.
Reservations:
Made without deposit; contact park.

Directions: Park is on the A91, 2 miles northeast of Stirling. O.S.GR: NS822968.

Grampian

755 Huntly Castle Caravan Park, Huntly

Top quality touring park within walking distance of Huntly.

Huntly Caravan Park was opened in '95 and its hard-working owners, Hugh and Debbie Ballantyne, are justly proud of their neat, well landscaped 15 acre site which is managed under contract for the Caravan Club (non-members are also welcome). The 76 level grass and 20 hardstanding touring pitches are separated and numbered, with everyone shown to their pitch. Arranged in three bays with banks of heathers and flowering shrubs separating them, 66 of the pitches have electric hook-ups (16A) and 15 are fully serviced with water and waste water also. Two of the bays have central play areas and all three have easy access to a toilet block, as has the camping area. Campers are provided with a covered cooking shelter (with work tops) should the weather turn inclement. The three heated toilet blocks are well designed and maintained, with washbasins (both in cubicles and vanity style) and large, free showers with lots of changing space. Each block also has a family shower room (even larger), dishwashing sinks with free hot water, chemical disposal facilities and a superb room for disabled visitors. Also one well equipped laundry room. The park also has 33 privately owned caravan holiday homes, plus 3 to hire. The Activity Centre near the entrance contains two indoor safe play areas (one for up to 2 yrs old, the other up to 9 yrs). In addition there are snooker and pool tables, table tennis, badminton and short tennis. There is a charge for these facilities which are also open to the public, with tea, coffee and ices sold (open weekends and all local school holidays). There is no shop on site but milk and papers may be ordered at reception and the town of Huntly is only 10 minutes walk with its shops and pubs. The castle is well worth a visit. The area abounds with things to do, from forest trails to walk or cycle, a falconry centre, malt whisky distilleries and an all year Nordic ski track. Fishing, golf or bicycle hire within ½ mile, riding 5 miles. Dogs are accepted with many good walks from the park. A member of the Best of British group.

Charges 2000:
-- Per standard pitch incl. 2 persons £8.95 - £9.75; electricity £2.00; awning £1.50; porch awning 75p; extra adult £2.00; child (5-16 yrs) £1.00; fully serviced pitch plus £1.50; tent incl. 2 persons £5.75 - £9.75.
-- VAT included.
-- Credit cards accepted.
Open:
24 March - 29 October.
Address:
Huntly,
Aberdeenshire
AB54 4UJ.
Tel:
(01466) 794999.
E-mail: enquiries@ huntlycastle.co.uk.
Reservations:
Contact park.

Directions: The site is well signed from the A96 Keith - Aberdeen road. O.S.GR: NJ526402.

753 Aden Country Park Caravan Park, Mintlaw, nr. Peterhead

Landscaped park in large country park with many attractions.

Aden Country Park is owned by the local authority and is open to the public offering several attractions for visitors including an Agricultural Heritage Centre, Wildlife Centre, Nature Trail, restaurant and craft shops, as well as open and woodland areas, with a lake, for walking and recreation. The caravan and camping site is on one side of the park. Beautifully landscaped and well laid out with trees, bushes and hedges, it is kept very neat and tidy. It provides 48 numbered pitches for touring units, with varying degrees of slope (some level) and all with electrical hook-ups (16A), plus an area for tents. There are also 12 caravan holiday homes in a row on the left as you enter. A modern, fully tiled sanitary block, with good facilities for disabled visitors, was very clean when we visited. It can be heated and provides free, pre-set hot showers, with dressing area, plenty of toilets and vanity type washbasins, with hairdryer for ladies, a baby bath and chemical disposal. Dishwashing and laundry facilities are together, with washing machines, tumble and spin dryers and an iron - all metered. Large dog walking area. Facilities for children include two games areas and various items of play equipment (with safety surfaces). There is a small shop (sweets and ice-creams) in the reception area, the restaurant in the Heritage Centre is available for meals and Mintlaw is ½ mile for shopping. Fishing 1 mile, riding 2 miles, golf 3 miles. The park is in a most attractive area and one could spend plenty of time enjoying all it has to offer.

Charges guide:
-- Per caravan or motor-caravan £8.65; tent £7.50; small tent or awning £3.50; electricity £1.75.
-- Reductions for OAPs out of season.
-- Credit cards accepted.
Open:
Easter - 25 October.
Address:
Old Deer,
Mintlaw,
Aberdeenshire.
Tel:
(01771) 623460.
Reservations:
Advisable for weekends; write to park for details.

Directions: Approaching Mintlaw from the west on A950 road, park is shortly after sign for Mintlaw station. From the east, go to the western outskirts of the village and entrance is on left - `Aden Country Park and Farm Heritage Centre'. O.S.GR: NJ985484.

WIDEN YOUR HORIZONS WITH CALOR GAS

Holidaymakers throughout the UK benefit from using Calor gas

Established in 1935, Calor Gas pioneered the development of liquefied petroleum gas (LPG) as a clean, efficient and convenient source of fuel for heating, cooking and lighting for caravanners and campers. Calor gas is a reliable, flexible fuel which has now been in use in caravanning and camping for over 60 years.

Calor Gas has developed strong links with the tourism and leisure sector and its support to the caravan industry is demonstrated through its close association with national organisations including the British Holiday and Home Parks Association, the National Caravan Council and the national Tourist Boards. A good example of Calor's support is the annual Calor Gas Caravan Park Awards scheme. The scheme encourages parks to improve facilities and services, providing caravanners and campers with all the ingredients for a first class holiday.

Calor also continues to work closely with major appliance manufacturers to develop new products and has recently launched its Calor Choice range of top quality, competitively priced

Calor-powered patio heaters enhance alfresco evenings

appliances. The range includes barbecues and patio heaters, designed to enable caravanners and campers to further enjoy their holidays with relaxed evenings of alfresco dining and drinking.

Appliances from the Calor Choice range are available from Calor's nationwide network of over 10,000 dealers and stockists, which supply gas and related products to all parts of the UK mainland and many of the surrounding islands. For details of your nearest Calor stockist, or for further information on the use of LPG in caravanning and camping please call Calor Gas free on *0800 626626*.

Comfort on the move with *Electrolux - The complete range of portable 3 way Refrigerators and Freezers*

Electrolux RC 1180
New portable fridge/freezer. 30 litres of fridge and 16 litres of 2 star freezer to cater for all your needs on the move. 3 way operation with noiseless Electrolux absorption technology.

Electrolux F 400
Portable 2 star-freezer - Frozen pleasure, wherever you want. Ice making facility. Piezo igniter. Thermostatic control for mains and gas operation. 39 litres.

Electrolux RC 1600
Cool Pleasure Unlimited. Anywhere. Anytime. Ice making facility. Piezo igniter for gas operation. Thermostat on mains operation. 35 litres.

Electrolux RC 3000
Cool comfort and complete freedom. The first absorption refrigerator with click on-wheels. Ice cube making facility. Push button piezo igniter. Thermostatic control on mains. 35 litres.

Keep Cool day and night. With Electrolux you can be at home everywhere. **1.** Portable refrigerators and Freezers from Electrolux have 3 way operation. **2.** 12v, 230v or LP Gas, the choice is yours. **3.** The RC 1600 is available in a 24volt version. **4.** All models are silent in operation. **5.** The only fridge for camping, your private bar under the awning, a Freezer to feed the Microwave, the limit is your imagination!

www.electrolux.com/caravan

Electrolux
THE SIGN OF COMFORT

Maritime Greenwich
The Story of Time, Space and the Sea

Explorers, Passengers, Trade & Empire, Nelson,
Harrison's clocks, The Meridian Line, Children's galleries.
Open daily 1000-1700.

Easy access from the M25 via A2 to Greenwich Park
or travel by Docklands Light Rail or River Cruise.
Information on 020 8312 6565 or www.nmm.ac.uk

754 Aberlour Gardens Caravan and Camping Park, Aberlour

Pleasant park within the large walled garden of the Aberlour Estate.

Mr and Mrs Moss, the owners, have made improvements to this sheltered, five acre, family run park on Speyside which provides a very natural setting amidst spruce and Scots pine. Of the 61 level pitches, 35 are for touring units leaving the remainder for holiday homes (1 for rent) and seasonal units. All pitches have electrical connections (10A) and 9 are 'all-weather' pitches. The toilet block can be heated and has vanity style washbasins (with shelves, mirrors, soap and towels), four large unisex showers on payment and facilities for visitors with disabilities. Laundry facilities, chemical disposal and motorcaravan service point. A small licensed shop stocks basics and has an information area. Children's play area. Public telephone. Dogs are welcome if kept under control. Caravan storage available. This is an ideal area for walking, birdwatching, fishing (salmon, 1 or 5 miles), pony trekking or for following the only Malt Whisky Trail in the world. Golf 4 miles, riding ½ mile, bicycle hire 1 mile, bowls 2 miles.

Directions: Turn off A95 between Aberlour and Craigellachie onto unclassified road and site is signed in 500 yds. Vehicles over 10' 6" high should use A941 Dufftown Road (site is signed). O.S.GR: NJ282432.

Charges 2000:
-- Per unit incl. 2 persons £6.75 - £9.25; tent £6.50 - £8.00; backpacker £3.00 - £3.75 (per person); extra person £2.00; child (5-16 yrs) £1.00; electricity £1.50 - £1.75.
-- No credit cards.
Open:
1 April - 31 October.
Address:
Aberlour-on-Spey, Banffshire AB38 9LD.
Tel/Fax:
(01340) 871586.
E-mail: abergard@ compuserve.com.
Reservations:
Advised for July/Aug; made with deposit.

766 Spindrift Caravan and Camping Park, Little Kildrummie, Nairn

Attractive, quiet, small family run park near popular resort.

Mr and Mrs Guillot have put a lot of thought into the landscaping of their park, making it into an absolute gem. Set in an elevated position overlooking the distant Monadlaith mountains and a short walk from the River Nairn, the popular seaside resort of Nairn with its shops, restaurants, beach and harbour is 2 miles away and it is said to take 30 minutes to walk via the riverside path. The park is surrounded by trees and is arranged on three terraces. The lowest level is used primarily for tents. With 40 pitches altogether, there are 28 electrical connections (16A), all on the highest terrace, although if you have a long cable, reached from the second level too. Part of the top level is set aside for motorcaravans (no dedicated service point). Two modern sanitary blocks are well equipped with free controllable hot showers, vanity style washbasins, hair dryers and chemical disposal. The large laundry room has separate dishwashing and laundry sinks with free hot water, a washing machine, dryer and iron. A thoughtful addition is a large table and chairs for the use of campers in inclement weather. The front porch of the owners house is used as reception (gas available), with tourist information and a telephone (left open at all times). There is no shop but the shops of Nairn are near. A bus passes the lane end (400 yds). Salmon fishing permits are available at the park. Bicycle hire, riding, golf and boat launching within 2 miles.

Directions: Follow the signs for Spindrift along the A976 which runs through Nairn. O.S.GR: NH863537.

Charges 2001:
-- Per unit incl. 2 adults and 2 children £7.50 - £9.50; small tent (2 adults) £6.50 - £9.00; extra adult free - £1.00; child free - 50p; awning free - £1.00; electricity (15A) £2.00.
-- No credit cards.
Open:
1 April - 31 October.
Address:
Little Kildrummie, Nairn, Highlands IV12 5QU.
Tel:
(01667) 453992.
E-mail: camping@ spindriftcaravanpark. freeserve.co.uk.
Reservations:
Advised for July/Aug. with £5 deposit.

769 Torvean Caravan Park, Inverness

Small, neat, select touring park for caravans and motorcaravans only.

Torvean is situated on the outskirts of Inverness beside the Caledonian Canal and within easy reach of the town's amenities which include an ice rink, theatre and leisure sports centre. Excursions to the coast and Highlands, including Loch Ness, are possible in several directions. The pitches on neat, level grass are well spaced out and clearly marked with a tarmac access road and street lighting giving a very neat appearance. There are 47 touring pitches (27 with 10A electrical connections, 18 fully serviced with fresh water tap, waste water disposal and electricity connection) and 10 caravan holiday homes for hire. Torvean offers a children's play area on bark, a well equipped launderette and public telephone. The two toilet blocks are of good quality with free hot water in washbasins set in flat surfaces with shelves and mirrors - ladies have two cubicles with washbasin and toilet and a hair washing cubicle. There are controllable hot showers on payment, hand and hair dryers, a suite for disabled people with toilet and shower and chemical disposal. A motorcaravan service point is next to the far toilet block. A dog walking area is provided. Golf adjacent, bicycle hire or fishing 3 miles.

Directions: Park is off the main A82 road on the southwest outskirts of the town by the Tomnahurich Canal Bridge. O.S.GR: NH638438.

Charges guide:
-- Per unit incl. 2 adults £9.00 - £11.50; electricity £2.00; extra adult £1.50; extra child (under 16 yrs) 75p; awning £2.00 - £3.00; small dog £1.00 (one only).
-- No credit cards.
Open:
Easter - end-October.
Address:
Glenurquhart Road, Inverness IV3 6JL.
Tel:
(01463) 220582.
FAX: (01463) 233051.
Reservations:
Made with first night's charge and £1 fee.

Highlands and Islands

767 Grantown-on-Spey Caravan Park, Grantown-on-Spey

Family run touring park with good sanitary facilities.

Gerald and Brenda Naylor take care of this excellent park which is owned by
Sandra McKelvie and her son John Fleming, and managed under contract for the
Caravan Club (non-members welcome). Peacefully situated on the outskirts of the
town, with views of the mountains in the distance, the park consists of well-tended
gravel (raked as soon as visitors leave so that it is perfect for the next occupier)
and grass pitches. Trees and flowers are a feature of this landscaped location.
There are 100 pitches for caravans or motorcaravans, of which 5 offer fresh and
waste water facilities and 16 have individual fresh water taps. A further 20 pitches
are available for seasonal occupation, and there is space for 50 or more tents.
More than 80 pitches have 10A electrical hook-ups. Gerald Naylor escorts visitors
to their pitch and will help to site caravans if necessary. Caravan holiday homes
are located in a separate area of the park. Sanitary facilities in two clean, modern
blocks include free hot water to individual washbasins and controllable showers,
covered dishwashing sinks behind each block, a laundry room with washing
machines, spin dryers and irons, and a chemical disposal point. The motorcaravan
service point features a drive-over waste water emptying facility and a fresh water
tap. Campers have access to a football field, games room (with table tennis and
pool table), two public telephone kiosks and a dog walk with hilltop views. There
is no on-site shop because the town is just a short distance away, however gas
cylinders, ice creams, cold drinks and various camping accessories can be
purchased at reception. Grantown is a pleasant touring base for the Cairngorms
and for the Malt Whisky Trail. Fishing, golf and mountain bike hire within 1 mile,
riding 3 miles. Winter caravan storage. A peaceful park with a warden on site at
all times.

Charges 2000:
-- Per pitch incl. 2
persons £7.00 - £10.50; 2
man tent and vehicle
£6.00 - £8.00; hiker's 2
man tent £5.00 - £6.00;
awning or extra pup tent
£1.50; extra person
£1.00; electricity £2.00.
-- VAT included.
-- Credit cards accepted.

Open:
31 March - 31 October.

Address:
Seafield Avenue,
Grantown on Spey,
Moray PH26 3JQ.

Tel:
(01479) 872474.
FAX: (01479) 873696.
E-mail: grantown
@aol.com.

Reservations:
Advised for peak periods
and made with £10
deposit.

Directions: Park is signed from the town centre. O.S.GR: NJ028283.

768 Glenmore Caravan and Camping Site, Glenmore, Aviemore

Forestry Commission site ideally placed for watersports and exploring the Cairngorms.

The Glenmore Forest site lies close to the sandy shore of Loch Morlich amidst
conifer woods and surrounded on three sides by the impressive Cairngorm
mountains. It is conveniently situated for a range of activities, including skiing
(extensive lift system), orienteering, hill and mountain walking (way-marked
walks), fishing (trout and pike) and non-motorized watersports on the Loch. The
site itself is attractively laid out in a fairly informal style in several adjoining areas
connected by narrow part gravel, part tarmac roadways with access to the
lochside. One of these areas, the Pinewood Area, is very popular and has 32
hardstandings (some distance from the toilet block). Of the 220 marked pitches on
fairly level grass, 137 have electricity (10A). There are two very basic toilet
blocks with heating and free hot water to the washbasins, but only one shower/
laundry block which is some distance from the majority of the pitches and reached
by an underpass. Opened by electronic key pad (you are given a number), it is a
large heated block with free hot showers, providing basic facilities. There is a
separate unit for visitors with disabilities. Next to the site is a range of amenities
including a well stocked shop, a café serving a variety of meals and snacks, and a
Forestry Commission visitor centre and souvenir shop (better than average quality
souvenirs). Barbecues are not permitted in dry weather. The Aviemore centre
providing a wide range of indoor and outdoor recreations is only 7 miles and there
are several golf courses within a range of 15 miles, as well as fishing and boat
trips. The new site managers live on site.

Charges 2000:
-- Per unit incl. up to 4
persons £7.70 - £9.20;
'select' pitch +£3.20;
electricity £2.20; back-
packer £3.80 - £4.50.
-- Less 20% all year for
disabled guests and
outside 7/7-28/8 for
senior citizens.
-- Credit cards accepted.

Open:
All year
except 1 Nov - 15 Dec.

Address:
Glenmore, Aviemore,
Inverness-shire
PH22 1QU.

Tel:
(01479) 861271.

Reservations:
Necessary for B.Hs and
peak times; made for
min. 3 nights with £30
deposit. Contact site
when open, otherwise
Forest Holidays, Forestry
Commission, 231
Corstorphine Road,
Edinburgh EH12 7AT.
Tel: (0131) 314 6505.
E-mail: fe.holidays@
forestry.gov.uk.

Directions: Immediately south of Aviemore on B9152 (not A9 bypass) take B970
then follow sign for Cairngorm and Loch Morlich. Site entrance is on right past
the loch. O.S.GR: NH975097.

770 Pitgrudy Caravan Park, Dornoch

Quiet park with marvellous views, in the heart of the Highlands.

Pitgrudy is in a rural situation with superb views over the Dornoch Firth and the surrounding Ross-shire hills. There are 40 touring pitches for caravans, motorcaravans or tents, mostly on slightly sloping grass and with electrical connections (10A). A few have hardstanding (unfortunately still on a slope) and six are fully serviced (drinking water, waste water disposal point and electricity). Located at the top of the park are 35 caravan holiday homes, 25 privately owned and 10 to hire. The whole park is on immaculately tended grass with tarmac roads. Sanitary facilities are provided in a modern, superior 'portacabin' style unit. Very clean and well equipped, the showers are controllable and free. A laundry has a washing machine, dryer and iron and there are separate dishwashing sinks. Chemical disposal. Gas is available but there is no shop – Dornoch, a pleasant little town, is less than a mile away with shops, restaurants, plus the cathedral. A safe sandy beach is 1 mile and the area is good for walking and golf (there are 7 courses within 15 miles of the park). Fishing 1 mile, bicycle hire or boat launching 3 miles, riding 5 miles. A member of the Best of British group.

Directions: At war memorial in Dornoch, turn north (park signed) on the B9168. Park is ½ mile on the right (45 miles north of Inverness). O.S.GR: NH795911.

Charges 2000:
-- Per unit incl. 2 persons £7.00 - £11.00; extra adult £1.00; child (under 16 yrs) 50p; awning £1.50; dog (max. 2) free; electricity £2.00.
-- No credit cards.
Open:
25 April - 30 September.
Address:
Poles Road, Dornoch, Highland IV25 3HY.
Tel:
(01862) 821253
(9 am. - 5.30 pm).
FAX: (01862) 821382.
Reservations:
Made with deposit and £1 fee. Enquiries to: GNR Sutherland, Caravan Sales, Edderton, Tain, Ross-shire IV19 1JY.

772 Woodend Camping and Caravan Park, Achnairn, Lairg

Delightful, peaceful and welcoming park overlooking Loch Shin.

Perfect for hill walkers and backpackers, Mrs Cathie Ross runs this small, simple park and provides a warm Scottish welcome. On a hill with panoramic views across the Loch to the hills beyond and all around, the large camping field is undulating and gently sloping with some reasonably flat areas. The park is licensed to take 55 units, although few pitches would be suitable for caravans or motorcaravans. Most of the 22 electrical hook-ups (16A) are in a line near the top of the field, close to the large, fenced children's play area which has several items of equipment on grass. The modernised sanitary facilities are kept very clean and are quite satisfactory, with hot water for showers, chemical disposal and dishwashing on small payment. A laundry with two machines and a dryer is just behind and a kitchen and eating room for tent campers. Reception and a shop are at the house. Fishing licences for the Loch are available. Besides fishing, there are opportunities for hill walking, mountain bikes can be hired in Lairg (5 miles) and there are several scenic golf courses within 20-30 miles. The famous Falls of Shin are 10 miles). Caravan holiday homes (5) to rent.

Directions: Achnairn is near the southern end of Loch Shin. Turn off the A838 single track road at signs for Woodend. From the A9 coming north take the A836 at Bonar Bridge, 11 miles northwest of Tain. O.S.GR: NC558127.

Charges 2000:
-- Per unit incl. electricity £7.00; tent £6.00.
-- No credit cards.
Open:
1 April - 30 September.
Address:
Achnairn, Lairg, Sutherland IV27 4DN.
Tel:
(01549) 402248.
FAX: as phone.
Reservations:
Not considered necessary.

773 Scourie Caravan and Camping Park, Scourie, nr. Handa Island

Family park with own restaurant, close to ferries for Handa Island Bird Sanctuary.

Mr Mackenzie has carefully nurtured this park, developing a number of firm terraces with 60 pitches. Perched on the edge of the bay in an elevated position, practically everyone has a view of the sea. The park has tarmac and gravel access roads, with well drained grass pitches and some hard-core hardstandings with 10A electricity. A few are on an area which is unfenced from the rocks (young children would need to be supervised here). Reception, alongside the modern toilet block, contains tourist information. The heated toilet facilities have free hot water to vanity style washbasins and controllable free showers (no divider or seat). There is a laundry room, chemical disposal and a motorcaravan service point. There are good facilities for disabled visitors on the park and at the restaurant, although the ramps leading to them are a little steep. The 'Anchorage' restaurant is at the park entrance (1/5-15/9). Trips to Handa Island (a protection area for seabird colonies) are available from here and Tarbet. The clear water makes this area ideal for diving. Fishing permits (brown trout) can be arranged. The village has a well stocked shop with post office; gas is available from the local petrol station.

Directions: Park is by Scourie village on A894 road in northwest Sutherland. O.S.GR: NC153446.

Charges 2000:
-- Per unit incl. 2 adults £8.00, 1 adult £7.00; extra adult £1.00; child (3-16 yrs) 50p; hiker and tent £5.00; extra tent, vehicle or awning £1.00; electricity £2.00.
-- No credit cards.
Open:
1 April - 30 September, but phone first to check.
Address:
Harbour Road, Scourie, Sutherland IV27 4TG.
Tel:
(01971) 502060.
Reservations:
Not made.

Highlands and Islands

764 Dunroamin Caravan Park, Lairg, Sutherland

Small, quiet park providing a suitable stopover while exploring northern Scotland.

Lewis and Margaret Hudson run this small park, close to the centre of Lairg and ideally suited for touring Sutherland and Caithness. Fifty level pitches are reserved for touring caravans, motorcaravans and tents on well-tended grass, and there are ten caravan holiday homes for hire. None of the pitches are marked so the owner directs caravans and motorhomes to the camping area and positions them correctly. Tent campers are able to select their own spot in a field behind the row of caravan holiday homes. There are 15 electrical hook-ups (10/16A) and 8 hardstandings, which are concrete below an inch of grass. A central sanitary block offers WCs, open washbasins with free hot and cold water, a shower (20p for 6 mins), and hairdryer (20p). Soap dispensers, paper towels, mirrors, shelves and coat hooks are also provided, and everything is kept clean and tidy. Other services attached to the block include a chemical disposal point at one end, a covered dishwashing sink at the rear, and fresh water tap and waste water disposal at the remaining end. There is no motorcaravan service point although tanks can be drained in a manhole near the entrance. The laundry is at the side of the main building to the right of the park entrance and comprises a washing machine, tumble dryer, spin-dryer, two deep sinks (free hot water) iron, and clothes airers. A public telephone is also close by. Tourist information and basic camping requisites, gas exchange and post cards are available at the reception; the nearest shop is 300 yds. A fully licensed restaurant next to the reception (open 8 am-8 pm) serves breakfasts, snacks and evening meals. Bicycles and barbecues can be hired from park. Local activities include a weekly ceilidh at the village hall, a multi-sports area, walking, fishing (permits are arranged at park) and watersports on nearby Loch Shin. Ferrycroft Country Centre is a 20-minute walk away. There are three buses daily to Inverness, and three trains daily further afield (timetable in reception). Dogs (max. two per unit) must be kept on a lead and exercised off site. This is a superb location for exploring the Shin Triangle.

Directions: On A836 (Lairg - Roagart road), park is on the south side of Lairg. Follow international camping signs. O.S.Landranger Sheet 16 586062.

Charges 2000:
-- Per unit incl. 2 adults £5.50 - £9.00; backpacker £4.50 - £7.00; extra person £1.00; extra car £1.00; electricity £2.00; awning £2.00; dog £1.00.
-- Less 10% for 7 or more nights.
-- VAT included.

Open:
1 April - 1 November.

Address:
Main Street,
Lairg,
Sutherland IV27 4AR

Tel:
(01549) 402447.
FAX: (01549) 402874.
E-mail:
dunroaming@hudson38.
freeserve.co.uk.

Reservations:
Made with £20 per week deposit, balance 4 weeks prior to arrival.

776 Reraig Caravan Site, Balmacara, Kyle of Lochalsh

Small, quiet park with views over to Skye, for caravans, motorcaravans and small tents.

This is a small, level park close to Loch Alsh and with a wooded hillside behind (criss-crossed with woodland walks). Mainly grass, it is sheltered from the prevailing winds by the hill and provides just 40 numbered pitches, 36 with electrical connections (10A) and some hardstandings. Large tents and trailer tents are not accepted at all. Small tents are permitted at the discretion of the owner, so it would be advisable to telephone first if this affects you. Awnings are not permitted during July and August in order to protect the grass. The ground can be stony so there could be a problem with tent pegs. The single sanitary block has been extensively refurbished (tiled floors and showers washbasins in vanity units, etc) and is kept immaculately clean. Washbasins are in vanity units with pine surrounds and very decorative mirrors, children have their own low basins, controllable hot showers are on payment (10p for 2 minutes), as are hair dryers, and a room at the end of the block provides sinks for clothes and dishwashing with free hot water. Use of a spin dryer is free. Chemical disposal and motorcaravan drainage point. Adjacent to the park is the Balmacara Hotel (with bar), shop (selling gas), sub-post office, off licence and petrol station. An attractive little park with well cut grass, Reraig makes a good base from which to explore the Isle of Skye and the pretty village of Plockton with its palm trees (remember Hamish Macbeth on TV?) Reservations are not necessary but it is advisable to arrive before late afternoon in July and August.

Directions: Take A87 towards Kyle of Lochalsh. Park is signed very soon after sign for Balmacara, on the right just before hotel and petrol station. O.S.GR: NG815272.

Charges 2001:
-- Per unit incl. 2 persons £7.80; extra adult £1.50; electricity (10A) £1.50; awning (May, June, Sept only) £1.50; backpackers/cyclists £6.50 per tent.
-- Credit cards accepted.

Open:
Easter - 30 September.

Address:
Balmacara,
Kyle of Lochalsh,
Ross-shire IV40 8DH.

Tel:
(01599) 566215.

Reservations:
Not necessary so not accepted by phone; if considered essential, by letter enclosing cheque/ PO for first night's fee (non-returnable).

196

771 Ardmair Point Caravan Park, Ardmair Point, nr. Ullapool

Spectacularly situated park on bay at Loch Kanaird.

Just three miles north of Ullapool and overlooking the little Loch Kanaird, just round the corner from Loch Broom, this park has splendid views all round. The 68 touring pitches are arranged mainly on grass around the edge of the bay in front of the shingle beach. Electrical hook-ups (10A) are available and some gravel hardstandings are on the other side of the access road, just past the well equipped second sanitary block. This block, with wonderful views from the large windows in the launderette and dishwashing rooms, provides good facilities including free hot showers and washbasins set in flat surfaces, plus large en-suite rooms for disabled people. Motorcaravans are not permitted on the grass pitches and must use the hardstandings. Tent pitches, together with cheaper pitches for some tourers are in a large field behind the other sanitary facilities (also good). Other amenities include reception, a restaurant and shop, housed in the same building, motor-caravan service point and a children's play area. Luxury timber chalets (separate from the camping park) accommodating up to six people are for hire. The park provides rowing and motorboats for hire and arranges fishing trips. Scuba diving is popular at Loch Kanaird because the water is so clear. Golf or bicycle hire 3 miles. Seals are regularly seen in the bay and the whole area is full of interest, including visits to Inverewe Gardens and the Isle Martin bird and seal colonies.

Directions: Park is off the A835 road, 3 miles north of Ullapool. O.S.GR: NH109983.

Charges 2000:
-- Per unit incl. two persons £7.50 - £10.00; awning £2.00; extra adult £2.00 - £3.00; child (over 5 yrs) £1.00; electricity (10A) £2.00.
-- Credit cards accepted.
-- VAT included.
Open:
1 May - late September, depending on weather, if in doubt phone.
Address:
Ardmair Point, Ullapool, Ross-shire IV26 2TN.
Tel:
(01854) 612054.
FAX: (01854) 612757.
E-mail: p.fraser@btinternet.com.
Reservations:
Recommended for July/Aug. (min. 2 nights).

774 Loch Greshornish Camping Site, Edinbane, Isle of Skye

Simple, spacious site overlooking the Loch in northwest Skye.

Mr and Mrs Palmer and Lesley Bisset took over this simple site with basic facil-ities in 1999. In a beautiful, peaceful setting with views over the loch to the low hills to the northwest of Skye, it is suitable for long or short stays. There are 30 level grass pitches for motorcaravans and caravans, 18 with 10A electric hook-ups. There are also places for up to 100 tents (but numbers never reach that level). The sanitary facilities have been refurbished and are light and airy, very well painted and spotlessly clean. They provide free hot water to showers (a little cramped) and washbasins, plus a dishwashing sink in the ladies' and another in the men's. A hair dryer is on payment. The only acknowledgement of any clothes washing needs is a tumble dryer in a little cabin outside. A new building houses reception and a small shop selling basic essentials, although it is to be expanded gradually to include an off-licence. The owners are offering bicycle hire (with safety helmets) and future plans include a children's play area. The local village has a hotel for drinks and meals; Portree, the nearest town, is 15 miles away.

Directions: Site is 15 miles west of Portree on the A850 Dunvegan road by Edinbane. O.S.GR: NG343524.

Charges 2000:
-- Per unit incl. 2 persons £7.00; extra person £3.50; child (5-16 yrs) £1.00; electricity £1.50; small tent £3.50 per person.
Open:
Easter - 12 October.
Address:
Arnisort, Edinbane, Isle of Skye IV51 9PS.
Tel:
(01470) 582230.
Reservations:
Advised for high season - contact site.

775 Staffin Caravan and Camping Site, Staffin, Isle of Skye

Simple hillside site with wonderful views in northeast Skye.

This very basic camping site is on the side of a hill just outside Staffin, where the broad sweep of the bay is dotted with working crofts running down to the sea. A marked walk from the site leads to the seashore and slipway (good for walking dogs but too far to be taking a boat). With 50 pitches, the site is quite sloping but there are 18 reasonably level pitches with irregular hardstanding for caravans and motorcaravans, all with electricity (16A). This is a site more suited to backpackers and small tents. The sanitary block is tiled with large, controllable, free showers and vanity style washbasins. Washing up sinks are unfortunately not under cover and have only cold water. There is also an older block but this is only open at very busy times. Chemical disposal facilities are out in the open. A large hardstanding area has a motorcaravan service point and gas is for sale. Staffin village is 400 yards with a large shop (six days a week), a restaurant, launderette, plus a public phone. Skye has many activities to offer and for the truly dedicated walker the Cuillins are the big attraction but the hills above Staffin look demanding! Fishing or boat launching 1 mile, bicycle hire 5 miles, riding 9 miles.Cottage for rent.

Directions: Site is 15 miles north of Portree on A855 (2 miles of single track at the start), just before Staffin on the right and up a slope. O.S.GR: NG496668.

Charges 2000:
-- Per caravan or motor-caravan incl. 2 persons £8.00; tent incl. 2 persons £7.00 - £7.50, 1 person £4.00; extra adult £3.00; child £1.00 - £1.50; electricity £1.50.
-- No credit cards.
Open:
1 April - 30 September (maybe October if fine).
Address:
Staffin, Isle of Skye IV51 9JS.
Tel:
(01470) 562213.
Reservations:
Maybe necessary for peak periods (made with £10 deposit).

Highlands and Islands

778 Faichem Park, Faichem, Invergarry

Small unsophisticated site near Loch Ness with wonderful views.

Faichem Park is situated on a hillside in a beautiful setting with glorious views over Ben Tee (2,955 ft). The road up to the site is of tarmac so it is now accessible to all except American motorhomes. For children there is the attraction of helping to feed the animals - sheep and lambs, chickens, many types of ducks and strange marvellous looking types of pheasants (Mr Wilson's hobby), the pony and the white 'runner' ducks which march around the park and farm. There are 30 pitches with plenty of space, including 14 with electricity and 10 with level concrete hardstanding. A log type cabin houses sanitary facilities which are older in style but very clean and well painted (key, £1 deposit). Hot water to the showers is metered but is free to the washbasins (with soap) and dishwashing sinks. Hair and hand dryers are provided. The chemical disposal unit is of a very high standard. Gas is available and eggs are sold at the farm but there is no shop (closest 2 miles towards Fort William). Four barbecues are positioned for visitors' use. The village is ½ mile with a hotel. Dogs are accepted (but care is needed with livestock) and there is an excellent area above the site for walks. TV reception is good. A flexible system for night-time allows campers to turn off lights close to their pitch if necessary. Pony trekking near, a pleasure cruiser on Loch Ness and the Great Glen water park (2 miles). Bicycle hire or boat slipway 2 miles, golf 7 miles. Pine lodges and a cottage to let.

Charges 2001:
-- Per unit incl. 2 persons £7.00 - £7.50; extra adult 50p; extra child 25p; electricity £1.50 - £2.00.
-- No credit cards.
Open:
15 March - 15 October.
Address:
Ardgarry Farm, Faichem, Invergarry, Inverness-shire
Tel:
(01809) 501226.
FAX: (01809) 501307.
E-mail: ardgarry.farm @lineone.net.
Reservations:
Advisable in main season and made with small deposit.

Directions: From A82 at Invergarry take A87 (towards Kyle of Lochalsh) for 1 mile. Turn right at Faichem sign and bear left up hill, farmhouse and reception is the first entrance on the right, site is second. From opposite direction on A87, left at Faichem sign, third on left for reception, second for park. O.S.GR: NH285023.

779 Invercoe Caravan and Camping Park, Invercoe, Glencoe

Family owned park in magnificent historical setting.

On the edge of Loch Leven, surrounded by mountains and forest, Iain and Lynn Brown are continually developing this attractively located park. It provides 60 pitches for caravans, motorcaravans or tents on level grass with gravel access roads (some hardstandings). You choose your own numbered pitch, those at the loch side being very popular, although the majority of the electrical hook-ups (10A) are to the back of the park. Five caravan holiday homes and three chalets are for hire. Adjoining the shop (May - end Sept) near the entrance is the nicely refurbished toilet block which can be heated and has free hot showers and vanity style washbasins (shower/wash room locked 10 pm. - 7 am). Dishwashing under cover, excellent laundry facilities with a drying room, and chemical disposal facilities are provided. The new motorcaravan service point is one of the best we have seen, comprising multi-drainage point, fresh water, dustbins, and chemical disposal point. Public telephone. Play area with swings. The only park rules imposed are necessary for safety because the owners prefer their guests to feel free and enjoy themselves. The village with pub and restaurant is within walking distance. There is much to do for the active with hill walking, climbing, boating, pony riding and sea loch or fresh water fishing in this area of outstanding natural beauty, with the Visitor's Centre at Glencoe just a couple of miles away.

Charges 2000:
-- Per unit incl. 2 persons £10.00; extra adult £1.00; child (over 2 yrs) 50p; awning £1.50 per car or boat on trailer £1.00; electricity (10A) £1.50; tent incl. 2 persons, no car £8.00.
-- Credit cards accepted.
-- VAT included.
Open:
Easter/1 April - end Oct.
Address:
Invercoe, Glencoe, Argyll PH49 4HP.
Tel/Fax:
(01855) 811210.
E-mail:
invercoe@sol.co.uk.
Reservations:
Recommended for electricity for peak season; made with £17 deposit and £3 fee.

Directions: Follow A82 Crianlarich - Fort William road to Glencoe village and turn onto the B863; park is ½ mile along, well signed. O.S.GR: NN098594.

780 Resipole Farm Caravan and Camping Park, Acharacle

Beautifully situated park on the loch shores, with good facilities.

This quiet, open park is marvellously set on the banks of Loch Sunart, 8 miles from Strontian, in the Ardnamurchan peninsula, with views across the water and is regularly visited by wild deer. It offers a good base for exploring the whole of this scenic area or, more locally, for fishing, boating (launching from the site's own slipway) and walking in the unspoilt countryside. There are 60 touring pitches here, more than half with hardstanding and electric hook-ups (10A), and 4 with all services. Tents are sited by the hedges. The central, modern sanitary block can be heated and provides free, pre-set showers, with dressing area, hooks and seat, washbasins in rows with mirrors, shelves, shaver points and hair dryers. All was very clean when seen, good dishwashing facilities are in separate rooms and there is excellent provision for visitors with disabilities. Other amenities include chemical disposal, laundry facilities and a public telephone. Adjoining the farmhouse is a well equipped bar and restaurant offering reasonably priced home made food in the evenings (vegetarians catered for). The park has its own 9 hole golf course. Riding 5 miles. Some caravans and cabins to hire. Caravan storage . Resipole Farm is well located for day trips to Mull via the Lochaline ferry.

Directions: From A82 Fort William road, take Corran ferry 5 miles north of Ballachulish and 8 miles south of Fort William. On leaving ferry, turn south along the A861. Park is on north bank of Loch Sunart, 8 miles west of Strontian. Note: the road is single track for 8 miles and care is needed. O.S.GR: NM676740.

Charges 2000:
-- Per caravan incl. 2 persons £9.00 - £10.00; motorcaravan or tent £8.50 - £9.50; cyclists (2 persons) £7.00; extra adult £3.00; child up to 5 yrs 50p, 6-12 yrs £1.00, 13 yrs upwards £1.50; electricity £1.50.
-- Credit cards accepted.
Open:
1 April - 31 October.
Address:
Loch Sunart, Acharacle, Argyll PH36 4HX.
Tel:
(01967) 431235.
FAX: (01967) 431777.
E-mail: info@ resipole.co.uk.
Reservations:
Advisable for hook-ups and made for any period with one night's fee.

781 Camping and Caravanning Club Site Oban, Barcaldine

Small friendly site in a sheltered location north of Oban.

This Club site at Barcaldine 12 miles north of Oban, is a small, intimate site taking 86 units. Arranged within the old walled garden of Barcaldine House, the walls give protection from the wind and make it quite a sun trap. There are 27 level pitches with hardstanding and 52 electrical hook-ups (16A). Being a small site, it has a very cosy feel, due no doubt to the friendly welcome new arrivals receive. Through the garden gate, one is immediately in the Barcaldine forest with its miles of forest tracks, perfect for both dog walking and mountain biking. The central toilet block can be heated and is kept very clean with free hot showers, hair dryers and plenty of washbasins and WCs. The laundry is next to the small shop for basic provisions and gas. Motorcaravan service point and an excellent unit for disabled visitors. Small play area with safety base. Unusual for a club site, is a lounge bar serving meals most evenings. The loch across the road is handy for sea fishing and a 20 minute walk takes you to a freshwater lake for fishing. Sea Life Centre 2 miles and a not too frequent bus passes the gate.

Directions: Park entrance is off the A828 road on south side of Loch Creran, 6 miles north of Connel Bridge. O.S.GR: NM966420.

Charges 2000:
-- Per adult £3.15 - £4.80; child (6-18 yrs) £1.55; non-member pitch fee £4.30; electricity £1.60 - £2.35.
-- VAT included.
-- Credit cards accepted.
Open:
April - end October.
Address:
Barcaldine by Connel, Argyll PA37 1SG.
Tel:
(01631) 720348 (no calls after 8 pm).
Reservations:
Necessary for high season and made with deposit.

782 Oban Divers Caravan Park, Oban

Scenic, peaceful and friendly park close to Oban.

Set most attractively in a 4 acre valley, yet close to Oban, this park has been thoughtfully developed as an extension to the garden of the owner's family home and diving business. There are only 45 pitches with 12 hardstandings, 34 electrical connections (10A) and plenty of space. Tents are placed mainly on a higher back terrace. Sanitary facilities are in two chalets, the smaller one near the tent pitches. The main chalet provides comfortable facilities with two ladies' washbasins in cabins and dishwashing, laundry and chemical disposal rooms. Small shop at reception with gas, covered barbecue with seating and a motorcaravan service point. An open fronted room is provided for tenters. Children's play items on gravel. The single track approach to the park has few passing places, so it is only suitable for smaller units. Bunk houses for groups to rent, two for up to six people, one up to twelve. Fishing 1 mile, bicycle hire 2 miles, riding or golf 3 miles. Definitely no dogs accepted. A member of the Countryside Discovery group.

Directions: From north follow A85 one way system through town to traffic island then take ferry terminal exit (Albany St). By Job Centre turn left and follow signs to Camping Glenshellach. From south into town to traffic island, then as above. Site is 2 miles on single track road with passing places. O.S.GR: NM841277.

Charges 2001:
-- Per unit £7.00; person 50p; electricity £1.50; awning or extra car £1.00.
-- No credit cards.
Open:
Mid March - end Oct.
Address:
Glenshellach Road, Oban, Argyll PA34 4QJ.
Tel/Fax:
(01631) 562755.
E-mail: info@ obandivers.co.uk.
Reservations:
Made with £10 deposit.

783 Glen Nevis Caravan and Camping Park, Fort William

Spacious touring park in wonderful situation by Ben Nevis range.

Just outside Fort William in a most attractive and quiet situation with views of Ben Nevis, this park is used by those on active pursuits as well as sightseeing tourists. It comprises eight quite spacious fields, divided between caravans, motorcaravans and tents (steel pegs required). It is licensed for 250 touring caravans but with no special tent limits. The large touring pitches, many with hardstanding, are marked with wooden fence dividers, 200 with electricity (13A) and 100 also have water and drainage. The park becomes full in the peak months but there are vacancies each day. If reception is closed (possible in low season) you site yourself. The four modern toilet blocks make a good provision with plentiful WCs, washbasins with free hot water and hot showers on payment (20p), with extra showers in two blocks; free hairdryers and units for disabled visitors. An excellent block in Nevis Park (one of the eight camping fields) has some washbasins in cubicles, showers, further facilities for disabled visitors, a second large laundry room and dishwashing sinks. There are ample water points around each camping area. Motorcaravan service point. Amenities include a self-service shop (Easter - mid Oct), barbecue area and snack bar (May - mid-Sept). The park's own modern restaurant and bar with good value bar meals is a short stroll from the park, open to all. Public telephones. Children's play area on bark. Site owned holiday park adjacent. Pony trekking, golf and fishing near. A well managed park with bustling, but pleasing ambience, watched over by Ben Nevis. Around 1,000 acres of the Glen Nevis estate are open to campers. Bellamy gold.

Directions: Turn off A82 to east at roundabout just north of Fort William following camp sign. O.S.GR: NN124723.

Charges 2000:
-- Per person £1.10 - £1.60; caravan £5.60 - £8.30; motorcaravan or tent £5.40 - £8.00; small tent £4.90 - £7.30; backpacker's tent: 1 person £3.20 - £4.70, 2 persons £3.90 - £5.70; awning 70p - £1.10; fully serviced pitch extra £1.30 - £2.00.
-- VAT included.
-- Credit cards accepted.

Open:
15 March - 31 October.

Address:
Glen Nevis, Fort William, Inverness-shire PH33 6SX.

Tel:
(01397) 702191.
FAX: (01397) 703904.
E-mail: holidays @glen-nevis.co.uk

Reservations:
Advised for July/Aug; contact park.

Glen Nevis Caravan & Camping Park
Glen Nevis
Fort William PH33 6SX
Tel: 01397 702191
holidays@glen-nevis.co.uk

This award-winning environmental park - **Calor 1998 Best Park in Scotland** - **David Bellamy Gold Conservation Award** - situated at the foot of Ben Nevis, Britain's highest mountain, offers modern, clean and well-equipped facilities including Motor caravan service point. Many pitches are fully serviced with electricity, water and drainage Showers, scullery, laundry. licensed shop, gas and play areas are all on park with our own spacious restaurant and lounge only a few minutes walk. Holiday Caravans, Cottages, Lodges on adjacent park. Colour brochures available.

784 North Ledaig Caravan Park, Connel, by Oban

Friendly park with splendid views, for caravans, motorcaravans and trailer tents only.

The views over the Sound of Mull here are magnificent and Mr and Mrs Weir have tried to ensure good views by staggering the pitches and not planting many trees. A member of the Caravan Club's 'managed under contract' scheme, non-members are also welcome. The park has 240 pitches, 230 with electricity(10A) and 228 with hardstanding. Around 120 are for non-members with caravans, motorcaravans or trailer tents. The main sanitary block is central - you may have a bit of a walk but a new block is planned. The current amenities are excellent and include full facilities for disabled visitors and for babies, both with access by key. There are free hot showers, washbasins in cabins for ladies (one for men), a well equipped laundry and dishwashing. Chemical disposal and motorcaravan service area. Further, well renovated sanitary facilities are behind the reception block, that also provides a well stocked, licensed shop. On land across the road is an award winning 30 acre nature reserve with ponds and walks (strictly no dogs). This is a quiet park which makes a good base for exploring the area, visiting the islands or simply relaxing on the shores of the loch. Fishing and sailing are possible from the site (there is a slipway for small boats), pony trekking close. Bicycle hire and golf 6 km. Buses pass the gate. Caravan storage. Bellamy silver.

Directions: Park is about 1 mile north of Connel Bridge, on the A828 Oban - Fort William road, 7 miles from Oban. O.S.GR: NM913456.

Charges 2000:
-- Per pitch £2.00 - £4.00; adult £2.60 - £4.00; child (5-17 yrs) £1.10 - £1.20; electricity £1.50 - £2.25; extra car, trailer or m/cycle £1.00.
-- VAT included.
-- Debit cards accepted (not credit cards).

Open:
27 March - 31 October.

Address:
Connel, by Oban, Argyll PA37 1RT.

Tel:
(01631) 710291.
FAX: as phone.

Reservations:
Any length, with £10 deposit incl. £1 non-returnable fee.

Highlands and Islands

785 Linnhe Lochside Holidays, Corpach, nr. Fort William

Quiet, well run park in a fine setting for caravans, motorcaravans and small tents only.

This park has a very peaceful situation overlooking Loch Eil, beautifully landscaped and with wonderful views. There are individual pitches with hardstanding for 65 touring units (12 seasonal) on terraces leading down to the water's edge. They include 32 special ones with electrical connection (16A), water and drain, plus 30 with electricity only (10A). A separate area on the lochside takes 15 small tents. There are also 64 caravan holiday homes and several centrally heated pine chalets for hire. The toilet facilities are of an excellent standard and can be heated in the cooler months, providing free hot showers, baths (£1), a dishwashing room and chemical disposal. A first class laundry, toddlers' play room and separate outdoor clothing drying room (charged per night) are also provided. Two well equipped children's play areas are on safe standing, there is a barbecue area, public phones, gas and a self-service, licensed shop (end May - end Sept). Fishing is free on Loch Eil and you are welcome to fish from the park's private beach or bring your own boat and use the slipway and dinghy park. Large motorhomes are accepted but it is best to book first. About 5 miles from Fort William on 'The Road to the Isles', the park is conveniently placed for touring the Western Highlands. Easily accessible are Ben Nevis and the Nevis range (cable car to 2,000 ft.), geological, Jacobite and Commando museums, distillery visits, seal island trips, the Mallaig steam railway and the Caledonian Canal. Bicycle hire 2½ miles, riding or golf 5 miles. Up to two dogs per pitch are accepted. Caravan storage. A member of the Best of British group. Bellamy silver.

Directions: Park entrance is off A830 Fort William - Mallaig road, 1 mile west of Corpach. O.S.GR: NN072772.

Charges 2001:
-- Per unit incl. 2 persons, with electricity £11.50 - £13.50, special pitch £12.00 - £14.50; small tent pitch £8.50 - £10.50; awning, extra tent or car £1.50; extra person £1.00; dog (max. 2, not on tent pitches) 50p.
-- VAT included.
-- Credit cards accepted.
Open:
All year except 1 Nov - 19 Dec.
Address:
Corpach, Fort William, Inverness-shire PH33 7NL.
Tel:
(01397) 772376.
FAX: (01397) 772007.
E-mail: holidays@ linnhe.demon.co.uk.
Reservations:
Made with £25 deposit for min. 3 nights.

786 Glendaruel Caravan Park, Glendaruel, Kyles of Bute

Peaceful family park set in former wooded gardens surrounded by the Cowal hills.

Glendaruel is in South Argyll, in the area of Scotland bounded by the Kyles of Bute and Loch Fyne, yet is less than two hours by road from Glasgow and serviced by ferries from Gourock and the Isle of Bute. There is also a service between Tarbert and Portavadie opening up the Mull of Kintyre. Set in the wooded gardens of the former Glendaruel House in a secluded glen surrounded by the Cowal hills, it makes an ideal centre for touring this beautiful area of Scotland. The park takes 35 units on numbered hardstandings with electricity (10A), plus 15 tents, on flat oval meadows bordered by over 50 different varieties of mature trees. There are also 28 privately owned holiday homes, plus 2 for hire, in a separate area. The toilet block is ageing but is kept very neat and tidy, can be heated and has a good supply of toilets, washbasins and showers (2M, 2F), hair and hand dryers and a washing machine and dryer. A covered area has picnic tables for use in bad weather and dishwashing sinks (H&C). Chemical disposal. Gas available. The converted stables of the original house provide an attractive little shop selling basics, local produce, venison, salmon, wines (some Scottish!) and gifts (hours may be limited in low season) and a games room with pool table, table tennis and video games. Behind the laundry is a children's play centre for under twelves and there is also a play field. Bicycle hire (adults only). Fishing on site (sea fishing and boat slipway 5 miles). Adventure centre (assault courses, abseiling and rafting) and sailing school close. Golf 12 miles. Dogs are accepted by prior arrangement. Glendaruel is a park for families with young children or for older couples to relax and to enjoy the beautiful views across the Sound of Bute from Tighnabruaich or the botanical gardens which flourish in the climate. The owners, Quin and Anne Craig, provide a warm welcome and will advise on where to eat and what to do - they are justifiably proud of their park and its beautiful environment. A member of the Best of British group. Bellamy gold.

Directions: Entrance is off A886 road 13 miles south of Strachur. Alternatively there are two ferry services from Gourock to Dunoon, then on B836 which joins the A886 about 4 miles south of the park - this route not recommended for touring caravans. Note: the park has discount arrangements with Western Ferries so contact the park before making arrangements (allow 7 days for postage of tickets). O.S.GR: NS001865.

Charges 2000:
-- Per unit incl. 2 persons £8.50 - £10.50; tent per person, no car £4.00 - £5.00; extra adult £1.50 - £2.00; child (4-15 yrs) £1.00 - £1.50; awning, extra tent, extra car, trailer or boat £1.50; electricity (10A) £2.00.
-- Special weekly rates and senior citizen discount outside July/Aug.
-- VAT included.
-- Credit cards accepted.
Open:
30 March - 28 October.
Address:
Glendaruel, Argyll PA22 3AB.
Tel:
(01369) 820267.
FAX: (01359) 820367.
E-mail: mail@glendaruel-caravanpark.co.uk.
Reservations:
Any length, with £10 deposit and £2 fee.

NORTHERN IRELAND

For information on all parts of Northern Ireland contact:

Belfast Welcome Centre
Tel: 028 9024 6609 Fax: 028 9031 2424
E-mail: info@nitb.com
Internet: http://www.discovernorthernireland.com

The natural beauty and variety of the countryside, the historic landscape and the friendly people are what holidaymakers remember best about Northern Ireland. In addition, a wide selection of good quality campsites, uncluttered roads, an abundance of pubs and restaurants and plenty to see and do wherever they go keeps visitors coming back for more.

As Northern Ireland is barely 85 miles from north to south and about 110 miles wide driving is something to be enjoyed. A matter of hours can transport you from the dramatic coastline and the nine Glens of Antrim to the rugged heart of the wild Sperrin Mountains, from the timeless land-scape and glittering lakes of Fermanagh to the foothills of the Mourne Mountains sweeping down to Carlingford Lough.

Irish miles: the old granite milestones that still peep out from behind the cow parsley on road verges, especially in County Down, are marked in Irish miles. An Irish mile at 2,240 yards is 480 yards longer than a standard English mile. Distances on road signs, however, are marked in standard miles!

For youngsters and the young-at-heart, action and adventure are never far away. Pan for gold, take a subterranean journey through underground caves, enjoy a literary break or leap from pre-history to the future, then have a go at kayaking, abseiling, archery, horse-riding or any one of the numerous sports and activities on offer throughout Northern Ireland. No matter where you pitch your tent, or park your caravan, you will find good company and great 'craic' just around the corner.

Ferry Services

The following ferry services are expected to operate between the UK mainland and Ireland in 2001:

Irish Ferries
(see advert between pages 224/225)
01233 211211 for brochures, etc.
or 08705 171717 for bookings/enquiries
www.irishferries.ie/index
Holyhead - Dublin
(ferry 3 hrs 15 mins, fastcraft 109 mins)
Pembroke - Rosslare *(ferry 3 hrs 45 mins)*

P&O Irish Sea
0870 24 24 777 www.porishsea.com
Cairnryan - Larne *(Super ferry 1 hr 45 mins,*
Superstar Express 1 hr - no caravans)
Fleetwood - Larne *(ferry 8 hrs)*
Liverpool - Dublin *(ferry 8 hrs, Super ferry 6 hrs)*

Sea Cat Scotland
08705 523 523 www.seacat.co.uk
Troon - Belfast *(2 hrs 30 mins)*
Heysham - Belfast *(4 hrs)*
Liverpool - Dublin *(4 hrs)*

Swansea Cork Ferries
(see advert between pages 224/225)
01792 45 61 16 www.swansea-cork.ie
Swansea - Cork *(10 hrs)*

Stena Line
08705 70 70 70 www.stenaline.co.uk
Fishguard - Rosslare
(Super ferry 3 hrs 30 mins, Lynx 99 mins)
Holyhead - Dun Laoghaire *(HSS 99 mins)*
Holyhead - Dublin Port
(Super ferry 3 hrs 45 mins)
Stranraer - Belfast
(Super ferry 3 hrs 15 mins, HSS 105 mins)

Norse Irish Ferries
02890 77 90 90
www.norse-irish-ferries.co.uk
Liverpool - Belfast *(8 hrs 30 mins)*

Visitors with Disabilities

For information and advice, disabled visitors to Northern Ireland are invited to contact:

Disability Action 2 Annadale Avenue, Belfast BT7 3JH
Tel: 028 9029 7880 Fax: 028 9029 7881
E-mail: hq@disabilityaction.org Internet: www.hq.disabilityaction.org

834 Drumaheglis Marina and Caravan Park, Ballymoney

Well kept site on the banks of the River Bann, convenient for the Causeway coast.

A caravan park which continually maintains a high standard, Drumaheglis is popular throughout the season. Situated on the banks of the lower Bann, approximately 4 miles from the town of Ballymoney, it appeals to watersports enthusiasts or makes an ideal base for exploring this scenic corner of Northern Ireland. The marina offers superb facilities for boat launching, water-skiing, cruising, canoeing or fishing, whilst getting out and about can take you to the Giant's Causeway, seaside resorts such as Portrush or Portstewart, the sands of Whitepark Bay, the Glens of Antrim or the picturesque villages of the Antrim coast road. For tourers only, this site instantly appeals, for it is well laid out with trees, shrubs, flower beds and tarmac roads. Electricity (5/10A) and water points are available on 52 pitches, of which 47 have hardstanding. The toilet blocks are modern and were spotlessly clean when we visited. They house showers which are free, individual wash cubicles, toilets and facilities for disabled visitors, plus four family shower rooms. There are razor points, hand dryers, dishwashing sinks, washing machine and dryer and chemical disposal point. A children's play area, barbecue and picnic areas are added facilities. Ballymoney is a popular shopping town and the Riada Centre is a leading leisure establishment with a health suite which incorporates a high-tech fitness studio, sports hall, etc. Bicycle hire and golf 4 miles, riding ½ mile. There is much to see and do within this Borough and of interest is the Heritage Centre in Charlotte Street.

Charges 2000:
-- Per unit incl. electricity £12.00, per 7 days
£72.00; unserviced £10.00, per 7 days
£60.00.
-- Credit cards accepted.
Open:
Easter - 1 October.
Address:
36 Glenstall Road,
Co. Antrim BT53 7QN.
Tel:
028 2766 6466.
Ballymoney Borough Council: Tel: 028 2766 2280; FAX: 028 2766 7659.
Reservations:
Essential for peak periods and weekends.

Directions: From A26/B62 Portrush - Ballymoney roundabout continue for 1 mile on A26 towards Coleraine. Site signed; follow International camping signs.

835 Bush Caravan Park, Bushmills

Family run park, an ideal base for touring the North Antrim Coast.

This select park that has recently been extended is only minutes away from two renowned attractions, the Giant's Causeway and the Old Bushmills Distillery. This fact alone makes Bush a popular location, but its fast growing reputation for friendliness and top class facilities makes it equally appealing. Conveniently sited just off the main Ballymoney-Portrush Road (B62), it is approached by a short drive. The site itself is partly surrounded by mature trees and hedging, but views across the countryside can still be appreciated. All roads around the site are tarmac and lead to the 43 well laid out and spacious pitches, with hardstanding and electric hook-up (16A), also grass area for tents. The sanitary block is opened by key and is modern, clean and equipped to a high standard. Walls and floors are fully tiled and facilities include controllable showers (by token) with curtain, divider, seat and hooks and there is excellent provision for people with disabilities. Additional facilities include a washing machine, dryer, dishwashing sinks and a chemical disposal unit. For children there is a central play area and for all ages a recreation room. Reception is housed in a mobile home to the left of the entrance. Unique features on site are murals depicting the famed scenery, sight and legends of the Causeway Coast. A further novelty is the Bushmills barrels used as picnic tables. The enthusiastic owners organise tours to the Distillery and coastal trips – a musical evening cannot be ruled out.

Charges 2000:
-- Per unit incl. all persons £10.00; frame tent £8.00; small tent £6.00; awning £1.00; electricity £1.00.
Open:
Easter - 31 October.
Address:
95 Priestland Road,
Bushmills,
Co. Antrim BT57 8UJ.
Tel:
028 2073 1678 or 028 7035 4240.
FAX: 028 7035 1998.
Reservations:
Advised for high season or weekends.

Directions: From Ballymoney A26/B62 roundabout proceed north on B62 towards Portrush for 6½ miles. Turn right onto B17 and site is 350 yds on the left.

Tourist Information:
Bushmills has the oldest licensed whiskey distillery in the world. It first received its license in 1608, though distilling has taken place here since at least the 13th century. To earn your free dram, you have to tour the distillery. You may just get a shot of all three types – the malt, Black Bush and regular Bushmills!

Antrim

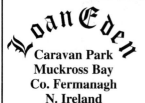

★ Award winning caravan park - Calor Green ★
★ Fully serviced pitches ★ Tent area ★
★ Immaculate sanitary facilities ★ Children's play areas ★

Caravan Park
Muckross Bay
Co. Fermanagh
N. Ireland

Tel: 028 6863 1603
Fax: 028 6863 2300

OPEN ALL YEAR - 5✓

★ Quality mobile homes for sale/hire ★
★ Horse riding tuition A.I. instructor ★
★ Special on site feature - barbecue in July ★
★ Extended facilities - new toilet block, 3rd play area,
new reception area, campers kitchen ★
★ Boat hire facilities ★ man made beach ★ Marina 5 mins walk
★ Scenic walks ★ Pony trekking ★
★ Village of Kesh - Lough Erne Hotel - Chef of the Year award ★

831 Carnfunnock Country Park Caravan Site, Drain's Bay, Larne

Touring site in magnificent parkland setting overlooking the sea.

What makes this site popular is its scenic surroundings and convenient location. It is 3½ miles north of the market town of Larne on the famed Antrim Coast Road and offers 28 level 'super' pitches, all with hardstanding, water, electricity (15A), drainage, individual pitch lighting and ample space for an awning. The site has a neat appearance with a tarmac road following through to the rear where a number of pitches are placed in a circular position. There is additional road lighting, a refuse area and allocated space for tents. A small building beside the entrance gates houses sanitary facilities (entry by key) which are kept clean, but now starting to show signs of wear. Facilities include shower units, facilities for disabled people, dishwashing, chemical disposal and motorcaravan service point. Run by the Borough Council and supervised by a manager, the surrounding Country Park is immaculately kept. The Visitor Centre includes a gift shop and information about local attractions and the restaurant/coffee shop is pleasant and looks towards the sea. Spending time around the parkland, you find a walled time garden with historic sundials, a maze, forest walk, children's adventure playground, putting green, 9 hole golf course, wildlife garden and miniature railway. There is also a summer events programme. Fishing and boat launching 400 yds.

Charges 2000:
-- Per caravan or motor-caravan £13.00; 5 nights £59.00; 7 nights £80.00 (electricity included); tent £7.00.
-- Credit cards accepted.
Open:
Easter - 30 September.
Address:
Coast Road,
Drain's Bay, Larne,
Co. Antrim BT40 2QG.
Tel:
028 2827 0541 or 028 2826 0088
FAX: 028 2827 0852.
Reservations:
Advisable for week-ends; peak periods and B.Hs.

Directions: From ferry terminal in Larne, follow signs for Coast Road and Carnfunnock Country Park; well signed 3½ miles on A2 coast road.

832 Curran Court Caravan Park, Larne

Well kept site convenient for ferry terminal, an ideal night stop.

Formerly run by the local borough council, the park is now managed by the Curran Court Hotel (opposite the park). Attractive garden areas add to the charm of this small, neat site which is very conveniently situated for the ferry terminal and only a few minutes walk from the sea. The 29 pitches, all with hardstanding and electricity connections (12A), give reasonable space off the tarmac road and there is a separate tent area of 1½ acres. The sanitary block is clean and adequate without being luxurious, with free controllable hot showers (2 for men, 1 for ladies) and there is a laundry room with dishwashing facilities. Plans are in hand for a new block, plus another 31 pitches. Children's play area with good equipment and safety surfaces. Bowls and putting are available on site and many other amenities are very close including a shop (100 yds), the hotel for food and drink, tennis and a leisure centre with swimming pool (300 yds). Bicycle hire 1 mile, golf 3 miles and boat launching 500 yds. Larne market is on Wednesdays. You may consider using this site as a short term base for discovering the area as well as an ideal overnight stop. The warden can usually find room for tourists so reservations are not normally necessary.

Charges 2001:
-- Per caravan or motor-caravan £8.50; tent £5.00; electricity £1.50.
-- Credit cards accepted.
Open:
Easter - 30 September.
Address:
Curran Road,
Larne,
Co. Antrim.
Tel:
028 2827 3797.
FAX: 028 2826 0096.
Reservations:
Not normally considered necessary.

Directions: Immediately after leaving the ferry terminal, turn right and follow camp signs. Site is just ¼ mile on the left.

850 LoanEden Caravan Park, Muckross Bay, Kesh

Family owned park by the shores of Lower Lough Erne, particularly suitable for enjoying fishing or riding.

The owners of LoanEden have built a reputation for their park, based on a friendly, caring attitude. First impression is an overall neat and tidy appearance, with well tended shrubs, flower beds and wide tarmac driveways. There are many privately owned holiday homes on the site, but these are kept separate from the touring area. The 24 touring and 12 long-stay pitches are level with hardstanding, water, electricity, drainage, rubbish bin and a grass area for an awning. The fully tiled central sanitary block is well equipped with soap dispensers, hand dryers and electric points. There are showers, facilities for disabled people, a laundry area with washing machines, dryers and sinks. A motorcaravan service point and a chemical disposal unit are situated near the long-stay pitches. For children there are two outdoor play areas and a new indoor room for football, netball, etc. The 'LoanEden Ramblers' club for 4-11 year olds provides activities in season (£1.50 per child). Young and old can enjoy pony and horse riding tuition under the supervision of the owners' daughter Victoria, an A.I. instructor and son Andrew who is an international rider. Fishing and bicycle hire nearby, golf 5 miles. There are ongoing plans to further extend this site. The owners organise barbecues and barn dances in aid of charity.

Directions: From Enniskillen take A32 Omagh road for 3½ miles and branch left on B82 Kesh road. Continue for 11 miles to village of Kesh. Cross over bridge at north end of village and turn immediately left to park in ½ mile on right.

Charges 2000:
-- Per caravan or motor-caravan incl. awning and electricity £12.00; tent £8.00; electricity £1.00

Open:
All year

Address:
Muckross Bay, Kesh, Co. Fermanagh BT93 1TX

Tel:
028 6863 1603.
FAX: 028 6863 2300.

Reservations:
Advisable for high season and B.Hs.

852 Share Holiday Village, Smith's Strand, Lisnaskea

Caravan park in village environment, offering range of activities for both able-bodied and disabled visitors.

This 30 acre park enjoys a quiet and beautiful location on the shores of Upper Lough Erne. The 5 acre touring park is a separate part of this complex, which offers all the benefits and self contained aspects of caravanning, plus the opportunity to enjoy all the sports facilities of the village. The 15 pitches have hardstanding, electricity and space for awnings. The sanitary blocks, which can be heated and are kept very clean, have washbasins, showers, washing up and laundry facilities, including a drying room with tumble dryers, and a chemical disposal point. An important factor here is that Share is committed to the provision of facilities and opportunities for both able bodied and disabled visitors. Caravanners can take temporary Leisure Suite membership for the duration of their stay (£2.50 per day, child under 5 free, and best booked and paid for in advance to ensure availability). If wanting to participate in the outdoor activities, an Activity Pass can be purchased covering sailing, canoeing, windsurfing, banana-ski, archery, mountain bikes, or you may prefer a Viking long-ship cruise. Package deals are available. A 2½ hour session costs £5 per person and includes all equipment and instruction. Fishing, bicycle hire and boat launching all on site. This centre is an approved British Canoe Union and Royal Yachting Association teaching school and has a 30 berth marina. A multi-purpose Arts Area has been added which provides a comprehensive range of art facilities.

Directions: From Lisnaskea village, take B127 sign to Derrylin and Smith's Strand and proceed for 3 miles. Site is clearly signed on the right.

Charges 2000:
-- Per caravan or tent £10.00; 2 man tent £7.00.
-- Touring caravan and campsite packages.
-- Credit cards accepted.

Open:
Easter - 31 October.

Address:
Smith's Strand, Lisnaskea, Co. Fermanagh BT92 0EQ

Tel:
028 6772 2122.
FAX: 028 6772 1893.
E-mail: share@dnet.co.uk.

Reservations:
Advisable in peak season and for B.H.s and with deposit (weekend or midweek £20, 7 days £50; activity passes 50% of total cost per person).

Down

843 Banbridge Touring Caravan and Camping Park, Banbridge

Conveniently sited touring park on main A1 Belfast - Newry road.

Banbridge is in an ideal place for a stopover if travelling between Southern and Northern Ireland, is within easy towing distance of the main ports or makes an ideal base for discovering many tourist attractions such as the Bronte Homeland or the Linen Trail. A small site, with 8 hardstanding pitches and electrical connections (6A), it is part of the Banbridge Gateway Tourist Information Centre complex. The centre is an attractive building of modern design surrounded by a well maintained garden area and car park. Housed inside, apart from the offices of the centre, a bureau de change and display areas for Irish crafts, are excellent sanitary facilities. Ultra modern, spotlessly clean and key operated, they include two showers, six washbasins, WCs, good facilities for disabled people and an outside, covered dishwashing area. There is also a chemical disposal unit and an extensive children's play area that has a safety base. The restaurant and coffee shop within the complex (10.00-16.30 hrs daily) serves lunch specials between 12.30-14.30, otherwise scones, cakes, etc. The touring park is located in the far left hand corner of the complex and is enclosed with ranch fencing, plus a security gate and barrier. The town of Banbridge is within 1 mile, with shops, restaurants, pubs and all services. Fishing, bicycle hire or golf within 3 miles.

Directions: Follow signs to Tourist Information Centre off the A1 Belfast - Newry dual carriageway, 1 mile south of Banbridge.

Charges 2001:
-- Per unit incl. electricity £10.00; tent £5.00.
-- Max. stay 5 consecutive nights.
-- Refundable key deposit (gate, showers) £20.
-- Credit cards accepted.
Open:
All year (except Christmas and New Year),but closed Sundays Oct - May incl.
Address:
200 Newry Road, Banbridge, Co. Down BT32 3NB.
Tel:
028 4062 3322.
FAX: 028 4062 3114.
Reservations:
Contact centre during office hours (summer: Mon-Sat 09.00-19.00, Sun. 14.00-18.00; winter: Mon-Sat 10.00-17.00, Sun. closed). It is essential to arrive during opening hours to obtain keys.

Banbridge Touring Caravan and Camping Park
Banbridge, Co. Down, N. Ireland

8 fully serviced pitches for Caravans. Adjacent to Banbridge Gateway Tourist Information Centre on main A1 Belfast/Dublin Euroroute.

All facilities available - toilets, showers, children's play area, restaurant, etc.

CARAVANS £10.00 per night. TENTS £5.00 per night. ELECTRICITY free

Arrivals by 6.00pm (summer) and 5.00pm (winter)

BANBRIDGE
DISTRICT COUNCIL

Telephone: (028) 4062 3322 for bookings

Delamont Country Park - Camping and Caravanning Club Site

This Club site is due to open in March 2001. All new, it has a rural setting on the southwest corner of Strangford Lough in the Lecale Area of Outstanding Natural Beauty. It will have some 65 hardstanding pitches, all with water and electricity connections.

842 Tollymore Forest Caravan Park, Newcastle

Well run site in forest setting at foot of Mourne mountains.

This popular park, for tourers only, is located within the parkland of Tollymore Forest. It is discreetly situated away from the public footpaths and is noted for its scenic surroundings. The forest park, which is approached by way of an ornate gateway and majestic avenue of Himalayan cedars, covers an area of almost 500 hectares. It is backed by the Mourne mountains and situated two miles from the beaches and resort of Newcastle. The site is attractively laid out with hardstanding pitches, 72 of which have electricity (6A). Toilet blocks, timbered in keeping with the setting, are clean, modern and tastefully decorated. They have free hot showers with benches and hooks, wash cubicles, facilities for disabled people, dishwashing and laundry area. Night lighting is adequate. Other amenities are a confectionery shop and tea room within close proximity. A small grocery shop is a few yards from the exit gate of the park and gas is also available here. The Head Ranger at Tollymore is helpful and ensures that the caravan site is efficiently run and quiet, even when full. Exploring the forest park is part of the pleasure of staying here. Of note are the stone follies, bridges and entrance gates. The Shimna and Spinkwee rivers flow through the park adding a refreshing touch and tree lovers appreciate the arboretum with its many rare species.

Directions: Approach Newcastle on the A24. Before entering the town, at roundabout, turn right on to A50 signed Castlewellan and follow signs for Tollymore Forest Park.

Charges 2000/2001:
-- Per unit incl. car and occupants £7.00 - £11.00, acc. to season; electricity £1.50.
-- Low season mid-week special rates.
Open:
All year.
Address:
Tollymore Forest Park (Administration), 176 Tullybrannigan Rd, Newcastle, Co. Down BT33 0PW.
Tel:
028 4372 2428.
Reservations:
Advisable in high season and for B.Hs. and made with £10 deposit.

856 Gortin Glen Caravan and Camping Park, Gortin, nr. Omagh

Quiet, well run friendly site in beautiful Forest Park surroundings.

Pronounced 'Gorchin', this excellent, truly peaceful site is deep in Gortin Glen with splendid views of the surrounding hills and forest. The very large Gortin Glen forest embraces the 405 ha. forest park which has a 5 mile scenic road offering breathtaking views, picnic areas, nature trails, wildlife enclosures and an indoor exhibit, all open to the public. Within the park is a camping area with 24 individually numbered pitches, all with hardstanding and electricity (13A). All pitches are spacious with room for an awning. In addition there are separate areas for tents and attractive self catering cottages. The sanitary block has four controllable hot showers (10p for 8 minutes) and good facilities for people with disabilities, which mothers may also use for children. There is a laundry room with two washing machines and two dryers, also a dishwashing area with free hot water. Leisure facilities include a TV/games room with table tennis and full sized snooker table, plus a children's play area with safety base and provision for ball games. A barbecue area is located behind the main block. Reception is well stocked with tourist information on local attractions which include the Ulster History Park, Ulster American Folk Park and Sperrin Heritage Centre. Shops are in Gortin village (3 miles).

Directions: From Omagh take B48 road signed Gortin. Proceed north for approx. seven miles and turn left immediately after Ulster History Park into site.

Charges 2000:
-- Per caravans £8.50 (£51 per week); tent £4.00 - £8.50, acc. to size (£24 - £51 per week); electricity £1.50; awning 50p.
-- Youth groups of 10 or more £1.50 per person, per night.
Open:
All year.
Address:
1 Lisnaharney Road, Lislap, Omagh, Co. Tyrone BT79 7UG.
Tel/Fax:
028 8164 8108.
E-mail:
gortinholidaypark @omagh.gov.uk.
Reservations:
Made with £15 fee for B.H. weekends.

For travel further afield, remember the other ALAN ROGERS' titles –
the GOOD CAMPS GUIDES for FRANCE and EUROPE

★ Independent site assessors make regular monitoring visits

★ Consistently revised and updated – sites included on merit only

★ Discount vouchers for selected sites, ferries and tourist attractions

Londonderry

860 Bellemont Caravan Park, Coleraine

Well kept park close to Coleraine and Portstewart; tents not accepted.

This brand new park makes an immediately favourable impression with its white concrete roads, its perfect grass areas and well laid out appearance. The gently sloping ground rises at the far right of the park to give views over Portstewart and towards the sea. To the left of the entrance and security gate are five privately owned caravan holiday homes. There are 30 touring pitches, all with hardstanding, electric hook up and water. These are spacious and well distributed around this open, parkland style setting. In a central position stands a gleaming white building, with flower tubs decorating the forecourt, which houses reception and heated sanitary facilities. These include washbasins, mirrors, electric points, soap and hand-dryer. Showers (token operated) are a good size and well equipped with seat, hooks, soap dish and changing space. For people with disabilities a separate unit comprises a shower, WC, washbasin, hand-dryer and seat. There is a laundry room with two washing machines, two dryers and iron (token operated), plus a dishwashing sink and drainer to the outside. Also outside is a chemical disposal unit with flush and hose. A play area for children with swings and slide on a bark surface is placed to the right of the park. Bellemont makes a good base for visiting the university town of Coleraine, the resorts and beaches of Portstewart and Portrush, or famous sights such as Dunluce Castle, Carrick-a-Rede rope bridge, the Giant's Causeway, plus the ports and harbours which follow the North Antrim coastline. There are no tent pitches and dogs are not accepted.

Directions: From Lodge Road roundabout on eastern outskirts of Coleraine follow A29 north to fourth roundabout. Continue towards Portrush and site is clearly signed on left after ¼ mile.

Charges 2001:
-- Per unit incl. all persons £10.50, with electricity £12.00; awning £1.50.
-- No credit cards.
Open:
Easter - 30 September.
Address:
10 Islandtasserty Road, Coleraine, Co. Londonderry BT52 2PN.
Tel:
028 7082 3872.
Reservations:
Contact site.

859 Tullans Farm Caravan Park, Coleraine

Well run family park in rural setting convenient for the Causeway Coast.

This quality park is one of the most popular in the area. It has a quiet, heart of the country feel, yet the University town of Coleraine is within a mile, the seaside resort Portrush and Portstewart 5 miles and a shopping centre a 5 minute drive. Tullans Farm has earned a reputation for its spotlessly clean toilet block and well cared for appearance. In a central position, fronted by a parking space, stands a long white building housing the sanitary facilities, reception, TV lounge and barn which is used for indoor recreation. The toilet and shower rooms, that include a family shower unit and facilities for disabled people, are spacious and modern . Extras are soap dispensers, hand and hair dryers, even flower arrangements. Next to the toilet area is a laundry and washing up room with sinks, washing machine, dryers and a large fridge. Around the park, roads are gravel and 20 of the 32 pitches are hardstanding; all have electric hook-ups (10A). Chemical disposal, water points, rubbish bins and receptacles for cans and plastic bottles are provided. For children there is an outdoor play area and in season the owners organise barbecues, barn dances and line dancing (funds in aid of charity).

Directions: From the Lodge Road roundabout (south end of Coleraine) turn east onto A29 Portrush ring road and proceed for ½ mile. Turn right at sign for park and Windy Hall. Park is clearly signed on left.

Charges 2001:
-- Per unit incl. all persons and electricity £11.00; awning £1.00; family tent £9.00; 2 man tent £6.00.
-- No credit cards.
Open:
March – 31 October.
Address:
46 Newmills Road, Coleraine, Co. Londonderry BT52 2JB.
Tel:
028 7034 2309.
FAX: as phone.
E-mail: tullansfarm@ netscapeonline.co.uk.
Reservations:
Advisable at peak times.

Alan Rogers' Discount

Saty 6 nights, get 1 night free

Tourist Information:

The scientific explanation for the Giant's Causeway, a promontory of 40,000 closely packed multi-sided basalt columns, is that it was formed after a volcanic eruption about 55 million years ago but myth has it that the giant Finn MacCool built it as a road to cross to Scotland – a similar but smaller causeway is visible on the island of Staffa. It is interesting that something that looks so geometrically exact can be natural. Sometimes it fails to live up to expectations – it is dwarfed by the surrounding towering cliffs.

SAVE MONEY AND TAKE IT EASY

- Choose from nearly 200 inspected sites across Europe
- Take advantage of superb cross-Channel rates
- Leave the hassle to us – travel in confidence, all fees paid in advance
- FREE comprehensive Travel Pack

PRICES FROM

£315

12 nights pitch fees with
ferry for car and caravan

THE ALAN ROGERS'
travel service

Call NOW for your FREE 2001 Reader's Travel Guide

01892 55 98 98

or just call us for an instant quote

www.alanrogers.com

NO STAMP
REQUIRED

The Alan Rogers' Travel Service
FREEPOST SEA 8263
90 - 94 High Street
Tunbridge Wells
Kent TN1 1BR

THE ALAN ROGERS'
travel service

insure4europe.com

Taking your own tent, caravan or motorhome abroad?
Looking for the best cover at the best rates?

Our prices considerably undercut most high street prices and the 'in-house insurance' of many tour operators whilst offering equivalent (or higher!) levels of cover. Our Annual multi-trip policies offer superb value, covering you not only for your European camping holiday but also subsequent trips abroad for the next 12 months.

Total Peace of Mind

To give you total peace of mind during your holiday our insurance policies have been specifically tailored to cover most potential eventualities on a self-drive camping holiday. Each is organised through Voyager Insurance Services Ltd who specialise in travel insurance for Europe and for camping in particular. All policies are underwritten by UK Insurance, part of the Green Flag group.

24 Hour Assistance

Our personal insurance provides access to the services of International Medical Rescue (IMR), one of the UK's largest assistance companies. Experienced multi-lingual personnel provide a caring and efficient service 24 hours a day.

European vehicle assistance cover is provided by Green Flag who provide assistance to over 3 million people each year. With a Europe-wide network of over 7,500 garages and agents you know you're in very safe hands.

Both IMR and Green Flag are very used to looking after the needs of campsite-based holidaymakers and are very familiar with the location of most European campsites, with contacts at garages, doctors and hospitals nearby.

Save with an Annual Policy

If you are likely to make more than one trip to Europe over the next 12 months then our Annual multi-trip policies could save you a fortune. Personal cover for a couple starts at just £79 and the whole family can be covered for just £99. Cover for up to 17 days wintersports participation is included.

Low Cost Annual multi-trip Insurance

Premier Annual Europe self-drive
Per couple including 17 days wintersports
£79 per couple

Premier Annual Europe self-drive
Per family including 17 days wintersports
£99 per family

Low Cost Combined Personal and Vehicle Assistance Insurance

Premier Family Package
10 days cover for vehicle, 2 adults plus dependent children under 16
£64 *

Premier Couples Package
10 days cover for vehicle and 2 adults
£52 *

*Motorhomes, cars towing trailers and caravans, all vehicles over 4 years old and holidays longer than 10 days attract supplements - ask us for details. See leaflet for full terms and conditions

Arrange your low-cost travel insurance today or ask for your FREE leaflet containing full details.

01892 55 98 44

Buy on line at www.insure4europe.com

This page provides a summary of the insurance we offer.
Please see policy document for full terms and conditions.

Thinking about a towbar?

Think Witter and you'll be in good company. With over 5 million sold, Witter are undoubtedly Britain's most popular towbar. Why? Because Witter towbars come with the additional security of the Shield of Safety that guarantees the bar for the life of the vehicle and not simply its warranty period.

The Witter Shield of Safety also symbolises a tradition of excellence started over 50 years ago. It continues today through investment in design, manufacture and quality standards. It brings you towbars made in the UK with an unrivalled reputation for strength, quality and reliability.

Look for the Witter sign at over 250 specialists throughout the UK where your towbar will be fitted with expertise and care.

The right direction

WITTER
TOWBAR SYSTEMS

The MOTOR Caravanners' CLUB

™

From the moment you join the club
YOU ENJOY ALL THESE PRIVILEGES AND SERVICES

- Monthly Magazine
- UK. & European Touring Service
- UK. Sites Guide
- Discounted Insurance Rates available
- Breakdown Recovery Service ™
- Camping Card (CCI) International
- "Snail" Know-How Booklets
- Discounted rates for Cross Channel Ferries and Overseas Travel Insurance
- Year round Social Events, Weekend Meets and Holiday Rallies

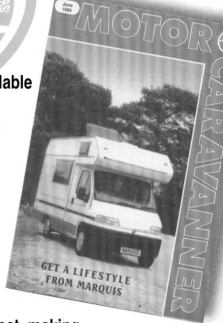

GET A LIFESTYLE FROM MARQUIS

It's a great club for enjoyment, interest, making friends, help and advice, weekend meets for you and all the family.

For membership details write:
THE MOTOR CARAVANNERS' CLUB LTD. FREEPOST (1292)
TWICKENHAM, TW2 5BR TEL: 0181 893 3883 (OFFICE HOURS)
E-mail: motorcaravanners@msn.com

Club
THE ROAD TO ENJOYMENT

F.I.C.C

If you're interested in the

ALAN ROGERS'
GOOD CAMPS GUIDE

you'll probably be
interested in

THE GOOD
MAGAZINE
GUIDE

For tests and touring
features 12 months of
the year choose
Britain's premier
caravan and
motorhome
magazines.

On sale at most good
newsagents or by
subscription –
telephone

01778
391134

REPUBLIC OF IRELAND

Irish Tourist Board
Tel: 020 7493 3201 Fax: 020 7493 9065
E-mail: info@irishtouristboard.co.uk
Internet: http:/www./ireland.travel.ie

'You're welcome' is not said lightly to the visitor who sets foot in Ireland, it is said with sincerity. On this `Emerald Isle' you will find friendly and hospitable people, spectacular scenery and a selection of good campsites to suit your particular needs. Whether you choose to be sited by a lough shore, at the foothills of a mountain range or close by golden sands, the scenery is stunning and the pace of life slow. With the help of information and maps available from the Tourist Office you discover for yourself, not only the beauty spots, but also many historic and interesting routes to follow. In such areas we have endeavoured to locate well run sites that range from family parks where children can find day long amusement, to the more simple site offering total relaxation, all of good quality.

A British visitor to the Republic of Ireland does not require a passport (and one may take the dog!). British currency is accepted in most outlets although we quote charges in Irish punts (IR£), currently valued at slightly below the UK£, or in Euros ( ).

Travel insurance is advisable when travelling in the south.

To telephone the Irish Republic from the UK, replace the first `0' given in the number with the country code: 00 353. For example: (094) 88100 becomes 00 353 94 88100.

The population of the Republic (26 counties) is just over 3.5 million. Dublin is the largest city with 1,058,264 inhabitants, Cork is the second with 420,510 inhabitants.

Signposts are mostly bilingual. Whilst Ireland has gradually converted to metric measurements, it should be noted that most of the black on white finger-post signs are in miles and the newer green and white ones are in kilometres.

Gas cylinders in the UK and Ireland are not compatible. In Ireland the Euro-system that has a click-on regulator is used. The cylinders used in Ireland have a different shape, weight and size to those used in Britain.

864 Knockalla Caravan and Camping Park, Portsalon

Family run park set amidst the breathtaking scenery of Donegal.

What adds to the popularity of this site is its location, nestling between the slopes of the Knockalla Mountains and Ballymastocker Bay. The fact that the beach here has been named 'the second most beautiful beach in the world' is not surprising. On entering this park, approached by an unclassified but short roadway, its elevated situation commands an immediate panoramic view of the famed Bay, Lough Swilly, Inishowen Peninsula and Dunree Head. The site is partly terraced giving an attractive, orderly layout with reception, shop and restaurant in a central position and the touring area sited to the left of reception. All 50 pitches have electricity and hardstanding, with a choice of just tarmac or with adjoining grass allowing for awnings. Tents are pitched on a lower level facing reception and to the far left of the tourers. Caravan holiday homes are placed around the right hand perimeter and to the rear of the park. The main sanitary block, a white, rough cast building, is situated in the touring section. Tastefully refurbished, it is kept clean and fresh and can be heated. There are washbasins, hand dryer, hair dryer, shaver points and showers (50p token) with hooks, soap dish, curtain divider and mat. Dishwashing area and campers' kitchen with hot water. A laundry service is operated by staff. Chemical disposal and motorcaravan service points. Gas is available. Children's play area and TV/games room. The park has a shop and café (both July/Aug, plus B.H. weekends) and specialities are home made scones, apple cakes, jams, etc. plus a takeaway or table service. Full Irish breakfasts are served. Golf 3 miles, fishing, riding and bicycle hire within 10 miles.

Charges 2000:
-- Per motorcaravan, caravan or family tent IR£11.00; awning IR£1.50; tent for 1 or 2 persons IR£8.00; extra person IR£3.00; electricity (5A) IR£1.50. -- No credit cards.

Open:
17 March - 17 September.

Address:
Portsalon, Co. Donegal.

Tel:
074 59108 or 074 53213.

Reservations:
Advisable for July/Aug and B.H. w/ends; contact park.

Directions: From Letterkenny take R245 to Rathmelton. Continue on R245 to Milford. Turn right on R246 to Kerrykeel. In village turn left towards Portsalon and at second crossroads turn right onto Portsalon/Knockalla coast road. Turn right to park at sign.

Sligo

869 Greenlands Caravan and Camping Park, Rosses Point

Park with excellent facilities in the sand hills adjoining a championship golf course.

This is a well run park at Rosses Point, just off the N15 road and 8 km. from Sligo town. It is thoughtfully laid out with small tents placed to the front of reception and the hardstanding touring pitches separated from the trailer tent pitches which occupy the rear. The ground is undulating and adds interest to the overall appearance. Your view depends on where you are pitched - look towards Coney Island and the Blackrock lighthouse which guards the bay, take in the sight of Benbulben Mountain or appreciate the seascape and the water lapping the resort's two bathing beaches. The sanitary and laundry facilities are modern and kept exceptionally clean, with tiled walls and floors, WCs, washbasins, hot showers (50p token), razor and hairdryer points, mirrors and hand-dryers. Also dish-washing and laundry sinks, washing machine, dryer and iron. Electric hook-ups (10A) are available for touring units. Chemical disposal and motorcaravan service point. Night security. An information point and a TV room are located beside reception. There is a sand pit for children and a ground chess and draughts sets. A mini-market, restaurant and evening entertainment can be found in the village. Fishing and boat launching 100 m, golf 50 m, bicycle hire 8 km, riding 14 km. This is an excellent base from which to explore the 'Yeats Country' and discover the beauty spots immortalised in his poems, such places as Lissadell, Dooney Rock, the Isle of Innisfree and the poet's burial place at Drumcliffe.

Charges 2001:
-- IR£: Per unit IR£10.00 plus 50p per person; hiker/cyclist incl. tent IR£6.50; awning or pup tent IR£1.00; electricity (10A) IR£2.00.
-- Euro: Per unit 12,70 plus 0,64 per person; hiker/cyclist incl. tent 8.26; awning or pup tent 1,27; electricity 2,54.
-- Weekly rates available.
-- Credit cards accepted.
Open:
Easter - mid-September.
Address:
Rosses Point, Co. Sligo.
Tel:
071 77113.
Reservations:
Contact park.

Directions: From Sligo city travel approx. 800 m. north on N15 road, turn left on R291 signed Rosses Point. Continue for 6.5 km. and park is on right after village.

870 Gateway Caravan and Camping Park, Ballinode, Sligo

Family run park, convenient for the beauty spots immortalised by the poet W. B. Yeats.

This is one of the northwest's most popular parks and it warrants the highest accolade for its excellent design and standards set. Its situation 1.2 km. from Sligo centre means this cultural city is easily accessible, yet Gateway's off-the-road location, screened by mature trees and fencing, offers a quiet relaxing environment. After the park entrance, past the family bungalow and to the left is parking space and the reception and services block which is fronted by columns. Incorporated in this building are three separate rooms – one for TV, snooker and board games, the second for satellite TV and the third for selected video viewing. A passage divides the elongated building which also houses showers, WCs, washbasins with shaver points, hand-dryers and baby changing units in both the male and female areas. Showers, room for disabled visitors (with WC and shower) are entered from the outside of this block which can be heated. In an adjacent building is a dishwashing area, laundry room, fully equipped campers' kitchen plus a large indoor games room and a toddlers room with playhouses and fixed toys. An outdoor children's play area faces reception. There are 30 fully serviced touring pitches with hardstanding and satellite TV connections, 10 grass pitches with electrical hook-ups for tents and 10 caravan holiday homes for hire. Touring pitches stand to the right and centre of the park, holiday homes to the left and rear, with tents pitched at the top left. Fishing or bicycle hire within 2 km, golf 8 km, riding 12 km. Evening relaxation could mean a 3 km. drive to romantic Half Moon Bay, or a drink in the fascinating surroundings of Farrells Brewery, which faces the caravan park.

Charges 2001:
-- Per unit incl. 2 persons IR£10.00; adult or child in July/Aug 50p; m/cyclist incl. tent IR£8.50; hiker or cyclist incl. tent IR£5.00; electricity (10A) IR£2.00.
-- 7 nights for price of 6 if pre-paid.
-- Credit cards accepted.
Open:
All year,
excl. 18 Dec. - 6 Jan.
Address:
Ballinode, Sligo,
Co. Sligo.
Tel:
071 45618.
FAX: as phone.
E-mail: gateway@oceanfree.net.
Reservations:
Contact site.

Directions: Site is 1.2 km. northeast of Sligo city, off the N16 Enniskillen - Belfast road. Approaching from the north on the N15, turn left at second traffic lights into Ash Lane, continue for 1.1 km. and turn left at traffic lights on N16 Sligo - Enniskillen road. Site entrance is on left in 50 m.

874 Cong Caravan and Camping Park, Cong, nr. Connemara

Family run touring park and hostel in a famous and scenic location.

It would be difficult to find a more idyllic and famous spot for a Caravan Park than Cong. Situated close to the shores of Lough Corrib, Cong's scenic beauty was immortalised in the film 'The Quiet Man'. This park, which is immaculately kept, is 1.6 km. from the village of Cong, near the grounds of the magnificent and renowned Ashford Castle. The owner's house which incorporates reception, shop and the hostel, stands to the fore of the site. The 40 grass pitches, 36 with electricity, are placed at a higher level to the rear, with the tent area below and to the side - the policy is for campers to choose a pitch rather than have one allocated. Sanitary facilities and the holiday hostel accommodation are entered from the courtyard area. These are tastefully decorated, kept spotlessly clean and heated when necessary. With a high standard of hygiene evident throughout, the facilities for the campsite include hot showers with curtains (50p), electric points, mirrors, hairdryers, washbasins, soap and hand towels. There is a dishwashing area, launderette service, chemical disposal, central bin depot, barbecue, games room and extensive children's play area. Catering is also a feature. Full Irish or continental breakfast, dinner or packed lunch may be ordered, or home baked bread and scones purchased in the shop. When not spending time around the village of Cong with its picturesque river setting and Monastic relics, there is much to keep the active camper happy. Watersports, cycling, walking, climbing, caving and scenic drives can all be pursued. Riding or golf within 2 km, fishing and boat slipway 500 m. Bicycle hire on site. Not least of the on site attractions at this park is a mini cinema showing 'The Quiet Man' film nightly all season.

Charges 2001:
-- Per pitch IR£6.00 - 7.00; adult IR£1.50; child IR£1.25; awning IR£2.00; electricity (16A) IR£2.00; hiker/cyclist incl. tent and 1 person IR£6.50.
-- Credit cards accepted

Open:
All year.

Address:
Lisloughrey, Quay Road, Cong, Connemara, Co. Mayo.

Tel:
092 46089.
FAX: 092 46448.
E-mail: quiet.man. cong@iol.ie.

Reservations:
Contact park.

`Camping Cheque'

Directions: Leave N84 road at Ballinrobe to join R334/345 signed Cong. Turn left at end of the R345 (opposite entrance to Ashford Castle), take next road on right (approx. 300 m) and the park is on right (200 m).

THE ALAN ROGERS'
travel service

Book this site with the experts
Call for an instant quote
01892 55 98 98

Low cost ferries
guaranteed!

875 Belleek Caravan and Camping Park, Ballina

Family owned park in a quiet woodland setting, only minutes from Ballina, a famed salmon fishing centre.

This is a park with excellent pitches and toilet block and a family committed to ensuring that it is immaculate at all times. From the entrance gate the park is approached by a road passing reception and leading to well spaced pitches with a very neat overall appearance. There are 58 pitches, 32 with hardstanding, 35 with electric hook-ups, and you have a free choice of pitch. Water points and rubbish bins are well distributed. The spotlessly clean toilet block is tastefully decorated with tiled floors, cream coloured, rough cast walls, pine ceilings and pot plants to complement modern washbasins, showers (50p token), WCs and baby sink. There are also razor points, hand dryers, facilities for disabled people, dishwashing and laundry sink, two washing machines and two dryers, and chemical disposal. In a separate building is a TV and games room with table tennis and a football game. A campers' kitchen and emergency accommodation with beds are also located in this building. There is a sink, free hot water, fridge, cooker, bench table and open fire. Reception includes a shop (June-Sept) and tea room serving delicious, home baked scones and fruit cake. A cooked or light breakfast, omelettes, sandwiches or salads can be ordered. There is a children's play area, a ball area, basketball and tennis courts. A feature is the new barbecue area. Sports facilities within a short distance of the park include pitch and putt, a swimming pool and tennis, with fishing 1 km, bicycle hire 3 km, riding 6 km. and golf 8 km. Other local attractions are the Blue Flag beach at Ross, Ceide Fields (Neolithic farm), Down Patrick Head, Mayo North Heritage Centre or a seaweed bath at Kilcullen's Bath House, Enniscrone. Mobile homes (10) and 2 luxury appartments for rent.

Charges 2000:
-- Per unit IR£6.00 - 7.00; adult or child IR£1.00; m/cyclist and tent IR£3.50 - 4.50; hiker or cyclist and tent IR£3.00 - 4.00; awning free - IR£1.00; extra car IR£1.00; electricity (10A) IR£1.50.
-- No credit cards.

Open:
15 March - 8 October; by arrangement all year.

Address:
Ballina, Co. Mayo.

Tel:
096 71533.
E-mail: lenahan @indigo.ie.

Reservations:
Contact park.

Directions: Take R314 Ballina - Killala road. Park signed on right after 3 km.

Mayo

877 Parkland Caravan and Camping Park, Westport

Popular park, enjoying the attractions of Westport House Country Estate.

In the grounds of an elegant country estate, this park offers the choice of a 'pitch only' or a 'special deal' (min. stay 3 nights) which includes free admission to Westport House and children's animal and bird park, plus other activities, such as boating and fishing on the lake and river, pitch and putt, 'slippery dip', ball pond and 'supabounce', hillside train rides and new flume ride. Stay one week or more and all the above are free, plus tennis, a par-3 golf course and 20% discount on bar food in the Horse and Wagon bar on the site. From Westport Quay, you enter the grounds of the estate by way of a tree lined road that crosses the river and leads to the site. In an attractive, sheltered area of the parkland, set in the trees are 155 pitches, 65 with hardstanding. There are 76 electric hook-ups. The gate is closed 11.30 pm.- 9 am. If late, vehicles must be parked in the car park. Toilet facilities, some at various points on the site, plus a 'super-loo' located in the farmyard buildings. Hot showers are free and there are facilities for disabled people. Also included are dishwashing and laundry sinks, chemical disposal, washing machines and dryers plus free ironing facilities. A well stocked shop is in the farmyard reception area and the bar offers food and musical entertainment (all 1/6-31/8). Early in the season the site may not be fully prepared, and only minimal facilities may be available. Within 5 km. of the estate are an 18 hole golf course and deep sea angling on Clew Bay. Westport is an attractive town with splendid Georgian houses and traditional shop fronts. No dogs are accepted.

Charges 2000:
-- Per unit excl. free facilities (see above), pitch only IR£16.00 - 24.50 (weekly IR£112 - 165); hiker or cyclist IR£12.00 - 13.00; electricity incl.. -- Specials (min. 3 nights) incl. free facilities from IR£129; weekly IR£275. -- No credit cards.

Open:
19 May - 9 September.

Address:
Westport, Co. Mayo.

Tel:
098 27766.
FAX: 098 25206.
E-mail: camping @westporthouse.ie.

Reservations:
Contact park.

Directions: Take R335 Westport - Louisburgh road and follow signs for Westport Quay, then turn right into Westport House Country Estate.

878 Knock Caravan and Camping Park, Knock

Clean, friendly park with many local attractions including religious shrine.

This park is immediately south of the world famous shrine, which receives many visitors. Comfortable and clean, the square shaped campsite is kept very neat with tarmac roads and surrounded by clipped trees. There are pitches for 38 caravans or motorcaravans, 20 tents and 15 caravan holiday homes (for rent). All pitches have hardstanding, 52 have electricity (13A). There is also an overflow field. An additional heated sanitary block, with good facilities for disabled visitors and a rest room attached, has 7 controllable hot showers (on payment) and adequate washing and toilet facilities. A laundry and dishwashing room is also part of this building. Chemical disposal and motorcaravan service points, and gas supplies. A children's playground is in the centre of the site. Because of the religious connections of the area, the site is very busy in August and indeed there are unlikely to be any vacancies at all for 14-16 August. Besides visiting the shrine and Knock Folk Museum, local activities include fishing (5 km), golf and riding (both 12 km). This is also a good centre for exploring scenic Co. Mayo.

Charges 2001:
-- Per unit IR£9.50 - 10.00; hiker or cyclist and tent IR£6.00 - 7.00; electricity (13A) IR£1.50. -- No credit cards.

Open:
1 March - 31 October.

Address:
Claremorris Road, Knock, Co. Mayo.

Tel:
094 88100 or 88223.
FAX: 094 88295.
E-mail:
info@knock-shrine.ie.

Reservations:
Any length, no deposit, but see editorial for Aug.

Directions: Take N17 to Knock site just south of village. Camp site well signed.

879 Carra Caravan and Camping Park, Belcarra, Castlebar

Small, unpretentious park in a pretty village setting.

This is an ideal location for those seeking a real Irish village experience on a 'value for money' park. Family run, it nestles at the foot of a wooded drumlin, and is surrounded by rolling hills and quiet roads which offer an 'away from it all' feeling, yet Castlebar the county's largest town is only an 8 km. drive. On the pleasant 1.5 acre park, the 20 unmarked touring pitches, 14 with electricity (13A), are on flat ground enclosed by ranch fencing and shaded in parts by trees. The basic sanitary block has adequate, well equipped showers (40p), etc. and there is a combined kitchen, dishwashing, laundry area with fridge/freezer, sink, table, chairs, washing machine and dryer. A comfortable lounge with TV is at reception. A novel idea at Carra are eight horse-drawn caravans for hire. Also of interest are the talks that the owner Sean and daughter Deirdre give on the area. There are recommended walks and maps provided. In the village are shops, a post office and 'Flukies' cosy bar . There is also a leisure centre, tennis courts, a free fishing area and a special walkway to the river. Golf 8 km.

Charges 2000:
-- Per unit incl. all persons IR£5.00; electricity IR£1.00. -- No credit cards.

Open:
10 June - 23 September (bookings may be accepted by arrangement outside this period).

Address:
Belcarra, Castlebar, Co. Mayo.

Tel:
094 32054.
FAX: 094 32351.

Reservations:
Contact park.

Directions: From Castlebar take N60 Claremorris road for 8.5 km. southeast and turn right at sign for Belcarra. Continue to village and site on left at end of village.

882 Hodson Bay Caravan and Camping Park, Kiltoom, Athlone

Peaceful, scenic park on shores of Lough Ree, in central Ireland.

This picturesque park is in a tranquil, wooded setting on the shores of Lough Ree on the River Shannon. Part of a 100 acre working farm, the site offers 19 pitches, with electricity for caravans and motorcaravans and 15 for tents, on flat grass. The central sanitary block, with good facilities for disabled people, was very clean when we visited and offers hot showers on payment 08.00 - 12.00 and 16.00 - 21.00 hrs, plus sufficient washing and toilet facilities. A dishwashing room at the rear of the block has two sinks and hot water (10p). The spin and tumble dryers provided are available for use after you take your laundry to reception where it is put through an industrial machine for you. The reception block provides a lounge area, a campers' kitchen and a TV room. The park has no shop but there is a mini-market at the top of the road. An hotel serving bar snacks and a carvery is close. You may fish, swim, go boating or just walk along the park's own path by the lough shore. Barbecues are permitted on site and by the lough. Horse riding and golf are available nearby. No dogs are accepted.

Directions: Leave N6 at Roscommon/Sligo junction on N61. After 4 km. turn right on minor road. Site clearly signed, end of this road (2.4 km).

Charges 2000:
-- Per adult or child IR£1.00; caravan or family tent IR£7.00; car IR£1.00; motorcaravan IR£8.00; small tent (1 or 2 man) IR£6.50; hiker/cyclist and tent IR£6.50; awning IR£2.00; electricity IR£2.00.

Open:
1 June - 1 September.

Address:
Kiltoom, Athlone, Co. Roscommon.

Tel:
0902 92448.

Reservations:
Made for high season with IR£5 deposit.

896 Lough Ree East Caravan and Camping Park, nr. Athlone

Touring park alongside river, screened by trees and reaching the water's edge.

Drive into the small village of Ballykeeran and this park is discreetly located behind the main street. The top half of the site is in a woodland situation and after the reception and sanitary block, Lough Ree comes into view and the remaining pitches run down to the shoreline. There are 60 pitches, 20 with hardstanding and 52 with electricity. The toilet block, with tiled walls, is clean without being luxurious. It houses WCs, washbasins, razor and hairdryer points, mirrors and hot showers (50p). Chemical disposal. Dishwashing sinks are outside and a new laundry room has been added. A wooden chalet with pool room and campers' kitchen stands behind the sanitary block. A restaurant and 'singing' pub are close. With fishing right on the doorstep there are boats for hire and the site has its own private mooring buoys, plus a dinghy slip and harbour. Golf or riding 4 km.

Directions: From Athlone take N55 towards Longford for 4.8 km. Park is in the village of Ballykeeran, clearly signed.

Charges 2000:
-- Per adult IR£2.50; child (under 14) IR£1.00; pitch IR£2.00 - IR£4.00; electricity IR£1.00.
-- No credit cards.

Open:
1 April - 2 October.

Address:
Ballykeeran, Athlone, Co. Westmeath.

Tel:
0902 78561 or 74414. FAX: 0902 77017.

Reservations:
Contact park for details.

889 Táin Holiday Village, Omeath

Fun packed holiday village, scenically set on Carlingford Lough.

This holiday complex is one of the most extensive in Ireland and is exactly what a family seeking entertainment might want. The touring park is within the 10-acre village, overlooking Carlingford Lough with views towards the Mourne mountains, whilst nestling at the foot of the Cooleys. The area for tourers is to the far right of the main buildings, entrance through a gate is by key (deposit). There are 87 pitches with hardstanding and electricity, plus 10 for tents. Young trees will eventually add more detail to this well laid out, but open site. The sanitary block is kept clean and can be heated. It houses WCs, hot showers, washbasins in cubicles and facilities for disabled visitors. Dishwashing and laundry sinks with hot water, washing machines and iron, chemical disposal and motorcaravan service facilities are provided. Included in the site fees is the use of the indoor leisure facilities. These include a heated pool (4-9 pm. daily) with slides, flumes and rafts, water play pool, an indoor play area with free fall, ball pool, climbing room and nets, also a sports hall, gym and games room, a jacuzzi, steam room and sun beds. Not least is a Science Interactive Centre. The licensed restaurant offers varied menus and there is a bar (all limited opening outside July/Aug). Outdoor activities include two adventure playgrounds, tennis and watersports. Fishing, bicycle hire or riding 2 km, golf 5 km. Caravan holiday homes to rent.

Directions: From Newry take B79/R173 road signed Omeath. Site is 1.6 km. south of Omeath village, on the left.

Charges 2000:
-- Per unit incl. 2 persons on fully serviced gravel pitch IR£19.00 - 21.00; tent on grass area IR£17.00 - 19.00; extra person IR£4.00 - 5.00.
-- Min. 2 nights in high season; for 1 night only prices are higher.
-- Credit cards accepted.

Open:
5 March - 31 October.

Address:
Carlingford Lough, Omeath, Co. Louth.

Tel:
042 9375385. FAX: 042 9375417.

Reservations:
Made with deposit (caravan IR£15, tent IR£10).

Low cost ferries guaranteed!

213

906 Green Gables Caravan and Camping Park, Geashill, Tullamore

Peaceful relaxing environment in the heart of Ireland's Bogland.

Green Gables enjoys a natural meadow-like setting in keeping with the wide open bogland countryside which enhances this county. This park is now maturing and offers top class facilities but most importantly, a friendly reception - in fact, here you experience Irish hospitality at its best. From the park entrance the drive leads to a parking area, clearly defined by a roundabout and a huge Ice Age stone from Boora Bog, known as 'Mona'. Reception, the Gables tea room and a patio area lie to the right, approached by a gateway and gravel path. The spotlessly clean sanitary block, a freshly painted, modern building, stands adjacent to reception. Its exterior is complemented with flower beds, shrubs and climbing plants which give a well cared for appearance. Facilities in the heated block include wash areas, attractive oval mirrors, hand towels, vanity unit, baby changing space and showers with hooks and seats. There are excellent facilities for disabled people, also a laundry area, washing up sink and chemical disposal. Motorcaravan service point and gas supplies available. Apart from 8 hardstanding pitches towards the rear of the park, the remainder are on grass. Electric hook-ups (10A) are provided on 14 and tents are catered for. The ground is gently sloping and the perimeter is surrounded by hedging. The village of Geashill is within 50 m. with old houses, stone walls, shops and three pubs. The proprietor at Hamilton's welcomes Green Gables campers in his pub where Irish culture abounds. Getting out of the village can mean taking a train from Portarlington station to Dublin city. If preferring the countryside there are cycle tours, the Grand Canal walking routes or a Bog Train tour through the historic bogland, one of Offaly's many attractions. Riding 5 km, fishing, bicycle hire or golf 10 km.

Charges 2000:
-- Per unit IR£8.00; small tent IR£6.00; adult IR£1.00; child 50p; hiker or cyclist and tent IR£5.00; electricity (10A) IR£1.50.
Open:
Easter - 31 September
Address:
Geashill, Tullamore, Co. Offaly.
Tel:
0506 43760.
FAX: as phone.
E-mail: ggcp@iol.ie.
Reservations:
Contact park.

Directions: From Tullamore take R420 east for 12 km. to village of Geashill. Site is on right at end of village.

911 Shankill Caravan and Camping Park, Shankill

Long-established park in pleasant rural surroundings convenient to ports.

This site makes an excellent overnight halt within easy reach of Dublin Port and Dun Laoghaire ferries. It also makes an ideal base for visiting Dublin with a bus departing from the site entrance every 15 minutes. The Dart fast train also leaves from Shankill village at 15 minute intervals. The site is located within a three minute walk of the village where you will find shops, restaurants, supermarkets etc. and, if a day at the seaside appeals, the resort of Bray is within a five minute drive. With lovely views of the Dublin mountains, the site is set in pleasant grounds with an abundance of mature trees, shrubs and well kept flower beds which gives it a park-like appearance. Additionally there are broad tarmac roads and night lighting. There are 82 unmarked pitches, 66 of which are for tourers. Some have hardstanding and 40 have electric hook-ups (10A). The two sanitary blocks, although showing signs of age and certainly not ultra modern, offer basic but adequate facilities which are kept clean with piping hot water to sinks and showers (50p payment). There is a separate chemical disposal unit, also laundry sinks, ironing facilities and dishwashing area. Reception staff are pleasant, helpful and willing to give advice on visiting the city or local tourist spots. Basic foodstuffs such as milk, bread etc. can be purchased at reception. Mobile homes for hire. No double-axle vans are permitted.

Charges 2000:
-- Per unit IR£6.50 - IR£7.00; adult IR£1.00; child IR£0.50; hiker or cyclist IR£5.50 - IR£6.00; electricity IR£1.00; awning IR£1.00.
Open:
All year.
Address:
Shankill, Co. Dublin.
Tel:
01 282 0011.
FAX: 01 282 0108.
E-mail: shankill-caravan@eircom.net.
Reservations:
Not possible in advance.

Directions: Site is 15 km. south of Dublin off the N11. From Dublin take N11 Wexford road for 15 km. and turn left at Bray, Shankill sign. Then follow signs to site on right.

To telephone the Irish Republic from the UK, replace the first `0' given in the number with the country code: 00 353.

eg. (094) 88100 becomes 00 353 94 88100.

910 Camac Valley Tourist Caravan and Camping Park, Dublin

Touring park with top class facilities convenient for ferry ports and Dublin city.

Opened in '96, this campsite is not only well placed for Dublin, but also offers a welcome stopover if travelling to the more southern counties from the north of the country, or vice versa. Despite its close proximity to the city, being located in the 300 acre Corkagh Park gives it a 'heart of the country' atmosphere. The site entrance and sign are distinctive and can be spotted in adequate time when approaching on the busy N7. Beyond the entrance gate and forecourt stands an attractive timber fronted building. Its design includes various roof levels and spacious interior layout, with large windows offering a view of the site. Housed here is reception, information, reading, TV and locker rooms plus heated sanitary facilities which include WCs, good sized showers (50p token) and central floor units with washbasins and mirrors. There are also shaver points, hand dryers, facilities for disabled people, baby changing room, laundry, washing up and chemical disposal. A second well designed and fitted sanitary block is operational, also a children's playground with wooden play frames and safety base. A shop and coffee bar open in June, July and August. There are 163 pitches, 48 for tents placed to the fore and the hardstandings for caravans laid out in bays and avenues with electrical connections, drainage and water points. Young trees separate pitches and roads are tarmac. There is an automatic gate and 24 hour security. Caravan storage. Dogs are not accepted in July/Aug. Fishing 8 km, bicycle hire 1.5 km, riding 9 km, golf 6 km. After a day of sightseeing in Dublin, which can be reached by bus from the site, Camac Valley offers an evening of relaxation with woodland and river walks in the park or a number of first class restaurants and pubs nearby.

Directions: From north follow signs for West Link and M50 motorway. Exit M50 at junction 9 onto N7 Cork road. Site is on right of dual carriageway (beside Green Isle Hotel) after 2 km. and is clearly signed. At City West business park, cross over bridge and return on dual-carriageway following camp signs - site is on left after 800 m.

Charges 2000:
-- Per unit incl. 2 persons IR£10.00 - 11.00, incl. up to 4 children IR£11.00 - 13.00; extra person IR£1.00; child (under 7 yrs) 50p; motorcyclist, cyclist or hiker with tent IR£3.00 - 4.00 per person; awning IR£1.00; extra small tent IR£3.00; electricity (10A) IR£1.00. -- Credit cards accepted.
Open:
All year
Address:
Naas Road, Clondalkin, Dublin 22.
Tel:
01 464 0644.
FAX: 01 464 0643.
E-mail:
camacmorriscastle@tinet.ie.
Reservations:
Advance bookings necessary. (max. stay operates at certain times).

`Camping Cheque'

913 Roundwood Caravan and Camping Park, Roundwood

Quality park in the heart of the Wicklow mountains.

This park, under new management, still maintains high standards and is neatly laid out with rows of trees dividing different areas giving an attractive appearance. There are 31 pitches for caravans and motorcaravans, all with electricity (5A) and 16 with hardstanding, plus 40 pitches for tents, arranged off tarmac access roads. There are several water points and rubbish bins handily placed around the park. The sanitary block is kept clean, with adequate washing and toilet facilities, plus spacious showers. The block also houses two dishwashing sinks with free hot water and good laundry facilities, but ask at reception as machines are not self-service. The facilities include a chemical disposal and motorcaravan service point. Bicycle hire is available and there is a children's adventure playground, a TV room, campers' kitchen and dining room. In the village of Roundwood you find shops, pubs, restaurants and takeaway food, also a Sunday market. There are excellent walks around the Varty Lakes and a daily bus service to Dublin city. Close by are the Wicklow and Sally Gap, Glendalough, Powerscourt Gardens, plus many other places of natural beauty. Fishing or golf 1 km. Apart from having a scenic location, this site is well placed for the ferry ports.

Directions: Turn off N11 Dublin - Wexford road at Kilmacanogue towards Glendalough and then 15 km. to Roundwood.

Charges 2001:
-- Per unit IR£7.00 - 8.00; adult IR£2.00; child (under 14 yrs) IR£1.50; electricity IR£1.50; hiker/cyclist IR£6.50. -- No credit cards.
Open:
31 March - 1 October.
Address:
Roundwood, Co. Wicklow.
Tel:
01 2818163.
FAX: as phone.
E-mail: dicksonn @indigo.ie.
Reservations:
Accepted without deposit and advisable for July/Aug.

Tourist Information:

Dublin the capital of Ireland since the late 17th century is stylish and energetic with a charm of its own, The old Ireland is still present in its castles, cathedrals and fine pubs but Dublin has seen a blending of cultures that has allowed for an amazing intellectual and literary life. From Swift and Burke to Joyce and Beckett, Dublin has produced so many great writers that nearly every street contains a literary landmark. Pubs shelter Dublin's public life and a world-renowned music scene for the Irish maintain a strong public life centred around music, sports, a laid-back attitude, and, of course, drinking.

Wicklow

914 Valley Stopover and Caravan Park, Kilmacanogue

Small, family run park located in quiet, idyllic setting and convenient for Dublin ferries.

This neat and attractive ¾ acre park in the grounds of the family home is situated in the picturesque Rocky Valley and could be used either as a transit site or for a longer stay. It will appeal to those who prefer the more basic 'CL' type site. There are 15 grassy pitches, 11 with electric hook-ups, 3 hardstandings, 2 water points, night lighting and a security gate. Toilet facilities, which were spotlessly clean when we visited, are housed in one unit and consist of two WCs with washbasins, mirrors, etc. and a shower (50p). There is a dishwashing and laundry sink, a spin dryer, chemical disposal point, a campers' kitchen and hot water is constantly available. A cooked full Irish breakfast is available for IR£3.50 in the family guest house. Staying put here you are only minutes from Enniskerry which lies in the glen of the Glencullen river. Here you can enjoy a delight of forest walks, or visit Powerscourt, one of the loveliest gardens in Ireland. If wanting to be at the sea, travel 6 km. to Bray and you are in one of the oldest seaside resorts in the country. Fishing 16 km, bicycle hire 7 km (can be delivered), riding 3 km, golf 7 km. Small caravan for hire.

Directions: Turn off Dublin-Wexford N11 road at Kilmacanogue - follow signs for Glendalough. Continue for 1.6 km and take right fork signed 'Waterfall'. Park is first opening on the left in approx. 200 m.

Charges 2000:
-- Per caravan or tent with car IR£8.00; motor-caravan IR£7.00; tent with bike IR£3.50; electricity £IR1.00; awning IR£1.00.
-- No credit cards.

Open:
Easter - 31 October.

Address:
Valleyview, Killough, Kilmacanogue, Co. Wicklow.

Tel:
01 282 9565.

Reservations:
Advised for July/Aug; contact park.

915 River Valley Caravan and Camping Park, Redcross Village

Family run park in small village in the heart of Co. Wicklow.

In the small country village of Redcross you find this well run and popular park. Being based here means you are within easy reach of beauty spots such as the Vale of Avoca, (Ballykissangel), Glendalough and Powerscourt, plus the safe beach of Brittas Bay. The 100 touring pitches at River Valley are mostly together in a dedicated area, all have electricity connections (6A) and offer a choice of hardstanding or grass - you select your pitch. A luxurious new sanitary block has a modern, well designed appearance making it a special feature. Facilities for disabled visitors are excellent, hot water is available for dishwashing and there is a laundry area, campers' kitchen, chemical disposal and motorcaravan service points. Within this 12-acre site children can find day long amusement, whether it be Fort Apache, the adventure playground, the tiny tots playground, or at the natural mountain stream where it is safe to paddle. There is also a pets corner with a 'fat belly' pig. Other amenities include TV, games room, three tennis courts, par 3 golf course and bowling green, plus a sports complex with badminton courts and indoor football and basketball. An attractive wine and coffee bar with a conservatory is an inviting asset, or an alternative may be the restaurant where home made, traditional dishes are on the menu (1/6-31/8). Gas is available. The late arrivals area has electric hook-ups, water and night lighting. There is a rally area, caravan storage and mobiles for hire. No dogs are accepted in July/Aug.

Directions: From Dublin follow N11 Wexford road. Turn right in Rathnew and left under railway bridge onto the Wexford-Arklow road. Continue for 11 km. and turn right at Doyle's Pub. Park is in Redcross village, under 5 km.

Charges 2000:
-- Per caravan, motor-caravan incl. 2 adults IR£10.00 - 11.00, small tent IR£9.00 - 10.00; extra adult IR£3.00; child (under 15 yrs) IR£1.00; m/cyclist, cyclist or hiker and tent incl.tent IR£5.00 - 6.00; electricity IR£1.00.
-- Credit cards accepted.

Open:
12 March - 13 September.

Address:
Redcross Village, Co. Wicklow.

Tel:
0404 41647.
FAX: 0404 41677.
E-mail: info@ rivervalleypark.ie.

Reservations:
Made with IR£10 deposit.

'Camping Cheque'

916 Moat Farm Caravan and Camping Park, Donard

Heart of the country experience within easy driving distance of Dublin or Rosslare.

Here is a true feel of the countryside - this site is part of a working sheep farm environment - that also offers incredible vistas across a scenic landscape. Driving into the village of Donard you little suspect that alongside the main street lies a pleasant, well cared for and tranquil five-acre site The entrance is approached by way of a short road where the ruins of a Medieval church sit high overlooking the forecourt and reception. Facing down the site is the sanitary block which is kept clean and includes spacious showers, facilities for visitors with disabilities, a well equipped laundry room and chemical disposal point. A recent extension on the site has added a new campers' kitchen and a large recreation/entertainment room with an open fire. Three large barbecues and a patio area are also provided. There are 40 pitches for caravans and tents. The pitches with hardstanding line both sides of a broad avenue and these are both spacious and incorporate awning space and all have electricity and drainage points. There is a separate area for tents. This site makes a good base for touring or going on foot, for this area is a walker's paradise with a 30 minute circular walk around the perimeter of the site. There is mountain climbing or sites of archaeological interest nearby. Bicycle hire 15 km, fishing 3 km, golf 13 km. Caravan storage available.

Directions: Park is 18 km. south of Blessington, 1 hour from Dublin via N4, N7 and N81 or 1½ hours frm Rosslare via N80 and N81. Site is clearly signed.

Charges 2001:
-- Per caravan, motor-caravan or family tent IR£8.00; adult IR£1.00; child 50p; tent (1 or 2 persons) IR£6.00; m/cyclist, hiker or cyclist incl. tent IR£5.00; awning free; electricity (10A) IR£1.50.
-- No credit cards.
Open:
All year.
Address:
Donard, Co. Wicklow.
Tel:
045 404727.
FAX: as phone.
E-mail: nuala@wicklowhills.com.
Reservations:
Contact site.

THE ALAN ROGERS'
travel service

Book this site with the experts
Call for an instant quote
01892 55 98 98

Low cost ferries
guaranteed!

908 Forest Farm Caravan and Camping Park, Athy

Farm site with good quality facilities, off Dublin - Kilkenny road.

This new site makes an excellent stopover if travelling from Dublin to the southeast counties. It is signed on the N78 and approached by a 500 m. avenue of tall pines. Part of a working farm, the campsite spreads to the right of the modern farmhouse, which also provides B&B. The owners have cleverly utilised their land to create a site which offers 64 unmarked touring pitches on level ground. Of these, 32 are for caravans, all with electricity and 10 with hardstanding and 32 places are available for tents. The red brick sanitary block, which is heated and has double glazing, occupies a central position on site. It offers quality amenities including a comfortable lounge/games room (a TV will be supplied on request). The shower and WC areas have freshly painted yellow walls and pine doors, plus top of the range fittings. Facilities include a spacious shower unit for disabled visitors and a family room with shower and WC. There is also a laundry room, with washing machine, dryer and spin dryer, and dishwashing sinks which are in the camper's kitchen. This is furnished with a fridge/freezer, cooker, table and chairs. Chemical disposal facilities are in a dedicated space separate from the main building. There is a basketball net, sand pit and picnic tables, also night lighting. Full Irish breakfasts are served at the farmhouse and farm tours available on request.

Directions: Site is 4.8 km. northeast of Athy town off the main N78 Athy - Kilcullen road.

Charges 2000:
-- Per unit incl. 2 adults IR£9.00 - 11.00; child 50p; 1 or 2 person tent IR£3.00 - 4.00 p/person; m/cyclist, hiker or cyclist incl. tent IR£3.00 - 4.00 p/person; electricity (13A) IR£1.50.
-- Stay 7 nights, pay for 6.
-- No credit cards.
Open:
All year.
Address:
Dublin Road, Athy, Co. Kildare.
Tel:
0507 31231 or 33070.
FAX: 0507 31231.
E-mail: forestfarm@eircom.net.
Reservations:
Contact site.

Alan Rogers' Discount

Less 10%

217

Laois / Kilkenny

920 Kirwans Caravan and Camping Park, Portlaoise

Friendly, peaceful park, ideal for exploring inland, rural Ireland.

One receives a warm welcome at this small 'homely' park, located on the edge of Portlaoise and surrounded by trees. The pitches are around the edges of a flat, firm grassy meadow and you site yourself sensibly, choosing morning or afternoon sun. Flowers and shrubs have been planted and secluded seating areas provided. The site offers 16 pitches with electricity (13A) for caravans or motorcaravans and another 14 for tents. There are a couple of static vans and mobile homes for hire. Water facilities are adequate with a long hose available. The sanitary block, near the entrance, is very clean and is adequate, without being luxurious. It offers hot showers on payment and additional facilities are being added. There are dishwashing facilities and a laundry with washing machine, spin and tumble dryers - the laundry is not to be used on Sundays. A TV and video room is provided and a rest room where one can make tea and coffee, plus a kitchen for groups, a playground, barbecue and a picnic area are on site. Supermarkets, shops, etc. are close by in Portlaoise, where there is a market on Thursdays. Laois is a beautiful inland county of Ireland, with picturesque small towns and many historical connections well worth exploring.

Directions: Approaching Portlaoise from the N7 Kildare - Limerick road, join the M7 bypass and branch off onto R445 signed Portlaoise centre. Continue to round-about in centre and follow signs for Limerick and Montrath. Site is on right approx. 1.5 km. from roundabout; watch carefully for campsite sign immediately by entrance.

Charges guide:
-- Per unit, incl. 2 persons IR£8.00 - 15.00; m/cycle and tent incl. 1 or 2 persons IR£5.00 per person; backpacker or cyclist IR£3.00 per person; child IR£1.00; extra adult, tent, electricity, dog, awning or boat all IR£1.00 - 1.50.

Open:
1 April - 15 October.

Address:
N7 Limerick Road, Portlaoise, Co. Laois.

Tel:
0502 21688.

Reservations:
Made for any length, with deposit.

923 Nore Valley Park, Annamult, Bennettsbridge

Small working farm site, set in picturesque and peaceful surroundings.

This lovely site is set on a grassy hillock overlooking the valley and the river Nore, with a woodland setting behind. Situated on a working farm, it offers 60 pitches, 30 for caravans and motorcaravans, all with electrical hook-up and hardstanding. The owners pride themselves on their home baking and farm produce and during high season cooked breakfasts are available in the small café (June-Aug). The reception area at the entrance is in an attractive courtyard and basic items such as milk, bread, camping gaz are available. A modern sanitary block houses facilities which are kept spotlessly clean and can be heated. These include free hot showers, WCs, washbasins and two units suitable for disabled visitors. There are dishwashing sinks with hot water, a laundry room with washing machine and dryer, chemical disposal and motorcaravan services. The original sanitary block in the courtyard is used mainly in the low season. A comfortable lounge is to be found next to the reception area, plus a games room with pool table. Crazy golf is a feature. Bicycle hire. Other facilities within the courtyard include a sand pit, pedal go-karts, tractor rides and a straw loft playing area for wet weather. At the front of the park is a fenced children's play area on gently sloping grass. This is an ideal park for families, offering children and adults alike the opportunity to feed the animals (goats, lambs, ducks, chickens, and donkey). The park is 11 km. from Kilkenny, renowned for its castle, history and crafts, and 3 km. from the village of Bennettsbridge, where there are shops and eating places. There is plenty of scope nearby for outdoor pursuits such as canoeing, pony trekking or golf (10 km), walking and fishing (4 km). Caravan storage available. Four mobile homes for hire. Note: the tractor rides, go-karts and the café are closed on Sundays.

Directions: From Kilkenny take R700 to Bennettsbridge. Just before the bridge turn right at sign for Stoneyford and after approx. 3 km. site is signed Nore Valley Park.

Charges 2001:
-- Per person IR£1.00; caravan IR£8.50; trailer or chalet tent IR£8.00; motorcaravan IR£7.50; family tent IR£8.00, 2 person tent IR£5.50; awning or extra small tent IR£2.00; electricity (6A) IR£1.50.
-- Credit cards accepted.

Open:
1 March - 31 October.

Address:
Annamult, Bennettsbridge, Co. Kilkenny.

Tel:
056 27229.
FAX: 056 27748.
E-mail:
norevalleypark@eircom.net.

Reservations:
Contact park.

924 Tree Grove Caravan and Camping Park, Kilkenny

Orderly, neat and welcoming touring park within walking distance of Kilkenny.

The entrance gate to this small family run site is easily spotted off the R700 road. It makes an ideal location for spending time in medieval Kilkenny, known for its elegance and famed for its beer and cats. Tree Grove has instant appeal because its young owners are friendly and have insisted on a logical layout to suit both the terrain and campers' needs. It is a terraced site with the lower terrace to the right of the wide sweeping driveway laid out with 11 hardstanding pitches for caravans. All 30 pitches have electrical hook-ups (10A) and plenty of water points are to be found. On a higher level, to the left is a grass area for hikers and cyclists with further caravan and tent pitches sited near the elevated sanitary block. If needed more grass pitches face reception, which is temporarily housed in a mobile unit. Whilst there are mature trees at the entrance and around the site perimeter, many young shrubs have been planted and flower troughs effectively placed. House plants add decoration inside the toilet block giving a cared for look to this modern building. Showers are free and a family room with shower, WC and washbasin can be used by disabled people. WCs and washbasins with mirrors, shaver and hairdryer points, are in separate spacious areas. Ladies' have a vanity unit with large mirror. An open, covered kitchen for campers with fridge, work-top, sink and electric kettle adjoins a comfortable games/TV room with pool table, easy chairs and magazine rack. Next to this is a laundry room with sink, washing machine, dryer and iron. Chemical disposal. On the patio there are bench seats with tables and umbrellas. Tents to rent on site. There is much to see and do around the ancient city of Kilkenny (1.5 km) with its cobbled streets and castle. Bicycle hire on site; fishing 500 m, riding 1 km. Golf 2 or 15 km. County Touring Routes are worth following.

Directions: Travelling north on the N10 Waterford/Kilkenny Road turn right at roundabout on ring road. Continue to 2nd roundabout and turn right onto R700. Site is 150 m. on right.

Charges 2001:
-- Per caravan, motor-caravan or family tent incl. 2 persons IR£8.50; extra person IR£1.00; 1 man tent IR£5.00; 2 man tent IR£6.50; car IR£1.00; awning IR£1.00; electricity (10A) IR£1.50.
-- No credit cards.

Open:
1 March - 15 November.

Address:
Danville House, Kilkenny, Co. Kilkenny.

Tel:
056 70302.
FAX: 056 21512.
E-mail: treecc@iol.ie.

Reservations:
Contact site.

930 Morriscastle Strand Caravan and Camping Park, Kilmuckridge

Family run park with direct access to sandy beach and convenient for Rosslare Port.

Whether you use this park as a stopover, or choose it as a longer stay destination, you will find it to be in a quiet relaxing location. Situated minutes from the pretty village of Kilmuckridge, there are 145 privately owned caravan holiday homes on site but these are unobtrusive and kept separate by high hedging. The entrance to the touring park is to the right of reception by way of a tarmac drive. This leads to the secluded, gently sloping, grass pitches which enjoy an open aspect overlooking marshland which attracts wild geese and ducks, whilst the sea brings in crabs, eels and fish. To the right of the site lie sand-hills and pathways to the beach which is supervised by lifeguards in high season. The 100 pitches are numbered and marked by concrete slabs, each has an electrical hook-up (6A) and drainage point. Spacing can be a little tight in high season when the park gets busy. There is good night lighting and two sanitary blocks house all toilet facil-ities. These include spacious WCs, washbasins, mirrors, shaver points, etc. Also unisex showers (on payment) with dividing wall, bench seat, hooks and soap dish. There is provision for disabled people, a baby bath, campers' kitchen, dishwashing area, launderette, chemical disposal and outside cold showers. Other on site facil-ities include a shop, snacks and takeaway in high season, also a games room, two tennis courts, football field and children's play area. Kilmuckridge is approxi-mately 3 km. with an assortment of shops, pubs offering nightly entertainment and top class restaurants, such as The Rafters, a picturesque spot which helps charac-terise this charming village. Golf 5 km. Dogs are accepted only in certain areas (not with tents).

Directions: Site is 25 km. east of Enniscorthy. Travelling south on N11 Dublin/Wexford road branch onto R741 at Gorey. Continue for 19 km. to Bally-edmund. Turn left at petrol station and follow signs for Kilmuckridge and site.

Charges 2000:
-- Per unit incl. 2 persons IR£10.00 - 11.00, incl. up to 4 children IR£11.00 - 13.00; extra person IR£3.00; child (under 7 yrs) IR£1.00; motorcy-clist, cyclist or hiker with tent IR£3.00 - 4.00 per person; awning IR£1.00; extra small tent IR£3.00; electricity (5A) IR£1.00.
-- Credit cards accepted.

Open:
1 May - 30 September.

Address:
Kilmuckridge, Co. Wexford.

Tel:
053 30124 or 053 30212 (off season 01 453 5355). FAX: 053 30365 (off season 01 454 5916).
E-mail:
camacmorriscastle @eircom.net.

Reservations:
Made with IR£10 deposit; contact site by phone or letter (use off season numbers Oct - April).

219

933 Casey's Caravan Park, Clonea, Dungarvan

Family run site with direct access to the beach.

Set on 20 acres of flat grass, edged by mature trees, this park offers 284 pitches which include 154 touring pitches, 118 with electrical hook-ups and 30 with hardstanding. The remainder are occupied by caravan holiday homes. The central sanitary block, operated on a key system, has good facilities kept spotlessly clean, a top priority for the owner. There are showers on payment (50p), free hot water to open style basins and washing up sinks (10p). Also housed in this block is a small laundry with machine and dryer. A further luxurious and modern block has been added with an excellent campers' kitchen, laundry room and toilet for disabled visitors. Chemical disposal. There is direct access from the park to a sandy, blue flag beach with a resident lifeguard during July/Aug. Facilities on the site include a large children's adventure play area with bark surface in its own field (not supervised by staff). Near the site entrance is a games room with pool table, table tennis and amusements, crazy golf and TV lounge. Gas is available. A highly recommended leisure centre is adjacent should the weather be inclement. There is no shop, but two village stores are near the beach. The park is 5½ km. from Dungarvan, a popular town for deep sea angling, from which charter boats can be hired and three 18 hole golf courses are within easy distance. Recommended drives include the scenic Vee, the Comeragh Drive and the coast road to Tramore. Dogs allowed on a lead. Full time security staff in high season.

Charges 2001:
-- Per unit IR£11.50 - 12.00; hiker or cyclist IR£4.00; electricity (5A) IR£1.00.
-- No credit cards.
Open:
27 April - 9 September.
Address:
Clonea, Dungarvan, Co. Waterford.
Tel:
058 41919.
Reservations:
Are made in low season, but not between 9 July - 15 Aug; contact park.

Directions: From Dungarvan centre follow R675 east for 3.5 km. Look for signs on the right to Clonea Bay and site. Site is approx. 1.5 km.

 ★★★★ # Casey's Caravan & Camping Park
Clonea, Dungarvan, Co Waterford Tel: 058 41919

Top class facilities	Two ablution blocks with laundry & kitchen
Playground	Games room and TV room
Electric sites for tents & tourers (5A)	EU Blue Flag beach
Dungarvan town 3½ miles	Two nearby shops with takeaway
Choice of scenic views to visit	Deep sea and river angling
18 hole golf course in easy reach	Adjacent hotel with 19 metre pool and leisure centre with bowling alley

---

934 Newtown Cove Camping and Caravan Park, Tramore

Small, well run, friendly park, 5 minutes walk from the beautiful Newtown Cove.

This park offers views of the famous and historic Metal Man and is situated 2.5 km. from Tramore beach and 11 km. from Waterford. Neatly set out on gently sloping grass with an abundance of shrubs and bushes, there are 40 pitches. All have electrical connections (10A), some hardstanding also, with access by well lit tarmac roads. There are around 50 privately owned caravan holiday homes. A modern building at the entrance houses reception, a small shop (1/7-30/8), TV room, games room and further sanitary facilities. The village of Tramore, with a wide range of shops and eating houses, is close. The main sanitary block is situated at the bottom end of the site and, although not very modern, offers good facilities which include a bathroom. Showers are on payment (50p for a token from reception). The block also provides a campers' kitchen with cooking facilities (20p), lounge and a washing up room and small laundry, with free hot water. A small children's play area set on sand is conveniently positioned in the centre of the park. A golf course is 800 m. and the choice of many delightful cliff walks in the immediate vicinity. Bicycle hire 1.5 km, fishing 400 m, riding 3 km. Dogs are allowed if kept on a lead. No bookings are taken and the park does not accept single sex groups.

Charges 2000:
-- Per unit incl. 2 persons IR£9.00 - 10.00; extra adult IR£1.00 - 1.50; child free - IR£1.00; hiker, cyclist or motorcyclist IR£3.50 - 4.50 per person; awning IR£1.00 - £2.00; electricity (10A) IR£1.50.
-- No credit cards.
Open:
Easter, then 1 May - 30 September.
Address:
Tramore, Co. Waterford
Tel:
051 381979.
E-mail: johngood@iol.ie.
Reservations:
Not necessary but for information contact park.

Alan Rogers' Discount

Pay 3 nights, stay 4th free (excl. July/Aug)

Directions: From Tramore on R675 coast road to Dungarvan. Turn left 2 km. from town centre, following signs.

939 Carrick-on-Suir Caravan and Camping Park, Carrick-on-Suir

Small, family run, town site in quiet and tranquil setting.

This memorable little site is not only conveniently situated off the main N24 between Waterford and Clonmel, but its owner, Frank O'Dwyer, is an excellent ambassador for his county. On his site campers are guaranteed the finest example of 'Cead Mile Failte' it is possible to encounter - personal attention and advice on where to go and what to see in the area is all part of the service. The entrance to the park is immediately past the O'Dwyers' shop, through a gate which is closed at 11 pm. The tarmac drive leads past tall hedges and well kept shrubs to the right and several caravan holiday homes (for hire) to the left. The touring park lies to the rear with scenic views to the wooded hills. At present there are 30 level pitches, 23 with electricity (10A) and several with hardstanding, but this number is to be extended. There are 7 water points, chemical disposal, a motorcaravan service point and good night lighting. What makes this little site distinctive is its excellent, well designed sanitary block which has a sparkling clean freshness. The building itself is white, as are all inside fittings, and the floor tiles, which are white with a black design. Facilities include WCs, showers, washbasins with mirrors, electric points, hand dryers and plenty of hot water each morning. Laundry room with washing machine and a dishwashing area also. Camper's kitchen with TV. Basic groceries, a selection of wines and gas are available from the family shop. Fishing 1 km, riding 6 km, golf 3 km. Carrick town centre is a five minute walk away where there are shops, pubs, restaurants, banks, sports facilities and all services, plus a castle which is open to the public. Within a short drive is the 'magic road', the Mahon Falls, a slate quarry or a romantic river walk. Carrick is well placed en-route to the west, only 1½ hours from Rosslare.

Charges 2001:
-- Per unit incl. 2 adults IR£9.00 - 11.50; tent IR£6.00 - 9.00; extra adult IR£2.50; child IR£1.00 - 2.00; electricity 6A IR£1.00, 10A IR£1.50; hiker/cyclist incl. tent IR£3.00 - 3.50; extra car IR£1.00.
-- No credit cards.
Open:
1 March - 1 November.
Address:
Kilkenny Road,
Carrick-on-Suir,
Co. Tipperary.
Tel:
051 640461.
E-mail:
coscamping@eircom.net.
Reservations:
Contact site.

Directions: Approaching town on N24 road, follow signs for R690 in the direction of Kilkenny. Site is north of town, clearly signed at junction with R697.

941 The Apple Camping and Caravan Park, Cahir

Fruit farm and campsite combination offering an idyllic country holiday venue.

In one of the most delightful situations imaginable, this small farm site for tourers only is located off the N24, midway between Clonmel and Cahir. Entrance is by way of a 300 m. drive which follows straight through the heart of the farm. Apple trees guard the route, as do various non-fruit tree species, which are named and of interest to guests, who are free to spend time walking the paths around the farm. When we visited, strawberries were being gathered - the best we had tasted all season. Reception is housed with the other site facilities in a large farmyard barn. Although a rather unusual arrangement, it is very effective. Showers, WCs and washbasins with mirrors, electric points, etc. are in functional units occupying two corners of the large floor space. Kept very clean, quite modern in design and with heating, there are simple extra touches such as green curtains and green coloured concrete floor which blend with the fittings to give an attractive well maintained appearance. Facilities for disabled visitors have been added. Also in the barn are dishwashing sinks with hot water, bench seating and a fridge/freezer for the use of campers. Chemical disposal and motorcaravan service point. The 32 pitches are in a secluded situation behind the barns and are mostly grass with a few hardstandings, with electricity connections to 24. Amenities include a tennis court, a basketball/football pitch and children's play area. No dogs are accepted. Public phone. Fishing, golf, bicycle hire and riding within 6 km. The towns of Cahir and Clonmel are of historic interest and the countryside around boasts rivers, mountains, Celtic culture and scenic drives.

Charges 2001:
-- Per person IR£3.75 - 4.25; child (0-12 yrs) IR£2.00 - 2.25; electricity (13A) IR£1.50 (no charge per unit).
-- No credit cards.
Open:
1 May - 30 September.
Address:
Moorstown, Cahir,
Co. Tipperary.
Tel:
052 41459.
FAX: 052 42774.
Reservations:
Contact site.

Alan Rogers' Discount

Free bottle of apple juice or fruit in season

Directions: Park is 300 m. off main N24, 9.6 km. northwest of Clonmel, 6.4 km. southeast of Cahir.

Tipperary / Limerick

938 Parsons Green Caravan and Camping Park, Clogheen

Small, family run park with excellent on-site facilities.

In a tranquil and scenic location, this open style site commands panoramic views toward the Vee Gap and Knockmealdown Mountains. Surrounded by low ranch fencing, it offers 20 pitches for caravans and motorcaravans with hardstanding and 14 on grass, all with electrical connections (6A), plus 20 pitches for tents. The sanitary facilities, to the top right of the site close to reception, are kept clean and include WCs, washbasins with mirrors and electric points, free hot showers and good facilities for disabled people (shower and toilet), plus a laundry area with washing machines, dryer and sinks, three dishwashing sinks and chemical disposal. A coffee shop is on site, ice cream, confectionery and gifts are sold and there is a takeaway. The village is within 500 m. (footpath and lighting) with shops, pubs, bank, post office, etc. The wide range of amenities on site includes a garden area, river walks, picnic area, an extensive farm museum, a pet field with selection of domestic and rare animals and birds, children's playground, minigolf, pony and trap rides, boating on the small lake and trout fishing river. TV/games room, campers' kitchen and function room. If not sitting back enjoying the scenic surroundings or participating in the many activities, there is much to see and do in this area. The manager of Parson's Green, would be more than pleased to pinpoint places of interest. Riding and golf 12 km. Caravan holiday homes (3) and chalets (2) for hire.

Charges 2000:
-- Per caravan, family tent or motorcaravan IR£4.00; small tent IR£3.00; adult IR£2.00; child IR£1.00; awning IR£1.00; electricity (6A) IR£1.00.
-- No credit cards.
Open:
All year.
Address:
Clogheen, Co. Tipperary.
Tel:
052 65290.
FAX: 052 65504.
Reservations:
Contact site.

Directions: Site is in the village of Clogheen, 200 m. off the R665, 24 km. west of Clonmel, 19 km. east of Mitchelstown.

945 Curraghchase Caravan and Camping Park, Kilcornan

Beautiful, tranquil park set in Curraghchase Forest.

Approached by a long, tree-lined avenue that sets it well back from the main road, this 39 acre park is set in 600 acres of beech forest (known as the Coillte Forest park), 21 km. from Limerick City. Touring pitches have hardstanding with drainage and electric hook-ups, plus a separate grassy area allocated for 40 tents. One large building houses a well stocked shop, TV lounge, a games room with table tennis and seating for an excellent campers' kitchen. Also within this building are the sanitary facilities which are basic. Hot water is free and showers are separated by a partition, sharing a large base with single drain and a communal dressing area with hooks and benches. Washing up sinks are available in the campers' kitchen and a small laundry with washing machines, dryers and iron. Chemical disposal. Behind the main block is a small `sun trap' picnic area. Children's play area with a bark safety base. Card telephone on site. Barbecues are allowed. There are many lovely forest walks, a nature trail and a number of rare orchids can be found. Within the forest are the ruins of Curragh (or Currah) Chase House, which was once the home of the poet Aubrey de Vere. Fishing, riding, golf and Adare village, with its interesting historical buildings and shopping facilities, are within 10 km.

Charges 2000:
-- Per caravan or family tent IR£10.00; tent incl. 1 or 2 persons IR£5.00; electricity IR£1.00.
-- Euros: Per caravan or family tent 12,70; tent incl. 1 or 2 persons 6.25; electricity 1.27.
-- No credit cards.
Open:
1 May - 10 September.
Address:
Coillte Forest Park, Kilcornan, Co. Limerick.
Tel:
061 396349 (or 061 337322 off season).
FAX: 061 338271.
E-mail: okeeffe_e@ ecoillte.ie.
Reservations:
Advisable in high season - contact site.

Directions: From Limerick city take N69 Foynes road; park entrance is at Kilcornan. Park also signed from Adare on the N20.

Tourist Information:

The West - even Dubliners will tell you that the west is the 'most Irish' part of Ireland. The West was hardest hit by the potato famine - entire villages emigrated or died. Today, every western county has less than half of its 1841 population.

948 Blarney Caravan and Camping Park, Blarney

Friendly, family run park easily reached from the ports of Cork and Rosslare.

There is a heart of the country feel about this 'on the farm' site, yet the city of Cork is only an 8 km. drive. What makes it so appealing is its secluded location and neatly laid out, open appearance. The terrain on the 3 acre park is elevated and gently sloping, commanding views towards Blarney Castle and the surrounding mountainous countryside. The 40 pitches, 30 of which have hardstanding and 10A electrical connections, are with caravans sited to the centre and left and tents pitched to the right. There are gravel roads, well tended young shrubs and a screen of mature trees and hedging marks the park's perimeter. Sanitary facilities are housed in converted farm buildings with the reception area and small shop abutting near the entrance. The toilet area is kept clean, showers are of a good size, free and have hooks, seat and soap rack, and there are now facilities for disabled visitors. The laundry room has stainless steel sinks, washing machine, dryer and ironing facilities and a washing up area is in the large campers' kitchen, which also has plenty of tables and seating. Other facilities include a shop (1/6-31/8), night lighting, chemical disposal, motorcaravan service point, TV lounge, phone room and an 18 hole golf and pitch and putt course. Caravan storage available. In the Blarney area, apart from the castle, house and gardens, there are shops, restaurants, pubs with traditional music and an abundance of outdoor pursuits such as walking, riding and fishing. A public bar and restaurant at 100 m. serves food all day.

Directions: Site is 8 km. northwest of Cork, just off the N20. Take N20 from Cork for approx. 6 km. and then left on R617 to Blarney. Site clearly signed at Esso station in village, in approx. 2 km.

Charges 2001:
-- Per caravan, family tent or motorcaravan IR£5.00 - 6.00; car and small tent IR£4.00 - 5.00; adult IR£2.50; child IR£1.00; hiker/cyclist and tent IR£3.50 - 4.00; m/cyclist IR£4.00 - 4.50 per person; electricity (10A) IR£1.50; awning IR£1.00 - 1.50.
-- 7 nights for price of 6, if pre-paid.
-- Credit cards accepted.

Open: All year.

Address: Stone View, Blarney, Co. Cork.

Tel: 021 4385167. FAX: as phone. E-mail: con.quill@camping-ireland.ie.

Reservations: Contact park.

949 Sonas Caravan and Camping Park, Ballymacoda, nr. Youghal

Pleasant family run park in an unspoilt rural area.

What sells Sonas is its delightful situation, overlooking Youghal Bay with direct access to the beach and a birdwatcher's paradise. In this peaceful and quiet location, 4 km. from Ballymacoda village, it is easy to sit back and relax at this family run site. Pleasantly laid out, the 20 touring pitches are mostly to the right, with 12 pitches for caravans and motorcaravans, all with electric hook-ups (10A) and 10 with hardstanding. It is also possible to choose a more isolated spot around the perimeter where at least 20 tents can be pitched. Immediately in view is the main amenity block with 70 privately owned caravan holiday homes placed beyond. This building, which has a fresh and clean appearance, houses all the facilities which include reception and small shop (1/6-30/8) selling basic groceries, confectionery and with tourist information. There is a TV room, campers' kitchen, laundry and dishwashing area (washing machine, tumble and spin dryers, sinks) and the sanitary facilities. These are opened by key and include showers (£1), WCs, washbasins, with electric points, mirrors, etc. and were clean when we visited. To the rear of the block is a unit for disabled people. Chemical disposal. Also on site are a tennis court, volleyball and football pitch and a new adventure playground. Fishing 1 km, boat launching 2 km, golf 15 km. If not keeping fit, birdwatching, fishing or enjoying the beach, which is a mixture of shingle and sand but safe for swimming, take time to visit the area's many attractions which include the Cobh Heritage Centre and the historic walled port of Youghal.

Directions: From Youghal turn left off the N25 to Ballymacoda. Park is 4 km. on left after village and is signed.

Charges 2001:
-- Per unit incl. 2 adults IR£10.00 - 11.00; small tent IR£8.00; cyclist or hiker and tent £4.00; extra adult IR£1.50; child (4-14 yrs) IR£1.00; awning IR£1.00; extra car IR£1.00; electricity IR£1.00; hardstanding IR£1.00.
-- No credit cards.

Open: 1 May - 30 September.

Address: Ballymacoda, Co. Cork.

Tel: 024 98132.

Reservations: Contact site.

Cork

950 The Meadow Camping Park, Glandore

Small, mature garden park on Ireland's garden route; for tents and motorcaravans only.

The stretch of coast from Cork to Skibbereen reminds British visitors of Devon before the era of mass tourism. This is rich dairy country, the green of the meadows matching the emerald colours of the travel posters. Thanks to the warm and wet Gulf Stream climate, it is also a county of gardens - and keen gardeners. The Meadows is best described not as a site, but as a one acre garden surrounded - appropriately - by lush meadows. It lies 1.5 km. east of the fishing village of Glandore. A further 5 km. west is the regional centre, Skibbereen, beyond which the landscape moves from unspoilt Devon to unspoilt Cornwall. The owners, who live on the park, have cunningly arranged accommodation for 19 pitches among the flower beds and shrubberies of their extended garden. Space is rather tight and towed caravans are therefore not encouraged. There are 6 hardstandings for motorcaravans with 5A electric hook-ups. Facilities are limited but are well designed and immaculately maintained. Among the homely features are a sitting room and a well equipped kitchen, and breakfast is available on request. Showers are on payment (50p); there are chemical disposal facilities, and a washing machine and dryer. American motorhomes are accepted with an additional charge according to length. No dogs are accepted. Fishing or riding 2 km, fishing, swimming, boat launching and sailing at Glandore (2 km).

Directions: Park is 1.5 km. east of Glandore, off N71 road, on R597 mid-way between Leap and Rosscarbery (coast road).

Charges 2001:
-- Per unit incl. 2 persons IR£10.00; extra person IR£3.00; child (under 12) IR£1.00; hiker or cyclist incl. tent IR£4.00 per person; electricity (5A) IR£1.00.
-- No credit cards.

Open:
15 March - 30 September.

Address:
Glandore, Co. Cork.

Tel:
028 33280.
E-mail: themeadow@ oceanfree.net.

Reservations:
Please phone site for details.

Alan Rogers' Discount

Less IR£1
per night

952 Barleycove Holiday Park, Crookhaven

Family owned park on the scenically renowned Mizen Peninsula.

This long established park enjoys an idyllic situation tucked between the golden sands of Barleycove and Crookhaven Harbour. It is within an 8 km. drive of Mizen Head, Ireland's most south-westerly point, and approached along a route of unspoilt rugged countryside, offering the ideal 'away from it all' environment. It is a well cared for park with an overall neat and tidy appearance. Mobile homes, some for hire, are sited around the perimeter and within a field to the right. The 85 touring pitches all have electricity hook-ups (5A). Some are on grass in bays of 12, divided by timber fencing and a number are unfenced, on hardstanding with drainage and rubbish disposal. Tents have a dedicated grass area. The three sanitary blocks are kept clean and well maintained. There are free hot showers, open style wash areas with light and electric points, plus a vanity unit and long mirror in the ladies. Other site facilities include a laundry, with washing machines, dryer and spin dryer, washing-up sinks, chemical disposal and motorcaravan service point. Reception, with bureau de change and tourist information, is at the park entrance. Alongside is a games room with table tennis, pool tables and games machines. Adjacent is a cafe/takeaway (July/Aug) with outside seating, also a well stocked mini market. Ice packs are available at reception. There is a tennis court (admission free) also pitch and putt (50p adult, 20p child). Activities for children are organised in the high season. A security gate and night watchman patrol operate. Dogs are not accepted. Apart from discovering the natural beauty of this peninsula, of interest is Mizen Head Signal Station visitor centre, reached by a suspension bridge. Alternatively, the local friendly pubs and quality seafood restaurant at Heron's Cove offer a memorable evening out.

Directions: Site is 35 km. southwest of Bantry. From N71 Bantry/Cork road join R591 (3.2 km. south of Bantry) and follow signs for Crookhaven via Durrus, Toormore and Goleen. Site on right before Crookhaven village.

Charges 2001:
-- IR£: Per family unit IR£10.25 - 13.00; 2 person unit IR£9.10 - 10.65; awning (high season only) IR£2.50; hiker, cyclist or m/cyclist with tent IR£3.16 - 4.00; hardstanding free - IR£1.00; electricity free - IR£1.00.
-- Euro: Per family unit 13,00 - 16,50; 2 person unit 11,50 - 13,50; awning (high season only) 3,00; hiker, cyclist or m/cyclist with tent 4,00 - 5,00; hardstanding free - 1,25; electricity free - 1,25.

Open:
Easter - 16 September.

Address:
Crookhaven, Co. Cork.

Tel:
028 35302 (low season 021 4346466).
FAX: 021 4307230.

Reservations:
Contact park

951 Eagle Point Caravan & Camping Park, Ballylickey, Bantry Bay

Spacious, well run park on a spectacular peninsula jutting into Bantry Bay.

Midway between the towns of Bantry and Glengarriff, the peninsula of Eagle Point juts into the bay. The first impression is of a country park rather than a campsite. As far as the eye can see this 20 acre, landscaped, part-terraced park, with its vast manicured grass areas separated by mature trees, shrubs and hedges, runs parallel with the shoreline. Suitable for all ages, this is a park devoted to tourers, with campers pitched mostly towards the shore. It provides 125 pitches (60 caravans, 65 tents) thus avoiding overcrowding during peak periods. There are three toilet blocks with free hot showers, all maintained and designed well above expected standards. Other facilities include electric hook-ups, bin area, laundry and dishwashing facilities, chemical disposal and motorcaravan service points, a children's play area, tennis courts, a football field to the far right, well away from the pitches, plus a supermarket at the park entrance. A wet weather timbered building towards the water's edge houses a TV room - the brightly decorated interior is guaranteed to brighten the dullest of days. Eagle Point makes an excellent base for watersports enthusiasts - swimming is safe and there is a slipway for small craft. Fishing on site. Bicycle hire 6 km, riding 10 km, golf 2 km. No dogs are accepted.

Charges 2001:
-- Per unit IR£11.00 - 14.00; extra adult IR£4.00; m/cyclist, hiker or cyclist IR£5.00 per person; extra car IR£2.00; electricity (6A) IR£1.00.
-- Credit cards accepted.
Open:
27 April - 30 September.
Address:
Ballylickey, Bantry, West Cork.
Tel:
027 50630.
E-mail:
eaglepointcamping @eircom.net.
Reservations:
Bookings not essential.

Directions: Take N71 to Bandon, then R586 Bandon to Bantry, N71 Bantry to Glengarriff. 6.4 km. (4 miles) from Bantry; park entrance is opposite Burmah petrol station.

`Camping Cheque'

957 Creveen Lodge Caravan and Camping Park, Healy Pass

Immaculately run, small hill farm park, overlooking Kenmare Bay.

The address of this park is rather confusing, but Healy Pass is the well known scenic summit of the road (R574) crossing the Beara Peninsula, which lies between Kenmare Bay to the north and Bantry Bay to the south. Several kilometres inland from the north coast road (R571), the R574 starts to climb steeply southward towards the Healy Pass. Here, on the mountain foothills, is Creveen Lodge, a working hill farm with a quiet, homely atmosphere. Although not so famed as the Iveragh Peninsula, around which runs the Ring of Kerry, the northern Beara is a scenically striking area of County Kerry. Creveen Lodge, which commands views across Kenmare Bay, is divided among three gently sloping fields separated by trees. Reception is to be found in the farmhouse which also offers guests a comfortable sitting room. A small separate block, which is well appointed and immaculately maintained, has toilets and showers, plus a communal room with a fridge, freezer, TV, ironing board, fireplace, tables and chairs. Full Irish breakfast is served on request. This park is carefully tended with neat rubbish bins and rustic picnic tables informally placed, plus a children's play area with slides and swings. To allow easy access, the steep farm track is divided into a simple one-way system. There are 20 pitches in total, 16 for tents and 4 for caravans with an area of hardstanding for motorcaravans. Electrical connections are available. This is walking and climbing countryside or, of interest close by, is Derreen Gardens. Fishing 2 km, bicycle hire 9 km, boat launching 9 km. Also available in the area are water sports, riding, `Seafari' cruises, shops and a restaurant.

Charges 2001:
-- Per unit IR£7.00; person IR£1.00; hiker or cyclist incl. tent IR£3.75 per person; electricity IR£1.00.
-- No credit cards.
Open:
Easter - 31 October.
Address:
Healy Pass, Lauragh, Co. Kerry.
Tel:
064 83131.
Reservations:
Write to site with an S.A.E.

Directions: Park is on the Healy Pass road (R574) 1.5 km. southeast of Lauragh.

To telephone the Irish Republic from the UK, replace the first `0' given in the number with the country code: 00 353.

eg. (094) 88100 becomes 00 353 94 88100.

FOSSA CARAVAN & CAMPING PARK

★ Ample hardstanding & electric hook-up ★ Separate tent area
★ Modern toilets ★ Shaving points ★ Hairdryers ★ Hot showers ★ Facilities for the disabled
★ Full laundry facilities ★ Campers kitchen ★ Free wash-up facilities
★ On site shop open 7 days Easter to Sept. ★ Restaurant (June-Aug) ★ Take away (July/Aug)
★ Children's playground ★ Tennis court ★ Games room ★ TV room ★ Bicycles for hire
★ Mobile homes for hire ★ Hostel accommodation

FOR FREE COLOUR BROCHURE WRITE TO:
Brosnan Family, Fossa Caravan & Camping Park, Fossa, Killarney, Co. Kerry, Ireland
Telephone: (064) 31497   Fax: (064) 34459

955 Anchor Caravan Park, Castlegregory

Secluded, mature park two minutes from a beautiful sandy beach.

Of County Kerry's three long, finger like peninsulas which jut into the sea, Dingle is the most northerly. Tralee is the main town and Anchor is 20 km. west of this famed town and under 4 km. south of Castlegregory on Tralee Bay. This five acre, family run park is in a secluded situation enclosed by shrubs and trees, with a gateway leading to the beach which is safe for bathing, boating and shore fishing. There are 30 pitches, all with electric hook-ups and some with drainage and water points. There is night lighting around the site and, although there are holiday homes for hire, these are well apart from the touring pitches. The sanitary facilities (entry by key), are kept clean (often three or four times daily in busy periods). Included are showers, two private cabins, toilet with handrail, dishwashing and laundry facilities, chemical disposal, clothes lines and central rubbish depot. Motorcaravan service point. Children enjoy two play areas which have sand pits and swings with rubber safety matting. There is also a games/TV room. Fishing 2 km, riding or bicycle hire 3 km, golf 4 km. In this area of great beauty, miles of sand abounds and taking in the panorama of mountain scenery from the top of the Conor Pass is a unique experience.

Directions: From Tralee follow the Dingle coast road for 19 km. Park is signed before Castlegregory.

Charges 2001:
-- Per unit incl. all
persons IR£9.00 - 10.00;
tent incl. 1 or 2 persons
IR£7.00 - 8.00; m/cyclist,
hiker or cyclist incl. tent
IR£7.00; electric
IR£1.00; awning IR£1.00.
-- No credit cards.
Open:
Easter - 30 September.
Address:
Castlegregory, Co. Kerry.
Tel:
066 7139157.
FAX: as phone.
Reservations:
Contact site.

956 Wave Crest Caravan and Camping Park, Caherdaniel

Dramatically located hillside park running down to Kenmare Bay on Ring of Kerry coast.

It would be difficult to imagine a more dramatic location than Wave Crest's. Huge boulders and rocky outcrops tumble from the park entrance on the N70 down to the seashore which forms the most southern promontory on the Ring of Kerry. There are spectacular southward views from the park across Kenmare Bay to the Beara peninsula. Sheltering on grass patches in small coves that nestle between the rocks and shrubbery, are 65 hardstanding pitches offering seclusion. Electricity connections are available (13A). Two blocks house the sanitary facilities and include hot showers (50p), toilet for disabled people and dishwashing sinks. There is also a laundry service, chemical disposal, central rubbish point, shop (open May - Sept) and children's play area. A unique feature is the TV room, an old stone farm building with thatched roof. Its comfortable interior includes a stone fireplace heated by a converted cast iron marker buoy. Beside the park is a small beach or there is Derrynane Hotel with its swimming pool and tennis court. Fishing and boat launching from the site, riding 1 km, bicycle hire or golf 10 km. Caherdaniel is known for its cheerful little pubs and distinguished restaurant. The Derrynane National Park Nature Reserve is only a few km. away, as is Derrynane Cove and Bay. This park would suit older people looking for a quiet, relaxed atmosphere.

Directions: On the N70 (Ring of Kerry), 1½ km. east of Caherdaniel.

Charges 2001:
-- Per unit IR£9.00; small
tent IR£8.00; adult
IR£1.00; child 50p; hiker
or cyclist incl. tent
IR£3.50 p/person;
m/cyclist incl. tent
IR£4.00; extra car
IR£1.50; electricity (13A)
IR£1.00.
-- Credit cards accepted.
Open:
All year.
Address:
Caherdaniel, Ring of
Kerry, Co. Kerry.
Tel:
066 9475188 or 9475483.
FAX: 066 9475188.
E-mail:
wavecrest@eircom.net.
Reservations:
Write for details.

959 Fossa Caravan and Camping Park, Killarney

Mature, well equipped park in scenic location, 5½ km. from Killarney.

A ten minute drive from the town centre brings you to this well laid out park which is recognisable by its forecourt on which stands a distinctive building housing a roof top restaurant, reception area, shop and petrol pumps. The park is divided in two - the touring area lies to the right, tucked behind the main building, and to the left is an open grass area mainly for campers. Touring pitches, with electricity and drainage, have hardstanding and are angled between shrubs and trees in a tranquil, well cared for garden setting. To the rear at a higher level and discreetly placed are 50 holiday homes (25 for hire). These are unobtrusive and sheltered by the thick foliage of the wooded slopes which climb high behind the park. The toilet facilities are modern and kept spotlessly clean. Showers are on payment (50p). A second amenities block is placed to the far left of the grass area beside the tennis courts. Other facilities, apart from a shop (April - Sept), restaurant (mid-May - end Aug) and takeaway (July/Aug), include a TV lounge, campers' kitchen, laundry room, washing up area, children's play area, picnic area, games room, bicycle hire, night lighting and security patrol. Fishing or golf 2 km, riding 3 km. Not only is Fossa convenient for Killarney, it is also en-route for the famed 'Ring of Kerry', and makes an ideal base for walkers and golfers.

Directions: Park is to the right (second park to the right) on the R562/N72, 5.5 km. west of Killarney on the road to Killorglin.

Charges 2001:
-- Per unit IR£3.00 - 3.50; adult IR£3.00; child (under 14 yrs) IR£1.00; 1 or 2 man tent IR£2.50 - 3.00; m/cycle and tent per person IR£4.00 - 4.50; electricity (10/15A) IR£2.00; awning IR£2.00.
-- Credit cards accepted.

Open:
1 April - 30 September.

Address:
Fossa, Killarney, Co. Kerry.

Tel:
064 31497.

FAX: 064 34459.
E-mail: campingholidays @ireland.com.

Reservations:
Advised in high season; made for min. 3 nights with IR£10 deposit.

`Camping Cheque'

THE ALAN ROGERS'
travel service

Book this site with the experts
Call for an instant quote
01892 55 98 98

Low cost ferries
guaranteed!

960 Glenross Caravan and Camping Park, Glenbeigh, Ring of Kerry

Immaculate small park on the edge of Glenbeigh Village.

Being situated on the spectacular Ring of Kerry and the Kerry Way gives this park an immediate advantage, and scenic grandeur around every bend of the road is guaranteed as Glenbeigh is approached. Quietly located before entering the village, its situation commands a fine view of Rossbeigh Strand, which is within walking distance. On arrival, a good impression is instantly created with the park well screened from the road and with new stone entrance and gates. Beyond the entrance stands a well maintained modern sanitary block which includes showers, and facilities for laundry and dishwashing. On site facilities include a games room, bicycle hire, public phone, a shelter for campers, a sun lounge and barbecue patio. There are 34 touring pitches including hardstanding pitches with electricity and, although there are six caravan holiday homes, the park is attractively laid out. Motorcaravan service point and chemical disposal. There is no catering on site but the Glenbeigh Hotel is popular and village shops are near. Watersports and tennis are near, riding and fishing 200 m. and golf 500 m. Not least is the Kerry Bog Village where you can go back in time in this reconstructed pre-famine village.

Directions: Park is on the N70 Killorglin - Glenbeigh road, on the right just before entering the village.

Charges 2001:
-- IR£: per unit IR£3.50 - 4.00; adult IR£4.00; child (under 14 yrs) IR£1.00; awning IR£1.00 - 1.50; electricity (10A) IR£1.70 - 2.00; m/cyclist and tent IR£5.00 - 5.25; hiker or cyclist and tent IR£4.50 - 5.00.
-- Euro: per unit 4,44 - 5,08; adult 5,08; child (under 14 yrs) 1,27; awning 1,27 - 1,90; electricity (10A) 2,16 - 2,54; m/cyclist and tent 6,35 - 6,66; hiker/cyclist and tent 5,72 - 6,35.
-- No credit cards.

Open:
5 May - 9 September.

Address:
Glenbeigh, Ring of Kerry, Co. Kerry.

Tel:
066 9768451 (May-Aug) or 064 31590 other times.
FAX: 064 37474.
E-mail: fwbcamping @tinet.ie.

Reservations:
Write to site for details.

Alan Rogers' Discount

Less 50p per night in low season only

Kerry

961 Mannix Point Camping and Caravan Park, Cahirciveen

Quiet and peaceful, beautifully located seashore park.

It is no exaggeration to describe Mannix Point as a nature lovers' paradise. It is situated in one of the most spectacular parts of the Ring of Kerry, overlooking the Portmagee Channel towards Valentia Island. Whilst the park is flat and open, it commands splendid views in all directions, it is right on marshland which teems with wildlife (2 acre nature reserve) and it has immediate access to the beach and seashore. The owner has planted around 500 plants with plans for around 1,000 more trees and shrubs. There are 42 pitches, 15 for tourers and 27 for tents, with electrical connections (6A) available. A charming old fisherman's cottage has been converted to provide reception. A cosy sitting room with turf fire, and 'emergency' dormitory for campers, is a feature of this site. Toilet facilities, now upgraded and immaculate, have well designed showers and free hot water. There is a modern campers' kitchen, laundry facilities with new washing machines and dryer, chemical disposal and motorcaravan service facilities. There is no television, but compensation comes in the form of a knowledgeable, hospitable owner who is a Bord Fáilte registered local tour guide. This park retains a wonderful air of Irish charm aided by occasional impromptu musical evenings. Watersports, bird watching, walking and photography can all be pursued here, but note that dogs are not accepted on site in July and August. Bicycle hire 800 m. riding 3 km, golf 14 km. Local cruises to Skelligs Rock with free transport to and from the port for walkers and cyclists. This is also an ideal resting place for people walking the Kerry Way.

Charges 2001:
-- Per adult IR£4.00; child IR£2.40; caravan or motorcaravan IR£2.40; tent no charge; electricity (6A) IR£1.20; m/cycle IR£0.75.
-- Book 7 nights, pay 6.
-- Reductions for groups if pre-paid.
-- No credit cards.
Open:
15 March - 15 October, the rest of the year also, if you write first.
Address:
Cahirciveen, Co. Kerry.
Tel:
066 9472806.
FAX: as phone.
E-mail: mannixpoint @mail.com.
Reservations:
Made with deposit of one night's fee.

Directions: Park is 250 m. off the N70 Ring of Kerry road, 800 m. southwest of Cahirciveen (or Cahersiveen) on the road towards Waterville.

962 Fleming's White Bridge Caravan Park, Ballycasheen, Killarney

Family run, 9 acre, woodland park on eastern outskirts of Killarney.

Once past the county border, the main road from Cork to Killarney (N22) runs down the valley of the Flesk river. On the final approach to Killarney off the N22 Cork road, the river veers away from the road to enter the Lower Lake. On this prime rural position, between the road and the river, and within comfortable walking distance of the town, is Fleming's White Bridge. The ground is flat, landscaped and generously adorned with flowers, shrubs and trees. There are now 92 pitches (46 caravans and 46 tents) which extend beyond a wooden bridge to an area surrounded by mature trees and where a new toilet block, one of three, is sited. Facilities include a shop (1/6-1/9), two TV rooms, a games room, campers' drying room and two laundries. Hot water is free, there are dishwashing sinks, chemical disposal facilities and a new motorcaravan service point. This is obviously a park of which the owners are very proud, and the family personally supervise the reception and grounds, maintaining high standards of hygiene, cleanliness and tidiness. There are six new luxury holiday mobile homes for hire, fishing (advice and permits provided), canoeing (own canoes), bicycle hire and woodland walks. Riding 3 km, golf 2 km. The park's location so close to Ireland's premier tourism centre makes this park an ideal base to explore Killarney and the southwest.

Charges 2001:
-- Per unit IR£3.50 - 4.00; small tent/car or motorcaravan IR£3.00 - 3.50; adult IR£3.50; child (under 14 yrs) IR£1.00; awning IR£1.00 - 1.50; electricity (10A) IR£2.00 - 3.00; m/cyclist and tent IR£5.00 - 5.25; hiker or cyclist and tent IR£4.50 - 5.00.
-- Credit cards accepted.
Open:
17 March - 31 October.
Address:
White Bridge, Ballycasheen Road, Killarney, Co. Kerry.
Tel:
064 31590.
FAX: 064 37474.
E-mail:
fwbcamping@eircom.net.
Reservations:
Advised for high season; write with IR£5 non-refundable reservation fee.

Directions: From Cork and Mallow: at N72/N22 junction continue towards Killarney and take first turn left (signed Ballycasheen Road). Proceed for 300 m. to archway entrance on left. From Limerick: follow N22 Cork road. After passing Super Valu and Killarney Heights Hotel take first right (signed Ballycasheen Road) and continue as above. From Kenmare: On N71, pass Gleneagles Hotel and Flesk Bridge. Turn right before Shell filling station into Woodlawn Road and Ballycasheen Road to continue 2 km. to archway.

THE ALAN ROGERS'
travel service

Book this site with the experts
Call for an instant quote
01892 55 98 98

Low cost ferries guaranteed!

963 White Villa Farm Caravan and Camping Park, Killarney

Small, welcoming park in scenic surroundings for tourers and campers only.

This is a very pleasing touring park on the N22 Killarney-Cork road. It is set in a 100 acre family operated dairy farm which stretches as far as the River Flesk, yet is only minutes away from Killarney town. Trees and shrubs surround the park but dominant is a magnificent view of the MacGillicuddy's Reeks. There are 25 pitches for caravans and tents, 15 with hardstanding and a grass area for awnings, electricity (10A), water points, rubbish disposal and night lighting. The toilet block, a sandstone coloured building to the rear of the park, is kept spotlessly clean and houses showers (50p), a good toilet/shower room for disabled visitors, laundry room and dishwashing sinks. There is chemical disposal, a motorcaravan service area and clothes lines, plus a campers' kitchen with TV. In a central position is a children's play area, areas for basketball and a novelty is old school desks placed around the site, plus an antique green telephone box. Bicycle hire on site. Walking through the oak wood, fishing on the Flesk or visiting White Villa's National Farm Museum are on site attractions. Leave the park and the scenic splendours, the allure of Killarney town and the National Park are 10 minutes away. Riding, golf and boat launching 5 km. Most dogs are accepted (max. 2 per pitch and not certain breeds).

Directions: Travel 3 km. east from Killarney town on N22 Cork road. Park entrance is 500 m. east of N22/N72 junction. From Kenmare take R569 via Kilgarvan to the N22, then as above. From Park Road roundabout follow 'N22 Cork' road signs and 'White Villa Farm' signs.

Charges 2001:
-- Per unit IR£2.00 - 3.00; adult IR£2.75; child under 14 yrs 75p, 14-18 yrs £1.25; m/cyclist incl. tent IR£3.50 - 4.00; hiker or cyclist incl. tent IR£3.25 - 3.50; electricity IR£1.50; awning IR£1.00 (July/Aug); extra tent IR£1.00 - 1.25.
-- No credit cards.

Open:
1 April - 16 October.

Address:
Cork Road (N22), Killarney, Co. Kerry.

Tel:
064 32456 or 31414..
E-mail: killarneamping @eircom.net.

Reservations:
Made with £10 deposit in Irish or UK currency.

964 The Flesk Muckross Caravan and Camping Park, Killarney

Seven acre park at gateway to National Park and Lakes, near Killarney town.

This family run park has undergone extensive development and offers high quality standards. Housed in one of Europe's most modern toilet blocks are well designed, heated shower and toilet areas, decorated in co-ordinating colours. Every detail has been added, including a vanity area with mirror and hair dryer and a baby bath/changing room. Pitches are well spaced and have electricity (10A), water, and drainage connections; 21 also have hardstanding with a grass area for awnings. Other on site facilities include petrol pumps, supermarket (all year), delicatessen and café (March - Oct) with extra seating on the sun terrace. There is also a laundry room, campers' kitchen with dishwashing sinks, a comfortable games room and chemical disposal point, plus night lighting and night time security checks. The grounds have been well cultivated with further shrubs, plants and an attractive barbecue and patio area. This is situated to the left of the sanitary block and is paved and sunk beneath the level road. Surrounded by a garden border, it has tables and chairs, making a pleasant meeting place which commands excellent views of Killarny's mountains. Fishing 300 m, boat launching 2 km. Winter caravan storage.

Directions: From Killarney town centre follow the N71 and signs for Killarney National Park. Site is 1.5 km. on the left beside the Gleneagle Hotel.

Charges 2000:
-- Per unit IR£3.00 - 3.50; adult IR£3.75; child (under 14 yrs) IR£1.00; small tent incl. 1 or 2 persons IR£2.50 - 3.00; hiker or cyclist IR£4.50 - 4.75; awning IR£1.50; electricity IR£1.75.
-- Credit cards accepted.

Open:
12 March - 31 October.

Address:
Muckross Road, Killarney, Co. Kerry.

Tel:
064 31704.
FAX: 064 34681.
E-mail: killarneylakes @eircom.net.

Reservations:
Advisable in peak periods, write to park.

FLESK MUCKROSS
CARAVAN PARK △

Family run, 7 acre park, situated at the gateway to 25,000 acres of National Park and lakes.
AA award winning sanitation facilities 1994/5
Just 1 mile (1.5 km) from Killarney town on the N71 south of Kenmare,
adjacent to Gleneagle Hotel and leisure centre

MUCKROSS, KILLARNEY   Phone: 064-31704
CO. KERRY, IRELAND   Prop: Johnny & Sinead Courtney   Fax: 064-34681

Kerry

965 Woodlands Park Touring Caravan and Camping Park, Tralee

Family run park in quiet setting minutes from Tralee centre.

Tralee is not only the Capital of County Kerry and gateway to the Dingle Peninsula, it is also Ireland's fastest growing visitor destination, with Woodlands its newest touring caravan park. Although only a 10 minute walk from the town centre, this park is located on a 16 acre elevated site approached by a short roadway and bridge which straddles the River Lee. Once on site the town seems far removed, for a countryside environment takes over. Hedging, trees, grazing fields and the distant Slieve Mish Mountain create the setting. The owners of Woodlands have ensured their park is designed and equipped to a high standard. A distinctive feature is its impressive yellow coloured building which houses an 'on top' family dwelling and ground floor services. This offers a spacious reception and information area, a café/snack bar, shop, games room, TV and adult room. The heated sanitary facilities, which are fully tiled with non-slip flooring, include sizeable showers (50p token), washbasins and provision for disabled guests. There is a campers' kitchen, dishwashing sinks, a laundry room with washing machines and dryer, also a chemical disposal unit. Fifty pitches with hardstanding, electricity, water and drainage plus night light lie to the left and centre behind the main building, and a grass area for 40 tents is to the right. Young shrubs, cordyline trees and flower beds have been planted around the park and a security barrier is in operation. For children there is a fenced adventure park, or alternatively, the nearby Aqua Dome offers half price admission after 6 pm. Interesting is the award winning 'Kerry the Kingdom' museum with its incredible time car trip through the Middle Ages. Not least are the blue flag beaches on the Dingle Peninsula. Evening entertainment in Tralee means a selection of 'singing' pubs, restaurants and the National Folk Theatre. Golf 6 km, riding 2 km.

Directions: Site is 1 km. southwest of Tralee town centre. From N21/N69/N86 junction south of Tralee follow camp signs for 2.4 km. to park, 200 m. off the N86 Tralee - Dingle road.

Charges 2000:
-- Per pitch IR£3.50 - 4.00; adult IR£3.50; child (under 14 yrs) IR£1.00; awning IR£1.50; small tent IR£3.00 - 3.50; m/cyclist with tent IR£4.50 - 5.00; hiker or cyclist with tent IR£4.00 - 4.75; electricity (10A) IR£1.75.
-- Incl. 2 persons IR£10.50 - 11.00; family incl. 2 children IR£12.50 - 13.00.
-- Credit cards accepted (Visa/Access).

Open:
15 March - 30 September.

Address:
Dan Spring Road, Tralee, Co. Kerry.

Tel:
(066) 7121235.
FAX: (066) 7181199.
E-mail:
wdlands@eircom.net.

Reservations:
Advisable for high season.

Woodlands Park

Touring Caravan & Camping Park
GRADE ★★★★

IRELAND'S BEST PARK AWARD 1999

Designed by campers, this family run park is located on a 16 acre parkland setting just a 10 minute walk from the centre of Tralee town, connected by bridge to the Aqua Dome (Ireland's biggest indoor waterworld). The facilities building has Euro style washrooms and shower blocks, Campers Kitchen, Laundry, Games Room, Café, TV Room and Reception. The 11 x 17 m. bays have hardstands and 10 amp electric with water and drains. Half price admission to the Aqua Dome after 6 pm.

How to find us: From N21, N22 turn left after McDonalds and follow signs. From N69 follow signs for Dingle until Tralee marina, then turn left and straight past Aqua Dome for 200 m.

Irish Caravan Council

Ireland, one of Europe's best kept secrets, is the Caravan and Camping destination for the discerning traveller. You take control of your holiday from start to finish, go as you please, and do as little or as much as you like. It's all on offer in Ireland: rugged coastlines, inland waterways, lakes and rivers, Celtic monuments, churches and castles, rolling hills and lush green valleys. Plus, of course, Ireland's legendary hostelries and the friendliest people you're ever likely to meet.

Pick up a copy of the 2001 Caravan and Camping Guide at your local tourist office today - it's a breath of fresh air.

Alternatively contact ICC direct at:
Fax: 00 353 98 28237.
E-mail: info@camping-ireland.ie
Website: http//www.camping-ireland.ie
Boite Postale: ICC, Box 4442, Dublin 2, Ireland

CHANNEL ISLANDS

Jersey
Jersey Tourism
Liberation Square, St. Helier,
Jersey JE1 1BB
Tel: (01534) 500700 Fax: (01534) 500899
www.jersey.com

Guernsey and Herm
States of Guernsey Tourist Board
PO Box 13, White Rock
Guernsey
Tel: (01481) 723552

Sark
Sark Tourism Office
Sark (via Guernsey), Channel Islands.
Tel: (01481) 832345.

A visit to the Channel Islands offers a holiday in part of the British Isles, but in an area which has a definitely continental flavour. Of course, you don't need a passport or to change your money, although the proximity of the islands to the French coast might tempt one to take a day trip. All the islands have beautiful beaches and coves, pretty scenery and fascinating histories. Jersey is probably more commercially orientated, with more entertainment provided, while Guernsey will suit those who prefer a quieter, more peaceful holiday. For total relaxation, one of the smaller islands, such as Sark or Herm, where no cars are allowed, might appeal. Shopping in all the islands has the advantage of no mainland VAT – particularly useful for buying cameras, watches, jewellery and clothes.

Camping holidays on the islands are limited to TENTS only - caravans and motorcaravans are not permitted due to the narrow and sometimes crowded nature of the roads. Trailer tents (with canvas roof and walls) are permitted but on Jersey advance reservations must be made. Contact the Island Tourism authorities for more detailed information. Some of the parks we feature offer tents and camping equipment for hire, which may prove a popular option for some, and cars are also easily rented on the main islands.

Since all the parks cater solely for tents, rather than caravans or motorcaravans, this means that there tend to be very limited waste water emptying points and almost no chemical disposal facilities.

We are advised that on both Jersey and Guernsey, that political pressure is being placed for a change of policy in order to develop tourism. Guernsey is trying for caravans on the basis that, once they are on site, then only the car will run around the island, while Jersey is pushing for motorcaravans under a certain length. Both developments are under consideration – contact the relevant tourist board for the latest information.

Travel between mainland Britain and the Channel Islands is not cheap, particularly if you take your car. However the Condor wave-piercing catamaran service has made travelling to the Channel Islands a very easy and much quicker proposition than ever before. We used this service, which now carries cars, and were most impressed, in respect of the speed (From Poole, Guernsey is only some 2½ hours travelling time, Jersey 1 hour longer), the comfort and the onboard service. These craft are surprisingly spacious with room to walk around (and even to go outside), a bar and snack bar and duty-free shopping facilities. Condor offer a range of fares, including a Family Saver deal. Condor may be contacted at:

Condor Ferries
Weymouth Quay, Weymouth,
Dorset DT4 8DX
Travel information and reservations:
Tel: (01305) 761551

Jersey Tourism - Events 2001
Jersey Jazz Festival, 5 - 8 April
Jersey International Food Festival, 12 - 20 May
Jersey Garden Festival, 9 - 14 July

Battle of Flowers,9 Aug
Battle of Flowers Moonlight Parade, 10 Aug.
Jersey International Festival 27 Sept - 13 Oct.

Jersey

971 Rozel Camping Park, St. Martin, Jersey

Rurally situated park in quieter northeast of island, close to picturesque harbour.

This family owned park is within walking distance of the famous Jersey Zoo and the pretty harbour and fishing village of Rozel where the north coast cliff path commences. The surrounding countryside is quieter than many areas of the island. A car is probably necessary to reach the main island beaches, although a bus service does run to St Helier from close by. The park itself is quietly situated at the top of a valley (the French coast can be seen on a clear day) and is surrounded by trees providing shelter. There are two main camping areas providing 100 pitches of which some 20 are used for fully equipped tents to hire. Some pitches, mainly for smaller tents are arranged on terraced areas. The remainder are on a higher, flat field where pitches are arranged in bays with hedges growing to separate them into groups. Parking is permitted by the tents and some electrical connections are available. Two heated sanitary buildings offer first rate facilities including excellent, free controllable showers with divider and good dry area, plentiful washbasins each with mirror, shelf and shaver point and a bathroom for disabled people with a shower, toilet and washbasin in the lower block with an access ramp. A family shower room is in the upper block; hand dryers and a small heater for cooler weather. Dishwashing facilities are under cover, hot water is free and there is a laundry and make up room, chemical disposal and a shop. Activities provided include play equipment, an attractive, sheltered swimming pool (June-Sept) with children's pool and sunbathing areas, crazy golf, games room, reading and TV room and bicycle hire. Torches useful. Public telephone. Fishing 1 mile, riding 3 miles, golf 4 miles. In addition to package deals for tent hire and travel, the site offers a good range of camping equipment for hire on a daily basis. Boats are accepted by prior arrangement. No dogs are accepted.

Charges 2000:
-- Per person £4.40 - £6.60; child (3-11 yrs) half price; electricity £1.50.
-- Tent hire and travel packages.
-- Credit cards accepted
Open:
1 May - 8 September.
Address:
Rozel, St. Martin, Jersey, Channel Islands JE3 6AX.
Tel:
(01534) 856797.
FAX: (01534) 856127.
E-mail: rozelcamping @jerseyhols.com.
Reservations:
Made for any length with £40 deposit; balance due 14 days before arrival.

Directions: On leaving the harbour by Route du Port Elizabeth, take A1 east through the tunnel and the A17. At fourth set of traffic lights turn left on A6. Keep in middle lane. Continue to Five Oaks and on to St Martin's church. Turn right, then immediately left at the `Royal' on B38 to Rozel and the park is on right.

972 Beuvelande Camp Site, St Martin

Family run park with outstanding sanitary facilities.

What a pleasant surprise we had when we called here - the new sanitary building gives campers facilities normally associated with top class hotels. Tiled top to bottom and spotlessly clean, there are free, controllable showers, washbasins in vanity units with mirrors and electricity points, plus two fully equipped bathrooms for disabled people, a baby room and chemical disposal. A licensed restaurant with covered terrace area is also situated in this building, open morning and evening at all times, but perhaps a few less hours at quiet times. There are 150 pitches, 60 with fully equipped tents for hire, but with plenty of space for those with their own tents. Some electric hook ups are available and cars may be parked next to your tent. An outdoor heated pool (41 x 17 ft) has a sun terrace and simple play equipment is provided for children. Plenty of dishwashing facilities and a laundry can now be found in the original sanitary building, and public telephones, a games room and TV room are provided. The well stocked shop is open 8 am. - 7 pm. during peak times and stocks gas. Ice pack and battery charging services are provided for a small charge. Torches would be useful. Car hire can be arranged and bicycle hire is possible from the site. Fishing, golf or riding within 3 km. This family run park prides itself on quality, cleanliness and hospitality.

Charges 2000:
-- Per adult £5.00 - £7.00; child 8-14 yrs £3.50, 2-8 yrs £2.50; dog £2.00.
-- Single sex groups not accepted.
-- No credit cards.
Open:
1 May - 15 September.
Address:
St Martin, Jersey, Channel Islands JE3 6EZ.
Tel:
(01534) 853575, 852223 or 851156.
FAX: (01534) 857788.
Reservations:
Made with £30 deposit; contact park for details.

Directions: On leaving harbour by Route du Port Elizabeth, take A1 east through the tunnel and the A17. At the fourth set of traffic lights turn left on A6. Continue to Five Oaks and on to St Martin's RC church, then right into La Longue Rue, right again Rue de L'Orme then left to site.

Book this site with the experts

THE ALAN ROGERS'
travel service

Call for an instant quote 01892 55 98 98

Low cost ferries guaranteed!

978 Fauxquets Valley Farm Campsite, Castel, Guernsey

Attractive, rural site with good facilities in quiet, sheltered valley.

Situated in the rural centre of the island, Fauxquets is in a pretty valley, hidden down narrow lanes away from busy roads and is run by the Guille family. A car would be useful here to reach the beaches, St Peter Port and other attractions, although there is a bus service each day (20 mins walk). It was once a dairy farm, but the valley side has now been developed into an attractive camp site, with the old farm buildings as its centre. Plenty of trees, bushes and flowers separate pitches and provide shelter around the various fields which are well terraced. The 86 good size pitches are mostly marked, numbered and with electricity, and there is lots of open space. There are 15 smaller places for backpackers. The site has 23 fully equipped tents for hire (no tour operators). Sanitary facilities are good with free, controllable hot showers, some washbasins set in flat surfaces, and others in cabins. There is a shower, baby bath and changing unit for children. Hairdryers and irons are free. Dishwashing facilities are under cover, with free hot water. Laundry room with washing machine, dryer and free iron. In converted buildings around the farmhouse is a small shop (Easter-15/9) with ice-pack hire and gas. The Haybarn licensed restaurant and bar provides (15/6-31/8) breakfast, morning coffee and evening meals. TV room, table tennis room, small children's play area and play field, nature walk, plus bicycle hire. Heated swimming pool (20 x 45 ft.) with a paddling pool and a shallow end. Fishing and boat launching 3 miles, riding and golf 2 miles. There is plenty of room to sit around the pool, including a large grassy terrace with sun-beds. Public telephone. A torch would be useful.

Directions: From St Peter Port harbour take 2nd exit from roundabout. At top of hill, turn left at 'filter in turn' into Queens Rd, then right at nest filter. Follow through traffic lights and down hill past Princess Elizabeth Hospital, through pedestrian lights and straight on at another set of lights at top of hill. Continue for ¾ mile, then turn right at sign for German Underground Hospital. Fourth left is pedestrian entrance, cars carry on for 400 yds to gravel entrance on left.

Charges 2001:
-- Per adult £4.50 - £5.20; child (at school) half price.
-- Fully equipped tents with fridge for hire.
-- Credit cards accepted.
Open:
Easter - 15 September.
Address:
Castel, Guernsey, Channel Islands.
Tel:
(01481) 255460.
FAX: (01481) 251797.
E-mail: fauxquets@campingguernsey.freeserve.co.uk.
Reservations:
Made for independent campers for any length, with £50 deposit. Tent hire details from site.

Alan Rogers' Discount

 Less 10% all season, excl. hire tents

Book this site with the experts

THE ALAN ROGERS' travel service
Call for an instant quote 01892 55 98 98

 Low cost ferries guaranteed!

977 Vaugrat Camping, St Sampson's, Guernsey

Neat, well tended site, close to beach, in northwest of island.

Vaugrat Camping is centred around attractive and interesting old granite farm buildings dating back to the 15th century, with a gravel courtyard and colourful flower beds. Owned by the Laine family, Vaugrat provides 150 pitches on flat grassy meadows, mostly surrounded by trees, banks and hedges to provide shelter. Tents are arranged around the edges of the fields, giving open space in the centre, and while pitches are not marked, there is sufficient room and cars may be parked next to tents. The site offers 25 fully equipped tents for hire. Housed in the old farmhouse, a listed building, are the reception area, plus in the main season a shop (with ice pack hire) and upstairs Coffee Barn, with views to the sea, where breakfast is served; one can sit here in the evenings. There is also a small games room with TV in the cider room complete with the ancient presses. The sanitary facilities are in two buildings, one in the courtyard, with hot showers on payment, washbasins and hairdryers (on payment). There is a room here for disabled visitors with shower, basin and toilet (although there is a 6" step into the building). A laundry room here has a washing machine, dryer and iron. The other block is near the camping fields and provides toilets and washbasins in a row, set in a flat surface, plus one cabin for ladies. Dishwashing facilities are in a room in this block with free hot water, with further sinks under cover outside. Chemical disposal. All these facilities are well kept and clean. A bus service is within easy reach and car or bicycle hire can be arranged. Fishing, riding and golf within 1½ miles. Hotel and bar near. No dogs are accepted. A torch may be useful.

Directions: On leaving St Peter Port, turn right on coast road for 1½ miles. At filter turn left into Vale Rd. Straight over at two sets of lights then first left by church. Follow to crossroads (garage opposite) turn right. Carry on past Hotel, then 2nd left for site. Site on left after wall (400 yds) with concealed entrance.

Charges 2001:
-- Per adult £5.50; child (under 14 yrs) £4.40; car or boat £1.05.
-- Families and couples only.
-- Fully equipped tents to hire.
-- Credit cards accepted.
Open:
1 May - 30 September.
Address:
St Sampson's, Guernsey, Channel Islands GY2 4TA.
Tel:
(01481) 57468.
FAX: (01481) 51841.
E-mail: adgould@globalnet.co.uk.
Reservations:
Made for independent campers for any length, with £10 deposit and balance on arrival. Hire details from site.

Herm / Sark

983 Seagull Campsite, Herm Island

Small site on beautiful, peaceful island with no cars.

This tiny site, and indeed the island of Herm, will appeal to those who are looking for complete tranquillity and calm. Reached by boat (20 mins and approx. £6 return fare for adults, £3 for children) from Guernsey, the 500 acre island allows only tractors on its narrow roads and paths (no bicycles either). One is free to stroll around the many paths, through farmland, heath and around the coast, where there are beautiful beaches. The campsite is a 20 minute uphill walk from the harbour, but your luggage will be transported for you by tractor. It consists of several terraced areas offering a total of 80 pitches, and 30 fully equipped tents for hire on flat grass areas. There are no electricity hook-ups. There is just a small, modern, but open, toilet block on site with WCs, hot showers (£1 payment - there is a shortage of water on Herm) and washbasins, plus shaver points, with a freezer for ice-packs. One may bring one's own tent and equipment or hire a tent and equipment (but not bedding, crockery and lighting) from the site. The harbour village is about ten minutes walk down the hill, where there is a small shop for provisions, gas, a post office, pub, restaurants and café. No dogs or pets are allowed. Torches useful. Fishing on the island. Herm is definitely not for those who like entertainment and plenty of facilities, but for total relaxation, with the absence of any bustle and noise it takes some beating!

Directions: Reached by boat from St Peter Port - report to Administration Office on arrival. Do not take your car as it is unlikely you will be able to park long term in St Peter Port.

Charges 2000:
-- Fixed site charge (irrespective of length of stay) incl. transportation of luggage £5.00.
-- Per adult £4.40; child (under 14 yrs) £2.20.
-- Equipped tents for hire.
-- Groups of single people not accepted.
-- Credit cards accepted.

Open:
14 May - first w/end in September.

Address:
Herm Island,
Channel Islands
GY1 3HR.

Tel:
(01481) 722377.

Reservations:
Made for any length with £20 deposit. Details of hire tents from above address.

987 Pomme de Chien Campsite, Sark

Tiny, family oriented site in superb 'away from it all' setting.

The `island where time stands still' is an apt description of Sark, one of the smallest inhabited Channel Islands, some 45 minutes from Guernsey by boat. There is no airport, no cars or motorcycles and (apart from a tractor-drawn 'train' up Harbour Hill) the only transport is by bicycle or horse-drawn carriage. However everything you are likely to need for a tranquil holiday is provided with several small shops, pubs, hotels, restaurants, a Tourist Office and even two banks! Situated five minutes from the shops and ten from the beach, the Pomme de Chien campsite on Sark is tiny in terms of the number of pitches, totalling only 20, of which 8 are occupied by large, fully equipped frame tents (of excellent quality) available for rent. The remainder are for campers with their own tents (no caravans, motorcaravans or trailer tents of course). The pitches themselves are large, on fairly level ground, but none have electricity hook-ups. A new sanitary block was added in 1999 with free hot showers (large, with bench and hook), toilets and washbasins. Dishwashing sinks are outside. This enhances the warm welcome of the owners Chris and Jill Rang and the famous charm of Sark. Although you cannot take your car to the island, transport by the Condor service via Guernsey means you can get there in a little over three hours either with your own small tent or of course you could hire one of the site's own fully equipped ones (equipment includes everything you're likely to need except bedding and a torch). Baggage can be transferred from the Harbour right to the site by tractor trailer (60p per item). Fishing (10 minutes walk, bicycle hire (5 minutes). Dogs are not accepted. Torches are necessary.

Directions: Take the tractor drawn 'train' up Harbour Hill (60p; you can walk but it is a ten minute hike). Once at the top take road leading off left, then second right, and follow lane to site entrance. Reception is at house with white gates.

Charges 2000:
-- Per adult £5.00; child £3.00.
-- Hire tents from £160 per week.
-- No credit cards.

Open:
All year - independent campers
June - Sept. for hire tents.

Address:
Sark, Channel Islands.

Tel:
(01481) 832316.

Reservations:
Write to site.

OPEN ALL YEAR

The following parks are understood to accept caravanners and campers all year round, although the list also includes some parks open for at least 10 months. These parks are marked with a star (∗) – please refer to the park's individual entry for details. It is always wise to phone the park to check as, for example, facilities available may be reduced.

England

002	Cardinney ∗	245	The Orchards ∗	390	Bosworth
006	River Valley ∗	249	Kite Hill Farm	392	Riverside
010	Leverton Place	260	Barnstones	394	Smeaton's Lakes
037	Budemeadows	262	Wysdom	407	Somers Wood
044	Dolbeare	275	Highclere ∗	412	Briarfields
071	Hidden Valley	281	Chertsey	413	Moreton-in-Marsh
080	Higher Longford	289	White Rose ∗	414	Winchcombe ∗
081	Riverside	293	Sheepcote Valley	421	Lickhill Manor
091	Ross Park ∗	294	Honeybridge	430	Poston Mill
092	Finlake	295	Washington	439	Westbrook
135	Quantock Orchard	303	Tanner Farm	440	Stanmore Hall
140	Isle of Avalon	304	Broadhembury	441	Beaconsfield Farm
142	Southfork	305	Pine Lodge	442	Severn Gorge
144	Baltic Wharf	307	Canterbury	443	Oxon Hall
145	Bath	309	Black Horse	454	St Helens ∗
148	Home Farm	326	Abbey Wood	462	Rawcliffe Manor
150	Long Hazel ∗	327	Crystal Palace	474	Jasmine ∗
151	Bath Chew Valley	330	The Grange ∗	528	Abbey Farm
152	Waterrow	331	Low House	529	Royal Umpire
167	Alderbury	340	Old Brick Kilns ∗	532	Bridge House ∗
170	Devizes	342	Two Mills ∗	535	HolgatesV
177	Binghams Farm	355	Old Manor	536	Willowbank ∗
181	Newlands	358	Ferry Meadows	556	Sykeside
202	Ulwell Cottage ∗	369	Bainland	557	Wild Rose
203	Wareham Forest	373	Skegness Sands	574	White Water
208	Merley Court ∗	376	Tallington Lakes ∗	576	Percy Wood ∗
227	Oakdene ∗	382	Darwin Forest ∗	580	Ord House
228	Lytton Lawn ∗	383	Firs Farm		
229	Sandy Balls	385	Rivendale ∗		

Wales

593	Cwmcarn	606	Tredegar House	659	Beddgelert
595	Afon Lodge ∗	633	Daisy Bank	660	Bryn Gloch
604	Pencelli Castle	637	Hendre Mynach ∗	668	James'

Scotland

692	Cressfield	702	Aird Donald	727	Auchterarder
693	Brandedleys	703	Gibson Park	768	Glenmor ∗
695	Brighouse Bay	705	Edinburgh	785	Linnhe ∗
697	Monks' Muir	724	Lomond Woods		

Northern Ireland

842	Tollymore	850	LoanEden
843	Banbridge	856	Gortin Glen

Republic of Ireland

870	Gateway ∗	911	Shankhill	956	Wave Crest
874	Cong	916	Moat Farm	961	Mannix Point
908	Forest Farm	938	Parsons Green		
910	Camac Valley	948	Blarney		

Channel Islands

987	Pomme de Chien

ADULTS ONLY

The following parks have made the decision not to accept children.

001 Chacewater Park (30 yrs+)
151 Bath Chew Valley Caravan Park
152 Waterrow Touring Park (18 yrs+)
168 Plough Lane Caravan Site
177 Binghams Farm Touring Park
342 Two Mills Touring Park
344 Gatton Waters Lakeside Touring Site (18 yrs+)
345 Little Haven Caravan & Camping Park
407 Somers Wood Caravan & Camping Park
461 Moorside Caravan Park (16 yrs+)
551 The Larches Caravan Park
633 Daisy Bank Touring Caravan Park

Opening 2001: Cheddar Bridge Park, Cheddar (01934 743048)

These parks have joined together to form an association – Adults Only Touring Parks. Their web site is: www.adultstouring.co.uk

The following parks also do not accept children at certain times or in certain areas of their site:

441 Beaconsfield Farm Touring Caravan Park (25 yrs) - high season only
380 Highfields Camping and Caravan Park - in one area only
440 Stanmore Hall Touring Park (21 yrs) - 31 grass pitches only

NATURIST PARKS

We feature just one naturist site in this guide: 024 Southleigh Manor Naturist Club.
029 Carlyon Bay provides a separate area for naturist campers.

NO DOGS !

For the benefit of those who want to take their dogs with them and for those who do not like dogs on the parks they visit, we list here the parks which have indicated to us that they do not accept dogs. If you are planning to take your dog we do, however, advise that you phone the park first to check - there may be limits on numbers, breeds, etc. or times of the year when they are excluded.

NEVER: these parks do not accept dogs at any time.

020	Newquay Holiday Park	598	Moreton Farm
025	Pentewan Sands	604	Pencelli Castle
087	Beverley Park Holidays	635	Barcdy
089	Grange Court	782	Oban Divers
138	Blue Anchor Park	860	Bellemont
149	Greenacres Camping	877	Parkland
212	Hoburne Park	882	Hodson Bay
213	Grove Farm Meadow	941	The Apple
230	Ashurst	950	The Meadow
305	Pine Lodge	951	Eagle Point
306	Yew Tree	952	Barleycove
312	Gate House Wood	971	Rozel Camping Park
410	Cotswold Hoburne	977	Vaugrat Camping
453	Northcliffe Holiday Park	983	Seagull Campsite
555	Limefitt Park	987	Pomme de Chien

SOMETIMES: these parks do not accept dogs at certain times of the year.

085	Galmpton	*not peak periods; max. 2 per unit*	452	Flower of May	*not main holiday times*
086	Ramslade	*not 21 July - 24 Aug*	629	Glan-y-Mor	*not 14 July-31 Aug*
208	Merley Court	*not 14 July - 31 Aug*	910	Camac Valley	*not July/August*
210	Sandford Park	*only after 2 Sept*	915	River Valley	*not July/August*
211	Pear Tree	*not July/August*	961	Mannix Point	*not July/August*

MAYBE: accepted at any time but with certain restrictions.

001	Chacewater	*not all breeds*	396	Silvertrees	*not certain breeds*
003	Ayr	*1 only (medium size)*	397	Glencote	*max. 2 per pitch*
006	River Valley	*certain areas*	420	The Boyce	*not certain breeds*
015	Sea View	*limited numbers/breeds*	440	Stanmore Hall	*max. 2 per pitch*
021	Hendra	*some areas only*	441	Beaconsfield	*max. 2 per pitch*
022	Trevornick	*one area only*	442	Severn Gorge	*max. 3 per pitch*
029	Carlyon Bay	*some areas only*	443	Oxon Hall	*max. 2 per pitch*
038	Wooda Farm	*not certain breeds*	452	Flower of May	*by arrangement only*
072	Easewell Farm	*max. 1 in high season*	463	Ripley	*max. 2 per pitch*
090	Widdicombe	*not certain breeds*	464	Goose Wood	*max. 2 per pitch*
092	Finlake	*in certain areas*	470	Nostell Priory	*max. 2 per pitch*
093	Ashburton	*not certain breeds*	476	Riverside	*max. 2 per pitch*
095	River Dart	*max. 2 per pitch*	530	Kneps Farm	*max. 2 per pitch*
102	Oakdown	*not certain breeds*	535	Holgates	*not certain breeds*
141	Broadway	*not certain breeds*	554	Fallbarrow	*1 per booking*
154	Batcombe	*max 1; not some breeds*	557	Wild Rose	*not certain breeds*
181	Newlands	*max. 2 per pitch*	571	Doe Park	*prior arrangement*
204	Manor Farm	*at owner's discretion*	576	Percy Wood	*not certain breeds*
225	Bashley Park	*max. 1 per pitch*	580	Ord House	*prior arrangement*
226	International	*certain areas only*	628	Aeron Coast	*max. 1*
228	Lytton Lawn	*max. 1 per pitch*	636	Pen-y-Garth	*prior arrangement*
229	Sandy Balls	*certain areas only*	665	Hunter's Hamlet	*max 2; not some breeds*
231	Hollands Wood	*certain areas only*	670	Ty Ucha	*not in certain areas*
247	Southland	*prior arrangement*	730	Blair Castle	*max. 2 per pitch*
257	Lincoln Farm	*max. 2 per pitch*	731	Twenty Shilling	*max. 2*
304	Broadhembury	*max. 2 per pitch*	764	Dunroamin	*max. 2*
330	The Grange	*max 2; not some breeds*	769	Torvean	*1 small dog only*
338	Clippesby	*max. 1 per pitch*	770	Pitgrudy	*max. 2*
340	Old Brick Kilns	*max. 2 per pitch*	785	Linnhe	*max. 2*
342	Two Mills	*max 2, not some breeds*	786	Glendaruel	*prior arrangement*
343	Kelling Heath	*max. 2 per pitch*	930	Morriscastle	*not in certain areas*
351	Lffens	*max. 1 per pitch*	963	White Villa	*max 2; not some breeds*
355	Old Manor	*max. 2 per pitch*			

FISHING

We are pleased to include details of parks which provide facilities for fishing on the site. Many other parks, particularly in Scotland and Ireland, are in popular fishing areas and have facilities within easy reach. Where we have been given details, we have included this information in the individual site reports. It is always best to contact individual parks to check that they provide for your individual requirements.

ENGLAND

South West
006	River Valley Country Park
017	Trevella Caravan & Camping Park
022	Trevornick Holiday Park
025	Pentewan Sands Holiday Park
038	Wooda Farm Caravan Park
075	Minnows Camping & Caravan Park
077	Clifford Bridge Park
079	Harford Bridge Park
081	Riverside Caravan Park
092	Finlake Holiday Park
095	The River Dart Country Park
097	Cofton Country Holiday Park
106	Yeatheridge Farm Caravan Park
109	Peppermint Park
137	Burrowhayes Farm Caravan Site
138	Blue Anchor Park
139	The Old Oaks Touring Park
142	Southfork Caravan Park
145	Bath Caravan Park
146	Lakeside Touring Caravan Park
148	Home Farm Holiday Park
154	Batcombe Vale Campsite
174	Golden Cap Holiday Park
176	Wood Farm Caravan Park
178	Freshwater Beach Caravan Park

South
201	Sandyholme Holiday Park
213	Grove Farm Meadow Holiday Park
229	Sandy Balls Holiday Centre
244	Adgestone Camping Park
245	The Orchards Holiday Caravan Park
261	Bo Peep Caravan Park
269	Wellington Country Park
281	Chertsey C&C Club Site
282	Horsley C&C Club Site
290	Horam Manor Touring Park
292	Bay View Caravan & Camping Park
303	Tanner Farm Touring Park
321	Lee Valley Caravan Park

East Anglia
340	The Old Brick Kilns Caravan Park
343	Kelling Heath Holiday Park
344	Gatton Waters Lakeside Touring Site
348	Little Lakeland Caravan Park

Heart of England
367	Lakeside Park
375	Foreman's Bridge Caravan Park
390	Bosworth Water Trust
392	Riverside Caravan Park
394	Smeaton's Lakes Touring Park
397	Glencote Caravan Park
410	Cotswold Hoburne Caravan Park
419	Kingsgreen Caravan Park
420	The Boyce Caravan Park
421	Lickhill Manor Caravan Park
430	Poston Mill Caravan Park
431	Luck's All Caravan Park
432	Broadmeadow Caravan Park

438	Fernwood Caravan Park
439	Westbrook Park
441	Beaconsfield Farm Caravan Park

Yorkshire
451	Thorpe Hall Caravan & Camping Site
461	Moorside Caravan Park
464	Goose Wood Caravan Park
466	Woodhouse Farm Caravan Park
470	Nostell Priory Holiday Home Park
472	Knight Stainforth Hall Caravan Park
473	Far Grange Park

North West and Cumbria
528	Abbey Farm Caravan Park
529	Royal Umpire Caravan Park
554	Fallbarrow Park
555	Limefitt Park
560	Pennine View Caravan & Camping Park

Northumbria
571	Doe Park Touring Caravan Park

WALES
592	The Bridge Caravan Park
593	Cwmcarn Forest Drive Campsite
597	Noble Court Holiday Park
631	Disserth Caravan Park
659	Beddgelert Caravan & Camping Site
660	Bryn Gloch Caravan & Camping Park
667	The Plassey Touring & Leisure Park

SCOTLAND
691	Hoddom Castle Caravan Park
694	Caldons Caravan and Camping Site
695	Brighouse Bay Holiday Park
700	Strathclyde Country Park Caravan Site
726	Ardgartan Forestry Commission Campsite
727	Auchterarder Caravan Park
766	Spindrift Caravan & Camping Park
771	Ardmair Point Caravan Park
772	Woodend Camping & Caravan Park
780	Resipole Farm Caravan & Camping Park
784	North Ledaig Caravan Park
785	Linnhe Lochside Holidays
786	Glendaruel Caravan Park

NORTHERN IRELAND
831	Carnfunnock Country Park Caravan Site
834	Drumaheglis Caravan Park
850	LoanEden Caravan Park
852	Share Holiday Village

IRISH REPUBLIC
877	Parkland Caravan & Camping Park
896	Lough Ree (East) CaravanPark
930	Morriscastle Strand Caravan Park
938	Parsons Green Caravan and Camping Park
951	Eagle Point Caravan & Camping Park
956	Wave Crest Caravan & Camping Park
962	Flemings White Bridge Caravan Park
963	White Villa Farm Caravan Park

BICYCLES & MOUNTAIN BIKES

We understand that the following parks have bicycles to hire on site or can arrange for bicycles to be delivered. However, we would recommend that you contact the park to check as the situation can change.

ENGLAND

West Country
009	Trethem Mill Touring Park
011	Calloose Caravan Park
014	Penrose Farm Touring Park
015	Sea View International
025	Pentewan Sands Holiday Park
026	Penhaven Touring Park
033	Killigarth Manor Caravan Park
036	Lakefield Caravan Park
069	Stowford Farm Meadows
078	Dartmoor View Holiday Park
100	Forest Glade Intl. Caravan Park
104	Old Cotmore Farm
135	Quantock Orchard Caravan Park
139	The Old Oaks Touring Park
140	The Isle of Avalon Touring Park
141	Broadway House Caravan Park
149	Greenacres Camping
178	Freshwater Beach Caravan Park

South
205	Rowlands Wait Touring Park
210	Sandford Caravan Park
213	Grove Farm Meadow Holiday Park
214	Mount Pleasant Touring Park
225	Bashley Park
227	Oakdene Forest Park
229	Sandy Balls Holiday Centre
235	Red Shoot Camping Park
258	Cotswold View Caravan Site

East Anglia
338	Clippesby Holidays
340	The Old Brick Kilns Caravan Park
356	Highfield Farm Touring Park

Heart of England
369	Bainland Country Park
375	Foreman's Bridge Caravan Park
380	Highfields Holiday Caravan Park
430	Poston Mill Caravan Park

Yorkshire
456	Golden Square Caravan & Camping Park
466	Woodhouse Farm Caravan Park
471	Rudding Caravan Park
472	Knight Stainforth Hall Caravan Park
536	Willowbank Touring Park

North West and Cumbria
555	Limefitt Park
557	Wild Rose Park

Northumbria
580	Ord House Country Park
581	Fallowfield Dene Caravan Park

SCOTLAND
695	Brighouse Bay Holiday Park
696	Crossburn Caravan Park
700	Strathclyde Country Park Caravan Site
723	Trossachs Holiday Park
724	Lomond Woods Holiday Park
786	Glendaruel Caravan Park

NORTHERN IRELAND
850	LoanEden Caravan Park
852	Share Holiday Village

IRISH REPUBLIC
874	Cong Caravan and Camping Park
908	Forest Farm Caravan and Camping Park
913	Roundwood Caravan & Camping Park
923	Nore Valley Park
952	Barleycove Holiday Park
959	Fossa Caravan & Camping Park
960	Glenross Caravan & Camping Park
962	Flemings White Bridge Caravan Park
963	White Villa Farm Caravan Park
964	The Flesk Muckross Caravan Park

CHANNEL ISLANDS
971	Rozel Camping Park
972	Beuvelande Camp Site
977	Vaugrat Camping
978	Fauxquets Valley Farm Campsite

There are facilities for the hire of bicycles within easy reach of many parks in this guide. When this information is available, and we have been given details, we have included this information in the individual site reports.

For the cyclist ...

Haynes Publishing's **Ride Your Bike** series of cycle guides takes you through the most scenic, traffic-free areas of Britain, including off-road rides for all abilities using numbered directions with routes clearly marked on Ordnance Survey Landranger mapping (spiral bound). *See inside cover pages for details.*

GOLF

We understand that the following parks have facilities for playing golf on site. Where facilities are within easy reach and we have been given details, we have included this information in the individual site reports. However, we recommend that you contact the park to check that the facility meets your requirements.

England
022   Trevornick Holiday Park
038   Wooda Farm Caravan Park
069   Stowford Farm Meadows
072   Easewell Farm Holiday Park
101   Lady's Mile Touring Park
107   Woolacombe Bay Holidays
175   Highlands End Holiday Park
225   Bashley Park
367   Lakeside Park
369   Bainland Country Park
407   Somers Wood Caravan Park
430   Poston Mill Caravan Park
452   Flower of May Holiday Park
471   Rudding Caravan Park

Wales
667   The Plassey Touring Park

Scotland
690   Seaward Caravan Park
691   Hoddom Castle Caravan Park
695   Brighouse Bay Holiday Park
769   Torvean Caravan Park
780   Resipole Farm Caravan Park

Northern Ireland
831   Carnfunnock Country Park

Irish Republic
877   Parkland Caravan Park
915   River Valley Caravan Park
948   Blarney Caravan Park

HORSE RIDING

We understand that the following parks have horse riding stables on site. Where facilities are within easy reach and we have been given details, we have included this information in the individual site reports. However, we would recommend that you contact the park to check that the facility meets your requirements.

England
036   Lakefield Caravan Park
038   Wooda Farm Caravan Park
069   Stowford Farm Meadows
092   Finlake Holiday Park
106   Yeatheridge Farm Caravan Park
137   Burrowhayes Farm Caravan Site
178   Freshwater Beach Caravan Park
227   Oakdene Forest Park
229   Sandy Balls Holiday Centre
262   Wysdom Touring Park

290   Horam Manor Touring Park
295   Washington Caravan Park

Scotland
695   Brighouse Bay Holiday Park
730   Blair Castle Caravan Park

Northern Ireland
850   LoanEden Caravan Park

Irish Republic
916   Moat Farm Caravan Park

BOAT LAUNCHING

We understand that the following parks have boat slipways on site. Where facilities are within easy reach and we have been given details, we have included this information in the individual site reports. However, we would recommend that you contact the park to check that the facility meets your requirements.

England
25   Pentewan Sands Holiday Park
175   Highlands End Holiday Park
269   Wellington Country Park
390   Bosworth Water Trust
421   Lickhill Manor Caravan Park
532   Bridge House Marina
554   Fallbarrow Park
695   Brighouse Bay Holiday Park

Scotland
700   Strathclyde Country Park
726   Ardgartan Forestry Site
771   Ardmair Point Caravan Park
780   Resipole Farm Caravan Park

784   North Ledaig Caravan Park
785   Linnhe Lochside Holidays

Northern Ireland
831   Carnfunnock Country Park
834   Drumaheglis Caravan Park
850   LoanEden Caravan Park
852   Share Holiday Village

Irish Republic
877   Parkland Caravan Park
896   Lough Ree Caravan Park
951   Eagle Point Caravan Park
956   Wave Crest Caravan Park
961   Mannix Point Caravan Park

REPORTS BY READERS

We always welcome reports from readers concerning parks which they have visited. Generally reports provide us with invaluable feedback on parks already featured in the Guide or, in the case of those not featured in our Guide, they provide information which we can follow up with a view to adding them in future editions.

However, if you have a complaint about a site, this should be addressed to the campsite owner, preferably in person before you leave.

Please make your comments either on this form or on plain paper. It would be appreciated if you would indicate the approximate dates when you visited the park and, in the case of potential new parks, provide the correct name and address and, if possible, include a park brochure. Send your reports to:

Deneway Guides & Travel Ltd, Chesil Lodge, West Bexington, Dorchester DT2 9DG

Name of Park and Ref. No. (or address for new recommendations):

....

....

Dates of Visit: ....

Comments:

Reader's Name and Address: ....

....

....

....

Gerry and Chris Bullock's Page

First of all who are Gerry and Chris, and why give them a page in this guide? Chris and Gerry have been motorhome owners for more years than they care to remember but, in the mid seventies Chris suffered a serious back injury which has worsened over the past ten years, taking away her ability to walk any distance more than within the motorhome or around the house, and otherwise she is wheelchair user. They have, therefore, over the years become 'experts' in finding parks with good facilities for the wheelchair user.

We felt that it might be useful for other readers of the guide to learn something of their experiences or indeed be able to tap their experience directly. They are very happy for us to include their address and phone number at the end of this article should you wish to contact them.

As you will be aware, we always include reference to facilities provided by the parks in our Guide but have not felt ourselves qualified to assess these facilities. Below we have listed what Gerry and Chris look at when they assess a park with few examples of what they have found.

Firstly, they look at the access to the sanitary blocks:

- Are they accessible for wheelchair users or walking disabled campers?
- Are door widths adequate for wheelchairs, are there steps for the walking disabled?

Secondly, what does the room offer?

- WC with handrails
- Handrails at the sinks
- Obstructions in the room
- Sink accessible by wheelchair
- Lights with cords
- The shower and its access
- Levers on taps
- Emergency alarm cord
- Handrails in the shower

Thirdly, access checks to other facilities.

- Washing up areas (even less abled persons like to help).
- Reception (Chris likes a chance to pay the bill!)
- Bars and restaurants (why can't we all enjoy ourselves?)
- Games room
- Clubs and other amenities

Fourthly, the pitches

- Where are they in relation to the facilities?
- Conditions of paths - gravel/tarmac/sleeping police men
- Terraced or level?
- Ground - level/sloping?

For example:

One park, recently assessed by Gerry and Chris, came out well with its ramped accesses to all bars, the shop, the takeaway and reception; also for the Radar key system for the sanitary facilities. It did not score so well with some of the paths and roads that connect the facilities - some were unmade and difficult for wheelchair users and their helper (this is an area the site now hopes to address). There were also some problems with the pitches as the park is based on heathland and is consequently somewhat bumpy. Perhaps the site will be able to specially level a pitch close to the facilities. At least their attention has been drawn to some of the problems experienced by wheelchair users and the walking disabled, which they maybe able to improve. They recommend both the Caravan Club and the Camping and Caravanning Club as having good, well designed and maintained facilities.

These are the sorts of things which Gerry and Chris look at so, if you have queries concerning sites and the suitability of their facilities or would like suggestions, or have any recommendations, please contact them. They would like to hear from you.

Gerry and Chris Bullock's address is:
97 Stalham Road, Hoveton, Norwich, Norfolk NR12 8EF Telephone. 01603 784152

NOTE. They advise that they are not looking at facilities for persons with special needs. They leave this to the such people as the Sue Ryder Foundation, etc. which cater very well in this field.

Following recent visits, Gerry and Chris have made the following comments:

England

011 Calloose Caravan Park

Good en-suite room for disabled visitors; roads tarmac; some parts steep; pitches level; access to large clubhouse; very busy site.

016 Newperran Tourist Park

Disabled washroom/wc (shower only suitable for persons able to leave wheelchair); roads tarmac; access to pool area; level site & pitches.

018 Carnon Downs Caravan Park

Excellent en-suite disabled room; level site; roadways tight packed gravel; level pitches; helpful owners.

021 Hendra Holiday Park

Good disabled rooms within non-handicapped facilities; shower has 6" high tray (but large transfer seat along one side); access to most other areas; hilly site; pitches level; very busy.

075 Minnows Camping & Caravan Park
Good disabled washroom/wc; slight sloping path; access to non-disabled facilities where showers are large enough to allow access and handrails are fitted; shingle roadways and pitches (owners will rake to assist); level pitches; book in advance; helpful owners.

088 Dornafield
Excellent disabled facilities; separate wc/washroom and shower rooms very well set out; tarmac roads some parts steep; very helpful staff; ramps not too steep; disabled friendly site; pitches level.

091 Ross Park
Good en-suite disabled room; shingle roads; pitches shingle (owners will rake if required to assist); access to tropical conservatory; level pitches; access to other areas; helpful owners.

144 Baltic Wharf Caravan Club Site
Good en-suite disabled room; tarmac roadways; level site; level pitches; access to riverside and to city; book in advance.

145 Bath Marina & Caravan Park
Good en-suite disabled room; tarmac roadways; level pitches; level site; access to other areas; hardstandings; book in advance.

203 Wareham Forest Tourist Park
Good en-suite facilities; hard-core roadways and hardstandings; speed humps; assistance needed with manual wheelchairs; slight ramp to disabled room; access other areas – level site.

229 Sandy Balls Holiday Centre
Excellent site for wheelchair users; en-suite facilities; Radar key; access to bar; hardstandings; level site.

258 Cotswold View Caravan Site
Excellent en-suite facilities; hard-core roadways; concrete paths; level site.

293 Sheepcote Valley Caravan Club Site
Superb en-suite facilities; tarmac roads; low kerbs; walking disabled facilities; level site.

27 Crystal Palace Caravan Club Site
Superb en-suite facilities; tarmac roads; access to reception; hilly site but all pitches level.

325 Lee Valley Campsite
Superb large en-suite facilities block; slight hill; tarmac roadways; key at reception; wheelchair accessible bus available; slight ramp.

330 The Grange Country Park
Good en-suite facilities; tarmac roadways; level site; slight ramp; access to bar/restaurant.

339 Dower House Touring Park
Good disabled facilities; level site; hardcore roadways; tree stumps; access to other areas.

340 Old Manor Caravan Park
Good disabled facilities; ramp not too steep; tarmac roadways; hilly site; level pitches.

343 Kelling Heath Holiday Park
Separate shower and toilet; slight ramp; roadway to touring site rough; good access other areas; main entertainment area all tarmac.

348 Little Lakeland Caravan Park
Excellent disabled room; access to all rooms including reception; pitches level; owners very helpful.

350 Woodhill Park
Superb separate shower and toilet; roadways hard-core; site slightly sloping.

340 The Old Brick Kilns
Excellent en-suite facilities; hard-core roadways; slightly hilly; shingle hardstandings.

347 Breckland Meadows Touring Park
WC and washroom only; hard-core roadways; flat; level site.

358 Ferry Meadows Caravan Club Site
Superb en-suite facilities; tarmac roadways; level site.

373 Skegness Sands Touring Site
Superb en-suite facilities; tarmac roadways; concrete paths; disabled friendly site.

365 Cherry Tree Site
Superb en-suite facilities; roadways hard-core; concrete paths.

411 Tewksbury Caravan Club Site
Superb disabled friendly site; excellent en-suite disabled room; roadways tarmac; facilities for walking disabled.

404 C&C Club Site Clent Hills
Superb en-suite disabled room; tarmac roads; steep hill out of site; pitches need blocks; some hardstandings.

442 Severn George Caravan Park
Superb separate disabled toilet and shower rooms; roadways hard-core; tarmac pitches level.

Ireland

906 Green Gables Caravan Park
Good en-suite facilities; concrete paths; hardcore roadways; some hard standings; access all areas including cafe and reception.

915 River Valley Caravan Park
Excellent en-suite disabled; all roadways and paths tarmac; all pitches level; disabled friendly site.

930 Morriscastle Strand
Good disabled room; site sloping; tarmac roadways; assistance on site with wheelchair.

TOWN and VILLAGE INDEX

Town and Village Index

CAMPSITE INDEX

page   *page*

REPUBLIC OF IRELAND

CHANNEL ISLANDS

New Parks: Parks that are new to the guide this year are highlighted in bold type in this index.

**For travel further afield, remember the other ALAN ROGERS' titles –
the GOOD CAMPS GUIDES for FRANCE and EUROPE**

★ Independent site assessors make regular monitoring visits

★ Consistently revised and updated – sites included on merit only

★ Discount vouchers for selected sites, ferries and tourist attractions

See www.alanrogers.com

NOTES

This page is for your own notes

THE NEW FOREST

NEW FOREST SEE MAP BELOW

DORSET

WILTSHIRE

PICCADILLY 166
DEVIZES 170
BATH 145
CHEW VALLEY 151
MENDIP HEIGHTS 143
GREENACRES 149
OLD OAKS 139
BATCOMBE VALE 154
LONGLEAT 169
BRISTOL
BALTIC WHARF 144
BROADWAY HOUSE 141
SLIMERIDGE FARM 153
HOME FARM 148
ISLE OF AVALON 140
QUANTOCK ORCHARD 135
SOMERSET
LONG HAZEL 150
SOUTHFORK 142
BINGHAMS FARM 177
FRESHWATER BEACH 178
EAST FLEET FARM 180
BLUE ANCHOR 138
TAUNTON
WATERROW 152
M5
FOREST GLADE 100
MONKTON WYLDE FARM 173
WOOD FARM 176
NEWLANDS 181
GOLDEN CAP 174
HIGHLANDS END FARM 175
BURROWHAYES FARM 137
HALSE FARM 136
LAKESIDE 146
MINNOWS 075
EXETER
WEBBERS FARM 110
OAKDOWN 102
COFTON 097
PEPPERMINT 109
LADY'S MILE 101
COAST VIEW 108
PARKERS FARM 096
DORNAFIELD 088
WIDDICOMBE FARM 090
BEVERLEY 087
GALMPTON PARK 085
WOODLAND 084
SLAPTON SANDS 083
OLD COTMORE 104
SPRINGFIELD 105
STOWFORD FARM MEADOWS 069
HIDDEN VALLEY 071
EASEWELL FARM 072
TWITCHEN FARM 073
WOOLACOMBE BAY 107
GREENACRES 070
DEVON
YEATHERIDGE FARM 106
BARNSTAPLE
OKEHAMPTON
DARTMOOR VIEW 078
CLIFFORD BRIDGE 077
HOLMANS WOOD 094
FINLAKE 092
LEMONFORD 098
ASHBURTON 093
RIVER DART 095
ROSS PARK 091
RAMSLADE 086
RIVERSIDE 081
A38
MOOR VIEW 082
HARFORD BRIDGE 079
HIGHER LONGFORD FARM 080
DOLBEARE 044
PLYMOUTH
WHITSAND BAY 035
POLBORDER HOUSE 032
LOOE VALLEY 042
KILLIGARTH MANOR 033
WOODA FARM 038
BUDEMEADOWS 037
LAKEFIELD 036
COLLIFORD TAVERN 030
GLENMORRIS 023
CORNWALL
TRELAY FARM 040
POWDERHAM CASTLE 028
POLRUAN 019
CARLYON BAY 029
PENTEWAN SANDS 025
PENGRUGLA 041
SEA VIEW 015
PENHAVEN 026
TRURO
TRETHEM MILL 009
TRERETHEN 043
SOUTHLEIGH MANOR 024N
TREKENNING 031
NEWQUAY 020
HENDRA 021
TREVELLA 017
TREVORNICK 022
CROFT FARM 046
LISKEY 013
CARNON DOWNS 018
MAEN VALLEY 008
NEWPERRAN 016
PENROSE FARM 014
SILVERBOW 012
LEVERTON PLACE 010
CHACEWATER 001
AYR 003
PENNANCE MILL FARM 045
TREVALGAN 004
POLMANTER 005
CALLOOSE 011
RIVER VALLEY 006
TRELOWARREN 039
SILVER SANDS 007
CARDINNEY 002

SALISBURY
ALDERBURY 167
ASHURST 230
LYNDHURST
HOLLANDS WOOD 231
BASHLEY PARK 225
SANDY BALLS 229
RED SHOOT 235
MERLEY COURT 208
HOBURNE PARK 212
LYTTON LAWN 228
THE INSIDE PARK 207
ROWLANDS WAIT 205
ULWELL COTTAGE 202

WALES, CENTRAL & SOUTHERN ENGLAND

HULL

HOME FARM 664

LAKESIDE PARK 367

CHERRY TREE 365

WOODHILL PARK 350

LITTLE HAVEN 345

TWO MILLS 342

CLIPPESBY 338

THE GRANGE 349

LIFFENS 351

LITTLE LAKELAND 348

QUEX 311

CANTERBURY 307

YEW TREE 306

DOVER

HAWTHORN FARM 310

BLACK HORSE 309

FOLKESTONE

KELLING HEATH 343

THE GARDEN 346

GATTON WATERS 344

THE OLD BRICK KILNS 340

NORFOLK 338

NORWICH

THE DOWER-HOUSE 339

MOAT BARN 333

LOW HOUSE 331

THE GRANGE 330

IPSWICH

SUFFOLK

PINE LODGE 305

BROADHEMBURY 304

WHYDOWN FARM 296

GATE HOUSE WOOD 312

TANNER FARM 303

HORAM MANOR 290

BAY VIEW 292

SHEEPCOTE VALLEY 293

BRECKLAND MEADOWS 347

FERRY MEADOWS 358

CAMBRIDGE

CAMBRIDGESHIRE

LEE VALLEY CARAVAN PARK 321

LEE VALLEY CAMPSITE 325

ABBEY WOOD 326

CRYSTAL PALACE 327

KENT

M20

SUSSEX

HONEYBRIDGE PARK 294

BRIGHTON

WHITE ROSE 289

WASHINGTON 295

WALESBY WOODLANDS 366

ORCHARD PARK 395

LINCOLNSHIRE

BAINLAND LAKES 369

SKEGNESS SANDS 373

RIVERSIDE 392

SMEATON'S LAKES 394

PILGRIMS WAY 370

FOREMAN'S BRIDGE 375

TALLINGTON LAKES 385

LEICESTER

OLD MANOR 355

HIGHFIELD FARM 356

LUTON

HIGHCLERE FARM 275

LONDON

CHERTSEY 281

HORSLEY 282

SURREY

M25

RAYLANDS 288

ROYAL UMPIRE 529

WILLOWBANK 536

ABBEY FARM 528

PRESTON

MANCHESTER

SHEFFIELD

DARWIN FOREST 382

DERBYSHIRE

NOTTINGHAM

THE FIRS 383

RIVENDALE 386

HIGHFIELDS 380

SILVERTREES 396

DERBY

COVENTRY

WARWICKSHIRE

BARNSTONES 260

BO PEEP 261

COTSWOLD VIEW 258

BUCKING-HAMSHIRE

OXFORD

READING

BERKSHIRE

WELLINGTON COUNTRY PARK 269

M3

M27

HAMPSHIRE

M4

LIME TREE 384

GLENCOTE 397

STOKE

FERNWOOD 438

THE PLASSEY 667

TY-UCHA FARM 670

PEN-Y-GARTH 636

BEACONSFIELD FARM 441

STAFFORDSHIRE

WOLVERHAMPTON

BIRMINGHAM

BOSWORTH WATER 390

SOMERS WOOD 407

CLENT HILLS 404

FLICKHILL MANOR 421

THE BOYCE 420

RANCH 418

MORETON-IN-MARSH 413

WINCHCOMBE 414

BRIARFIELDS 412

COTSWOLD 257

LICOLN FARM 410

WYSDOM 262

GLOUCESTERSHIRE

PLOUGH LANE 168

HOBURNE 410

WILTSHIRE

SOMERSET

DORSET

DEVON

CHICHESTER 232

ISLE OF WIGHT

SOUTHLAND 247

ADGESTONE 244

APPULDURCOMBE GARDEN 248

KITE HILL FARM 249

HEATHFIELD FARM 250

THE ORCHARDS

SOUTHAMPTON

NORTH WALES

BARCDY 635

PENYBONT 634

BRON-Y-WENDON 669

HUNTERS HAMLET 665

JAMES 668

OXON HALL 443

SHROPSHIRE

STANMORE HALL 440

SEVERN GORGE 442

FFOREST FIELDS 632

HEREFORDSHIRE

POSTON MILL 430

LUCK'S ALL 431

KINGSGREEN 419

TEWKESBURY 411

BROADMEADOW 432

GLOUCESTER

THE BRIDGE 592

NEWPORT

BALTIC WHARF 144

BRISTOL

M5

MID WALES

DISERTH 631

DASH BANK 633

WESTBROOK PARK 439

CWMCARN FOREST DRIVE 593

TREDEGAR HOUSE 606

CARDIFF

OCEAN VIEW 630

GLAN-Y-MOR LEISURE 629

AERON COAST 628

RHANDIRMWYN 607

BRYNICH 603

PENCELLI CASTLE 604

ABERMARLAIS 596

SOUTH WALES

NOBLE COURT 597

AFON LODGE 595

SWANSEA

PEMBREY 594

FRESHWATER EAST 599

MORETON FARM 598

LLWYNGWAIR MANOR 608

GWAUN VALE 600

CENARTH FALLS 601

HOLYHEAD

CADNANT VALLEY 661

BRYN GLOCH 660

BEDDGELERT 659

LLANYSTUMDWY 658

HENDRE MYNACH 637

HOME FARM 664

SEE SOUTH WEST ENGLAND AND NEW FOREST MAP

EXETER

254

SCOTLAND & NORTHERN ENGLAND

SCOURIE 773
WOODEND 772
DUNROAMIN 764
ARDMAIR POINT 771
PITGRUDY 770
STAFFIN 775
LOCH GRESHORNISH 774
SPINDRIFT 766
TORVEAN 769 *INVERNESS
ADEN COUNTRY PARK 753
ABERLOUR GARDENS 754
RERAIG 776
HIGHLANDS AND ISLANDS
GRANTOWN-ON-SPEY 767
GRAMPIAN
HUNTLY CASTLE 755
FAICHEM PARK 778
GLENMORE 768
*ABERDEEN
A93
LINNHE LOCHSIDE 785
GLEN NEVIS 783
BLAIR CASTLE 730
RESIPOLE FARM 780
INVERCOE 779
NETHER CRAIG 728
A90
OBAN 781
NORTH LEDAIG 784
HEART OF SCOTLAND
*DUNDEE
OBAN DIVERS 782
TWENTY SHILLING 731
AUCHTERARDER 727
CRAIGTOUN MEADOWS 729
ARDGARTAN 726
TROSSACHS 723
WITCHES CRAIG 732
GLENDARUEL 786
LOMOND WOOD 724
EDINBURGH 705
EDINBURGH
MONKS' MUIR 697
*GLASGOW
MORTONHALL 699
DRUM MOHR 698
STRATHCLYDE 700
SLATEBARNS 704
ORD HOUSE 580
CROSSBURN 696
WAREN 575
GIBSON PARK 703
DUNSTAN HILL 577
CULZEAN CASTLE 701
SCOTTISH LOWLANDS
PERCY WOOD 576
NORTHUMBERLAND
CALDONS 694
CRESSFIELD 692
BROWN RIGG 578
HODDOM CASTLE 691
PARK OF BRANDEDLEYS 693
FALLOWFIELD DENE 581
*NEWCASTLE UPON TYNE
AIRD DONALD 702
BRIGHOUSE BAY 695
SEAWARD 690
THE LARCHES 551
M6
A1(M)
WATERFOOT 561
DOE PARK
TEESIDE
COVE 562
WILD ROSE 557
DOE PARK 571
BARNARD CASTLE 572
CUMBRIA
SYKESIDE 556
LIMEFITT PARK 555
PENNINE VIEW 560
CONSTABLE BURTON HALL 469
SKELWITH FOLD 552
WESTMORLAND 559
STREET HEAD 468
WALLS 553
FALLBARROW PARK 554
HOLGATES 535
RIVERSIDE MEADOWS 476
WOODHOUSE FARM 466
YORKSHIRE
KNIGHT STAINFORTH HALL 472
RIPLEY 463
WOOD NOOK 467
RUDDING 471
*YORK
BRIDGE HOUSE MARINA 532
HOWGILL LODGE 475
KNEPS FARM 530
LANCASHIRE
*BLACKPOOL
PIPERS HEIGHT 531
*PRESTON
*BRADFORD
ROYAL UMPIRE 529
WILLOWBANK 536
ABBEY FARM 528
M62

WHITE WATER 574
NORTHCLIFFE 453
ROSEDALE 477
ST HELENS IN THE PARK 454
VALE OF PICKERING 460
CAYTON VILLAGE 455
GOLDEN SQUARE 456
FLOWER OF MAY 458
JASMINE PARK 474
THORPE HALL 451
FOXHOLME 458
GOOSE WOOD 464
MOORSIDE 461
FANGFOSS OLD STATION 465
FAR GRANGE 473
*YORK
RAWCLIFFE MANOR 462
M62
*HULL
NOSTELL PRIORY 470

IRELAND

KNOCKALLA 864
BELLEMONT 860
BUSH 835
COLERAINE
TULLANS FARM 859
LONDONDERRY A2
DRUMAHEGLIS 834
CARNFUNNOCK 831
N15
STRABANE
BALLYMENA
A36
LARNE
CURRAN 832
DONEGAL
GORTIN GLEN 956
BANGOR
LOANEDEN 850
OMAGH
COOKSTOWN
BELFAST
GREENLANDS 869
SLIGO
N16
ENNISKILLEN
ARMAGH
BELLEEK 875
GATEWAY 870
N17
SHARE 852
BANBRIDGE GATEWAY 843
NEWRY
TOLLYMORE FOREST 842
PARKLAND 877
N5
CARRA 879
KNOCK 878
CAVAN
DUNDALK
TAIN 889
CONG 874
N17
HODSON BAY 882
LOUGH REE (EAST) 896
GALWAY
ATHLONE
N6
CAMAC VALLEY 910
DUBLIN
GREEN GABLES 906
NAAS
SHANKHILL 911
N18
KIRWANS 920
PORTLAOISE
ROUNDWOOD
VALLEY 913
914
N7
FOREST FARM 908
MOAT FARM 916
WICKLOW
RIVER VALLEY 915
CURRAGHCHASE 945
LIMERICK
N24
N8
N9
TREE GROVE 924
KILKENNY
NORE VALLEY 923
N11
MORRISCASTLE STRAND 930
ANCHOR 955
TRALEE
WOODLANDS PARK 965
N21
N20
TIPPERARY
APPLE 941
CARRICK-ON-SUIR
CLONMEL 939
WEXFORD
FOSSA 959
KILLARNEY
GLENROSS 960
N8
PARSONS GREEN 938
WATERFORD
ROSSLARE
MANNIX POINT 961
THE FLESK 964
WHITE VILLA FARM 963
FLEMING'S WHITEBRIDGE 962
N22
BLARNEY 948
CASEY'S 933
NEWTOWN COVE 934
WAVE CREST 956
CORK
N25
SONAS 949
CREVEEN LODGE 957
EAGLE POINT 951
BARLEYCOVE 952
THE MEADOW 950

VAUGRAT 977
SEAGULL (HERM) 983
ST PETER PORT
FAUXQUETS VALLEY 978
POMME DE CHIEN (SARK) 987

GUERNSEY

ROZEL 971
BEUVELANDE 972

JERSEY
ST HELIER